THE STRUGGLE FOR CRETE

The Struggle for Crete

20 May – 1 June 1941

A STORY OF LOST OPPORTUNITY

I. McD. G. STEWART

'In many of its aspects at the time it was fought the Battle of Crete was unique. Nothing like it had ever been seen before.'
> Winston Churchill in *The Grand Alliance*

'The unique nature of the operation for the division must be borne in mind.'
> Colonel Ernst Haidlen, Staff Officer to the 7th Air Division

London

OXFORD UNIVERSITY PRESS

NEW YORK TORONTO

1966

Oxford University Press, Ely House, London W.1

GLASGOW NEW YORK TORONTO MELBOURNE WELLINGTON
CAPE TOWN SALISBURY IBADAN NAIROBI LUSAKA ADDIS ABABA
BOMBAY CALCUTTA MADRAS KARACHI LAHORE DACCA
KUALA LUMPUR HONG KONG

Printed in Great Britain by
Eyre and Spottiswoode Limited, Her Majesty's Printers
at The Thanet Press, Margate

DEDICATED TO THE MEMORY OF

2nd Lieutenant L. M. Stewart M.C.
of The Suffolk Regiment
killed on Active Service 30 November 1940

Another of those who saw the issue early
and needed no advice
to join the fight

CONTENTS

vii

CONTENTS

PART THREE

CRISIS

PART FOUR

VICTORY AND DEFEAT

MAPS

1•

ILLUSTRATIONS

ACKNOWLEDGEMENTS

Before all others my thanks are due to Mr. D. M. Davin, Fellow of Balliol College, Oxford, who not only made available to me the whole of his numerous papers on Crete but has been equally generous in hospitality and advice throughout the six years that it has taken me to write this book.

I should also like to offer particular thanks to Mr. F. W. Deakin, Warden of St. Antony's College, Oxford, who was the first to hear of my intended effort, and whose specific encouragement has included a meticulous and burdensome study of my proofs, together with Brigadier H. B. Latham who, before his retirement from the Historical Section at the War Office, was most kind in giving me his advice. Later I had further help from his successor, Lieutenant-Colonel W. B. R. Neave-Hill, and also from Brigadier J. Stephenson, Director of the Royal United Service Institution, and from the authorities in charge of the Imperial War Museum, the Bodleian Library, and the Blackpool Public Library. At all times Mr. C. A. Potts, of the Ministry of Defence Library, has supplied me with the latest news about fresh sources of information.

Friends who have been kind enough to read and comment upon the typescripts and proofs include Dr. J. A. R. Pollock, who submitted intermittently to this trial for more than four years, Miss M. R. Hulme, whose detailed and constructive criticisms were continued over much the same period, Air-Vice Marshal R. I. Jones, Mr. Guthrie Moir and Dr. P. R. Duncan.

From the German side I was given highly important facts and impressions by Major-General Walter Gericke, now Commander of West Germany's first Airlanding Division, whose book *Da Gibt es Kein Zuruck* admirably conveys the atmosphere of the battle, and by Colonel A. Wittman who kindly sent on to me the relevant numbers of the Mountain-Troop Journal *Die Gebirgstruppe*. They will understand that the hard assessment that I have made, inevitably, of some aspects of German behaviour in no way diminishes my recognition of the distinction and gallantry of their personal conduct.

The maps were drawn with much skill by G. Hartfield Limited, and Mr. B. H. Kemball-Cook, now Headmaster of Bedford Modern School, and Mr. Savvas Theodosian made expert translations from the Greek.

ACKNOWLEDGEMENTS

Many people, some of whom I have never met, responded with the utmost courtesy to my requests for information and for permission to quote from their writings. Most of them are identified in the footnotes. I am very grateful to Colonel Neville Blair, Lieutenant-Colonel J. D. L. Boyle, Major-General Ian Campbell, Mr. F. S. Charles, Sir Geoffrey Cox, Dr. C. R. Croft, Mr. Henry Daston, Lieutenant-Colonel A. Duncan, Brigadier Sir Bernard Fergusson, Major R. W. Fleming, Captain T. A. Francis, Mr. E. R. M. Gawne, Admiral J. H. Godfrey, Major-General F. C. C. Graham, Mr. Robert Harling, Mr. Edward Howell, Captain Sir Basil Liddell Hart, Mr. Robert Lush, Mr. Christopher Makin, Mr. W. E. Murphy, Mr. W. W. Oakley, Major T. V. Rabbidge, Captain A. W. F. Sutton, Mr. Evelyn Waugh, and Wing-Commander V. C. Woodward.

I must emphasize, however, that nobody shares responsibility for my views on the battle.

Finally I should like to acknowledge the efforts of Mrs. M. Barnett and Miss L. Mould, who at various times have helped me with my typescripts, and of my secretary, Mrs. C. E. Longden, who with no undue complaint has borne the weariest part of the enterprise.

PART ONE

THE ISLAND OF LEGEND

'The fundamental axiom in modern war is that an exact knowledge of weapons and equipment is necessary at the highest level of all as the essential basis, not only of strategy and tactics, but even, one may say, of policy itself.'

Professor A. V. Hill, House of Commons, 24 February, 1942

1

Hitler Strikes South

In the spring of 1941 the British cause against Germany was about to enter the period of its lowest fortune. Already things were bad enough. Hitler held the dominion of Europe after a series of victories unmatched by Napoleon. One after another the old continental allies had gone, some persuaded by fear or cupidity into uneasy accommodation with the conqueror, others crushed by expert force of arms. Among them had fallen the greatest of 1914-18; nearly a year had passed since France had paid a delayed price for the valour that had sustained her at the last gasp a generation earlier. In her place no new friends had appeared. The people of America, woefully misled by their ambassador in London, watched from the ringside, sceptical, wary and withdrawn. Russia actively aided the enemy. Far away, within the countries of the Empire, young men were gathering for the fight; few had yet been in action. At home thousands of recruits had begun to swell the beaten and fugitive Expeditionary Force that had escaped across the Channel. But nothing could disguise the fact that the army remained small, ill-equipped, and largely untrained.

Amidst so much catastrophe there had been some consolation. During the previous autumn a small company of fighter pilots, at high cost to themselves, had won reprieve from the imminent prospect of invasion. And with the turn of the year good news had come from the Middle East. Despite the threat looming within sight of Dover, the Prime Minister had been swift to recognize that the operations developing in North Africa had become second in importance only to the defence of Britain. Greatly daring he had not waited even for the conclusion of the vital conflict in the skies over southern England before sending reinforcement to Egypt.

This was to prove one of the vital decisions of the war. By the end of November 1940 the equivalent of an armoured division and two infantry divisions had set out upon the long and hazardous journey round the Cape of Good Hope. Within three months the first of these troops, together with a handful of hardened regulars from Palestine and India, had brought a sharp rebuff to Mussolini. In the Western Desert and in Abyssinia, General Wavell, the Commander-in-Chief in Cairo, had contrived a series of well-planned victories over greatly superior numbers of Italians. These achievements were now to be followed by fresh disaster.

For the Germans this had been a winter of enchantment. Their arms seemed touched with magic. One after another the traditional enemies, so formidable in the past, had gone down almost without a struggle. Every day the newspapers chanted their practised chorus of success. Poland, Norway, Denmark, Holland, Belgium, France – all now lay crushed beneath the mighty *Wehrmacht*; they were beginning to leave out Denmark which no longer seemed to add very much. And what reason could there be for not enlarging the list indefinitely? England next of course. Then Russia. After that the decadent Americans and the rest of the New World. Finally, it would have to come, the treaty partners in the Far East, the Yellow Men, Japan. Even the doubters were silenced. Not that they had ever been less than enthusiastic about the slaughter and enslavement of the nations of Europe. But there had been a handful of elderly people, survivors from the trenches of the First World War most of them, who had been unable to restrain some anxiety about the rate at which it was all happening. Like Napoleon's mother they had felt reservations. '*Pourvu que ça dure* . . . ' was the thought that had nagged at them. Now they, too, were greatly reassured.

Such was the general sentiment. It was not shared by all who had been in the front line. Some of the soldiers were already beginning to think of the comforts of home, and a few hundred pilots had reason to suspect that the war against England was not yet finished. Moreover, the High Command understood that in the Battle of Britain the *Luftwaffe* had suffered defeat; the elaborate arrangements for a victory march down the Champs-Elysées had been a little premature.

Hitler himself was under no illusion. After the failure of his peace overture, made in the Reichstag on 19 July, he had persisted, in doubt and reluctance, with preparations for a landing on the English coast. But by 18 September he could see that Goering's pilots had failed to gain the necessary mastery over the

Royal Air Force. There could be no hope that England might be invaded in 1940. He was forced to recognize that this must mean the end of his plan for a short war, the conception upon which all his strategy had been based. Suddenly the prospect of victory by direct conquest had receded far into the future, since if invasion were not accomplished this year it could be attempted only after a complete re-orientation of German power in the direction of new air and sea forces. There would, of course, be no real difficulty. But in the meantime much could be expected to happen. Not only would the British continue to make fervent efforts to help themselves. There was also the likelihood that they would receive increasing aid from the United States. He was thus bound to conclude that he must now ensure for his European empire the supplies in food and war material that would enable it to compete with the industrial resources of the western world. Above all he had become more than ever dependent upon the continued delivery of the grain and oil that had recently been made available to him by the unnatural liaison with Russia.

This was a matter of some delicacy since he and his henchmen had already decided to attack their new-found friends in the east; indeed fulfilment of the traditional German policy of the *Drang nach Osten* had always been his main purpose, disguised though it might be as expediency demanded. From the moment of victory in the west his thoughts had turned to this central item in his programme of conquest. Now was the time to seize the *Lebensraum* so long coveted by his predecessors, while in the same stroke settling for good all difficulties about supply. At a series of conferences in the Berghof on 29, 30 and 31 July he had announced his intention to the startled but fascinated members of his Staff. The thing might wait if England were successfully eliminated that autumn. On the other hand, as General Halder, the Chief-of-Staff to the Army, noted in his diary, 'in the event that invasion does not take place' the destruction of Russia might do much to discourage America by increasing Japanese power in the Far East. If they started in May 1941 they would have 'five months in which to finish the job'.[1]

Here was emerging once again the danger of a war on two fronts, that classic German predicament to which Hitler had ascribed so many of Prussia's difficulties in the past, and which he had himself solemnly undertaken to avoid. But there was a way in

[1] Halder, 31 July 1940

which the risks might be lessened. If he could continue to beguile
Stalin into a false sense of security it might be possible to strike a
crippling blow against Britain in the Mediterranean before he
started his great onslaught to the east. Thus, as the year 1940
drew to an end Hitler, like Churchill, was turning his eyes
southward towards the Mediterranean.

Raeder and Goering, his Commanders-in-Chief of the Navy and
of the *Luftwaffe*, had already suggested this line of approach. At
first it had all seemed simple enough. The aim would be to close
the Mediterranean at each end. And in June, at the time of the
French collapse, Franco had declared that Spain would be 'ready
under certain conditions to enter the war on the side of Germany
and Italy',[2] a contribution which should account for Gibraltar.
Before the end of the month the Joint Planning Staff in London
had come to accept the probability that Hitler would move
through Spain. 'At any time that Germany chooses,' it reported,
'and whatever line Spain may take, the naval base at Gibraltar
can, therefore, be denied to us. We believe that sooner or later
Germany will take this action'.[3] A few weeks later Churchill had
sought to forestall the blow by persuading the colonial French to
invite a British landing in West Africa, an attempt which foun-
dered, on 23 September, in the affair at Dakar.

Franco, however, was a realist. More significant to him than
any other event that autumn had been the failure of Germany to
invade England. He was also impressed by the limitation placed
by the Royal Navy upon his oil imports from America. In the
words of Chester Wilmot 'He could obtain sufficient oil from
Britain and America to stay at peace; could he extract from
Hitler enough to go to war?'

On 23 October Hitler met the wary Spanish leader at Hendaye,
and found him surprisingly intransigent. Nevertheless, in January
the Führer felt constrained to make a further approach; with no
better success. General Student, the Commander-in-Chief of the
airborne forces, had reported that Gibraltar could not be taken by
parachute attack alone. For this reason, says Student, 'the plan
was changed into the bigger one of capturing Gibraltar by an
attack from the mainland. Eight divisions from France were to race
through Spain. This depended on the Spanish agreeing to let us
through. Hitler did not want to take the risk of having to fight a

---

[2] Chester Wilmot, p. 59
[3] Gwyer, Official History, *Grand Strategy*, Vol. III, Part I, p. 7

way through Spain. He tried to persuade Franco, but Franco would not agree.'[4]

Even worse than this rebuff was the obstruction to Hitler's plans caused by the activities of his old friend and supporter Mussolini.

For more than a year Mussolini had been reduced to a role in which he could do little but contemplate, with increasing jealousy and distrust, the dazzling exploits of his rival in the north. 'For Mussolini,' wrote Ciano, his Foreign Secretary and son-in-law, 'the idea of Hitler waging war, and, worse still, winning it, is altogether unbearable'.[5] He was also highly incensed at the manner in which Hitler, who for many years had accorded him respect if not deference, was now more and more inclined to leave him out of his confidence. Only at the last moment had the Germans told him of their purpose in Poland. No less galling was the manner in which Hitler had sent his troops into Rumania on 17 October, a mere three days after an Axis meeting in the Brenner Pass at which he had let fall no hint of any such intention. This was no way to treat a man who regarded himself, in Ciano's phrase, as 'the Dean of Dictators'.[6]

Mussolini determined, therefore, to find some means of restoring his dignity. 'Hitler always faces me with a *fait accompli*,' he told Ciano, 'this time I am going to pay him back in his own coin. He will find out from the papers that I have occupied Greece. In this way equilibrium will be re-established.'[7]

Such was the motive, characteristically petulant and ill-judged, which a few days later led him to invade Greece from Albania. No more than three divisions were available for the attack, a force the Germans were quick to recognize as 'entirely inadequate'.[8] Almost without thought he had entered upon a course which was to lead to fiasco within a week, and bring grave consequences both to himself and his partner.

Hitler soon realized that the spectacle of Italian confusion on the Albanian frontier had 'accentuated the tendency of certain nations to avoid becoming entangled with us and to await the outcome of events'.[9] Moreover, he saw that if the British should now be invited to Greece their aircraft would be able to threaten

[4] Liddell Hart, *The Other Side of the Hill*, p. 166   [5] Chester Wilmot, p. 63
[6] Ibid., p. 63   [7] Ibid., p. 63
[8] Jodl and Schniewind, Nov. 1940, quot. Chester Wilmot, p. 64
[9] Chester Wilmot, p. 66, Hitler to Mussolini, 20 Nov. 1940

the Rumanian oil refineries at Ploesti, the source of something like two-thirds of the special fuel required by the *Luftwaffe*. This he could scarcely endure. Nothing was more vital to him than oil. 'I am determined, Duce,' he wrote, 'to react with decisive forces against any British attempt to establish a substantial air base in Thrace'.[10] He therefore decided, sometime in November, that he must contrive to establish bases in Rumania and Bulgaria, and from these attack Greece in the following spring.[11]

By this time, Mussolini's aggression, following so soon upon the German entry into Rumania, had aroused Russian doubts about Hitler's intentions in the Balkans. These suspicions were sharply increased as soon as it became clear that his troops were stealthily moving towards Bulgaria. Hitler knew that he must not press the Russians too far. It was essential to preserve Stalin's wavering confidence until the moment when he could attack him. He was therefore forced to attempt conciliation. In accordance with his usual technique, this included a formal offer of alliance. Hitherto Stalin had 'tried his very best to work loyally'[12] with him. Now he was becoming less gullible, or perhaps more aware of the risks of playing for time. He still had no inkling of his immediate danger. Nevertheless, through Molotov, and in a memorandum which he sent to Berlin, he made counter-proposals which were a test of German good faith. He was prepared to give Hitler a free hand in the west in return for a guarantee of Russian bases in Bulgaria and the Dardanelles, coupled with the withdrawal of German troops from Finland, an exchange which would have deprived Germany of access to the oil sources in Iraq and Iran, and at the same time rendered an attack eastward infinitely more difficult.

Hitler was outraged. Indignantly he complained to Raeder 'Stalin is nothing more than a cold-blooded blackmailer'.[13] But the moral was clear. He could no longer rely upon Russia for the supplies that would enable him to build up his strength for the conquest of Britain. He concluded that the attack upon Russia must be made sooner rather than later.

And so he came to a decision. At the earliest possible moment he would strike east. This was the moment so long anticipated in *Mein Kampf*. For many years he had been obsessed with thoughts of the rich Ukranian plains and the Caucasian oil that lay beyond

---

[10] Chester Wilmot, p. 66, Hitler to Mussolini, 20 Nov. 1940
[11] Gwyer, Official History, *Grand Strategy*, Vol. III, Part I, p. 7
[12] Churchill, Vol. II, p. 511   [13] Führer Naval Conferences, 8 Jan. 1941

them. Now he would take this prize. Already, on 18 December, he had issued to his Commanders-in-Chief his famous Directive No. 21. It began:

The German Armed Forces must be prepared, even before the end of the war against England, to overthrow Soviet Russia in a rapid campaign (Operation Barbarossa).[14]

All was to be ready by 5 May 1941. He was confident that by the autumn he would have crushed all effective resistance, and established 'a screen against Asiatic Russia along the general line Volga-Archangel'.[15] The concept might fall somewhat short of Clausewitzian orthodoxy. But it seems unlikely that he was aware of any contradiction. No doubt he felt that in occupying western Russia he would also ensure the destruction of the enemy forces. He knew that Roosevelt, now re-elected, might eventually bring America into the war at the side of Britain. But Russia should be defeated long before opposition from the west could become formidable. Thus he would avoid the worst consequences of a war on two fronts. Count von Schulenburg,[16] the German Ambassador at Moscow, must not know of the new development lest the knowledge impair the efficiency of his reassurances to Stalin.

In the meantime, before the start of the Russian campaign, it should still be possible to inflict serious damage on the British position in the Middle East.

If we encompass the fall of Gibraltar [he had written to Mussolini, 20 November], we shall bolt the western door of the Mediterranean and ensure the final establishment of the authority of Pétain over North Africa. . . . By the judicious employment of our air forces the Mediterranean should become, in three or four months, the tomb of the British Fleet.[17]

There was no need to point out that, for the present, his main purpose in this theatre of operations would be to safeguard his southern flank; he had not told Mussolini of his designs on Russia. From choice his intervention in the Mediterranean would certainly not, at this stage, have included a diversion of troops sufficient to occupy Greece.

By the beginning of February 1941 he was ready to acknowledge that there would be no decisive results in the Mediterranean until he had completed his campaign in the east. Franco, impressed by

---

[14] Hitler War Directive No. 21   [15] Ibid.

[16] Schulenburg was executed by the Gestapo on 10 Nov. 1944

[17] Chester Wilmot, p. 66, Hitler to Mussolini, 20 Nov. 1940

the defeat of Graziani's Army in Cyrenaica, and by such events as the bombardment of Genoa by the Royal Navy, was proving increasingly difficult. 'The logical development of the facts,' he remarked, 'has left the circumstances of October far behind'.[18]

Thus, for Hitler, the winter had been full of surprising frustrations. 'He had been double-crossed by Mussolini,' observes Chester Wilmot, 'blackmailed by Stalin and jilted by Franco.' Some of his advisers, in particular Raeder, were insistent that he should at least make an attempt to reduce Malta. But he determined that all else must now be made subsidiary to the assault against Russia.

While Hitler thus reluctantly found his attention diverted more and more towards the scene of Mussolini's disastrous adventure in Greece, the members of the British Cabinet had also begun to look with interest in the same direction. They did so in a mood of bland optimism induced by the victory they had seen achieved by the Royal Air Force against the *Luftwaffe*, and encouraged by the resounding news of Wavell's exploits in the desert.

On 19 April 1939, before the outbreak of war, the British Government had guaranteed the independence of Greece as part of a final and forlorn attempt to discourage Germany from the course upon which she was by then so clearly determined. During the next few months events had unfolded in the sad fashion then prevailing among all the small nations of Europe that felt themselves threatened by the dictators. The Greeks, under the Fascist government of Metaxas, had become ever more punctilious in avoidance of any action that might seem to give the slightest offence either to Italians or Germans. But shortly before dawn on 28 October they were made sharply aware that this had availed them nothing. Mussolini delivered his ultimatum and attacked from Albania at the same moment.

Immediately the Cabinet in London found itself faced with a decision. The guarantee to Poland had done nothing to stave off disaster for the unfortunate Poles. By contrast, the ferocity and success with which the Greeks now turned upon their Italian attackers soon began to win the admiration of the free world. For the first time one of the chosen victims was outdoing the aggressor in dealing blow for blow. Now that it had come to the point could anything be done to help her?

[18] Chester Wilmot, p. 74, Franco to Hitler on 26 Feb. 1941

There were many factors to be considered. Certainly it was time to be fighting again somewhere. And it would be helpful if the Greeks could be kept going. To this might be added the warming thought that a small foray in Greece might perhaps be undertaken without any great risk – provided, of course, that it was only against Italians; a Blenheim squadron had in fact been sent to Athens within three days of the Italian attack. On the other hand, if the Germans should come in, this would make a difference. What particular difference, in terms of man-power, air strength, and armoured forces, was something that nobody was disposed to inquire into very closely. It was no doubt too painful, in November 1940, to reflect that the Germans were estimated to have available at least 150 divisions,[19] supported by 6,000 front-line aircraft,[20] eager for new slaughter and conquest after their triumph in western Europe, and for all that was known, inactive and uncommitted. Wavell, at that time, could scarcely dispose of 25,000 front-line troops to meet the formidable advance of the 200,000 Italians who had already begun to dribble across the border west of Mersa Matruh in their advance towards Alexandria.

Finally, there was the question of national honour. In a series of telegrams the Prime Minister discussed this aspect of the situation with his Foreign Secretary, Mr. Anthony Eden, who was visiting Wavell's Headquarters in Cairo. There was a danger, he pointed out on 2 November, that the 'whole Turkish position' might be 'lost through proof that England never tries to keep her guarantees'.[21] It seemed likely that if no effort were made in Greece the effect upon British prestige in the Balkans, indeed throughout the world, might well be calamitous.

At the beginning of November the Chiefs of Staff, endorsing an appreciation by the Joint Planning Staff, decided that the national honour could not stand unsupported against overwhelming tanks and aircraft. They knew nothing of Wavell's projected counter-stroke in the Western Desert. Nevertheless, at the instigation of Sir John Dill, the Chief of the Imperial General Staff, they opposed

---

[19] Churchill, Vol. III, p. 338, says that '164 divisions rolled eastward' into Russia on 22 June 1941

[20] Ibid., p. 695. The Air Ministry estimated the German front-line strength to have been some 6,000 machines on 1 May 1940. It was believed, or at least hoped, that replacement had been slightly less than destruction during the subsequent eight months

[21] Churchill, Vol. II, p. 474, Prime Minister to Mr. Eden (at G.H.Q. Middle East) 2 Nov. 1940

the idea of sending an expeditionary force to Greece. At the same
time they emphasized that Crete, by far the largest and most
important of the Greek Islands, should be firmly secured as a
naval and air base. This simple and unsophisticated military
assessment is of interest in the light of later events.[22]

But suppose that the Germans should decide to take a hand in
Greece. There was reason for believing that nothing could stop
them. This consideration might not make an agreeable topic for
the Government, but it surely demanded the closest scrutiny by
the three Armed Services. The Middle East Joint Planning Staff
had referred to the possibility in a paper issued on 30 October.
They suggested that in such circumstances it would be necessary
to place 'a brigade group' in Crete. They also expressed their views
about the naval base at Suda Bay, maintaining that ' . . . if the
mainland should be occupied by German forces Suda could not
be used by the Royal Navy by daylight',[23] an opinion which even
at that time might have been thought to be no more than a firm
statement of the obvious.

On 8 January, a month after the beginning of the great advance
in the desert, the Chiefs of Staff decided that to send substantial
forces to the Balkans in the face of a German intervention would
be to invite a second and even more disastrous 'Dunkirk'. That
same day, according to Churchill, the Defence Committee, under
his own formidable chairmanship,

. . . agreed that in view of the probability of an early German advance
into Greece *through Bulgaria* it was of the first importance, from the
political point of view, that we should do everything possible, by
hook or by crook, to send at once to Greece the fullest support within
our power.[24]

And on 10 January the Prime Minister, fortified by the agree-
ment of General Smuts, despatched to Wavell explicit orders to
help Greece:

Nothing must hamper capture of Tobruk, but thereafter all operations in Libya are subordinated to aiding Greece . . . we expect and
require prompt and active compliance with our decisions, for which
we bear full responsibility.

With this telegram, so he was to write later, the Chiefs of Staff
were 'in accord',[25] despite the opinion which they had expressed
a mere two days earlier.

[22] Davin, p. 6   [23] Middle East Joint Planning Staff Paper 30, 30 Oct. 1940
[24] Churchill, Vol. III, p. 14   [25] Ibid., p. 17

Such vacillation was typical of the time. At this stage, as Churchill was to point out later, the Cabinet intentions 'did not amount to the offer to Greece of an army, but to special and technical units'. Nevertheless, these special units included, as the commander in Cyrenaica saw with dismay, most of the desert air force.

Meanwhile the Greeks, already attacked by the Italian cat, maintained their painful concern not to provoke the German tiger. Wavell, together with Air Marshal Longmore, who was commanding the Royal Air Force in the Middle East, flew to Athens on 13 January. For four days they conferred with Metaxas and General Papagos, the Greek Commander-in-Chief. Despite the Fascist tendencies of his régime Metaxas had been staunchly determined that his country should defend itself to the utmost whatever the politics of the invader. He was now dying of a cancer of the throat. From Wavell he heard that the only help that could be sent to Greece immediately would consist of a single artillery regiment and perhaps some sixty armoured cars. This offer he declined as too small to be of any value. It could only provide a pretext for a German attack. Metaxas had some hope that the Germans might hesitate to affront Russia by moving through Bulgaria. A few days later he was dead.

Papagos had been no more enthusiastic. British intervention 'would not only fail to produce substantial military and political results in the Balkans, but would also, from a general allied point of view, be contrary to the sound principles of strategy'. The 'two or three divisions' which might reach Greece by the end of March would 'come in more useful in Africa'.[26] There was thus still no call upon Britain for the full implementation of her guarantee.

Not until the middle of February 1941 could the Greek leaders bring themselves to accept the inevitable. But by now the intensity of German preparation in Rumania and Bulgaria made it certain that a further onslaught, this time from the Germans, was about to fall upon their tormented country. They therefore invited the Foreign Secretary to Athens, and with him Sir John Dill.

The two men went first to Cairo. Here Eden found encouragement for his own sanguine views and the C.I.G.S. contrived to overcome his misgivings. The city was in the full flush of triumph

[26] Papagos, p. 315

after the victory over the Italians in Cyrenaica. None of the three Commanders-in-Chief revealed any uncertainty. Even Wavell raised no demur. A few weeks earlier he had pointed out: 'As in the last war Germany is on interior lines and can move more quickly to attack Greece or Turkey than we can support them.'[27] But now, on 12 February, he signalled obediently to Churchill:

We will do our best to frustrate German plans in the Balkans.[28]

The great hope was that a show of British strength might provoke action by Yugoslavia, and even perhaps by Turkey. The Foreign Secretary cabled home on 20 February:

We are agreed we should do everything in our power to bring the fullest measure of help to Greeks at earliest possible moment. If the help that we can offer is accepted by the Greeks we believe that there is a fair chance of halting a German advance and preventing Greece from being overrun.

Some indication of the dream world which the Service Chiefs in Cairo had now begun to share with the politicians is afforded by the sentence with which Eden concluded his cable to London:

Limitation of our resources, however, especially in the air, will not allow of help being given to Turkey at the (same) time if Greece is to be supported on an effective scale.

This was undeniable. There were at that moment less than seven squadrons in Greece. But it may be questioned whether such language could be consistent with the slightest understanding of the air resources available in the Middle East, or of the transcendent influence which German air power must continue to exert upon every battlefield until it could be met on level terms.

On the same day a final admonition arrived from Churchill. They should not feel themselves 'obligated to a Greek enterprise' if in their hearts they felt that it could only lead to 'another Norwegian fiasco'.[29] But nothing could check the optimism of Eden. With the C.I.G.S. he again flew to Athens where he was informed that the Greeks were determined to resist this new threat of invasion whether given help or not. He needed no further encouragement. On 23 February he once more offered the support of an Expeditionary Force. This time it was accepted amidst protestations of mutual satisfaction.

As the critical moment approached, the outlook appeared progressively less inviting. The Turks were cautious, observing

---

[27] Terraine, p. 137   [28] Churchill, Vol. III, p. 59   [29] Ibid., p. 63

that the best time for them to enter the war would be after they had been attacked, and by now Admiral Cunningham, the Naval Commander-in-Chief in the Mediterranean, was doubtful if the formations that could be committed, 'particularly naval and air', would be 'equal to the strain'. He told the First Sea Lord that he felt sure that the Chiefs of Staff had been 'badly misinformed as to the numbers of fighter squadrons available'. But the spell cast by the Prime Minister was still upon him. He felt the decision to be 'absolutely right'.[30]

Not even Churchill could feel very cheerful by early March. On the 6th he wrote gloomily to Eden: '. . . We do not see any reasons for expecting success, except that of course we attach great weight to opinion of Dill and Wavell'. Here he was imputing to the soldiers a persuasion that had been his rather than their own. Indeed the shrewd sceptical Wavell, unbendingly taciturn as always, and reluctant perhaps to underline discouragements that might appear sufficiently obvious, was making little more than an acquiescence in political orders. On the other hand he had not offered the reasoned protest which the Prime Minister had invited. De Guignand, one of his staff officers, felt that he had himself failed to appreciate the true situation.[31] Certainly he never afterwards sought to evade responsibility. With a casual honesty unusual in defeated generals he wrote many years later 'The Service Chiefs recognized the dangers of the Greek expedition, but believed that there was a reasonable chance of defending Greece against German attack.'[32]

Thus Churchill was given no professional warning that the project was beyond the strength of the forces in the Middle East, and it was upon the freedom and integrity of such advice that he depended in his direction of the war. He was ready enough to chide and harry his commanders when they seemed to him to be dilatory, or to dismiss them when he judged it necessary, but he seldom overruled them, and unlike Lloyd George he backed them to the utmost while they held responsibility. Never, at any stage of the struggle can he have felt less inclined to restrain a local, and highly successful, Commander-in-Chief who promised 'a reasonable chance' of striking an effective blow against the enemy.

There was little enthusiasm from the Dominion governments,

[30] Heckstall-Smith and Baillie-Grohman, p. 32
[31] De Guignand, *Generals at War*, p. 15
[32] In an article for the *Army Quarterly*, Jan. 1950

and still less from Blamey and Freyberg, the generals who would be in charge of the Australian and New Zealand contingents that were to make up the core of the expedition. But they were under military orders, and subject to a Service loyalty that must necessarily be more restrictive than that appropriate to a Commander-in-Chief. On 15 March Blamey sent a message to Mr. Menzies, the Australian Prime Minister, whose reluctant involvement in the Greek decision was later to play a part in his loss of office:

> The plan is, of course, what I feared: piecemeal despatch to Europe. I am not criticizing the higher policy that has required it, but regret that it must take this dangerous form. However, we will give a very good account of ourselves.[33]

And Freyberg was afterwards to point out 'the difficulty of a subordinate commander criticizing the plans of superior officers'.[34]

Thus, at all levels, whether from lack of comprehension of the new forms of war, or out of obedience to Service tradition, those professional voices that might have spoken against the expedition remained silent.

Churchill himself now had few illusions. On 29 March he told Menzies, who was in London, that the 'real foundation' for the expedition was fear of the 'overwhelming moral and political repercussions of abandoning Greece'.[35] This was a motive cogent and worthy enough. But it was somewhat different from the windy talk of a Balkan front. The truth was that it had become plain that the Greek leaders, some of whom might have preferred the Germans to their own Communists, could not bring themselves to face the political consequences of a withdrawal from Albania. They preferred not to think about the Germans. This meant that there no longer existed any prospect even of delaying an advance into northern Greece from Yugoslavia and Bulgaria. Nor would there be enough troops available to man the projected Aliakmon line further south. Only Eden had no doubts. To Churchill's suggestion that perhaps it might be better, after all, to concentrate upon an advance to Tripoli he had replied on 7 March: 'In the existing situation we are all agreed that the course advocated should be followed and help given to Greece.'[36] And on 21 March he telegraphed to the Minister in Belgrade:

. . . so long as Yugoslavia is resolute to refuse passage, it should now

---

[33] Long, p. 19   [34] Ibid., p. 20   [35] Ibid., p. 19   [36] Churchill, Vol. III, p. 93

be difficult for the Germans to direct the attack on Greece with good prospects of success.[37]

A fortnight later he could still find reasons for confidence. While visiting forward troops near Katerini he noted that 'much work' had been done on the defences and that the position was 'naturally very strong'.[38]

One hope proved justified. In Belgrade there came a brave last minute *coup d'état*. Since the war the German documents have shown that the attitude to Germany of the Regent, Prince Paul, was less sympathetic than had been supposed. But for weeks he had been tempted by Hitler's suggestion that Yugoslavia should join the Tripartite Pact. In return his country might hope to be spared invasion. Moreover, there was the promise of reward at the expense of Greece. On 17 March his government had asked that account should be taken of 'Yugoslavia's interest in a territorial connexion with the Aegean Sea through the extension of her sovereignty to the city and harbour of Salonika'.[39] Hitler agreed. It would cost him nothing, and he was eager for his quick settlement in the Balkans. All the greater, therefore, was his fury when a few days later, on the 27th, a rising of young officers forced Paul into abdication. Without waiting for contact with the new government he ordered the immediate occupation of Yugoslavia and the postponement 'up to four weeks'[40] of the attack on Russia. By 6 April the plans for this awkward and unwanted operation were complete. On the same day he decided that the Russian invasion should begin on 22 June.

Thus his southern commitment had grown. He found himself embarking upon a campaign considerably more arduous than the minor operation which he had been contemplating against Greece. And it was important that all should be disposed of in the shortest possible time.

He accordingly increased his Balkan Force from eighteen to twenty-eight Divisions, of which twenty-four were already intended for 'Barbarossa'. Included among them were about a third of the mobile formations required for the first big encirclement movements in the east. After the war General Von Thoma, who had been Chief of Mobile Forces of the Army High Com-

[37] Avon, p. 227   [38] Ibid., p. 235

[39] Documents on German Foreign Policy 1918, Series D, Vol. XII (1937–1945) 1 Feb.–22 June, 1941

[40] Ibid.

mand, was to say that only 2,434 tanks had been available for the eastern front in June 1941, and that 800 of them had been brought back from the Balkans.[41] Bad weather must in any case have delayed the move into Russia, but Blumentritt, who was Chief-of-Staff of the Fourth Army in Poland, believed that it was 'the friction in the Balkans' as well as 'the exceptional weather' that 'caused the loss of four precious weeks',[42] and Hitler himself was to maintain of his Russian campaign that he had 'only failed by a short head – exactly five weeks'; he had 'lost them because of the confidence' which he had placed in his 'dearest and most admired friend Mussolini'.[43] Thus it may well be that the revolution in Belgrade did something to turn the course of the war by contributing to Germany's failure in Russia. For this British policy can claim little credit. The Serbs had been influenced slightly, if at all, by what was happening further south. Theirs had been a sudden patriot gesture rather than a considered political enterprise. Still less had it any military significance.

In Greece the news of this flash of defiance inspired a brief and final flare of optimism. Even Churchill felt a sudden, unreasoning renewal of confidence.

When a month ago [he cabled to Mr. Fadden, the acting Prime Minister of Australia], we decided upon sending an army to Greece it looked rather a blank military adventure dictated by *noblesse oblige*. Thursday's events in Belgrade show the far-reaching effects of this and other measures we have taken on whole Balkan situation. German plans have been upset, and we may cherish renewed hopes of forming a Balkan front with Turkey, comprising about seventy Allied Divisions from the four Powers concerned.[44]

These hopes had no contact with reality. Nothing could halt the march of events. On 6 April the Germans attacked Yugoslavia and Greece, simultaneously, and without warning. Two days later 17,000 civilians lay dead beneath the ruins of Belgrade, and the crawling lines of Yugoslav transport, with their ox-drawn wagons and heavy-laden soldiers, had been scattered and destroyed by the *Luftwaffe*. At the Piræus, near Athens, the only substantial harbour installations in southern Greece had been wrecked by bombing. It was already clear to General Wilson, who was in command of the British and Empire army in Greece,

---

[41] Chester Wilmot, p. 77, *n.* 1   [42] Ibid., p. 77
[43] The *Daily Telegraph*, 19 Oct. 1962, p. 14, quot. F. W. Deakin
[44] Churchill, Vol. III, p. 152

that the best he could hope for was to get his force out of the country with as much dignity as possible. They would kill a few Germans on the way back, but there could be no hope of orderly withdrawal through a defended bridgehead. Nobody had thought of organizing one.

Within a few days yet another British Expeditionary Force was struggling to contain itself within the chaos of defeat. And this time almost entirely without air support. In Norway the Germans had themselves been isolated at the end of a long sea communication, and at Dunkirk a dwindling reserve of Spitfires and Hurricanes, unseen and unappreciated by the hard-pressed soldiers, had succeeded in keeping most of the German planes at bay. Both evacuations had been carried through in daylight. In Greece no such cover was possible. A few dozen Hurricanes fought with skill and daring until no airfields remained to sustain the survivors. They could not prevent the destruction of the ports, nor protect the infantry from the searching pursuit of the Messerschmitts and Stukas. For the ground forces movement on the roads was possible only at night.

In general it did not go badly. The Anzac corps, including the 6th Australian and 2nd New Zealand Divisions, withdrew 300 miles in just over a fortnight, under constant threat from flanking movements by German armour, but again and again disengaging successfully at the last moment to spend the nights in headlong lorry drives to the south. Every visible movement was attacked from the air.

For two days [wrote an Australian correspondent to *The Times* on 19 April], I have been bombed, machine-gunned, and shot at by all and sundry. German Stukas have blown two cars from under me and strafed a third . . . all day and all night there have been waves of Germans in the skies. Eighteen Messerschmitts strafed us on the road last evening. Bullets ripped the trucks and one was destroyed, but nobody was lost except the truck. Before that, the convoy I was in was attacked seven times in two hours, but not once was the convoy disorganized or broken up. The Germans are using a fantastic amount of aircraft, more than I ever saw in Norway under similar conditions of terrain. Goering must have a third of his air force operating here and it is bombing every nook and cranny, hamlet, village and town in its path . . .

The Royal Air Force was given a last opportunity to demonstrate that it was superb in quality even when almost negligible in numbers. On 20 April fourteen Hurricanes, attacking more than a hundred aircraft over Athens, shot down fourteen of the enemy for the loss of half their own machines.

The troops were cynical but not dismayed. For a few days after their arrival in Greece there had been some hopes for the new front. But the incessant air attacks, and the subsequent retreat, had come as no real surprise. All knew that it was futile to hope for anything better until the army could be provided with air support. The enemy radio made much play with the current London musical hit *Run, Rabbit, Run*. This was regarded as fair comment, rather better than might have been expected from the Germans. Certainly it was a pity to be leaving Greece so near to Anzac Day, 25 April. But the Australians and the New Zealanders were not worrying about that. Next time it would be different.

The worst regret was for the unfortunate Greeks. The troops had quickly come to feel both affection and admiration for these people who had not paused to count the cost before seeking to defend themselves with their primitive equipment against the most powerful war machine the world had ever known. Unreasonable though the sentiment might be, they could not leave them now without some sense of guilt. They would not have been surprised to hear reproaches and accusations of betrayal. Yet all the way to Athens, and on down the roads to the beaches, they met only kindness and expressions of goodwill. The young men of Greece were still far away to the north where they had won such gallant success in their mountain battles against the Italians. Soon they must be cut off from the rear by this unprovoked assault from their new enemy. But their women and children, and the old men, gathered in the doorways of their shattered homes, asking only that the British should return. A colonel of the 1st Armoured Brigade described the scene as the long column of battered trucks entered Athens:

No one who passed through the city with Barrowclough's brigade will ever forget it. Nor will we ever think of the Greek people without the warm recollection of that morning – 25 April, 1941. Trucks, portées and men showed plainly the marks of twelve hours battle, and the hundred and sixty miles march through the night. We were nearly the last British troops they would see and the Germans might be on our heels; yet cheering, clapping crowds lined the streets and pressed about our cars, so as almost to hold us up. Girls and men leapt on the running boards to kiss or shake hands with the grimy, weary gunners. They threw flowers to us and ran beside us crying: 'Come back – You must come back again – Goodbye – Good luck'.[45]

To all this the men replied with rough fervour that they would indeed be back. But they felt the emptiness of their reassurance. What would happen in the meantime? What would the Germans do to these people?

And so the army took to its boats – from the open beaches near Athens, or from the coast of the Peloponnesus. As so often before, in the early stages of so many continental wars, the Navy came to rescue the harried and pursued survivors of an inadequate army. The main evacuations were carried out in brigade groups. Within a few minutes brisk young naval officers had come ashore to issue their instructions. Soon cheerful seamen were greeting their jaded guests with cups of cocoa.

At the same time small parties of all Services seized their chance in vessels of every kind, some of them manned by the Merchant Service, and some by resolute Greeks. Night after night, freighters, tankers, tugs, passenger steamers, caiques, and even rowing boats, slipped away between the darkened shapes of the Greek Islands, making what haste they might to escape before the bombers should catch them at dawn. Many came to disaster. In an effort to embark her full number the transport *Slamat* delayed too long. At first light she was sighted, and quickly sunk by dive bombers. Two destroyers, *Diamond* and *Wryneck*, picked up the survivors, but were themselves both sunk at noon. From the three ships there remained alive one naval officer, forty-one ratings, and eight soldiers.[46] Most of the wounded below decks, and many of the civilians on board suffered a cruel death when the *Hellas* was bombed and burnt to the water line while still in the Piraeus.

Before the end of April the last organized parties of the British had left Greece, bearing with them such weapons as they could carry and leaving their dead upon the ground.

Most of them went no further than Crete. In order to make the best use of the limited shipping it had been decided to use the island as a staging area. The convoys were given protection by the remnants of the air contingents. From the three Cretan airfields the young pilots continued to fight with the utmost resolution

[45] Waller, Lieut.-Col. R. P., *Journal of the Royal Artillery* July 1945, 'With the 1st Armoured Brigade in Greece'

[46] Cunningham, p. 354

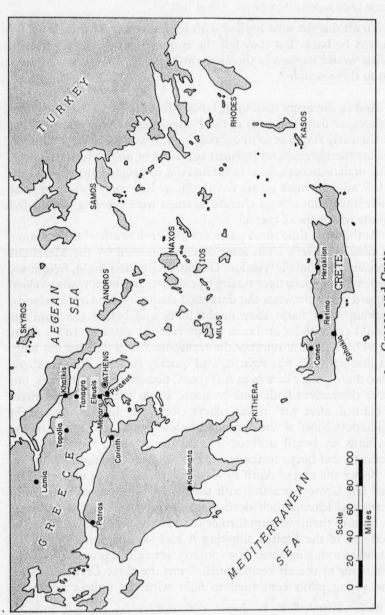

1. Greece and Crete

against overwhelming odds. But they could not do much. Left largely to their own resources the ships made shift to protect themselves by manoeuvre, and by firing every weapon that could be mustered. In this way they came through, most of them, seldom however without fresh dead and wounded to be laid among the casualties from Greece.

Behind the campaign in Greece there had lain the centuries-old tradition that Britain, the great sea power, should be able to raid the continent at will, choosing such points as might seem to offer advantage, sure in the confidence that the Navy would secure withdrawal if the enemy pressure should become too strong. 'At Dunkirk,' declares Chester Wilmot, 'Hitler restored to Britain the strategic freedom of action which she had lost twenty-five years before.'[47]

Not that it is easy to see how this freedom of action could have availed very much had it not later been for the efforts of the Russians; Correlli Barnett has pointed out that 'The Sommes and the Passchendaeles' of 1939–45 were fought at 'Leningrad, Stalingrad and Moscow'.[48] Nor was it only the vast commitment in France, and the primary need to destroy the mass of the German Army, that had forced a change in British policy during the earlier war. Another influence had been that of improved land communications. Ancient traditions had flickered to life in the attack on the Dardanelles – until the threat of German support along the railway through Bulgaria had finally impelled Bonar Law and others to the conclusion that Gallipoli must be evacuated.[49] Before the end of the Second World War the new factor of air power, now working in favour of the western allies, and operated in conjunction with naval strength, was to revitalize the old strategy.

But in the spring of 1941 none of this was perceived in London, where present limitations were understood no better than future possibilities were foreseen. A year later, in the House of Commons, a civilian voice was to reveal something of this failure. 'The fundamental axiom in modern war,' said Professor Hill on 24 February 1942, 'is that an exact knowledge of weapons and equipment is necessary at the highest level of all as the essential basis, not only of strategy and tactics, but even, one may say, of policy itself.'

[47] Chester Wilmot, p. 65   [48] Corelli Barnett, *The Sword-bearers*, p. 211
[49] Beaverbrook, *Politicians and the War*, p. 255

At the time of their Balkan campaign, Hitler's massive ground forces were invulnerable on the mainland of Europe, their advantage of interior lines, so potent twenty-five years before, now magnified ten-fold by the support of the ubiquitous *Luftwaffe*. This truth had not been apparent to Wavell, nor to the Chiefs of Staff in England, nor to the Cabinet. Above all it had not enforced itself upon Churchill himself, whose personal mirage, with less reason than in 1915, had once again enticed him into a perilous landing from the Aegean. None of these had yet learnt that for so long as the enemy held air superiority any serious venture upon the occupied coast of Europe must end in costly disaster.

Never for a moment had there existed the slightest prospect of 'halting a German advance'. Nor does it require the knowledge of hindsight to appreciate this fact. It should have been plain in the light of what was already known of enemy strength, and from the experience that had been gained from the defeats suffered in Norway and France. All the more so in that it was not yet suspected that Germany had begun to mobilize for the move against Russia. Acceptance of the truth need not have precluded all action in Greece. Immediate measures to harass and delay the enemy were both possible and desirable provided that the Greeks had been ready to accept the situation in such terms. Nearly three years later Eden sought reassurance upon the subject of Greece after a happy day spent with his old friend 'Jumbo' Wilson. The General proved 'rocklike' in saying that the campaign had been 'right militarily', an answer which no doubt gave the comfort intended, but revealingly Wilson then added that they would have done better to 'travel lighter',[50] a comment which at once made nonsense of the presumption of permanence upon which the whole enterprise had been based.[51] In his pessimistic signal of 6 March the Prime Minister had exposed his dawning realization of the extent to which such help was likely to be limited. 'If on their own they resolve to fight,' he had said of the Greeks, 'we must to some extent share their ordeal'. The pity was that able and responsible men, in their eagerness to do more, should have allowed themselves to be seduced by empty fancies. And it was unwise to have

[50] Avon, p. 408

[51] In *The Business of War*, Sir John Kennedy, who was Director of Military Operations from 1940 to 1943, says that at the time of the campaign he noted in his diary that Wavell had committed 'major mistakes', as, for example, 'in Greece where he would have sent five divisions (one of them armoured) and lost them, had the Germans given him a little more time'

permitted those fancies to become so widely known. Later many would be ready to proclaim their earlier wisdom. No leading figure was very wise at the time. General Brooke was to maintain that he had always 'lamented'[52] the fact that Dill, his predecessor as Chief of the Imperial General Staff, had given sanction to the attempt to take on the Germans in Greece. Such an attempt had violated the sacred military principle of concentration.

Neither he, nor anyone else of importance, had ever said that without an air force it was impossible.

Thus far only the troops had learnt this simple lesson. It was characteristic of the first two years of the war that with increasing remoteness from the front line the less appeared the importance of the *Luftwaffe*. In Cairo there was still appearing a War Office Instruction that talked of 'Forming Two's' as a precaution at the sight of enemy aircraft. And much favoured in official circles was the story of the man who had brought down a Messerschmitt with a rifle. The soldier who had been in action did not find this advice impressive. If he had an effective weapon he fired it; if not, he dived for cover.

Upon every man who had been in Greece the experience had wrought a potent influence. Those who went on to Crete brought with them the beginning of an obsession about enemy aircraft. For weeks the German planes had dominated their actions, their thoughts, and their conversation. Later, precipitate retreat had weakened their confidence. Freyberg had noticed a 'loss of trust in themselves'. Even the ebullient Australians had been shaken by the air attacks despite their recent memories of victory in the Western Desert.

Paradoxically there was not a soldier who regretted that he had fought in vain. Admiration for the unfortunate Greeks remained universal. And a blow had been struck for honour at a time when honour appeared to have passed for ever from the calculation of nations. This was something to be noted by Europe and the world; indeed by all who remained free or hoped to regain freedom. Nor did the troops feel any chagrin at having been thrown off the Continent. They knew it had not been their fault. And obscurely they understood that it had happened many times before. In fact it always started that way. But they always got back in the end.

The value of the Greek enterprise is still discussed. Certainly

[52] Bryant, *The Turn of the Tide*, p. 203

Hitler had been forced, much against his will, into a campaign to secure his southern flank. This diversion, coupled with bad weather, delayed his attack upon Russia. But the credit lies with the Greeks themselves, for their valiant fight against the Italians, and with the Serbs for the *coup d'état* which replaced the government of Prince Paul. The first, and more important, of these events had been wholly spontaneous, an expression of national feeling that owed nothing to any outsider, and it is scarcely to be supposed, despite the claims made later by Eden, that diplomatic encouragement can have contributed much to the resolution of the renegade ministers in Belgrade. Both Greeks and Serbs had feared rather than welcomed the prospect of British support, making every effort, until the last moment, to propitiate the Germans. Better than their sanguine friends in Egypt they understood the meaning of the 150 divisions backed by 6,000 front line aircraft that waited, eager and uncommitted, beyond their northern borders.

This was the overwhelming strength that Eden and Wavell had sought to oppose with their two and a half divisions and their handful of Hurricanes and Gladiators. Blind to all reality, despite the experience of Norway and the Low Countries, they had convinced themselves that the venture offered 'a fair chance', whatever the Germans might do. Inevitably its military achievement was negligible. The best that can be said is that the presence of a British force on the mainland may have served to confirm Hitler in his conviction that Yugoslavia and Greece must be destroyed, thus perhaps contributing in a minor way to the postponement of 'Barbarossa', an effect undreamed of by Eden and Wavell at the time of their decision. Even this is doubtful. Hitler was to describe the intervention as the 'capital error'[53] which alone made possible the German reconquest of Cyrenaica, an observation which may be taken to indicate that the prospect of British air bases in Greece would by itself have sufficed to impel him to subdue the Balkans.

Disaster in the desert was not to be the only consequence of attempting the impossible in Greece. Soon another great prize was to be lost unnecessarily. But one thing it might be thought to have shown beyond misunderstanding – the new importance of aircraft. Here was a weapon that was changing the aspect of war no less completely than had the long bow, gunpowder, the flint-

[53] Deakin, p. 19

lock musket and the machine-gun. Yet the Commanders-in-Chief in Cairo, equally with the military leaders and the government at home, had failed to recognize what was happening. Nor did they now. To make it plain, one more lesson was required. The scene of this demonstration was to be the historic island of Crete.

2

A 'Second Scapa'

The War Cabinet in London had long been distantly aware of the inconvenience that might attend an enemy occupation of Crete. On the other hand, from the point of view of the Navy, Suda Bay would make an admirable fuelling base in the Eastern Mediterranean. During the early months of 1940 Greece was not yet at war, and it was important that the British should not be the first to violate her neutrality. At that time Italy offered the only immediate threat. It was agreed, therefore, that if Italy should invade Greece, a small French force from Syria would take the island into protective occupation. The collapse of France destroyed this understanding.

Six months later Italy duly launched her attack upon Greece. Later Churchill was to maintain that, from this moment, 'One salient strategic fact leapt upon us – CRETE! The Italians must not have it. We must get it first and at once.'[1] He could quote a formidable documentation to show that this was how he had felt at the time. Certainly the authorities in the Middle East had not lacked instruction.

On 29 October, twenty-four hours after Mussolini's troops had begun to cross the Albanian frontier, he was telegraphing to Mr. Eden, who had just met General Smuts in Khartoum:

We here are all convinced that an effort should be made to establish ourselves in Crete, and that risks should be run for this valuable prize.

And on the same day:

It seems of prime importance to hold the best airfield possible and a naval fuelling base at Suda Bay. Successful defence of Crete is invaluable aid to defence of Egypt. Loss of Crete to the Italians would be a grievous aggravation of all Mediterranean difficulties. So great a prize is worth the risk, and almost equal to a successful offensive in Libya. Pray after an examination of whole problem with Wavell and Smuts, do not hesitate to make proposals for action on large scale at

[1] Churchill, Vol. II, p. 472

expense of other sectors, and ask for any further aid you require from here, including aircraft and anti-aircraft batteries. We are studying how to meet your need. Consider your return to Cairo indispensable.[2]

Two days later a small force went ashore at Suda Bay bringing twenty anti-aircraft guns and a few naval pieces for coast defence. On 3 November the Prime Minister again telegraphed to Eden:

Gravity and consequence of Greek situation compels your presence in Cairo. However unjust it may be, collapse of Greece without any effort by us will have deadly effect on Turkey and on future of war. Greeks probably as good as Italians, and Germans not yet on the spot. Establishment of fuelling base and airfield in Crete to be steadily developed into permanent war fortresses (is) indispensable.[3]

And again that day, remembering perhaps his own efforts as First Lord of the Admiralty to prepare the great naval base at Scapa Flow in the years before 1914, he remarked, in a note to General Ismay, his personal staff officer, that he would like to see Suda Bay a 'second Scapa'.[4] Four days later he told Dill that the Cretan Division should be allowed to join the Greek forces on the mainland. The primary defence of the island, he believed, must depend upon the Navy. Nevertheless he did not agree that the two British and three remaining Greek battalions would be sufficient garrison. He felt that they should be reinforced by another 'three or four thousand additional British troops and a dozen guns'.[5] He insisted, moreover, that a reserve Cretan Division, fully equipped with small arms, should be formed and trained in the island:

Every effort should be made to rush arms and equipment to enable a reserve division of Greeks to be formed in Crete. Rifles and machine-guns are quite sufficient in this case. To keep a Greek division out of the battle on the Epirus front would be very bad, and to lose Crete because we had not sufficient bulk of forces there would be a crime.[6]

On 26 November he was writing to General Wavell:

... All good wishes to you ... and to the Admiral, who is doing so splendidly. I rejoice to hear that he finds Suda Bay 'an inestimable benefit'.[7]

[2] Davin, p. 6
[3] Churchill, Vol. II, p. 476, Prime Minister to C.I.G.S., 3 Nov. 1940
[4] Ibid., p. 472   [5] Ibid., p. 473
[6] Ibid., p. 477, Prime Minister to C.I.G.S., 7 Nov. 1940
[7] Ibid., p. 484

To Wavell the matter appeared less straightforward. He had other preoccupations. Unknown as yet to the Prime Minister, he was already preparing the great offensive that a few weeks later was to smash Mussolini's Desert Army. He wanted to avoid diversion from this central purpose. Crete seemed to be in no danger, even if Mussolini should succeed in overrunning the Greek mainland, a prospect which every day became less likely. Any aircraft sent to the island must be extremely vulnerable on the primitive landing grounds. Moreover he would need every plane to support his advance on Sidi Barrani. While the Cretan Division remained in the island it would surely be sufficient to send some infantry battalions. As for the anti-aircraft defences, he must do what he could, but Malta itself, at the very centre of the Mediterranean war scene, had not yet been equipped according to the anti-aircraft requirements that had been agreed upon two years before.

Such were the views he expressed at a conference in Cairo at the beginning of November. They were cabled home by Eden who plainly agreed with them. He had particular reason for doing so since he had now been told of the impending initiative in the Western Desert.

But the Prime Minister was not impressed. On 1 December, still indefatigable on the subject of Crete, he was addressing a detailed inquiry to General Ismay:

Exactly what have we got and done at Suda Bay (Crete) – i.e. troops, A.A. guns, coast defence guns, lights, wireless, R.A.F., nets, mines, preparation of aerodromes etc. ?

I hope to be assured that many hundreds of Cretans are working at strengthening the defences and lengthening and improving the aerodromes.[8]

These exhortations from the highest level brought little response. The months passed. No arms came for the Cretans. No reserve Cretan Division was formed. The inhabitants were not mobilized for the construction of the defences. Such activity as there was had neither vigour nor purpose.

This failure must be ascribed to the lack of higher direction. At Wavell's Headquarters no plan was devised for the defence of the island. None was even discussed. There was therefore no guidance over policy for the local commanders who followed each other in rapid succession. Nor was there any further advice from the Chiefs of Staff in London who no doubt felt, as Churchill certainly did, that all was going ahead under the informed encouragement of the command in the Middle East.

Some explanation can be found in Wavell's preoccupation with his western flank. To Churchill this consideration had come to mean little more than continued security against the Italian threat from Tripolitania. His first concern now lay with the Balkans. But Wavell was still looking towards Tripoli. After his startling success in Cyrenaica he had hoped to press his advantage in North Africa. This ambition was sharply extinguished by the obligation to mount the expedition to Greece. Moreover, with the turn of the year, he had incurred the added responsibility for the campaign in East Africa.

For three months everything prospered. But on 31 March Rommel's newly arrived tanks erupted into the extended British line south of Benghazi, drove back to the Egyptian frontier the thinned and dilapidated armoured units, isolated Tobruk, and captured the two leading desert generals, including O'Connor, the victor of Sidi Barrani. Within a fortnight Wavell was forced to divert an infantry brigade and a regiment of artillery to Iraq in order to deal with the revolt by Rashid Ali. For the rest of April he was reluctantly absorbed by the events in Greece, while in Syria there continued to develop the train of events that was to culminate in the distasteful campaign against the Vichy French. Throughout these months most of his supplies and reinforcements could reach him only after making the long and increasingly precarious journey round the Cape.

It is easy to see, therefore, that to him the fortification of Suda Bay had meant something less abstract than the 'steady development' recommended by Churchill. Every gun he sent to Crete meant one gun less in Greece or Malta or the Western Desert. And in these places things were happening. Crete, during the winter of 1940, was still an obscure island in the Mediterranean where the local citizens dozed in their wicker chairs while taking the afternoon sun. Very naturally he did not wish to tie up there large numbers of unemployed troops.

These uncertainties are reflected in the changes that were made in the command of the island. Between November 1940 and April 1941 six officers commanded in Crete, one of them coming round twice. None of them knew what he was expected to do. Brigadier

Tidbury, who was appointed on 3 November, was ordered to defend the whole island, in particular Suda Bay, with the help of the local Cretan Division. A few days later the Cretan Division departed for the mainland leaving him with an infantry battalion, two commando units, the original gunners, and the citizens of Crete. He appreciated that any attack would almost certainly be largely airborne, and that it would be likely to fall upon Suda Bay, Maleme, Retimo and Heraklion. He suggested that defences should be dug night and day. His stay, however, was brief. Such energy was not to be seen again for four months.

The officers who succeeded him were not told whether they were supposed to think in terms of the whole island. The main instruction now was to create an administrative base and to defend Suda Bay. Crete was to be a transit camp held by garrison troops. Yet no autonomy was permitted. Even the boots were sent back to Egypt for repair. And all proceeded at laggard pace. Not even the ominous march of events in the north brought any change.

Today the reason for this neglect is clear. Wavell had not, at first, believed the island to be in danger. Despite the approach of the Germans, he was relying on the Navy and the hundred miles of sea.

It seems unlikely [he wrote on 24 April, as the first British troops were leaving Greece] that the enemy will attempt a landing in force in Crete from the sea. An airborne landing is possible but not probable, since the landing force would be isolated without sea support. Scale of air attack on Crete will, however, undoubtedly be heavy, especially in view of presence in island of King of Greece and Government.[9]

There is nothing to suggest that he had heard of the conclusion reached earlier by the Middle East Joint Planning Staff that day-light supply through the northern ports would become impossible if the Germans should occupy the mainland.[10] To judge by their lack of activity none of the island commanders thought of this independently, though to do so should have required no great powers of deduction.

At last, somewhat late in the day, amidst the turmoil of the withdrawal from Greece, the Middle East Joint Planning Staff issued a paper about Crete. On 21 April it recommended that

[9] Connell, p. 419

[10] See above, p. 10, footnote 23. Middle East Joint Planning Staff Paper 30, 30 Oct. 1940

three brigade groups of fresh troops would be necessary for the defence, together with more artillery, especially anti-aircraft batteries, and a Royal Air Force fighter strength maintained at two squadrons.

The commanders of the three Services in Cairo were now under extreme pressure from all sides. For guidance they turned to the Prime Minister, asking for his ruling on priorities. Characteristically, he did not shirk this challenge. In an unflinching directive he summed up his requirements:

... Victory in Libya counts first, evacuation of troops from Greece second. Tobruk shipping, unless indispensable to victory, must be fitted in as convenient. Iraq can be ignored and Crete worked up later.[11]

His hope, and reasonable expectation, was that in Crete the basic planning and organization for defence had been completed during the preceding six months. For the moment the island would have to become a receptacle for whatever could get there from Greece.

Since the beginning of the previous November, there had been a slow increase in the strength of the occupying force. By the middle of April the main body of a battalion of the 2nd Black Watch had been detached east along the coast to Heraklion. Two more regular battalions, the 1st Welch, and the 2nd York and Lancs, were in the vicinity of Canea, together with the 16th Heavy and 36th Light Anti-Aircraft guns, twenty-four searchlights, a field company of Engineers, and a Field Ambulance.

Air support remained an illusion. Up to 17 April the Officer Commanding the Royal Air Force in Crete was a Flight Lieutenant. Like his colleagues in the army he had been given no specific orders. The only aircraft belonged to a squadron of the Fleet Air Arm which had performed notably in the attack on Italian shipping at Taranto and was now stationed at Maleme, twelve miles west of Canea, where there was a primitive airfield. Here it had inherited a strange collection of Brewsters, Fulmars, and Gladiators. These machines sat solidly among the sand-dunes like exhibits in an open-air museum. The Brewsters could not fly; some fundamental internal affliction had remained undiagnosed since their departure from America. The Gladiators and Fulmars

11 Churchill, Vol. III, p. 201, Chiefs of Staff to Commanders-in-Chief, 18 April 1941, 'issued by the P.M. and Minister of Defence'

took to the air only after the greatest exertions. Such was the
Fighter Defence of Suda Bay.

Wiser than the soldiers the higher Air Command had begun to
see something of the truth. On 4 January the Joint Planning Staff
in London, reverting to the view they had expressed at the
beginning of November,[12] had accepted a memorandum from the
Chief of Air Staff declaring that 'the foundation on which we
should base our defence of Greece is Crete, which must be held at
all costs'.[13] This was sense. Indeed the observation gleams like a
jewel among the dross. There was about it something of Wellington's conception in the Peninsula. His vision had always lain far
to the north, in France itself. From the moment of his arrival in
Portugal he had looked forward to the moment when he would
reach out at the enemy in pursuit beyond the Pyrenees to 'touch
them vitally' in the valley of their own Garonne. But first he must
have his base, his toehold on the Continent. Here he would build
his refuge nourished from the sea, the source of all his strength.
He had taken his time about it. For many months the bewildered
Portuguese were 'set digging on the tumbled skyline above
Torres Vedras'.[14]

There had been little digging in Crete. No airpens had been
built, and no preparation made for demolitions. Every available
aircraft had been sent to Greece, but where were the 'many
hundreds of Cretans' that Churchill had demanded, together with
ground staff and technicians, preparing for the time when the
planes themselves should arrive? And what was being done about
the roads? And about new landing installations in the south?

To examine these questions, it is necessary to look at Crete
from the point of view of a commander who might, that winter,
have been invited to plan its defence.

The island is long and slender, some one hundred and sixty
miles in length, and an average of thirty miles in width. It lies east
and west across the outlet from the Aegean Sea, nearly two
hundred miles south of Athens. A savage mountain chain runs
from end to end, its highest peaks falling precipitously into the
waves along the southern coast; this face is thus fully exposed to
the weather. In 1941 it contained no harbour of any size; at
Palaiokhora in the west, and at Sphakia and Tymbaki further to

[12] Middle East Joint Planning Staff Paper 30, 30 Oct. 1940
[13] Davin, p. 19   [14] Guedalla, p. 194

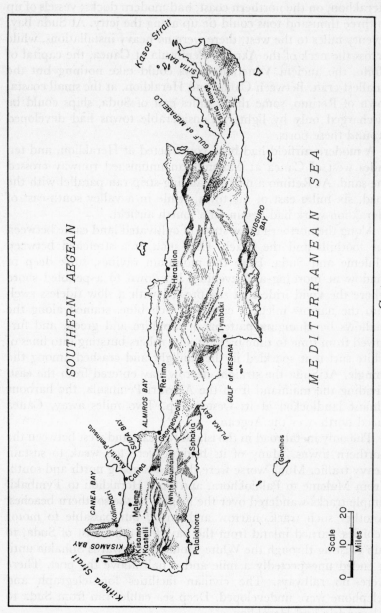

2. Crete

the east, there were fishing ports accessible only to small boats. Heraklion, on the northern coast, had modern docks; vessels of up to three thousand tons could tie up along the jetty. At Suda Bay, seventy miles to the west, there were no heavy installations, while across the neck of the Akrotiri Peninsula at Canea, the capital of Crete, the ancient Venetian quays could take nothing but the smallest craft. Between Canea and Heraklion, at the small coastal town of Retimo, some thirty miles east of Suda, ships could be discharged only by lighter. Considerable towns had developed around these ports.

A modern airfield had been constructed at Heraklion, and ten miles west of Canea at Maleme, an unfinished runway crossed the sand. At Retimo a narrow landing-strip ran parallel with the road, six miles east of the town, while in a valley south-east of Heraklion work had begun on a fourth airfield.

Along the northern coast strips of cultivated land came between the foothills and the beach. One such area stretched between Maleme and Suda. Here the mountain ravines, sunk deep in shadow at morning and evening, led down to a pebbled shore where the vivid iridescent sea pressed with a slow tideless swell into the narrow inlets, a carpet of rich blue, stained along the shallows by changing patterns of sapphire and green, and furrowed from time to time by long slow rollers bursting into lines of white surf that sparkled in the sunlight and crashed among the shingle. At Suda the straight narrow bay entered from the east, dividing the mainland from the Akrotiri Peninsula, the harbour almost landlocked at its western tip. Two miles away, Canea faced north over the Aegean.

The only metal road in the island ran east and west between the northern towns. Many of its bridges were too weak to sustain heavy traffic. Much worse were the roads going north and south. From Maleme to Palaiokhora, and from Heraklion to Tymbaki, simple tracks wandered over the heights to the southern beaches. Another such track, narrow and dusty, but passable to motor vehicles, turned inland from the bay, five miles east of Suda, to run twisting through the White Mountains towards Sphakia until it ended unexpectedly a mile and a half above the port. There were no railways. The civilian facilities for telegraph and telephone were undeveloped. Deep sea cables ran from Suda to Alexandria and Heraklion.

With little to go on, Brigadier Tidbury had assumed that any assault would come largely by air. There was no advice from the Planning Staffs upon the extent to which the development of such an attack might be dependent upon the use of landing-grounds. Nevertheless, it was reasonable to assume that the Germans would at once attempt to capture the airfields, together with the ports along the northern coast. At the same time, they would no doubt seek to block movement on the roads and all sea communication with the island. From southern Greece it should be possible to achieve much of this by command of the air. Even to reach the northern harbours, it would be necessary for the ships bearing essential supplies from Egypt to make a perilous passage through the straits to the east or west before beginning to run down the coast. Convoys docking after dark would then need to make the return journey during the following day. Moreover, they would certainly be subjected to intensive and continued bombing while unloading. A foretaste of what might be expected was provided at the beginning of April when the port of Piraeus was finished off on a single moonlit night.

All this should have been perfectly plain from the moment when British troops first set foot on the island. It had required greater prescience than was available at that time within the General Staff to foresee that before long, whether given an excuse or not, some part of the enormous, and temporarily inactive, German Army was likely to come bursting down into Greece, and that such a stroke must inevitably succeed. Yet even if this development had been no more than remotely possible, instead of overwhelmingly probable, it had still been the plain duty of Middle East Command to make calculated preparation for the defence of Crete.

In fact, there had cried aloud the need for five simple, immediate measures: the improvization of landing facilities at the southern fishing ports; the completion and improvement of the roads leading north from these ports; the construction of fighter air-strips, with camouflaged protection pens, in two or three of the mountain-locked plains in the south, where they would be remote from the nerve centres of the island's defence; the mining or destruction of the airfields in the north; and, finally, the arming of the Cretans.

On 5 September 1941, in his despatch on Operations in the Middle East, Wavell was to maintain that although the 'value of the island was fully appreciated' effective preparations had been rendered impossible by 'the constant shortage of troops and material'. He added that 'practically all able-bodied men in the island were serving in the Greek forces in Albania'.

This explanation is inaccurate. There had been immediately available not only 15,000 Italian prisoners-of-war, but 400,000 patriotic Cretans, nearly all of whom wished for nothing better than to do what they could to help during the period of waiting, and to take part with relish in the fighting if it should come. Their energies might have been harnessed and employed with but negligible diversion of men and material from other theatres of war. In 1945, an engineer officer making a return visit to Crete came to the conclusion that 'two or three good Engineer works officers' could have directed the work on the roads. They would have needed a 'minimum of equipment'.[15] And in July 1947, writing in the *Army Quarterly*, Brigadier Brunskill, who had been Freyberg's Quartermaster in the island, maintained that 'a road right through to Sfakia . . . could have been put through by a field company in a month to six weeks with some road-making equipment'.[16]

The time allowed had proved to be a full six months. Yet almost nothing was done, no policy determined or even considered, and no more than vague and conflicting instruction given to a rapid succession of local commanders. Crete became first a minor garrison area, after that a dumping ground, and at last a battle-field. It was never 'the fortress' that had been promised, never remotely a 'Scapa'.

From the first, the Greek campaign had set its imprint upon all activity in Crete. Later, the War Cabinet and the Commanders-in-Chief in the Middle East were to claim that they had thought of Greece, the Aegean, and the Eastern Mediterranean as one theatre of war. The fact remains that, in deciding what priorities they should accord within this theatre, they had allowed themselves constantly to be enticed by visions of political reward. Thus they fell into errors of military judgement. The general who was to command in Crete found that the aftermath of Greece was a governing factor in all his difficulties. Yet this was not the 'inevitable corollary of the Greek tragedy'.[17] In Crete all might

[15] DP, Freyberg to Churchill, letter dated 25 March 1949, ref. to Major F. M. Hanson
[16] Long, p. 317, footnote 4
[17] John Connell, *New Statesman*, 18 Aug. 1961, p. 213

have been done secretly and subtly, exploiting the geographical features that rendered it so suitable for defence, the fear being that the Germans, seeing their peril too soon, might not attack at all, and the hope that they would come confidently and in strength to break their teeth upon an unsuspected rock.

The story of Suda Bay is sad [was Churchill's comment in 1949] . . . how far short was the action taken by the Middle East Command of what was ordered and what we all desired! . . . it remains astonishing to me that we should have failed to make Suda Bay the amphibious citadel of which all Crete was the fortress. Everything was understood and agreed, and much was done; but all was half-scale effort. We were presently to pay heavily for our shortcomings.[18]

Looking back now, it is possible to see in better perspective the extreme and complex pressures that were crowding upon the Commander-in-Chief of the Army in the Middle East. Wavell's biographers make much of the fact that a shortage of every form of equipment still did much to cripple his vast command. Woollcombe points a contrast with the generalized exhortations of Churchill: 'How admirable in sentiment, how right was every injunction, from home, from the summit.'[19] And Connell maintains: 'Any amount of planning, any amount of drive could not have replaced the men who were training or fighting elsewhere, or the guns, the transport and the equipment which did not exist.'[20] But these comments take no account of the essential difference between Crete and the mainland: the difference was a wide stretch of the southern Aegean.

Unlike the forlorn campaign in Greece, the original failure in Crete did not stem from lack of resources. It was a failure of vision and of decision. During November 1940, Wavell had warned the War Office that 'the Germans must intervene' if the Italians should get into difficulties against Greece. He knew that for many months to come the Middle East would remain desperately short of aircraft. This handicap alone must have been fatal to any attempt to form a front on the mainland. A proper sense of reality should have at once revealed, as it had to the Chief of Air Staff, that, in the face of such overwhelming strength on land and in the air, the only logical counter-stroke lay in a resolute and calculated occupation of Crete; the mountainous island might yet remain inviolable, a constant threat to Hitler's southern flank, a

[18] Churchill, Vol. II, p. 485   [19] Woollcombe, p. 119   [20] Connell, p. 449

second Torres Vedras behind its hundred miles of sea. This he failed to understand. Instead he encouraged the professional absurdity of sending two divisions and a brigade group to Greece. He forgot Crete during six months in which thought and planning were more important than anything else. At first all his attention had been centred upon the campaigns that he was directing with such brilliance and success in the Western Desert and Abyssinia. Then suddenly the burden of the Greek venture upset the balance of his widely stretched forces. Still he did not see the danger that must threaten Crete if the Germans should come to the aid of Mussolini. By the end of March he had reached a state of mind in which he dared not look too far ahead. Threats and crises from every quarter were following upon one another almost daily. The present was always difficult enough. Too much foresight might reveal only too clearly the shape of further misfortune to come and this was scarcely to be borne. Better concentrate on the present. It is easy to understand such an attitude. Its effect, nevertheless, could not fail to be disastrous.

Night after night the ships from Greece used the shelter of darkness to make full speed to the south. In the wardrooms, on the decks, and all about the cabins and holds, the men of Wilson's army lay collapsed in sleep. Few were awake to see the line of snow-covered mountains that rose at dawn from the sea. Still flinging their white plumes of spray, the cruisers and destroyers raced through the lifting mists to close upon a rocky shore. Here they swung west, at slackening pace, past a small island topped by ancient fortifications, to enter a long narrow bay enclosed between steep and rugged cliffs. The sun rose behind them as they slid quietly over the dappled water, through an outer and then an inner boom, and finally into a land-locked harbour, crowded with a great variety of small vessels.

Now the soldiers came to crowd the rails. On their right, they saw the cruiser *York* lying aground with her stern awash. Huddled behind the quays was a cluster of grey-white houses. Cool groves of green olive reached down to the shores. This, they were told, was Suda Bay. They had arrived in Crete. Many had not heard the name before.

But they were well pleased with the news. The island itself seemed to welcome them. They felt refreshment in the tang of the morning air, and looking back into the white haze, in half expectation of pursuit by the Stukas, they saw only the sunlight sparkling from the surface of the inlet. In cheerful disarray, they scrambled ashore from the lighters and formed up in raggle-taggle columns along the wharf. Reaction was upon them. They could not find their officers. There were no orders. After a while they streamed away, laden and chattering like passengers from an excursion train entering a holiday resort, to trudge along a white dusty road that twisted between powdered hedgerows and grey stone walls, through glades of oak and olive, and past scattered whitewashed houses. Their military appearances were not improved by the increasing heat of the day. From time to time aircraft buzzed discreetly in the brilliant blue sky. At this, conversation ceased as they measured the ground, ready to hurl themselves if need be behind a wall or into a ditch. They knew very well that two planes together were unlikely to be British. But to their surprise they saw only Hurricanes.

At length they came to a garden suburb with wayside cafés set among the trees that fringed the street. Here they clustered around the elderly men and women who had come to greet them carrying ice cream and baskets of oranges. After they had eaten they rested in the shade, their gear lying about them while they drank the local red wine. It was night before they reached the transit areas, and already cold again before they had settled down, huddling themselves in such cover as they could find, with their backs pressed against the narrow trees.

Their thoughts were of Greece, of their own escapes, and of the fate of friends. Their ears still echoed with the scream of planes and the crash of bombs. They had no care for the future. This was a moment sufficient in itself, to be accepted gratefully and without speculation, in brief isolation from the future and the past. They had no suspicion that within a month they would be playing their parts in a battle unique in the history of the world, matching their own ground forces, still largely disorganized and ill equipped, against assault by an enemy entirely airborne, and thus inevitably deprived at first of heavy weapons, but supported by omnipotent and absolute air power. Such a contest had never been seen before. Nor was it ever to be repeated in similar form during the Second World War. And now it is certain that it can never be seen again as long as men and war exist.

On 27 April General Wilson reached Crete. Wavell at once

telegraphed to ask him whether the island could be held, on the assumption that any attack would be largely airborne; the garrison would have to consist in the main of such troops as happened to arrive from Greece; there could be no hope of aircraft reinforcement 'for some time to come'.[21]

In his reply Wilson referred immediately as did everyone in those days who had recently been in the front line, to the fact that the enemy air superiority was going to make things extremely difficult. Air protection would be needed 'for the vital points and for the morale of the civilian population'. Since he had just been told that no more aircraft were available this was a clear hint that it might be unwise to attempt a defence. He added that he feared that the domination of the enemy in the air must virtually cut off seaborne supply and reinforcement. Unless 'all three Services' were 'prepared to face the strain of maintaining adequate forces up to strength', a continued occupation must remain 'a dangerous commitment'.[22] He ended by saying that full information about the southern anchorages would be available after reconnaissance which it was hoped to carry out soon, a comment likely to chill anyone who remembered that British troops had been in the island for six months.

Indeed there was much to be said for an immediate withdrawal to Egypt. For those on the spot the bitter fruits of the long months of vacillation were only too plain. Every movement on the island, and in the waters around it, would be made under overwhelming and unopposed air attack.

Others, too, saw the prospect of occupation in a changed light. To the Prime Minister the island remained 'a valuable and highly offensive outpost', but for the Service Commanders it had lost much of its former attraction. Air Marshal Longmore now had available in the whole of the Middle East only ninety bombers and forty-three single-engined fighters. His present ambition, and that of Portal, the Chief of the Air Staff, extended no further than the fervent hope that the surviving pilots from Greece might be reassembled in Egypt. Whether or not they had ever heard of Ploesti, and the oil-wells that were proving such a source of concern to Hitler, any prospect of raiding so far into the Balkans had receded into the remote future. In like fashion, Cunningham's hope of 'a fuelling base' had taken on a very different aspect now

[21] Long, p. 206
[22] Davin, pp. 39 and 458

that German fighters would be swarming continually from the mainland; much more immediate were his apprehensions of what enemy aircraft based on Crete might do to his supply line in the Mediterranean. The Joint Planning Staff continued to demonstrate their confusion over the whole situation by asking Wavell about the prospects of defending the island from two aspects, as a fuelling depot, and as a base to be denied to the enemy.

Thus even at this date [says the author of the *Official New Zealand War History*], it seems to have been possible for them to believe that the two cases were in some essential respect different.[23]

By this time, Wavell was nearing the climax of his long misunderstanding with the Prime Minister. His chief biographer has maintained that he had, for many years, been 'suspicious of professional politicians',[24] and in particular of Churchill, whom he had held in some measure responsible for the unhappy 'Curragh' incident of 1914. The two had met for the first time in August 1940, during the early days of the Battle of Britain. The occasion proved unhappy. At a series of conferences, Churchill was genial but, at the same time, increasingly provocative. 'Impervious,' as ever, 'to the climatic conditions of other people',[25] he challenged Wavell's dispositions, and was free with suggestions to 'move this battalion here and that battalion there'.[26] The general's response was no less typical of his own character. Dour and monosyllabic, he confined himself to the barest factual assertions, conceding nothing even to the news that he was to be sent most of his country's armoured forces at a time when invasion across the Channel seemed certain and imminent. 'I do not think Winston quite knew what to make of me and whether I was fit to command or not,' he wrote later, adding, 'Winston has always disliked me personally'.[27] But, rather than dislike, the feeling had been first one of incomprehension, and then of disappointment. At this moment of supreme national crisis, the Prime Minister was looking for evidence of a zest and invention to match his own. What he saw was 'a good average colonel'.[28] Their incompatibility was complete. Later that year, the desert victories brought a temporary softening to their relationship, but there was no end to the flow of detailed importunities from London. Wavell never

[23] Davin, p. 35   [24] Connell, p. 254   [25] Bonham Carter, p. 392
[26] Avon, p. 131   [27] Connell, p. 255-6   [28] Avon, p. 133

found, nor indeed sought, the 'right tone of enthusiastic and evasive response'.[29] By the beginning of April 1941 almost every cable carried some fresh source of mutual irritation.

For several weeks there had been sharp conflict over the situation that was developing in Iraq. Unwilling to spread his forces further, and fearful of 'political repercussions'[30] in Palestine and Egypt, Wavell protested his reluctance to move to the relief of Habbaniya, the air force training base in the Iraqi Desert. At this, Churchill made an exception to his usual attitude of ultimate deference to the views of his generals. The Commander-in-Chief in Cairo was 'directly overruled'[31] by the War Cabinet.

Certainly Wavell, despite his earlier misplaced confidence, was now no happier about Crete. He realized all too well that virtually no preparation had been made for the island's defence. Indeed, within the space of a week, his unthinking optimism had changed abruptly to something like despair. This was a feeling that he was scarcely able to conceal. 'At the eleventh hour,' wrote the officer who was later to command in Crete, 'General Wavell knew quite well himself, and if he were in any doubt, Generals Wilson and Weston told him, that without air support Crete could not be held'.[32] But he was also aware that if the Germans got it they would be able to use their occupation to increase their threat against Syria and Iraq. His dilemma was sharpened by the fact that he felt 'doubtful if troops could be removed before enemy attack',[33] a reservation which may be judged no very obvious indication for remaining, since, if withdrawal were thought inevitable, the sooner it were attempted the better, before the *Luftwaffe* could become fully organized upon its Greek bases.

While the Service Chiefs continued to exchange their doubts and uncertainties the matter was settled for them by the Prime Minister. On 28 April, already savouring in advance the prospect of an encounter which seemed at last to offer him genuine cause for confidence, he signalled to Wavell:

It seems clear from our information that a heavy airborne attack by German troops and bombers will soon be made on Crete. Let me know what forces you have in the island and what your plans are. It

[29] Taylor, A. J. P., *The Observer*, 8 Nov. 1964
[30] Wavell to Chiefs of Staff, 5 May 1941   [31] Churchill, Vol. III, p. 236
[32] DP, Freyberg comments on the battle for Crete, 31 Oct. 1949
[33] Ibid.

ought to be a fine opportunity for killing the parachute troops. The island must be stubbornly defended.

This time Wavell was ready enough with his acquiescence. He must have known that the slightest demur would have brought his instant dismissal.

In all this the Prime Minister was to prove right. Although firmly set upon 'aiding Greece', he had invited a critical Service assessment of the prospects that might be expected from a full-scale campaign. So far from exposing the folly of such a venture, Wavell had done much to encourage it. From the first, Churchill had insisted upon the importance of the defence of Crete. Yet such preparation as was made remained both ill-judged and dilatory. Finally, nothing less than his direct intervention had sufficed to overcome Wavell's hesitations in Iraq, a move that quickly proved no less successful than it had been vital.

Today few would deny that he was no less right to insist upon giving battle to the Germans in Crete. A sounder strategy would have seen the island as the centre-piece of any approach to the Balkans. Yet no great difficulty was visible from London, even after the débâcle on the mainland. It was reasonable enough to assume that use had been made of the period of occupation. For many months ahead there might be no better opportunity than this to fight the Germans. And what, after all, was the alternative? There was none that could be taken without disgrace. No other course remained beyond another abandonment of friends, one more hasty scuttle at the first breath of contact with the forces of Hitler.

But would they come at all? Would they defy all national precedent and dare to attack an island under the nose of the British Navy? The answer to these questions had already been determined.

Hitler had been reluctant to become further involved in the Mediterranean. With the occupation of Greece nearing completion, he felt that he had done all that was necessary to safeguard his southern flank before striking east. But General Löhr, the commander of Air Fleet IV, who was responsible for the campaign in Yugoslavia and Greece, now told him that the Ploesti oilfields might still be threatened by bombers stationed in Crete. And Halder, although aware of 'the dangers of extending too far', had long foreseen an air-landing in Crete as a first step towards domination of the Eastern Mediterranean. In the end it was Student who succeeded in changing his mind, after first gaining the support of Goering. Student was confident that he could capture the island by the use of airborne forces alone. 'Goering – who was always so easy to enthuse –', he told his interrogators after the war, 'was quick to see the possibilities of the idea, and sent me on to Hitler. I saw him on 21 April. When I first explained the project Hitler said, "It sounds all right, but I don't think it is practicable." But I managed to convince him in the end.'[34] Hitler was ready enough to be persuaded. He was attracted by the flamboyancy and novelty of the enterprise, and by the prospect of the impression that its success would make upon the world.

Both Student and Halder felt that the operation could be a stepping-stone to the Middle East, perhaps into Egypt itself. The German Naval authorities entertained similar hopes. Nevertheless the Operation Instructions refer somewhat less ambitiously only to the capture of 'a favourable base for the operational air force for attacks on Egypt and the Suez Canal'. Hitler himself continued to regard the enterprise as valuable chiefly for the added security which it would provide for him in the south.

On 25 April it was decided. From his Headquarters Hitler issued his Directive 28 ordering 'an operation to occupy the island of Crete'. The code name would be 'Mercury'. From this moment, all preparations were pressed forward with drive and ruthlessness.

A day later Wavell entrusted the defence of Crete to General Weston, who had arrived less than a month before in charge of a detachment of Marines. Weston was a regular officer, intelligent, courageous, and capable of gaiety, but a man of moods, subject to fits of sudden despondency which flawed his bearing and judgement. At this moment he showed himself at his best.

Within hours of his appointment, on the night of 26 April, he issued an Operation Instruction in which he made some important points. He began by saying:

The area in the vicinity of our defences is considered unsuitable for parachute troops, and effective air operation against the island can only be carried out after a landing ground has been captured.

Maleme and Heraklion were therefore 'vital to the defence of the island', as was Suda Bay, the only channel of supply to the

34 Liddell Hart, p. 167

area of Canea and Maleme. Although it was desirable to hold Retimo, its retention was of less importance since the landing strip there was relatively isolated. It would no longer be possible to maintain a battle fleet in Suda Bay. For this reason an attempt at seaborne invasion by the enemy could not be 'ruled out'.

He then added:

It is the intention of the Middle East Command to make use of existing aerodromes for the defence of the island to the fullest possible extent. Air support will be 'limited until evacuation of Greece is completed and our air forces have been reorganized'.[35]

Two days later Wilson was to give him the news, straight from Cairo, that in fact no air reinforcement could be expected.

Thus from the outset Weston had appreciated that it was, for the enemy, a transcendent necessity to capture an airfield quickly in order to land airborne troops upon it. It is strange that this basic conception, soon to prove of paramount significance to both sides, was nevertheless allowed to become confused among lesser considerations.

In this Operation Order there is also revealed for the first time the Middle East attitude towards the airfields. They were to be used 'to the fullest possible extent', but 'for some time to come' there would be no more planes to fly from them, an equivocation that was to remain uncontested, and to prove a cruel handicap to the defence. It was true that for some months the production of aircraft in England had been rising rapidly. On 21 January, Mr. Justice Singleton had reported to the Prime Minister, with fair accuracy as was to be shown later, that the strength of the German Air Force compared with the British was roughly four to three. Throughout February and March the improvement had continued.[36] And on 30 April the Prime Minister was to tell Cunningham of his hope that sixty-four Hurricanes and nine Fulmars would arrive in the Middle East by 25 May. More planes, in particular some scores of fighters, might reach Egypt in June.

But nobody would accept the fact that hopes of this kind were no longer relevant to the impending battle in Crete.

There was little excuse for this refusal to face the truth. Before the end of April, Intelligence was already forecasting that invasion

[35] Creforce Operation Instruction No. 5, 26 April 1941   [36] Churchill, Vol. III, p. 37

was 'imminent'.[37] On the 30th, Wavell expected it 'within the next few days'.[38] The time squandered during the previous six months was now fast running out. Even if hundreds of aircraft were soon to reach Egypt, they would never be able to land in Crete if, by that time, the enemy should have seized and consolidated a landing ground as a bridgehead. And even if a few planes should arrive earlier, there was no hope that they would be able to fly effectively from airfields which had few anti-aircraft guns, and no other facilities for protection or camouflage.

Weston had seen the situation more clearly than anybody else. Yet all that he could do was to calculate for the immediate future. Troops were still arriving from Greece in every kind of disarray. He made shift to feed them and to reorganize them, short as they were of every kind of equipment.

At the same time, he made preliminary dispositions designed to protect his vital points. First, he set the New Zealanders to guard the vulnerable area near Platanias, between Canea and Maleme, while placing the scattered groups of the 6th Australian Division, together with his own Marine detachment, along the southern and eastern approaches to Suda Bay. To Heraklion he sent two battalions of the British 14th Brigade, under Brigadier Chappel, who had preceded him in command of the island. From this brigade he retained the 1st Welch, together with various reduced units from Greece, to guard the base area at the neck of the Akrotiri Peninsula. He also began to make contact with some scattered and half-formed Greek battalions. Two of these he placed at Retimo, and two at Heraklion. The rest he kept in the vicinity of Canea and Maleme.

He was not optimistic. He knew that there could be no air defence, and he considered it probable that the Germans would be able to improvise daylight landings from the sea under cover of the *Luftwaffe*. Nevertheless, he had set about his difficult task with vigour and insight. Within four days he learnt that his tenure of office was to be even briefer than that of his predecessors.

On 30 April, Wavell arrived from Cairo to see for himself. At once he called a conference of senior officers. These included Generals Wilson and Weston, Air Commodore D'Albiac, who had been the Air Officer commanding in Greece, and Wing

Commander Beamish, a famous captain of the Irish Rugby team, who was to take over the Air Force in Crete. There were also present Sir Michael Palairet, the British Ambassador to Greece, General Heywood, in charge of the Greek Military Mission, and General Freyberg, who had just arrived from Greece with two brigades of the 2nd New Zealand Division. All could see that the demeanour of the Commander-in-Chief was far from cheerful.

Later Freyberg was to recall the scene:

We met in a small villa between Maleme and Canea and set to work at 11.30. General Wavell had arrived by air and he looked drawn and tired, and more weary than any of us. Just prior to sitting down General Wavell and General Wilson had a heart to heart talk in one corner, and then the C.-in-C. called me over. He took me by the arm and said, 'I want to tell you how well I think the New Zealand Division has done in Greece. I do not believe any other Division would have carried out those withdrawals as well.' His next words came as a complete surprise. He said he wanted me to take command of the Forces in Crete and went on to say that he considered Crete would be attacked in the next few days. I told him that I wanted to get back to Egypt to concentrate the Division and train and re-equip it and I added that my Government would never agree to the Division being split permanently. He then said that he considered it my duty to remain and take on the job. I could do nothing but accept. With that over we sat down round the table on the flat-topped roof in the open air under an awning. The only subject on the agenda was the defence of Crete. . . . There was not very much to discuss. We were told that Crete would be held. The scale of attack envisaged was five to six thousand airborne troops, plus a possible seaborne attack. The primary objectives of this attack were considered to be Heraklion and Maleme aerodromes. Our object was to deny the enemy the use of Crete as an air and submarine base.[39]

It was agreed that something would have to be done about the possibility of landings from the sea. Wavell promised to speak to Cunningham about it. But he was 'at his wit's end for aircraft'.[40] For the present there could be no hope of more air support.

[39] Freyberg Report, quot. Davin, p. 40   [40] Ibid, p. 43

3

General Freyberg

Here was one more challenge for Bernard Freyberg in a career that was already legendary. Perhaps for a moment he allowed himself memories of another Aegean spring. Almost exactly twenty-six years before, on 23 April 1915, he and other members of the Royal Naval Division had carried their friend Rupert Brooke to his hill-top grave on the island of Skyros. A few hours later, his body stained brown, he had swum two miles, alone in darkness and bitter cold, to a beach on the Gallipoli Peninsula, planting decoy flares within the Turkish positions before turning back into the black and empty water to be rescued at last, almost dead with exhaustion, by friends in a naval cutter. A photograph of him taken at this time shows a calm, fair young man, with the physique of a heavy-weight boxer, and a look of steadiness about the mouth and the eyes.

While still a child he had emigrated with his parents from England to New Zealand where the family had settled in Wellington. At school he became well known as a swimmer. Later he spent some years wandering about the world, but at the start of the First World War he at once travelled to London. Soon he was revealing on the Turkish beaches a taste for personal glory in battle. This was not the easily recognized ambition of the commander who cares nothing for the deaths of those who win him his reputation. Rather was he driven, like Nelson, by some demon that urged him constantly to the centre of the fray, yet seemed to increase rather than lessen his compassion for the human failings of his men. And, like Nelson, he freely acknowledged his longing for acclamation and the trappings of fame.

From the Dardanelles, Freyberg returned to England, severely wounded in the stomach, but already widely known. By the autumn of 1916 he was commanding the Hood Battalion of the Naval Division during the dying spasms of the Somme offensive, and on 14 November he achieved the renown which he had been seeking. After twenty-four hours of fighting he led his men to the capture of Beaucourt, a village in the enemy line west of Bapaume. While organizing the defence of the position against counter-attack he was wounded for the fourth time in the action. This was an injury that almost killed him. Indeed, the stretcher-bearers who found him, lying upon his face, deeply gashed across the neck and shoulder, thought at first that he was dead. Then 'his mouth moved' and one of them heard him say, as he had said to others that day, 'I wouldn't mind losing an arm for a V.C.'[1] Within a few days he learnt that this award had been granted. On 23 November *The Times* military correspondent wrote that the tale of his exploits was 'beginning to spread through the Army'. By the end of the war, still only twenty-nine years old, he was a brigadier.

He had gained much in return. For the first time, he had found himself among men who were interested by ideas and words as well as deeds. This world delighted him, not as a substitute for what he had known before, but as an enrichment and enlargement of his experience. On level terms he met men who were world figures in art and politics, and he began to read widely; soon he was something of an authority on the works of Jane Austen.

In the years that followed he was less happy. For a time he stayed on in the British Army. But here he met disappointment. He was, by temperament, ill suited to the egotism and complacency of the times. Seeking lesser diversion he found that success did not come as easily as before. In an attempt to swim the English Channel, he was forced to surrender to an ebb tide when only four hundred yards from the foot of the cliffs at Dover.

The outbreak of the Second World War quickly restored his old zest. He was chosen to lead the New Zealand Expeditionary Force, the 'athlete's heart' with which the War Office had thought to pension him off a few years earlier, now recognized by all concerned as no more than a medical whim, or perhaps a tactful fancy invoked at a time when it had seemed that distinguished middle-aged generals would no longer be needed. It was an admirable appointment. Time had softened his hunger for individual honour, extinguishing for ever the simple vanities of his youth. Like Sir Andrew Russell, his predecessor in the First World War, he wished for nothing better than to lead his own countrymen in a cause that was worthy of them.

[1] Mr. J. R. Bushell, to the author, 22 May 1962

By the time of his arrival in Crete Freyberg was fifty-two – the age at which Marlborough had rallied his Grand Alliance with the four great victories yet to come – rather more lined in the face than twenty-five years before, but little heavier, and still capable of swimming further than any man in his new command. Here indeed was a soldiers' general. He would have fitted well into the pattern of a medieval battle fought between armies of a few thousand, the captain on each side constantly visible to encourage the waverer and the faint-hearted among his supporters. The figure of Harold at Hastings was perhaps not unlike him. And Prince Rupert, in his extreme youth, had shown against the Roundheads the same qualities of impetuous daring, later to be tempered by sagacity in his middle years. Freyberg's troops of 1914–18 had always known that in times of crisis he would be sure to appear among them, standing casually amidst the firing, or at the roadside to offer them a cheerful word as they moved past him in retreat. Moreover, they had been grateful for his awareness that there is a limit to the bravest spirit. Constantly he had sought to preserve them from being asked to do the impossible.

All this the new generation of New Zealanders quickly understood. First in training, and later during their brief campaign in Greece, they came to feel that he was on their side to protect them against the manoeuvres of politicians and the vagaries of high level strategists. Unlike Montgomery he seldom revealed to them the details of a coming battle. If things were going to be difficult, his instinct was that of a father doing what he could to shelter them from unpleasant things to come. All he asked of them was their confidence. This they gave him completely. Those who failed to come up to his standards he was quick enough to dismiss, but to all the rest he offered constant and kindly encouragement. While training in England, the 5th Brigade had marched past him one evening at the end of an arduous four-day route-march. As it went by, each platoon, widely separated from the next, heard with satisfaction the comment: 'Best platoon so far.'[2]

On the day before the conference with Wavell, Freyberg had sailed to Suda Bay in a warship that was bound for Alexandria. His only purpose in leaving the convoy had been to visit the two New Zealand brigades which he understood to have landed in Crete. Like everyone else, he had greatly appreciated the meals,

[2] DP

hot drinks, and brief chance to sleep that had been provided by the Royal Navy He was still very weary. His whole intent for the immediate future had been the reconstitution of the 2nd New Zealand Division in Egypt.

Now all was abruptly changed by the unwelcome order from Wavell. The future of the Division, the only force that New Zealand could put in the field, must first hang upon the outcome in Crete. He had one consolation. For many years he had enjoyed the friendship of the Prime Minister in England. Between these two there was a bond of mutual affection and admiration. Long before, in 1914, Churchill had secured the commission to the Naval Division of the young New Zealander who had travelled across the world to England. After 1918, in recognizing the exploits of his protégé, Churchill had come to refer to him as 'the Salamander',[3] the title earned in the wars against Louis XIV by that firebrand soldier Cutts, who was said by Macaulay to find the most savage encounter 'a party of pleasure'.[4] In September 1940, Churchill had 'toyed with the idea of giving him a far greater scope'.[5] It was he who had proposed to Wavell that Freyberg should be appointed to the command in Crete. Such patronage by the ceaselessly exigent genius in Downing Street sometimes brought trials of its own A few days later, Freyberg was to find awaiting him a special emissary from the Prime Minister bearing a list of suggestions how best the defence of the island might be conducted. But nothing could shake Freyberg's devotion. He knew very well upon whom, for many months already, the hopes of the world had depended.

Although he had no illusions about the difficulties that awaited him, he was taken aback by the discoveries that he made during the first few hours. Force Headquarters, he found, were in the process of moving into a quarry on the high ground that ran between Suda Bay and Canea, along the neck of the Akrotiri Peninsula Here everything was in confusion. The Marine officers of Weston's staff were moving out. There was nobody to replace them.

He still had with him Colonel Keith Stewart, his own Chief of Staff from the New Zealand Division, but there were no trained Intelligence officers.

---

[3] Churchill, Vol. III, p. 242
[4] Macaulay, *History of England*, Vol. III, p. 362   [5] Churchill, Vol. III, p. 242

I did not know the true state of disorganization until I went to Crete Headquarters [he wrote later to Churchill]. Although there was an Officers' Mess, there were no staff officers or clerks, in fact there was no headquarters. . . . I had to start by taking men from units to make the headquarters staff, and although they all tried hard, they were not in the accepted term a staff. One of the greatest mistakes in the evacuation from Greece was the failure to evacuate from Greece to Crete a headquarters staff of which there were at least four.[6]

There was here an ironic parallel with the situation that had faced the Prime Minister himself twenty-seven years earlier. At that time First Lord of the Admiralty, he had paid a visit to the beleaguered city of Antwerp on the flank of the German advance into Belgium. Typically he had offered to resign from the Government in order to take over command of the garrison. But he had insisted that, in addition to 'full powers of a commander of a detached force in the field', he would require a 'complete staff proportionate to the force employed', as 'all the officers' were already active 'in positions of urgency'.[7] Freyberg could make no such stipulation. He had to do what he could. Everything – staff, intelligence, and organization, as well as supplies and installations – would have to depend upon what he could improvise for himself.

There was little that anyone could tell him about Crete. He asked for the defence plan and found that none had been made. From local maps, and from the Cretans, he quickly learnt some of the essential facts. They were not reassuring. 'Crete', he was to write in his report, 'faced the wrong way, with its three aerodromes, two harbours, and roads, all on the north coast.'[8] Such information as he had was often misleading. He told Wavell that he was 'confident' that he could 'push a road quickly through to Sphakia', the small port on the south coast. Nobody had yet discovered that this road ended on top of an escarpment hundreds of feet above the beach. Nor was there any information about the small southern ports at Palaiokhora and Tymbaki.

It was not in his character to seek excuses for himself in deriding the shortcomings of others. Yet he must have felt immediately

[6] DP, Freyberg comments on draft history of Second World War, Vol. III (*The Grand Alliance*) by Sir Winston Churchill (hereafter called 'Churchill Draft'), 25 Mar. 1949

[7] Beaverbrook, p. 48

[8] Davin, p. 41

that, if he should fail in this hard and unexpected duty, there would be little memory for earlier delays and neglect, even if it should prove that they had rendered success impossible. It would be upon himself that the blame would fall.

Nor could he draw much comfort from what he learnt about the men that he was to lead. The strength of the forces in Crete during these confused days at the end of April can never be known. It seems probable that there were about 30,000 British and Imperial troops, together with some 10,000 partially armed Greek and Cretan infantrymen, many of them recruits of a few weeks standing.

These numbers are misleading. The battalions from Greece were much depleted by casualties, and by the detachment of groups that had been carried on to Egypt during the turmoil of evacuation. Most of the infantrymen had managed to hold together, but some had been forced to leave their small arms on the embarkation beaches in order to make more room on the ships. Others had been directed to leave their rifles in a central storage dump as they came ashore in Suda Bay, an order which most had evaded; it could only have been made in ignorance of the tradition and instinct of fighting soldiers. Soon after their arrival they had taken up the defence positions chosen by Weston.

Thousands of men, mixed indiscriminately, and almost entirely without equipment, were gathered in transit areas at the foot of the mountains. Here were gunners without guns, drivers without vehicles, and signallers without apparatus for signalling; something might yet be made of them if they could be provided with rifles. Less promising were the numerous clerks and orderlies. Not that anyone was paying very much attention to them. It was assumed that most, if not all, of these troops would be moving on to Egypt as soon as transport became available.

There remained the 'odds and ends', as Freyberg called them, whose 'morale was low'. This was a kindly euphemism. Many were deserters loudly protesting that they should not have been sent to Greece; the laxities of retreat had proved too much for them. For the moment they had become immune to military discipline. Some had taken to the hills and were living off the countryside. At night they came down into the villages, where they drank the local wine as though it were beer, and shouted and fought in the cafés. The nights had begun to ring with shots and cries. Several of the Greeks had been injured, and at least one killed. It was behaviour unlikely to endear the British Forces to the Cretan population.

Finally there were the civilian refugees from Greece, and a sad and dispirited assortment of Cypriots, Palestinians, and Yugoslavians.

Most of the soldiers had been quick to make the best of things, cooking in old petrol containers, and eating out of tin cans. Some were dressed in rags, and lice had begun to appear.

> We had a long fight with them [wrote one Australian]. The boys would do a day in underpants while the women washed their clothes, and they are great washerwomen; but until the great day when we were given a shirt and shorts each, the lice were always with us. I had a blanket and greatcoat, but for a week or more shared the blanket with three others. We would sleep in a row with greatcoats on and the blanket over our feet. . . . I slipped into Canea and bought a brush and razor. Except for a table knife that was all my equipment.[9]

From this variegated assembly of troops, the chance remnants of defeat, Freyberg had now to fashion a force capable of meeting the Germans in the full tide of their success.

No doubt his thoughts turned first to his own New Zealanders. And here at once he met calamity: the 6th Brigade was missing. After relatively slight loss in the fighting it had arrived late in Suda Bay; but the men had not been put ashore. Instead the convoy had sailed straight on to Egypt under naval orders. If he had known that his Division was to defend Crete he would have held on to this brigade at all costs. The incident well illustrated the increasing failure of foresight and planning that was paralysing the High Command. Not for nothing had the Middle East Headquarters in Cairo become known universally as the 'Muddle East'. Once again all had been left to chance. Crete would be defended by whatever troops happened to be left behind there after the Navy had pleased itself with its sailing arrangements.

About 9,000 New Zealanders remained in the island. Of these the most important elements were the infantry of the 4th and 5th Brigades, augmented by the Maori Battalion, and weakened by the loss of about a thousand men, killed, wounded, or taken prisoner in Greece. They made up the biggest formed group of infantry. Moreover Freyberg knew them well. After the fall of

France, the 5th Brigade had been sent to England to continue training under his command during the critical autumn of 1940. Later it had joined the other two brigades in Egypt. Within a fortnight, the newly formed Division had moved to Greece where it had met the enemy for the first time. In the difficult conditions of the withdrawal it had done all that was possible. There had been no great losses. Although Freyberg had felt some anxiety over morale after such a precipitate retreat, few of the men would have admitted to any failure in confidence. But what they needed now, as did all the troops who had fought in Greece, was time for the battalions to be brought back to strength and to be re-equipped.

In the New Zealand Division was concentrated the whole intense war effort of a small nation. The spirit that sustained it from home had been expressed in the words of Mr. Michael Savage, Prime Minister at the outbreak of the war, when he had said: 'Where Britain goes, we go. Where she stands, we stand.'

As individuals, the New Zealanders could on occasion be notably less explicit in their admiration for all things British. They had seen evidence enough of the confusion and incompetence which still impeded the conduct of the war. And, like the Australians, they had largely renounced the traditions and group loyalties of social class. Increasingly they were beginning to feel an insular pride in their own achievements. They were men of peace who had taken to war. Many of them had been farmers. Few had known the shallow sophistications of life in a large city. In the whole country there had been only some eight regular staff officers. As in all territorial units, every man's action now lay under the merciless scrutiny not only of his fellows but, indirectly through them, of all his friends, neighbours, and relatives at home. The standards that they set for each other were hard. Already they had begun to evolve for themselves a discipline and military professionalism, different in superficialities, but in essence no less intense than that of the Brigade of Guards.

They had little experience of battle. Until a month before, none of the junior officers, N.C.O.s, or other ranks had ever been in action. In Greece, their chief concern had been to impose brief delay upon the enemy while taking shelter in daylight from the *Luftwaffe*. They had not yet tasted success in attack. Nor had they ever needed to stand and fight it out over a period of days. The colonels, who were in their middle forties, had all fought in the struggle of 1914–18. Without exception they were brave and capable leaders. So much was guaranteed by the fact that they had survived intensive selection in gaining their present appointments. Like their troops, however, they had only lately begun to learn about modern war. There was no reason to suppose that this would matter very much, especially in view of the certainty that in Crete they would have to rely largely upon defence. None could have guessed that the handicap would affect them more than their men.

Paradoxically enough, the presence in Crete of so many New Zealanders added greatly to Freyberg's anxieties. The special responsibility that he bore towards them weighed heavily upon him. He sought no privileges for them, and was about to place them in the forefront of the battle. But in spite of the overriding claim now made upon him by his appointment to command all troops in Crete, he could not fail to be conscious that here, for the second time in a month, the New Zealand Division had been placed in the gravest jeopardy. New Zealand was standing to lose proportionately far more than any other member of the Empire. As always, he was ready to face any danger. But he would have preferred to do so without this particular concern for his fellow countrymen. In fact, he heartily wished them all in Egypt. For a few days he toyed wistfully with the hope that there might be time to replace them before the battle should start. Very soon he realized that this hope was vain. They would have to take their chance in Crete. For himself, there could be no avoiding this additional burden.

In number, the Australians about equalled the New Zealanders. They had, however, suffered rather more severely in Greece. During the retreat they had been given less opportunity for timed withdrawal, and the organization of those who reached the island was even more chaotic. Among them were representatives of all the units that had made up the 6th Australian Division. The senior Australian officer, Brigadier Vasey, found that he could muster five depleted infantry battalions. He felt that they should remain as part of the defence force, together with some artillerymen who might reasonably hope that guns would arrive for them, a few machine-gunners, and a field ambulance. The remainder, some 5,000 men, should be transported as quickly as possible to Egypt, though doubtless it would be necessary to form composite battalions of all the stray infantrymen who might be available.

He had good reason for believing that some of these unattached troops should be removed.

On the whole [he wrote to Australian Corps Headquarters], the discipline of the unarmed and more or less unemployed personnel is fair. There have been a few major incidents including an alleged murder, but so far we have always been able to apprehend the culprits.

He had set up Courts Martial, but he hoped that the legal officer would review the proceedings 'with a kindly eye'.[10]

The Australians had some claim for indulgence. After their successes in Wavell's surprise attack on the Italians, first at Bardia and Tobruk, and later in the pursuit to Agedabia, they had been suddenly wrenched out of the Western Desert like dogs off a bone. Not more than a day or two had been allowed them to savour their triumphs in Alexandria. Almost at once they had been sent to Greece to fight in what appeared to many of them to have been some crack-brained politicians' venture. Now they found themselves in this paradisial island. The Germans had apparently forgotten them. It was natural that they should feel in the mood for a well-earned holiday. To most this meant simply that they could get their boots off and lie in the sun, or swim lazily among the rocks in the warm Mediterranean, not greatly perturbed by the lack of those 'swimming drawers . . . as many as possible'[11] for which Headquarters in Suda had made urgent application. Only a few had gone on the loose in the way described by Brigadier Vasey.

It was true, however, that those who had done so were contriving to flaunt their intransigence with a panache that nobody else could match. The sight of a dozen Australians on tour in a stolen truck, their tunics undone, cowboy hats on the backs of their heads, a rifle in one hand and a bottle of *krassi* in the other, was sufficient to give the impression that most of the deserters came from the Australian Division. The rest of the troops, already perhaps a little jealous of tales from the desert, began to feel that the heroes of Bardia might be overdoing it. Indeed, to the British the Australians were still something of a puzzle. Was it possible to be quite as wild as this and still fight under orders when the time came? The sober, efficient New Zealanders were easier to understand.

But it was plain that the Australians and the New Zealanders had one characteristic in common. Reputation meant nothing to them. The whole world might be acclaiming German military genius. About this they knew little and cared not at all. Certainly the enemy had a lot of aeroplanes. Maybe his soldiers were good too. This was something they would soon be able to judge for themselves. In the meantime they remained unimpressed. It was an attitude of mind that in war is useful at any time. Never, perhaps, has it been of greater value than in the spring of 1941.

The heart of the British contingent consisted of those elements of the 14th Brigade that had already been stationed in Crete for several months. Of the three regular infantry battalions, the 1st Welch remained in the Canea area. Two companies of the 2nd Black Watch had moved to Heraklion in the middle of March; at the end of April, Weston sent the rest of the battalion to join them, together with the 2nd York and Lancs. The presence on the island of the soldiers from these famous regiments, with their immaculate dress and confident bearing, provided a welcome and encouraging contrast after the disorders of the retreat.

Every man was very grateful to the Welch Regiment [one of the Maoris was to write of their reception in Crete], not only for the refreshment its men were issuing, but for sense of stability at the sight of the disciplined organization it provided.

Also in the Suda area, after sailing direct from Egypt, was an advance party of 2,000 Royal Marines of the Mobile Naval Base Defence Organization; these men were trained primarily for static fighting. From Greece had come just over 400 survivors of the 1st Rangers, motorized infantry formed from the 9th Battalion of the Kings Royal Rifle Corps, together with 279 of the Northumberland Hussars. All the vehicles had been left behind. Several thousand more British servicemen, from every kind of broken unit, lounged among the olive groves, many of them unarmed.

This motley collection of soldiers was unlike any other formation that would fight the Germans in the Second World War. It had neither the equipment nor the organization of the expeditionary forces which had landed in Norway and France, and it was no less different from the drilled and efficient conscript armies that were later to represent the Allies. Most of the troops in Crete were

half-trained, poorly armed, and older, many of them, than their
successors. Yet they possessed one salient virtue; the great majority
had volunteered. They had done so without illusion. Unlike those
young men who had responded in 1914 to Kitchener's appeal,
they felt no trace of jingoistic patriotism. Politicians they regarded
with hearty contempt. Only Churchill had spoken for them.
Through him they had recognized what was at stake. Knowing
nothing in detail of that system of mass murder of women and
children that was already the official policy of the enemy, they
had yet come to sense from afar something of the cold infamy of
the Germans under Hitler. Thus they saw the war as a sour
necessity. Since there could be no escape, they had gone to meet
it with zest and confidence, expecting that it would bring them
diversion and adventure. But this was not what they were seeking.
A few may have hoped to escape the consequences of a bar-room
brawl in Sydney, or the tongue of a nagging wife in Bradford.
Most were there because they scorned to shelter behind the efforts
of others while awaiting coercion to defend their own freedom.
Fundamentally they were, perhaps, better than any that were to
follow.

Lastly, Freyberg had the support of the Greek soldiers who had
contrived to escape from the mainland, together with the meagre
armed forces of Crete itself. Before the end of April, representatives
of the Greek cabinet had approached Weston with a request that
all Greek and Cretan forces should come under British command.
It was indeed the only course open to them, since there was no
other hope of equipping or even feeding them. Freyberg had
accepted the situation, while admitting to Wavell that it was no
doubt 'very irregular'. But this was not the moment to consider
the niceties of international protocol. A day or two later, King
George arrived with his Cabinet. He at once issued a Royal
Proclamation in which he handed over control of the fragment
that remained of his Army.

No less serious than the condition of the troops was the lack of
equipment. None of the heavy material had been brought out
from Greece. This meant that there could be no unit transport,
few guns, no tools for digging, and of course no tanks. Moreover, at
every level staff organizations had broken up, with the loss of all
the essential instruments of administration and communication.

3*

The air force consisted of the Fleet Air Arm squadron and their museum pieces at Maleme, together now with the gallant survivors from Greece, who had caused first alarm and then sensation when they had flown in with six Hurricanes; many of the troops had never before seen a British monoplane. The airfields themselves were certain to prove a liability rather than an asset, until such time as protection could be organized for them and aircraft provided to fly from them.

Nor was there any undertaking that the Navy would be able to interfere with seaborne landings. From the moment when he first heard of his new command, this had been Freyberg's chief anxiety. All that he had been able to learn from Cunningham was that the island could not be supplied through the northern harbours: 'We cannot maintain Crete from the northern ports Suda Bay and Heraklion,' Cunningham had told him: 'It is too dangerous. Our losses will be too great.'[12] The warning, issued by the Joint Planning Staff in November of the previous year – and thereafter forgotten, apparently, by themselves, as well as by everybody else – was now seen to have been justified. The Admiral had added that perhaps something might be done from the south. But first it would be necessary to construct landing installations, together with roads leading northwards. In the meantime, there was the problem of providing food for 30,000 troops, together with a population of nearly half a million.

Such were the bare facts that Freyberg was able to acquire during the first hours after taking over his command. He did not find them very heartening. There was worse to come.

In the late afternoon of 1 May a message, dated 29 April arrived direct from the War Office in London. Marked 'Secret and Most Immediate', it contained the substance of an appreciation made two days earlier by the War Cabinet Joint Intelligence Sub-Committee.

According to this [says Davin], attack was certain, probably by sea and air simultaneously. Three hundred transport aircraft were being collected. . . . The area from Larissa to Athens was being stocked up with fuel and supplies. An airlanding division was already in the Balkans and the aerodromes round Athens were available. As many as 3,000 fully equipped troops could be carried in the first wave, and, if gliders were used, the numbers could be raised to 4,000.

[12] DP, Freyberg comments on battle for Crete, 31 Oct. 1949

There might be two or three sorties each day from Greece and perhaps from Rhodes. It was also believed that the Germans would have 'ample' shipping, for tanks as well as men, and that the scale of the seaborne invasion would depend only upon the extent to which it could evade the Navy. Italian naval reinforcement was another possibility.

For the air attack 'the enemy was estimated to have about 285 long-range bombers in the Balkans and about 30 in Rhodes; about 60 twin-engined fighters which would not need extra petrol tanks; about 270 single-engined fighters which would need extra tanks if based north of the Corinth Canal; and 240 dive-bombers with a similar limitation. But both dive-bombers and single-engined fighters could operate from Rhodes without extra tanks'.[13]

The General could 'scarcely believe' his eyes.[14] He realized at once that if this appreciation were even to approach the truth there could be no hope of defending Crete successfully with his present force and equipment. Moreover, he was aware that although this highly unpalatable fact might already be clear enough to Wavell in Cairo, who had every reason to know that almost nothing had been done to prepare the island for its coming ordeal, it was certainly not yet understood in London, nor indeed in Australia and New Zealand. It was time, he felt, to 'introduce a little reality into the calculations for the defence of Crete'.[15]

He therefore at once prepared a message for Cairo:

Forces at my disposal are totally inadequate to meet attack envisaged. Unless fighter aircraft are greatly increased and naval forces made available to deal with seaborne attack I cannot hope to hold out with land forces alone which as result of campaign in Greece are now devoid of any artillery and have insufficient tools for digging and inadequate war reserves of equipment and ammunition. Force here can and will fight but without full support from Navy and Air Force cannot hope to repel invasions. If for other reasons these cannot be made available at once urge that question of holding Crete should be reconsidered. I feel that under terms of my charter it is my duty to inform N.Z. Government of situation in which greater part of my Division is now placed.[16]

At the same time, he drew up a similar message for his Government in Wellington telling them in plain terms of this development:

Feel it my duty to report military situation in Crete. Decision taken

[13] Davin, pp. 31 and 33 [14] DP [15] Davin, p. 42 [16] Churchill, Vol. III, p. 243

in London that Crete must be held at all costs. Have received appreciation scale of attack from War Office, which is as follows:

[Here he gave the figures of the War Office estimation]

In my opinion Crete can only be held with full support from Navy and Air Force. There is no evidence of naval forces capable of guaranteeing us against seaborne invasions and air force in island consists of 6 Hurricanes and 17 obsolete aircraft. Troops can and will fight but as result of campaign in Greece are devoid of any artillery and have insufficient tools for digging, little transport and inadequate war reserves of equipment and ammunition. Would strongly represent to your Government grave situation in which bulk of N.Z. Division is placed and recommend you bring pressure to bear on highest plane in London to either supply us with sufficient means to defend island or to review decision Crete must be held. I have of course made my official representation on this matter to C.-in-C. Middle East.[17]

In another signal, he explained to his Defence Minister that he had felt himself bound to accept the command in Crete, although he would have preferred to set about the immediate reorganization of the New Zealand Division in Egypt. As a 'temporary measure' only, so he hoped, he was putting the 4th and 5th Brigades in the charge of Brigadier Puttick.

The troops still had no suspicion of the ordeal to come. Under the benign influence of a perfect Mediterranean spring they were rapidly recapturing their physical vigour. Nearly all of them supposed that they would soon move on to Egypt. It seemed unlikely that Hitler would venture across such a stretch of sea. Instinctively, rather than out of any knowledge of history, they understood that for centuries no enemy had dared a pursuit by water, and unsupported attack from the air was scarcely to be imagined. Indeed, there was very little evidence that the Germans had any interest in Crete. Already the best of the infantry were beginning to hope that they might attempt an invasion. There seemed to be little prospect of it, but if it should happen what a chance for revenge after the humiliations of the mainland.

In close contact as ever with the feeling of his men, the General was well aware of this swift resurgence of unquestioning optimism. He was glad of it. Certainly he would do nothing to injure it. Only three people in Crete knew the truth of the position, his Chief of Staff, the personal assistant who typed his messages, and his cypher officer.[18] Nobody else, not even his brigadiers, should know the anxieties of his own heart. To Cairo and Wellington he had sent messages which expressed his belief that there was no real hope of holding Crete. Now he wrote for the troops a special Order of the Day. Under his rank and titles it said:

The withdrawal from Greece is now being completed. It has been a difficult operation. A smaller force held a much larger one at bay for over a month and then withdrew from an open beach. This rearguard battle and the withdrawals has been a great feat of arms. The fighting qualities and the steadiness of the troops were beyond praise.

Today the British forces in Crete stand and face another threat, the possibility of invasion. The threat of a landing is not a new one. In England, we faced it for nearly a year. If it comes here it will be delivered with all the accustomed air activity. We have in the last month learned a certain amount about the enemy air methods. If he attacks us here in Crete, the enemy will be meeting our troops on even terms and those of us who met his infantry in the last month ask for no better chance. We are to stand now and fight him back. Keep yourselves fit and be ready for immediate action. I am confident that the force at our disposal will be adequate to defeat any attack that may be delivered upon this island.[19]

At this moment he received a special message from an old friend:

Congratulate you on your vitally important command . . . every good wish.

It was signed 'Winston'.

The two cables and the Order of the Day were brought to him for signature at midnight. He signed them one after the other, feeling that he had done his best to state the position clearly and that he could now go about his job with a clear conscience. Little more than twenty-four hours had passed since Wavell had told him of his new appointment. It had been a busy day for the General.

[18] DP, Freyberg comments on Churchill Draft, 25 Mar. 1959
[19] Davin, p. 42

4

The 'Muddle East'

These messages soon provoked response from both London and Cairo. On 2 May Wavell signalled to Dill, admitting for the first time that a 'difficult problem' had arisen in Crete. 'Enemy air superiority' was likely to prove a critical factor. In particular, it must threaten the supply of the island by sea. There were no good roads north and south, and no harbours on the south coast, although, 'with time', it might be possible to develop landing facilities. Until this was done it would be impossible to find food for the civilian population. The present garrison was 'three British Regular battalions, six New Zealand battalions, one Australian battalion, and two composite battalions of details evacuated from Greece'. Greek forces were 'weak in numbers and equipment', and also 'mostly untrained and unarmed'. There was no artillery and the anti-aircraft defences were 'inadequate'. He went on to refer to the 'great shortage of transport', and outlined the many other problems, concluding with the admission that there were 'at present no modern aircraft in the island',[1] and that it was difficult to see how any protection from the air could be provided.

He was underestimating the number of men who had arrived from Greece. But the matter was of little practical importance since, with the exception of the Australians, most of the additional troops were certain to prove more of a hindrance than a help to the defence.

This news from Cairo cannot have given great encouragement to the War Cabinet. All the same, Churchill at once did his best to reassure the Government in New Zealand, where there was now great anxiety. And in a message to Mr. Fraser, the New Zealand Prime Minister, who had just arrived in Cairo on his way to England, he offered his congratulations upon the efforts of Freyberg's men in Greece, expressing his pleasure that they should

[1] Churchill, Vol. III, p. 244

have arrived 'in such good order' in Crete. The defence of the island, he pointed out, was of vital importance. He was very glad that General Wavell had accepted his suggestion to give the command to Freyberg, who would be sustained 'in every possible way'. Although it was possible that the enemy might be 'only feinting at Crete' all information pointed to an airborne attack in the near future. This, he commented, 'ought to suit the New Zealanders down to the ground, for they will be able to come to close quarters, man to man, with the enemy, who will not have the advantage of tanks and artillery, on which he so largely relies'. If the Germans should succeed in getting a landing, that would be no more than the beginning of their troubles. The defence would be able to 'reinforce far more easily', and the Navy would 'certainly do their utmost' to prevent any seaborne attack. There was not going to be much help from the Royal Air Force which, in the Middle East, was 'scanty and overpressed . . . simply because of the physical difficulties of getting aircraft and their servicing personnel to the spot by the various routes and methods open to us'. Every effort was being made to overcome these difficulties. Things would probably be 'better in the Middle East in a month or so'.[2]

No doubt this was a political message in which the Prime Minister was expressing more optimism than he felt. Certainly he had not yet understood the significance of unresisted strength in the air. But he can scarcely have failed to realize that the ports at Suda and Heraklion were now very likely to share the fate of the Piraeus. His suggestion that it would be possible to 'reinforce far more easily' must therefore be taken to show that he had not seen the implications of Wavell's admission that nothing had been done to provide for supply from the south of the island. Indeed, he was to admit later that realization of the 'halting manner' in which the defence of Crete had been prepared had come to him as an unhappy surprise. Even now he was according to the Navy a responsibility with precedence over that of Crete. Only two days previously, on 1 May, in telegraphing his congratulations to Cunningham about the successful evacuation of Greece, he had mentioned the approaching prospect of a battle in Crete, but at the same time he had emphasized that 'above all' it was necessary to 'cut off seaborne supplies from the Cyrenaican ports'.[3]

Under these handicaps it was unlikely that the Navy would be

[2] Churchill, Vol. III, p. 245   [3] Ibid., p. 243

able to reinforce the island more effectively than would be possible to the enemy if he should now succeed in exploiting his air strength to establish a landing-field bridgehead. And as for things being 'better in the Middle East in a month or so' – it was becoming more obvious every day that long before there could be any improvement the battle would be over.

Wavell also replied directly to Freyberg. First he reported that, from information reaching the Middle East, it was felt that the London estimate of the scale of attack was 'excessive'. Something like '150 single-engined fighters and 40 twin-engined fighters'[4] might be more accurate. On 2 May he gave the important assurance that the Royal Navy would do all that it could to help. Air support remained 'difficult', but arrangements were being made to send artillery, tools, and other equipment. The War Cabinet had given 'definite instructions' that Crete must be held. The difficulties were appreciated, but all the Commanders-in-Chief still believed the scale of enemy attack predicted by the War Office to be 'exaggerated'.[5]

The harassed Commander-in-Chief in Cairo was now striving to make amends for the previous failure in planning and foresight, and to do what still could be done. Freyberg recognized this and was grateful.

The C.-in-C. Middle East did everything that was humanly possible to get us every available bit of equipment, artillery, and defence stores [he was to say in the report that he wrote soon after the battle]. They did their utmost to send us every bit of equipment they had.[6]

After these reassurances, Freyberg was able to feel that his difficulties were being taken seriously. He had made his attempt to introduce 'a little reality' into the situation. Now he gave no further thought to the outside world, but resolutely set about making the utmost use of his restricted resources. 'In war, as a rule, there is a shortage of something or other' wrote Marshal Chuikov after his defence of Stalingrad. 'Many people . . . used to mention the fact in order to emphasize . . . their own merits.'[7] To Freyberg, such an attitude was no less contemptible than to the redoubtable Russian.

Despite the many urgent demands that pressed upon him, he

⁴ Davin, p. 33   ⁵ Ibid., p. 42
⁶ Freyberg Report, quot. Davin, p. 43   ⁷ Chuikov, p. 332

was, from the start, much concerned with the Greeks, and with the Cretans themselves. He attended several conferences with the Greek Commander, and with the King, who was now intent upon placing all that remained of his adopted country's resources at the disposal of the British. King George's origins were Danish, but he had been educated in Prussia, an experience that had left him with a profound distaste for everything German. Later he had lived at Brown's Hotel in London.[8] Now he had become, in every sense, a patriot Greek, a staunch and courageous man, undismayed by his misfortunes, and already recognized by Hitler as a determined enemy. Soon he was to win the admiration of the New Zealanders, among them Freyberg, who paid tribute to him for his 'unfailing help'[9] at this difficult time.

Still less could he be anything but delighted with the local inhabitants. The Cretans come of a fierce and ancient race. At Knossos, near Heraklion, are to be found the ruins of a civilization which flourished four thousand years ago, echoes of which still persist in the mythology which tells of Theseus and his struggles with the Minoan monster. In those days Crete was the centre of the western world. As the centuries passed it became the scene of bitter conflict between the peoples that strove for supremacy along the Mediterranean shores. Greeks, Romans, Arabs, Phoenicians, Venetians and Turks all fought in Crete. Not until 1913 did the Cretans win freedom from the hated Turk. In 1941 many old men still lived who had striven in that cause. These veterans had never ceased to see Crete as a battlefield. Every cross-roads, and every pass through the mountains, served to remind them of the exploits of their youth. Some had spent a period of exile in America. Little trace now remained of this long journey from home. Their traditional black turbans and their bristling moustaches, their lined brown faces, their breeches and top boots, their cummerbunds, belts and daggers gave them the appearance of brigands – with the bearing of kings. Soon many of them, and many women too, were to show once more that they valued their fierce island patriotism more than their lives.

There were few young men. Most were lost among the shattered armies on the mainland. The wives and grandmothers, in accordance with long tradition, were clothed entirely in black, only their faces and hands revealed. But the younger girls and the

[8] Spencer, p. 176   [9] Davin, p. 468, Mr W. E. Murphy

children wore modern European dress, their bright frocks bringing colour to the scene as they stood in the sunlight beside their dark doorways.

Neither Freyberg nor anyone else could know that there had already begun to stir among the Cretans a spirit of resistance no less ferocious than that which, almost a century and a half earlier, had animated the common people of Spain in their struggle against Napoleon: a resistance that must at first be forced to operate under a cruel handicap. A few years earlier, the Metaxas régime, fearing rebellion among these independent islanders, had demanded the surrender of all weapons. At this moment of danger, surpassing any in their history, the men of Crete, who had always borne arms, found themselves largely defenceless.

The force of local Cretans was made up of three garrison battalions of partially trained soldiers, together with eight territorial battalions of recruits. These troops were widely scattered about the island. Few carried weapons. The worn rifles that they possessed were of five different types; the machine-guns were relics from the First World War. How valuable now might have been the men of the ardent Cretan Division, with their knowledge of every rock and byway along the coast. Six months earlier, still with no thought of danger to their own homes, these men had threatened a hunger-strike in fear of missing their hour of glory in Albania. Now they were far away in the North. Taken from the rear by the Germans, they had already been handed over in captivity to the despised Italians. It has been seen that, despite Churchill's instructions, none of the island commanders had attempted to arm and train the men who remained behind. On 27 November the number of 'Greek troops available' had been estimated at 3,733. Between them they had 'only 659 rifles'.[10] Since that time nobody had thought of giving them any more.

There had been no lack of volunteers. Within days of his arrival in the island Freyberg had received an unexpected offer. In careful translation the message said:

We too, the convicts, look towards you with gratefulness and hope for the future of our nation, and kindly ask you to stand by our King and Government, so that they will take care of us when we get out of prison and see that we also do our little bit in winning this sacred struggle of ours for People's Liberty, which is put under the darkness of Tyranny.

[10] DP, Freyberg comments on Churchill Draft, 25 Mar. 1949

We wholeheartedly put ourselves under any service, dangerous or not, provided that the cause of our Allied effort is fulfilled.

Trusting we shall enjoy your proper attention,

We remain,

Respectfully yours,

The convicts of the Island of Crete.[11]

If recruitment had been started during the previous November, as Churchill had suggested, it would have been possible to train two complete divisions of Cretans; in Freyberg's words: 'The entire population of Crete desired to fight.' Rifles for them could have been brought to the island without difficulty on any day during the previous six months.

In training and arms the Greek battalions were little better. Several of them had been called up no more than six weeks earlier. Some of Freyberg's staff were ready enough to point out that the tatterdemalion characters who had been able to make their way to Crete, together with these few lately recruited islanders, were unlikely to be of much military value. With so few weapons available it might be unwise to risk wasting them on the untrained recruits of a beaten ally. The General did not agree. Certainly the Greeks, with their pitiful equipment, had failed to stand against the motorized columns of the Germans backed by an overwhelming air force. But here in Crete, in a scattered fight among rocks and trees, there would be a chance for any resolute marksman to come into his own. Moreover, Freyberg knew well that in this battle, as in all battles, morale would play a vital part. He therefore resolved that such local forces as there were in the island should be encouraged to feel themselves welcome and honoured participants in the struggle. Every effort must be made to supply them at least with rifles. First he organized some 9,000 men into seven 'Greek Regiments' and a 'Garrison Battalion'.[12] On 3 May he asked Middle East Headquarters for the despatch 'immediately' of '13,220 rifles and after that 19,800'.[13] In the meantime, liaison officers, interpreters and instructors were appointed. The forces of King George would remain in their own units, brigaded within the British war establishment.

These good intentions were frustrated by the continued lack of weapons. German raids had greatly reduced production from the Birmingham factories, and to this had been added the diffi-

[11] DP   [12] Davin, p. 480 et seq.   [13] DP

culty of supply across the Mediterranean. Even for their own ancient firing-pieces, the ammunition available for the Greeks seldom exceeded three rounds per man. The Cretan Police, about 1,000 strong, were more fortunate. Both armed and disciplined, they were likely to prove the most effective of the home forces.

But nothing could daunt the universal will to resist. Like his troops, Freyberg had quickly discovered an unexpected sympathy with these allies. 'We have no business here', Moore had written from Salamanca in 1808, 'but being here it would never do to abandon the Spaniards without a struggle'.[14] By the middle of May, Freyberg was beginning to think in similar terms of these new friends in Crete.

He decided to maintain the disposition of his immobile patch-work army largely as it had been left to him by Weston. The New Zealanders, with the support of two Greek battalions, would defend the ten-mile stretch of coast west of Canea. Another Greek battalion, stiffened by a small New Zealand detachment, was appointed to guard the little harbour of Kastelli in Kisamos Bay, some fifteen miles beyond Maleme. Weston was given the Suda Area. This included Canea, the harbour and environs of the bay, and the Akrotiri Peninsula. With his polyglot command were the 1st Welch Battalion, the Marines, a Greek regiment, some Australians, a few stray gunners and engineers, Palestinians, Cypriots, and civilian refugees from Yugoslavia, together with thousands more men from miscellaneous units of all kinds. The reduced battalions of the 19th Australian Brigade, one of them at less than half strength, were sent to join the Greeks at Georgeou-polis, fifteen miles west of Retimo town. Heraklion remained the responsibility of the 14th British Infantry Brigade under Chappel. It had the support of an Australian and three Greek battalions.

Thus he aimed to protect the three airfields with their adjoining ports. The widely separated garrisons might have to fight in isolation, since the connecting road was exposed to attack both from the air and the sea. Each must succeed equally in repulsing the enemy. Ultimately the fall of one must mean the fall of all. If the Germans should secure an airfield they would be able to use heavy troop-carrying planes to bring in fully-armed infantry, together with guns, transport and light armoured vehicles; and, despite the optimism of the War Cabinet in London, it was

14 Hibbert, *Corunna*, p. 63

becoming increasingly likely that more men and material could be landed in this way than could be expected to complete the sea passage from Egypt. Later the daylight protection of the *Luftwaffe* must enable a few vessels from Greece to evade the Royal Navy and creep into any harbour that might be captured.

It was therefore vital that the defence should be able to concentrate quickly against any such danger point. But here Freyberg came against an insoluble problem. It was not merely that, to judge by the Greek example, the exposure of vehicles on the roads during the day might soon become impossible. More immediate was the fact that he had very little transport. Even at night the movement of stores was greatly hampered. The vehicles and Bren-carriers belonging to formations that had not been in Greece were shared out among all the rest. A few were scraped together in the hope that the New Zealand 4th Brigade might be equipped as a mobile reserve. The handful that remained were not enough even to supply the battalions. The whole of the newly improvised New Zealand 10th Brigade could claim only a single truck.

Freyberg was painfully conscious of the handicap imposed by this immobility. In the face of enemy landings from the air, his force was likely to be as cumbrous as a fat man trying to protect an orchard from a group of marauding small boys. He feared that the Germans might exploit their control of the air by seizing some flat stretch of ground and using it to build a landing strip. If they did this far away in the south it should be possible to contain them, for a time at least. But he felt that they might try it much closer at hand, perhaps even in the shallow valley which lay south-west of Canea itself, a position that would give them direct access to the town and Suda Bay. At this time he could see no limit to what they might attempt. Neither he nor anyone else understood that light airborne forces, operating at such close range, would scarcely be able to defend themselves while undertaking a major construction effort as well.

If only they could be granted a little time. But time was a factor that might work both ways. Freyberg had no idea that the enemy was about to attack Russia.

There seemed no need for Germany to hurry the final capture of Crete [he wrote later]. We, for our part, were mostly preoccupied by seaborne landings, not by the threat of air landings. We felt that if they succeeded in getting a lodgment they could build up and take Crete.

The 'greatest hope was that they would not commit enough troops for the job'.[15] At the Conference on 30 April he had told Wavell that he felt that 'a seaborne landing was the greatest threat'.[16]

On 29 April Wilson and Weston had made a similar appreciation:

The enemy's approach to the island [is] comparatively easy. He [can] provide air protection for a seaborne expedition. This, of course, from the enemy point of view, would merely make the reduction of the Island a matter of time.[17]

Nobody sought to dispute this view.

In the light of all existing knowledge at the time [observes Commander Kemp in his *Official History of the War at Sea*], it appeared most unlikely that an airborne invasion by itself could succeed without seaborne support, and it was on the Mediterranean Fleet's capacity to destroy the enemy reinforcing troop convoys that the hopes of the defence lay.[18]

Freyberg was reminded of the situation he had seen in England after the fall of Dunkirk. Large numbers of potentially excellent troops were temporarily disorganized and poorly equipped. Many were only half-trained. But to get at them the enemy would have to come by air or sea. Or both. There were, however, two essential differences. In England not every man had needed to be in the front line; from organized bases training and re-equipment could go forward swiftly and constantly. And in England there had been an air force. Over the coast, even over the Channel, the Germans had never been able to achieve more than a transient and local air superiority.

There could be no such opposition when the *Luftwaffe* turned on Crete. Not much had been seen of it yet. But plainly this was a respite that would not last long. What could there be to resist it? Fighter aircraft were promised indeed, for June perhaps. What was to happen in the meantime? For the troops on land it would be difficult enough. But what about the Navy? Here again there arose directly the threat of landings from the sea. In the War Office appreciation of 29 April, Freyberg had been told that the Greek shipping was 'ample for seaborne operations', and that

[15] DP, Freyberg comments on Churchill Draft, 25 Mar. 1949
[16] Ibid.   [17] Ibid.   [18] Kemp, p. 133

'lighters for transport tanks' were 'also believed available'. Indeed the 'scale' of an enemy seaborne attack was thought to be 'dependent' only upon the 'extent' to which it could evade the Navy. Precise information was lacking. But the tip of the mainland reached to within sixty miles of western Crete, and Athens itself lay only a hundred and eighty miles north of Canea. It therefore seemed certain that an invasion flotilla, starting before dawn, would be able to make the whole journey in daylight. How then could the Royal Navy hope to intervene, without the support of land-based fighter planes, in the face of an overwhelming onslaught from the air? Was it not possible that the Germans might regard the situation as offering them a double prize, not merely the capture of the island, but also the destruction of the Mediterranean Fleet?

These were vital matters that urgently required the attention of Middle East Headquarters in Egypt. In addition to accurate Intelligence they demanded the technical opinion of naval experts:

A comparatively junior commander such as I was at the time [Freyberg was to write after the war], or any commander, coming in at the last minute, should not be faced with these inter-Service problems which depend upon questions of availability and supply of troops, equipment, ammunition, aircraft, and shipping, of which he has little knowledge, and over which he has no control.[19]

From his quarry on the Akrotiri Peninsula, with the help only of his amateur staff, he could not hope to make an accurate judgement.

Wavell had little to offer. At that time such matters were beyond the capacity of his Headquarters. There still was little technical exchange between the Services. No thought was given to the problems that the enemy might encounter in an attempt to land an invasion flotilla. Yet in fact there was abundant reason to suppose that such an operation, undertaken at short notice, from a tideless sea against an unknown and almost wholly rocky coastline, was likely to prove hazardous and uncertain even if only lightly resisted. Inspection of the northern beaches by naval officers might have done much to lessen anxiety about a sea attack. It would have become apparent that only vessels of shallow draft would have been able to approach the shore, and even these with much difficulty. This was quickly understood by the New

[19] DP, Freyberg comments on battle for Crete, 31 Oct. 1949

Zealander, Colonel Kippenberger, who had been given an improvised brigade west of Canea:

> I did not understand why our commanders were so worried about a seaborne invasion, the principal reason being that none of them had been down to look at the coast. Just before going to Greece I attended a combined training course at Kabrit and had learned something about steep beaches, shelving beaches, etc. I went down to the coast in my sector. There was only one place where any vessel drawing three or four feet could have got within a chain of the coast. In many places there were rocks which would have made a landing impossible. There was a little bay near the 7th General Hospital where there was a perfect landing beach but everywhere else it was extremely difficult and on the first night I had no hesitation in thinning out the single company which I thought sufficient to cover my sector of the beach.[20]

If the character of the coast had been fully understood it must at once have raised the question of how many flat-bottomed craft might be available to the Germans, and above all what might be the speed at which they would be able to sail. Once they had left the protection of the islands they would need to achieve a full six knots if they were to reach Crete before dusk. After night had fallen they would lose the protection of the *Luftwaffe*.

At no time did there reach Freyberg any hint that thought was being given to these questions in Cairo. He was left with a deepening impression that the 'fear was a seaborne landing bringing tanks'.[21]

As for the weight of the expected airborne attack, here again the War Office prediction was far from clear. It had spoken of '3,000–4,000 parachutists or airborne troops in first sortie. Two or three sorties per day possible from Greece and three or four from Rhodes if Rhodes not used as dive bombers' base'. What did this mean? A maximum of some ten thousand a day? Or double that number if they came from Rhodes as well? How long would they come for? How many parachutists were there? And what was the distinction between parachutists and other airborne troops? Were some to come by glider and some by troop-carrying aircraft? In particular, would it be possible for troop-carrying aircraft to bring infantry reinforcement before the capture of an airfield? Would they start crash-landing all over the place in the first minutes of the attack?

20 DP, Brig. H. K. Kippenberger to Brig. H. B. Latham, 27 Aug. 1952
21 DP, Freyberg comments on Churchill Draft, 25 Mar. 1949

Without some guidance on these problems Freyberg could only plan in the dark. How greatly now must he have felt the lack of a trained staff to interpret and balance the confused information that was arriving from England and Cairo.

In the meantime the sun shone over Crete. April came to an end and the days of May followed in tranquil succession. Along the coast west of Canea the New Zealanders spent many hours swimming in the sea. Most of the unattached troops were still resting in the transit areas among the ravines south-west of Canea. Here they bathed, sunned themselves, and washed their clothes in the icy torrents that tumbled out of the mountains. All around them the spring flowers had burst into luxurious colour. Tamarisk and oleander, geranium and rhododendron sprouted among the pools and grottoes, while above them the bare slopes of the mountains were speckled with daisies, poppies and flowering thistles. As the days grew warmer the evening dew brought with it the scent of wild thyme.

In a diminishing stream, stragglers continued to arrive by caïque from the mainland. It became known that the evacuation attempt from Kalamata had failed. There was much discussion of the recent campaign. Tales were retold of Servia and Katarine, of the delaying action at Mount Olympus, of the confused night in Larissa, of the long withdrawal through Lamia and Thebes, and of the German parachute landing across the Corinth Canal. The mood was one of increasing disillusion. The men did not feel that the war would be lost. Indeed much was said to the effect that things would be better now that the British and Empire troops were on their own with no allies to falter at a critical moment. 'We're in the final now', was the catch-phrase of the moment. But they realized with bitterness how wide was the gap between the facts and the palliatives of the official bulletins. Inevitably there was mounting resentment against those remote directors of the war who had exposed them to such impossible odds while continuing blandly to flaunt a total ignorance of the new factor of air power. What seemed inexcusable was that misleading public hopes of effective aid to Greece should have been blazoned about the world when in fact none had ever existed. It was disconcerting to feel that after two years of fighting the nation's leaders were so ignorant of the realities – and so shameless in exposing their incomprehension. Like those disillusioned

French soldiers who had taken part in Nivelle's abortive offensive on the Aisne in 1917 they felt that they had been deceived, and worse still, deceived by fools. Many years later Churchill was to write words appropriate to these weeks of 1941:

The British people can face peril and misfortune with fortitude and buoyancy, but they bitterly resent being deceived or finding that those responsible for their affairs are themselves dwelling in a fool's paradise.

One man was exempt from this increasing weight of contempt, although he had been the first to instigate the venture in Greece and second to none in the extent of his initial self-deception. But instinctively the troops felt that where there was such abundance to be thankful for it was also easy to forgive. About Churchill no one had the slightest doubt.

There was not yet any thought of fighting in Crete. The men were sure that soon they would all be going on to Egypt. For the present, they still felt inclined to relax. There were no Military Police to restrain them. From the transit camps they went on shopping expeditions, buying cheese and honey in the markets of Canea and returning to sit at ease in the village squares, drinking their *krassi*, the raw local wine, and exchanging with the Cretans their few words of Greek and English. *Kalimera* and *Kalispera*, Good morning and Goodnight, became the key to social intercourse, and also the word *nero*, later to become for every soldier the most important word in his vocabulary, the word that means 'water'. Quickly, too, they fell into the way of the English soldier abroad. The women began to wash shirts and underwear, and many homes now found a man to do some of the rough work about the house. At Galatas, a picturesque hill-top village three miles south-west of Canea, a radio blared tirelessly into the little square, playing again and again a popular ditty about Mussolini, the old men, the women, and the children marking the end of each verse with an appropriate throat-cutting gesture. Very soon the troops had learnt to do it too. Those who had fought on the mainland, remembering what they had seen during the long journey to the coast, felt a sudden spirit of kinship with these stout-hearted people. No longer did they think of themselves as mere agents of a political gesture in defence of an alien land. To their own surprise they had been caught up in admiration for this staunch Mediterranean race of which had known nothing. Here was a feeling for freedom to match their own, backed by a courage and resolve that had already been expressed in deeds, despite the brutal inequalities imposed by modern weapons.

At night it was still very cold, and the troops from Greece had only the clothes they had been wearing during the evacuation, together with the single blanket which had been issued to them since their arrival. Nor had there been any improvement in their primitive eating and cooking utensils. But these deficiencies scarcely seemed to matter. They swam in the sea, ate oranges and lay in the sun. In the evenings there were long slow conversations in the olive groves among the croaking frogs, with sometimes the nostalgic notes of a familiar tune hesitantly played on a mouth-organ. Everywhere there was the atmosphere of holiday.

Weather fine [a soldier of the New Zealand 23rd Battalion wrote in his diary], am very happy and in the best of health. (26 April) . . . went down to the sea for a swim. All we do is eat oranges and swim. Having a marvellous time. God! I am as fit as a fiddle – a real box of birds (29 April) . . . on fatigues all day, carting wood and water for the cookhouse. We are having a grand time. The grub is rather awful though (30 April) . . . went for a long march over the hills for the day and took our grub, with about a dozen oranges each. Boy! I am feeling fit. Never been so well off before (2 May) . . . this holiday we're having seems too good to last. These swims in the old Mediterranean are great (7 May).[22]

Each day the sun grew warmer and the sea more inviting. At noon the silence was broken only by the whirring of the cicadas, by the rattle of the trucks that passed occasionally along the coast road, and by one other sound, scarcely heard and little regarded; hour after hour, from somewhere far above within the perfect blue of the sky, there waxed and waned the drowsy hum of a reconnaissance plane.

[22] Ross, 23 Battalion, p. 59

5

The Enemy

The Germans also had their difficulties. They were entering upon an adventure for which there were no precedents. Such minor air-landing operations as they had attempted hitherto had been conducted within close range of strong motorized relief forces. Now they were sending their airborne troops to an island that was separated from the inhabited mainland by more than a hundred miles of open sea, upon which the control of the Royal Navy, even if it were hotly contested in daylight, remained at night undisputed. And there was no clear indication of the enemy strength that might await them.

The manner in which the German High Command sought to deal with these problems is shown in *Operation Crete (Einsatz Kreta)*, the report on the battle that was issued by the Headquarters of XI Air Corps on 11 June 1941. This important document has been too little regarded by historians. There is no reason to doubt that it contains the essential truth so far as the German staff knew it at the time. In few important particulars does it differ from what soon became apparent to the defence. The numbers of men engaged, the timings and outcome of the various actions, the estimated numbers of casualties suffered and prisoners taken, all are largely in accord between the two sides. Only in the matter of the landing techniques employed by the airborne forces is there to be found any significant divergence. And here no detached judgement can fail to infer that the German account is in the main accurate, and that most of the discrepancies can be traced back to the wild tales that spread among the men of Freyberg's army during the first days of the fighting. Rumour founded upon fear and prejudice is the normal accompaniment of battle. In Crete it was natural that much of it should be believed. It has remained too long unrefuted.

For years Goebbels had permitted no uncalculated word to reach the German Press. But *Operation Crete* was a highly secret military assessment issued at a time when German strength was so overwhelming as to have no need of self deception. Moreover, the attack was seen at first as a prototype for similar operations upon a larger scale. As such it was subjected to critical, searching and informed appraisal by professional colleagues who would have been quick to recognize and decry any attempt at dissimulation. Basically it must be accepted as true, and the same may be said, with due allowance for some inevitable self-justification, of the diaries compiled by the divisional, brigade and battalion commanders who took part.

From *Operation Crete* there emerges a clear picture of the German Order of Battle. Overall responsibility lay with General Löhr, the commander of the Air Fleet IV. The first assault was to be delivered by the glider and parachute troops of the 7th Air-landing Division, part of XI Air Corps. The bridgeheads would then be reinforced by the 5th Mountain Division, followed by elements of the 6th Mountain and 5th Armoured Divisions. Some of these forces would be brought in by troop-carrying aircraft which would land on the captured airfields. Others would follow by sea in such assorted vessels as could be mustered.

About 22,750 men were to engage in some three or four days. Originally it had been intended that the 22nd Airborne Division should be used in support; despite its name this division was formed of infantry accustomed to travel by air; it contained no parachutists and had no gliders. But since it was required for the invasion of Russia it was decided that the Mountain Troops should be used instead, although most of them had never entered an aircraft. Air transport would be provided by 500 troop-carriers from XI Air Corps, the slow and cumbrous Junkers 52 that three years before had bombed the Republicans in Spain. They would be accompanied by 70, if possible 80, gliders. Much of the preliminary exploration and bombing of the island would be left to VIII Air Corps under the command of General Freiherr von Richtofen who could dispose of 280 bombers, 150 Stuka dive-bombers, some 200 single and twin-engined Messerschmitt fighters, and a few reconnaissance machines: a total of about 650 aircraft. The air strength available thus amounted to some 1,330 planes and gliders as compared to the War Office estimate of 885, a number judged by Wavell to be 'exaggerated'.[1]

---

[1] Davin, p. 83–85 (In his Diary Halder noted on 28 May 1941 that there were 600 troop carriers, Ringel, p. 128, claims that eventually 650 took part)

To mount an attack on this scale presented a formidable task. And time had become a vital factor. Victory must be complete before the starting-date for the invasion of Russia; on 30 April this was confirmed as 22 June.[2] If necessary, the Balkan Army would detach more of its resources; most of the tanks were being rushed northward, but sixteen divisions were still available in Greece. The Italian Navy might be persuaded to help. A few weeks earlier it had been hit a staggering blow off Cape Matapan, and had later made no attempt to interfere with the British evacuation of the mainland. But it was hoped that with the *Luftwaffe* above it, it would become more venturesome.

Intensive efforts were made to ensure the arrival of the necessary supplies. All material had to be transported in stages by coastal steamer, since the Balkan roads and railways, at best quite unsuited for the passage of heavy traffic, had been further damaged during the fighting. 'The most vulnerable bottle-neck,' says *Operation Crete*, was 'the supply of the airfields with petrol and oil'. This could only be done by using barrels obtained 'with great trouble'. No less grave was the condition of the airfields themselves which were few, small, and dusty, and lacking the installations that were necessary for the many hundreds of planes that would have to fly from them. Savagely, the civilian population was driven to repair these deficiencies.

In immediate charge of all this activity was General Kurt Student, the source and inspiration of the whole enterprise. In 1909 he had entered the German Army as a second lieutenant, but from his earliest days he had been captivated by the thought that aeroplanes must soon play a vital part in the conduct of war. By 1913 he had already joined the infant German Air Force, and in the war that began a year later he was twice wounded while serving as a pilot. After further brief service in the army he had returned to the *Luftwaffe* in 1934, becoming Inspector of Parachute Troops four years later. Soon he was appointed Commander of the newly formed Air Division.

He was now something of a national figure, and his new responsibilities brought him into close touch with Hitler. Indeed, it was Hitler who had suggested to him that parachutists might be used against the bridges on the Albert Canal in May 1940. This

---

[2] Long, p. 193, 'From a detailed monograph prepared in Mar. 1952 by the Enemy Documents Section of the Historical Branch of the U.K. Cabinet Office'

operation was a success. A small force of 500 men captured the crossings intact, while, at the same time, German ground forces were unable to prevent the destruction of the bridges over the lower Meuse. Even more striking was the *coup* against Eben Emael. Using gliders for the first time, two officers and seventy-eight men swept silently onto the platform of the fort, holding the garrison in subjection for twenty-four hours until the arrival of mechanized infantry.

Student was severely wounded in Holland, but the renown of these exploits had brought him a prestige which was resented by some of his colleagues among the German generals. They felt, as they were later to feel about Rommel, that he owed more to public acclaim, and to close association with Hitler, than to ability. General Meindl, who commanded the Storm Regiment of the air-landing troops in Crete, was to say of him that he had 'big ideas but not the faintest conception as to how they were to be carried out'.[3] Baron von der Heydte, one of his battalion commanders, was more discerning. He saw him as a 'non-political type of German officer . . . a soldier and only second a German soldier . . . austere in his manner, unable to fill others with his enthusiasm'. But von der Heydte also gave him credit for an ability and coolness which inspired confidence, together with important qualities of military intuition, his main strength lying in his 'ability to appreciate the enemy's situation accurately, even when actual information about the enemy is wrong'.[4]

He was soon to have every need of this faculty, perhaps the supreme virtue required for a general in the field.

On 25 April, the day on which it had been decided to attack Crete, the men of the 7th Airlanding Division were still far away in their German training quarters. In much secrecy they were quickly assembled and put on trains for the south, passing through a silent hostile Prague, across Hungary, and then, amid scenes of increasing enthusiasm, into Bulgaria. Von der Heydte, who was later to write a book about the battle, noticed this improvement in their reception as they moved further from the frontiers of Germany. He had forgotten, perhaps, that it was their closest neighbours who knew them best. As they continued down into Greece, travelling now in motor transport, they met some of the tank regiments on their way back. The soldiers, burnt brown by

[3] Shulman, p. 58   [4] DP

the sun, did not miss the chance to shout their comments that it was a little late in the day to be coming to Greece.

During the summer of 1940, the German airborne troops had acquired a vast and sinister reputation, not only among the nations of Europe, but in the eyes of the world. It was understood that there were many thousands of them, perhaps hundreds of thousands. Not many people had seen them, but there was always someone who knew all about them, even if he had not caught sight of them himself. In Poland and France, so it was said, parachutists had been dropped in hordes, sometimes wearing their own uniforms, but often disguised as French or English soldiers, even as priests, postmen or market women. The disintegration of the defences was thought to have been greatly hastened by the sudden emergence of these sinister agents. This was accepted in the highest quarters. On 21 May 1940, the Dutch Foreign Minister had told a Press Conference in London that the parachutists who had attacked his country had been dressed as nuns, monks, and tram-car conductors.[5]

Second to none in the credence which they gave to these myths were the Chiefs of Staff in London. A year after the campaign in France they still believed the Germans to have available at least 'half a dozen'[6] parachute divisions.

The facts were very different. Although airborne forces had played some part in the campaigns of 1940, their main influence had been upon morale. In Poland they had not been in action. Later their feats of arms had been spectacular, but not critical in any military sense, and in number they were much fewer than was supposed. There had been no addition to the original Air-landing Division. No disguises had been worn. Nor was any such device to be used against the Western Allies until the abortive counter-stroke through the Ardennes in September 1944.

But, in these early months of 1941, the threat of German attack from the air was still invested in mystery. To the War Cabinet in London, to the High Command, and to the troops themselves it appeared as a great and yet unmeasured menace. Indeed it had taken upon itself an air of fantasy, mingled with the added threat of the unknown. This was the atmosphere that had helped to turn the French retreat into rout. In Crete its influence upon the subalterns and other ranks, with their robust disinclination to remain long impressed by something once seen, was to prove less

[5] *The Times* on 22 May 1940   [6] Churchill, Vol. III, p. 253

than upon the senior officers, with their preoccupations about communication and control.

Although relatively small in numbers, the German Air Division nevertheless represented, in Churchill's words, 'the flame of the Hitler Youth Movement . . . an ardent embodiment of the Teutonic spirit of revenge for the defeat of 1918'.[7] Here was the 'spear-point of the German lance'.[8] Already it might have been launched against England if British air power had been broken in 1940. Or against Malta. Instead, its whole weight was now to be thrust at Crete.

The men who were to take part in this unparalleled onslaught were nearly all young. According to von der Heydte the average age in his battalion was little more than eighteen years.[9] Many were ardent Nazis; euphemistically von der Heydte describes them as 'the idealists'. In fact they were child fanatics in whom every youthful passion had been transmuted into a single perverted devotion towards Hitler and his vision of Germanic world conquest. Their meagre education had consisted of indoctrination into the Nazi view of history. They had seen the terror of neighbours and the sudden disappearance of unbelievers, and had been delighted to participate in these events. Eagerly they had worked for the régime as informers. To win their spurs as future leaders of the New Order in Europe, they had shown themselves adept at chivvying Rabbis and breaking Jewish shop windows. Now, in this glowing springtime of German success, it seemed that a limitless extension of these easy pleasures awaited them. Nothing could ever go wrong. They were young men possessed.

Not all the parachutists were like this. There were the characters to be found in every army, the ambitious, the men determined on promotion at whatever cost to others, and also not a few of the gay adventurers, a type which corresponded very closely with that of the volunteers who at that time were beginning to form the new Special Units in the British Army. Two or three friends, often the best of their age, had joined the parachutists from an infantry battalion, much to the chagrin and annoyance of their officers.

I liked the adventurers best [says von der Heydte]. They jumped easily into life and they found it worth living for, whatever it brought along, provided it did not become monotonous. Their heads were

[7] Churchill, Vol. III, p. 252   [8] Ibid., p. 253   [9] von der Heydte, p. 25 *et seq.*

4

filled with nonsensical pranks but also with good ideas. You could go horse stealing with them, but you could also take them on any patrol. They were born parachutists. Many of them had committed some offence, only to become honest with us. Others had run away from home solely to prove themselves men.

They were not unlike the young soldier that Freyberg had been at that age.

Von der Heydte himself has been described as belonging to that 'soft-spoken, extremely intelligent class of Germans, whose protestations of innocence of everything National Socialist, almost bit off the tongue they held firmly wedged in their cheek'.[10] This may well be true. Nevertheless, with an ambivalence characteristically German, he reveals himself no less, in his book about Crete, as a man of sensibility.

Several factors served to swell the self-confidence of the young parachutists. They were aware of belonging to an *élite*, that classic stimulus to military courage. In the cafés of the garrison towns, the girls were always interested in the badge that showed the golden plunging eagle, symbol of a new and glamorous form of warfare. Moreover, they knew that their leaders, even the most senior of them, would be sharing with them the same risks, and that these officers represented not only the new men, the ex-rankers and professional Nazis, but others who bore names long honoured in German military tradition, names such as von Plessen, Bauer and Blücher. Typical of the first sort was Colonel Ramcke, who, like Massena had started life as a cabin-boy, making his first parachute jump at the age of fifty-one, and of the second, Lieutenant Count von Blücher. Finally, the parachutists had the courage of ignorance. Few of them had been in action.

Their training had taught them to leave their aircraft, about twelve men from each Junkers 52, at a height of two to four hundred feet, hitting the ground with a forward roll in five to twelve seconds. For the jump they wore special crash helmets, and knee-length camouflaged overalls of green and yellow, with straps between their legs. Canvas padding protected their knees and elbows. In their haversacks were two days' rations of bread and chocolate, with thirst-quenching tablets, cooking utensils, and a blanket. A small water bottle and a jack-knife hung from their belts.

During the drop they held a Schmeisser machine pistol, and

[10] Shulman, p. 236

sometimes two or three grenades. They could carry little ammunition. After landing and breaking free from their harness,
their first need was to muster in groups and equip themselves
from the canisters which were parachuted down among them. In
this way they were provided with rifles, machine-guns, mortars,
grenades, light field guns, and ammunition of all kinds, an
armament which would give them something like double the
fire power of their opponents in the British Infantry battalions.
But first they must reach the canisters. In the face of a resolute
hidden enemy this might not be easy. Little less important were
the water containers, the food, and the medical stores which
were also thrown from the planes. And in Crete there were to be
tents, chairs and tables. Nothing had been forgotten. In addition
to his standard issue of contraceptives, each man had been given
a short glossary of German-English phrases phonetically spelt,
among them the useful sentence 'If yu lei yu uill bi schott'.[11] All
was ready for a great and enjoyable occasion.

The Parachute Battalions, each containing 550 men divided
into four companies, were organized in regiments, or brigade-
groups, about 2,000 strong. The numbers in each battalion of the
Storm Regiment, the first of the *élite*, were increased to 600.
Some 600 of the men in this regiment were transported by about
seventy gliders, a *staffel* of fifteen gliders for 145 men. They
carried rifles, machine-guns, grenades and mortars, and were
therefore able to get into action much more quickly than the
parachutists. Only one special skill was required of them – that
they should disembark on arrival with the utmost dispatch, an
accomplishment for which they felt every incentive, since the
gliders, although impressive when in the air, were extremely
fragile, constructed out of wood with canvas stretched over
narrow ribs of steel. These machines were capable of cruising
some fifty miles after release from fifteen thousand feet, the range
depending upon the strength and direction of the wind. Their air
speed was about seventy miles an hour. With the use of flaps it was
easy enough to put them down safely in open fields or on to a
broad road. But they at once broke up if they hit rough country.[12]

In the hope of overcoming the limitations imposed by this novel

[11] Guedalla, *Middle East*, p. 131

[12] Based on Brief Notes on the German Army, G.S.I.G.H.Q. MEF Dec. 1941, together
with *Einsatz Kreta*, the Battle Report of XI Air Corps. But figures given by the
German writer Franz Kurowski suggest that, whatever their establishment, fewer
than 60 gliders landed in Crete. (See later, chapter 9, footnotes 1, 4, 5.)

form of warfare, Student had trained his men to achieve a sudden landing in the middle of an enemy's defences, thereafter making use of the available fortifications to repel counter-attack, while at the same time achieving the maximum disruption of communications. The first of the shock troops would usually arrive by glider. Here the great advantage was the silence in which fully equipped men could be launched immediately upon the objective. Within a few minutes the glider force would be supplemented by parachutists dropped a few hundred yards away. While still half paralysed, the enemy should be at the mercy of any orthodox frontal attack.

This technique had worked very well in Holland. So far it had not been attempted against men who were both resolute and prepared. Another factor was that of timing. The parachute landing on the Corinth Canal, carried out on the morning of 26 April, shortly before the end of the campaign in Greece, had been safe enough but just too late to be effective, a consideration likely to arise only during an enemy retreat. It was plain that in Crete there must be one problem that would be critical – the provision of adequate support and supply.

Earlier that spring, Keitel and Jodl, like Goering and Raeder, had suggested that the parachutists might best expend their bursting energies upon the capture of Malta, 'since this seemed to be the only way to secure permanently the sea-route to North Africa'.[13] Student had not been enthusiastic. In so small an island there was a danger that the enemy might effect 'a quick switch of reserve forces'.[14] By contrast, the long northern coastline in Crete 'favoured invaders from the air'.

This was the concept that Hitler had accepted. It was now embodied in the order of the battle. The men of the 7th Airlanding Division would deliver the first assault. Since they would be unable to maintain themselves for long against serious opposition they must very quickly be reinforced. This would be done by heavy transport planes putting down with infantry loads on the captured runways. At the same time, troops would be landed from the sea on the open coast.

Thus it was vital that at least one airfield should be captured at the earliest possible moment. Many writers have maintained that it was always part of the German intention to land troop-carriers

[13] Warlimont, p. 131   [14] Student, p. 60

upon beaches and upon other open spaces. In 1952, Christopher Buckley expressed this view in a description of the battle published by Her Majesty's Stationery Office. It is disproved both by *Operation Crete* and by Student's own comments. The Germans understood that to crash land these heavy machines would be disastrous. There was never any thought of putting them down except upon an established airstrip. Nor did Student ever consider the possibility of constructing a runway. Without heavy weapons, his lightly-armed men would be hard enough put to it to defend their captured objectives. Certainly they would have neither energy nor material for anything else.

Anxious to exploit his command of the air, Student first proposed six simultaneous landings along the north coast, at Kastelli, Maleme, Canea, Georgeoupolis, Retimo and Heraklion, together with a seventh operation against the Askifou Plain which lay isolated high within the White Mountains thirty miles south of Suda Bay. It was evident, however, that this would cause too much dispersion of aircraft. Löhr then suggested that all arms should be concentrated against the Sector Maleme-Suda. Student objected. He felt that planes from the eastern airfields might be used by the defence against such an isolated landing. In this, he was paying unconscious tribute to the gallant efforts of the handful of R.A.F. pilots. Had he known that no more aircraft would be available to fly from these fields for many weeks to come he might well have agreed with Löhr. But, as he judged the situation at the time, he felt it necessary to put out of action all the airfields simultaneously by a widely spaced onslaught, capturing them for his own use, and at the same time paralysing communication within the whole system of the defence.

Since facilities in Greece could not sustain an operation on this scale, Goering put forward the new idea that two sorties should be made on the same day. This was accepted. The Maleme-Suda Sector would be attacked at 8.15 a.m. By 2 p.m. the Junker groups were to be ready to take off again 'punctually and in close formation'.[15] At about 4 p.m., this second sortie would begin to drop parachutists at Retimo and Heraklion. Thus it should be possible to ensure maximum concentration of aircraft at the critical moment for each phase of the operation. Some 9,000 parachutists of the 7th Airlanding Division would take part, together

[15] *Einsatz Kreta*, Battle Report of XI Air Corps. The report insists that the airlanding troops were to capture the 'three usable airfields'. It contains no hint of planned crash-landings or of improvised landing strips.

with 600 men,[16] all members of the Storm Regiment, who were to go by glider. As soon as an airfield had been captured the troop-carriers were to return with the first 5,000 men of the 5th Mountain Division. The sea expeditions would serve as a precaution against the expected destruction of the runways, while at the same time bringing in light tanks and heavier guns than could be carried by air. It was intended that a flotilla should 'reach the open coast west of Maleme on the afternoon'[17] of the first day. Another would be directed to the east of Heraklion on the second day. Each would carry 'one infantry battalion of Mountain Troops, heavy weapons without transport, and supplies'.[18] Also to travel by sea were 2,000 parachutists for whom no space could be found in the aircraft.[19, 20]

It was unlikely that the attack would achieve surprise. But Student hoped to prepare the way by an intensive onslaught from the air delivered by bombers and by low-flying aircraft machine-gunning from all directions. The surviving defenders should then be so dazed and demoralized that his men would be upon them before they knew what was happening. He decided to use most of the gliders at Maleme, with a few more to attack important points in the Canea-Suda area. They would be followed immediately by drops of parachutists in the vicinity of the three airfields and near Alikianou, south-west of Canea. Recognition and communication between the land and air forces had been worked out and practised with the greatest attention. Almost every officer had radio-transmission within his unit; for the glider troops there would be two wireless transmitter sets to each platoon of thirty men.[21]

There is nothing in the German documents to suggest that the sea invasion was planned with the meticulous care that had been lavished upon the preparations for the airborne assault. General Ringel, Commander of the 5th Mountain Division, was to observe that the only navigational equipment available for the naval expedition had consisted of 'a 1/500,000 map and a pocket compass'.[22] *Operation Crete* maintains that 'from the very first the early establishment of shipping communications between the mainland and Crete for the follow-up of heavy weapons, motor-

---

[16] For estimation of enemy strength see p. 161, footnotes 1, 2, 3, 4
[17] *Einsatz Kreta*, Battle Report of XI Air Corps   [18] Ibid.   [19] Davin, p. 85
[20] von der Heydte, p. 42. Ringel, p. 64, says 'some companies of Parachute Infantry' with support units. *Einsatz Kreta* is discreetly silent about the parachutists who were sent by sea.
[21] DP, Report by Brig. E. Puttick   [22] Harmeling, p. 24

transport and supplies had been considered a condition for the success of the operation'.[23] From this it would seem that the Planning Staff was thinking of sea 'communications' rather than invasion, with the ports required only for the peaceful nourishment of the garrison after victory had been achieved. 'At the earliest' the clearance of the harbour entrances 'by Italian minesweepers' could not be 'concluded' until the 'third day of operations'.[24] Little was said about the sea operation to the men of the Airlanding Division. Indeed, in his orders to his senior officers, Student envisaged the capture of the administrative centre at Canea and Suda, together with Retimo and all the airfields, by the evening of the first day. Reinforcement should thus present no difficulty.

The pilots who were carrying out reconnaissance had reported that 'the island appeared lifeless'.[25] No infantry positions could be detected within the olive groves. And little shipping had been seen. It was supposed that the troops from Greece were being evacuated by night, and that the garrison that remained was in a strength of 'one division, composed of two infantry brigades and one artillery regiment', in addition to 'remnants of the British Greek Army'.[26] Nothing was definite. As Halder noted in his diary on the 16th:

There are no clear reports of the conditions and difficulties to be expected in Crete.[27]

Student had been misled both by his air reconnaissance and by his Intelligence. The three airfields had been identified, but the country around them had not been observed with accuracy. The wide shallow valley, south-west of Canea, already chosen as a landing area for parachutists, was described as 'a high plateau'.[28] Had he suspected the truth he must have found it highly disconcerting. Certainly it would have forced him to revise his scheme of attack. Not only was he mounting an air-landing operation on a scale far greater than had ever been seen, much more significantly he was attempting it, as had never been done before, without the prospect of immediate support by motorized infantry. Nor, to his regret, had he been given control over VIII Air Corps. And in one way his plan was highly vulnerable.

---

[23] *Einsatz Kreta*, Battle Report of XI Air Corps   [24] Ibid.   [25] Student, p. 60
[26] *Einsatz Kreta*, Battle Report of XI Air Corps   [27] Halder, 16 May 1941
[28] *Einsatz Kreta*, Battle Report of XI Air Corps, Appendix 3, orders for Operation MERKUR ('Mercury'), signed 'Student'

On the first day he was committing almost all his parachutists, including the two thousand who were to go by sea. Among these were a company of the II Battalion of 3 Parachute Regiment, and a company of the Engineer Battalion. Some of these men had responsibility for heavy equipment not easily carried by air, but it remains extraordinary that he should have been willing to deprive himself of the special services of parachute riflemen, or indeed of any troops who had been trained to jump from aircraft. He was holding a mere 400 parachutists in reserve. This meant that if the Airlanding Division did not succeed immediately in capturing at least one airfield they would be facing disaster. Except by sea there would be no hope of bringing them reinforcement. Nor was it likely, if they should fail, that better fortune would attend a sea invasion carrying some 4,500 men to land on consecutive days upon sectors of defended coast eighty-five miles apart.

Nevertheless, he had no misgivings. To those few members of his staff who were in the secret he explained what he meant to do. Soon the date for the attack was fixed for 18 May. With the greatest confidence, he set about perfecting the details of this battle upon which he had staked his reputation.

6

' Colorado '

Between these adversaries, separated by nearly two hundred miles of the blue Aegean, there could be no preliminary exchange, no sudden skirmish or patrol contact. Indeed, the parachutists did not know why they had been brought to Greece. Clearly there must be something afoot. Would it be Cyprus perhaps, or Crete, or Persia, or even Egypt itself? They could only guess. Nor were the men of Freyberg's army any better informed. As the days followed upon one another in tranquil succession they still scarcely believed that they would be attacked.

The General himself had few doubts. From London he heard of feverish German activity upon the airfields of southern Greece, and of the progressive occupation of islands in the Archipelago, two of them, Kithera and Milos, less than a hundred miles away. Every day brought some new portent from the north. But by now he had shaken off his early pessimism and was beginning to feel that it should be possible to defeat any attack that might be made by airborne forces alone. In this new vein of confidence he cabled to the Prime Minister on 5 May:

Cannot understand nervousness; am not in the least anxious about airborne attack; have made my dispositions and feel can cope adequately with the troops at my disposal. Combination of seaborne and airborne attack is different. If that comes before I can get the guns and transport here the situation will be difficult. Even so, provided Navy can help, trust all will be well.

When we get our equipment and transport, and with a few extra fighter aircraft, it should be possible to hold Crete. Meanwhile there will be a period here during which we shall be vulnerable.

Everybody in great form and most anxious to renew battle with our enemy, whom we hammered whenever we met him in Greece.[1]

Characteristically, he then protested that the New Zealanders had been 'greatly and justly incensed at not being mentioned

[1] Churchill, Vol. III, p. 246

4*

adequately in B.B.C. and Press accounts of the vital and gallant part played by them in Greek rearguard action'.[2] The Prime Minister smoothed this down in his most tactful form.

It is only gradually that we have learned and are learning the full tale [he wrote], and the more the accounts come in the more we realize the vital part you played in a task of honour and indeed of fame. Throughout the whole Empire and English-speaking world the name of New Zealand is saluted.[3]

But Freyberg knew that the ships of the Royal Navy would be able to return to the Aegean in daylight only at their mortal peril. His fears of seaborne invasion tended to increase rather than lessen as the days went by. Soon they became reflected in the minds of his subordinate commanders. In particular they made their greatest impression upon those officers whom he knew best, and with whom he had still the closest contact, his old friends the brigadiers and colonels of the New Zealand division, whose responsibility it was to guard the stretch of coast that lay between Canea and Maleme.

For defence against a sea invasion he must depend largely upon the Navy. Closer at hand there confronted him the situation created by the presence of those thousands of troops who would be incapable of fighting. He was also responsible for the safety of the King of Greece and his Government. These matters were vexatious rather than essential, but they impeded him in his con-centration upon the vital problem of supply, and upon decisions affecting the disposal and tactics of his force in the light of his Intelligence information.

Among the men evacuated from Greece were many casualties, together with over a hundred nursing sisters. The 7th General Hospital, which had been established on a small promontory three miles to the west of Canea, was already overflowing; on 26 April the New Zealand medical organization alone had dealt with 700 wounded and sick, hundreds of them lying in the open under the olive trees. He sent them all to Egypt, together with the nursing sisters, by the first available boats. On 4 May he asked for the removal of some 14,000 troops who had no equipment, and were likely soon to become demoralized. These men were living under primitive conditions, camping in the open air with little organized sanitation.[4] He feared that their appearance and behaviour might all too easily impair the excellent relationship that had so quickly become established between the greater part of his force and the Greeks and Cretans.[5]

During the next few days many sailed for Alexandria, but some 5,000 were left to become embroiled in the battle. With them remained the 15,000 Italian prisoners of war.

Little less embarrassing was the presence of King George of Greece. Amid his other troubles, Freyberg faced the possibility that the King might be captured by parachutists. With a slight failure of tact he explained that he could bear with equanimity the thought that his Royal Highness might be killed or wounded in the fight for his country: the graver possibility was that he might be taken alive. Clearly there was no place in Crete where he could be safe. For this reason Freyberg felt that he and his party should leave for Egypt at once. From London the advice was far from helpful. At first it had been insisted that the King and his Government should be exposed to no 'undue risk'.[6] But now, shortly before negotiations for their departure were complete, a cable arrived bearing a decision concerted by the War Cabinet and the Foreign Office. It came from Wavell, urging 'very strongly that the King and Government should remain even if the island were attacked'.[7] This was also the view of Sir Michael Palairet who had been the British Minister in Greece.

With much misgiving Freyberg agreed. In the event of a parachute landing they would at once leave their house, in the outskirts of Canea, and take to the hills with a small armed bodyguard. If necessary, they could then be guided to the south coast and picked up by destroyer.

All plans hung upon the maintenance by sea of the supply line with Egypt. First there was the question of food. In peacetime Crete was not self-supporting. Now, in addition to the civilian population of 400,000, there were the British and Empire forces, amounting to about 30,000 men, the Greeks who had escaped from the mainland, and 15,000 Italian prisoners. It was no less necessary to receive weapons and ammunition, tanks, motor vehicles, and all the other equipment that must be needed if the

[4] DP   [5] Ibid.   [6] Davin, p. 468, Mr. W. E. Murphy
[7] Ibid., p. 469

fight were to have any hope of success. From his Quartermaster Freyberg learnt that if a small reserve were to be established the daily intake required immediately was something in the region of '30,000 tons a month',[8] of which it was hoped that 750 tons a day would come through Suda, and the rest through Heraklion. For maintenance alone it would be necessary to land 'between five and six hundred tons a day',[9] most of it at Suda. Much more would be needed, in the form of motor fuel, if it should become possible to establish upon the island any significant number of aircraft. Apart from the difficulties that could be expected from the enemy bombers, the dock facilities were inadequate to deal with such a weight of stores. On 2 May his Quartermaster told him that it would soon become necessary to organize the clearance of supplies by making use of small ports and beaches as an alternative to Suda Bay.[10]

By the end of the first week of May the Germans had almost completed their redeployment of the *Luftwaffe*. Bombers began to attack the shipping and the docks in raids that increased daily in number and ferocity. While the bells in Canea jangled a brief warning, the troops on the isthmus of the Akrotiri Peninsula would see a line of planes flying from the north towards the coast beyond Maleme. Briefly the distant hum of engines would die away, returning a few minutes later, suddenly urgent, and accompanied by the sharp cracking of the anti-aircraft guns as the Stukas reappeared over the southern mountains to fly in a leisurely circle above the harbour, a score or so at a time, before peeling off, one after another, to plunge with their crescendo whine through the puffs of smoke onto the ships. At the last moment each flattened out below the level of the masts to streak like black arrows across the peninsula neck and down to the safety of the sea north of Canea.

For a long time this assault did surprisingly little damage. The weakened batteries, constantly menaced by machine-gunning fighters, were not yet silenced, and the beached cruiser *York*, half hidden amidst the drifting smoke and fountains of water, continued to throw back fire at her attackers. But, before the middle of May, the raids were being pressed at intervals of scarcely an hour. Inevitably, at last, ship after ship was sunk or set blazing.

For the gunners it was a bitter ordeal. But the experience of the workers on the docks was far worse. Against this continuing

[8] Davin, p. 46   [9] Ibid.   [10] DP

avalanche of bombs they felt themselves helpless. Many had enlisted as shipping clerks. The strain upon them was great. 'A man may stick to his post in the excitement of battle,' wrote Captain Stephanides, who was acting as Medical Officer to the dock-operating companies, 'or he may stand up to dive-bombing if he has a weapon in his hands and feels that he can hit back. But no man can face dive-bombing for very long when engaged in the prosaic task of unloading coils of barbed wire or crates of bully beef and he is still less enthusiastic if he is handling boxes of high explosives or tins of aviation spirit, and he knows there is a ship full of the same stuff beneath his feet.'[11] There was irony in this situation. Only at the docks was there yet any danger. The infantrymen, in their battalion positions along the coast, still lived in comfort and safety, apart from those few of them who had once worked as stevedores, and who now volunteered to help at Suda. Soon it was realized that little could be done if attention were paid to the air-raid warnings. Orders were therefore given that unloading would continue until the moment when bombs began to fall.

Despite these measures, which brought increasing dead and wounded each day, there soon developed the situation that had been foreseen by the Middle East Planning Staff in their memorandum of 30 October 1940. Now it was true that, with the mainland in German hands, 'Suda could not be used by the Royal Navy by daylight'. Nor indeed, at any time, by slow merchant ships incapable of reaching comparative safety before dawn. At best there was the hope that destroyers, or an occasional cruiser, might arrive at Suda Pier before midnight to dash away three hours later. Such efforts could produce no more than a bare hundred tons each twenty-four hours. And as the Germans started to bomb at night even this became increasingly precarious. Other devices were tried. On 19 May the anti-aircraft barrage was concentrated to form a protective umbrella above the pier while two ships discharged simultaneously.

But already there had been a disastrous interruption to the flow of supplies. Few convoys had so much as reached the island. Attacked on the open sea, many ships carrying the most vital equipment had been sunk, or forced to turn back. By 15 May the *Luftwaffe* had established a total blockade in daylight. In the course of three weeks 27,000 tons of war munitions had left Egypt

[11] Stephanides, p. 48

for Crete. Of these, less than 3,000 tons had been landed. And much that did survive the desperate journey was found to be sickeningly inappropriate. 'Right up to the battle,' reported Lieutenant Elletson of the Ordnance, 'we were finding crates of table-cloths, and if we had indented in five copies for some special and vital type of replacement we would as like as not find ourselves given a veterinary box for the care of sick mules in Afghanistan'.[12]

Freyberg had been quite plain about his priorities. On 7 May a message had reached him from the Commander-in-Chief Middle East. After some preliminaries Wavell had promised to make the 16th Infantry Brigade available 'if shipping allowed'.[13] He felt, however, that it might be better first to equip the unarmed troops already in the island. He had then made the important offer of heavy and light tanks which he felt 'might intervene effectively' if they were kept carefully concealed. Finally he had asked for a complete statement of the most urgent requirements in troops, equipment and vehicles. He would do everything that he could to help.

On the same day Freyberg replied in a long cable. It began:

First. Agree not desirable at this juncture to attempt to land 16th Inf Bde and broadly speaking do not require additional personnel of any arm as a first priority. Prefer concentrate on landing essential equipment and stores. Second. Agree infantry tanks with crews and light tanks valuable also carriers. Third. Ample artillery personnel available also sights and directors without stands. 25pr ammunition could be unloaded . . . if guns available. Otherwise hasten despatch of 75 mm guns. Tractors and artillery signal equipment will also be needed. Fourth – other weapons required. Vickers guns and belts complete at least 24. Tripods for existing guns 30. Bren guns with magazines all possible to meet existing shortage of 300 and magazines for existing 300 guns. Rifles and bayonets 5,000 for British plus 500 for Greeks . . .[14]

There followed a long and detailed list of further requirements in the form of motor vehicles, grenades, ammunition, and signal equipment, together with various workshop materials.

[12] Lieut. R. Elletson to the author, 1963
[13] Davin, p. 48   [14] Long, p. 215

It may be noted that in this signal the request for rifles and bayonets was no more than '5,000 for British plus 500 for Greeks'. Clearly it was intended that these should be additional to the '13,220 rifles and after that 19,800' already specified on 3 May as necessary for the Greeks alone. Perhaps these further figures caused misunderstanding among the Quartermaster Staffs in Egypt. Whatever may have been the explanation the fact remains that by the time the battle began several thousand British soldiers, and nearly all the Greeks and Cretans, still did not possess a British rifle. Many were left to face the Germans without a weapon of any kind. Nor does this cable make clear the true urgency of the need for signalling equipment. Indeed nowhere in the course of the exchanges between Freyberg's Headquarters and the Middle East is there to be found any real insistence upon the need for field wireless apparatus.

Of about a hundred field guns that were despatched from Egypt less than half reached Crete, and of those which arrived, 'some,' in Freyberg's words, 'came without their instruments, some without their sights, some without ammunition, and some of the ammunition without fuses'.[15] Eventually forty-nine guns were delivered, each with three to four hundred rounds of ammunition. They were distributed to Heraklion, Retimo, Georgeoupolis, Suda Point, Suda and Maleme, where they were sited to cover the airfields, docks, and possible beach landing areas, with a considerable proportion of them arranged in depth to guard the approach upon Canea from Maleme. But these guns could not easily be moved. They did little to allay Freyberg's apprehension that the Germans might succeed in landing amphibious tanks upon the beaches. It would then be important to meet them at once with heavy weapons. The Greek experience had shown that anti-tank rifles alone would be useless.

If they come as an airborne attack against our aerodromes [he wrote to Wavell on 11 May in a letter carried by a liaison officer], I feel sure we should be able to stop him if he attacks after the 16th. If however he makes a combined operation of it with a beach landing with tanks, then we shall not be in a strong position. . . . I know you will do all you can.[16]

Here was a danger that the defence might counter with tanks of their own. It was clear that they could play a vital part not

[15] DP   [16] Connell, p. 454

only against lightly-equipped airborne forces but also in counter-
ing any heavy armour that might come ashore.

This had been emphasized from the first by the Prime Minister,
who now inquired of the Chiefs of Staff whether it might be
possible to send some heavy tanks directly to Suda Bay by divert-
ing the *Clan Lamont* from the Tiger convoy, which during the
second week in May, in response to his own initiative, was making
its successful passage of the Mediterranean from the west. Such a
course was considered inadvisable by the Staffs in Egypt since it
must mean endangering the rest of the ship's cargo. Thus was
bred a regiment of infinitely greater risks in the unforgiving future.
Of this incident Alan Clark remarks that these few tanks, later to
be 'squandered in the ill-conducted "Battle-axe" offensive in the
Western Desert', might have 'altered the scale of events in
Crete'.[17] This view enjoys the advantage of hindsight. At the time,
no doubt, Wavell saw the matter in a different light. So far from
knowing that he was about to 'squander' his precious tanks in a
failure he may have believed that, with the help of every tank
that he could find, he would be able to make 'Battle-axe' a
success, and thus extinguish in its early stages the main German
threat to the Middle East.

Nevertheless, Churchill's instinct was right. Tanks could make
a vital contribution in Crete.

He was now cabling to Wavell almost daily. On 10 May the
House of Commons had been devastated by bombing, but there
was no hint of calamity at home in the rumbustious encouragement that reached the Middle East. Two days later he again
revealed his concern upon the subject of tanks in a signal asking
whether 'at least another dozen "I" tanks with skilled personnel
should not go to help (against) "Scorcher" '.[18] (This was the code
name that had been adopted for the anticipated German onslaught upon Crete; 'Colorado' was the pseudonym for the
island itself.)

And on 14 May:

All my information points to 'Scorcher' any day after the 17th.
Everything seems to be moving in concert for that and with great
elaboration. Hope you have got enough in 'Colorado', and that those
there have the needful in cannon, machine-guns, and armoured
fighting vehicles. It may well be that in so large and complicated a

[17] Clark, p. 44   [18] Churchill, Vol. III, p. 249

plan zero date will be delayed. Therefore reinforcements sent now might well arrive in time and certainly for the second round, should the enemy gain a footing. I should particularly welcome chance for our high-class troops to come to close grips with those people under conditions where enemy has not got his usual mechanical advantages, and where we can surely reinforce much easier than he can. I suppose Admiral is with you in every detail of this, and that you and Tedder have concerted the best possible air plan, having regard to other tasks. All good wishes.[19]

A day later, on the 15th:

I am increasingly impressed by the weight of the attack impending upon 'Colorado', especially from the air. Trust all possible reinforcements have been sent.[20]

These messages reveal that the Prime Minister had still not understood how great had been the lack of foresight and preparation during the six months' occupation. Or perhaps he could not believe it. He must have heard that it was rapidly becoming impossible, as the Planning Staff in Cairo had long foreseen, and Cunningham had confirmed on 30 April, for ships of any kind to come into the northern ports during daylight. Evidently he was reluctant to believe that nothing whatever had been done to anticipate this situation. At the same time he was not making sufficient allowance for the influence of the *Luftwaffe*, a factor of which the Navy had good reason to be increasingly aware. Writing of this time, Cunningham was to remember that for many months the fleet had been 'dogged by shadowing aircraft'[21] based on Sicily and North Africa. Now 'four hundred dive-bombers' had started to cover Crete from Greece. Already both reinforcement and supply were nearly cut off by this German domination of the air, coupled with the absence of south coast landing facilities. As for the 'best possible air plan', this was to prove a simpler matter. On 19 May it was to be resolved. By that time it concerned the disposal of the three Hurricanes and three Gladiators that remained serviceable.

Like the guns, those few armoured vehicles which survived the journey quickly proved a disappointment to those who were about to use them. The 'I' tanks had been rejected from the Desert Army on account of mechanical faults which were still unrepaired. The

[19] Churchill, Vol. III, p. 249   [20] Ibid.   [21] Cunningham, p. 350

light tanks were in much the same condition. Lieutenant Farran of the 3rd Hussars described them as 'battered ancient hulks', which had been 'hastily patched up in Waadian workshops'. There were 'no proper fittings to the cooling system for the guns', and the wireless sets had 'arrived so late' that there had been 'no time to fit them' before the embarkation.[22]

A typical reception awaited Farran and his men in Suda Bay. At first all was deceptively calm

. . . except for the wreck of the cruiser *York* in the middle of the harbour there was no sign of war. Suddenly the sky filled with our old screaming enemies, whistling down from the sky like buzzards to the kill. A squadron of Stukas had come in at a great height from the direction of the mainland, catching the anti-aircraft gunners unawares, deadly bombs fell all around us, shaking the old ship at her anchor, and we sought sanctuary beneath a table in the saloon. We realized that we had been hit when a loud explosion threw us against the cabin wall. . . . A bomb had fallen upon one of the three-tonners on the after-hatch to pass straight through to the bottom of the ship. . . . She was filling fast and had already heeled over a little.[23]

For the next few days he and his men were doing what they could to get the tanks ashore.

A few in the upper hold were salvageable, but all the others and all the transport except the trucks on the deck were under water. Worst of all the wireless sets were a total loss. The harbour was being constantly bombed and we found great difficulty in persuading the Navy to give us steam to work the winches. After much thumping on the table in the office in Suda we persuaded them to bring a tug alongside to give us steam. Stripped to the waist we performed the unaccustomed role of dockers to unload tanks on to a lighter on the other side of the wreck. It was a terrifying job working in the bowels of the ship to our knees in water, at a time when the harbour was being heavily bombed. Every bomb, however far away, sent concussion waves through the sea to crash against the hull.[24]

It was not until 18 May that the few rescued tanks were able to move out to their battle stations west of Canea. As they left Suda Bay a ship blew up and showered them with wood fragments. The glow from the burning vessel lighted their way along the goat tracks to the road.

The significant truth was slow to gain acceptance in Egypt and

[22] Farran, p. 85   [23] Ibid., p. 86   [24] Ibid.

slower still to reach London. By 15 May Wavell was sufficiently encouraged to send a spirited reply to the Prime Minister:

Have done best to equip 'Colorado' against beetle pest. Recent reinforcements include six 'I' tanks, sixteen light tanks, eighteen A.A. guns, seventeen field guns, one battalion. Am preparing small force, one or two battalions, with some tanks, to land south of 'Colorado' as reserve. Propose also holding Polish Brigade as possible reinforcement. But problem landing reinforcements is difficult.[25]

He added that Cunningham, Tedder and he had 'concerted plans' as far as possible. It was going to be a hard struggle, but they hoped to make 'Scorcher' a 'red-hot proposition'[26] for the enemy.

At last there was a real sense of urgency. Lack of transport still imposed a crippling handicap upon its distribution, but each day brought some addition of war material, and at last it began to arrive in rather better quantity. Much of it remained highly unselective. Some scores of modern 25-pounder guns had recently been sent to Egypt. None went on to Crete. The ships that reached the north coast, scarred by their perilous passage across the Mediterranean, continued to deliver the wrong cargoes to the wrong ports. Despite the utmost effort it seemed at first that no progress was being made. Not until the middle of May did the defences begin to appear more formidable, with wire springing up everywhere 'like mushrooms in a night'.

In his report Freyberg was later to describe this period of intensive activity. He was travelling long distances from Sector to Sector and was able to admire the cheerful spirit of improvisation that he found wherever he went.

The gunners [he noted] were either British Regular Army, Australians or New Zealanders; men of infinite resource and energy; they set to work and one lot made a sighting appliance out of wood and chewing gum. Another lot of gunners made out charts which enabled them to shoot without sights or instruments. Nobody groused . . . and everybody got on with the job.[27]

The brigadiers and battalion commanders also saw that their equipment was beginning to approach establishment level. 'We should now be ready to receive the enemy', felt Brigadier Hargest, out at Maleme, 'our defences are nearly as good as we can make them, but material promised us has not come to hand – wire and carriers etc. With it, and a few days, we shall be ready.'

Much of this optimism was illusory. The supply of guns, tanks, vehicles and stores of all kinds, even of ammunition, was never to reach the level that was required. In particular the Germans were to enjoy a great advantage in mortars, grenades, and light automatics, weapons ideally suited to fighting in close broken country.

Ironically the deficiency that was to prove by far the most damaging was also the only one which might, with sufficient thought, have been wholly remedied. A single plane, flying if necessary direct from England via Gibraltar, could have brought enough wireless sets to equip every unit in the island down to company level.

As Freyberg had explained to Wavell in his signal of 7 May, he was not asking for troops. Already he had more than he could equip. Admittedly many of them were likely to be of little value, once the lines of battle had become established. But while the parachutists were in the air, and during the first few minutes after they had hit the ground, there must be a great opportunity for any clerk or cook who could aim a rifle. Sensibly, the more independent characters among the unattached specialists had soon given up mourning for their lost apparatus and had set about preparing themselves as best they could. Most of them remained in the Suda area. Here they were formed into composite battalions. But they were still much handicapped by the universal shortage of weapons.

From the first, Freyberg had realized how greatly he must depend upon good Intelligence. Only with some foreknowledge of the enemy strength and intentions would he be able to devise a plan that might give hope of success to his static, heterogeneous, and widely dispersed forces. In this he was not disappointed. Much information continued to reach him from London and Cairo. Copies of these reports cannot now be traced, but their main tenor is reflected in an appreciation of the likely German plan of attack, 'based on previous German air attacks and on Intelligence reports',[28] which was issued to Sector Commanders from Force Headquarters on 12 May.

[28] DP, Intelligence appreciation of German Plan for attack on Crete issued by B.G.S.H.Q., 12 May 1941

Much of this document was to prove remarkably accurate.

Although we can claim credit for the excellent dispositions that were made [Freyberg wrote after the war], in fact they were forced upon us by the wonderful Intelligence reports that were supplied from the United Kingdom.[29]

According to Churchill:

At no moment in the war was our Intelligence so truly and precisely informed. In the exultant confusion of their seizure of Athens the German staffs preserved less than their usual secrecy, and our agents in Greece were active and daring. In the last week of April we obtained from trustworthy sources good information about the next German stroke.[30]

Yet there is a curious inconsistency about this appreciation, a combination of correct and meticulous detail with one or two considerable errors and one glaring omission. The result might be taken to suggest that military secrets leaking from somewhere very close to the inner direction of the war in Germany were becoming distorted and misunderstood in the process of their interpretation in London. Today it is easy to suspect that in the background there may have lurked the strange figure of Admiral Canaris.

It has become widely accepted, although not admitted officially, that for several years this Naval Officer betrayed his country's secrets to Britain. From 1935 he had been the head of the *Abwehr*, the German organization which bore responsibility for military Intelligence. As with all Intelligence systems, contacts were maintained abroad, and deceptions practised upon friends and enemies alike. Canaris, however, quickly saw the nemesis that was threatening Germany. Before long he was working actively, and with surprising lack of caution, in the plots against his Führer.[31] In the end the dissimulations of this rash apostate were to lead him to his death – by slow asphyxiation, at dawn one morning in 1945, naked upon a communal scaffold according to the ritual which so much appealed to Hitler.

His German biographer, Karl Abshagen, recognizes that Canaris had long doubted the capacity of the *Wehrmacht* to beat England, and that he felt a particular sympathy with the Greeks. 'For years Canaris had had good friends in Greece, so it was very painful to him to hear of the attack against Greece . . . at the beginning of May 1941 . . . Canaris flew to Athens. The main

[29] DP, Freyberg comments on Battle for Crete, 31 Oct. 1949
[30] Churchill, Vol. III, p. 240   [31] Clark, *Barbarossa*, p. 272

motive for his trip was to do what he could for his friends who were in the city.'[32] Abshagen says no more.

Indeed this may well be all that he knew. Others, no doubt, are better informed. Certainly it is with a new piquancy that one can read today, in *Operation Crete*, that 'on 10 May an attempt was to be made by Admiral Canaris's organization to establish touch with . . . supposedly pacifist circles'[33] among Greeks and Cretans who were thought to be in favour of ending the war. The report adds that it had been hoped to 'surprise the enemy tactically by the method, strength, and timing of the operation',[34] an attempt that had not succeeded. Indeed 'the deployment of the Parachute Troops and the JU-groups in the Athens area, and the loading and clearing of ships', had been 'known to the enemy Intelligence service in every detail'. Later 'offences against security on the German side' were suspected but had 'not been discovered'.[35]

The appreciation of 12 May predicted that the first enemy objectives would be the aerodromes at Heraklion, Retimo, and Maleme. On the second day, Suda and the town of Heraklion would be seized and their ports used for the landing of further troops and heavy equipment. This sequence of events would begin with heavy air attack, directed particularly upon the anti-aircraft guns, and intensified for several days. The air-landing itself would be preceded by onslaughts from fighters and medium bombers upon the airfield perimeters. 'Almost immediately' there would follow the first wave of parachutists, who would be dropped 'all round' the airfields within a distance up to about a mile. They would carry light weapons, and would probably make extensive use of smoke. That troop-carriers, the heavy Junkers 52, might attempt to land in open country, away from the airfields, was thought to be no more than 'possible'. With more confidence it was suggested that these heavy planes, bearing their loads of infantry, would attempt to land on the established runways 'within half an hour . . . irrespective of the success or failure of the parachutists'. Some '5,000 troops' would take part in the first sortie. Later in the day another 1,500 men would probably be 'dropped at various key points to prepare the way for the capture of Heraklion and Suda Bay ports, and to cause general disorganization and confusion'. The possibility of 'sea landings on beaches' was not to be overlooked. But any actions of that sort

[32] Abshagen, p. 180   [33] *Einsatz Kreta*, Battle Report of XI Air Corps
[34] Ibid.   [35] Ibid.

would be 'of secondary importance to those from the air'. It was
noted that the aerodromes had not been bombed, nor had the
ports been mined; the implication was that the Germans intended
to use both themselves. The appreciation concluded:

It will be noted that the entire plan is based on the capture of the
aerodrome [*sic*]. If the aerodromes hold out as they will, the whole
plan will fail.

This was tantamount to expressing confidence that the Germans
would find it impossible to carry into effect any attempt to put
down their heavy carriers directly on to an airstrip before its
capture.

Thus the German objectives were identified exactly. And also
the fact that there would be a second sortie to Heraklion later
upon the first day. There were two errors. It was suggested that
the Junkers 52 might attempt to crash-land in open country,
although this was regarded as no more than 'possible', and it was
thought that they would attempt to land on a runway 'within half
an hour' whatever might have happened to the parachutists.

More significant was the omission. Once again no effort had
been made to guess at the total number of parachutists available
for the operation. To have been told this would have served
Freyberg better than all the rest of his information put together.
The first estimate had been of '3,000–4,000 parachutists or airborne troops in first sortie', with 'two or three sorties per day
possible from Greece and three or four from Rhodes if Rhodes not
used as a bomber base'. Now there was this figure of '5,000 troops'
in the first sortie with another 1,500 men to be dropped at key
points later in the day, but no indication how many more there
might be to come. And nothing was said about the number of
airborne infantry who, nevertheless, were expected to arrive
'within half an hour of the beginning of the attack'. Once again
the distinction between parachutists and airborne infantry had
been blurred. How many parachutists were there in Greece?
How many were there in each such division? And how many
airlanding divisions had arrived in Greece?

It was scarcely possible that the troop-carriers could be flown
directly from further north. Certainly there was abundant
evidence of the preparations that were being made upon the
Greek airfields.

How many parachutists then? These young men were living in

encampments close to Athens. Some of them, abandoning the elaborate security precautions that had accompanied their passage through the Balkans, were strolling in the town itself.[36] Sources capable of revealing so much should surely have been able to provide the answer. Indeed it seems probable that there was here a grave failure on the part of the Intelligence Service at home, and that this vital information was reaching London with all the rest, only to become confused and distorted somewhere in its transfer to Crete, where it was about to take on supreme importance.

Nor was Freyberg given detailed advice about the manner in which the German airborne forces might be expected to press their attack. After the war Student was to tell the historian Liddell Hart that the 'Operation Orders' for his actions in Holland had been captured by the Dutch on an aerodrome near The Hague:

From these valuable documents the British Command quickly ascertained the principles of attack, tactics, and training methods, of the new German airborne troops which they used in an exemplary manner for their own defence. Unfortunately these facts remained unknown to me until they were discovered from captured documents in Crete. They were one of the most important causes of the heavy German losses on Crete.

Had I previously known how much the enemy already knew about us I would have used different tactics for the attack on the aerodromes and thus avoided the British defences.[37]

Elaborating upon this Clark says that it was a 'training manual' that was captured on the aerodrome and that its contents were 'thoroughly disseminated through the British Army'.[38] The truth was very different. No doubt the story proved useful to Student when later he was called upon to explain his 'heavy' losses. But whether or not a parachutist's papers were found in Holland there is nothing to suggest that they brought much enlightenment to Intelligence. There was, for example, no mention of gliders in the appreciation of 12 May. Indeed, the knowledge that it revealed of air-landing methods in general was notably less than that of the specific plan of attack against Crete. Freyberg had made his dispositions close to the three airfields, and to his base

[36] Gericke, p. 23

[37] DP, letter from Student to Liddell Hart, 28 Nov. 1948

[38] Clark, p. 60

in Suda Area. In this, however, he was following a policy already laid down by his predecessors, indeed dictated by lack of transport and by the necessity of fighting from fixed defences, rather than by any insight into Student's tactical conceptions. 'For my part I was committed to the main dispositions that existed,' he wrote later, 'because I could not move our garrison about on account of the lack of transport as well as tools for digging'. As for the troops, their anticipations were scarcely to exceed a vague impression, derived from the tales of the previous year, that the Germans were likely to descend from the heavens wearing some kind of fancy dress. In December 1941 the establishment and methods of the German Airborne Forces were to be described fully in a Secret Document. But the facts had been learnt in Crete.

The Intelligence view scarcely expressed the feeling of Freyberg himself. He was still under the spell of the strange mystique exerted at this time by the *Luftwaffe*. And it may be well to recall that not only those soldiers who had taken part in the retreats, but others who had been much less closely exposed to the German planes, even the most exalted, had been affected in the same way. Within weeks of his retirement from the post of C.I.G.S., General Ironside, a figure in many ways not unlike Freyberg, had been telling the Home Guard Commanders, 'We have got examples of where there have been people quite definitely preparing aerodromes in this country . . . we want to know from you what is going on. Is there anything peculiar happening? Are there any peculiar people?'[39] And Sir Alan Brooke, soon to succeed Ironside in the highest office within the Army, was confiding to his diary that there was 'ample room for a series of parachute landings in the large London parks'. The more he examined these possibilities the more he 'realized the chaos that such landings would create'.[40] On 4 June 1940 Churchill himself, in the House of Commons, had spoken in terms of parachutists 'taking Liverpool or Ireland'.[41] British knowledge of airborne attack had made little progress since the previous summer, matching the ignorance of amphibious landings that was later to handicap the Germans and Italians. The basic conception was still that of a limitless cascade of armed nuns and tram-car conductors. Nor had there been any examination of landing techniques by aircraft. Rather

[39] *Spectator*, 23 Nov. 1962, p. 825
[40] Bryant, *The Turn of the Tide*, p. 198   [41] Fleming, p. 67

was there a universal inclination to endow every type of German flying-machine with something more than natural powers. The opinions and reactions of Freyberg can be judged fairly only in the context of this prevailing atmosphere.

Nevertheless Intelligence had seized correctly upon the flaw in the German plan; the attack would fail if the aerodromes held out. Weston had arrived at the same conclusion. Freyberg was less inclined to see air attack exclusively in terms of the airfields, merely accepting that 'their loss would jeopardize'[42] the defence, partly because his information could set no limits to the number of the parachutists that might be used against him, and partly because he remained convinced that the troop-carriers would be able to crash-land in open country. As will appear, both in his actions and his words, he was to persist in these misconceptions, encouraged in them by false reports that circulated during the fighting, reports that later came to be widely believed. At the same time, he remained confident that, whatever techniques they might employ, he would be able to 'stop' the airborne troops if they came unsupported.

'We, for our part,' he admitted to Churchill after the war, 'were mostly preoccupied by sea-landings, not by the threat of air-landings'.[43]

While retaining his own ideas about the *Luftwaffe* he had lost none of his preoccupation with the threat of invasion from the sea. And in this there had never been anybody in the Middle East to disagree with him, whatever might be the assumptions of the authorities in London; Cunningham still could give him little assurance that the Fleet would be able to fulfil its obligations against transport flotillas crossing the Aegean in daylight.

Thus he was entering upon the struggle with no idea how many parachutists the Germans might have available, and with a reluctance, natural enough in the light of the beliefs then prevailing, to accept the Intelligence view that the enemy planes would be unable to land until after the capture of an airfield. At the same time he remained acutely apprehensive of invasion from the sea, an anxiety from which better staff work in Egypt might have relieved him. In fact he was rejecting the best of his advice while accepting the worst. Much that was to happen in Crete can be explained on this understanding.

[42] DP

[43] DP, Freyberg comments on Churchill Draft, 3 Mar. 1949

The general instructions given to the officers in command of the Sectors were that they should deploy one-third of their available strength in or around the airfields, the remainder being held back outside the perimeters, with counter-attack forces always in hand. The troops should be told all that was known of German air-landing methods. Matters of detail would be settled within each Sector. Coast defence must be a particular concern between Maleme and Canea, but there were many factors that would apply equally in all parts of the island. Nothing was more important than the matter of concealment; the Germans must not discover what sort of opposition they would encounter. This could best be achieved by the use of deep, narrow, slit trenches constructed at right angles round the trunks of the olives. In the words of a British officer each of these 'separate dust-grey growths' preserved a 'character' of its own with the same 'distinct personality'[44] as the individual Greeks themselves. The broad spread of leaves prevented air observation, while at ground level the gnarled and twisted trunks left open a good field of fire. And it had been shown in Greece that trenches dug among the roots gave protection against everything short of a direct hit by a bomb.

The use of anti-aircraft fire was left to the discretion of the local commanders. If the guns were to blaze away at every plane in sight it was certain that they would be destroyed before the time when they would be most needed, the moment of the air-borne attack itself. On the other hand some attempt must be made to protect the essential targets – the airfields and the docks. There was therefore much to be said for tailing off their action progressively, thus suggesting to the enemy that the aircraft defences were being eliminated. This was the plan adopted at both Heraklion and Retimo. At Maleme the artillery remained under separate direction from Canea, the four coastal defence guns controlled from the Royal Marine Headquarters, and the anti-aircraft defences, together with the other field guns, from the Gun Operation Room. At this distance there was no direct guidance for the British and Australian crews of the ten Bofors guarding the airfield. Moreover, the effective range of these weapons was little more than 800 yards. For this reason they had been set up close to the runway. Here they were in the open and clearly visible to the enemy pilots.

At every stage of the action swift counter-attack would be

[44] Fielding, p. 84

necessary. The enemy would be at their most vulnerable during the first few minutes after landing. So much was obvious. Yet here again there were differences. Should the infantry leap upon them immediately, exposing themselves from the first? Or should they stay in their slit trenches waiting for counter-attack under company or battalion orders? To the trained infantry these first minutes must offer their greatest opportunity. At Heraklion, Chappel insisted that counter-attack should be spontaneous. Here the initial responsibility would lie with the corporals and sergeants. 'Section Commanders,' wrote Captain Rabbidge, who was commanding a company of the 2nd York and Lancaster Battalion, 'had orders to work on their own and to attack the enemy the moment they landed'.[45]

Among the New Zealanders there was less certainty. Some maintained later that Freyberg himself had warned them 'not to rush out'[46] when the parachutists came down. Indeed it was clear that the improvised units would quickly lose their organization once they had left their slit trenches. On the other hand, dependence upon battalion orders must mean delay.

Each of Freyberg's defence centres contained its vital pair of enemy objectives – an airfield and a harbour. Inland the ground rose steeply towards the mountains. Along the coastal strip, vine-yards and patches of ground bearing withered growths of rye and barley were divided by stone walls or by hedges of savage cacti, and crossed by ravines that wound between terraced slopes. Everywhere luxurious growths of vegetation flowered among boulders and jutting outgrowths of rock. Narrow, twisting roads, lined by poplars, wandered between villages. Farm-houses nestled under the rising slopes. Larger buildings, a monastery perhaps, or a barracks, an olive-oil factory, or a prison stood somewhat apart. Close to the shore, prosperous flat-roofed villas were set among shrubberies of magnolia and bougainvillaea, with gates of trellised iron and balconies that looked out over the shingle. To the eye of a pilot it must have been obvious that not even a light aeroplane could hope to land in such broken country, except perhaps at one or two points where there was a brief stretch of sand along the shore.

[45] Capt. T. V. Rabbidge, letter to the author, 23 Sept. 1961
[46] Lieut. J. W. C. Craig in Davin, p. 100

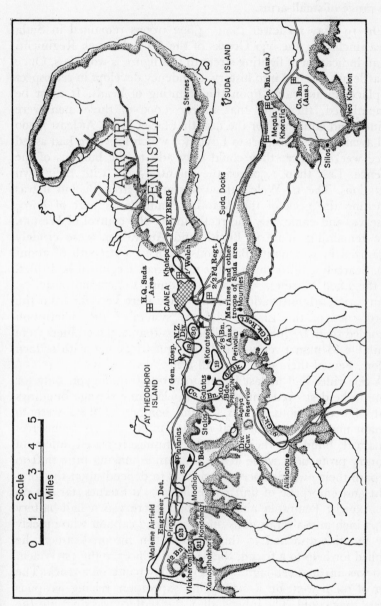

3. Suda–Maleme Area: 19 May

In all three Sectors a low hill surveyed the airfield from within the range of small-arms.

On 19 May no fewer than 14,822 troops remained in Suda Area, including the 930 Greeks of the Second Greek Regiment. As an indication of fighting strength this figure is worthless. Once a battle has receded into history a tendency develops in retrospect to place undue value upon the counting of heads. It must be remembered, therefore, that barely 3,000 of these men were trained and equipped for the task that faced them. At least 5,000 still awaited the transport to Egypt for which Freyberg had asked three weeks before; they could only add to the burdens of the defence. Less than 1,500 of the infantry were with their own battalions. The 1st Welch alone was at full strength, but it was guarding the neck of the Akrotiri Peninsula as part of Force Reserve, and came only indirectly under the control of Weston. The remaining infantry, British and Australian, were crudely organized in Composite Battalions, each in a strength of about 500. Scarcely half the men in the 2nd Greek Regiment had rifles. Of the 2,000 Marines, some were manning the coastal batteries. Many were administration troops. They were very far from the 'hard core of the island's defence system',[47] the description accorded them by John Connell. No less than 2,500 gunners were available to man twenty-four heavy guns together with sixteen Bofors. Few of them carried small arms.

A few rifles had at last begun to arrive from Egypt, only for some to be destroyed immediately in elaborate storage buildings that offered obvious targets for the bombers. Others were to remain undistributed. Several of the gunner officers themselves remained blind to their danger, refusing repeated offers of infantry protection, while at the same time making little shift to prepare their own defence. Much was to depend upon the foresight and enterprise of unit commanders. At Sternes, far out on the Akrotiri Peninsula above the bay, there was a half-battery of 3.7 inch anti-aircraft guns under a young captain who quickly saw the risk attached to this isolation. In his predicament he applied for help to a friend, the Medical Officer to the 1st Welch, who was fortunate enough to be able to lay hands on a truck. The pair of them went on a marauding expedition, seizing weapons where they could. The other half of this battery was dug into the cornfields in the southern outskirts of Canea. For approximately

[47] Connell, p. 450

180 men there was the regulation small-arms equipment, a Lewis gun and about a dozen rifles, with pistols for the officers. But there were infantry detachments not far away. They felt no apprehension.

Weston placed his own Marines, together with most of his nondescript troops, in immediate defence of the docks. Here there was a gap of about a mile between the foothills and the water's edge; three miles further east the mountains closed directly upon the bay, the coast road winding across the face of the cliff. He dispersed his half-strength and improvised battalions among the olives between Canea and Suda, with the 2nd Greeks further to the south-west where Periviola lay among the orchards below the hills. On 19 May the King of Greece, together with his Government, moved into the village.

In the Maleme Area of the Western Sector 7,702 New Zealanders waited along the coast between the rivers Tavronitis and Kladiso, among them the infantry of the 4th and 5th Brigades, together with the freshly improvised 10th Brigade, some two-thirds of the original New Zealand Division. They were commanded by Brigadier Puttick, an experienced regular soldier of fifty-one who had led a battalion in the First World War; a few months earlier, he had played a leading part in the formation and training of the Division in New Zealand, only to find himself superseded when Freyberg emerged from retirement in England.

The total strength within Maleme Area came to close on 12,000. But this included 3,500 men of three Greek regiments, many of whom had no weapons, together with various assorted units, such as the Royal Air Force ground staffs at Maleme, that would be unlikely to contribute much to an infantry fight. Moreover, not all, even of the New Zealanders, were under Puttick's orders. Most of the 4th Brigade had been allotted to Force Reserve. His immediate claim upon it was limited to a single battalion and a few machine-guns. As artillery support, he had some thirty assorted pieces varying widely in type and value, and towards the middle of May there arrived, salvaged from the wrecks at Suda, ten of the 3rd Hussars' light tanks. On the night of the 14th two heavy infantry tanks, carrying with them many high hopes, ground their way out to the airfield where they were reverently tucked away in prepared shelters that had been dug under the southern slopes.

Puttick was thus forced to make his essential dispositions with no more than two weakened brigades, the 10th indeed a brigade by courtesy title only. He had to defend the airfield at Maleme from airborne attack, while standing between Canea and Suda and any air-landing that might be made under the hills to the south. At the same time he must watch the coast; it was assumed that parachute assaults would be swiftly followed, if not accompanied, by invasion from the sea.

His problems were much increased by the size and character of the ground that he had to cover. West of Canea there were ordered rows of vines and fields of sparse barley. But soon the plain broke into a series of rolling hills entered by a broad valley that passed for five miles diagonally inland, south-west of Galatas, as far as the village of Alikianou; this was the valley that had been identified by the German pilots as a 'high plateau'. It was criss-crossed with narrow patches of cultivation thickly interspersed with groves of olives, the fruit, at this season of the year, beginning to form its tight green buds. Three miles from Canea, the local prison, a substantial white building with solid walls and out-houses, stood in a circle of open ground. From the heights of Galatas, a mile to the north, it was possible to catch a glimpse of it through the trees. A mile beyond it, and still some two miles short of Alikianou, Lake Aghya, a narrow strip of glistening water, lay north of the road. The whole area had become known as the Prison Valley.

The coast road led west over Canea Bridge, crossing the drying stream of the Kladiso half a mile above the sea. A mile past the river the tents and marquees of the 7th General Hospital were exposed upon a flat treeless promontory; huge red crosses had been marked out across the withered grass. South of the hospital, a side road led away at right angles from the Galatas turn to dip and wind up the slopes towards Galatas. Further along the coast Platanias extended back onto high ground, facing across the water to the island of Theodhoroi. Next came Modhion, some-what inland. The road now became enclosed within dark and menacing walls of bamboo. Some ten miles from Canea it led into a scatter of small houses, an olive oil factory on the right, and low white-walled crofts half hidden among the trees. For the Cretans who lived there, and soon for the New Zealanders themselves, the name 'Maleme' served and still serves, for this group of buildings. But in the Operation Orders of both sides a distinction is made

The chief authors of the Campaign in Greece with their Force Commander: Rt. Hon. Anthony Eden, General Sir Archibald Wavell, Lieut-General Sir H. Maitland Wilson

(Imperial War Museum)

New Zealanders and friends in a village in Crete

(Historical Publication Branch, N.Z. Dept. of Internal Affairs)

'Parachutists!'   (from Mourellos *Battle of Crete*)

between the substantial village of Pirgos, lining the road itself, and Maleme, a cluster of four or five cottages some five hundred yards further south.

At the far end of Pirgos the bamboos thinned to reveal first a small church and walled cemetery, and then the airfield, on the right of the road, and somewhat below it. The single runway, less than half a mile long, was laid out obliquely across the sand. Beyond it the Tavronitis emerged from a deep pebbled gully between the hills, dividing into shallow runnels that wandered to the sea among boulders and short green whins.

As it left the airfield the road twisted inland and was then carried across the river by a substantial bridge bearing an iron balustrade and supported by stone pillars. It led to the small port of Kastelli, fifteen miles away on the southern shore of Kisamos Bay. Beyond the river clumps of bamboo rose above the thick scrub. But between the road and the shore, within the fringe of sand dunes, the land was flat. Puttick saw that this territory was suitable for parachutists. His instructions gave him no direct responsibility for it, but he knew that he could not leave it out of his calculations.

From the Tavronitis to Canea the distance was a full twelve miles. Such rough country should favour a defence in depth. At the same time there must be many patches of dead ground, as for example in the river beds, where enemy groups might find shelter.

With so much territory to cover it was impossible for the New Zealanders to be strong everywhere. Plainly the enemy would attempt to capture the airfield at Maleme. But Puttick could not afford to give priority to its protection. Freyberg had impressed upon him the danger of invasion from the sea. Moreover, it seemed likely that parachutists might drop in the Prison Valley. Perhaps even troop-carriers might land there despite the many plantations of olive; Puttick had caught from Freyberg the feeling that enemy planes could be expected to crash-land almost any-where. Finally there was the question of communication with the administrative centre in Canea. This could only be maintained along the coast road.

Compromise was inevitable. He decided that the 5th Brigade should guard the airfield, together with the coast as far east as Platanias. The 4th Brigade, still at the disposal of Force Reserve, he kept back west of Canea Bridge. Between the two he put his improvised 10th Brigade, basing it on Galatas. Here it should be able to block any immediate threat against Canea and Suda from a German landing near the Prison.

He could scarcely feel much satisfaction in these dispositions. Between the 5th Brigade and the rest of his Division there was a six mile gap across high broken ground. And if the Germans should come down in the Prison Valley they would be able to make their descent almost unmolested during that vital period when they would be at their most vulnerable. The problem was to find any remedy which would not lead to a fatal dispersal and lack of control. Already almost every man was committed. Indeed, if anything should go wrong, he had in his Divisional Reserve only a single battalion to put it right. And it was not going to be easy to organize a large scale counter-attack in daylight, under the searching *Luftwaffe*, even if his communications should allow him to deliver the necessary orders. Certainly the telephone lines would not last long. To supplement them he would have to rely upon radio transmitters. And of these there were not enough to supply so much as one to every battalion.

In the Retimo Sector the possible enemy objectives were again widely separated. The enemy might attempt a landing at Georgeoupolis on Almiros Bay, twenty miles east of Suda, or at Retimo itself, a further ten miles along the coast. Here the port was of little account, but better suited to attract the Germans was the primitive landing strip five miles beyond the town.

To defend the whole of this area Brigadier Vasey had the weakened 19th Australian Infantry Brigade and two Greek regiments. Like all their fellow-countrymen in the island, the Greeks were potentially excellent soldiers, but they were untrained and ill-equipped. More formidable was a battalion of Cretan Police. In all there were some 6,700 men, of whom 3,630 were Australian, with fourteen guns, and another pair of the infantry tanks. Vasey decided to send two of the Australian battalions, together with most of the Greeks, eight of the guns, and both the tanks, to guard the landing-strip at Retimo. He gave the command of this detachment to one of his young officers, Lieutenant-Colonel Ian Campbell, who had been a staff major in Libya and had subsequently led the 2/1 Battalion in Greece. Vasey himself stayed at Georgeoupolis with his two remaining battalions, one of them at less than half strength.

Only at Heraklion was the problem comparatively simple. Here the port and the airfield could be included within an oval perimeter some five miles in length. Once again the position was well suited to defence. Low hills less than a mile to the south commanded the airfields. Moreover, Brigadier Chappel had at his disposal, in the augmented 14th Brigade, three regular British Battalions, fresh and at full strength, and a battalion of Australian infantry, reduced in numbers but full of confidence after their success in Cyrenaica. There were also three regiments of Greeks, together with some hundreds of armed gunners and R.A.F. men. The total complement was just over 8,000 men, all but the Greeks reasonably well armed, supported by twenty-nine guns of varying types, including ten Bofors, six light tanks and the usual ration of two infantry tanks. Nor was the shortage of transport quite so severe as in the other Sectors. There were enough three-ton lorries to put one battalion on wheels. Freyberg had recommended that this transport should be used to create a mobile reserve that could be sent to Retimo or Almiros 'to scratch the enemy as a diversion while Force Reserve Brigade come in and attack him'.[48]

This was a compact, well-organized defence area. It had need to be. For here at Heraklion was a major danger point. The airfield and harbour were the best in the island. If the enemy should succeed here he would conquer Crete. Moreover, the road connections might well be cut during the fighting. It was not unlikely that the Germans would make no more than diversionary attacks at other points along the coast while concentrating the mass of their strength at Heraklion. With these possibilities in mind Freyberg had, from the start, felt particular anxiety about this Sector. It was here that he had made his first detailed tour of inspection, in the course of the visit developing some doubt about the ability of Chappel, whom he referred to on 18 May, in a message to Wavell, as reasonably good, but not perhaps sufficiently inspiring to command so large a force.[49] Little could be seen to justify such misgiving. Preparations were made with method and purpose. The 2nd Leicesters arrived on 16 May, the only infantry reinforcement from Egypt that was to reach any of the Sectors before the battle. Freyberg could feel with justice that, although he might still have some doubts about its commander, at least much had been done to strengthen the garrison for its task.

[48] DP   [49] Ibid.

During the second week of May it became clear that the island might be attacked at any moment. The infantry battalions had resumed vigorous training. And it was plain that the unfortunate people on the docks at Suda were having a rough time. But the troops still found it hard to take seriously the prospect of invasion. In the evenings they bathed, with few planes to interrupt them, and at night the cafés rang with cheerful talk. Hundreds of men wandered about without orders. Officers whose units had disappeared, or who were left perhaps with their batman as sole representative of a company, spent much time in paying social visits to old friends in other battalions. From time to time they could be heard to announce their intention of moving on to Egypt, somewhat in the manner of guests at a party who want to be in time to see the cabaret at the next night club.

There were some who regarded the future with less confidence. Down at Suda two American journalists from Athens were sitting on their bags day and night declaring to all who would listen their unshakeable intention of leaving the island by the first available boat. Widely quoted was their depressing comment, 'Gee, I guess you boys have surely got it coming to you'. Nobody was much disturbed by these birds of ill-omen. But one morning they were gone. And on 13 May, soon after dawn, machine-gunning Messerschmitts, in groups of five, swept for an hour across the airfield at Maleme.

The Last of the Royal Air Force

There are no villains among the defenders of Crete. Some of the brigadiers and colonels are seen to delay for hours, and even for days, over decisions that now appear with startling clarity as urgent and vital. But those who fail in this way do so in a manner strangely at variance with their usual behaviour. Within a week, most of them have recovered their usual vigour of thought and action. Never again do they fall into such uncertainty as confines them during the early fighting upon this sunlit Mediterranean island.

The explanation lies in the fact that in this battle their situation was unique. Unprecedented dilemmas faced them at a time when they were themselves still in the grip of fatigue. New methods were required. Suddenly their experience had become a liability. Inevitably, some of the steps they took were to prove wrong. No less certain is it that all criticism, offered in the light of after knowledge, must properly be joined in tribute to men who gallantly bore their responsibilities in the field.

Much that has since appeared puzzling can be readily understood by anyone who cares to explore the road leading west from Canea to Maleme. On the map all is simple. But what can be seen of the airfield from Platanias? Is the runway in sight even from Pirgos? Suppose that the sky be filled with clouds of smoke and dust, what then would be apparent to an observer on the southern heights? And the road itself, the single thread connecting Maleme with the base at Canea, how closely does it lend itself to ambush? These were the questions, with others like them, that confronted the senior officers of the New Zealand Division. The extent to which their significance was recognized, and the responses which they evoked according to individual character and capacity, were to determine the course of the fighting.

The New Zealand 4th Brigade, still directly under Freyberg's orders for use as a mobile reserve, was commanded by Brigadier Inglis, a man of forty-seven, who had served for four years in the infantry between 1915 and 1919. He had been sent from Egypt at Freyberg's request. As a soldier, there still clung to him something of the attitudes that he had learnt in his civilian profession as a lawyer. Highly intelligent, quick-thinking and volatile in argument, he was also pugnacious and opinionated, adept at proving to his own satisfaction that any failure with which he might be associated could not relate to any inadequacy of his own. It is a skill that colleagues seldom find endearing.

Now he found waiting for him the New Zealand 18th and 19th Battalions. He would also have under his orders the New Zealand 20th, and the 1st Welch, when they were not required directly by Puttick or by Force Headquarters. All these units were at approximately full strength, apart from the 19th which had a complement of 565 officers and men. Ancillary formations under his command included ten light tanks of the 3rd Hussars, a troop of Royal Artillery, and a platoon of machine-gunners.

He could thus count on having at least two, and perhaps four, good infantry battalions, together with the tanks, a useful force to destroy concentrations of lightly-armed parachutists. Armoured vehicles landed from the sea might well prove more formidable. There was, of course, no telling where counter-attack would be needed. The approaches to Maleme and Alikianou, the various outskirts of Canea, and finally to Almiros Bay and Retimo, had all been reconnoitred. For transport, so it was said, there would be enough vehicles to carry the whole brigade, a hope which, in the words of the *New Zealand Official History*, contained 'a touch of optimism, if not fantasy'. Until it was called upon it would lie as quietly as possible west of Canea, taking no notice of planes, and shooting only at any parachutists who might favour it personally.

The 10th Brigade did not come into existence until the morning of 14 May. Appointed to lead it was that Colonel Kippenberger who had already observed that the nature of the coast would confront the enemy with formidable difficulties in any landing attempted from the sea. He was an active man of forty-four. In Greece he had commanded the 20th Battalion – apart from a lively few hours during the retreat which he had spent on the run behind the enemy lines.

Kippenberger had served in the ranks with the earlier New

Zealand Expeditionary Force, and had been severely wounded in 1917. On his return to civilian life he had become, like Inglis, a lawyer. But he had always been interested in war, both in its history and its practice. Later he had taken a commission in New Zealand's tiny Territorial Army. Now he was to find widening opportunity as a leader in battle. He was the embodiment of the citizen soldier, a thoughtful, kindly man, dedicated to the waging of necessary war and already increasingly ruthless in the standards that he imposed upon himself and others. His judgements were analytical. Failure he found hard to forgive. In a man of such human breadth and wisdom there could occur surprising lapses of sympathy and insight. Only with his friends could he relax, liking nothing better than to spend an occasional hour with his pipe over a game of chess. He was a man of contrasts, blending aggression with humility, asceticism with savour for life.

As yet he was only beginning to feel his way as a commander. Moreover, the heterogeneous polyglot 10th Brigade would have tested the powers of a Marlborough. Its military value rested largely upon the 'Composite Battalion', a miscellaneous collection of some 750 men mostly gunners and truck drivers. He thought them 'good material'. But they were 'wholly untrained in infantry work'. In addition, he had 190 men of the New Zealand Divisional Cavalry, a platoon and a half of machine-guns, and a battery of three Italian 75 mm. guns 'without sights and with little ammunition'. Still less obvious were the military virtues of two Greek Regiments; they had few weapons and no more than a handful of rounds to go with them. Not unnaturally, he regarded these troops with scepticism, describing them as 'malaria-ridden little chaps from Macedonia with four weeks' service'. He noted that, 'The 8th Greeks had fired ten rounds each from their ancient Steyers, 6th Greeks none, and neither battalion could be said to have any military value'.[1] He had no wireless sets, very few tools for digging, and for transport only his single truck.

He placed his Composite Battalion along the hills from the sea to screen Galatas from the west, its southern flank, the Divisional Petrol Company, touching the road that led down through the olives from Galatas to the Prison. Further south, the 6th Greeks, who had only three rounds per man, covered the direct approach from the Prison Valley to Canea and Suda at a point where the Alikianou-Canea road passed through a gap in the hills. He did

[1] Kippenberger, p. 49

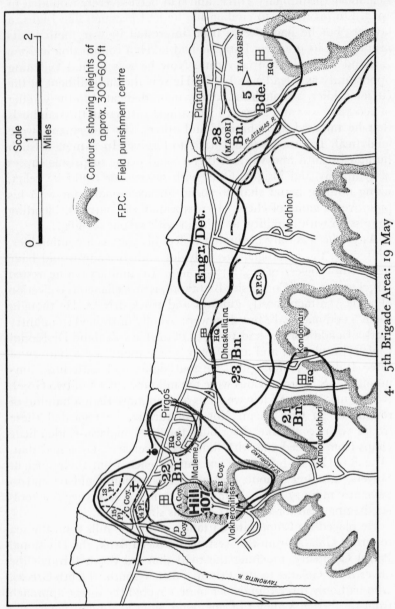

Scale

Miles

0 1 2

Contours showing heights of approx. 300–600 ft

F.P.C. Field punishment centre

Platanias

28 (MAORI) Bn.

PLATANIAS R.

5 Bde.

HARGEST

HQ

Engr. Det.

Modhion

F.P.C.

HQ Dhaskaliana

23 Bn.

Kondomari

HQ

21 Bn.

Xamoudhokhori

Pirgos

HQ Coy.

Maleme

22 Bn.

SFAKORIAKO R.

13 Pl.

15 Pl.

C Coy.

14 Pl.

D Coy.

A Coy.

Hill 107

B Coy.

Vlakheronitissa

TAVRONITIS R.

not occupy the Prison itself, partly because he had not enough troops, and partly out of fear that it would prove too vulnerable to air attack. North of Lake Aghya he placed the 190 men of the Divisional Cavalry detachment, with the 8th Greeks immediately south of them, across the road, and in the hills east of Alikianou.

These Greeks were in a strength of about 900. He felt the 'Greek C.O.' to be 'quite useless'. As 'actual commander' he left Major Clifford Wilson, one of his best young officers, together with some N.C.Os. The Greeks were untrained and could scarcely be called equipped. Moreover, they would be cut off by any landing in the Prison Valley. Not surprisingly, Wilson felt a little lonely.

I did not tell him [says Kippenberger in a book that he wrote after the war], that I had argued elsewhere that 8th Greek Battalion was only a circle on the map – and that it was murder to leave such troops in such a position, and had been told that in war murder sometimes has to be done. We had lunch together in a spotlessly clean little parlour and then said goodbye . . . [2]

Despite these forebodings the 8th Greeks were to be heard of again.

He did what he could to fortify his position, and to organize and encourage the men of his motley force. But he found it difficult to be optimistic about their potentialities. Nor did he think it agreeable that he should be instructed on the morning of the 19th to send twenty-four non-commissioned officers to assist in training Cretan recruits four miles away in Alikianou. He decided that 'meanwhile' he would ignore the order.

The 5th Brigade was commanded by Brigadier James Hargest. Like all his contemporaries in the New Zealand Division, he had fought with distinction in the First World War. When it was over he had returned to farming, and had later taken up politics. From 1931 he had been a member of the New Zealand Parliament. In contrast with the tall lean young men who surrounded him, he was plump and stocky, dressed habitually in large baggy shorts. To the British he seemed a genial and impressive figure. But the New Zealanders, like everyone else in Crete, had ceased to think highly of politicians. Geniality in a Member of Parliament was a suspect quality. It could be said of him that he had turned his

[2] Kippenberger, p. 50

back upon such frivolities, indeed had given up security, and prospects of personal advancement, in order to fight again at the age of fifty. Cautiously his fellow countrymen were prepared to allow him some credit, but some of them wondered whether he might not be getting a little old for it.

The Operation Instructions for his brigade were explicit:

a) 5th Inf Bde will maintain a defensive line running east and west from PLATANIAS to TAVRONITIS RIVER with special regard to defence of MALEME aerodrome.

b) In the event of the enemy making an airborne or seaborne attack on any part of the area, to counter-attack and destroy him immediately.

c) The whole essence of the bde's work is a spirited defence.[3]

For these tasks he had available his four battalions of the re-doubtable 5th Brigade, trained in England under the guidance of Freyberg himself during 1940, and strengthened now by a detach-ment of 364 New Zealand Engineers armed as infantry, together with two platoons of machine-gunners, a total of just over 2,800. As at Suda, however, appearances far exceeded reality. All the battalions were under strength; the 21st, which had been isolated and scattered near Mount Olympus, could muster no more than 376 officers and men. By 19 May, they had been re-equipped to something approaching establishment level, but they needed more automatic small arms, and they were still very short of grenades and mortars. This was a serious handicap. In such close and broken country both types of weapon would clearly be of par-ticular value. Seven French and Italian 75 mm. field guns, and two 3.7 inch Howitzers, were available in support.

Hargest entrusted the immediate defence of the airfield to the 22nd Battalion under Lieutenant-Colonel Andrew. Most of the rest of his brigade he spread out along the coast to the east. Near Dhaskaliana, a mile short of Pirgos, and two miles from the airfield, he concentrated the 23rd Battalion, at something like its full strength, under the command of Lieutenant-Colonel Leckie, a schoolmaster who had served with the Canterbury Mounted Rifles from 1916 to 1919. Between these two fine battalions there had developed a sense of rivalry that went somewhat deeper than normal mess-tent banter. A few months later the officer who had taken over the brigade found that 'the battalions had an odd

[3] 5th Brigade Operation Instruction No. 4

hostility towards one another which sprang from old antipathies between earlier commanders'.[4]

It was arranged that the 23rd would counter-attack if the 22nd should appear in any danger of losing its hold upon the airfield. In the meantime, Leckie was likely to be much concerned on his own account for the defence of his area together with the adjoining coastline. Brigade Headquarters, and 28th (Maori) Battalion, were at Platanias. The Engineers filled the gap along the coast between the Maoris and the 23rd, while the much reduced 21st Battalion was centred on Kondomari across the foothills south of Dhaskaliana.

At Maleme itself a heavy responsibility fell upon Andrew, a silent thin-faced man of forty-four, with grizzled hair and a black moustache. For courage, his record could not be surpassed; in the First World War his service had been distinguished by the award of the Victoria Cross. Later, he had stayed on as a regular soldier in the tiny cadre of the New Zealand Army. His professional views were wholly orthodox. Now his orders were to fight a battle of static defence, maintaining the protection of the airfield 'at all costs'.[5] It was a task for which his qualities appeared to suit him perfectly.

The first of his problems arose from the fact that the distance across the runway from the sea to the foothills was little short of a mile. This meant that if visibility should be impaired by dust and smoke it would become impossible to command it by aimed fire from the heights. He decided that one of his companies would have to dig in on the perimeter itself. Another would defend the line of the Tavronitis above the bridge, while the others occupied the Pirgos-Maleme village and the high ground to the south. With this disposition he would need to cover an area that was more than a mile by a mile and a half in size. The available strength of his battalion was a mere 620 officers and men. He would therefore have no troops left to form a reserve.

Immediately south of the airfield and the road, the steep elongated Kavzakia Hill rose to a height of about three hundred and fifty feet, the red soil bursting from bare tumbled slopes between clumps of meagre scrub; but the face that presented west above the river was thickly covered by substantial growths of olive. This height was soon to be known by both sides as Hill 107.

[4] Kippenberger, p. 113
[5] Henderson, 22 *Battalion*, p. 37. One of his platoons had been detached to guard the radar station at Xamoudhokhori

It was plain that its possession would decide the fate of Maleme. Here Andrew established his command post in a hollow somewhat back from the crest, but the broken country and the trees 'made it impossible to find a spot which gave a good view of all the battalion area'.[6] Added to his battalion strength were two platoons of heavy machine-guns; he sited them to fire into the undefended space beyond the Tavronitis. His two tanks were dug into the hillside below his Headquarters.

The ten Bofors still stood out nakedly upon the perimeter, and a mile above the bridge a forward platoon of 21st Battalion lay concealed in the river bed. There remained, in mounting apprehension, a mixed collection of Fleet Air Arm and R.A.F. troops, 339 officers and men in all. Few showed much enthusiasm for their prospective rôle as infantry. An effort was made to coax them into learning something that might help them to defend themselves; the New Zealanders offered to instruct them in musketry. But 'they did not want to learn'.[7] Of all the specialists in Crete they continued to be the most disdainful of the cruder forms of fighting. In their quarters, along the east bank of the river above the bridge, they played cards and hoped for the best. Andrew had made the reasonable request that all the troops at Maleme should come under his command, but it was felt in Canea that nothing could be held to justify so revolutionary a liaison of arms.

He fully understood the necessity for concealment from the air. While an occasional plane still remained available, he investigated this matter in the best possible way by persuading a pilot to fly him over his battalion position. As a result, he was able to suggest some improvements in camouflage. He had been given some wire but, like every other commander in the island, he was acutely aware of the shortage of automatic weapons, grenades and mortars. And he must certainly have felt anxiety about his communications. Telephone line had been taken out to the companies, but there was neither equipment nor time to dig it in, and not the slightest hope that it would survive bombardment. He had one wireless set.

To a great extent, this disposal of his brigade had been forced upon Hargest by his need to compromise between the competing demands of the airfield and of the coast. No guidance had been given to him to suggest that one of them might be more important

[6] Henderson, 22 *Battalion*, p. 35   [7] Lieut. A. W. Sutton, D.S.C., of the Royal Navy

than the other. Nor did he discern any priority for himself. He had probably learnt from Puttick that Freyberg was not inclined to ascribe to the airfields the importance claimed for them by Intelligence. Nevertheless, the runway at Maleme was a mere eight hundred yards long, while invasion from the sea might fall unpredictably upon any section of a dozen miles of coast. Wherever he kept his battalions, it was likely that he would have to move them in order to concentrate them against invasion from the sea, while at least he could be certain of being ready on the spot if they should make their first onslaught upon the airfield. Logically, therefore, there was much to be said for holding his main force at Maleme. At the insistence of Puttick, he had moved the main body of his brigade somewhat to the west. Yet he still kept his Headquarters at Platanias, five miles away, while the 23rd Battalion remained at Dhaskaliana, a full two miles short of the Tavronitis. From here, the runway itself was hidden by the shoulder of the hills, by the fall of ground towards the river, and by the thick tangles of bamboo and olive that closed in upon the road as it passed through the village. This meant that even in clear daylight nothing could be seen of the runway from the main position of the 23rd, and little enough of Hill 107.

Thus the 22nd lay isolated and vulnerable two miles beyond any support, somewhat like the head of a snail poked far out from within its protective shell. And here was a naked head that could be withdrawn only at the peril of the body as a whole – since to abandon the airfield would be to expose the rest of the brigade, and indeed the entire force in Crete, to German reinforcement brought in by troop-carrier.

Whatever might be this risk, Hargest did not account it sufficient to justify any further thinning of the defence along the beach. Nor did he use any of his troops, apart from the single platoon of the 21st Battalion, to man the hollow of the river bed. Still less did he feel able to spare so much as a company to occupy the coastal strip further to the west. All that he could do to protect this area would be to cover it by artillery fire, and by the heavy machine-guns on Hill 107.

An alternative policy had been discarded. At Kisamos Kastelli, fifteen miles further west, was stationed the 1st Greek Regiment, over a thousand strong. If the Germans were to land here they would have neither an airfield nor good harbour facilities; reinforcement must inevitably be slow, and it was unlikely that they could present any immediate danger. Freyberg had therefore suggested that these Greeks should be moved into the area west of the Tavronitis. The *New Zealand Official History* says that there was 'no transport' for them, and adds that 'before I Greek Regiment could be moved the permission of the Greek authorities had to be obtained'.[8] This takes no account of the fact that by the beginning of May Freyberg had been given command of all Greek forces in the island. Nor does it accord with his later recollection. In 1952 he wrote:

It is a mis-statement to say that we could not move the 1st Greek Regiment without permission from the Greek authorities. As far as I can remember the facts were these: Owing to policy matters holding me at H.Q. and the fact that Heraklion was looked on as most important aerodrome, I inspected their defences first, and it was not until late in the period of preparation that I got to Maleme. . . . I discussed the whole question with General Puttick, and I was in favour (and so, I think, was he) of moving the 1st Greek Regiment up to the area west of the aerodrome. It was only when he looked at the surface of the ground, and took into account the shortage of tools, that we realized that it would be impossible to do it and have them dug in before the attack came.[9]

The move was cancelled, a decision which may be taken to suggest that Freyberg was already underestimating the importance of the airfields. Certainly it is difficult to understand how such objections could have been judged adequate to justify the neglect of a tactical area from which there might develop a deadly threat to the defence of the runway. The distance could have been covered comfortably in a night's march; the men had very little to carry. And some trenches had already been prepared. They were to remain unoccupied.

It is easy to see that Hargest's disinclination to spread his force west of the Tavronitis need not have been dictated solely by anxiety for the protection of the coast between Maleme and Canea. He must also have felt great concern about his communications with the rest of the New Zealand Division. All effective contact depended upon freedom of passage along the exposed coast road. A determined enemy landing by air or sea at any point along this road would immediately cut off both reinforcement and essential supplies. Indeed, he might well be

8 Davin, p. 60

9 DP, Freyberg comments on D. M. Davin's draft of New Zealand War History on Crete, 1952 (undated) (hereafter called 'Davin Draft')

tempted to fight the coming battle with half his attention at
Maleme and half cast back over his shoulder to the rear. As
it was, he still had the whole of his brigade in hand at little more
than an hour's march from the airfield or from any point of the
coast between the Tavronitis and the Galatas Turn.

But success would hang upon one transcendent factor: there
must be flexibility of command, with the utmost vigour of
organized counter-attack, wherever it might be required, at the
earliest possible moment.

Much had now been settled. One vital problem remained. A
handful of aircraft could still leave the ground. But they were too
few to offer any hope that they might intervene effectively in the
battle. What should be done with them then? More important,
since there would soon be no planes to fly from them, should not
the airfields be destroyed? Here was a matter of crucial significance, already too long neglected. From the start it had evoked
attitudes which tell a dismal tale of self-delusion and shuffled
responsibility.

On 22 April Air Marshal Longmore had himself flown to the
island, and had estimated that a squadron of Hurricanes, with a
hundred per cent rate of replacement, might be able to protect
Suda Bay. Five days later Air Marshal Portal, the Chief of the
Air Staff, was telling the Chiefs of Staff Committee that, unless
the Navy 'attached great importance to holding the island' it
would be 'better to keep the fighters in Egypt'. By 5 May he had
become 'emphatic' that it would be 'dangerous to send aircraft to
Crete at the expense of the Western Desert and elsewhere'.[10]
Wavell had never pretended that there was any immediate hope
of air reinforcement.

During the next few days some of the most gallant feats of the
war were performed in the skies above Crete. The pilots from
Greece had come to the island after weeks of exhausting struggle
during which they had seen the deaths of many friends. Their
ground staffs had lost their familiar maintenance equipment. All
had left Greece in the confident hope of rest and refreshment in
Egypt. Instead, they were called upon again to fight immediately
at odds of thirty to one while lacking even the ground installations,
and the basic requirements in engine lubricants and machine-gun
ammunition, that had been available in Greece. During the

[10] Clark, p. 40

seventeen days that followed the evacuation, a further ten Hurricanes were flown from North Africa to join them. Most were quickly destroyed. Last minute attempts to construct protection pens under the hillsides achieved nothing. For the few pilots who survived, it became certain that death could be delayed no more than briefly from one flight to the next. And this without the encouragement that is essential to every fighting man if he is to sustain a forlorn resistance – the conviction of playing a vital part in a critical battle. Not for them the triumph and exhilaration that had inspired their comrades in the Battle of Britain. In Crete it seemed plain that nothing they might do could alter the course of the conflict on land. Their sacrifice was no more than a gesture, their resistance a token resistance. Only their deaths were real. Yet they fought with desperate valour.

At first Freyberg could not bring himself to believe the grim truth. In his buoyant message of 5 May he had referred to the 'equipment and transport . . . with a few extra fighter aircraft' with which it should be 'possible to hold Crete', associating these requirements in a way which showed his continued refusal to accept the fact that the two were not equally attainable. And it seems likely that he was encouraged in his false hopes. On 13 May he sent to the Middle East a report of a meeting that he had held with his Air and Naval Commanders. In view of expected Hurricane replacements it had been agreed that fighters should be used to combat the enemy air attack.[11]

But now these fancies were quickly destroyed. German air activity suddenly increased and was ruthlessly pressed against opposition which was already beyond giving an effective reply.

There was a whine and a roar, [says Aircraftman Comeau, of the attack at Maleme on the morning of the 13th], and thirty Me 109s flashed out of the sun. The air crackled with their exploding cannon shells. The erks were racing for cover followed by a fusillade of bullets as Sergeants Ripsher and Reynish trundled their Hurricanes along the strip at a desperate full throttle – Sutton harnesses flapping, nothing fastened up. The Messerschmitts shot overhead, while the two men sat with their backs to the oncoming fighters, fighting to gain height, struggling to gain a little more speed out of the lumbering Mark Is as they lifted their undercarriages . . .

Half a dozen Messerschmitts were flying straight down the strip as

Squadron-Leader Howell in the third Hurricane opened his throttle. Eaton in his gun-pit hung onto the Lewis, blazing wildly at them. Yet another wave of aircraft skimmed the beach. There were so many Messerschmitts it was impossible to keep track of them. Everything was yellow tracer and crackling cannon, thumping Bofors and rifle shots. One-o-nines swept past the C.O. on either side of him before he was airborne. Others came in on his starboard quarter just as he came 'unstuck'. Two Germans flashing past his nose left him their slip-stream. The Hurricane dropped violently in the bumpy air, then, miraculously unscathed, carried on. It kept low and headed for the protection of the hills.

To the east Sergeant Reynish was holding his machine in a vertical bank with three Messerschmitts trying to turn inside him. He was more than a match for them. Then he was on the tail of one of them – the 109 turned slowly on its back out of control and dived into the hills. But by now there were twelve Messerschmitts in pursuit of the Hurricane, and they all disappeared from view over the hills.[12]

Three and a half hours later, Squadron-Leader Edward Howell, flying a Hurricane for the first time in his life, came back to land safely. Reynish was rescued from the sea. Between them they had shot down six of the enemy.

On the following day, at Heraklion, forty German planes were attacked by two Hurricanes which had arrived from Egypt during the previous night. One got down in a forced landing, the other disappeared. At Maleme another replacement Hurricane arrived in the middle of a raid. Comeau heard the

. . . Merlin engine's thoroughbred drone as the aircraft skirted the hills. The pilot must have seen that the 'drome was under attack but nevertheless prepared to land. He was probably out of fuel. We followed his passage breathlessly. One-o-nines crowded above and behind him. Then . . . wheels down . . . full flap . . . he swung out to sea on his final approach. He was coming in down-wind. Agonizing seconds passed. 'He's going to make it!' Ken yelled in my ear. Then the aircraft was falling like a plummet. It hit the sea with a mighty splash. The waters closed over and were calm once more. . . . The 109s . . . screamed past in triumph.[13]

Flight-Lieutenant Woodward, who had fought in the great air victory over Athens, twice had his plane set on fire before he

[12] Comeau, p. 62   [13] Ibid., p. 72

could reach the end of the runway at Maleme. On two further occasions he contrived to get it into the air, and to escape alive, after desperate twisting flights up and down the valleys.[14]

From their slit trenches the troops watched these hopeless combats in admiration and anguish.

Freyberg knew at last that he would have to fight his battle without fighter defence. The truth that should have been accepted from the start could be denied no longer. At every level the ugly thought had been evaded. Wavell had deceived himself in pretending that the battle might be delayed until more planes could reach the Middle East. The Air Chiefs had talked in terms of planes that did not exist. Freyberg himself had been living on dreams when he had spoken of 'a few extra fighter aircraft' in his message to the Prime Minister. Even if by some miracle of engineering contrivance it might have proved possible, within a few days, to construct effective shelters for them there had never been any prospect that a sufficient number of aircraft could arrive in time. It had never really mattered that 'sixty-four Hurricanes' might arrive in Cairo by 25 May. From every Intelligence source, including those which had begun to reveal the concentration against Russia, it had become increasingly plain, since the end of April, that the Germans would certainly attack before that date. Even to the blindest optimist it should have been obvious that effective air cover for the island must be impossible within a period of many weeks to come. No doubt the best that had been hoped was that a handful of Hurricanes, thrown against the slow-moving troop-carriers, might have been able to cause damage and disorder before falling to their own destruction among the German fighters. By the middle of May even this possibility was seen to have been no more than a mirage. Of the British planes that remained not one could expect to leave the ground in the presence of the enemy.

This was the reality that Freyberg had finally to accept. In the end it was with relief that he gave the necessary orders. At least he would be able to spare those few pilots who survived. Maintenance staffs would be retained in the hope that aircraft might eventually return. In the meantime any machine that could fly would be sent back to Egypt. On 17 May three Hurricanes and three Gladiators took off for Cairo. The Official Naval Historian says of this decision that 'the air battle' was thus 'lost by default

[14] Flight-Lieut. V. C. Woodward, to the author, 1960

before it had begun',[15] a comment which might be taken to imply, quite wrongly, that there remained some viable alternative.

But now there must be a consequence. At the last moment, with no anti-aircraft weapons, indeed without serious thought of counter-measures, the troops in Crete must be exposed, as no troops had ever been exposed before, to the utmost rigours of unopposed attack from the air.

And what of the airfields, each of them, while it remained intact, an open invitation to the enemy troop-carriers and a source of mortal danger to the defence?

Minor obstructions had been set up during the previous few days, barrels filled with earth, and petrol containers that could be ignited by machine-gun fire. These might perhaps prove helpful against a direct landing by enemy planes, but they could be cleared within minutes if the fields should be captured by parachutists. At Maleme, the Staff Captain of the New Zealand 5th Brigade had prepared plans for demolition of the runway. He had '300 mines available for use'.[16] Hourly he waited for the orders that would tell him to go ahead. He waited in vain.

After the battle, Freyberg was to maintain that he had received specific instruction not to destroy the airfields and that he had complied with reluctance.

The source of this decision remains a mystery. But it would appear to have had the approval of the Chiefs of Staff, for on 6 June they were to issue a detailed minute in which they attempted to justify the fact that the airfields had been left intact. By this time many voices in the Press and in Parliament were clamouring for an explanation. To judge by their minute, it might be supposed that the attitude of the Chiefs of Staff had been governed by the feeling that so gigantic an operation as the mining of the runways in Crete had been scarcely possible. Few people could have any idea of the extent and complexity of the task of laying mines and charges to destroy an airfield, and of the resources in skill and material that were needed to carry it out. Not only was it necessary to have expert engineers, but also a great quantity of explosive and detonators with a good deal of transport. Technically it would all have been very difficult. Moreover, the best prepared demolitions often went wrong. Somebody might even have made a mistake in firing the charges.

[15] Kemp, p. 137   [16] DP, Capt. W. W. Mason

Certainly it would have taken a long time, and if the airfields had been captured any damage could easily have been repaired by the enemy. Finally, there had been the need to retain them for operations. It had to be remembered that they had been used 'to within twenty-four hours of the German attack'.[17]

It is scarcely surprising that the Prime Minister made no use of this deplorable document when he came to face the House of Commons four days later.

No doubt it would have been difficult to carry out extensive demolitions in 'twenty-four hours'. But the decision should have been taken much earlier, at the beginning of May at the latest, by which time the developing situation was already plain. With the willing help of the Cretans, it would then have been easy to block the fields with trenches, stakes and tree trunks. There was no necessity to shatter them into a likeness of the surface of the moon. The timed detonation of mines need have been no more than an attractive embellishment. Intelligence had thought it 'improbable' that any substantial help would reach the parachutists by air until after the runways had been put into operation. And the parachutists would be fighting for their lives, with no time or equipment to set themselves up as labour gangs. All that was required, therefore, was sufficient obstruction to render it impossible for troop-carrying aircraft to be landed within a matter of two or three days, even if the airfields should temporarily fall into the hands of the enemy. As for the insistence that the Germans could readily repair any damage, this at once disposed of the argument that the fields need remain out of action once the assault had been beaten off. If they had been in service again within a week or two that would have been time enough, long before aircraft reinforcements from Egypt could be available.

Finally, the claim that they had been used until the last 'twenty-four hours' – by a single Gladiator perhaps, or by two Hurricanes on a good day – reveals thinking blind to all reality. It well reflects the failure of comprehension within the High Command at that time, the ignorance of the factor of air power, the lack of such qualities of imagination as might have done something to compensate for that ignorance, and above all, the incapacity to see that, in Crete, all had hung upon the outcome of the next few days, and not upon some benign development of events in the future. The Chiefs of Staff in London had been

[17] Chiefs of Staff, 6 June 1941. Ref. Davin, pp. 35 and 51, and Buckley, p. 161

indulging in a wave of wholly illogical optimism about the impending struggle. In August 1939 they had greatly exaggerated the German strength in the air. This had led them to accept an estimation of half a million civilian dead in the first fortnight. A few months later they had seen the *Luftwaffe* faced and rebuffed above south-east England. They had forgotten that the Royal Air Force, stretched but triumphant, had held the enemy planes at a distance. Swarms of Messerschmitts had not flown continually, and unopposed, across the tree-tops of the Green Park. They still did not suspect the overall ascendancy that could be conferred by overwhelming strength in the air. In general, their view had been that in Crete there must be a splendid opportunity to beat hell out of the Germans. From this safe distance, nobody had felt that the destruction of the airfields really mattered very much.

Freyberg had known how serious was the threat from the *Luftwaffe*. But, since he believed that the troop-carriers would be able to crash-land indiscriminately, he was not according supreme importance to the airfields themselves. He was not happy about them; indeed he had ordered the blockage of the runways under construction at Kastelli Pediada. But he did not contest the official view that the airfields at Heraklion and Maleme were still needed by the Royal Air Force for operational purposes, even after it had become clear that such a view was worthless. He suggested to Beamish that, at the very least, the airstrip at Retimo should be rendered unserviceable; if it were left intact he would have to find a garrison to station there. Beamish maintained that Retimo was needed as a satellite landing-ground to Heraklion and Maleme. Freyberg let it go at that. Later he was to say, 'I wanted to mine all airfields. I was not allowed to. I don't think that the decision rested with Group Captain Beamish. It was taken on a much higher plane – I believe by the War Cabinet.'[18]

Here he showed a strange and uncharacteristic acquiescence. It was quite foreign to him, when responsibility was his, to defer to anybody in a course of action which he believed to be wrong, whether it might be suggested by a Group Captain in Crete, the General Staff in London, or by Churchill himself. In all his past his attitude had been, as it was to be again, precisely that recommended by another general as appropriate to a commander, that he 'should not wait for pressure or suggestions, or even orders.

---

[18] DP, Freyberg comments on Gavin Long's draft of Australian War History on Crete, 5 Dec. 1949 (hereafter called 'Long Draft')

He should anticipate these things and put clearly before his government how he views the situation and the action he proposes to meet it'.[19]

Why then did he not destroy the airfields? It would seem likely that the reason was three-fold, lying partly in the misguided optimism that induced him to believe too long that effective air reinforcement might be sent from Egypt, partly in his pre-occupation with what he conceived to be the paramount danger of invasion from the sea, and partly in his conviction that the Germans would, in any event, be able to land their airborne troops in great numbers whether they had taken possession of an airfield or not. Whatever the explanation it is difficult not to conclude that in this matter his vision had deserted him. He was still very weary after the campaign in Greece. Exhaustion, which never could dim either his courage or his generosity, had for the moment laid a cloud upon his judgement.

Towards the middle of May, a feeling of tension and expectation began to spread along the coast. The rollicking parties had left the village squares and the market place at Canea. The few soldiers who appeared in the streets wore arms and helmets and went quickly about their business. In the defence areas, after each delivery of equipment from Egypt, the men worked all night, wiring positions and digging emplacements. From the first, danger had lurked about the harbour at Suda. Later it had appeared in the neighbourhood of the airfields. Now it began to visit every house and olive grove. Fighter planes roared suddenly from behind the hills to scream machine-gunning along the roads. It became unsafe to drive a truck without the help of spotters to watch in all directions. Men died abruptly and unexpectedly. A surgeon and his anaesthetist were killed by a bomb while bathing near the hospital. Soon this threat from the air began to exert an effect more potent than it could yet achieve in dead and wounded. For the soldiers who had been in Greece it was an ominous reminder, for the new arrivals a promise that they too must now face this menace of which they had heard so much. The slit trenches began to take on an immense significance, conferring a protection which seemed almost magical. One hot afternoon, hundreds of planes returning from Suda swept, bombing and machine-gunning, a few feet above the neck of the Akrotiri Peninsula to plunge down

[19] Nigel Nicolson on General Dill, *New Statesman*, 28 Nov. 1959

a narrow ravine to the sea. In their trenches, lining the banks, less than thirty yards from the planes which were often below them, were the men of the Welch Regiment. Quickly the little valley filled with dust and reeking cordite. But not a man had been hit. For a minute or two there was a lull. Four soldiers and a Cretan civilian left their trenches to stretch their legs and visit friends. In an instant a straggler Messerschmitt had swept upon them, scattering their limbs and brains about the trees and rocks.

These deaths were typical of others. The sight of such incidents made men reluctant to move in the open. Where was the sense of getting above ground simply to be killed by a casual bomb? They induced an atmosphere that affected men at every age, veterans of the First World War, who had begun by saying that air attack was nothing to compare with artillery bombardment, no less than the boys fresh from school. This experience was new. Its very strangeness made it impressive. Already it was clear that it must embarrass every movement of transport. Now a greater danger began to appear. At this rate the Germans might well achieve their object, and arrive to find the defenders paralysed like rabbits. 'I don't like to see these men cowering in their trenches,' remarked the Quartermaster of the Welch, himself a survivor of 1917, 'they've got to get out of them some time and they might as well start to learn how to do it now.'[20]

Amidst so much natural luxury something of the atmosphere of holiday still lingered. Every day the sun mounted in a sky of perfect blue softened only by a faint haze above the sea, while a narrow tracery of cloud lay motionless upon the rim of the horizon. Sometimes a sharp storm would send rivulets gurgling for a few hours down the hillsides, while raindrops sparkled from the flowers and shrubs, and steam rose from the freshly scented earth until the sun returned to dry the dust and set it lifting again along the white roads. At every opportunity men continued to bathe in the sea, much to the astonishment of the Cretans who never went near it. There were other diversions. An enterprising journalist among the New Zealanders had begun to produce a news sheet, *Crete News*, and on the radio the traitor commentator 'Lord Haw Haw' was referring increasingly to Crete. 'The island of doomed men,' he called it. The 1st Welch were gratified to hear their regiment described as 'famous for its rugby footballers', a discrimination somewhat resented by the New Zealanders who

[20] To author, Capt. W. E. Cooper

felt that they too knew something about the game. At night, there was a rivalry of choirs among the trees. In this none could outdo the Welshmen, company challenging company in practised harmony through the darkness. One day they were given a different reminder of things to come; a Greek orange seller, a well-known figure about the Battalion lines, was found to be carrying written details of troop numbers and dispositions.[21]

All were aware of facing the unknown, that 'real destroyer of courage'.[22] But there was little anxiety. The men disliked the impotence imposed upon them by the *Luftwaffe*, but for the attack itself they felt curiosity rather than fear. As the bombing of Maleme increased from day to day a New Zealand soldier wrote in his diary, 'Boy, the fun has started. All the boys are just waiting on this invasion by parachutists which is to take place sometime'.[23] This, indeed, expressed a feeling that was becoming widespread. Within the organized infantry battalions the discouragement they had felt in Greece was fast disappearing. As Churchill had expected the trained men, those who had practice and confidence in the use of their arms, were beginning to look forward with relish and anticipation to fresh encounter with the enemy.

The German preparations were now approaching their climax. On a bright summer morning during the third week in May, Colonel von der Heydte was ordered to report at eleven o'clock for a conference with General Student. The meeting was held at the Grande Bretagne, the hotel in the centre of Athens where, a month earlier, Wavell had been forced to recognize that his Greek venture had failed, and that evacuation was inevitable.[24]

One look at the hermetically-sealed and shuttered room in the Hotel Grande Bretagne [wrote von der Heydte], where the commanders of all the paratroop regiments and battalions were gathered to receive their orders, was sufficient to dispel the secret of our target; a large map of Crete was prominently displayed upon the wall.

In a quiet but clear and slightly vibrant voice General Student explained the plan of attack. It was his own personal plan. He had devised it, had struggled against heavy opposition for its acceptance, and had worked out all the details. One could perceive that this plan had become a part of him, a part of his life. He believed in it and lived for it and in it.[25]

[21] De Courcy, *History of the Welch Regiment*, p. 138   [22] Moorehead, *Gallipoli*, p. 132
[23] Ross, *23 Battalion*, p. 64   [24] De Guingand, *Generals at War*, p. 137
[25] von der Heydte, p. 40

This was the attack which Student had concerted with Goering and Löhr, the scheme which would enable his airborne troops to apply in action, the great majority of them for the first time, the principles in which he had so carefully trained them.

When the General had finished, the corps intelligence officer rose to speak. He sketched a broad picture of the enemy's situation. On the island were the remnants of two or three Greek divisions, much weakened by the battles of the mainland, and a British force of divisional strength consisting mainly of dominion troops under command of the well-known General Freyberg. A portion of the population would be sympathetic towards a German attack. There was also on the island a secret resistance group which would be prepared to fight alongside the Germans and would make itself known to us by the code words 'Major Bock'.[26]

Student could not, of course, let fall any hint of priority between Sectors. But in fact there is no reason to suppose that he regarded this as a problem, since he confidently expected swift success in all three. Although he was sending the Force Commander to land in the area of 3 Parachute Regiment south-west of Canea he may well have placed his main hopes upon Heraklion. The 5th Mountain Division had been given detailed information about the town and its surroundings.

For several days Freyberg had been receiving from Cairo a series of messages suggesting, not very helpfully, that the attack might after all be made against Cyprus. This was yet another of the possibilities that tormented Wavell, who at the same time was forced every day to recognize more clearly the indications of a threat to the Levant. On the 19th he heard from Churchill that he was to prepare a force to capture Syria from the Vichy French. Vainly he protested against this fresh commitment. Once more he was overruled. For the moment the project was to remain secret, known only to himself and to his staff, one further addition to his crowding anxieties.

The world at large was no longer in any doubt that Crete was about to become the scene of a critical battle. The prospects were freely discussed in all the western newspapers. Indeed the Prime Minister had told the House of Commons, on 7 May, that Crete, like Tobruk, would be defended 'to the death and without thought of retirement'.

[26] von der Heydte, p. 43

On 18 May he had cabled to Wavell:

Our success in 'Scorcher' would of course affect whole world
situation. May you have God's blessing on this memorable and fateful
operation, which will react in every theatre of the war.[27]

And to Freyberg:

We are glad to hear of the strong dispositions which you have made
and that reinforcements have reached you. All our thoughts are with
you in these fateful days. We are sure that you and your brave men
will perform a deed of lasting fame. The Royal Navy will do its
utmost. Victory where you are would powerfully affect world
situation.[28]

The reinforcements had been meagre enough. Yet Freyberg
was becoming more confident. He had expressed his new hopes in
a signal to Wavell on 16 May:

I have completed plan for defence of Crete and have just returned
from final tour of defences. I feel greatly encouraged by my visit.
Everywhere all ranks are fit and morale is high. All defences have been
extended, and positions wired as much as possible. We have forty-five
field guns placed, with adequate ammunition dumped. Two infantry
tanks are at each aerodrome. Carriers and transport still being unloaded and delivered. 2nd Leicesters have arrived, and will make
Heraklion stronger. I do not wish to be over confident, but I feel that
at least we will give excellent account of ourselves. With the help
of Royal Navy I trust Crete will be held.[29]

This optimism may well have reflected some lessening of
personal anxiety. He had not ceased to be painfully aware of the
allegiance which he owed to his own New Zealanders. Nor can
that awareness have been lessened by the knowledge that for a
week the New Zealand Prime Minister, who was still in Cairo,
had been pressing to see him. But this demand had now been
relaxed and the messages that came from his Home Government
had contained nothing but encouragement and congratulation
upon his appointment to command the island; from him at least,
with a restraint that did them honour, they were withholding
expression of their acute anxiety. Equally happy was the sage
dispensation by which his only son, who had been serving as a

private with the New Zealand 23rd Battalion, had been selected
for officer training, and promptly sent protesting to Egypt.

His latest information, issued to the Battalions on the 16 May,
forecast that the attack would begin on any day from the 17th to
the 19th. The scale and method of the onslaught was estimated in
terms very similar to those of 12 May:

   . . . there would be an airborne force of some 25,000 to 35,000 men,
and a seaborne force of 10,000 men. The first attack would be launched
by 100 bombers and heavy fighters. Then 600 troop-carriers would
follow up and there would be successive waves of paratroops. The
seaborne attack would be escorted by the Italian Navy. And the
objectives of the enemy would be Maleme, Canea, Retimo, and the
Aghya Valley.[30]

Again no attempt was made to break down the numbers of
'airborne' troops into parachutists and men discharged from
landed troop-carriers. Nor is there any record that Freyberg, or
any other member of his amateur staff, ever asked specifically for
this information. The fact that he did not do so may be taken to
reveal that he saw no reason to make this vital distinction. This
time nothing was said about Heraklion. Wisely he decided to
draw no particular conclusion from that. As can be judged from
the signal that he returned to Wavell on 16 May, this final
appreciation tended to confirm him in his feeling that airborne
attack alone might very well be dealt with, and that landings
from the sea, above all if supported by tanks, must be regarded
as the chief danger.

It may be wondered whether it occurred to him, as he awaited
the onslaught, that the ordeal which faced him would be very
different from any that he had known before, and that it would
demand of him qualities totally unlike those that had led him to
his old triumphs. This would be no compact action with men to
be inspired by the appearance of their commander walking
nonchalantly among them whenever the fire might be hottest. In
his quarry on the peninsula above Canea he would be stranded
and frustrated, at the mercy of his precarious communications,
while his troops fought along eighty miles of coast in a series of
distinct engagements each of which could lose the battle. Here
there would be little opportunity for a warrior king. Instead a
subtler faculty would be required of him, one that was well

[30] Davin, p. 77

recognized in his adversary, the 'ability to appreciate the enemy's situation accurately, even when actual information about the enemy is wrong'.[31]

For more than a week the parachutists had been relaxing in their tented camps beside the airfields of Southern Greece – at Almiros, Dadion, Topolia, Tanagra, Eleusis, Phaleron, Megara, Corinth and Mylene.[32] The favoured members of the Storm Regiment had been granted passes to visit Athens, where they noted with interest that columns of Mountain Troops were marching down to the docks at the Piraeus. They found themselves a little resented for their privileged airs by cynical fellow soldiers who had already begun to think in terms of home, and family, and the pleasures of peace. When asked what they were doing in Greece they replied, with brash confidence, that they had no idea, but that the world would know before long.[33]

At midday on 19 May they heard that their objective was to be Crete. The orders, lacking nothing in clarity, told them that they were to attack on the following day.

With strong formations of parachutists and assault troops XI Air Corps will capture by storm the three usable airfields upon Crete, at Maleme, Retimo and Heraklion, and will then be reinforced by further formations of parachutists and mountain troops both from the air and by sea.[34]

The capture of *usable* airfields. Here was revealed the incontrovertible basis of the plan which Student had outlined to their commanders. To it were added such details as were available concerning their particular objectives. They were told that little opposition was expected, no more than a small occupation force, backed, perhaps, by a few demoralized survivors of the beaten army from Greece. All seemed very simple. By the time the Stukas had finished there would probably be very little left for them to do. Nevertheless, that night they did not sleep well.

On the same evening Freyberg reported a further great increase in enemy air activity. He informed Wavell that he was expecting to be attacked at any moment. Some hours later he heard that two German pilots had told Cretans who had rescued them from

[31] DP, von der Heydte's assessment of Student
[32] Gericke, p. 29   [33] Ibid., p. 23   [34] Ibid., p. 30

the sea that the invasion would come at dawn. This time he issued no special warning. No doubt he feared he might again be wrong. During the night one more message arrived from Cairo. It proved to be well within the tradition of its predecessors. 'There are some indications,' it said, 'which point to delaying attack on you or even possible diversion elsewhere'.[35] If this should happen no one was going to be able to say that Middle East Headquarters had not thought of it first.

The soldiers had spent the day cheerfully busy about their affairs. Hour after hour the planes had swept the tree-tops, wheeling about their objectives in leisurely groups of ten to fifteen and returning as they pleased to survey the scene. Apart from an occasional chasing shot from a Bofors, they were unmolested. The infantry kept in cover and held their fire, encouraged to realize that the pilots did not know where to find them. Casualties remained light. Among the troops on the perimeter at Maleme no more than six men were hurt. Even the guns were largely un-damaged. At Suda the 'umbrella' protection by anti-aircraft fire above the jetty met with some success.

By 7 p.m. the last of the planes had faded down the evening sky. It was quiet again in the villages where the Cretans had always welcomed these strangers who had come from unimagin-ably far to fight the common and universal enemy. With their Greek allies, the men from Britain and the Britons from the Antipodes awaited the unknown in a mood of measured con-fidence not without gaiety. There was quiet laughter still among the coloured fields at Heraklion, along the bush-covered slopes at Retimo, and in the olive groves around Canea. At Galatas music from the radio echoed hour after hour down the narrow street, and the sound of an accordion came from the R.A.F. Camp on the bank of the drying river bed at Maleme.

Along the hundred miles of coast from Kastelli to Heraklion the soldiers drank tea and ate their bully-beef stew, talking briefly of the chances and escapes of the day.

There was a remarkably fine sunset that evening [one of them remembered later]. The sun appeared to be sinking into a sea of blood against which the black branches of olive trees were strikingly sil-houetted. Had I foreseen what was so soon to come, I might have read an omen in this grim outlining of the symbol of peace against the crimson ocean which seemed to be flooding the whole world. But the

[35] Connell, p. 456

angry glow gradually faded and the calm stars appeared one by
one – symbols too of a peace as distant and as unattainable as the
heavens themselves.[36]

For his more prosaic comrades there were no symbols, and no
premonitions. As darkness fell they lay down beside their slit-
trenches, twisting close into their blankets, with a final glance
perhaps at a letter from home, before seeking sleep in the cold
night.

[36] Stephanides, p. 56

PART TWO

ATTACK FROM THE AIR

'Hardly anyone behaves on this day as you might have expected him to do.'

Alan Moorehead: *Gallipoli*

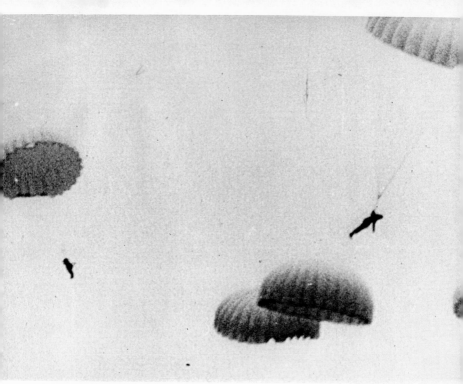

'Each man carried a death' *(Imperial War Museum)*

Parachute landing *(Imperial War Museum)*

Exposed British gunners in action *(Imperial War Museum)*

Parachutist on the road below Hill 107 *(Imperial War Museum)*

8

'Scorcher': 20 May

At 3 a.m. the glider troops and parachutists of Germany's 7th Airlanding Division stumbled out of their tents into a night full of noise and movement, the confused shouting of orders almost drowned by the reverberation of many engines. As the sky lightened they could see that the racing propellers had raised tall clouds of brick-red dust through which there now began to penetrate the level rays of the early sun, flashing for a moment upon some cabin window or aluminium super-structure. Heavily laden with their equipment, the men gathered in groups beside their allotted aircraft before climbing aboard.

A little after 6.30 a.m. the heavy Junkers, some of them drawing gliders, started to rush in succession down the rough runways. Soon they had lifted above the murk of the airfields to assemble over the city of Athens. Below them the Acropolis gleamed white in the sunlight. The Greeks stood at their doors and windows, watching and listening in awe and hatred while the hundreds of planes, like a migration of vast birds, crossed and circled before wheeling south over the glittering water.

Inside the gliders, jerking and pitching at the end of their tow-lines, it was dark and stiflingly hot. Nothing could be seen through the thick cellophane windows. The troops found themselves looking at the bright segments of sea and sky that slid across the narrow tears in the fabric. Many were sick, overcome by the movement and the rank oppressive atmosphere. After about an hour the lines were cast off. In the sudden silence, broken only by the rushing of the wind, the great machines began to dip towards their targets. The men fastened their helmets and sat rigid in their seats, each alone with his thoughts.

The defenders of Crete at first saw nothing remarkable about the new day. They stood to their arms among the olive groves while the dawn slowly lit the sky, sharpening the black shadows of the mountains, and touching the sea first to silver and then to blue. It was still very cold. At about seven o'clock groups of enemy aircraft attacked along the coast between Suda and Maleme. This was much as usual. The men came off guard and went to breakfast. Half an hour later, just before eight o'clock, fresh streams of bombers came in from the north in far greater numbers than before. Once more the air raid 'red' warning rang out over Canea. It was never to be heard again. There was now to be no end to air attack in daylight.

For some minutes, the men at Canea and Suda were aware of nothing but the planes that screamed continually above their heads. But soon they heard through the noise a sound that was new to them, a faint urgent drubbing from far to the west. For the first time, and the last, all the Bofors at Maleme were firing together.

Above the airfield, on the forward slope of Hill 107, Squadron-Leader Howell was crouching in his slit trench. At a quarter to eight he had heard the thunder of many aircraft:

As yet we could not see them. But slowly it became apparent to me that this was bigger than the usual blitz. Nevertheless, I could not believe that it would be more than a blitz. It seemed so suicidal for them to try dropping paratroops in broad daylight on to prepared positions. It was suicidal for many, but I underestimated the determination of our enemies.

In any event, our orders were clear. We were not to move till it was apparent that invasion was occurring. So we watched the skies as interested spectators watching the teams come out on the field for a rugger match. The first formations of bombers – Junkers 88's – were in sight now and wheeling in to run up over us. We watched them closely, with a more personal and apprehensive interest now. They were clearly going to pass straight overhead. That meant we were the target. We waited till we heard the whistle and whine of several scores of heavy bombs on their way down, and then we went flat in the bottom of our trench. The bombs struck in twelves, earth spouted to the heavens, the crump and shock of impact crept closer up the hill. The noise was indescribable. The ground shuddered and shook under us as the bomb pattern passed over and beyond.

The whole area was shrouded in thick choking dust, and earth and stones were falling everywhere. We could not see more than a few yards. But we heard the whistle of more bombs on their way down and we kept below ground . . . bombs bursting close to us shook in the sides of the trench. We were covered in earth. Our eyes and mouths were full of grit. And still it went on. We were shaken . . . till our teeth felt loose and we could hardly see. Debris continued to crash around us and the sides of the trench crumbled. We lost count of time.[1]

The slit trenches maintained their remarkable protection for those able to use them. But the bombardment was going far to achieve its purpose. Enveloped in swirling dust and sand the men on the perimeter could see no more than the occasional rushing shape of an aircraft. The luckless gunners, exposed in the open, quickly suffered the fate which from the first had seemed inevitable to all but their own officers. Howell heard

. . . long bursts of cannon and machine-gun fire as low-flying fighters came in to attack the anti-aircraft gun pits. These were already silent under the terrific weight of attack with the exception of one Bofors gun down by the beach. This went on firing for some time till a host of Stukas and Me 108s fastened on it and shot and blasted it out of existence.[2]

No less helpless were the heavy coast defence guns as the planes stole upon them from over the mountains at their back.

Suddenly the torrent of bombs ceased. There was silence, 'eerie, acrid and ominous'.[3] From his vantage point Howell could see that patches of blue sky had begun to appear through the dark clouds of drifting dust. He noted the time. It was eight o'clock. Then he saw the gliders. Silent as ghosts after the deafening screams of the fighters and bombers, huge, black and menacing, they were sliding down from the mountains, banking in long slow turns with a faint hiss of wings, before swooping to their landing places. Some moved in, grim and purposeful above the sea. As he watched, one of them dropped suddenly to crumple against a rock, while another, still airborne, smashed full tilt against the ironwork of the bridge. Others landed safely in the river bed; he could see figures running from them to disappear among the bushes.

Many of the troops were still dazed, perhaps by cerebral concussion rather than by simple fear. Howell felt 'numb and unable to appreciate the significance of the scene'.[4] Two airmen who were with him had been affected in the same way:

Dust was still in the air and it lay thick on everything. Our mouths were dry and full of grit and we were covered with dirt. My ears and

---

[1] Howell, p. 14   [2] Ibid.
[3] Henderson, 22 *Battalion*, p. 41, Sgt. A. M. Sargeson
[4] Howell, p. 15

head were still singing and I was unable to think clearly . . . I chatted about trivialities to the men. They too were badly shaken and automatically shrank down at every aircraft that went over.[5]

Few of the gliders, and scarcely any of the troop-carriers, had fallen to the anti-aircraft guns; only seven transport planes were destroyed out of the 500 that took part in the operations of the first day between Maleme and Suda.[6] But soon the troops who were higher up the hill began to see what was happening. As their wits cleared they opened rapid fire. Now the gliders began to crumble, drilled with bullets, while still in the air. From several that had held their course and seemed to land without gross damage there came no movement; every man sat dead in his place. Some turned aside to be torn apart in a rending crash among unforeseen rocks and trees. Many lay surrounded by the tumbled bodies of those who had sought to escape from them. At best each landing ended in jarring shock, amid splintering wood and the hazards of catapulting ammunition boxes and equipment. Often they came to rest under the very muzzles of enemy weapons. In the R.A.F. Camp Aircraftman Comeau stood transfixed beside his tent as a glider burst at him out of the bushes, one wing slithering above his head to wedge itself against the hillside. He emptied his rifle into the open doorway, blocking it with dead and wounded, before making his escape up the bank.

The German air reconnaissance, which had visualized the Prison Valley as a 'high plateau', may well have proved equally misleading about the terrain at Maleme. Certainly any detached observer who looks today at the steep broken country, at the precipitous slopes, and the tree-lined gorge of the river with its terraced ledges and stone walls can scarcely fail to wonder at the boldness of this assault, and to marvel that any of those who took part in it should have survived.

Within a few minutes some sixty gliders, all that were available for the operation, had landed at Maleme, in the Prison Valley, and upon the Akrotiri Peninsula. Already many of the men who had ridden in them were dead.

Before the last had touched ground they were followed by the parachutists, each of them now entering into their common experience, first the lurch into the void, then the giant tug as the

[5] Howell, p. 16   [6] *Invasion of Crete*, a report issued by Air Fleet IV, 20 Nov. 1941

parachute opened, followed by the fall, twisting and turning in the wind, a glimpse of snow-capped mountains, and of the furrowed sea with its rim of surf – at last, in quick succession, the green hills and squat white houses, fields and plantations, trees, rocks and sand. All were sharing the ruthless hazard of the parachutist, the time when skill and courage are of no avail, when chance rules all, the journey with no return. The fire crackled up at them with an intensity far beyond their fears. For many this brief climax of exaltation and terror was to be their last moment of life.

Among the defenders there was again sudden, brief stupefaction. Much had been expected. Yet imagination had failed to picture the drama and magnitude of the reality. Some had never seen a parachute before. The great balloons, about a dozen from each plane, themselves seemed immensely large and ominous. Stranger still were the voices that came from the sky as the Germans shouted to each other in warning and encouragement. Howell watched 'as if in a dream'. To Lieutenant Thomas of the New Zealand 23rd Battalion the parachutists seemed

. . . unreal, difficult to comprehend as anything at all dangerous. Seen against the deep blue of the early morning Cretan sky, through a frame of grey-green olive branches, they looked like little jerking dolls whose billowy frocks of green, yellow, red and white had somehow blown up and become entangled in the wires that controlled them. . . . I struggled to grasp the meaning behind this colourful fantasy, to realize that those beautiful kicking dolls meant the repetition of all the horrors we had known so recently in Greece.[7]

These indeed were dangerous dolls. In the words of the *Official New Zealand History*:

Each man dangling carried a death, his own, if not another's.[8]

Suddenly the men on the ground were seized by wild excitement. An intense fire rippled out of the olive groves. The swinging marionette figures jerked and crumpled as the bullets tore into them from below. 'You'd see one go limp,' remembered a New Zealander, 'then give a kick and kind of straighten up with a jerk, and then go limp again, and you knew he was done for'.

Many crashed through the branches of the trees and at once lay still. Hundreds fell within the area of the New Zealand 23rd Battalion, two miles east of the airfield. From his command post,

[7] Thomas, p. 7   [8] Davin, p. 187

in a gully near the road, Lieutenant-Colonel Leckie himself killed
five. His adjutant shot two more while still sitting at his packing-
case desk. On the following day a Staff Officer visiting this Headquarters was to find 'bodies everywhere, every ten–twelve yards.
One stepped over them as one went through the olive groves.
And some very good-looking fellows there were too.'[9]

For a fortnight, Leading Aircraftman Denton had been
standing guard with a machine-gun in a gun-pit close to the
runway, crouching and twisting as the explosions tore at the earth
around him. His orders were to hold his fire until the moment of
the invasion. Now his chance had come. Finding himself in the
middle of a crowd of descending parachutists he fired until his
gun burnt out, then picked it up and walked back through a ring
of enemy corpses to one of the defended positions on the slopes
behind him.[10]

Out on the open field Flight Lieutenant Henry Daston, in a
deep underground shelter, was in charge of the main wireless
observation post. He could not see what was happening, but after
receiving the information that aircraft were approaching in much
greater numbers than usual he heard 'a series of thumps' on the
ground overhead. Soon the enemy announced themselves by
throwing grenades into the dug-out. One of his men was killed
and the other two injured by splinters. The three of them were
then driven out of the dug-out at gun-point and forced to walk
west towards the river. A moment later the two wounded men
were cut down by a burst of fire. Daston was hit, but not fatally.
He was allowed to limp on across the stream bed.[11]

From Maleme to Suda, men were fighting for their lives, many
in savage combat with a single adversary, at a range of a few
yards. Typical of hundreds of encounters, now being fought to
the death amid the sunlit orchards and ravines, was the experience
of Lieutenant Thomas. Soon after the beginning of the attack he
was told to lead his platoon on a search for parachutists across the
valley between Dhaskaliana and Hill 107. He noticed that outside
the battalion perimeter all at first seemed 'unnaturally still'.

[9] Davin, p. 187.
[10] Described in a letter from Lieut. A. W. F. Sutton, D.S.C., to Rear Admiral Mediterranean Aircraft Carriers in June 1941
[11] Mr. Henry Daston to the author, January 1960

Ahead of his men he climbed a high bank onto one of the terraces. A few yards away were two Germans. One he killed with a shot fired from the hip, and the second with a blow from his rifle butt. While he still held his rifle by the muzzle a third rushed at him through the trees:

His tommy-gun was pointing straight at me. For a split second my mind shot off to a foolish thought that this fellow did not know that all tommy-guns fire high in bursts. Then the urgent danger of the position registered like panic.

He dropped to the ground, grabbed a revolver from one of his victims, pointed it at the charging figure, and pulled the trigger.

Nothing happened. It was jammed. The big German stopped about three paces from me. As I cringed closer to the still twitching corpse he raised his tommy-gun to his shoulder. Slowly, deliberately, and coldly, he took aim. I saw his right eye screw up as he focussed the sights. The barrel steadied. I was frozen stockstill. I could not move. Then in a flash it was all over. Simultaneously, I saw his shoulder jar as he pulled the trigger, and a red splodge appear on his forehead. Something plucked at the corpse by my face. I saw the German topple to the ground, his face covered in blood. Corporal Rea Thompson, his rifle smoking, was looking at me with inquiry from over the edge of the terrace.[12]

The platoon returned to find the battalion area littered with crumpled parachutes, their gay colours lending an air of macabre festivity to the scene of carnage. On all sides lay the bodies of dead Germans, most of them still in their harness, the sheets and cords entangling them in death like strange earth-bound seaweed. Others hung from the branches of the trees. Thomas had lost two of his own men, but he had brought back with him the discs of twenty-nine dead Germans, together with three prisoners.

It quickly became clear that the parachutists were highly vulnerable to immediate counter-attack. At ranges of anything over two hundred yards their machine pistols were much less effective than rifles. With aimed fire they could be picked off as they ran frantically in search of cover. But the eager New Zealanders were uncertain of their instructions. Some sprang out at once. Others waited reluctantly for orders that were slow to arrive from battalion and company level. At Maleme they had good reason to stay in their trenches, but further afield some of the enemy were left unmolested to search for their heavier weapons;

12 Thomas, p. 11

every minute improved their chances. No such inhibitions were felt by the prisoners in the Field Punishment Centre near Modhion. When parachutists came down nearby the lieutenant in charge gave orders to get 'into them' immediately.[13] At once every man 'went hunting'. Within an hour these 60 hard characters had celebrated their own release by killing 110 of the enemy.

To the other ranks taking part, whether in attack or defence, an endearing feature of airborne operations is the certainty that, for a time at least, their senior officers will be exposed to the same dangers as themselves. At Galatas, Colonel Kippenberger found himself in the thick of things from the start. He was finishing his breakfast under the trees near the village square when it struck him as 'a bit unusual' that an enemy fighter should be 'tearing up and down the main street'. He felt that the cooks must have noticed it too, since 'the porridge was mere oatmeal and water'. He was 'still grumbling' about this when an exclamation that 'might have been an oath or a prayer' diverted his attention to something else:

Almost over our heads were four gliders, the first we had ever seen, in their silence inexpressibly menacing and frightening. Northwards was a growing thunder. I shouted 'Stand to your arms!' and ran upstairs for my rifle and binoculars . . .

When I reached the courtyard again the thunder had become deafening, the troop-carriers were passing low overhead in every direction one looked, not more than 400 feet up, in scores. As I ran down the Prison road to my battle headquarters the parachutists were dropping out over the valley, hundreds of them, and floating quietly down. Some were spilling out over our positions, and there was a growing crackle of rifle-fire. I pelted down the road, outpacing the two signallers who had started with me, and scrambled up the steep track to the battle post, a pink house on a little knoll east of the road. As I panted through the gap in the cactus hedge there was a startling burst of fire fairly in my face, cutting the cactus on either side of me. I jumped sideways, twisted my ankle, and rolled down the bank. After whimpering a little, I crawled up the track and into the house, and saw my man through the window. Then I hopped out again, hopped around the back and, in what seemed to me a nice bit of minor tactics, stalked him round the side of the house and shot him cleanly through the head at ten yards. The silly fellow was still watching the gap in the hedge . . .[14]

[13] Davin, p. 129, Report by Lieut. W. J. T. Roach   [14] Kippenberger, p. 52

Kippenberger decided to move his command post to the Head-quarters of the Composite Battalion, a mile to the north-east of Galatas. By ten o'clock he had learnt that in this area, where landings had been comparatively light, fifty-five parachutists had been killed or captured, while south and east of the village 155 had fallen to the 19th Battalion which had also taken nine prisoners. Further south, the Germans had dropped in strength across the Prison Valley. Here they had quickly dispersed the unfortunate 6th Greeks who had only their three rounds per man. Ammunition for them had arrived 'some days' before but had not been distributed. For this some of the New Zealanders were inclined to blame the Greek Colonel. Later that morning, he was shot by troops of the 19th Battalion who believed him to be 'throwing grenades'[15] at them. The truth remains obscure. In 1941 the British and Empire forces were ready to see fifth columnists everywhere. And certainly there were individual Greeks who sought to help the enemy. But in Crete there was confusion enough to account for almost any mistake or failure. Today, any such accusation of treachery at once becomes suspect in the light of what is now known of the stoic gallantry of Greek behaviour as a whole.

Before noon, a strong threat from the Prison Valley had developed against the Galatas heights. The Germans were moving up through the trees on both sides of the road and had overrun the old Brigade Headquarters. Already there seemed to be little hope for the 8th Greeks at Alikianou.

The New Zealand 18th Battalion was part of the 4th Brigade. Its Commanding Officer, Lieutenant-Colonel Gray, had set three of his companies to face west, astride the coast road, about a mile short of the Galatas Turn. Soon after nine o'clock a corporal of this battalion saw 'large troop-carrying planes lumbering through the air, while from their bellies dropped little dots, which were steadied in their descent by the sudden billowing of parachutes'.[16] Most of them could be seen falling into the 7th General Hospital.

Gray was a man of independent spirit, less popular on that account among his superiors than in the estimation of his own men. That morning he was quick to lead the counter-attack.

Gathering up everybody at Bn Hq, even to the cook [he wrote

[15] Kippenberger, p. 55   [16] Davin, p. 146, Report by Cpl. E. A. Howard, M.M

later], we went up on the ridge in the direction of the enemy. Arrived there, one saw the parachutists still descending and the last planes just turning away to go home. The parachutists dropped from an average height of about 300 feet, and took about half-a-minute (*sic*) to come down. Many had reached the ground. They were dropping on a ridge about 700 yards or so away, among olive trees, and there was an intervening ridge between ours and theirs.

Down and on to the next ridge. There we stood for a few moments shooting at the last ones in the air. Then on again to get in among them. I looked round. My batman, George Andrews, the RSM, and Cpl. Dick Phillips, one of the orderly room clerks, were with me. I felt the others were coming. There was nothing for it but to go on and trust to the rest following.

I saw a parachute hanging in a tree and detected a movement round the left side of it. Fired quickly with my rifle – every officer in the battalion had a rifle. Then, advancing very softly and quickly up to the parachute, I looked round the side to see a Hun lying on the ground beside a gaily coloured container fastened to the parachute. He moved, so I shot him at once to make sure, and then moved cautiously from cover to cover.

I shot another hiding behind a tree, and wounded him. He was very frightened, but I told him to lie still and he would be looked after. Took his pistol away and gave it to Dick Phillips who was just on my right. No sooner had I handed it to him than he was shot through the knee. Two Huns about 30 yards away hiding behind a tree were shooting at the two of us. Two careful ones immediately despatched them both. There were plenty of bullets flying around but one had no time to bother about them. I saw George Andrews sitting on the ground taking careful aim at some cactus bushes behind us. 'Steady on George,' I said, 'You will be shooting one of our own chaps'. 'No bloody fear, it's a Hun,' he said, and fired. 'Got him.'[17]

By this time the parachutists had occupied the Hospital Peninsula and had seized a Field Ambulance which had been set up close to the Galatas Turn. They had also captured several hundred patients, who had first realized what was happening when the sound of guttural voices outside their tents broke the silence that followed the bombing and machine-gunning.

The large red crosses must have been plainly visible from the air, but Student's Operation Orders referred to the 'tented encampment west of Canea', within which there had been identified a 'Hospital Barrack'. The size of the establishment in relation to what they believed to be the total occupation force,

[17] Davin, p. 147, Report by Lieut.-Col. J. R. Gray

only a third of what it was in fact, must have appeared to their Air Reconnaissance to be too large to contain only a hospital; and it was a strange place to be used in this way, a tactically important area, giving immediate access to Canea, and bounded by a sandy beach suitable for landings from the sea. The defence had no right to claim protection for such a position merely by using it for the sick and wounded.

Now the Germans found themselves in a dilemma. Most of their prisoners would clearly soon be fit to fight again. No doubt they were greatly tempted to slaughter them all. This they refrained from doing. They shot the doctor in charge of the Field Ambulance and left him to die in his slit trench,[18] but after that there was no more deliberate killing. During the morning, they collected as many as could be forced to walk, about 300 in all, many without shoes and still dressed in pyjamas or hospital blue, and began to march them in a long column across the road and up the slope towards Galatas where they hoped to find support.

In this they were disappointed. Gradually they met mounting pressure from the New Zealanders, to whom the prisoners identified themselves as best they could, while at the same time shouting instructions about the positions of their guards. There was an impression, scarcely confirmed by the members of the hospital party, that they had been used as a protective screen. Several more were killed during the skirmishing among the trees. The rest were released. By late afternoon the episode had ended. All the Germans had been killed or captured.

Everywhere, men were depending for their lives upon the extent to which they had succeeded in begging or stealing weapons. Some managed well enough. Of the eleven New Zealanders manning one of the guns east of Maleme only one had a rifle, but the battery as a whole was able to defend itself with gusto.

B.H.Q. now receive a 'carrier' load right in our front garden [wrote its commander], and we get into the fun. One Hun is only about 25 yards away in grape vines. A few rounds are fired. . . . Another poor devil gets his on the wing. His 'chute catches in an olive tree and he finishes up by leaning on a rock wall, head on hands almost as if he had been meditating by the wall when death caught up to him. Dead Germans everywhere – 'chutes caught in trees and still fluttering in the wind . . . [19]

[18] Davin, p. 148, Report by Lieut.-Col, J. R. Gray
[19] Davin, p. 130, Report by Maj. W. D. Philp, D.S.O.

Even a single parachutist at once offered a deadly threat to men without rifles. East of Galatas, close to the Alikianou-Canea Road, a Light Troop of Royal Artillery were well placed to fire down the Prison Valley or onto the beaches. But these gunners were 'entirely without personal weapons'.[20] Infantry protection from the New Zealand 19th Battalion had been offered and refused. Within a few minutes they were overrun. An N.C.O. managed to put three of the guns out of action, but a fourth was later used by the enemy.

The isolated 3.7 inch heavy anti-aircraft guns at Sternes were defended with the arms that had been acquired in such unorthodox fashion by the captain in charge. The other half of this battery, safe enough, so it seemed, in its position so close to Canea, had been 'the last detailed for the issue of rifles and protective wire'.[21] It was less fortunate. An enemy glider loomed out of the dust clouds and came skidding down on to the road beside the emplacements, its nose breaking through a stone wall. There was a savage clash. The Lewis gunner was killed immediately as he lay at the roadside. The dozen rifles cracked briefly, and a few pistol shots came from the command post. But the fire power of the ten men from the glider soon crushed all resistance. The Germans then lined up their unarmed adversaries and shot them to death against the sandbags. For themselves, there remained time to put the guns out of action before they were killed by a party of Marines supported by Welch carriers. Two or three who tried to escape into a surrounding cornfield died in the flames when the dry straw was set ablaze.[22] Of the 180 gunners seven had survived.[23]

News of this bizarre encounter spread rapidly. Nobody felt much inclined to blame the enemy. A few men, isolated and greatly outnumbered, could scarcely be expected to hold prisoners. Rather must they have found it impossible to believe that the British would be so incapable of defending themselves. Anger was reserved for the High Command, in particular for the authorities in England, and for the Army Staffs in the Middle East. After nearly two years of conflict, against an airborne attack that had

[20] Davin, p. 152, Report by Pte. W. H. Bishop

[21] DP

[22] Described to the author by survivor shortly after the battle

[23] *Einsatz Kreta*, Battle Report of XI Air Corps

been fully foreseen, these experts had sent their troops into battle equipped with a weapon establishment that was three decades out of date.

But more profitable than resentment was the sudden realization that the fighting in Crete would owe little to civilized convention. It was understood that no one could expect immunity. Doctors and stretcher-bearers discarded their Red Cross armlets and found weapons where they could, prepared to shoot if necessary while they attended the wounded. British and Greeks alike ransacked the Venetian warehouses in Canea where they found large stores of British rifles and Italian machine-guns that had not been distributed. On every side men searched for guns, many providing for themselves entirely from the bodies of their dead enemies.

All along the coast, between Maleme and Suda, the battle was following a common pattern. The shrieking of the planes, the stunning concussions, the choking clouds of grit and dust, had been followed almost immediately by the brief dazed silence, and then by the sudden crackle of small arms, as bullets leapt from familiar houses and orchards. But now the danger lay no less heavily upon the unseen enemy. The *Luftwaffe* pilots could not distinguish between friend and foe. At noon Kippenberger had noted that 'numerous enemy fighters were about but were uncertain as to who was who and were doing little damage'.[24] The air had become neutral. For a time the struggle below would be beyond the influence of air power. Here was a factor that might have been foreseen, and which could still play a vital part if it were understood in time.

Chance brought to the defenders one strange stroke of fortune. It was rumoured that the Germans were wearing British battle-dress. This was later found to be untrue. But an immediate order was issued instructing all ranks to wear shorts. In their heavier uniforms, the Germans were at a disadvantage. They found it 'incredibly hot'. Their equipment, one of them wrote later, was 'unsuitable for that type of fighting . . . everything was too heavy'.[25]

Hour after hour the struggle continued. Man stalked man

[24] Kippenberger, p. 55
[25] DP, Oberfeldwebel F. Teichmann, interviewed by W. G. McClymont, 31 Dec. 1945

among the olives, through luxuriant gardens of scented jasmine and mimosa, from wall to wall across the narrow fields of barley, and from behind the rocks and boulders that littered the terraced hillsides. Almost every encounter was mortal. The cold of the morning had turned quickly to sweltering heat. From a cloudless sky the sun blazed down upon the sweating soldiers who quickly came to exhaustion as they struggled up and down the steep ravines or dashed for cover among the rocks. And the wounded grew desperate for water.

9

Maleme: 20 May

The capture and protection of the narrow airfield at Maleme had been entrusted to the *élite* Storm Regiment, commanded by Major-General Meindl, a tough career officer who had distinguished himself at Narvik. He had available three Parachute Battalions, together with some 330 troops carried by glider. The exact strength of the force is not known. From *Operation Crete* it is possible to estimate a total of about 2,300 men.[1] But in 1965 the German writer Kurowski published figures which suggest that some of the units may have been under establishment, and that only 1,860 parachutists[2] were allotted initially to this Sector. Moreover, it is clear that some were left behind[3,4] on the first morning as the result of delays in Greece.

[1] No official German information on the strength of the Storm Regiment is available. Indeed there is no certainty about the numbers in the 7th Airlanding Division itself. After the battle *Einsatz Kreta* reported that 13,000 '7th Airlanding Division and 'Corps troops' had been in action, but it is not clear what is meant by 'Corps troops', nor how many of them, in addition to the 2,000 parachutists, had been committed to the sea invasion. The figures given here are calculated from information set out by Davin, p. 90, and from the article 'Parachute Engineers in the Battle of Crete' in *Wie Wir Kämpfen*, the German Air Force Handbook 1944, together with information on the Airlanding Division in *Brief Notes on the German Army*, a pamphlet issued by G.S.I. G.H.Q. M.E.F. Dec. 1941. An estimate of 2,460 for the Storm Regiment was made on behalf of the New Zealand Department of Internal Affairs by C. R. Monaghan, archivist to the New Zealand War Historian (DP). On the other hand Kurowski, p. 242, gives '1,860 Parachutists' as the *Kräftverhältnis* at Maleme, 2,460 at Suda (Prison Valley), 1,380 at Retimo and 2,360 at Heraklion, a total of 8,060. There is some reason to believe that this may be as near the truth as can now be calculated from German sources. It may be noted that although his total for the western sectors is less than has been accepted by British, New Zealand, and Australian historians that for Heraklion and Retimo combined is greater. Moreover, Kurowski claims that his figures, together with exact numbers that he gives for some of the companies and battalions at Maleme, were approved by Walter Gericke who led IV Battalion with distinction in Crete (see later), and in 1962 became Commander of the first West German *Luftlande-division*. Kurowski does not specifically mention glider troops as distinct from their fellows under Meindl's command, but if 330 be added to his estimate, and the obvious assumption made that his figure of '1,860 parachutists' includes only the men who had been expected to arrive on the first day, the strength of the Storm Regiment at Maleme on 20 May would still remain less than has been generally accepted.

[2] Kurowski, p. 242   [3] *Wie Wir Kämpfen*   [4] Kurowski, p. 93

Meindl decided, in accordance with the Student technique, that he must place his gliders close to the perimeter of the airfield, and thus immediately on top of what he took to be the main defence positions. The parachutists would be released a mile or two further away, a distance which should give them time to muster, and to collect their weapons. Nine of the gliders, bearing about 80 men, including a skeleton Regimental Staff under Major Braun, were to come down along the river bed of the lower Tavronitis with the road bridge as their objective. Another group of gliders, commanded by Major Koch, who in May 1940 had led one of the successful attacks against the bridges on the Albert Canal, was to carry the Headquarters staff and two companies of I Battalion, each made up of 108 men. Lieutenant von Plessen would land with one of these companies at the river mouth, while the other, together with Major Koch and the Battalion staff, would put down across the slopes of Hill 107 and occupy the high ground south of the airfield before attacking the perimeter itself. Of the three parachute battalions, each in a strength of about 600, II Battalion under Major Stentzler, and IV Battalion under Captain Gericke, were to fall along a coastal strip extending three miles west of the river. Two detached companies would protect the flanks, one higher up the valley, near the village of Voukolies, three miles from the coast, and the other a little beyond the main body of II Battalion. Still further west a small detachment of 72 men, under Lieutenant Muerbe, would attack Kastelli. III Battalion, under Major Scherber, was to be aimed at a two-mile stretch of the coast road immediately east of Pirgos.[5]

Thus the airfield would be subjected to a converging attack. The plan must entail considerable dispersion. Against serious opposition the Regiment might soon find itself in difficulty.

And the opposition was indeed serious. The drop itself was accurate enough. But there was no protection for the men of von Plessen's glider company among the sand dunes along the shore. From Hill 107 the heavy machine-guns poured down a steady fire which rippled about their feet as they dashed hither and thither among the whins. Only in the stream bed was there some shelter. This advantage was quickly exploited by the

[5] *Einsatz Kreta*, Battle Report of XI Air Corps, which, however, does not reveal the numbers in the Koch and Plessen companies. Nor does it say how many gliders were used to carry them, although this information is provided for all the other glider groups. The figure 108 is taken from Kurowski, p. 36, who gives the strength of I Battalion at Maleme as *Stab, 3. und 4. Kompanie mit jeweils* 108 *Mann*.

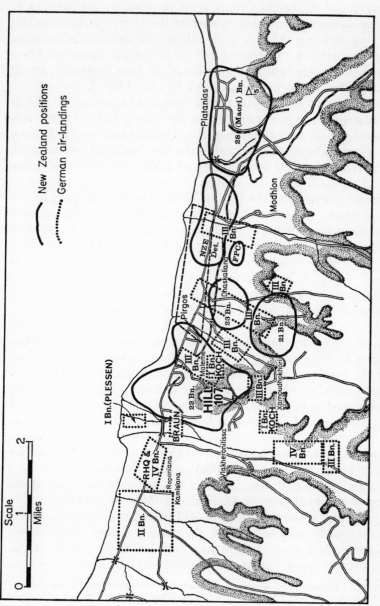

5. German Landings at Maleme: 20 May

New Zealand positions

German air-landings

Scale

Miles

28 (Maori) Bn.

Platanias

Modhion

NZE
Det.

FPC Bn.

Dhaskaliana

III
Bn.

23 Bn.

IV
Bn.

III
Bn.

21 Bn.

Pirgos

III
Bn.

Maleme

I Bn.
KOCH

III
Bn.

22 Bn.

HILL
107

10

BRAUN

Vlakheronitissa

Xamoudhokhori

III Bn.

I Bn.
KOCH

I Bn.(PLESSEN)

RHQ &
IV Bn.

Roponiana

Kamisiana

IV
Bn.

III Bn.

II Bn.

survivors of the Braun Group, some of whom seized the R.A.F. Camp on the eastern bank, scattering the airmen in disorder and driving them up the hill, while others captured the bridge after darting between the cement pylons below the roadway. Once across, they were held by the bullets of the New Zealand C and D Companies. Braun and von Plessen had been killed.

On Hill 107 failure was almost complete. Many of the gliders were smashed to pieces as they hit the ridges. Koch was severely wounded, and most of his men either killed or driven back down the slopes. Those who escaped to the west, reduced to a handful, were rallied by their medical officer[6] in the bed of the river a few hundred yards above the bridge.

Even sharper was the distinction in fortune that awaited the parachutists. Those landing west of the river, among bamboo plantations and fields of scrub barley, suffered little worse than damage to their heavy weapons and to their motor-cycles, most of which were wrecked among the trees. There was no firing to greet them. A few Cretans had lingered in the village of Roponiana, a small cluster of houses half hidden among the bushes at the western end of the bridge. But none carried arms. All were forced to flee to the hills.[7] To the Germans it seemed that the defenders must have been taken by surprise, and for this reason had not had time to occupy 'the well-prepared positions on the heights between the bridge and Kolimbari'.[8] The truth was simpler; this was the gap in the defences which had from the first caused so much misgiving to the officers of the New Zealand 5th Brigade, and in particular to Andrew and the 22nd Battalion.

Very different was the fate of Colonel Scherber's III Battalion. Some of these parachutists fell south-east of Pirgos where they came under fire from the Headquarters Company of the New Zealand 22nd Battalion. Most of the rest of them came down among the 23rd close to Dhaskaliana. Many were killed before they hit the ground. Those who still moved within the perimeter were quickly attacked before they could collect their heavier weapons. And some of them were pursued further afield. It was against these parachutists that Thomas had led his patrol, and the

[6] Both the main glider groups were now commanded by doctors, the Plessen company by Oberarzt Dr. Weizel, from 10.30 a.m., and the Koch survivors by Oberstabarzt Dr. Neumann, see Kurowski, pp. 42 and 45. Medicine in Germany had, of course, long become a preserve of Nazism.

[7] People of the village to the author 1961

[8] *Einsatz Kreta*, Battle Report of the XI Air Corps

men of the Field Punishment Centre had celebrated their return
to society. About 400 of the 600, including the Battalion Commander, died immediately.[9] All the officers were either killed or
wounded. In the pocket of one company commander was found a
unit roll containing 126 names. Within an hour or two 112 of
these had been accounted for among the dead. More fortunate
were a few members of two companies which in error had been
scattered across the valley west and south of Pirgos. In this region,
isolated groups were able to establish themselves.

Meindl himself jumped at half past eight. It was soon plain to
him that the Koch gliders had failed. And gradually there must
have come the disconcerting realization that something had gone
wrong with Scherber and III Battalion on the eastern side of the
airfield. He saw at once that the key to the situation lay in
possession of the southern heights. If he could not take them
his action would fail. And he must have them quickly, before his
enemies could reinforce. Already he had lost something like
half his regiment. He could rely only upon the two parachute
battalions that had descended unharmed in the west, both of
them reduced in strength by the flank detachments.

In this crisis he acted with speed and vigour, sending two
companies of II Battalion, under Major Stentzler, upon a long
encircling movement to come upon Hill 107 from the south, while
at the same time making arrangements to exploit the early success
at the road bridge. For this direct approach he had available,
though certainly not in hand, the unwounded survivors of the
glider force, scarcely a hundred strong, a company from II
Battalion, and three companies of IV Battalion, perhaps 700
men.

At this moment IV Battalion, a mixed unit consisting of 'heavy
machine-gun, anti-tank, mortar, and pioneer companies, with no
specialist infantry',[10] was short of its pioneer company, which had
been dropped at Voukolies. Captain Gericke, the Commander,
a resolute and intelligent man in his early thirties, had become
the senior officer in the vicinity of the bridge after the death of
Braun. Quickly he collected the scattered parachutists, using
captured transport to help bring them forward to mustering
point along the western bank of the river.

[9] *Einsatz Kreta*, Battle Report of the XI Air Corps

[10] Col. Walter Gericke in a letter to the author, 21 Jan. 1960

Soon Meindl learnt that the pioneers had become involved in hard fighting with Greeks and villagers. His western detachment was also engaged, and no word had come from Muerbe. Thus he could feel secure neither to the south nor the west. Moreover, every hour that passed made it more certain that disaster had befallen Scherber in the east. This must mean that the enemy were in strength on the far side of the airfield, less than two miles away, and might be expected to counter-attack from that quarter at any moment. Whatever hopes he may have had of help from the sea he knew that he would be given little airborne reinforcement unless it could be landed by troop-carrier on the runway. He must therefore capture the southern heights before night should come to aid the enemy.

While he still contemplated these prospects he was himself twice wounded, first slightly in the hand, and then severely, by a burst of machine-gun fire through the chest. Still conscious, he was carried to an improvised casualty centre among the bamboos. Here he was able to remain in control of his Regiment until late in the afternoon.

No account of the struggle in Crete can be of any value if it should fail to convey the atmosphere of these first hours at Maleme. During the bombardment, the 620 officers and men of the New Zealand 22nd Battalion had been crouching in their slit trenches at the heart of the inferno. At first they did not know that the attack had begun.

It was impossible for all but a few men to observe the landing of the gliders [says the War Diary of the 22nd Battalion], as a blanket of dust and smoke, rising to several hundred feet, covered positions.

These were the conditions in which men had fought before the days of smokeless powder. Under the same handicap, Wellington's foot-soldiers at Waterloo had searched the slopes before them while the lines of French cavalry vanished and reappeared among the belches from the guns. And thus the men of Gough's 5th Army had found suddenly that the Germans were among them in the misty valley of the Somme on the morning of 21 March 1918. It is a situation classic in war, the more familiar since armies became vast, anonymous and mobile. Bursts of firing give sudden, un-expected notice of the enemy. Sense of direction becomes lost. Only the steadiest discipline can stand against this challenge to nerve and confidence. At Maleme it was made doubly disconcerting by the abruptness of its onset, and by the continued menace from the air.

The staff of C Company Headquarters failed to notice any of the gliders that were landing all about them on the southern edge of the airfield, and from Battalion Headquarters both the bridge and the river gorge were hidden by the dust and the swell of the hill. Andrew was one of the first to realize that gliders were taking part in the attack. 'Gliders landed *during* the bombardment,' he wrote later. There were, he thought, 'certainly more than fifteen'. And he added

At first we thought the crashing was from bombers brought down, but as the dust and smoke cleared saw what it was. In some cases the crews from the gliders covered the drop of the parachutists. The parachutists began to drop as the last bombs burst – or so it appeared to me from a look-out above Bn Hq.[11]

This was the news that reached Hargest at Platanias. In the 5th Brigade War Diary there is an entry, timed at 08.30 hours, saying, 'Five gliders reported landing in Tavronitis river bed just west of aerodrome and below bridge'. The source of the message cannot now be traced. Captain Dawson, the Brigade Major, remembered that it was sent by telephone.[12] It therefore seems probable, since the line to the 22nd was not cut until about 9 a.m., that it came from the Headquarters dug-out on Hill 107.

Andrew could only guess at the weight of the enemy attack. And the guess that he made was wrong. At 10.55 a.m. he sent Hargest an estimate that a total of 400 paratroops had landed in the area, 100 near the airfield, 150 to the east, and 150 'west of river and on beach'.[13]

He did not know that 1,000 men had landed unharmed behind the curtain of dust, many of them less than a mile away. Before the battle he had sent three observers to watch from the heights above Roponiana. None had returned. Today it can be seen how great might have been the part played here by a wireless transmitter. If any one of these men had survived for an hour to witness that silent and sinister spectacle along the shore west of the Tavronitis he would have been able to send back news that must have transformed Andrew's conception of the battle.

[11] DP, Comment by Lieut.-Col. L. W. Andrew
[12] Ibid. Comment by Capt. R. B. Dawson
[13] 5th Brigade War Diary, 10.55 a.m., 20 May 1941

Not even the troops on the western face of Hill 107 had noticed what was happening. For now every eye had taken on a short-range focus – on a hint of movement in the nearest bush rather than upon a glimpse of parachutes in the distance. Misleading tales were drifting east as far as Puttick's Headquarters. There was an impression that the Germans had dropped all over the battalion area. Yet scarcely three score, and none designedly, had fallen directly upon Hill 107 or within half a mile of the runway. More sinister in their ultimate effect were stories of 'troop-carriers' landing inland under the mountains and along the beach.[14]

At last, through the lifting dust, the men of the 22nd began to see their enemies. Figures dressed in green emerged from the river bed. Others appeared among the bushes in the hillsides, and from the houses in Pirgos. Most of them found it impossible to make progress. The New Zealanders were much handicapped by their lack of automatic weapons, and by the shortage of mortars. But they enjoyed one great advantage. Against their well-sited defences the Germans were being drawn forward in their need to enter the perimeter, forced to expose themselves openly in unknown terrain, unsupported by heavy weapons, and with no immediate hope of direct help from their aircraft. Only here and there did they achieve some small local success. Creeping forward out of the dead ground near the river mouth, the Plessen troops cut off 15 Platoon of C Company from the north and south. Here twenty-two men, under Lieutenant Sinclair, some of them armed with 'grenades of jam tins filled with concrete and plugs of gelignite',[15] had been set to defend a front of some 1,500 yards on the western edge of the airfield. At 11 a.m. Sinclair was severely wounded in the neck. Those of the platoon who could still shoot continued to hold off the enemy until the evening. South of Pirgos another platoon, part of Headquarters Company, was isolated and overrun. These men, too, had been handicapped by their shortage of weapons. 'No machine-guns,' was the comment of a Section Commander who survived, 'no hand grenades, 8 rifles, and 2 bayonets'.[16]

But the main line of the entrenchments remained unbroken. On the southern ridges A and B Companies had been little troubled by the Koch gliders. To the north-east the reduced Headquarters Company was successfully defending the villages of

[14] N.Z. Division War Diary, see below, p. 219   [15] Henderson, *22 Battalion*, p. 40
[16] Davin, p. 105, *n*. 3

Maleme and Pirgos, while D Company, under Captain Campbell, though heavily beset, still held on along the east bank of the river, and from the smouldering hill-side above the canal a hundred yards further back.

Only in the R.A.F. Camp, where the code books had been captured intact,[17] and at the bridge itself, had the enemy made some progress. And late in the afternoon the Gericke Group, forcing an opening between the scattered platoons of C Company, began to encroach upon the north-west perimeter, and to exert increasing pressure along the road and onto the northern face of the hill. The flat red sand of the field itself, lit by the afternoon sun shining through the dust, remained empty of movement, swept by the bullets of both sides, and marked only by the scattered wrecks of British fighter planes.

A mile to the south, Stentzler's two companies were moving slowly and painfully through the broken foothills. At first they had been much impeded by the isolated New Zealand platoon in the river bed. Further east, in the outskirts of Vlakheronitissa, they collided with a patrol from the 21st Battalion. Later they were harassed by sharp-shooters of the R.A.F. and the Naval Air Establishment firing from the reverse slopes of Hill 107. It was almost dark before they began to make contact with A and B Companies of the 22nd Battalion. By this time they were much exhausted. Throughout the day they had been forced to struggle over difficult country under a burning sun in a heat that far exceeded 100° F. The sweat poured down their faces, and their heavy parachute clothing stuck to their backs. Many had cut away the material of their trouser legs. Frequently they found it necessary to turn aside in search of water. When at last they began to stumble up the rearward slopes of Hill 107 they were in no condition to offer an immediate threat to the defenders.

Andrew remained unaware of these successes. That morning his Headquarters had been heavily attacked by the bombers; he had himself been wounded by a splinter. All around him dense growths of grape and olive had almost disappeared. His Intelligence sergeant noted that the ground between the sandbags was now 'regularly covered by small bomb craters'. Telephone

---

[17] *Einsatz Kreta*, Battle Report of the XI Air Corps, appendix II, para. 4, says: 'The main source for the enemy order of battle is contained in a list of code names dated 20 May 1941, which was captured on the first day of the attack and which gave all units and formations, including the Greek battalions'

communication with his companies had gone during the preliminary bombing. The line to Brigade Headquarters had lasted
only for a few minutes. For an hour the radio link had been lost
too. Outwardly, he retained all the stoicism that had won him
his V.C. To Squadron-Leader Howell, who visited him a few
minutes after the beginning of the battle, he seemed calm and
confident, indifferent to the flying bullets. But it is easy to imagine
his growing bewilderment.

At about 9 a.m. he reconnoitred part of the way down a
gully towards the R.A.F. Camp. Much of the undergrowth was
alight. Through the smoke and dust he was unable to make out
what was happening to D Company, and the camp itself was
hidden by the convex slopes. He therefore returned to his
command post, expecting that he would be able to maintain a
delayed contact by runner. Soon this liaison also failed. By late
afternoon, there had been no news for many hours either from
D Company, on the western face of the hill, or from Headquarters
Company, which had been cut off by a small group of glider
troops and parachutists established in a brick house south of
Pirgos. Down on the perimeter of the airfield, C Company had
apparently disintegrated; so far as he knew there remained only a
single platoon, near the road below Battalion Headquarters.

Less surprising was the absence of any sign of effective support
from the 339 mixed troops of the R.A.F. and the Navy. Since his
own companies were finding the opposition so formidable he can
scarcely have expected that aircraftmen, naval ratings and clerks
would be able to offer much help. In fact, several parties of these
men were fighting with great determination. A group of about
forty, under three naval officers, had become firmly established
on a knoll overlooking the R.A.F. Camp,[18] and many individuals
had killed at least one German. But in general it was true that,
without training, often without weapons, and with little officer
control, they were incapable of effective resistance. Some had
been killed or wounded and others taken prisoner. Most were to
spend the day streaming back as best they could.

Why did none of the runners get through? Certainly their task
was perilous.

I endeavoured to contact H.Q. Coy myself [wrote Andrew], and

[18] Lieut. A. W. F. Sutton, R.N. Almost certainly it was of this group that Andrew
wrote later that about forty naval and R.A.F. troops, under two officers, had 'put
up a good show'. (DP)

was fired at by Germans in the valley and under trees between Bn H.Q., H.Q. Coy and 'B' Coy. I went to ground and before withdrawing counted eight enemy.[19]

But D and C Companies were only a few hundred yards away and the runners had spent more than three weeks upon these hills. All the tracks had been reconnoitred. Moreover, deadly as was the danger that threatened every move in the open, it has to be recognized that this was a risk which the Germans were facing all the time. So too were the aircraftmen, inspired by their hope of safety further east. It may be that the Company Commanders saw no great need to waste men upon these desperate missions, assuming that it would be easy enough to re-establish their contacts after dark. Or perhaps, as for so much else, the *Luftwaffe* was responsible. After the war, Major Leggat, second-in-command of the 22nd at Maleme, was to suggest that some damage to morale had been caused by the heavy enemy bombing of the previous four days.[20] German aircraft still roared about the sky. For many hours they were unable to intervene. Nevertheless, the defenders found it hard to believe in this sudden immunity.

This failure of contact within his battalion now became for Andrew his absorbing anxiety. The War Diaries reveal his uncertainty. Wireless communication with the 5th Brigade had been restored at 10 a.m. He then reported that he was being heavily attacked. At 10.55 a.m. he added that he had lost touch with his forward companies. By 2.55 p.m. he was telling Hargest that his Headquarters had been penetrated, and at 3.50 p.m. that his 'left [*sic*] flank had given way',[21] although the general situation was believed still to be under control.

Heavy mortar fire, searching the summit of Hill 107 from the vicinity of the R.A.F. Camp, now forced him to pull back his Headquarters some two hundred yards into his B Company area. According to the *New Zealand War History* there is no evidence that he made it clear to Hargest that the enemy had made their important thrust across the Tavronitis Bridge.[22] The assumption must be that he had no specific knowledge of it. Indeed it may be that the continued absence of information from his forward companies was forcing him to the conclusion that the enemy

[19] DP, Comment by Lieut.-Col. L. W. Andrew

[20] Ibid. Brig. K. L. Stewart reporting interview with Maj. J. Leggat on 13 Sept. 1948

[21] Ibid. Entry in 5th Brigade War Diary   [22] Davin, p. 135

had in fact advanced from the west on a much broader front. This deadly and increasing pressure must have seemed all the more sinister in relation to the relatively small numbers of the enemy that had been seen to land. Already he had asked for artillery to supplement the fire that his two heavy machine-gun platoons had been able to bring down on the enemy beyond the Tavronitis. He now sent up flares, the agreed signal to show that he had urgent need of the pre-arranged counter-attack from the 23rd Battalion. Observers had been appointed to watch for them. But the flares were not seen. At 5 p.m. he explained directly to Hargest over the radio telephone that aid from the 23rd had become a compelling necessity. Hargest replied that the '23rd could not attack as they were engaged with paratroops'.[23]

At this Andrew decided that he must use his own last reserve – the two heavy tanks, together with the available survivors of C Company. They were joined by one of the gunner officers and six of his men. At a quarter past five the little party, about twenty strong, advanced into the evening sun, keeping to the left of the road behind the two tanks.

For the Germans this was a nasty moment. Most of their heavier weapons had been lost in the drop. Their reports make it clear that counter-attack by tanks was what they feared most. Among the parachutists at the bridge there was sudden anxiety as they heard the churning of tracks on the tarmac.[24] Their light weapons had no effect upon the two heavy shapes that appeared round the shoulder of the hill and rolled towards them out of the dust.

But their fears were brief. Mechanical failure soon brought the attack to disaster. In the first tank it was discovered, somewhat belatedly, that the two-pounder ammunition would not fit the breech block. The driver was forced to stop on the road. The second tank pushed on boldly down the steep bank into the river bed, then turned towards the sea, firing in all directions. Daringly it pressed its way under the bridge. Today the concrete pylons are scored by many hundreds of bullet flecks, not only upon their eastern but also upon their western surfaces. Many of these marks are near the ground, twelve feet below the level of the road. It is easy to picture the Germans rushing for shelter round the walls as the tank passed through. But two hundred yards down-

[23] DP, Narrative by Lieut.-Col. L. W. Andrew
[24] Harmeling, p. 24

stream its adventure ended. Here it stuck among the river boulders. The crew were forced to abandon it. In the meantime, the small infantry detachment had been caught in a storm of fire from the front and from the slopes on their left. Only a handful returned unwounded. The officer of the gunners was killed.

Much has been written of this episode, and about the part played by the tanks in other phases of the battle. Most of these accounts are coloured by what was later revealed of German apprehensions. Student had expected that his troops would meet armoured vehicles; the threat proved greater than he supposed. After the war he was to say: 'The few British tanks that were there shook us badly at the start – it was lucky that there were not more than two dozen.' And Gericke, in a book describing the part played by the Storm Regiment, admits that 'panic threatened to break out' among his men at the bridge.[25] Less attention has been paid to the limitations imposed upon any tank action in Crete by the nature of the country, and by the unresisted activities of the *Luftwaffe*. Nor is it accurate to suggest, as Clark has done, that only heavy weapons could stop the Infantry Tanks in the open. The two at Retimo were both to be crippled by mortars.

All the same, to lightly armed troops, they appeared formidable indeed. Certainly it was their own imperfections, coupled with the fact that there were only two of them, that defeated them at Maleme. A few months previously machines like these, in better repair, had supported the Australian Infantry with great success at Bardia and Tobruk. Moreover, on this afternoon at Maleme, they were protected by attack from the air by the dust haze, and by the intermingling of the troops on the ground. It can be supposed that a decisive success might have been obtained at this moment by a small force of perhaps half a dozen heavy tanks bursting from cover in a sudden foray against the bridge. Such a venture could have succeeded in restoring the line of the Tavronitis, and done much to destroy the concentration west of the river.

It was not Freyberg's fault that there were only two Infantry Tanks at Maleme. No more than six had been available for the whole island. He had made the best possible use of them. To have held them in a central reserve would have been futile; with many

---

[25] Gericke, p. 59, adds that there were sudden cries of 'Tanks from the east', and that 'a few men jumped up and ran back'

miles of primitive roads to cover under air attack they could not have hoped to reach any critical scene of action. He was right to divide them between the three airfields. Later, although there had been no foreseeable reason for doing so, he came to regret that he had not placed them all at Maleme.[26]

The better course would have been to have concealed the ten light tanks of the 3rd Hussars close to the Maleme perimeter. It was natural enough that he should wish to hold them back at the Galatas Turn as part of Force Reserve. But if they had been hidden within the 23rd Battalion lines south of Dhaskaliana they could have been ready for action on the airfield, the one area in which they would have had room to play an effective part in defending a vital objective.

At about 5.45 p.m. Andrew heard from Captain Johnson of C Company that the tanks had failed and that one, if not both, of the two perimeter platoons had been overrun. He still had no news from D and Headquarters Companies. It was this absence of information that weighed upon him most heavily. One pointer might have served to encourage him. The Intelligence report had suggested that enemy troop-carriers would come down upon the airfields 'within half an hour'. Yet no planes had landed. From this, had he known it, he could have drawn the conclusion that some of his men were still firing from the perimeter. But he did not know it. From his Headquarters, withdrawn now upon the reverse slope of Hill 107, he could not see the runway.

And so he came to believe that all three of his forward companies had been engulfed, and that the enemy could press in strength across the Tavronitis at any point. There was nothing to relieve his doubt and apprehension. All around him the dead and dying lay among the undergrowth while the mortars churned and crashed in rapid succession. The Messerschmitts were renewing their attacks upon the summit and Stentzler's troops, after their arduous march in the sun, had started to exert pressure from the south upon A and B Company. If these Germans should get behind him, every man in his battalion might be lost. No doubt it was fear of this that led him to tell Hargest over the radio telephone, after he had reported the failure of the counter-attack, that if no reinforcement could reach him he must make a limited withdrawal. Hargest replied, 'If you must, you must'.[27]

[26] DP, Freyberg comments on Davin Draft, 1952   [27] Davin, p. 110

It was now 6 p.m. But a few minutes later Brigade Headquarters signalled that two companies were to be sent in support.
'From the gist of the message,' commented Andrew later, 'I
expected the companies almost immediately.'[28]

Now that help was promised, he decided that he must try to
hang on a little longer. Perhaps, in the meantime, some sort of
information might reach him from his lost companies. And he
must have been wondering what had happened to the 23rd
Battalion behind him to the north-east, the direction from which
he had been promised immediate assistance if it should be needed.
He can only have concluded that it had been engaged all day in a
desperate encounter of its own. Indeed this was what he had been
told by Hargest.

Yet the truth was that the rest of the Brigade had suffered very
few casualties. For the 23rd the day had gone particularly well.
They had shattered Colonel Scherber's III Parachute Battalion to
almost complete destruction. At 9.45 p.m. Hargest was to report
to Puttick at Divisional Headquarters that 'hundreds of dead
Germans'[29] were lying about the rocks and gullies of the 23rd
Battalion area, and within the lines of the 7th Field Company
along the shore; the losses of the 23rd had been no more than
seven dead and thirty wounded. Long before this, he had known
that no immediate danger threatened any of his three eastern
battalions. At midday Leckie had reported that the situation was
'under complete control';[30] he was ready to support the 22nd if it
should require help.

All that afternoon the men of the 23rd had waited in their slit
trenches, unmolested except by an occasional sniper, while they
tested the weapons of their enemies and savoured their triumph
of the morning. Through the dusk and smoke nothing could be
seen beyond the villages of Pirgos and Maleme, and the sound of
the infantry weapons was drowned by the scream of the planes
which continued to search the road. No one came back to tell
them what was happening two miles to the west. Leckie may have
had some anxieties for Andrew, but he still waited for orders.

At 2.25 p.m. he received positive instruction from Hargest to
stay where he was. The message said:

Will not call on you for counter-attack unless position very

[28] DP, Narrative by Lieut.-Col. L. W. Andrew
[29] New Zealand Division War Diary   [30] DP

serious. So far everything is in hand and reports from other units satisfactory . . .[31]

After this he can have had no reason for doubting that all was well. Nor did anything unsettle him in that belief. There were no further drops of parachutists. Hour after hour went by. The sun began to set beyond the haze that hung above Maleme. And still no call came.

After a lively start the 21st had been no more active. Without difficulty, it had held its position along the vineyard ridges which stretched north and south between Kondomari and Xamou-dhokhori, killing or taking some seventy parachutists who had fallen within the lines. During the early afternoon a platoon had been sent exploring westwards towards the Tavronitis. But in a sharp encounter with the Stentzler group it was held up at Vlakheronitissa, half a mile south of Hill 107.

Lieutenant-Colonel Allen, the battalion commander, who had been working on his farm when the Germans invaded Poland, had no wireless apparatus, and no telephone, since the line had been cut immediately. He was therefore out of contact with Brigade Headquarters, and could communicate with Leckie only by runner. Left entirely to his own resources he felt reluctant to abandon his original position lest there should be further drops of parachutists. He might, perhaps, have reflected that an increase in the number of Germans within his present area need not be of any great importance. Far more serious must be the tangible threat offered by this group of Germans that he now knew to be advancing from the south upon the vital strongpoint of Hill 107. The situation was not wholly unforeseen. His orders gave him discretion, if he should judge it necessary, to press forward with his whole strength in the direction of his detached platoon in the river bed. Such an advance, undertaken at this moment, could have established contact with the 22nd, and relieved pressure upon it from the south.

He did not do it. He felt that he could not take this initiative while knowing nothing of what was happening elsewhere. And so the 21st Battalion, no less than the 23rd, was to pass the day in relative inactivity, unaware of the desperate encounter that was being fought less than two miles away across the hills to the north-west.

Until well into the afternoon, Hargest had been given every

[31] Ross, *23 Battalion*, p. 67

reason for satisfaction with the news that was reaching him. That morning he had been in Platanias when gliders began to come in low overhead, passing west towards Maleme. To reach his Battle Headquarters he had been forced to run from cover to cover under machine-gunning planes.[32] The first reports were reassuring enough, and for six hours there was no change. Some loss of contact within the battalions had been accepted as inevitable. No doubt he was still thinking in terms of the 150 parachutists that Andrew had reported as having landed beyond the Tavronitis. He had no inkling that this estimate was more than a thousand short of the truth.

What is surprising is that the tenor of the messages that now began to come from Maleme did little to shake this confidence. By five o'clock, Andrew was asking urgently for the prearranged counter-attack by the 23rd Battalion, only to be told that support from this quarter was impossible since the 23rd was 'engaged with paratroops'. This, of course, was not true. During the afternoon there had been a temporary breakdown in communication with the 23rd. But there had never been any reason to suppose that Leckie had encountered a serious set-back. Hargest must have used the phrase simply to spur Andrew into further activity upon his own account. He would have done better to remember that Andrew was a man of great courage and experience. There was good reason to accept his reading of the situation at its face value. Certainly two companies, one from the 23rd, and one from the 28th, were a poor substitute for the battalion counter-attack which had been envisaged in the original plan. Moreover, the Maoris would have five miles to go.

News of the failure of the two tanks produced no spurring forward of these troops. Nor did it lead to any increase in their strength.

By 9 p.m. neither company had reached the 22nd Battalion area. Darkness was gathering upon the hills above the airfield. And for some time the German pressure had been easing. Yet Andrew felt no lessening of his anxieties. He now told Hargest directly over the radio speaker that he 'would have to withdraw to B Company ridge'. There is no record of this critical conversation. It is recalled by Andrew, the surviving participant.[33] What is clear is that it provoked no reaction. Hargest sent no

[32] Davin, p. 132   [33] DP, Narrative by Lieut.-Col. L. W. Andrew

further reinforcement. And about an hour later he reported to Puttick that the brigade situation remained 'quite satisfactory'.

All this is very puzzling. Hargest knew that to abandon the fortified strongpoint on Hill 107 must mean that the airfield would be lost until the heights could be recaptured. It therefore seems scarcely possible that he could have appreciated what Andrew was saying through his weakening transmitter. Had he heard him correctly, he would surely have told him to hold on come what might. Indeed, he might have been expected to go forward himself soon after six o'clock, no doubt within the protection of the Maori Company, in order to see whether the situation was as bad as Andrew appeared to think it even at that time. The presumption that he had not realized what was happening at Maleme is further strengthened by his continued confidence. Even now none of his staff suspected that anything might be going wrong. 'We knew that things were confused,' says Dawson, 'and that 22nd Battalion was taking a hammering, but we did not feel that they were bad'.[34] And a few days later Hargest was to write in his diary:

The infantry seemed cheerful except 22nd, which was badly knocked about. I sent the 23rd to their assistance, but Andrew decided to fall back a little off the prominent feature above the aerodrome . . .[35]

a comment which suggests that he had not understood what Andrew was proposing to do. But neither, of course, had he 'sent the 23rd'. He had sent one company of the 23rd.

Although it seems probable that he had not grasped the extent to which the 22nd was being forced off the airfield he can scarcely have failed to realize, from Andrew's repeated messages to him, that the battalion was in very serious difficulty. Why then did he hesitate so long to commit those of his troops that were still unengaged? In particular, why did he not that evening despatch the 23rd Battalion upon its prearranged rôle? If ever the defenders were to move in daylight, now was the time. From where he was he could not see, but he might have deduced, that the *Luftwaffe* was hesitating to intervene in the areas of the parachute drops.

The answer no doubt is that, in his own words, he believed the airfield to be 'where we were strongest'.[36] And he may have felt that Andrew was exaggerating his difficulties. He must have been

[34] DP, Narrative by Capt. R. B. Dawson
[35] Ibid., Hargest's Diary
[36] Ibid., Hargest's Diary, entry for 24 May 1941

wondering how any great pressure could develop from a force of
no more than 150 parachutists. Before the battle he had feared for
the area west of the Tavronitis, but once the attack had started
he had been told that all the serious landings had been made close
to the airfield and east of it. Moreover, it seemed that the Germans
everywhere had been roughly handled. In these circumstances he
probably felt that he could afford to hold most of his brigade in
reserve, in the expectation that they would very soon be called
upon to deal with further attacks both from the air and from the
sea. He was also paying much attention to a sketch map, taken
from a German officer, which showed arrows pointing northward
from the Prison Valley to the coast. It seems likely, therefore, that
he was already much concerned, and with good reason, about
the threat to his communications.

Still there remains the question: Why did he not go forward
himself to see what was happening? The protection of the airfield,
although neither Puttick nor Freyberg himself had accorded it
absolute priority over defence of the coast, nevertheless remained
a key task for his brigade. In retrospect it is easy to say that he
should have done so. But this kind of battle was new to him. Nor
did there develop later in the war any simple answer to the
problem of control during the mixed fighting that follows airborne
operations.

The author of the *New Zealand War History* has examined the
actions of Hargest on 20 May and has speculated upon the
reasoning that lay behind them. He concedes that Hargest was
weary after the battle in Greece, and that he was facing a difficult
problem. But he concludes that he 'began with a battle plan
which gave his battalion commanders too much choice of rôle with
too little guidance on which rôles were prior'. And he adds:

> . . . in the battle itself he failed to give his commanders firm
> directions . . . he would have been better able to deal with the break-
> down of communications had he taken up beforehand an advanced
> H.Q. much closer to Maleme, the vital point . . . once things had begun
> to go wrong his wisest course would have been to go forward as far as
> possible to see for himself what the situation was.[37]

Ultimately the failure had been one of human communication.
In character the two men most concerned were utterly apart. At
Maleme, Andrew, the professional soldier, puzzled, brave, and

[37] Davin, p. 138

7

inarticulate, had spent the day anxiously peering into the dust clouds in search of his scattered companies, conscious only of the mystery of this mounting pressure from beyond the Tavronitis. At Platanias, Hargest, the politician returning to arms, remained calm, optimistic – and totally uninformed. Between the two stretched a gulf that could have been bridged only by personal encounter. Their frail exchanges across the radio telephone brought them no real contact. Had they met face to face all might have been different. Hargest must surely then have been impressed by the gravity of the situation, and by the need for urgent measures to meet it.

Today, it can be seen that his failure to mount a substantial counter-attack was influenced less by misgiving about the risk, than by failure to realize the magnitude of the need. It never occurred to him that in failing to move now he might be laying up for himself, and for his brigade, indeed for the whole force in Crete, hazards that were to prove infinitely greater.

Thus on the evening of 20 May the mass of the New Zealand 5th Brigade, including more than 1,600 unwounded infantry, the core of the New Zealand Division, were allowed to settle for the night in misguided and short-lived tranquillity. Scattered among them, hunted, thirsty, and exhausted, a few dozen surviving Germans crouched in such cover as they could find while a bare two miles to the east, pinned upon the outskirts of the vital airfield, the men of the 22nd Battalion were locked in a death grip with an enemy scarcely more numerous, and considerably wearier, than themselves.

10

The Prison Valley : 20 May

Student had decided to drop the greater part of his Centre Group in the Canea-Suda area, as part of the first sortie, while the Storm Regiment attacked Maleme. During the early afternoon most of 2 Parachute Regiment would attack Retimo. The task of the Group as a whole was nothing less than the capture of Canea, Suda and Retimo by nightfall on the first evening. A detachment from Retimo was to move west to join the rest of the Group at Suda. Thus it was intended that the command centre of the island should be seized, and organized resistance paralysed, within the first few hours. The clearance of mines from Suda should be 'concluded' on about 'the third day'.[1]

The first part of this ambitious programme was entrusted to a force which may be estimated at about 3,000 men.[2] It consisted largely of 3 Parachute Regiment augmented by a Parachute Engineer Battalion, and by some detachments armed with heavy infantry weapons. There would also be about 270 glider-troops from the Storm Regiment carried in some thirty gliders. In command of the Group, and also of the Airlanding Division, was the fifty-year-old Lieutenant-General Suessmann, another veteran of the First World War who had only recently joined the airborne forces; against Poland he had led an infantry formation, later taking part in the campaign against Norway; he had spent some time swimming in Oslo Fiord after the sinking of the *Blücher*. Travelling by glider he was to land with his Headquarters close to Lake Aghya.

His dispositions were simple. He decided to use most of his gliders to neutralize the anti-aircraft batteries around Suda. Like

[1] *Einsatz Kreta*, Battle Report of XI Air Corps

[2] Based on *Einsatz Kreta*, Battle Report of XI Air Corps, and Davin, p. 140 *et seq.* Some of the aircraft were unable to leave the runways in Greece. See p. 184 this chapter. An estimate of 3,570 for the Canea–Galatas–Alikianou area was made by C. R. Monaghan, Archivist N.Z. War Histories. But Kurowski, p. 242, maintains that there were only '2,460 parachutists' for 'Sector Suda'

Meindl he divided them – fifteen to attack the guns on the Akrotiri Peninsula, and a further nine for the battery and wireless station south of Canea. The four battalions of 3 Regiment, together with their supporting companies, would be dropped south-west of Canea, III Battalion a few hundred yards east of Galatas, II and I Battalions near the Prison, north and south of the Canea-Alikianou Road, and the Engineer Battalion north of Alikianou.

The gliders were in trouble from the start. During the flight they lost cohesion, and when they arrived over Suda they were faced with heavier anti-aircraft fire than had been expected. Casting off at 6,000 feet, some of the pilots of the Akrotiri section, commanded by Captain Altmann, found it impossible to identify their allotted landing points. Four of the machines were destroyed by fire from one of the Welch companies. Others were smashed among the rocks. The men who got out alive found themselves too widely scattered to give each other cover. The survivors had the mortification of discovering that the guns had been moved. They were able to do a little sniping. But in the end forty-eight out of 150 men were killed, thirty-six wounded, and the rest captured.[3]

The smaller section, under Lieutenant Genz, did rather better; it was from one of these gliders that ten men were able to kill almost all the 180 virtually unarmed gunners serving the half-battery of heavy guns south of Canea. But the rest of them achieved little. Pressed increasingly by the Marines, and by the Welch Bren-carriers, they failed to reach the wireless station. Later in the day, they received radio instruction to withdraw to the Prison. Rather less than half got there, after a night of adventure. They were greatly helped by their commander, who spoke English, and was able to bluff his way in the darkness through the Greek and British posts.

For several hours, confusion was caused by the few Germans who remained scattered about the outskirts of the town, the more so since it was believed that some of them might be wearing British battle-dress. All troops passing check-points were stopped and made to prove their identity. Weston himself, on a visit to Force Headquarters, was challenged at a Welch road-block. His reaction to this strict compliance with his own order was to

[3] *Einsatz Kreta*, Battle Report of XI Air Corps

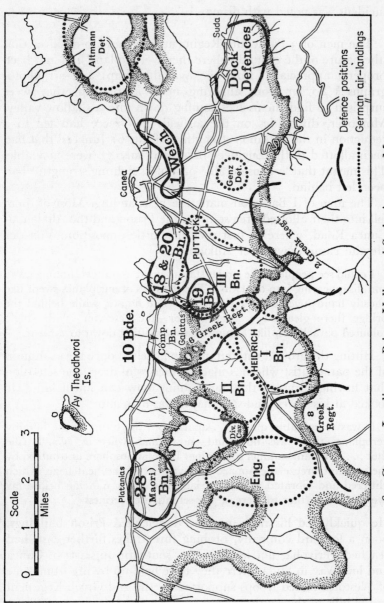

6. German Landings at Prison Valley and Suda Area: 20 May

upbraid the lieutenant in charge; by those who saw it the small incident was noted with dismay.[4]

The men of 3 Parachute Regiment were now to discover that 'the nature of the ground' where they were to land had 'not been properly appreciated from the available maps and air photographs'.[5] So far from alighting upon a 'plateau' they were surprised to find themselves coming down into a shallow valley. Moreover, difficulties on the airfields in Greece had led to a reduction in the battalion strengths. Of the '61 Junkers' that had been allotted to the Engineer Battalion 'only 47' were available. This meant that 'a considerable part of its fighting strength'[6] had been left behind.

The men of I Battalion made the best landing. Most of them fell into their allotted area south of the Prison and the Alikianou-Canea Road, where at first they met little opposition. Von der Heydte came down over Alikianou:

I could see people in the streets staring up at us, others running away and disappearing into doorways. The shadows of our planes swept like ghostly hands over the sun-drenched white houses, while behind the bridge there gleamed a large mirror – the reservoir – with single coloured parachutes, like autumn leaves, drifting down towards it.[7]

Hitting the ground without mishap he felt at once the exaltation of the parachutist who has made a successful drop, the sensation that having survived thus far nothing now can harm him. He looked at his watch and saw that it was 8.15 a.m.

It was remarkably quiet . . . apart from the drone of the homing aeroplanes there was no sound – no human voice or even a rifle shot . . . a radiant summer's morning. In an atmosphere untroubled by the smallest breeze the apparent movement of the heat haze, which glittered and vibrated as if a myriad ghosts were dancing before my eyes, served further to increase the sensation of eeriness.[8]

He quickly led his men into the undefended Prison buildings. Soon a forward company, probing three miles further east, had reached Perivolia, not far from the southern outskirts of Canea and half-way to Suda. Here they were held up by fire from some of Weston's mixed troops supported by the 2nd Greek Regiment in the hills to the south.

[4] Observed by author   [5] *Einsatz Kreta*, Battle Report of XI Air Corps
[6] *Wie Wir Kämpfen*   [7] von der Heydte, p. 59   [8] Ibid., p. 62

Most of II Battalion dropped along the northern slopes of
the valley and among the olives close to Galatas. Replacing a
company which was to 'reach the regiment as quickly as possible'[9]
after travelling by ship were two companies with anti-tank
guns. From the moment of leaving their planes the men of this
battalion suffered heavy casualties. According to Karl Neuhoff, a
company Sergeant-Major, about '350 men . . . survived the initial
landing and organizing period'.[10] Only three men from his own
machine reached the ground unhurt.

Nearly all of those who came down near Galatas itself were
killed at once. One company dropped a mile to the south. These
were the Germans who, at about 10 a.m., moved up through the
trees on both sides of the road leading to the village until they
encountered Kippenberger's Petrol Company. Greatly encouraged by Captain McDonagh, the New Zealanders put up a
stout resistance, killing many of their enemies, among them the
German commander. Nevertheless, at this vital point, the defence
soon found itself subjected to dangerous and increasing pressure.
McDonagh himself fell, mortally wounded. His men were forced
back, but managed to hold again a few hundred yards below the
village walls.

III Battalion became widely scattered. Instead of forming a
concentrated group east of Galatas, as had been intended, the
companies were spread over a distance of nearly three miles
between the Hospital Peninsula and the foothills west of Perivolia.
Some of the men in the south were able to join the advance
of I Battalion. But nearly all the others, including the members of
the company which had attacked the 7th General Hospital, were
destroyed during the day. By nightfall, the few survivors were
scattered and ineffective, except in the rôle of solitary snipers.

At the south-western end of the Prison Valley, the Engineer
Battalion had landed uncomfortably among the cactus north of
Alikianou. Here they encountered no British troops. Instead
they were greeted by the 8th Greeks, and by the local Cretan
inhabitants, who quickly revealed the true temper of the native
population. From all sides, men, women and children, armed with
shot-guns and with every primitive sort of weapon, poured out in
defence of their homes. At the same time, the 8th Greeks held on
fiercely in their positions along the hillsides, and from the houses
within the village. There were less than a thousand of them, but

[9] Davin, p. 143, *n.* 2   [10] Ibid., p. 142

later the Germans were to maintain that at Alikianou they had been opposed by '4,000 Greeks, partisans and British'.[11] Both the Greeks and the Cretans seized the arms which showered down among them from the sky. Soon the Germans found themselves facing an increasing fire from their own machine-guns. Both sides suffered heavy loss. On the following day, a New Zealand officer was to count 'more than 100 dead Germans in one small area alone – near the road to Alikianou and a mile or two from the village'.[12] The Greek Colonel, of whom Kippenberger had expected so little, was killed, together with most of his staff. When night came, the Greeks still held out on the ridges, at the road-bridge, and in the village of Alikianou itself. It was very much more than Kippenberger had expected of them. More, indeed, than he was ever to understand.

The impetuous Farran had been waiting with his three tanks near the Galatas Turn. When the attack began, every instinct told him that he should drive into the parachutists wherever he could find them. Without waiting for orders he drove inland up the twisting road, through Galatas itself, the street now filling with Greeks crying for ammunition, and on towards the Prison Valley. Soon he had passed the New Zealand Petrol Company. The men gave him a grin and a thumb's up sign. 'Just to look at their confident smiling faces was good for the spirit.'[13] But once among the olives in the valley he found that there was little that he could do. The Germans were invisible within the 'long black shadows'.[14] He lost a track from his tank and was lucky to make his escape.

Back in the village about 200 survivors of the 6th Greeks had found a leader. On the previous evening, a tall fair-haired officer of the Queen's Regiment, now attached to the Greek mission, had arrived at Kippenberger's Headquarters upon what was intended to be a brief official visit. His name was Captain Michael Forrester. In appearance and behaviour he had struck his cynical hosts as being almost too English to be believable. Now, in the Brigade Major's phrase, he 'nonchalantly forgot about reporting back'. During the next week his exploits at Galatas were to impress even the New Zealanders. First he quickly rallied the

---

[11] *Wie Wir Kämpfen*

[12] DP, Comments by W. E. Murphy on draft of book (*Greece and Crete* 1941) by Christopher Buckley (hereafter called 'Buckley Draft')

[13] Farran, p. 89   [14] Ibid., p. 90

demoralized Greeks, found arms for them, and re-established
them down the slope south of the houses, with the Petrol Company
on their right and the New Zealand 19th Battalion on their left.
By midday they had recovered their spirits, chasing German
patrols from the middle of their new position in the course of a
yelling counter-attack. Later in the day they were reinforced by
the Divisional Cavalry, who had retreated from their isolated
position in the foothills two miles north of Alikianou bringing
with them news that the 8th Greeks appeared to be 'hopelessly
dispersed and disorganized'.[15]

But the cavalrymen had not been close enough to see the
fighting.

Shortly before 9 a.m. four of the gliders of 7th Airlanding
Division Headquarters came down as planned into a clearing
near Lake Aghya, only to encounter tough vine stumps, invisible
from the air, which tore them apart and killed most of the
occupants. One glider failed to arrive. Its fuselage, the wings
wrenched away by some unexpected towing stress, caused perhaps
by a passing Heinkel III, had crashed on to a rock in the Aegean.
There were no survivors. Among the dead was General Suessmann.

Control of the Centre Group, and of the Airlanding Division,
now passed to Colonel Richard Heidrich, the Commander of
3 Parachute Rifle Regiment, a solitary, single-minded man of
forty-five whose life had been wholly devoted to the profession
of arms. For a time he had served under Rommel as an instructor
in tactics at the Military School in Potsdam, later transferring to
the airborne troops in command of the first German Parachute
Battalion; according to one of his officers he was 'the type of
soldier for whom the war was an unpleasant interruption to training'.[16] For the moment there was nothing he could do with the
Division as a whole. Indeed it was clear that he was going to have
trouble enough with his own Regiment. As he stood in the morning sunlight he saw that the 'plateau' was a valley and that the
attack had miscarried. Von der Heydte appeared to be well-
established in the south, and no pressure had developed from the
north. But before he could advance upon Canea and Suda he
must capture the occupied heights on his left flank.

By the middle of the afternoon he had collected a force of about
400 men. He sent them off in a ragged line towards Galatas. The

[15] Kippenberger, p. 57   [16] DP, von der Heydte's description

attack failed. Half a mile beyond the Prison, below the sharp incline to the walls of the village, they came to a swell of ground known to the New Zealanders as Pink Hill. Here the Petrol Company held on grimly among the trees. There had been no time for the Germans to collect heavier weapons. Armed only with their machine pistols they could do little against the New Zealand rifles and Brens.

In the afternoon [says Neuhoff], between 14.00 and 15.00 hours we advanced to attack the hill of Galatas. We proceeded without opposition, about half way up the hill. Suddenly we ran into heavy and very accurate rifle and machine-gun fire. The enemy had held their fire with great discipline and had allowed us to approach well within effective range before opening up. Our casualties were extremely heavy and we were forced to retire leaving many dead behind us. . . . This first attack on Galatas had cost us approximately fifty per cent casualties about half of whom were killed.[17]

Towards evening Heidrich withdrew the troops that were covering his southern flank and used them to support a further advance. He had not lost sight of the fact that the heights remained the key to the situation. Nor had he surrendered the initiative. This time he was able to gain a foothold on Pink Hill as the Petrol Company withdrew, while a few hundred yards further to the south-east, on the summit of another low hill, some of his men established themselves among the gravestones of a cemetery. But Galatas itself remained inviolate behind its forbidding walls.

Already the engagement in the Prison Valley had reached a crisis. If the defence were to counter-attack, now was the time to do it, while the enemy were still scattered and short of weapons, and before they could be reinforced.

At noon Kippenberger had been able to get through to Puttick over the telephone with the news that the 10th Brigade was holding its position, apart from the disintegration of the 6th Greeks. He also feared the worst for the 8th Greeks near Alikianou. At 2.15 p.m. he sent Puttick a wireless signal insisting that 'a vigorous counter-attack would clear the Prison'.[18] Later that afternoon he pressed again for 'infantry with which to counter-attack'.[19] It was a reasonable request; his own men were obviously ill-suited to full scale action in the open; indeed all the troops in the southern part

[17] Davin, p. 143, *n.* 3, interrogation of Karl Neuhoff
[18] New Zealand Division War Diary   [19] Kippenberger, p. 57

of his area were hard pressed to hold their positions; at the same
time his desire to do something quickly to clear the Valley had
been spurred by reports from the 19th Battalion that the enemy
were making a landing-ground.

As the afternoon lengthened, he became increasingly
despondent about his brigade's prospects. Little of this appears in
the book that he wrote after the war. Nevertheless, the signal
which he sent to Divisional Headquarters at 7 p.m. was a mounting catalogue of anxiety. It had begun to seem to him that he
could rely only on Lieutenant-Colonel Blackburn and the 19th.
He even proposed that if no help could reach him he would need
to abandon the heights at Galatas and withdraw to a position
across the coast road.

Div Cav Det arrived without loss and is in Galatas. No word of
of 8 Greeks. 6 Greeks have disappeared. Landing at 17.00 hrs mainly
stores but prisoner says many more tps will arrive tonight.

Blackburn reports position intact but small parties in rear not
disposed of.

Pressure on my left has been increasing. Left Coy has retired 200 yds
causing next Coy to come back. Casualties about 60 incl 4 off and are
continuing steadily. Rations and amo alright water short. Loss all on
left. Can carry wounded to Maleme Rd if trucks can be sent up.

If no counter-attack can be mounted to clear Prison area where
enemy are clearing landing field suggest that after dark I should
withdraw to shorter line N-S astride Maleme (Coast) road retaining
contact with Blackburn.

Wire to you has been down for two hours and enemy are at present
within short range of exchange.

Please advise position and instruct. Don't think this line would hold
against serious attack tomorrow.

Have had to thin out beach defence.[20]

In most of this he was mistaken. Like everyone else, Kippenberger was a victim of the communication difficulty. All the
same, by his standards, this was an alarmist message. It was true
that most of the 6th Greeks had 'disappeared'. No doubt it was
reasonable, on the strength of the gloomy opinions brought back
by the Divisional Cavalry, to fear that the same fate must have
befallen the Greeks at Alikianou. And for what it might be worth
he was right to pass on the prisoner's tale that 'many more'
parachutists would arrive that night; it was for the Intelligence

staff to assess the value of such a story. Much more serious in its effect was the scare that he now raised about the construction of an airstrip. It was unfortunate that he should have allowed himself so quickly to have become convinced by what can have been no more than superficial reports. After the war he was to deny that he had authorized this reference.[21] Indeed, a glance at the thick growth of olive that covered the floor of the Prison Valley might quickly have dispelled such an apprehension. It is scarcely likely, however, that so singular a comment could have become included by chance in his signal to Divisional Headquarters. As it appeared, the phrase '. . . Prison area where enemy are clearing landing field' had about it the ring of authority and truth. Divisional and Force Headquarters were bound to take it seriously. It could only serve to strengthen Freyberg and his commanders in their belief that enemy troop-carriers would put down upon improvised landing-strips, if not in open country.

Yet, in his request for immediate counter-attack, Kippenberger was right. He did not know how severely the Germans themselves had been mauled during the day, but he understood that if those in the Prison Valley were to be eliminated by force, and not merely starved out, delay could only make the task more difficult. Moreover, he knew that Puttick still held in reserve the New Zealand 4th Brigade.

He was now to learn that the Divisional Commander had no intention of committing his reserve in this way. Indeed, Puttick had at first been disposed to ignore the Prison Valley. Only now, on hearing of the landing-ground threat, did he feel impelled to order Inglis to send a single battalion.

The signal which reached the Commander of the 4th Brigade at 8.30 p.m. was nothing if not optimistic:

10 Brigade reports construction of landing-ground in PRISON area 0553. 4 Inf Bde will counter-attack with one bn Lt tks and carriers to clear PRISON area of enemy. When attack completed 19 Bn will come under comd 10 Bde to hold posn on left of 1 Comp on line previously held by 6 Gk Bn down to incl rd CANEA-ALIKIANOU.[22]

At 4 p.m. the 19th Battalion had reported to Divisional Headquarters that between 900 and 1,150 men had landed in the

[21] DP, Comments by Sir Howard Kippenberger, Editor in Chief of the N.Z. War Histories, and author of *Infantry Brigadier*, commenting on Buckley Draft. In Crete his rank was that of Colonel

[22] Davin, p. 168

Prison Valley. Although this was an underestimate the *New Zealand War History* figure of 1,800 is probably too high. At least, 540 had been killed or wounded, leaving perhaps 1,000 men fully active. Further east only 310 scattered survivors remained out of 1,060. Three miles to the west the Engineer Battalion had suffered 150 casualties and was still isolated.[23] Puttick may well have believed that the Germans near the Prison could have no more than 800 men capable of fighting. This would have been a reasonable assessment on the strength of the numbers seen to fall by the 19th Battalion. But it scarcely adds wisdom to his decision to use only a single weakened battalion for the counter-attack.

His order was to be interpreted by the two Brigade commanders, and by the commander of the 19th Battalion, in a way which did credit to their robust sense of realities. From the wording it would appear that he had intended that the 18th or 20th Battalion should make the attack, with the 19th following up to occupy the position which had originally been held by the 6th Greeks across the Canea-Alikianou road. Inglis himself recognized as much in maintaining later that he did not want to have one of his 'free battalions dispersed or pinned down'.[24] For this reason he chose to use the 19th itself, which, in its position east of Galatas, was two miles south-west of the other two battalions. He seems not to have stopped to consider whether the 19th might not already be playing a vital rôle in covering the left flank of the 10th Brigade.

The *New Zealand War History* maintains that it was too late to bring up the 18th or 20th from their positions on the coast road west of the Hospital Peninsula. But against this it might be said that the journey for the 18th, straight up the Galatas road to the proposed start line north-west of the village, would in fact have been easier than the approach across country that was necessary for the 19th. The *War History* adds that the order 'clearly envisages the employment of 19th Battalion'. So indeed it does, but the general sense would appear to indicate that Puttick intended this battalion to occupy its new line only after the attack had been completed. Inglis chose to interpret his orders in a way that would enable him to keep at least two of his battalions together. He was 'still nourishing hopes of a brigade counter-attack . . . next day'.[25]

[23] Davin, p. 173, *n.* 1
[24] DP, Letter from Inglis to Kippenberger, 12 Feb. 1951
[25] Ibid.

For this action he was being allowed to use only one of his battalions. In such strength, and at this hour, failure was almost certain. No doubt he reflected that it would not be his fault. At least he would do the thing in a way that should spare his brigade further fragmentation.

Kippenberger now learnt for the first time that an attempt was to be made to mount the attack for which he had been asking all day. It was to start from his brigade area. Moreover, he was the only officer with any knowledge of the local situation. But neither Puttick nor Inglis had consulted him. He was told that the transfer of the 19th to 10th Brigade should occur 'when attack completed'. Nevertheless, he at once assumed, as did its Commanding Officer, that he should take charge of the battalion immediately.

Already dusk was falling. It was too late for any detailed preparation. Moreover, both Blackburn and Kippenberger felt that they could not spare more than two companies of the 19th without fatally weakening the left flank. Thus the stature of the expedition became further diminished. In the end the group that set out doubtfully into the darkness consisted not of a brigade, which four hours earlier would probably have succeeded in isolating the Prison and bringing support to the Greeks at Alikianou, nor even of the force envisaged by Puttick, the fresh battalion accompanied by seven light tanks and 'carriers', which in daylight might have cleared much of the valley, but simply of two infantry companies supported by Farran and his three tanks.

Despite his own reservations, Inglis had not hesitated to speak to Blackburn in terms of 'clearing the landing ground'. Not unnaturally Blackburn was reluctant to talk on this scale. Farran and the two company commanders understood that they were to reach the olive trees north of the Prison and there cover the potential landing-ground with fire. This they succeeded in doing, finding their way with difficulty in the black night. At the cost of some casualties they killed about twenty Germans. Before dawn Kippenberger sent runners to call them back.

Operation Crete suggests that these night manoeuvres may have achieved more than Kippenberger appreciated at the time. The enemy were induced to withdraw from the 'vital Galatas height'.[26] This description, it may be assumed, refers to Pink Hill, which the two companies had crossed during their advance. The

[26] *Einsatz Kreta*, Battle Report of XI Air Corps

evacuation, says *Operation Crete*, was due to 'a misunderstanding', but it adds, 'the enemy immediately followed up with tanks'. As a result 'a critical situation'[27] developed on this flank. No doubt the New Zealanders, together with Farran and his tanks, had contributed to the misunderstanding. In the Prison Valley, as at Maleme, the parachutists had been much alarmed at the sound of armoured vehicles advancing against them, even in the darkness, while they were still short of heavy weapons.

Heidrich judged the threat sufficient to demand the recall of von der Heydte's battalion from Perivolia. He brought it back to block the valley south of the road. At the same time he ordered the Engineer Battalion to close up from Alikianou.

That evening the situation must have seemed to him little short of disastrous. There was nothing that he could do in his inherited rôle as senior officer at Divisional Headquarters. He had only the scantiest information from Greece, and none of his own plans was in sight of realization. Scattered among the olive groves on the far side of Galatas, III Battalion had lost half its strength. Even von der Heydte's men had begun to suffer increasing casualties. From behind him came sounds of battle in the dropping area of the Engineer Battalion. Plainly the Canaris organization had been wrong about the attitude of the Cretans.

Earlier that day, Divisional Headquarters had ordered that 'an area supposed to be suitable for the landing of Junkers 52 planes . . . on the high plateau near Alikianou' should be reconnoitred 'as soon as possible'.[28] This may have been the source of the rumour that was to cause so much concern to Kippenberger and Puttick, and ultimately to Freyberg himself. For Heidrich, looking at the tree-grown valley, the words must have held a special mockery. He was a sanguine and bitterly determined fighter. That night, however, the best that he could hope was that the remnants of 3 Parachute Regiment, this collection of little more than a thousand unwounded men concentrated near the Prison, would prove 'just sufficient' to enable him to 'hold the position against the expected attack from Galatas'.[29]

For Puttick, the problems of the day had been more complex

[27] *Einsatz Kreta*, Battle Report of XI Air Corps
[28] *Wie Wir Kämpfen*. Not, however, with any suggestion that plane-landings were to play a part in the battle. See above, p. 87, *n*. 15
[29] *Einsatz Kreta*, Battle Report of XI Air Corps

since they had offered him more choice. By early afternoon a pattern had begun to emerge from the chaos of noise, smoke and dust. It was clear that the main weight of the enemy assault was falling, as had been predicted, upon Maleme and the Prison Valley. This left the three battalions of the 4th Brigade relatively unscathed – the 19th, east of Galatas, and the 18th and 20th in their position between Canea Bridge and the Galatas Turn. These were the troops that had been designated as the main part of Force Reserve. Urgently, therefore, the problem now arose of when and where they should be used for counter-attack.

When the battle began they had still been under Freyberg's orders. At 11 a.m. he returned them to Puttick, retaining only the 1st Welch, dug into the terraces around Force Headquarters on the east side of Canea.

This was a bold step. The Intelligence forecast was proving remarkably accurate. If the Germans continued to follow their expected programme there would soon be further heavy drops of parachutists at Heraklion and Retimo – probably too, in the Canea-Suda area where so far only a few had appeared.[30] Nor had Freyberg forgotten the promised invasion from the sea. Despite all these threats he had nevertheless, at this early stage, surrendered direct control of his Force Reserve to the local commander of the area in which the Germans had already landed. Nothing could better illustrate his own recognition of the transcendent need for immediate counter-attack. It may be that he was already inclined to believe that the main German effort would come from the west of Canea. On the other hand he may very well have decided that, if necessary, he would have to form a new reserve. One thing is clear. On the evidence of this decision he was determined that his only striking force should be fully employed during those first few hours in which it could expect to enjoy a brief advantage.

A great responsibility thus fell upon Puttick, and it is necessary to ask why he let the day pass without committing the 4th Brigade as a whole, and indeed delayed the use even of one battalion of it until late into the evening. By the early afternoon, it was known that few Germans remained alive east of Galatas. From hour to hour, Brigadier Inglis and his battalion commanders awaited the

[30] Photographs in the Australian War History show some dozens of parachutes falling over Suda Bay. They may have carried supplies. Certainly very few parachutists landed in this area, and none by German design

order to counter-attack, while, from all sides, suggestions for such action began to come in to Divisional Headquarters.

The first specific request had been made at 2.15 p.m. by Kippenberger in the course of the telephone conversation in which he declared that 'a vigorous counter-attack would clear the Prison'. Several other senior officers were later to claim that they had sought to persuade Puttick to use the 4th Brigade in this way, among them Inglis, and Brigadier Stewart, who had brought from Freyberg the order restoring the Brigade to Divisional command. But Puttick, in Stewart's words, 'wouldn't budge'.[31] Throughout the day he maintained that he must hold back his reserve lest the whole Division should become cut off from the rear by a further drop of parachutists, or a landing from the sea, in the vicinity of Canea. It seems probable that he was further restrained by a reluctance to make any move in daylight. For nearly a week it had been almost impossible for a vehicle, or small group of men, to cover thirty yards without attracting the immediate attention of machine-gunning fighters. Like everyone else on the island he had come under the spell of the absolute power exerted by the enemy in the air. He had failed to make the inference that, on this particular day, the *Luftwaffe* must find it impossible to intervene for so long as the airborne troops remained mixed with the defenders.

Nothing could induce him to change his mind, neither the importunings of his brigadiers, nor the evident constraint upon the enemy planes, nor even his own increasing concern about the Germans in the Prison Valley, the only enemy lodgment in the whole of his divisional area for which his officers were expressing any concern.

Everywhere else the situation appeared to be under control. At 10 a.m. Hargest had reported that the 5th Brigade had things 'well in hand'.[32] Two hours later, in a message that reflected the same confidence, he had referred only to 'guns searching across river west of the 22nd Battalion where parachutists in olive groves'.[33] At 5.15 p.m. he said that he was sending two companies to support the 22nd. But since he had already claimed that his other three battalions had dealt with the enemy in their areas this mention of a mere two companies, presumably all the support that he thought to be needed, must in itself have served to assure Puttick that nothing much could be going wrong at Maleme.

[31] DP   [32] New Zealand Division War Diary   [33] Ibid.

Finally, at 9.45 p.m., a signal from the 5th Brigade summarized the day's fighting in optimistic terms. 'Hundreds of dead Germans' were lying within and around the lines of the 23rd Battalion. Casualties in the 22nd had been 'severe', but reinforcement had been sent to them. 'In general the situation' was 'quite satisfactory'.[34]

Not until midnight did there begin to reach Divisional Headquarters some whisperings that all was not well at Maleme. Only then can Puttick have begun to suspect that before long Hargest too would be asking for help.

After the war he explained his reluctance to use the 4th Brigade on 20 May. From the first he had 'believed that the Galatas front was only a foundation for the real front at Maleme and that so long as the 10th Brigade held fast it was doing all that was necessary'.[35] There was therefore no need to take the ground held by 3 Parachute Regiment. Any attack made towards Alikianou in daylight would have had no heavy weapons to support it, and there would have been no tools with which to dig in if it should have succeeded. Nor would it have been possible to destroy the Germans. Since they had 'nothing vital to defend',[36] they would have resisted only long enough to inflict maximum casualties before falling back into the hills. The New Zealanders would then have found themselves exposed to the full onslaught of the *Luftwaffe*.

These explanations overlook two points. First, he did not, that evening, believe that the Germans in the Prison Valley had 'nothing vital to defend'. It was because he feared that they might be building a landing-strip, erroneously as it turned out, that he was eventually persuaded to mount a counter-attack of sorts. And secondly, a concerted move through the valley by the whole of the 4th Brigade might have been the best way of reinforcing Maleme from the south-east.

In 1951, Inglis wrote that this was what he had always wanted. At 2 p.m. he had met a war correspondent, who was returning by Bren Carrier from a visit to Platanias. He thus learnt that the 5th Brigade Headquarters was 'out of touch with its units' and 'flapping'. This had been enough to convince him that the battle was 'out of control'[37] at Maleme. 'The immediate situation', as

[34] New Zealand Division War Diary
[35] DP, comments by Sir Edward Puttick on Davin Draft
[36] Davin, p. 167   [37] DP, letter from Inglis to Kippenberger, 12 Feb. 1951

he then saw it, 'was to clear and secure the Prison Valley and the Alikianou area,' where, so he understood, there were 4,000 Italian prisoners of war whom the enemy might arm and use.

I expected to follow this up by regaining Maleme if the situation there had to be restored. On 18 May I had spent the day reconnoitring the Prison Valley, Alikianou, a route from the latter place through the hills to reach Maleme from the S and SE, the Maleme area itself, and the coastal area between there and my own positions. ... I was prepared to carry out the first operation, the Prison Valley party, in daylight for enemy air activity had slackened off considerably.

The attack would have been made with the 18th and 20th Battalions, helped by mortars borrowed from the Welch. In the second stage of the operation, if that should have proved necessary, he had intended to make a night approach through the hills to Maleme 'with the double object of separating the two German groups and surprising the Maleme Area'. All this he had suggested directly to Puttick. But the Divisional Commander had remained 'strongly opposed to the whole idea'.[38]

On hearing these recollections, so closely argued in retrospect, Puttick denied that Inglis had ever said anything to him about counter-attack in the Prison Valley.[39] He had hesitated to engage the Reserve only to ensure that it might eventually be used with the utmost effect. In a letter to Kippenberger, written in 1952, he maintained that he would have been ready to send it to support Hargest at Maleme on the first evening. But he had been given no reason to suppose that it was required:

I thought and still think that, whatever the reason, 5 Bde at Maleme on day of attack almost completely failed to carry out its rôle, and in fact lost the aerodrome with little more than one-fourth of its infantry force employed.

On General Maitland Wilson's advice I instructed Hargest to move one bn much closer to the aerodrome, to give immediate help to Andrew's bn, but from the narrative it seems that even this bn was hardly used in its main rôle.

I had expected that in the circumstances the whole bde (less dets up to a coy per bn to police their areas etc.) would have made an all-in C/A on Maleme, and had this resulted in any difficulty in the areas vacated by the bns, the Div Reserve would have been used.[40]

[38] DP, letter from Inglis to Kippenberger, 12 Feb. 1951

[39] Davin, p. 164, n. 2

[40] DP. In a letter to Brig. H. B. Latham, dated 27 Aug. 1952, Kippenberger quotes a letter from Puttick

But this contention that he would have been prepared to help Hargest, if he had been given any hint that the 5th Brigade was in difficulties, ignores the fact that he nevertheless preferred to let the 4th Brigade remain idle rather than use it in the Prison Valley where it was plainly needed. His decision had not been easy. There were no precedents to guide him. For all that anyone knew, thousands more parachutists might arrive at any moment. And it was true that a sudden reinforcement of the landing which had apparently been defeated at Maleme, or some fresh appearance of the enemy on the coast, or behind him in Canea, must offer a worse immediate danger than that presented by the Germans near the Prison. It is understandable that he feared to make the classic error of committing his reserve too soon. Yet this very uncertainty should itself have been a spur to swift and vigorous action. This airborne attack was no ordinary operation, no straightforward punching of a hole through a fortified line by forces fully prepared and equipped, the sort of situation which, if the flanks held, might be permitted by the defence to mature for days or even weeks in the expectation of exhausting resistance in the salient before the delivery of a fully mounted counter-stroke. On the contrary, the parachutists at this moment were relatively weak. With every hour that passed they would grow more formidable, as their organization improved and their concentration enabled them to call again upon their air support; and at any moment their strength might be dramatically increased by airborne reinforcement. Recognizing that this must be true of every lodgment made by the enemy, Freyberg had handed over control of a potent striking force, virtually the only reserve in the island. Rather than not use it at all, even although the *Schwerpunkt* were still not apparent, Puttick should surely have urged it against the biggest collection of the enemy within reach.

Before the battle, Freyberg had emphasized that the airborne troops must be subjected to organized counter-attack as soon as possible after their landing. Yet here in the Prison Valley, as at Maleme, the long day had been allowed to pass while the scattered Germans, bereft for a few vital hours of that air support upon which they had come to count so dearly, made desperate shift to collect themselves and their weapons under the guns of a static defence. Scarcely two miles away, three New Zealand battalions waited, unengaged. With them were a platoon of machine-guns and the light tanks of the 3rd Hussars.

One consideration alone might be taken to explain, if not to justify, Puttick's restraint. From the first, so he was to claim, he had recognized that the 'real front'[41] would be at Maleme. The virtue of this judgement must be measured by the speed and resolution with which he came to use his reserve in the defence of the airfield once he knew it to be threatened.

[41] Davin, p. 166

11

Heraklion and Retimo: 20 May

At Heraklion the day began quietly. During the morning, a flight of Messerschmitts circled about the harbour and the airfield, but early in the afternoon, Major Nicholls, a company commander of the Leicesters, heard from his colonel that the 'trouble' appeared to have 'died down'. He would therefore be able to take his platoon commanders away from their men for the afternoon in order to show them over the area. 'Get off about two o'clock,' he was told, 'and be back by four-thirty p.m.' Before long he was to feel that 'the horoscope issued to Battalion Headquarters' could not 'have been in very good working order that morning'.[1]

He duly set out on a round of visits, taking with him his three lieutenants. They went first to the south-west of the town, visiting the Greek batteries. On their way back through Heraklion they dropped in on the Royal Marines, who were manning the Bofors. Next they drove across the airfield to pay their respects to the Black Watch. It was not until 3.30 p.m. that they dismissed the trucks and began to stroll back to their company lines which were nearly two miles away. At this moment they became suddenly aware of a familiar roar swelling in from over the sea. Within a few minutes the sky had filled with aircraft.

Here is a minor mystery. Seven hours after the beginning of the battle the battalions in Heraklion still knew nothing about it. It must be presumed that both the telephone and the submarine cable had been out of action.[2] Indeed, the Germans suspected a breakdown in the Heraklion communications at this time. If Chappel had heard of the German attack in the west he must surely have issued a special alert. He could have had no con-

[1] Underhill, *The Royal Leicestershire Regiment*, p. 55, Maj. A. W. D. Nicholls

[2] Capt. C. R. Croft, a member of the Brigade Staff, returned to the Headquarters 'rather hurriedly' as the attack started. In a letter to the author dated 26 Feb. 1963, he wrote, 'I do not think the cable to Cairo was working then'. It seems the cable to Canea was not working either, and that any attempt to 'listen in' had failed

ceivable reason for not doing so. Even had he wished to keep it secret it seems likely that it would have leaked from Brigade Headquarters during a period so long as seven hours.

It has been assumed that the news must have reached Heraklion much earlier. The *Official Australian War History* maintains that '. . . by eleven a.m. the defenders knew that paratroops had landed on the main body of Creforce round Suda Bay'.[3] Plainly this cannot be true. It is inconceivable that Major Nicholls and his platoon commanders should have spent the afternoon in social exchanges throughout the area without hearing about it. In fact the *Regimental War Histories* show that notification began to reach the battalions at about 3 p.m. It made no difference. The parachutists were to be well received.

From the first it had been clear than the Heraklion Sector should be easier to defend that the area allotted to the New Zealand Division west of Canea. It was smaller. Both the airfield and the harbour could be enclosed within a perimeter four miles in length and less than two miles broad. Now the defenders were to enjoy further advantages.

The German time-table was going wrong. Towards midday chaos had developed upon the airfields in Greece. This had been caused partly by dust clouds above the runways, and partly by devoted Greek attention to the civilian telephone system upon which the Germans were relying for their co-ordination of flights. There thus began serious failures in the timing of the Junkers in their second sorties. The parachute drops were not only delayed but spread in series over a period of several hours.

The formations started in incorrect tactical sequence [says *Operation Crete*], and arrived over their target areas between sixteen and nineteen hundred hours not closed up but in successive formation and at the most by squadrons. The bulk of the forces had to land without fighter protection. Moreover in the end, the force delivered was 'some six hundred men less than had been intended'.[4]

Almost equally serious was the failure of German Intelligence, which had appreciated the numbers of the garrison at less than half the true strength. Even after the battle, during which the defenders were to be reinforced by the 2nd Argyll and Sutherland Highlanders, the Germans believed that they had been opposed

[3] Long, p. 280

[4] *Einsatz Kreta*, Battle Report of XI Air Corps. (It was about 5 p.m. before the drops began)

by no more than 'three British and two Greek battalions with a tank detachment'.

The capture of Heraklion had been entrusted to Colonel Brauer, in command of I Parachute Regiment, reinforced by a battalion from 2 Regiment, together with two added companies. There were no gliders. The strength of this force, the whole of which it had been intended to commit during the first afternoon, was 2,600 men.[5] Of these, one battalion was to capture the airfield, attacking it from both sides, while another would storm the harbour from the west. The two remaining battalions would cover the approaches from east and west. Colonel Brauer himself was to drop with the eastern of these battalions, three miles from the airfield. On the following day, the sea flotilla would reach the coast close to the town carrying a battalion of Mountain Troops, together with heavy weapons, and several hundred parachutists for whom there had been no space in the aircraft.

These expectations were to be disappointed. All through the late afternoon the Junkers straggled south, flying low above the brilliant sea while the westering sun lit their windows from the right. It was perhaps as well for the parachutists that they had no suspicion of the reception that awaited them.

By 20 May the strongly reinforced 14th Brigade had reached a strength of just over 8,000. The heart of this force was made up of four good battalions, the 2nd Leicesters, the 2nd York and Lancs, the 2nd Black Watch, and the 2/4 Australian Battalion, a total of 2,799 fully trained infantry. There were also about a thousand ancillary British troops, together with three partially equipped Greek battalions, and transport sufficient to lift some 600 men. Finally there was the usual modest ration of half a dozen light tanks, backed by two Matildas.

The airfield lay close to the beach, three miles beyond the ancient walled town, and overlooked from the east by steep hills topped by the radar station. Between the two, the road was flanked to the north by a rough meadow known as Buttercup Field, and to the south by the Greek Barracks, a tall modern structure painted yellow standing out from the olives and growing

---

[5] This total is estimated from *Einsatz Kreta*, coupled with reports from Heraklion that some 2,000 parachutists arrived during the first day (quoted by Wavell in his Despatch on Operations in the Middle East dated 5 Sept. 1941), together with the admission in *Einsatz Kreta* that the number landed was 'some 600 men less than had been intended'. Kurowski, p. 242, says 2,360

corn which covered much of the coastal plain. About a mile south-west of the crossed runways were two small conical hills, the evocative 'Charlies', an 'Australian slang term', as the *Australian War History* soberly observes, 'meaning breasts'. Another mile inland was the somewhat larger Apex Hill. Four miles south of the harbour, drowsing in the sunshine of a warm upland valley, were the ruins of Knossos.

Chappel had been ordered by Freyberg to defend the airfield and the town, with its harbour, from the air and sea. At the same time, he was to be ready to support the Australians at Retimo if they should become cut off from the west. 'Everything must be done,' Freyberg had told him, 'to ensure that communications with us are maintained'.[6]

Brigade Headquarters, protected by a small guard of armed gunners, had been established north of the road and west of Buttercup Field. The Black Watch were dug in upon the perimeter of the airfield itself, and the Australians established upon the two Charlies, which they had embellished with sangars of rock and stone. In the town itself, facing west and south, were the three Greek battalions, with the York and Lancs close behind them. The Leicesters, in reserve, filled the small gap south of Brigade Headquarters. The whole force lay within a defensive perimeter fortified in depth. Communication was likely to be as primitive as elsewhere in Crete, once the telephone lines had gone. But this need not prove so grave a handicap as in the west. The whole of the prospective battle area lay within three miles of the command post.

Chappel's orders were simple. The anti-aircraft gunners would reveal themselves only when they saw fit, in general reserving their efforts for the main attack. They would then fire not only upon the planes in the air, but also upon any troop-carriers which might succeed in landing upon the airfield. All other troops were ordered to remain concealed until the preliminary air bombardment had ended. Once the enemy began to land they were to be 'attacked immediately'.[7] Organized counter-attack upon the airfield would be carried out by the Leicesters, and by the tanks which lay hidden close to it.

As the planes swept across the coast, Nicholls and his three

[6] DP

[7] Maj. T. V. Rabbidge to author 23 Sept. 1961. The 14th Infantry Brigade War Diary was lost in the fighting

lieutenants dashed across Buttercup Field to one of the Charlies. Breathlessly, they scrambled up the side and wedged themselves among the rocks.

Here they stayed 'for an hour or more', as Nicholls remembered later, watching

> . . . one of the finest air displays of the whole war. From our perch the whole of Heraklion and its defences were laid out before us. The view we had of the town, the batteries position and the airfield, was of the wicket from the top of the pavilion at Lords. We watched speechless as bomb after bomb was dropped on the Black Watch around the airfield, on the Bofors positions, and what we now know were dummy aircraft round the airfield. Each and every bomb seemed to hit its target, and each one sent a pang of anguish through us as we watched. There was no opposition, and when the bombs had dropped, the pilots cruised around. Many times we heard planes flying below us, and it seemed as though we could stretch out a hand and touch the pilot as he went by. After the break in the bombing the strains of the 'general alarm' on a bugle floated up to us from the Black Watch position. Two of us said we had heard it, and two said they had not, but the truth was that none of us wanted to hear it, as the bugle call was for action stations in the event of an enemy parachute landing, and here we were, company commander and three platoon commanders, a good mile away from our positions and quite half of the distance to be covered over the bare open buttercup field.[8]

They got back safely, to be greeted by their colonel who had also been enjoying his afternoon, relaxing in his bath in a Heraklion hotel; fortunately it had not been difficult to find him; only one hotel in the town could offer so luxurious an amenity.

Despite the impression which it made upon Nicholls and his platoon commanders, this preliminary air attack had lacked the weight and concentration of the onslaught in the west; very few casualties had been caused; the troops remained unshaken; there was little dust. Within a few minutes, as the drone of the departing bombers lessened and died, the patchwork of cornfield, vineyard and buttercup was again bright in the late afternoon sun.

At this moment, looking out to sea, a soldier of the Leicesters saw 'a host of little flashes of light, like the twinkling of stars. It was the sunlight on the "blisters" of the Ju 52 parachute aircraft. Soon the snaking lines of troop-carriers could be seen flying

[8] Underhill, *The Royal Leicestershire Regiment*, p. 55, Maj. A. W. D. Nicholls

low over the sea . . . quite suddenly the air seemed filled with parachutes.'[9]

As at Maleme and Canea the men who watched felt admiration as well as awe.

A young Australian wrote later:

I was spellbound by the futuristic nature and the magnificence of the scene before me. . . . It wasn't long before they were coming in along about five miles of coastline and as far as the eye could see they were still coming. They were about 100 feet above the water and rose to about 250 feet as they came over the coastline, dropped their parachutists, dived again and turned back to sea. I saw many Huns drop like stones when their parachutes failed to open. . . . I saw one carried out to sea trailing behind the plane, with his parachute caught in the tail.[10]

And then they heard the guns. A regular pounding mingled with the roar of the planes. From their scarred emplacements, better hidden and better controlled than at Maleme, the Bofors were at last enjoying the reward of their long patience and deception.

If ever there was a fillip to morale [says Nicholls], this was it. These guns which we had seen battered twice a day for the past two days were not out of action but had merely waited patiently for their target, and there it was sitting on the end of their barrel. The sound of these guns put life into us all and we cheered. We had only to wait a short time before one Junkers was hit just as it was about to disgorge its load. It crashed. Perhaps the death of those parachutists was preferable to the death suffered by those who came down with their parachutes on fire, going faster and faster as they neared the earth, only to be followed up by our platoons as they landed. One had the misfortune to land on top of company headquarters as we lay concealed within some standing corn. He drifted slowly to earth as I watched. When he was about ten feet from the ground seven or eight Tigers, each with bayonet fixed, rose and approached him. That was the first time I had heard a man scream with fright.[11]

The *Black Watch Regimental History* makes clear the extent of the German catastrophe.

This was the moment so long awaited, but the scale of it, the fullness of the sky with the black blobs and white canopies exceeded the maddest dreams. . . . Every soldier picked his swaying target and fired and picked another and fired again. Many Germans landed dead

[9] Underhill, *The Royal Leicestershire Regiment*, p. 56
[10] Long, p. 281 [11] Underhill, *The Royal Leicestershire Regiment*, Maj. A. W. D. Nicholls

many were riddled as they hung in trees and telephone wires, some tangled with each other and fell like stones, one was cut up by another aircraft, many fired their tommy-guns at their enemies beneath them as they floated down, many arrived with their hands up in token surrender – and then threw the grenades concealed in them as soon as they touched the ground. Of the first flight to drop, all of whom came down by the Charlies or the Greek barracks, it seems that the majority were killed in the air or in the first few minutes. . . . Those who had fallen in the turnip fields were running about madly to get at the cylinders which held their weapons, and they offered easy targets. Others had fallen in vineyards and cornfields and were now calling to each other to establish contact. A good number of the aircraft were going down in flames; an entry in the War diary at 7.7 p.m. records 'Eight of them at one time'.[12]

For more than three hours the drop continued. By 7.30 p.m. about 2,000 men had left the planes, most of them falling into a murderous fire from all arms.

Worst of all was the fate of II Battalion which had been set to capture the airfield. Of the eastern companies, falling close to the Black Watch Command Post, only one of the officers survived, with about sixty of his men. The western group was 'destroyed within twenty minutes', overwhelmed by a storm of small arms fire from the Australians and the improvised infantry near Brigade Headquarters. Those who were still alive, says *Operation Crete*, then 'succumbed to the immediate attack of several light and medium tanks'. At 6.15 p.m. the Leicesters were sent by Chappel to comb the area of Buttercup Field. Only five men, the survivors of two companies, succeeded in rejoining their colonel from west of the airfield by swimming back along the coast. Within an hour the losses of II Battalion had reached twelve officers and 300 men killed, and another eight officers and 100 men wounded.

The two battalions which landed west and south of Heraklion also suffered heavily in fierce encounters with the Greeks outside the city, and with a company of the York and Lancs, under Captain Rabbidge, which had been brought forward to line the west wall of the town. 'We were on top of the wall,' Rabbidge was to write in 1961, 'and the Germans got up to the moat – only the boiling oil was missing'.[13]

Small parties of parachutists succeeded in forcing an entry

---

[12] Fergusson, *The Black Watch and the King's Enemies*, p. 79

[13] Maj. T. V. Rabbidge, letter to author 23 Sept. 1961

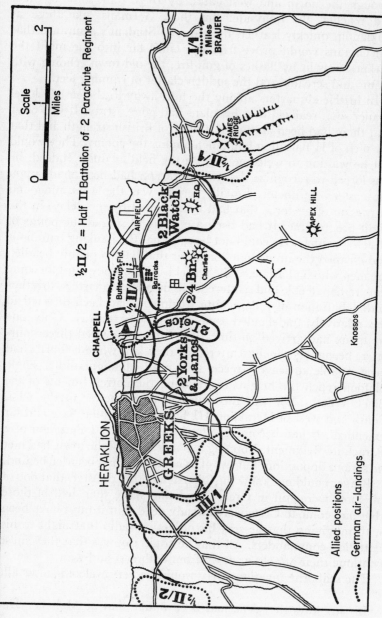

7. Heraklion: Evening, 20 May

through the north and west gates. By 10.30 p.m. some of them had reached the quayside. But these Germans, like those at Alikianou, quickly learned the value of Student's assurance that the Cretans would prove friendly. Until far into the night the darkness was lit by flashes of gun-fire, the old town echoing with shouts and screams and the sudden clatter of running feet.

In his Headquarters among the hills away to the east Colonel Brauer soon realized that his plans had gone astray. It was clear that there had been an underestimate of British strength and that the men of II Battalion had fallen among the enemy. They would not be waiting to welcome him on the field at dusk. Indeed, he was forced to recognize that no impression had been made upon the eastern perimeter. Equally serious was the weakening and dispersion of his force that had been caused by the delays in the flight programme. It had been a mistake to spread the points of attack so widely. He could not be sure that the flanking battalions had escaped the immediate slaughter that had so plainly befallen the men who had attacked the airfield. At best they must for some time remain feeble and scattered. His own Headquarters, together with I Battalion of 1 Parachute Regiment, had been directed to the relatively undefended zone east of the runway. Only one company had arrived on time. Two others appeared three hours later, becoming widely scattered as they fell, while a fourth had been unable to leave Greece. Not until midnight did a single platoon reach the heights overlooking the entrenchments of the Black Watch. Nor was the situation much better in the west. South and west of Heraklion III Battalion, landing 'late and far extended', [14] had become engaged immediately. I Battalion of 2 Parachute Regiment, dropping two miles west of the town, had met no serious opposition. But two of its companies had been left behind.

Brauer could not know the full extent of the disaster, that 600 of his force were still in Greece, and that more than half of those that had come to Crete were already dead. But it must have been with misgiving that he sent his orders by radio that night to his battalion commanders. All that he could say was that they must continue their attacks at dawn from both east and west.

The seaborne invasion party would be very welcome after all.

In two ways the scene had been unlike that at Maleme. The parachutists had nowhere fallen abruptly in large numbers, and

[14] *Einsatz Kreta*, Battle Report of XI Air Corps

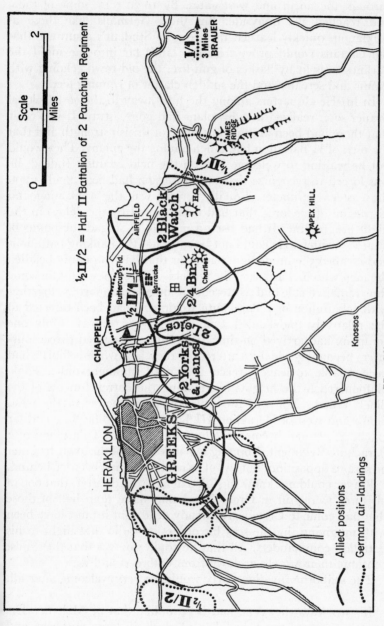

HERAKLION

CHAPPELL

GREEKS

2 Yorks & Lancs

2 Leics

2 Black Watch

½ II/1

Buttercup Fld.

AIRFIELD

Barracks

2·4 Bn

H.Q.

I/II/1

AMES RIDGE

BRAUER

I/4
3 Miles

III/1

Knossos

Charles

APEX HILL

½ II/2

——— Allied positions

········· German air-landings

Scale

0   1   2
Miles

7. Heraklion: Evening, 20 May

through the north and west gates. By 10.30 p.m. some of them had reached the quayside. But these Germans, like those at Alikianou, quickly learned the value of Student's assurance that the Cretans would prove friendly. Until far into the night the darkness was lit by flashes of gun-fire, the old town echoing with shouts and screams and the sudden clatter of running feet.

In his Headquarters among the hills away to the east Colonel Brauer soon realized that his plans had gone astray. It was clear that there had been an underestimate of British strength and that the men of II Battalion had fallen among the enemy. They would not be waiting to welcome him on the field at dusk. Indeed, he was forced to recognize that no impression had been made upon the eastern perimeter. Equally serious was the weakening and dispersion of his force that had been caused by the delays in the flight programme. It had been a mistake to spread the points of attack so widely. He could not be sure that the flanking battalions had escaped the immediate slaughter that had so plainly befallen the men who had attacked the airfield. At best they must for some time remain feeble and scattered. His own Headquarters, together with I Battalion of 1 Parachute Regiment, had been directed to the relatively undefended zone east of the runway. Only one company had arrived on time. Two others appeared three hours later, becoming widely scattered as they fell, while a fourth had been unable to leave Greece. Not until midnight did a single platoon reach the heights overlooking the entrenchments of the Black Watch. Nor was the situation much better in the west. South and west of Heraklion III Battalion, landing 'late and far extended', [14] had become engaged immediately. I Battalion of 2 Parachute Regiment, dropping two miles west of the town, had met no serious opposition. But two of its companies had been left behind.

Brauer could not know the full extent of the disaster, that 600 of his force were still in Greece, and that more than half of those that had come to Crete were already dead. But it must have been with misgiving that he sent his orders by radio that night to his battalion commanders. All that he could say was that they must continue their attacks at dawn from both east and west.

The seaborne invasion party would be very welcome after all.

In two ways the scene had been unlike that at Maleme. The parachutists had nowhere fallen abruptly in large numbers, and

[14] *Einsatz Kreta*, Battle Report of XI Air Corps

few had been unopposed. There was no group to correspond with those 1,000 men who had arrived unseen among the sand dunes west of the Tavronitis.

By nightfall the main defences had been cleared. Small parties of the enemy still lurked near the docks and in the town, but the airfield was secure and no attempt to crash-land had been made by the troop-carriers. Already a thousand enemy dead had been counted within the perimeter.

The evening's work had demonstrated the value of immediate counter-attack at platoon and section level. Rabbidge noted that it was 'the excellence of the corporals and their leadership'[15] that had made the success possible. With no chance to collect themselves, almost half the parachutists had been destroyed within the first few minutes of leaving their planes. And at relatively small cost. An Australian company had killed ninety for the loss of only three dead. But among the fallen, to the second of two wounds, was Young of the Leicesters and the Scotland rugby team, who earlier that afternoon had taken cover with his friends on the Charlie to watch the preliminary air attack.

There would be more hard fighting next day. In the east the sky was lit repeatedly by flares as the Germans sought to make contact with each other, and from the town the sounds of bitter conflict continued unbroken. Communication with the west along the coast road was blocked. And over all there hung the question of how many parachutists there were still to come. Yet Chappel cannot have failed to be aware of the surge of confidence among his men. The Black Watch were 'tired but delighted with themselves and with the feeling that the months of heart-breaking preparation, the digging, the incessant improvement of position had been so utterly worthwhile'.[16]

Against his better judgement, Freyberg had been persuaded not to destroy the airstrip at Retimo.[17] This was now to be the second objective of Student's Centre Group. He had chosen to launch upon it two of the battalions that had landed across the Corinth Canal augmented by some strong ancillary detachments, in all some 1,500 men[18] commanded by the fifty-two-year-old Colonel

---

[15] Maj. T. V. Rabbidge to author 23 Sept. 1961

[16] Fergusson, *The Black Watch and the King's Enemies*, p. 81   [17] See Chapter 7

[18] The figure 1,700 given by Wavell in his Despatch is probably slightly too high. Kurowski, p. 242, says 1,380, and Long 1,500; the details in *Einsatz Kreta* accord with this estimate

Sturm, an arrogant character who had been in action with the parachutists both in Northern Holland and at Corinth.

In drawing up his plan of attack, Sturm had divided his force into three groups. About 550 men, including two companies of I Battalion of 2 Parachute Rifle Regiment together with a Machine-gun Company, under Major Kroh, were 'to land east of the airfield and capture it'.[19] A larger group, based on III Battalion of the same regiment, with a Machine-gun Company and heavy weapons, about 800 men commanded by Captain Wiedemann, would drop three miles to the west in order to take the town from the east. Sturm himself was protected by a Headquarters Company about 200 strong. Like Brauer, he had no gliders. Only 'weak resistance' was expected. He should quickly be able to detach some of his men west to join up with the rest of Centre Group at Suda.

This formidable assault was directed upon the garrison which had been entrusted to Ian Campbell, the young Australian Lieutenant-Colonel who a few weeks before had been a major in the Western Desert. In addition to his two Australian battalions, each reduced to a strength of just over 600 men, he had 90 Australian gunners and two platoons of machine-guns. There were also 800 Cretan Police, a well disciplined and effective force, together with about 2,300 Greeks, many without rifles, and few of them carrying as much as ten rounds of ammunition.

The Australians had their small arms. In every other respect their equipment was inadequate. 'There were only five rounds for each anti-tank rifle,' says the *Australian War History*, and 'eighty bombs for each of the four 3-inch mortars. The medium machine-gunners had but sixteen belts of ammunition to a gun. Uniforms and boots were in need of repair'.[20] Even for the rifles there was a shortage of ammunition. And, as everywhere in Crete, there were not enough grenades, and very little signals apparatus.

On arriving at Retimo, Campbell had faced the same tactical problems as Puttick and Chappel. The outcome of the battle must depend upon possession of the low foothills which abutted upon the narrow coastal plain.

The airfield lay south of the road, about five hundred yards from the beach and five miles east of the town. Curling around its eastern limit was a steep broken plateau which Campbell named Hill A. From here, branching away at right angles, a narrow ridge

[19] *Einsatz Kreta*, Battle Report of XI Air Corps   [20] Long, p. 257

Fighting in the dust at Maleme

(Imperial War Museum)

Parachutists attack at Maleme

(from Kurowski, *Der Kampf um Kreta*)

The Bridge at Maleme; Hill 107 in background; early June 1961

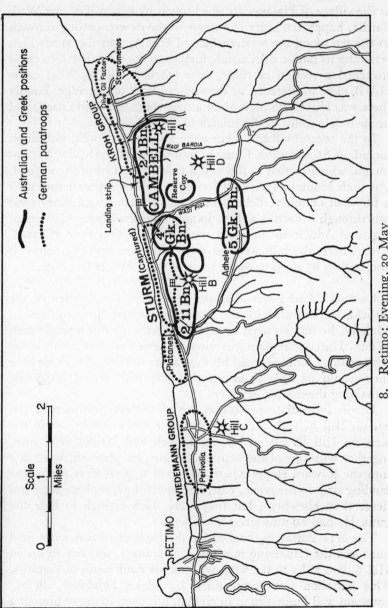

Australian and Greek positions

German paratroops

Scale

Miles

0   1   2

RETIMO

WIEDEMANN GROUP

Hill C

Perivolia

Hill B

2/11 Bn.

4 Gk. Bn.

STURM (Captured)

Plátanes

5 Gk. Bn.

Adhele

KROH GROUP

Landing strip

Reserve Coy.

CAMBELL

2/1 Bn.

Hill A

Hill D

WADI BARDIA

WADI PIGI

Olive Oil Factory

Stavroménos

8. Retimo: Evening, 20 May

led three miles to the west, immediately south of the road, as far as the village of Platanes. It was broken by two gullies, the Wadi Bardia, happy reminder of success in the desert, cutting through to the sea along the western face of Hill A, and the Wadi Pigi, retaining its native title, a mile further to the west. Between them stretched a section of ridge, now labelled Hill D. Next came Hill B, close to Platanes, at the western limit of the ridge. Finally there was Hill C, no more than a mile short of Retimo itself, and immediately south of the suburb of Perivolia.

In the coastal villages there were a number of solid buildings, including St. George's Church, south-west of Perivolia. Stavromenos, which nestled in the hills a mile to the east of the airfield, was built around its olive oil factory, a substantial structure with a fifty-foot chimney. Behind the coastal ridge a subsidiary road ran through a narrow valley, joining the small house clusters of Pigi and Adhele to the coast road at a junction near Platanes. Everywhere, the hills were covered with trees and undergrowth and broken by steep terraces, some of them twenty feet high.

Campbell had given absolute priority to the defence of the airfield. In contrast with the problem that had faced Andrew at Maleme, he had no need to expose directly upon it a single man or gun. The coastal plain was nowhere more than half a mile wide. This enabled him to spread his men along the foothills. From here they would be able to sweep the field with aimed fire while remaining themselves in cover.

For its immediate protection, he placed one company of the 2/1 on Hill A, with the remaining companies strung out to the west on Hill D. Six of his old French and Italian field guns, together with one of the heavy machine-gun platoons, were dug into the forward slopes where they had a good view across the landing strip to the north, east, and west; the trees here were less dense than elsewhere, but they were thick enough to hide the guns. He had no anti-aircraft artillery.

The 2/11 Battalion, backed by the support of two more field guns and the remaining machine-gun platoon, was drawn up on Hill B, two miles to the west, with its left flank south of Platanes. This battalion was commanded by Major Sandover, an accountant and businessman in civilian life, soon to prove himself a dauntless and resourceful soldier.

A battalion of Greeks filled in the gap between the Australians, while the rest of the Greeks and the two Infantry Tanks remained hidden behind the ridge. He left the town of Retimo to the Cretan Police.

Communications remained primitive. There were telephone lines to the companies, and a single cable between Hills A and B. But exchanges between the battalions were likely to depend upon runners. There was also a line to Force Headquarters. When this was lost there could be no contact with Canea except through the single radio transmitter. A reserve supply of food, sufficient to last for about ten days, had been established in a dump three miles to the south, at the end of the branch road that led into the hills.

Campbell decided to retain the command of his own battalion while taking charge of the whole garrison. Indeed he had little choice. The 2/1 was holding the vital area. Moreover, it was very short of officers; the second-in-command had been lost in Greece; others had been detached to help the Greeks; neither battalion could spare any officers to form a brigade staff.[21]

These handicaps in no way discouraged the Australians, who were the most battle experienced soldiers in the island. Their misfortunes during the unequal struggle in Greece had done nothing to destroy the confidence they had gained in the desert. At first, they had seen little immediate prospect of further fighting. And they had quickly grown tired of darning their socks. In their usual exuberant form, some of them had shown a tendency to brawl in the Retimo cafés while under the influence of the notorious *krassi*. They needed firm personal command. This they got from Campbell, who put the town out of bounds and set up small parties of military police.

It soon became clear that the Germans could not find them from the air. Among the luxuriant foliage on the terraces they were able to disappear as completely as snakes in a jungle. On 16 May aerial photographs found in a crashed reconnaissance plane showed that only one defence position had been identified. It was quickly changed. Movement on the roads in daylight remained difficult. Messerschmitts patrolled ceaselessly. But Campbell found that he could get round his posts successfully in a series of watchful bursts by motor-cycle. At night he returned to his command post on Hill D. Like Andrew at Maleme, he had chosen a position that looked down directly upon the airfield.

[21] Letter to the author, dated 5 May 1960, from Maj.-Gen. Ian Campbell

No doubt he would have been greatly interested to know the strength of the four German assault groups in relation to the British and Empire troops who were to meet them in the different Sectors. At Maleme, in the first encounter, the proportion of Germans to the New Zealanders of the 5th Brigade would be about four against five, rather greater than the proportion meeting the New Zealand Division as a whole. At Heraklion, the strength of the parachutists making their jump on the first day would be about half that of the men from Britain and Australia. Only at Retimo would the enemy outnumber by some hundreds the Australians who cheerfully awaited their arrival.

At 9 a.m. on 20 May a group of heavy Junkers flew low along the coast in the direction of Canea. The troops watched them with interest, deducing that the attack was beginning further west. For their own turn, they had to wait another seven hours. At 4 p.m. the terraced slopes were searched by a flight of about twenty Messerschmitts and light bombers. Again it was plain that the natural camouflage afforded almost complete protection.

No bombs had fallen among the Greeks. Nevertheless, there was now mounting tension among the raw levies between the two Australian battalions. A few of them began to move away up the ridge from their position in the centre of the line. Campbell at once sent across some of his N.C.Os. This proved effective. The Australians were able to lead their apprehensive allies back to their old positions, where they stayed with them.

At 4.15 p.m. it began. Troop-carrying planes began to stream in from the north. After crossing the coast a few miles to the east they turned and flew back along the beach, dropping their parachutists from a height of about four hundred feet. The guns blazed at them. Seven at once came down into the shingle. Others were enveloped in flames as they flinched away over the sea. By the end of an hour 161 had been counted. According to the German plan the whole operation should have been completed within a few minutes.

Again the Germans were handicapped by dispersion as much as by the prolongation of the drop. The eastern group was put down over a five mile scatter. Many of these parachutists were injured as they crashed into broken, rocky country. Only two companies fell as planned. These landed close to the eastern edge of the airfield. Here they were immediately engaged by the

Australians from Hill A. All the officers of one company were killed, including their commander, who had acquired fame for his part in the airborne action against Holland. Scrambling about the terraces, the survivors found it difficult to reach their weapon containers. But after about two hours they were joined by the eastern companies led by Major Kroh. And, by this time, they had been strengthened by some members of the western group who had overlapped their appointed landing area.

Hill A was now attacked by a German force which greatly out-numbered the single Australian company which had been set to hold it. On the broken summit, some two hundred by three hundred yards in size, there raged a series of fierce individual battles, each largely isolated from the others by the steep terraces and by the entanglement of rocks and trees. The seventy-five millimetre guns were lost, the gunners, as usual, having no rifles for their own defence. Nearly all the machine-gunners were killed. By 9 p.m. only three isolated infantry posts still held out on the northern slopes. The rest of the company, although strengthened by a platoon sent across by Campbell, had been forced back to the southern neck of the hill. Above the combatants, the German planes circled harmlessly, the pilots peering down in bewilder-ment, unable to distinguish any pattern in the anonymous flashes among the trees below.

Further west the second group found their enemies awaiting them with fervent anticipation. Many were killed as they fell into the vineyards across the front of the 2/11 Battalion. 'In one party of about twelve every man' was seen to have been 'riddled with bullets as he floated down'.[22] The Greeks now found their courage greatly fortified by the presence of their Australian N.C.Os. A small party of them, led by Corporal Smallwood, rushed forward to capture twenty Germans as they hit the ground. These eastern elements of Wiedemann's Group were soon 'mostly destroyed',[23] apart from those who managed to join Kroh at the foot of Hill A. But those who reached the ground alive quickly vanished among the thick cover. The defenders were forced to leave the protection of the rocks and slit trenches in order to attack them. Seeing this, Sandover drove forward with his whole line at dusk. By nightfall, he had taken eighty-four prisoners, some of whom gave him the comforting news that there were no more airborne troops to come; among his other accomplishments he could speak German.

[22] Long, p. 260   [23] *Einsatz Kreta*, Battle Report of XI Air Corps

Few of those parachutists who had come down within reach had survived. Most were scattered in small groups between the road and the sea.

Further down the coast, some hundreds of Wiedemann's troops had landed out of range of Sandover's weapons. They could be seen drawing together and moving towards Perivolia where they were to meet stout resistance from the Cretan Police. At the time it was thought that there were about 500 of them. Today it can be judged that they must have been somewhat fewer.

At 5.15 p.m., no more than an hour after the start of the battle, Campbell decided to commit his tanks to the task of clearing the airfield and harassing the Germans on Hill A. They set off down the Wadi Pigi before turning to the right, across the field and along the main road, to a position from which they could take the Germans from the north. But they fared no better than the tanks at Maleme. One became stuck in a gully on the edge of the airfield, and the other, after gaining the east side of Hill A and firing a few shots, fell into a wadi eight feet deep. Both crews were killed or captured.

There was now a danger that the Germans on Hill A might turn west. To meet this threat, Campbell brought up his reserve company to face them across the Wadi Bardia. This ensured that any further move would be exposed to fire from most of his own 2/1 Battalion. He knew well, however, that he could not afford to wait for this advantage. At the earliest possible moment he must recapture the hill itself.

At Retimo the onslaught had lacked the intensity of the attack launched upon the New Zealanders at Maleme. As at Heraklion, the preliminary air attack had been notably less severe, neither so heavy nor so well directed. It had caused no damage, and had raised no more than a few thin patches of dust to drift above the road. The parachutists had been plainly in sight from the start, and the landings prolonged and scattered.

But more significant than these failures in the German plan had been the manner in which Campbell had seized his opportunity. Unprejudiced by memories of the First World War, he had launched his men upon immediate counter-attack. From every side his troops had leapt upon those Germans who had reached the ground alive inside the lines of the defence. Within an hour he had committed his reserve, sending his tanks into the open across

the airfield. Here was a calculated risk bravely taken. The last of
the enemy troops had fallen only a few minutes earlier. Time
remained for many more to be dropped before nightfall. Yet he
had seen that any that might follow must be rendered the more
formidable by every German who remained in action to greet
them, and that if Hill A were to be lost, with it must soon go
control of the runway itself. He had therefore determined that this
was no time for half measures. Already the issue was for all or
none. In this reasoning there lay both courage and logic. Here
was the crucial dilemma which was reducing Hargest and Puttick
to hesitancy and impotence. Soon it would confront Chappel,
and ultimately Freyberg himself.

He had some reason for satisfaction. Many Germans had been
killed or taken, and there had been none of the promised attempts
to land troop-carriers. But the heights that overlooked the airfield
remained the key to the situation. And as darkness fell the most
important of them was largely in the hands of the enemy. Moreover his tanks had failed, a sad disappointment to those of his men
who had seen them in action at Bardia.

He had been unable to discuss his difficulties with Freyberg.
Inevitably the telephone line to Canea had gone dead. At 6 p.m.,
in a radio message, he had asked for assistance, explaining that he
was 'heavily engaged on both flanks' and would 'appreciate
help'.[24] He was hoping for support from the rest of his brigade
which was still stationed, so far as he was aware, twenty miles to
the west at Georgeoupolis. He had no illusions. Although, by
then, the battle had not lasted two hours, he well understood that
his situation was critical. Another six hours were to pass before he
received a reply. But by midnight he heard that he could expect
no reinforcement. From Freyberg an answer had come at last
over the radio telephone. It said simply: 'Regret unable to send
help. Good luck.'[25]

He was on his own. If the situation were to be saved he would
have to do it himself. Delay could only make the danger worse.
He resolved that he would collect every man that he could find,
and with them counter-attack on Hill A at dawn.

---

[24] Letter to author, dated 5 May 1960, from Maj.-Gen. Ian Campbell
[25] Ibid.

12

The First Night: 20–21 May

That morning Freyberg had watched the developing scene
from a spur above his Headquarters on the Akrotiri Peninsula.
To the west he could follow the line of the coast as far as the
heights of Platanias and Theodhoroi Island. Above the haze the
sky was clear, and etched against the blue were the planes.

I stood out on the hill [he wrote later] with other members of my
staff enthralled by the magnitude of the operation. While we were
still watching the bombers we suddenly became aware of a greater
throbbing in the moments of comparative quiet, and looking out to
sea with the glasses, I picked out hundreds of slow-moving troop-
carriers with the loads we were expecting. First we watched them
circle counter clockwise over Maleme aerodrome and then, when
they were only a few hundred feet above the ground, as if by magic
white specks mixed with other colours floated slowly to earth.[1]

As he returned to his quarry six gliders, making for their
objectives on the Akrotiri Peninsula, swept in silence above
his head.

Throughout the anxious day he sought to follow the course of
the battle. To guide him he had little more than his eyes, and his
own seasoned instinct. From the first he was tormented by the
numbing failure of his communications. Most of the telephone
lines had been damaged by the bombing. Others had been cut
by the parachutists. Since few of the battalions, and none of
the companies, possessed a wireless set vital messages were being
delayed for many hours on their way to the battalion and
brigade commanders. Sometimes, as was happening at Maleme,
they failed to get through even by runner. In the end a tangled
profusion of information reached his amateur staff at Force
Headquarters, many of the facts already disparaged or ignored,
and the wildest rumours accepted as truth.

His despatches to the Middle East reflected the day's alarms. At

[1] Long, p. 221

nine o'clock he signalled that the attack had begun. German troops were landing by parachute and glider. More were approaching as he ended the message. He could not tell how many. Two hours later he believed that about a thousand of the enemy had dropped in the Canea-Suda area. Another wave could be seen in the sky south of Canea. And now there was a reference to parachutists landing among the foothills south-west of Retimo. The origin of this rumour remains obscure. It was false, but it well illustrates the problem that confronted him. That morning this report must have seemed no less convincing than all the rest.

The first news from the New Zealand Division began to come in at about 9.30 a.m. Freyberg heard that parachutists had dropped on the airfield, and within the lines of the 22nd and 23rd Battalions. 'Smoke and noise and broken cable'[2] made it difficult to know exactly what was happening, but the 23rd appeared to be in no trouble. There was a suggestion that the Germans might be wearing khaki battledress. A few minutes later Puttick added that 'troop-carriers' were thought to be 'landing three miles south Maleme and in river bed west of aerodrome'.[3] Almost immediately, at 9.50 a.m., he confirmed this message: 'Large number troop-carriers reported landing under mountains SW of reservoir.'[4] And within an hour: 'Germans are clearing area for troop-carriers vicinity 1,000 yds. of Prison.'[5]

Parachutists had indeed fallen among the 22nd and 23rd Battalions. But of the rest not a word was true. Above all, the 'troop-carriers' were gliders, apart perhaps from one or two of the seven Junkers brought down that day by gunfire at various points along the coast between Maleme and Suda.[6] Here was the myth, still preserved in many accounts of the battle, that was to grow and flourish in the cause of the enemy, its persistence reflecting the conviction with which it was believed at the time. In a book on Crete, written at the request of the Government and published by Her Majesty's Stationery Office in 1952, Christopher Buckley says of these first hours, 'It can hardly be contended that the failure adequately to wreck Maleme itself was itself of decisive significance . . . the Germans were landing their troop-carriers in the bed of the Tavronitis on its western side'.[7] And later, referring again to this same morning, 'Meanwhile troop-carrying aircraft

[2] New Zealand Division War Diary   [3] Ibid.   [4] Ibid.   [5] Ibid.
[6] Report by Air Fleet IV, 20 Nov. 1941, *The Invasion of Crete*   [7] Buckley, p. 170

continued to land on the beaches. Nearly forty had come in by midday'.[8] The danger, he adds, was 'not at first appreciated . . . because it was difficult to realize the extent to which the enemy was prepared to go . . . in crash-landing carriers on the beaches or elsewhere'.[9] On reading this the Editor-in-Chief of the *New Zealand War Histories* made the comment: 'If the Germans chose to crash-land all over the place what could the defence do about it more than was done?'[10]

Thus, eleven years after the battle, historians were still failing to distinguish between gliders and powered aircraft. In fact all the gliders had been engaged within the first few minutes. No engined plane had landed by design anywhere on Crete, nor was any to do so during the first twenty-four hours of fighting.

But if these misconceptions were to endure so long after the war how much less was the hope that the truth could reach Freyberg amid all the confusions of the time. The Intelligence report had suggested that the 'Junkers 52 were likely to attempt landings upon the airfields, within an hour . . . irrespective of the success or failure of the parachutists'.[11] That they might attempt the same thing in open country had been thought unlikely. But Freyberg himself had always felt that they would try it. And now, already, he had reason to believe that he was right. For him these reports must have held particular significance. They lent impressive weight to his assumption that the airfields themselves, although their loss must 'jeopardize the defence', were of no paramount importance.

Next he heard alarming news from closer at hand. The 7th General Hospital had been seized, and 'parachutists were pushing east along the road to Canea'. This threat quickly came to nothing. Early in the afternoon he learnt that the hospital site had been reoccupied, and that the situation throughout the Canea-Suda area was well under control. Instead there came another uncertainty – the fate of the King of Greece and his ministers. Parachutists and gliders had been seen to come down close to the house where they had been staying. Nobody knew whether they had been able to reach the shelter of the mountains. Three days later, the royal party was to leave Crete from the south coast. But by this time Freyberg was to find himself absorbed in greater anxieties.

[8] Buckley, p. 183   [9] Ibid., p. 184   [10] DP, Kippenberger comments on Buckley Draft
[11] See above, p. 104

Puttick was underestimating the weight of the enemy attack. At 1.25 p.m. he signalled to Force Headquarters:

Captured officer prisoner reports that parachute landing in Duke (New Zealand Division) area made by 1,500 men and that they are very disturbed by reception they got.[12]

In giving this number, less than a third of the true figure, the German officer, whether by accident or design, was serving his side well. Nevertheless Puttick could have improved upon this assessment. The 19th Battalion had counted 1,000 parachutists in the Prison Valley, Andrew had seen 400, and further substantial groups were known to have come down near Dhaskaliana, east of Galatas, and on the Hospital Peninsula. What Puttick could not know was that another 1,000 men had landed unseen beyond the Tavronitis.

By the middle of the afternoon uncertainty about the enemy strength was increasing, but Freyberg knew that lodgments had been made at Maleme, and in the vicinity of the Prison, where, so he had been told, the Germans were building a landing strip. It can be supposed that he was already thinking of counter-attack in the Prison Valley. He had restored the 4th Brigade to the New Zealand Division in anticipation of just such a situation. Indeed, something of his feeling appeared in a signal that he sent to Cairo reporting that the enemy had begun to prepare a 'landing-ground' in the valley north-east of Alikianou. He was 'taking action'.

But he did not intervene directly. Stewart had not been relaying an instruction when he attempted to persuade Puttick to commit the 4th Brigade in the Prison Valley. He had sought, without succeeding, to obtain a direct order for immediate counter-attack, but 'General Freyberg would not issue orders that the Brigade was to be used for such an attack. He preferred to make the Brigade available and leave it to Divisional Command how and when to employ it'.[13]

After the war Puttick was to write that although he had been in constant touch with Freyberg throughout the day he had heard 'no suggestion' that the Prison area should be attacked, and that if the General had thought such an attack desirable it was 'most unlikely' that he would not have mentioned it, or indeed 'ordered

[12] New Zealand Division War Diary
[13] DP, Narrative by Brig. K. L. Stewart

it'.[14] Inglis, too, was to maintain that, in the course of conversation with Freyberg long afterwards, he had come to believe
that the General had not been in favour of using the 4th Brigade
in the Valley.[15]

These impressions should not be allowed to obscure the salient
fact that Freyberg had handed over its control. Even less than
Puttick he had gathered no hint of the threat that was developing
at Maleme. Here at least, if nowhere else, all seemed well. Later
he admitted, 'It can be argued that we might have succeeded
in re-establishing our hold on the Maleme aerodrome on the
night of the 20th with an all-in attack. Unfortunately, owing to
faulty communications and other causes, we did not know the full
damage that had been done.'[16] But this does not mean that he
had been content that the brigade should do nothing.[17] He had felt
that Puttick was better placed to decide upon the manner in
which it should intervene. In 1950 he told the New Zealand War
Historians, 'When I released the reserve (to) General Puttick
I envisaged his using them for an immediate counter-attack'.[18]

He was to learn with dismay that two battalions, and most of
the tanks, had spent the day without stirring from the olive groves
west of Canea Bridge.

Perhaps he should have remembered that Puttick had all the
professional soldier's inclination to wait for orders, and might
therefore be reluctant to accept at its face value the heavy
responsibility entailed in the control of the island's only reserve.
No doubt he came to regret his reluctance to insist that the whole
of the 4th Brigade should move that afternoon against the biggest
collection of Germans within reach.

Why, at least, did he not intervene as evening approached, and
it became clear that Puttick had sent no orders to Inglis? It is
possible that he was restrained by his special relationship with the
New Zealand Division, the formation which he was to command
for most of the war, dedicating to it the allegiance which had
called him out of retirement. From the first it had been agreed
that the senior officers should be allowed a high degree of independence; indeed this understanding was later to play a big part
in their success. If, therefore, he should now betray any particular

---

[14] DP, Puttick comments on Davin Draft
[15] Ibid., Inglis comments on Davin Draft
[16] DP, Freyberg comments on Long Draft, 5 Dec. 1949   [17] Davin, p. 165
[18] Ibid., Freyberg comments on Davin Draft, 1952 (undated)

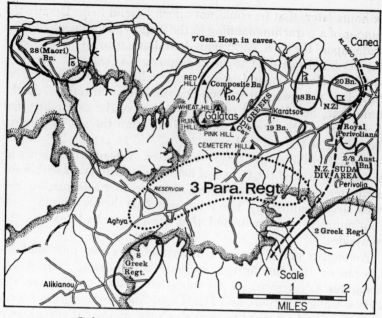

9. Galatas and Prison Valley: Evening, 21 May

concern with the New Zealanders he must weaken the authority of the man who was standing in for him. Puttick and his officers would be quick to recognize any such tendency; might already subconsciously be on the look-out for it. There was thus good reason for him to feel that he should preserve some detachment from his old friends. It was an attitude that was to have much bearing upon the battle in Crete.

Soon after 4 p.m. he learnt that parachutists were falling upon Retimo and Heraklion, about one regiment strong, so he believed, 'in each place'. He could not yet know that they had been delayed, and were arriving in scattered and reduced packets. The reports told of desperate fighting in both Sectors.

By 6 p.m. Campbell had already told him that the Australians at Retimo were 'heavily engaged'[19] on both sides; reinforcement was needed. This was disconcerting news. He was well aware that in numbers and equipment this Sector was the weakest of all. It can only have been after much painful consideration that he decided,

[19] Letter to the author, 5 May 1960

six hours later, that he could not afford to send help. Despite the rumour of a parachute landing in the vicinity, no attack had been made upon the two Australian battalions near Georgeoupolis. But he dared not send them to Retimo. No doubt he felt that, with the New Zealand 4th Brigade already handed over to Puttick, it was essential to keep this small force in reserve. At the same time, he remained constantly aware of the possibility that the enemy might attempt to disembark from the sea in Almiros Bay between Retimo and Suda.

From Heraklion the news was better. Towards midnight, he heard that most of the Germans had been cleared from within the perimeter defences. Nevertheless, this cheering information had been accompanied by the admission that heavy fighting was continuing in the town, and that the enemy had reached the quaysides.

Among so much that was uncertain there was one solid re-assurance; the Intelligence estimate was proving remarkably accurate. As foreseen, the Germans had landed at Maleme, the Prison Valley, Retimo, and Heraklion. And nowhere else. More-over, they had attacked in very much the manner that had been expected – except in one important detail. They had apparently made no attempt to crash-land upon the airfields. But this was a point that Freyberg did not appreciate. Indeed he was probably not aware of it, although direct questioning to Heraklion and Retimo might have made it plain enough. Such reluctance on the part of the Germans was highly significant. He might have deduced from it that they would be unable to land upon runways that remained swept by infantry fire.

He did not reach this conclusion. Nor did he perceive the dilemma in which the attackers must now be placed if their plan should depend upon the capture of an airfield. Indeed his im-pression was entirely in the other direction. All the failures of his information, in particular the fact that gliders were being mistaken for powered aircraft, were tending to prolong in his mind the view that the enemy would be able to operate at little disadvantage even without the possession of a prepared landing-ground.

What he did know was that the Germans had as yet captured no vital objective, although many thousands had landed during the day. Already it was certain that a great number had been killed or wounded, while losses among the defenders had been

much less. But if there was reason here for satisfaction there was
none for confidence. It seemed that Campbell's two weakened
battalions at Retimo might already be breaking up. And close at
hand there was the threat from the Prison Valley. It is not certain
that he had yet seen a copy of the pessimistic message sent by
Kippenberger to Puttick at 7 p.m.; many of the records kept at
Force Headquarters have been lost. But at this time he still had
good communication with the New Zealand Division. It seems
likely, therefore, that before midnight he must have learnt at least
the gist of what Kippenberger had reported. And here was this
trusted and resolute officer expressing the fear that his improvised
10th Brigade would be unable to hold any further attack in the
morning. Even the key point at Galatas might have to be abandoned. In similar fashion Haig had signalled to Sir John French,
on 26 August 1914, that the position of his 1st Corps was 'very
critical',[20] although in fact it was scarcely in contact with the
enemy, at a time when the 2nd Corps, on his left at Le Cateau,
was closely threatened by six infantry divisions and a Cavalry
Corps; as at that grim moment of the retreat from Mons, the effect
of Kippenberger's fears was to attract attention to the wrong place.

Only from the 5th Brigade had the news been uniformly good.
The messages passed on by Puttick from Hargest had radiated
confidence throughout the day. There had been a great slaughter
of parachutists east of the airfield. The 22nd were said to be engaged
in some fighting on the perimeter, but Andrew had estimated that
only 100 parachutists had landed on the field itself, with no more
than a further 150 west of the river. There should be no difficulty
here. By a singular stroke of fortune, so it appeared, the Germans
had not discovered that undefended gap west of the Tavronitis
which had caused so much concern. No doubt they knew all
about it now. But it seemed reasonable to hope that any further
attack delivered from that quarter would find the 5th Brigade
increasingly confident and secure. Not surprisingly, Freyberg
'did not realize that the aerodrome was in danger'.[21]

He understood well enough that the margin of safety was
narrow in the battle as a whole. At 10 p.m. he sent to Cairo a
despatch that was touched with misgiving:

Today has been a hard one. We have been hard pressed. So far
I believe we hold the aerodromes at Maleme, Heraklion, Retimo, and

[20] Terraine, p. 87   [21] DP, Freyberg comments on Davin Draft, 1952 (undated)

the two harbours. Margin by which we hold them is bare one and it
would be wrong of me to paint optimistic picture.[22]

The fighting had been very heavy, but large numbers of Germans
had been killed. The scale of the air onslaught had been severe,
and communications were very difficult.

At this moment Second-Lieutenant Cox, one of his staff officers,
appeared with a captured German document. Cox had been a
journalist in civilian life. After his arrival from Greece he had
brought out two numbers of *Crete News*. But that morning,
with the beginning of the attack, he had joined Freyberg's improvised intelligence staff. While looking through a bundle of
German documents captured during the day, he had come
suddenly upon a faded undercopy of the Operation Order for
3 Parachute Regiment. Fortunately he could read German,
sufficiently at least to show him the significance of this find. He
took it at once to the General's dug-out, and with the aid of a
torch, missing out here and there a word that he did not understand, he read out a rough translation.[23]

The Order was dated 18 May. It gave a summary of the
German objectives, revealing the fact that the attack was to be
carried out by XI Air Corps, supported by VIII Air Corps. A
'Central Group' was to take Canea and Suda with 3 Parachute
Regiment in a first wave, and Retimo with a second wave, also in
brigade strength, which was to come in eight hours later to
occupy the town and airfield before using captured transport to
move against Suda and Canea from the east. A Western Group
was to drop at Maleme as part of the first attack, before joining
the Central Group. Reinforcements would arrive by sea in the
Maleme area. The local objectives of 3 Parachute Regiment were
then given in detail, with the exact instructions that had been
issued to the four battalions taking part. A ring was to be established around Canea with forces pressing on to Suda. Galatas was
to be stormed, and the Canea-Maleme road blocked. Canea itself
would then be occupied. All this before darkness on the first day.[24]
Not surprisingly the document was stamped with a warning that
it must be burnt and not taken into action.

Freyberg now had a detailed summary of the enemy plan. The
accuracy with which it foretold the pattern of the fighting already
seen left little doubt that the document was genuine. He must

[22] Buckley, p. 209

[23] Mr. Geoffrey Cox to the author, 1962   [24] Davin, p. 180

have felt greatly encouraged as he made a last moment addition to his signal to Cairo. An important enemy order had been found among captured documents. This revealed the chief German objectives, none of which had been attained.[25]

Here indeed was cause for both comfort and reflection. The order could help him to a firm and accurate estimation of the strength already committed by the Germans. By 11 p.m. he was telling Cairo that it was 'certain' that one Parachute Regiment had attacked Maleme, and another the area south-west of Canea. The force attacking Retimo was believed to be 'stronger than that against Heraklion'.

It was also clear that 3 Parachute Regiment had misfired. The Germans had underestimated the strength of the defence. Reasonably it could be hoped that they were making the same misjudgement in the other Sectors. Another point of interest was the absence of any suggestion that an invasion flotilla might enter Almiros Bay. On the other hand, there was still good reason to be chary of moving Vasey's reduced 19th Brigade from Georgeoupolis, since it might be called upon at any moment to block an enemy force erupting from Retimo, where Campbell's Australians were evidently outnumbered in a desperate struggle with opposition that appeared to be no less powerful than that engaged at Maleme and in the Prison Valley. Finally, there was the threat of a sea-borne landing near the mouth of the Tavronitis, an indication that in this area Hargest might soon find himself hard put to it to maintain his apparent success.

There is no evidence to show that Freyberg felt that this document called for any immediate change of emphasis in his conduct of the defence. Rather did it appear to Cox that his reaction was little more than a feeling that 'Here was something interesting to send on to Wavell'.[26] Its main effect upon him was to increase the anxiety that he already felt for a tank-landing strike from the sea against the heart of his defence system.

And yet there was one further conclusion, weightier than all the rest put together, that he might have drawn from this important find. It has been seen that thus far the minds of Freyberg and his staff had been full of the tales of 'troop-carriers' landing in the Tavronitis river bed, on the beaches, and under the hills to the

[25] Davin, p. 181

[26] Mr. Geoffrey Cox to the author, 1962

south. They could not know that not a single German had arrived in Crete by any means other than parachute or glider, with the exception, perhaps, of a handful of survivors from the few planes that had been brought down. This fact had been obscured by mistaken reports. The captured Order now suggested a different view. In it there was no hint of heavy aircraft attempting to land in open country. On the contrary, all the emphasis was upon the necessity to seize airfields within the first few hours. Taken in conjunction with the knowledge, now beginning to reach his Headquarters, that the heavy planes were finding it impossible to land under fire on the runways, the supreme importance to both sides of these airfields should at last have become clear. All day, the defence had been cruelly deprived of accurate information. Here was a windfall indeed. Illuminated by the flash of intuition it might reveal much. But intuition had nothing to offer that night in the quarry dug-out above Canea.

And no help came from Egypt. To one vital question there was still no answer, either from Cairo or from London. How many parachutists were there still in Greece? Did Freyberg ask specifically for this information? Did he perhaps repeat such a request, as he might well have done, again and again? There is no evidence that he did. And for this there is a ready explanation. Intelligence had forecast that the main airborne assault would be made by infantry delivered by heavy troop-carrying planes. But it had also been assumed that these planes, almost from the start, would burst down upon the airfields, if not into open country as well, 'irrespective of the success or failure of the parachutists'. Within such a conception, the parachutists themselves assumed less importance. The distinction among the 'airborne' forces, whether dropped from the air, or landed by troop-carrier, mattered little. And the significance of the airfields dwindled.

How different would all have appeared to Freyberg that evening if he had known the mechanical limitations of powered aircraft, and had there been provided for him a reasonably accurate estimate of the number of parachutists available for the operation.

The truth has been seen. Student had sent into this first assault some 9,000 parachutists and glider troops, and had committed another 2,000 to the seaborne invasion. This was very nearly the whole trained airlanding force the Germans possessed. It was true that about 1,000 of those who were to go by air, most of them destined for Heraklion, had failed to take off in consequence of the confusions on the Greek airfields, but it would be difficult, if not impossible, to switch the plans for these men within the next day or two. That evening, so far as Student knew, no more than two-and-a-half companies of parachute riflemen and anti-tank troops remained available in his airborne reserve, together with some Headquarters detachments, a total of less than 400 men.

Thus, at this moment, a supreme opportunity lay unrecognized before the defence. Student had dissipated his Airlanding Division, the highly trained *élite* of the German Army, in scattered attacks about the island. Thousands of its young men now lay dead in the olive groves, and among the buttercups and barley. His glider troops, and four of his parachute battalions, one each at Maleme, Galatas, Retimo and Heraklion, had been shattered, reduced within the space of fifteen minutes to a few dozen fugitive survivors. Other battalions had suffered little less severely. Yet he still had not captured an airfield. Now he had left only his tiny airlanding reserve. If these few hundred men should fail on the morrow, the only possible relief for the Division would have to come by sea.

News of the fighting quickly reached England. In the course of a morning session of the House of Commons the Prime Minister announced that 'a serious battle' had begun in Crete. He was confident that 'most stern and resolute resistance' would be offered to the enemy.

Before the House separated he again interrupted its proceedings to say that, 'after a good deal of intense bombing' enemy troops had 'landed by gliders, parachutes, and troop-carriers' in the Canea-Maleme area. They were 'wearing New Zealand battle-dress'. A message sent at twelve o'clock had claimed that the military situation was 'in hand'. It was thought that the enemy were attempting to capture the aerodrome at Maleme. So far this had failed. He went on to tell the Members: 'A later report at three o'clock says that there is continuous enemy reconnaissance, accompanied by sporadic bombing and machine-gunning, chiefly against anti-aircraft defence. The military hospital between Canea and Maleme, captured by the enemy, has now been recaptured. There is reported to be a fairly strong enemy party south of the Canea-Maleme Road which has not yet been mopped up. Heraklion was bombed, but there has been no landing so far.

I must apologize to the House for intruding on them, but I thought they would like to hear how the action has so far developed.'

That evening, as they left the cities in their darkened trains, or sat at home beside their wireless sets, men and women discussed the news from the Middle East with a feeling of cautious optimism. The Greek business had been a disappointment, but an island should be different. They remembered that the *Luftwaffe* had found it heavy going in daylight over England. And recently Wavell's men had been doing well against the Italians. This time, perhaps the Germans would get more than they bargained for. Nobody, neither the journalists, nor the Service Ministries, nor Churchill himself, knew that in the skies above Crete there was no air defence.

With the coming of night, a strange silence fell upon the battlefields. An hour before sunset, the fighters and bombers had departed to the north. As it grew darker, the splutter of small arms slackened. Soon that too ceased. Only at Heraklion was the clamour of battle still echoing through the streets of the old town.

But if there was quiet there was little rest. Slowly the darkness came alive with silent movement. On all sides men had lain hidden among their enemies, threatened through every moment of the long day with discovery and death. Each now sought escape and the comfort and support of friends. Anonymous shapes stumbled about the broken slopes, and sudden flame splashed against the darkness as volleys echoed among the ravines, outraging the subdued murmurs of the night.

There were some who could not move. In the confusion, the wounded had been quickly lost. Squadron-Leader Howell lay in misery at the bottom of his slit trench half-way down the northern face of Hill 107. Both his forearms had been shattered by bullets. At first he had drifted through periods of unconsciousness. Late in the afternoon he had tried to shoot himself, but the broken tendons had failed to pull the trigger of his pistol. Now he lay back, scarcely breathing, against the earth of the trench wall. West of the Tavronitis, among the bamboos, General Meindl grew more breathless as the blood filled his chest. And at the bottom of a gully, near the coast road, Lieutenant Davin, later to become the New Zealand Historian of the campaign, was nursing wounds sustained in a dispute with a parachutist.

At Maleme frogs croaked incessantly among the sedges by the river, and there was a mournful braying from a group of donkeys still tethered among the trees beyond the bridge. In the narrow ravine, where the scent of wild flowers lay like incense about the unburied dead, the night was to pass without fighting. But a few hundred yards to the east, upon the scarred heights of Hill 107, and along the borders of the airfield, much was happening in obscurity scarcely touched by the young moon.

As dusk closed over the slopes, Andrew had still been waiting for the arrival of the reinforcement promised him by Hargest. After 5.45 p.m. he had heard no more from C Company, and from D and H.Q. Companies, since early morning, there had come not so much as a word of warning or farewell. Both appeared engulfed within this strange tide flowing from the west. An entry in the 22nd Battalion War Diary made at 9.0 p.m. shows how destructive was this absence of information:

By this hour the enemy was between C Coy and Bn HQ. He had worked up the eastern ridge and so cut off the line of communication with D Coy. Maleme village[27] was in his hands and no contact had been made with HQ Coy. A D Coy man reported that all the rest of D Coy was either killed or prisoners of war. The enemy was holding the area between Vlakheronitissa and Xamoudhokhori in force and threatened to push between our East and West ridges.

The men in Battalion Headquarters felt themselves almost surrounded. To Andrew it now seemed clear that the support of two companies would not be enough. If he were to stay on Hill 107 he would be subjected at daylight to a concentrated hammering from the air. At the same time, he could expect attacks from at least three sides by an enemy whose strength had already proved great enough to disintegrate his full battalion. Before long his last two companies would surely go the way of the others. He had done his best to explain it all to Hargest over the radio telephone. And indeed there had been nothing very surprising about it. This was the moment that had been foreseen, the crisis for which Leckie and the 23rd had rehearsed their counterstroke. Yet he had been promised only this meagre reinforcement, and that after many hours delay, half the support to come from as far back as Platanias. The inference seemed plain. This must be all that could be spared. And if this were true, if nothing more could be done, even to save the airfield itself, it could only be

[27] Maleme here means Pirgos, see Chap. 6, pp. 114-15

assumed that the brigade as a whole must be fighting for its life. In these circumstances, he began to think of moving back while there was still time.

Between 9 and 10 p.m. he was joined by the first of the reinforcing companies. It came from the 23rd. Here at last was a chance to hear news of the rest of the brigade. It is easy to picture the eagerness with which he must have questioned Captain Watson, the company commander. What had happened to the 23rd? Why hadn't they come? What had gone wrong? Watson was well placed to answer. Two hours earlier he had visited Leckie's Headquarters to receive his instructions. It can scarcely be doubted that he must now have told Andrew that the 23rd was feeling very pleased with itself, that it had made a great slaughter of Germans at very little loss, and had spent the day awaiting the call for further action.

Whatever may have been Andrew's thoughts on hearing this news, at once hopeful yet inexplicable, it did nothing to lessen his discouragement. About three-quarters of an hour had passed since he had told Hargest of his intention to 'withdraw to B Company ridge'. He had then sent runners to carry this order to all the companies. Already A Company had begun to come back from Hill 107.

But he had not yet entirely abandoned the position. He ordered Watson to take his men into the old A Company trenches close to the summit. This they did after a sudden spurt of firing in the darkness had killed their officer guide. Soon they were joined by the detached platoon of the 21st Battalion, retiring after its successful day in the river bed.

It now became plain that in its new position the truncated battalion was worse placed than it had been before. On B Company ridge there was little natural cover, and no tools were available to improve the defences. If the men stayed here they would be at the mercy of the bombers in the morning, and the whole position would be surveyed by the Germans as soon as they had occupied Hill 107.

Once again Andrew was faced with a bitter choice. He must go either forward or back. No doubt he again considered the puzzling news of Leckie and the 23rd. It was enough to show him his problem in a new light. Should he, after all, return to the heights above the airfield? He still could do so. By leaving Watson

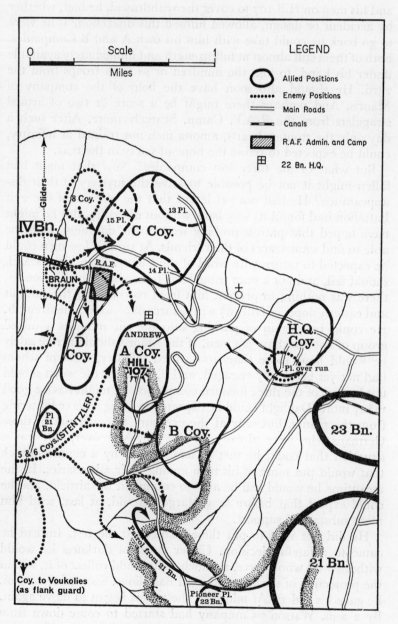

10.   Maleme: 9 p.m., 20 May

and his men on Hill 107 to cover the withdrawal, he had, whether by accident or design, allowed himself this discretion. If he were to go back he could take with him his own A and B Companies, both of them still almost at full strength and immediately available under his hand, to join the hundred or so fresh troops from the 23rd. He should also soon have the help of the company of Maoris. And perhaps there might be a score or two of armed stragglers from the R.A.F. Camp. Scarcely more. After such a day only the stoutest hearts, among men not trained as infantry, could be expected to refuse the hope of safety in the rear.

But what of the three lost companies? Now that night had fallen might it not be possible to solve the mystery of their disappearance? He had not yet learnt that the platoon of the 21st Battalion had found its way back without difficulty. But he might have hoped that patrols probing west in the darkness would be able to find some traces of their friends. At worst a few men could be expected to return with word of the enemy. Even if the search should fail, and not a man come back from above the Tavronitis, there was nothing to prevent him from reoccupying the summit and eastern slopes of Hill 107 with a force of considerable strength. He could be certain of packing into the slit trenches a mixed group of not less than 300 men. If the Maoris should arrive safely he would have more than 400 armed infantry, most of whom had not yet been fully engaged, and if, after all, the worst should not be true of the three forward companies, he might have a good many more. Daylight could be expected to bring a fierce battering from the planes, but only at the exposure to equal risk of those Germans who were already on the hill. Moreover, this was a situation that could be met to some extent by a counter-attack that would put more of his men among their adversaries. In the meantime he would still be able to command the airfield, and he could expect that before long Hargest would, at last, send him more substantial support.

He did not wait to put these chances to the test. Instead he came to a fateful decision. Under cover of darkness he would withdraw his whole force, as much as he could collect of it, within the protection of the 21st and 23rd Battalions. Soon after 10 p.m. he gave his orders. At midnight the troops began to move again. By 2 a.m. Watson's Company had started to come down from Hill 107. Last of all went Andrew himself. There was still no sign of the Maoris, nor indeed of anyone else.

Today it is easy to say that Andrew was wrong. The judgement is worthless unless it take full account of his difficulties, while acknowledging that he was confronted by a dilemma as then unknown in the history of war. Neither his courage nor his experience had prepared him for this trial.

Superficially his obligation may seem to have been not very different from that of many another commander told to stand in defence of some key position. Often enough in such circumstances groups of determined men have hung on for days in isolation, without hope for themselves, while continuing to play a great, and sometimes decisive, part in turning the course of a battle. In the years that followed, the virtues of such fighting were to be demonstrated again and again. Andrew's record, no less than his temperament and his reputation as a dedicated disciplinarian, proclaimed him ideal for the leadership in such a heavy task.

What went wrong then? Once again the historian comes upon that mystery which lies about the actions of so many of the older commanders in Crete. 'Hardly anyone behaves on this day as you might have expected him to do,'[28] says Moorehead of the Gallipoli landing. So it was on this 20 May in Crete. Andrew, Hargest, even Freyberg, all had acted in a manner quite outside their ordinary characters. The explanation may partly lie in some inflexibility of attitude persisting from their memories of the First World War. More important was the doubt and uncertainty that had been induced in them by the overwhelming German strength in the air, the power that had disrupted communication, and which carried the constant reminder that enemy reinforcement might be delivered anywhere at any moment. In facing this unexampled onslaught, Andrew had been deprived of the one modern device that could have helped him most. Unlike the commanders who opposed him he had not been given the wireless sets that would have enabled him to keep contact with his companies. And so, when his runners were cut down, and his flare signals lost in the smoke and dust, he had come to believe, despite his great experience of war, that no news must mean bad news.

Some further explanation for this too ready acceptance of withdrawal can be traced to the attitude of Freyberg himself; it has been seen that the General regarded the immediate protection of the airfields as no more than a part of the defence against

[28] Moorehead, *Gallipoli*, p. 128

landings from the air, while believing that all forms of air attack would be subsidiary to invasion from the sea. Puttick and Hargest were soon to reveal their acceptance of this doctrine. Reasonably, therefore, it can be assumed that neither had impressed upon Andrew the paramount necessity to keep some sort of fire playing on the runway. Admittedly he had been told that the 22nd must maintain its defence 'at all costs',[29] but phrases such as this are part of a currency too readily cheapened by high commanders. If he had understood all that hung upon it, there can be no doubt that he would have held the 22nd at Maleme until it had been relieved or utterly destroyed.

Now it is possible to see the other side of Hill 107, and to know the truth that was hidden from him. It was far less grim than he supposed. At 10 p.m. there remained of his battalion not merely the two companies with which he had contact, but at least another 180 unwounded men, still in their trenches, eager to fight, and confident of victory.[30] One of the reinforcing companies had already arrived to support them, and as he might have expected, in the light of the reassuring news of the 23rd, the Maori company was now close at hand. This made a total of almost 700 trained New Zealand infantry, many of them still occupying their old defence positions on the perimeter and along the western face of Hill 107 above the Tavronitis. Drifting among them were hundreds of armed men from other units.

Only the two platoons lost in the early afternoon had gone from the three forward companies. All the others, though several were cut to less than half their strength, still held their positions.

Along the eastern bank of the Tavonitis Campbell had forty-seven unwounded men of D Company, together with about sixty Marines and R.A.F. troops. In such a mêlée the break in contact with Battalion Headquarters had not been unexpected. Despite the presence of a few Germans on the slopes to his right, and the harassing fire from the west, he had been 'quite happy'[31] all the afternoon. At the centre of the enemy penetration, sheltering in

[29] Henderson, *22 Battalion*, p. 37

[30] Davin, p. 117 and p. 118. Also footnote on p. 319 which gives casualties for the 22nd as 261 on 25 May. Some scores of these men had still been in action on the night of the 20th. Since the battalion had started the day at a strength of 644 it can be calculated that at least 450 men were still unwounded at the time of the withdrawal. The Battalion War History gives the total killed in Crete as 62

[31] DP, Capt. D. Campbell

the narrow concrete canal cut into the hill-side three hundred yards from the bridge, Sergeant Sargeson and eight survivors of 18 Platoon held firm among the Germans who crawled all around them.

Down on the airfield perimeter C Company had lost Sinclair and 15 Platoon, in their widely separated gun-pits north of the bridge, but along the shore 13 Platoon was still in its trenches, and Captain Johnson had the rest of his company in hand south of the road. 'The surviving men were in excellent heart,' he was to say later, 'in spite of their losses. They had NOT had enough. They were first rate in every particular way and were as aggressive as when action was first joined.'[32]

In and around Pirgos, Lieutenant Beaven and Headquarters Company had enjoyed a most successful day. About 120 parachutists had landed near them, some coming down 'in the narrow streets and on the flat-roofed houses'. Most had been killed. Of those who had got into the village 'a few stayed but only the dead ones'.[33] Unknown to him, his isolated southern platoon had been destroyed, but in the rest of his company the casualties by 4.50 p.m. had been no more than one dead and five wounded. Eight Australian gunners, who had swum to join them after being cut off by parachutists further up the beach, had done excellent work with a small German field gun presented to them during the day by a passing Junkers. Determined to defend themselves against the parachutists whom they had seen falling further east they had fired upon all movement in this direction, and had thus discouraged the patrols from the 23rd which were trying to make contact with them. But at nightfall Beaven was feeling rather pleased with his company and with himself. He was only slightly disconcerted at the fact that there had been no news all day from anyone else.

As darkness fell, the German commanders at Maleme knew that they had failed. They had not captured the airfield. In the east, a whole battalion had disappeared. Further inland, Stentzler had achieved some success, only to be held up half a mile short of Hill 107. On the heights themselves little was left of Koch's glider troops. 'After heavy losses,' says *Operation Crete*, the 'remnants fought their way to the bridge'.[34] But if they had succeeded in

---

[32] Davin, p. 118, report by Capt. S. H. Johnson
[33] Henderson, *22 Battalion*, p. 47, Private N. N. Fellows
[34] *Einsatz Kreta*, Battle Report of XI Air Corps

doing this Gericke must surely have met some of them during the day. This he was to deny:

I never met Captain Koch in the Maleme Sector. He was wounded on Hill 107. Neither did I have any radio contact with his battalion. Until the evening of 20 May we knew nothing of the true state of affairs on Hill 107.[35]

In fact it seems likely that almost the only survivors who had escaped westward were those who had been collected by their medical officer in the river bed higher upstream, and these men were too few, and too shaken, to turn back between the platoons of Campbell's D Company.

Nevertheless some of those cut off were still effectively in action. Several small parties, established within the hollows that scored the slopes, were in radio contact with Meindl's Headquarters. One lieutenant reported that his twenty-eight men were being strongly attacked. He asked for help and was told that they must break out to the south-west. They found it impossible. But by staying where they were they achieved far more than they could have done by rejoining their comrades beyond the Tavronitis. No doubt it was the continued action of these pockets of airborne troops between Pirgos and Vlakheronitissa that, by nightfall, had convinced Andrew and his staff that the enemy had 'worked up the eastern ridge'. The manner in which they were able to exploit their situation, confident in the knowledge that they would be rescued as soon as possible, well illustrates the value of their radio equipment. How swiftly might the battle have been transformed if Andrew had enjoyed the same contact with his company commanders.

The survivors of the smaller group of glider troops, those remaining of the ninety men led by Braun until he was killed, had begun to climb through the shattered undergrowth that covered the north-west face of the hill. They were able to take advantage of the confusion caused by the unfortunate men from the R.A.F. Camp who were 'milling about'[36] among the stripped trees and the bomb craters, their blue uniforms all too easily mistaken for those of the enemy. But the Germans did not get far against Sergeant Sargeson and his gallant platoon.

By noon the mixed force based upon Gericke's IV Battalion had assembled in the dead ground north and south of the bridge. All around them, in the river bed, among the tents of the encamp-

[35] Letter to the author, 21 Jan. 1960   [36] Henderson, _22 Battalion_, p. 35

ment on the eastern bank, and dotted about the dunes at the river mouth, they could see the wrecked gliders and scattered bodies of the Braun and Plessen detachments. But these new men were fresh after their unresisted drop, well-armed and fully organized. While their mortars plastered the slopes, they began to press forward south of the road. Soon they came under the lee of the north-west face of the hill, out of the view of the defenders on the summit. The sudden appearance of the tanks did little to check them, their first dismay turning to elation as this threat so quickly faded. But every foot of their advance was fiercely resisted by the New Zealanders of Captain Johnson's C Company. By nightfall they had succeeded in doing no more than infiltrate across the western perimeter of the airfield, while opening a small gap, a few hundred yards deep, down the narrow cultivated strip between the road and the hill. For this success they had been forced to pay a high price. 'Captain Gericke had succeeded with his Storm Troops,' says *Operation Crete*, 'after suffering heavy casualties, and as the result of superhuman efforts, in seizing the northern slope of Hill 107'.

How many Germans had in fact set foot upon the hill cannot now be told with certainty. But their strength can be roughly gauged from Gericke himself. In his book he says that word came back to the 'adjutant' at the bridge reporting that 'those out in front on Hill 107' had 'no water and no ammunition'. Whereupon eight weary men were roused from sleep and detailed to provision them. Laden with ammunition, and pushing their water-cart, they set out along the road. 'A little beyond the bridge they turned right' in order to reach the 'captured tent position'. All around them they could hear the cries of the English wounded. With great difficulty they began to push their water-cart up the slopes, their knees weak, and 'the heat of the day still heavy in their bones'. At last they came upon a German post 'established on an outcrop of rock'.[37] They went no further. Before dawn they had returned gratefully to the road carrying with them two wounded men.

From this it would appear that it was by no means the 'northern slope' of the heights that had been captured, but merely this small north-western shoulder overlooking the bridge. It was here that Howell still lay in his trench. Later he was to hear from the Germans that they had 'only twenty-seven men that night'.[38] For

[37] Gericke, p. 73 *et seq.*   [38] Howell, p. 20

the small penetration on to the hill itself this may well have been the correct figure.

Only now did Gericke learn of the fate of the Koch glider troops and of III Battalion: 'At dusk we made contact with scouts from the units commanded by Captain Koch. An officer and a few men from III Battalion (Major Scherber) were also able to fight their way through to me. From verbal reports I was able to build up a picture of the situation.'[39] He had 'made contact with Major Stentzler immediately after the landing', and so was aware that II Battalion had made a successful drop. Later he had learnt through Meindl's Headquarters, if not from Stentzler himself, that part of it was approaching Hill 107 from the south.

By nightfall, therefore, he knew the best and the worst of his situation. He had supported the Braun Group after their capture of the road bridge, and had won positions along the western perimeter of the airfield, together with a section of the north-west slopes of Hill 107. But this small advance, so much less than had been expected, had cost 'heavy casualties'. Those of his men who had not been wounded were much exhausted by their exertions in the blazing heat. He greatly feared counter-attack during the night.

From German sources it is possible to make a rough estimate of the strength of the Storm Regiment on the night of 20 May. In the east, beyond Pirgos, III Battalion had been lost, its commander killed with 'almost 400'[40] of his men. Nearly all the glider troops were dead or out of action. Only the 'remnants'[41] of the Koch Group had succeeded in making their way back to the bridge. Scarcely more than a score or two of Braun's ninety men had survived the fire of Sargeson's platoon to reach cover on the hillside. In the west the seventy-two men of the Muerbe Patrol had all been killed or captured by the Greeks under the direction of Major Bedding, a New Zealander. The two flanking companies were both now more than five miles away to the west and south, and were heavily involved among the Greeks and Cretans.

Here and there Germans remained active as far east as Platanias. Some of them, it has been seen, had formed small

[39] Letter to the author, 21 Jan. 1960 [40] *Einsatz Kreta*, Battle Report of XI Air Corps
[41] Ibid.

parties in radio contact with Meindl. But many were wounded.
And others were still alone. They cannot have numbered more
than a few dozen, since nearly all were members of Scherber's
ill-fated III Battalion of which all but 200 had died immediately,
and more had been killed, wounded or captured later. While
daylight lasted they had fought with the utmost resolution in the
midst of their enemies, contriving to inflict more damage than
they knew, indeed to an extent far disproportionate to their
numbers; they had tied down movement and communication
among the New Zealanders at a time when speed and mobility
were vitally necessary to the defence. But now there was not much
fight left in them. Exhausted, thirsty, and short of ammunition
they were in no mood to attract further attention to themselves.
The day had been time enough for heroism.

Thus the German force at Maleme had been whittled down
until it consisted only of two small groups separated by about a
mile of broken hills. Gericke's men, with the surviving glider
troops included, had begun the day some 700 strong. They were
now greatly diminished in numbers and striking capacity.
Stentzler's two companies, on the other side of Hill 107, had been
under heavy fire since before noon. They too were much reduced
by casualties. The total strength that faced the New Zealanders,
from both sides of the hill, can scarcely have amounted to 600
unwounded men. Probably it was considerably less. No other
Germans remained within striking distance.

In planning his attack, Meindl had dispersed his troops no less
widely than Hargest had separated the elements of the 5th
Brigade. This was the result. That morning he had set out from
Greece with some 2,300 men. These few were all that remained to
deliver the crucial assault.[42] Many were suffering acutely from
thirst after their strenuous exertions in the burning, waterless hills.
All were short of ammunition and dismayed by the loss of so
many of their friends in the face of a resistance that had come as a
complete surprise. For the moment they felt themselves incapable
of further attack unless reinforced.

Nowhere were the Germans less active than along the lower
slopes of Hill 107. Their experiences during the day had convinced

---

[42] After the war the N.Z. historians estimated German strength at nightfall on the
20th as '300 to 500 scattered east of the Tavronitis, a thousand odd across the river'.
Kippenberger to Brig. H. B. Latham, 27 Aug. 1952

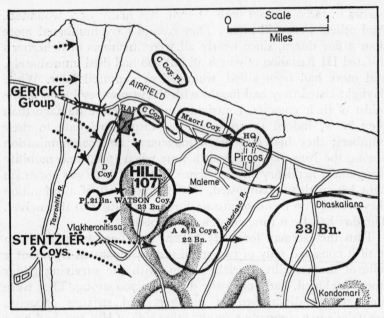

11.   Maleme: 1.30 a.m., 21 May

them that here their enemies must be well established. After
darkness had fallen they at first made little attempt to explore
towards the summit. Yet now, at last, movement for both sides had
become relatively easy. If Andrew had dared to hang on for one
more hour he could have had full information from his three lost
companies with more than half the night still to come.

The commanders of these companies had been quick to discover
their new freedom. None of Andrew's runners had succeeded in
getting through to them with the orders for retreat. But they soon
learnt for themselves that the rest of the battalion had abandoned
Hill 107. Each was now forced to decide what he should do next.

There followed a strange and fateful quadrille in which
Watson's company, alternating with representatives from the
Maoris, from D Company, and from Headquarters Company,
each unbeknown to the others, advanced and retired upon the
empty hilltop. By 9.30 p.m. A Company had already left the
forward positions. About an hour later the trenches were taken
over by the relief from the 23rd. Not long afterwards two runners
from Headquarters Company arrived at the old Battalion

Mountain Troops leave Junkers 52: Hill 107 in background

(Imperial War Museum)

Mountain Troops from Junkers 52 reach shelter under Hill 107

(Imperial War Museum)

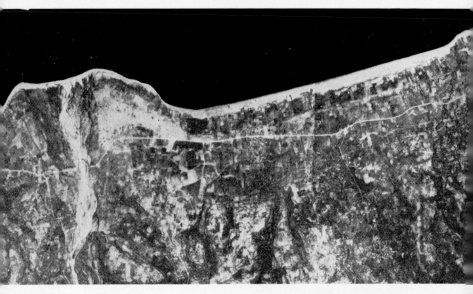

Aerial photographs of Maleme area and airfield

(*Historical Publications Branch, N.2. Dept. of Internal Affairs*)

Command Post, only to find nobody there. They did not meet any of Watson's men, who must still have been nearby. At 2 a.m. Watson moved off the hill to follow Andrew.

Soon after this, Campbell, of D Company, while searching the hill for water, was painfully surprised to find that among the dead there remained only a number of wounded, none of whom could tell him where the battalion had gone. Much disconcerted, he returned to his position above the Tavronitis. Including the troops from the R.A.F. Camp, he had collected some 110 unwounded men. He knew very well how vital was the line that he held, despite the penetrations that had been made on each side of it. When the fighting had died down he had confidently expected that before long he would be supported by a counter-attack. But what was he to think now? The fact that Andrew had left no messages suggested that he must have departed in a hurry with no immediate hope of return. Perhaps he had been recalled by Hargest. Had there then been some disaster further back? Had the 23rd been wiped out?

While he still pondered what course to take, the Maoris, under Captain Rangi Royal, were at last approaching Hill 107 after a long and serpentine march of twelve miles. They were 114 strong. Shortly after 7 p.m. they had left Platanias and gone straight down the coast road, killing twenty of the enemy for the loss of two dead, in a sharp bayonet skirmish on the way.[43] They had then turned south, looking for B Company ridge, but near Xamoudhokhori they had lost their way and instead found themselves back on the main road.

This led them further west. At about 1.30 a.m. they passed through the long central street of Pirgos, receiving no response to their shouts despite the fact that Headquarters Company was still there. Moving on they passed the Cemetery, with its small church, on the right of the road, and came at length to the edge of the airfield itself. Here they encountered a few Germans who had made their way east in the darkness across the empty runway and were now shouting and whistling to keep contact with each other. At this point they were no more than two hundred yards from the Headquarters of the 22nd Battalion's C Company. Moreover, the position of C Company Headquarters and 14 Platoon was 'marked clearly on the maps in the hands of other battalions and even as far back as Creforce Headquarters'.[44]

[43] Cody, *Maori Battalion*, p. 94   [44] Henderson, *22 Battalion*, p. 54

But Royal assumed, naturally enough, that the airfield had been captured, and that his first responsibility still must be to find Andrew. After some delay, his guide, who had boldly explored the dark hillside, returned to say that he had found the old 22nd Command Post, only about five hundred yards away, and that the slit trenches were empty. At this, Royal turned back through Pirgos and south down the Xamoudhokhori Road. On the way he met Andrew who told him that he had been sent no help from the rest of the brigade. When the position had 'deteriorated further' he had been forced to 'pull out'.[45] On hearing of the Maoris' wanderings he commented briefly that they were 'damned lucky to be alive'.[46] He did not ask whether they had seen any sign of Headquarters Company, or of the Germans, in Pirgos. Nor did the news that his old Command Post had still been empty an hour before induce in him any change of mind.

During the evening, Royal had collected a number of supporters, including some Australian gunners. They had increased the strength of his party to about 180. Most of them he had just led to within five hundred yards of the unoccupied summit of Hill 107. Andrew told him to take them all back to Platanias.

A few minutes after the Maoris' guide had left the hill-top Campbell reached the decision that he must retire. He sent two of his platoons to the south, including Sargeson's heroic survivors from above the bridge, in the hope that they might find their way on a long detour to Canea, or if need be to the south coast. With the rest, a mixed group of about eighty-five men, he set out eastward to cross the summit of Hill 107 for the last time. Nobody tried to stop them as they stumbled among the bomb craters and the shattered trees, past the wrecked gliders and the bodies of the dead and dying. Once again the slit trenches and the sandbagged emplacements lay empty for any who should care to occupy them.

At 4.45 p.m., in his message reporting the failure of the tanks, Captain Johnson of C Company had told Andrew that Sinclair's platoon had apparently been overrun, together with the western section of the platoon along the beach. He could 'probably hold out until dark, but reinforcements would be needed then'.[47] To this Andrew had replied, in the last word to come through from

[45] DP. 'These may not have been his exact words but they give the sense of what he said to me' (Capt. R. Royal)

[46] Cody, *Maori Battalion*, p. 95   [47] Henderson, *22 Battalion*, p. 54

him, that the company must continue to 'hold on at all costs',[48] ironically the phrase that had been used in his own orders.

As soon as it became dark Johnson began a series of attempts to make contact with the other companies. These efforts failed. The Maoris came and went within easy shouting distance of the small copse in which he was sheltering with his weary party of survivors. He heard nothing of them. At 4.20 a.m. he discovered that the enemy had moved on to the slopes behind him. He had scarcely fifty men, many of them wounded. It seemed that he could serve no purpose by staying longer, and that if he did not go soon they would all be captured.

Later he was to describe his departure:

a) At 04.20 hrs when I ordered withdrawal I despatched a runner to advise 13 Pl of this order. At the same time I ordered every man to remove his boots and hang them about his neck. . . .

c) At 04.30 hrs we moved off in single file, the wounded inter-dispersed along the line of our march, through the southern wire of the copse, past the snoring Germans on our right, through the vineyards which separated C Coy from A Coy's reserve platoon and HQ area up to A Coy's deserted HQ on to the road, up the hill past a grounded glider, until we reached the forward boundary of B and A Coy's position.[49]

Clearly the Germans had not yet occupied the eastern face of the hill. Finding 'no sign of any opposition' Johnson now told his men to put their boots on. Without further difficulty they reached B Company ridge, picking up 'two or three sleeping members of 22 Battalion who were unaware that any withdrawal had taken place'.[50]

Even more expressive of the atmosphere of this strange night were the silent encounters that had been taking place in Pirgos. The Maoris had twice passed through the village without making contact with any of the members of Beaven's Headquarters Company who still held it. Their Regimental history says that they saw 'vague figures who, so far as they knew, were probably Germans, but neither party molested the other'.[51] Later some of Beaven's men were to maintain that they had seen the Maoris on the road. They did not declare their presence at the time. Such was the overwhelming inclination felt by the contenders of both sides to live and let live after the terrors of the day. Few felt

[48] Henderson, 22 Battalion, p. 54   [49] Davin, p. 119, report by Capt. S. H. Johnson
[50] Ibid.   [51] Cody, Maori Battalion, p. 95

impelled to enquire about the identity of unknown shadows moving in the darkness.

Beaven himself, after six of his runners had disappeared, went upon a fruitless search for B Company. On his return, at about 3 a.m., he decided that he must move out. All remained quiet. He was able to bring with him all his wounded, including the stretcher cases.

The men of the 22nd were much puzzled by this withdrawal. They were weary, thirsty, and hungry. But they had been conscious of success. It irked them to leave prepared positions which they had defended so hotly, and which they knew to be of great importance. And they resented the need to abandon so many of the wounded. 'The hardest part,' said one of them, 'seemed to be having to leave mates behind'.[52] All the same they were not greatly disconcerted. Before long, no doubt, they would return. They were confident that their leaders knew what they were about, and that all would yet be well.

At last the enemy began to understand what was happening. As he came back over the hill Campbell's Sergeant-Major had tossed a grenade 'for good luck'[53] among some Germans. This prompted them to take a more active interest. Gericke refers to a 'counter-attack', and claims that the New Zealanders were able to achieve only 'small local gains'.[54] From this it would seem that some of his men, feeling themselves so weak in their hill-side posts, may, for a moment, have turned back in panic. But, after a while, they realized that they were not being attacked. With great caution a few began to feel their way upward. As they crossed the first crest they came upon a line of empty trenches. Then another.[55] Suddenly it dawned upon them that the New Zealanders had gone. Astonished and exhilarated they went on faster. Before long, still scarcely able to believe their good fortune, they were joined by Stentzler's men from the other side of the hill. Without fighting, they had occupied the vital heights from which there had poured upon them such a murderous fire all through the previous day. A few minutes earlier they had been lying uncomfortably on the stony slopes, cramped, cold and discouraged, anxious at the thought of the further ordeal that awaited them in the morning. Now they had in their possession the key to Maleme airfield.

[52] Henderson, *22 Battalion*, Frontispiece, 'Doc.' Bradford
[53] Davin, p. 118   [54] Gericke, p. 76   [55] Ibid.

It began to grow light. A gentle breeze ruffled the fresh dust around the bomb craters, stirring the tattered branches of the olives near the old R.A.F. Camp. As the darkness lifted, the drone of a plane could be heard from far out at sea, faintly at first, a changing pulse on the wind, familiar yet fading and for a moment uncertain, then suddenly unmistakable. Out of the grey sky came a single Junkers 52. With a roar it swung about Hill 107, then curved lower, increasingly confident, across the runway itself, skimming the shore a few feet above the trenches that had been held until an hour or two before by C Company's beach platoon. At last it hit the ground and lurched safely to a stop among the sand runnels at the mouth of the river, the first powered aircraft to land of intent upon Crete since the start of the battle.[56] On board was a staff officer sent by Student to find out whether the plight of his troops at Maleme was as desperate as it appeared to be everywhere else.

At about this moment the New Zealanders of the 23rd Battalion became aware of a long line of figures approaching them through the trees from the west. Soon they were dismayed to recognize their friends of the 22nd.

---

[56] Kurowski, p. 70, claims that two Junkers 52 were sent by Student to Maleme 'before midday' on the 20th, and that they were able to take off again 'though damaged', with the news that the airfield could not yet be used. No German report refers to such an incident, but Henderson, p. 54, says that 'two Ju 52s attempted to land' late in the afternoon; they were driven off by small-arms fire.

PART THREE

CRISIS

'It is a most strange and grim battle that is being fought. Our side have no air . . . and the other side have very little or no tanks. Neither side has any means of retreat.'

Winston Churchill, House of Commons, 22 May 1941

'The English have uncontested control of the sea; we have uncontested control of the air.'

General Halder's Diary, 28 May 1941

13

Student Chooses Maleme: 21 May

At his Headquarters in Athens, General Student waited for
news. At first all had seemed to be going very well. For some
hours he continued to find encouragement for his belief that there
would be little resistance. The pilots returning from Maleme were
full of confidence. They reported that their drop had been made
successfully and that they had seen 'no anti-aircraft defence'.[1]
Only at Heraklion was there any sign of gunfire from the ground;
here a sharp response had been evoked by a trial flight of
Messerschmitts. For a moment he was tempted to switch his
eastern landing force away from this Sector. Not until 12 a.m.
did he decide to 'make no alteration in the plan to land troops at
Heraklion'.[2]

Then suddenly all was changed. From Heidrich he heard that
3 Parachute Regiment could make no headway towards Suda.
Next he learnt that General Suessmann, the Force Commander,
had been killed while still within sight of the Piraeus. The signals
sent by the Storm Regiment were more detailed[3] but scarcely
more cheerful. The gliders had failed in their assault upon the
heights around Hill 107, and in the Pirgos area Major Scherber
and III Battalion had disappeared. The afternoon brought no
improvement. No recognition flares could be seen from the glider
landing areas on the Akrotiri Peninsula. A rumour that the airfield at Maleme had been captured was quickly seen to be false.
Nor was there any consolation from the east. By eight o'clock in
the evening he knew that the Heraklion detachment, arriving in
scattered formation during the late afternoon, had fallen into a
hornet's nest. At Retimo things were even worse; heavy firing
could be seen among the trees; wireless contact had not been
established with Sturm; there seemed to be little prospect that

---

[1] 5th Mountain Division War Diary   [2] Ibid

[3] From the start the Regiment had 'unbroken radio contact with Athens', Gericke
to the author, 21 Jan. 1960

any of the troops in this Sector would be able to turn west to help
the attack upon Suda.

And now, in ominous succession, he heard of the deaths of old
friends, men with whom he had shared the hopes and enthusiasms
of the newly formed Airlanding Division. Braun and von Plessen
both were dead. Koch, one of Goering's companions, was thought
to be dying, and Meindl had been severely wounded. There was
no comfort anywhere.

As it grew dark there was mounting tension and anxiety in the
operations room on the second floor of the Grande Bretagne
Hotel where the oppressive heat of the day was scarcely relieved
by the chill of the night air. The heavy furnishings contrasted
with the paraphernalia of command.

On the wall [says von der Heydte, describing the scene from
recollections given to him by members of the General's staff] was the
large map of Crete dotted with little paper flags marking the positions
of the German and British units according to the latest information,
while in the bottom right-hand corner were arrayed further ranks of
little flags like companies awaiting the order to march. On the broad
table in the centre of the room, which was illuminated with un-
necessary brilliance, stood three field-telephones amid a confusion of
wires, a stack of papers, two black files, and, in the centre a large
ash-tray piled high with stubs and the remains of half-finished
cigarettes.

At this table sat the General, working almost throughout the night
waiting and waiting for the first news which would bring him confirmation that he had been right in proposing the attack on the island
to Goering a month previously. Everything had seemed so simple in
prospect, so feasible and so certain. He had thought that he had taken
every possibility into consideration – and then everything had turned
out contrary to plans and expectations.[4]

Indeed it was plain that the enterprise hung by a thread.
Despite the heavy losses none of his objectives had been reached.
Above all else stood the failure to capture an airfield. He was
forced to recognize that he had miscalculated, and that the
resistance everywhere was proving far stronger than he had
expected. Since 1938, he had prepared his Division for just
such a venture as this, enjoying to the full the privilege which had
enabled him to take picked volunteers from the rest of the Army.
Only at his insistence had it been committed to an island battle
remote from infantry support. Now, in the space of a few hours, it

[4] von der Heydte, p. 110 *et seq.*

was disintegrating under his hand. On him lay the chief responsibility. If it should be lost, nothing but the fickle favour of Hitler could save him from the jealousy of his fellow generals. No doubt he was aware of the whispers and the covert glances of men who would not be sorry to see him fail. Already there were suggestions that it might be better to accept defeat. At a quarter to twelve his Intelligence officer asked if he should make preliminary arrangements for the 'breaking off' of the engagement if this should be thought 'advisable'.[5]

But Student had the courage that goes with dedication to an idea. He remained convinced that, come what might, his new air technique must in the end prove equal to his hopes. As the night lengthened, he wrestled alone with his problem, his pale face, dominant forehead and high-pitched voice lending him the air of a prosperous businessman rather than a general. He knew that the situation was 'critical'[6] and he feared for his communications. His first thoughts were for Retimo:

Unfortunately the wireless apparatus carried by 2 Parachute Regiment had been badly damaged in the fall. This meant that . . . there could be no radio contact between Athens and Rethymnon. Two attempts to drop replacements went astray. Still trying to make contact, I then sent a Fieseler 'Storch' which managed to get across the sea and reach the vicinity of Rethymnon but was then captured. Despite all these efforts, we still could not get radio contact; all we had was air reconnaissance and signs laid out by the troops.

With the other three attacking groups at Maleme, Chania and Heraklion, radio contact was good from the first . . . the parachute regiments came through soon after dropping and then gave their regular situation reports to Athens. This was decidedly useful! Already, on that evening of 20 May in Athens, I had so complete a picture of the situation on the island that I was able to reach a new and decisive resolution, namely that the '*Schwerpunkt*' of the attack must lie at Maleme, and that the island would have to be rolled up from the west.'[7]

Here, perhaps, he is claiming a greater confidence than he felt at the time, but it is true that he had kept his nerve better than the whisperers who surrounded him, and that he came at last to his 'decisive resolution', choosing the one course that might still

[5] Clark, p. 100
[6] DP, letter from Student to Capt. B. H. Liddell Hart, 28 Nov. 1948
[7] Student replying to questions put to him by Gericke at the request of the author. Gericke to the author, 21 Jan. 1960. Von Richthofen also claimed some credit, Gundelach, p. 427

retrieve his earlier mistakes and save the battle. 'I decided to use the mass of the parachute reserve still at my disposal for the final capture of Maleme aerodrome.'[8]

This was to put it a little high. The difficulties on the Greek airfields were proving a blessing in disguise, saving him from the full consequences of his intention to use almost the whole of his airborne forces on the first day. Providentially, two companies of the 600 men who had failed to take off for Heraklion were 'still available'.[9] He gave orders that they were to join the two and a half companies that he had left uncommitted. But a total of something like 650 parachutists can hardly be accounted a weighty reserve.[10] And not all, even of these men, could be sent immediately. He decided to drop them 'in the early afternoon',[11] after an air bombardment lasting an hour – two and a half companies west of the airfield, and two 'in the enemy's rear east of Pirgos with the task of capturing the position Pirgos-Maleme from the east'.[12] Already a whole battalion had been lost in this area, but he felt, so he was to claim later, that the New Zealanders would by now have moved every man west in an attempt to protect the runway and the heights. It is, perhaps, no less likely that he had not understood the extent of the earlier disaster.

There was now little that he could do but contemplate the fate of his Division. Like Freyberg, he felt a burning need for precise information. To get it he would send one of his aides to Crete: 'During the night I sent for Captain Kleye, a bold go-getting character on my staff, and told him to take a Junkers 52 and land at Maleme in order to get a personal feeling of how things were going with the Storm Regiment.'[13] It was a technique that General Montgomery was later to make famous.

Within minutes Kleye was in the air. It was his plane that came down at first light among the sand dunes north-west of the runway. 'He managed to land on the airfield,' wrote Student, 'and also to get off again although fired at by the enemy. In this way he was able to bring back the important information that the western edge of the airstrip lay in dead ground.'[14]

Here was the first hint of the dramatic change that had taken

[8] Davin, p. 182   [9] *Einsatz Kreta*, Battle Report of XI Air Corps
[10] Although it was double the 'half a battalion' given by Clark, p. 101, as the strength of the 'remaining parachutists', and was probably further increased by more left-overs. See below, p. 259, *n.* 23
[11] *Einsatz Kreta*, Battle Report of XI Air Corps   [12] Ibid.
[13] Gericke, letter to the author, 21 Jan. 1960, quoting Student   [14] Ibid.

place during the night. Kleye did not stay long enough to discover that the New Zealanders had withdrawn, and that the vital heights south of the airfield had fallen, as though by magic, into German hands. But Student's quick instinct told him that this safe landing was the sign that he had been looking for, and that he had been right in deciding to gamble everything upon Maleme. He lost no time in exploiting the opportunity that had been revealed. Very soon six more Junkers had 'put down along the beach at Spilia, three kilometres west of the airstrip, bringing with them the urgently needed ammunition.'[15]

Colonel Andrew reached the 23rd Battalion lines at about 2 a.m. The shock and surprise caused by his arrival can be imagined. Until that moment, Leckie had believed everything to be going well. Now he was suddenly faced with the disastrous news that the airfield was lost. There could be no guidance from the Brigade Commander, still three miles back at Platanias; once more the signal link had broken down. Most of this critical night was to pass with Hargest unaware of what had happened. From his telephone conversations with Andrew during the afternoon, he had understood only that the 22nd might be formed to 'fall back a little'. Had he known, at 2 a.m. on the following morning, that his battalions were now standing on a line nearly two miles east of the airfield he would have found less cause for equanimity. But it was not until 3 a.m., 'in pyjamas and sleepy',[16] after being awoken by a liaison officer, that he heard of the true position from Leggat who had travelled back in a Bren-carrier.

In his absence a grave responsibility had fallen upon the battalion commanders. Half the night still remained. Could anything be done to recapture the vital heights, and with them the landing-strip itself, before morning?

At about 3 a.m. the three colonels met at the Headquarters of the 23rd, near Dhaskaliana. Major Philp, of the Artillery, who had been invited to join them, noted the haggard and exhausted appearance of Andrew. It made him realize that the 22nd must have been through a 'rough passage'. Moreover, it was apparent that all that its commander could tell them was that his battalion had dissolved in the face of increasing pressure from the west.

---

[15] Gericke, letter to the author, 21 Jan. 1960, quoting Student

[16] DP, Major J. Leggat, second-in-command, the 22nd Battalion

The 'details of enemy strength and dispositions' were 'just not known . . .'[17]

Leckie brought no more ebullience to the discussion, despite the almost total slaughter that the 23rd had wrought upon its own parachutists. His inclination, as he later revealed, was to blame Andrew, his old rival, for having withdrawn.[18] More profitably it might have occurred to him that here was a moment of opportunity, indeed of obligation, for his own men and for himself. Hargest had said that his battalion would not be called upon for counter-attack unless the position should become 'very serious'. It was serious enough now. Yet he did not urge that this was the moment for the 23rd to restore the position. Perhaps it had become easier for him to recognize that Andrew was the senior man. 'I well remember,' wrote Philp, 'that all looked to Col. Andrew'.[19] But less than an hour earlier Andrew had been telling the Maoris as they came back from Hill 107 that they were 'damned lucky to be alive'. Now the weight of his silence fell upon them all. This was a man whom they knew and respected, a professional soldier of proven valour. That he should thus have despaired of three of his companies must surely mean the enemy strength was formidable indeed. Leckie and Allen may well have asked themselves whether they would be likely to fare any better. Might it not be that they too would founder upon this inexplicable German strength in the west? Was it not perhaps, already, too late to do anything that night? Especially since they had always thought in terms of counter-attack from the south. From this direction Bren-carrier approaches through the hills had been reconnoitred, but one of the officers who knew them was dead and the other wounded.[20] The country was difficult, and few of the troops had explored it outside their own area. In the darkness, and with little time before dawn, these factors assumed additional importance. Certainly there was much to give them pause.

On the other hand, if they did nothing, it was plain that on the following day the Germans would use the airfield to land reinforcement by troop-carrier. And soon after dawn the fighters and bombers would return. Counter-attack would then be more difficult. There was every incentive for facing almost any risk in

[17] DP, Narrative of Maj. W. D. Philp
[18] Ibid., Leckie staunchly supports Hargest maintaining that he was 'let down'
[19] Ibid., Philp Narrative
[20] Ibid., Maj. T. Fyfe and Lieut. D. M. Davin, letter to the author from D. M. Davin

an attempt to get back on to Hill 107 before morning. Might it not be possible to discard all previous ideas and save time by moving straight down the road through Pirgos? As Andrew knew, the Maoris had done this less than two hours before, reaching the edge of the runway almost without sight or sound of the enemy.

Those who took part in the conference do not recall any discussion of these alternatives. The 21st Battalion Diary contains no more than the laconic entry: 'Conference of C.Os. at 23 Bn HQ. Decided to hold our position next day. 22 Bn to reorganize.'

Soon after it became light, the weary Andrew himself reached Brigade Headquarters. Hargest at once agreed that it had been right to establish the new line east of Pirgos. Clearly there would have to be a counter-attack, but this must wait. Nothing could be done in daylight. In the meantime, it would be necessary to look out for fresh landings from the air or from the sea – not forgetting those nasty-looking arrows on the captured enemy maps, all of them pointing north towards Platanias. He still did not go forward himself.

It has often been said that there is little to be gained from speculation in detail upon what might have been in war. The 'must haves' are better avoided. None can tell what effect upon the whole might have resulted from the shift of one piece in a mosaic of imponderables. 'The historian is not concerned to fight past battles over again,' says one writer, 'still less to fight them differently. His duty is to explain.'[21] Yet such a view may perhaps, on occasion, prove somewhat sterile. It can also be profitable to 'examine the causes of mistakes and assess to what extent they were inevitable or avoidable',[22] provided always that the utmost endeavour has been made to picture the situation as it presented to those who were there at the time.

Lately it has become fashionable to write of battles largely in terms of the mistakes made by each side. Nothing could be simpler. It is seldom difficult to point out that the commanders were wrong. But from this it may be too readily concluded that they were all fools. In this form of literature little distinction is made between actual and after knowledge, and there is scant concern with the atmosphere prevailing at the moment when the crucial decisions were made. Such matters as the hour of day or night, and whether the officer concerned had recently dined at

[21] A. J. P. Taylor, *New Statesman*, 5 Oct. 1961   [22] Barclay, p. 149

leisure with his staff or scarcely slept or eaten for days, are
accorded little recognition by the writers in this genre.

Judged in these terms, those responsible for the failures at
Maleme cannot escape criticism. It is, however, no less clear
that every soldier must expect that history will take hard account
of his lost opportunities, even those that could have been per-
ceptible only to the eye of faith or inspiration.

Certainly there are questions that must be asked about this
first night at Maleme. Would it not have been possible to mount
an effective counter-attack starting by dawn at the latest? Should
this not at least have been attempted, even at the grave risk of
failure? And need it have failed? The scattered elements of the
22nd Battalion, supported by the Maoris recalled from the
Platanias Road after their long route march, could have been left
to take over the area of Dhaskaliana, while the 23rd and the 21st
together moved westwards through the darkness. Among the
22nd there would have been plenty of men eager to serve as guides
in the hope of seeing the rescue of their friends.

Here was a force of 850 fully-trained infantry. Andrew and his
fellow colonels did not know that it outnumbered the enemy
available to meet it by at least four to three, but they had reason
to guess that the German strength might be less than their success
suggested. And the men of the 21st and the 23rd were in excellent
form. Scarcely touched in casualties, better armed than before,
and brimming with confidence after their successes of the day, they
had settled to sleep in the belief that victory was at hand. Time
enough remained to assemble them on the Kondomari side-track
and to bring them west along the coast road before deploying
them in a counter-attack starting from Pirgos. On their way
forward they would have been welcomed by the stragglers of the
22nd, and joined with fanatical enthusiasm by the armed Cretans
who prowled in anger about the villages. Their knowledge of the
ground, though less than it should have been, would have surpassed that of their enemies. It is scarcely to be doubted that they
would have succeeded in swarming onto the heights and reaching
the shelter of the slit trenches and bomb craters along the
Tavronitis. Infiltration into these positions, rather than the
immediate destruction of the Germans, would have been the
object. As the Russians were to find at Stalingrad, close contact
with the enemy was the best protection from the *Luftwaffe*. Under
the morning sun, friend and foe would have been caught in a

maelstrom in which it would have been difficult, if not impossible, for the pilots to identify any target between Pirgos and the river bed. In this way the airfield could have been subjected to concentrated fire from small arms. No more was required. Time would now have been on the side of the defenders.

For most of the night Gericke believed the New Zealanders to be in secure possession of Hill 107. At four o'clock in the morning, Student's revised plan, embodied in an order from XI Air Corps, told him that the airfield was to be captured 'at all costs'.[23] But he feared counter-attack before the parachutists could arrive.

In all probability [he was to write later] my battalion, the IV Battalion of the Storm Regiment, would not that night have been able to withstand an energetic counter-attack in battalion strength.[24]

Thus the stroke which the Germans had feared and expected, the action for which the men of the 23rd had so long held them-

---

[23] Gericke, p. 74 and Kurowski, p. 90. Gericke read the order 'by the light of a pocket torch'. It went on to say that the attack would be supported by further falls of parachutists 'in rear of the enemy at Maleme and Pirgos'. The German official reports do not give exact timings. But in his letter to the author of 21 January 1960, Gericke quotes Student as saying 'By the evening of the 20th I already had a picture of the situation that was sufficiently clear to enable me to arrive at a new decision, namely, to lay the *Schwerpunkt* of the attack upon Maleme and to roll up the island from the west towards the east'. It was not until later, 'in the night', that he sent for Capt. Kleye. It seems, therefore (and there is no evidence to contradict it), that he decided to concentrate on Maleme, and had ordered the parachute reinforcement, before hearing the result of Kleye's fact-finding flight; he was, of course, hoping that the first of his delayed seaborne flotillas would arrive on the beach at Maleme before nightfall on the 21st. The order that reached Gericke at dawn mentioned specifically only 'two companies of parachutists'. Both were from the 11/2 Parachute Regiment, the whole of which had been intended for Heraklion. Although *Einsatz Kreta*, in retrospect, refers confidently to the additional two-and-a-half companies that landed west of the airfield it may well be that some at least of these troops too had become available by accident rather than by design, and that Student did not learn of this further stroke of good fortune until after he had sent his order to the Storm Regiment. Kurowski, p. 93, maintains that at Topolia, on the evening of 20 May '550 parachutists came from all sides of the vast airfield' to report to Ramcke saying that their 'machines had fallen out at the start' that morning. Ramcke passed on news of this 'reserve' to Student who, 'a little later' ordered him to drop them at Maleme on the following 'afternoon'.

It is possible, therefore, that the parachute reinforcement at Maleme on the 21st may have been substantially more than the four-and-a-half companies recorded in *Einsatz Kreta*, and that even this strength had owed more to good luck than good judgement, Student and his staff can have had little wish to call attention in their report to the fact that their originally inadequate parachute reserve had been increased only by the happy accident of the delays on the Greek airfields. The implication is that the strength of the Storm Regiment at Maleme, until well after daylight on the 21st, may have been considerably less than the 2,300, itself perhaps an exaggeration (see chapter 9, footnote 1), that can be estimated from the Order of Battle

[24] Gericke, letter to the author, 21 Jan. 1960

selves prepared, remained undelivered. It might well, before the return of daylight, have decided the struggle for Crete.

During these vital hours, Hargest and his senior officers at Maleme had surrendered time and opportunity in a manner that did outrage to their courage, and mocked the eager devotion of their men. In the failure of communication between Andrew and Hargest had lain the beginnings of disaster. If he had suspected the extent of Andrew's predicament upon Hill 107 Hargest could scarcely have failed to come forward to Dhaskaliana before nightfall. Even at 3 a.m. on the following morning he might still have grasped his battalions and turned back the retreat; had he learnt of Andrew's arrival he could have reached the 23rd Battalion dug-out by carrier within half an hour. It was cruel misfortune that both radio and telephone contact should have broken down once more. But the very frailty of this link, with its failure lasting hour after hour during the night, should have impelled him to discover for himself whether Andrew had been exaggerating his difficulties, and to decide whether indeed it remained safe to assume that there was no need for the 23rd to counter-attack. As a company commander in the First World War he had been famous for his zeal in visiting his front-line posts.[25] The years had not lessened his courage. It was his judgement that had failed. Forced to make their own decision, while cut off from all knowledge of what was happening around them, the battalion commanders had proved no more equal to the situation.

All were men of resolution, well seasoned in war. What, then, is the explanation? The answer must be that Crete was different from anything that they had known. The ruthless, unceasing bombardment that had preceded the landings, the mystic, omniscient, searching quality of overwhelming attack from the air, the drifting dust clouds shrouding the scene, above all, the lack of those radio sets which for twenty-four hours had been serving the enemy better even than their aircraft, these factors had combined to lay a spell upon their usual vigour of thought and action.

Soon after dawn news of the retirement from Maleme reached the Headquarters of the New Zealand Division. Neither Puttick nor Hargest thought of attempting counter-attack in daylight. Such was the attitude induced in them by the *Luftwaffe*. They

[25] Aitken, p. 103

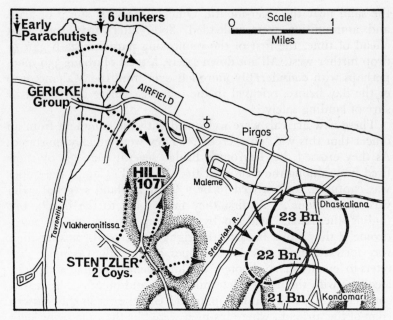

12.   Maleme: 8 a.m., 21 May

knew that possession of the airfield must greatly strengthen the
enemy. Tacitly it was accepted that this could not be prevented.
The artillery would do what it could. Nothing more was possible
until after the return of darkness. The movement of reserves to the
west was not considered.

The men of the Storm Regiment felt their spirits rising with
the sun of the new day. There was still no sign of the expected
counter-attack, and now they would again have the *Luftwaffe*
to help them. In their penetration along the road from the
Tavronitis Bridge Gericke's troops soon found that, instead of
killing machine-gun fire, only occasional shots came from the
slopes on their right. Gradually they understood that, in some
miraculous fashion, these heights had fallen to their comrades
during the night. They could now be sure of occupying the
runway. But for the moment they dared not move far. Although
every hour brought improvement they were still very conscious
of their weakness.

At about 8 a.m. the six Junkers sent by Student thudded into the sand near the river-mouth. Quickly the vital stores of arms and ammunition were unloaded. Soon afterwards, somewhat ahead of time, the first of the reinforcing parachutists began to drop further west. All got down safely, a total of about 350 men, perhaps with considerably more left over from the Maleme drop of the day before, released in the one area where they could be sure of landing safely.[26]

These new arrivals were welcomed with the comment from an officer that this was 'no exercise'.[27] They were quickly mustered. As they crossed the Tavronitis Bridge several were hit by shots fired from among the trees near the old R.A.F. Camp; the sniper was captured, and proved to be a 'New Zealand sergeant' who was 'quite alone'.[28] At first they moved left to the beach, but finding themselves held up by fire from 'houses on the aerodrome'[29] they came back to the right of the road, picking their way forward along the lower slopes of the hill. *Operation Crete* refers to 'enemy sharp-shooters' holding 'well camouflaged defence localities with the utmost determination', and mentions 'repeated counter-attacks'. Not until 4 p.m. did Gericke reach the 'eastern edge of the airfield', where his men were 'for the time being held upon this line'.[30] Further inland the advance was no less cautious. It was 5 p.m. before it reached the old 22nd Regimental Aid Post, in a fold of the hills about five hundred yards south of the eastern end of the runway, and the capture of Maleme village, still nearly half a mile short of Pirgos, was not claimed until after 7 p.m.[31]

Such comments, exaggerated though they must be, suggest that stragglers from the 22nd, backed by armed Cretans, were still offering resistance a full mile in front of the New Zealand line. There were no 'houses on the aerodrome', but determined men could find cover within the walled cemetery, and among the straggle of scrub and bamboo stretching out from Pirgos village.

Over the whole area west of Modhion, the German pilots, deceived by the Nazi flags, and aware that many parachutists had fallen in the vicinity, were hesitating to press their attacks. Here an infantry encounter would have been fought on level terms.

[26] DP. According to Sgt.-Maj. F. Teichmann, interviewed by W. G. McClymont in Dec. 1945, a 'first group' of parachutists arrived early in the morning. Almost certainly these were some of the men who had been left behind. They would now be able to play a far more effective part than they could have done if they had been dropped on the day before as intended. See also above, p. 259, *n.* 23

[27] DP, Sgt.-Maj. F. Teichmann   [28] Ibid.   [29] Ibid.

[30] *Einsatz Kreta*, Battle Report of XI Air Corps   [31] Kurowski, p. 95

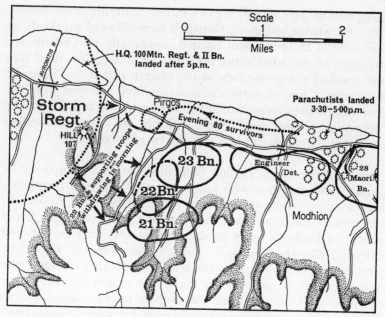

13.   Maleme: 7 p.m., 21 May

Instead, not even skirmishing parties had been sent forward to make the Germans pay dearly for their advance over the exposed slopes. All contact had been broken at a time when it should have been maintained at any cost. The 5th Brigade, and indeed the whole of Puttick's Division, had begun the day in total passivity, neither daring a return into the hills south-west of Pirgos, nor attempting any concentration for a counter-blow that might begin at dusk. From their positions between Dhaskaliana and Kondomari the New Zealanders could see nothing of the parachutists, still hidden by the shoulders of the hills, by the gentle swell of ground, and by the plantations and dense growths of bamboo which stretched from Pirgos to the shore. The men of the 23rd and 21st Battalions, still joined by stragglers from the 22nd, lay in the shade of the olives among the German corpses while a mile in front of them their few hundred enemies doubtfully and cautiously felt their way forward under the blazing sun, hour by hour extending their grip upon the defence positions lately held by Andrew and the 22nd.

At about 3 p.m. the view to the west was further obscured by rising dust as the *Luftwaffe* began a furious battering of the villages. After the planes had gone, Gericke's men followed up slowly on each side of the road, still resisted, apparently by Cretans and stragglers of the 22nd, from some of the houses. Not until they had reached the cross-roads at the eastern exit from Pirgos did they meet a line of entrenchments; as they emerged from the dust clouds they were brought abruptly to a standstill by two companies of the 23rd. Optimistically the New Zealanders estimated that their fire had cost the enemy 200 dead.

Some three hours earlier Student's last two companies of parachutists, the men who had been switched from Heraklion, had began to come down along the road between Pirgos and Platanias. Unable to reach their weapon containers, they fared almost as badly as their predecessors in this area on the first morning. Gericke saw with dismay that some of the white parachutes were falling into the sea; he knew that the men who hung from them must drown under the weight of their heavy equipment. Those who made the drop on land fell into the arms of the Engineer Battalion and the Maoris. For a few minutes there was a savage fight, Schmeisser and Spandau against rifle, Bren and bayonet, with many desperate individual encounters.

At one stage I stopped for a minute or two to see how things were going [reported one of the New Zealand officers], and a Hun dropped not ten feet away. I had my pistol in my hand . . . and without really knowing what I was doing I let him have it while he was still on the ground. I had hardly got over the shock when another came down almost on top of me and I plugged him too while he was untangling himself. Not cricket I know but there it is.[32]

No man dared pause to accept surrender. Major Dyer of the Maoris saw a German firing from the mouth of a well.

As we got to him he crouched down shamming dead. I told the Maori to bayonet him. As he did so he turned his head away, not bearing the sight . . . we rushed out among the Germans scattered every 15 or 20 yds. . . . One at about 15 yds. instead of firing his tommy-gun started to lie down to fire. I took a snap shot with a German Mauser. It grazed his behind and missed between his legs. My back hair lifted but the Maori got him (I had no bayonet). We

---

[32] Davin, p. 188, Narrative by Capt. J. N. Anderson. Ringel, p. 95, thought the 'bestial Maoris' most unfair. But a few days later his men were able to console themselves by murdering some hundreds of hostages

rushed on. . . . Some tried to crawl away. A giant of a man jumped up with his hands up like a gorilla, shouting 'Hants Oop!' I said: 'Shoot the bastard' and the Maori shot him. That was because many others were firing at us and a Spandau from further off. Suddenly bullets spluttered all round my feet . . .[33]

Few of these Germans survived. Out of one company all the officers and N.C.Os. were lost, while from the other only one officer, together with about eighty men, succeeded in gaining the outskirts of Pirgos. Small groups found cover in the houses, and among the clumps of bamboo between the road and the sea, where they waited for the protection of night.

While the New Zealanders were still engaged in this struggle they heard a new thunder of heavy aircraft. Moving in above the sea was a huge concentration of troop-carrying planes.[34]

Here was the beginning of the vital second stage of the German plan. During the morning no better news had reached Student from Heraklion, and Retimo had remained silent. But towards noon he had been encouraged to hear that his troops had occupied the heights south of the landing-ground at Maleme. The success of Kleye's adventure had demonstrated that it was possible for a heavy plane to land in the north-west corner of the airfield. He had therefore ordered that during the late afternoon a special formation of Junkers 52, carrying a mixed battalion of Mountain Troops together with a Regimental Headquarters, in all about 800 men, should 'force an air-landing on airfield Maleme'.[35]

At about 5 p.m. the operation began. Kurt Meyer, a war correspondent, later recorded the sensations he had felt while his pilot searched for a place along the runway:

The look-outs on each side sweep back the great doors so that the wind almost throws us from our seats. At half the height of the mountains we follow the line of the surf. The pilot has turned away as much as he can in order to upset the fire of the English. Machine-gun tracer dances below us and over the waves. Much too short . . . now the earth is just beneath us with houses, a strip of beach, wine gardens and surf. Impossible to land. Once more we turn back over the water. Heavy artillery fire covers the landing ground. Brown fountains of earth leap up and shower the machines which have already landed

---

[33] Davin, p. 190, Narrative by Lieut.-Col. H. G. Dyer

[34] Ibid., p. 189, Capt. F. Baker

[35] *Einsatz Kreta*, Battle Report of XI Air Corps. 'None of us had heard of Maleme,' says Ringel, p. 85

with earth, smoke and dust. . . . Now the pilot comes in again. This time he makes the attempt along the strip of shore in Maleme Bay. However this too isn't going to be easy. All the surface is irregular. Here and there there are broad strips of sand cut through by the courses of small rivulets. Between them lie thick clumps of reeds and smashed machines. We can't get down here. Shall we have another try on the landing-strip? Out of the question. Obstacles everywhere. English and German aircraft lie mixed with one another along the runway . . .

Our pilot turns away. He's got to land. At all costs, too, he must get his machine home safe again. The devil take this Crete. Hello, now we've caught it. Machine-gun bullets tear through the right wing span. The pilot grits his teeth. Cost what it may he has got to get down. Suddenly there leaps up below us a vineyard. We strike the ground and bounce. Then one wing grinds into the sand and tears the back of the machine half round to the left. Men, packs, boxes, ammunition are flung forward. Nothing we try to hold supports us. We lose the power over our own bodies. At last we come to a standstill, the machine standing half on its head.[36]

The danger was less than it seemed. The pilots were handicapped more by the congestion than gun-fire. Not under orders, but as a last resort when there seemed to be no more room in the vicinity of the airfield, a few brought their machines down along the shore towards Platanias, where no doubt the prospects looked better than west of the river mouth. They quickly discovered their mistake. Six of these great planes were 'set on fire before the occupants had the chance of alighting'.[37]

But at Maleme all but a dozen of the Junkers came down safely on the runway or close beside it. As they skidded to a halt the troops leapt to the ground and ran through the clouds of dust to take shelter under the lee of the hill. Although many of them, as Gericke noted, were 'greatly shaken' by what had been for most their first journey by air, their losses had not been great.

The New Zealand machine-guns could do little. They were now nearly a mile and a half from the runway, and the men who fired them could not see their targets. The range was also too great for the mortars. The only effective fire came from the artillery, despite a gruelling ordeal inflicted from the air. Groups of Messerschmitts swarmed above the guns, directed by observers who watched for the muzzle flashes from vantage points on Hill 107; before long one troop had lost half its men in dead and wounded.

[36] Meyer, from *Battle for the Strongpoint of Crete*   [37] Davin, p. 189, Capt. F. Baker

With great resolution the survivors continued to serve their weapons, taking shelter only as each attacking fighter began its run. Their performance convinced the Germans that this fire must be silenced.

Nevertheless, the defenders were much inclined to exaggerate its effect. Only nine guns were in action, all of them Italian 75 mm. field pieces that had been captured in the desert. With these weapons, several of them faulty, the gunners could achieve far less than would have been possible with their own cherished 25-pounders. Those best placed to judge had the fewest illusions. A lieutenant, observing for a troop of three guns, saw shells bursting upon stationary planes, and among groups of men as they disembarked. But he allowed himself no extravagant hopes. 'A few, not many', of the Junkers had 'burst into flames'.[38]

The Commander of the 5th Mountain Division was later to write of 'an indescribable inferno, machines everywhere mixed up together even on top of one another, wrecks, bomb craters . . .'[39] And *Operation Crete* admits that 'a number of Junkers remained shot to pieces or burnt out on the beach or on the airfield', while adding that 'extensive losses of Mountain Riflemen were avoided through the presence of mind of the pilots'.[40] The Diary of the 5th Mountain Division says that the operation was carried out 'without heavy casualties', although 'about twenty aircraft' were wrecked. More than half, indeed, were able to return that same afternoon to their bases on the Greek mainland.[41]

Thus the bulk of a Mountain Battalion, together with a Regimental Headquarters, perhaps 650 men, had been landed safely by the troop-carriers. At 7 p.m. they were joined by the tough and uncompromising Colonel Ramcke, now to succeed Meindl in charge of the Maleme Sector. His first order was to Gericke, telling him to 'press on regardless, on both sides of the road, and to keep on going into the darkness, in order to ensure that the enemy can no longer reach the airfield with heavy infantry weapons'.[42]

While he was still waiting anxiously for news of this operation a curious message reached Student:

Enemy columns approaching on road from Palaiokhora to the north. Head of column has reached . . . 10 k. south of the airfield. Heavy

[38] DP
[39] Gen. Ringel, quoted by Wittmann in *Die Gebirgstruppe*, Vol. II, 1954, p. 31
[40] *Einsatz Kreta*, Battle Report of XI Air Corps   [41] von der Heydte, p. 116
[42] Kurowski, p. 95

fighting with Group West. Stukas and bombers urgently requested.

The signal was signed 'Group West'.[43]

Palaiokhora was one of the small ports on the southern coast about thirty miles from Maleme. There was of course no column on this road. Partisans in the area were actively engaged with the southern company of parachutists, but it is scarcely conceivable that they exposed themselves in columns. Later Group West was to deny that any such message had been sent. Indeed, its origin remained a mystery to the Germans. Gericke felt that the British might have been using a captured transmitter.[44] Today it is tempting to speculate upon the possibility that the German system of signals may have been penetrated by an agent in Athens. But it would seem more likely that the message was sent by some alarmist who later preferred to conceal his identity. Certainly the story greatly perturbed Löhr who, for an hour or two, turned his Stukas away from the valley east of Pirgos and sent them roaming in vain up and down the gorges to the south. Student, with his flair for interpreting events at a distance, was less impressed. The report did not distract him from his conviction that the only real threat now lay in the east. Once assured that most of the troop-carriers had landed safely he began to feel that 'the crisis . . . had been overcome', and that any further difficulties should quickly be settled with the help of the seaborne reinforcements due to arrive at Maleme late that evening.

Neither Hitler nor Goering shared this confidence. Both had been dismayed by the losses of the first day. Goebbels did not allow any mention of the landing to appear in the press or on the radio. To the Germans already in Crete, and to those waiting to leave Greece, the significance of this was clear. There must be doubt about the outcome. 'Not a word about Crete,' wrote one of them, 'that tells us a lot'.[45] That night there was again much apprehension among the staffs in Athens.

On the evening of the second day of the invasion [says the War Diary of the 5th Mountain Division] the situation appeared to be balanced on a knife-edge . . . a heavy concentrated British counter-attack would force the defenders to fight for their lives.

There is no evidence that Ramcke shared these anxieties. Yet the situation which faced him as he took over his new command

---

[43] *Einsatz Kreta*, Battle Report of XI Air Corps. Ringel, p. 97, felt that 'British troops and tanks landed overnight at Palaiokhora might appear at dawn at Maleme'

[44] Gericke, p. 104   [45] Wittmann, p. 32

gave little reason for optimism. Certainly he knew that help was on its way. At any moment the first of the sea flotillas should appear upon the horizon. This would bring him an augmented Mountain Battalion, together with more parachutists and units of artillery with heavy weapons, a substantial reinforcement of 2,331 men. These should be followed next day by at least another two battalions of Mountain Troops arriving by air. But during the coming night he was bound to be highly vulnerable. His force was still small and lightly armed. It was clear that there had been few survivors among the parachutists that dropped east of Pirgos earlier that afternoon, and the men of the Gericke and Stentzler groups had been further reduced in the course of their advance by the stray snipers, and by the costly engagement around the Pirgos cross-roads. Casualties among the officers had been very severe. Meindl had returned with Kleye to hospital in Athens, the commanders of I and III Battalions together with Braun, the Brigade Major, were dead, and the adjutant had been injured in his parachute fall.[46] The 650 Mountain Troops were now the strongest group that he had available. That night the number of Germans who remained unwounded at Maleme, including the two companies now almost out of contact among the hills to the south and west, and taking account of all headquarters, medical and other ancillary formations, can scarcely have reached 1,800.

With this force he had to block the eastern approach to the airfield, while at the same time maintaining his grip upon the southern heights. No less important was the need to nourish the detachments that guarded his flanks. The Muerbe party had disappeared. At any moment there might emerge from the scrub west of the river mouth the enemy which must be presumed to have destroyed them. To the south, five miles along the winding road that led up the valley towards Palaiokhora, the company which had dropped near Voukolies on the first morning remained closely invested by the Cretans; he had been greeted on his arrival with the news of the 'enemy columns' that were said to be approaching along this road. He could not afford to neglect this threat. To meet it he called on the much reduced battalion at Pirgos. Reluctantly Gericke sent back to the bridge a party containing 'parts of' a company under a lieutenant. These men struck south into the mountains.

There was also the need to silence the guns. The engines of war are effective no less for what men fear of them than for what they do. Freyberg's conviction that the troop-carriers were capable of landing in open country had infinitely increased their value to the enemy. At this moment Ramcke believed that the artillery fire was the greatest threat to his operation, despite the relatively slight destruction that had been achieved by the shell-bursts. His anxiety was sufficient to convince him that these guns must be knocked out, even at the cost of detaching some of his precious troops from the protection of the airfield itself. No doubt he drew confidence from the fact that neither tanks nor infantry had made any attempt to burst in among the Junkers as they arrived. In fact the withdrawal of the New Zealanders, not only from Hill 107 but also from Pirgos, was a clear hint that they might have little further resistance to offer. The broken ground and the trees made it certain that any further approach by tanks would have to be made on the road. In such thick country armoured vehicles would scarcely dare to move in darkness, and it should now be possible to block them in the village if they came at first light; a few minutes later they could safely be left to the *Luftwaffe*.

Fortified, perhaps, by such reflections, he reacted with singular boldness to the challenge of his new command. At 9 p.m. he told Colonel Utz of the Mountain Regiment to take over the protection of the airfield from the south and west, while at the same time preparing for a wide sweep through the hills towards the guns. The move would start at dawn on the following morning.

These orders carried the scent of victory. Here indeed was aggression, almost a feeling of contempt for the opposition. Already he was subordinating the immediate defence of his perimeter to the attack. The captured ciphers may well by now have given him a clear hint that he was opposed by a much greater strength than had been expected, and before leaving Athens late that afternoon he must have heard that the formidable Heidrich Group had been contained in the Prison Valley, from which it followed that the New Zealanders behind Pirgos were still in contact along the coast with substantial reserves around Canea. Yet so lightly did he estimate the danger from this quarter that he was content to guard the two miles of his vital eastern flank with the weary remnants of the Storm Regiment, further weakened by the detachment of part of another company, and reinforced only by the survivors of the parachutists who had jumped that day. This mixed group from the Air Division, perhaps 900 strong, was all that he judged necessary to hold on during the night. It was a disposition that took little account of the twenty-four hours that had passed since the beginning of the battle, time enough for an alert defence to have organized an infantry reserve sufficient to infiltrate through such a screen and regain positions commanding the airfield.

If Ramcke had been able to see beyond the line of bamboos at Pirgos his confidence would have increased still further, for among the New Zealanders all was still uncertain. At Platanias there was none of the drive and purpose that he had imposed upon his own small force. Puttick and Hargest had not yet come to grips with the realities of their situation.

No less misguided than their determination to do nothing in daylight was the decision which they had now reached upon the strength in which they should make their counter-attack at night. That morning, at 11 a.m., Hargest had agreed with Puttick over the telephone that it should be carried out by the 5th Brigade, with the addition of one further battalion. Later that afternoon, after it had become clear that a substantial number of troops had been landed upon the airfield to supplement the fresh drops of parachutists observed earlier in the day, he reported that the situation was developing into 'a major offensive from the west of the aerodrome'. And he added that he was becoming increasingly apprehensive about the threat to his rear from the Germans who had been identified in the vicinity of Lake Aghya. Nevertheless he asked only for a further small detachment of 120 men to take over from the Maoris protection of the Platanias area. Even this request was refused by Puttick, who had lost none of his preoccupation with the Prison Valley and with coast defence.

Whatever doubts the Divisional Commander might have felt about committing his reserve on the first afternoon he could have no justification for withholding it now. His attitude at this moment does little to support his claim that he had earlier foreborne to use the 4th Brigade against the Germans in the Prison Valley for the reason that he had realized from the first that it might be needed for the more important task of clearing the airfield. It can only be assumed that he had not understood what was happening at Maleme. Since the action began he had not moved west from his Headquarters near Canea Bridge. Nor was the significance of the situation any clearer to Hargest, who was still at Platanias. Despite his apprehensions about a 'major offensive' by the enemy he was asking for only one battalion to help his counter-attack. Such were the views of the men on the spot.

In the light of such judgements by his local commanders, Freyberg still had no clear indication that the situation in the west had taken on particular urgency. Late that afternoon he held a conference of his brigadiers. It was attended by Puttick, Stewart, Vasey, and Inglis, but not by Hargest. All agreed that two battalions should be used for the recapture of Maleme, the 20th from the 4th Brigade coming in to support the Maoris. At the same time Freyberg decided to bring west from Georgeoupolis the 2/7 Australian Battalion, the last of Vasey's 19th Brigade, since the 2/8 had already joined a group of improvised infantry based on a transit camp near Perivolia.

That morning Vasey had intended to use the 2/7 to support his two battalions at Retimo. Later he had gathered that it might be needed for the counter-attack on the airfield; it was well fitted for such a task, about 580 strong, and full of confidence after its successes at Bardia and in Greece. But he had protested that this would entail the final splintering of his command. Now he learnt that instead it was to take over from the New Zealand 20th the defence of the coast west of the Kladiso River, a rôle that was assuming great importance. Throughout the day there had been increasing information to indicate that a German flotilla was at sea, and that a landing would be attempted that night. Lieutenant-Colonel Walker, the commanding officer of the 2/7, who also attended the conference, did not like the new arrangement. He foresaw that confusion might arise in the darkness, a consideration quickly dismissed by Inglis, who told him that 'a well-trained battalion'[47] would be able to carry out the relief in an hour.

Nobody was much concerned about what the Germans might have been doing at Maleme. Nobody asked whether two battalions would be enough.

Yet more troops were available – and not only within the New Zealand Division. Suda Area had been no more than lightly touched by the invasion. More than 14,000 men remained unengaged under Weston's command. It has been seen that thousands of these were of negligible value, disorganized and largely un-

47 Long, p. 235

armed. But thousands more were capable of maintaining a static defence, and among them, as yet little reduced by casualties, were the 854 men of the Welch Regiment, a striking force second to none in the island. Nor was there any thought of molesting the Germans in the Prison Valley. Rather was there now good reason for leaving them where they were. Coast defence and the recapture of Maleme had assumed the greater importance. It would be a pity to fail in either task for the lack of sufficient men committed.

Nevertheless, Freyberg decided not to call on any of the troops from Suda Area. It was a considered choice.[48] His brigadiers appeared to be reasonably happy about the west, happier indeed than he was himself. But more pressing and real to him was his awareness of the need to keep his administrative base intact, coupled with his increasing concern over information which foretold, from hour to hour and with growing certainty, that the enemy was about to land from the sea.

He had reason enough to be chary of using his reserves. False reports had continued to reach him from all sides. A study of these messages today gives some idea of the difficulties that must have weighed upon him in his attempt to direct this modern battle with no trained staff, and only the most primitive of communications.

Early in the day it had twice been signalled to Force Head-quarters that another drop of 300 parachutists had been made south-west of Canea. At about the same time he was told that at 4.30 that morning a man had seen a party of Germans landing on the beaches near the hospital. The exact numbers were unknown but it was thought that there must have been 'between fifty and sixty rafts or boats'.[49] His staff thought it wise to signal to the New Zealand Division:

Two separate reports state that enemy is landing troops from pontoons in vicinity area Seventh General Hospital.[50]

Not long afterwards another rumour was being refurbished. It came from the 10th Brigade:

Escaped warden confirms Commandant provided prisoners assisting construction landing ground west of prison.[51]

[48] Davin, p. 206
[49] New Zealand Division War Diary   [50] Ibid.   [51] Ibid.

In 1951 Christopher Buckley still believed this tale:

German parachutists [he wrote] were already busily at work by the end of the first day preparing alternative landing grounds, notably one in the Prison area.[52]

The truth was that no more parachutists had landed near Canea, nor anywhere in the west, apart from the few who had come down on each side of Maleme. No boats had approached the coast at any point. As for the Greek Commandant of the prison, who spoke German, he had indeed welcomed the invader with the utmost friendliness. But his prisoners, though doubtless sufficiently uncomfortable, were not assisting in the construction of a landing-ground since such a project had been recognized from the first as impossible.

From this tangle of deceptive rumour few certainties emerged. Although it seemed clear enough, not least from the captured German order, that the enemy intended to make a landing from the sea, little was known of the enemy airborne forces already in action.

At first a further 2,000 parachutists were thought to have fallen in the Maleme Sector during the second day.[53] Later it was realized that many of the parachutes had been bearing supplies. That evening the figure was amended to a count of 500 west of the Tavronitis and another 500 between Pirgos and Platanias. This was near enough. But how many of the heavy Junkers had come somewhere to earth was the subject of the wildest conjecture. The underestimations of the first day had now been succeeded by grotesque exaggeration. The Intelligence Section at Force Head-quarters decided that sixty troop-carrying planes had 'landed in the river valley and on the beaches west of the aerodrome before 0900 hours'. By nightfall it was believed that 'six hundred planes'[54] had come down in the general vicinity of Maleme; a mere 'thirty'[55] were thought to have landed on the airfield itself.

These figures contrast strangely with the truth. After the war

[52] DP, letter from Christopher Buckley to D. M. Davin, 1951 (undated)

[53] DP

[54] DP. The idea seems to have originated in a signal from N.Z. Div. to Creforce recorded in the N.Z. Div. War Diary. This says '5th Brigade estimate 600 troop-carriers landed their area yesterday'. The signal is dated 23 May, an error perhaps for 22. Later Freyberg was to refer to 'Six hundred planes' as the number believed to have landed at 'Maleme aerodrome or its environs during the day' of the 21st. It is possible, of course, that he may himself in retrospect have confused the two days

[55] New Zealand Division War Diary

the official New Zealand historians were to decide that sixty-six planes had put down on the airfield during the second afternoon.[56] In all, therefore, with the addition of those that had crashed along the beach towards Platanias, about eighty of the Junkers had landed troops. Earlier, Kleye had arrived on his special mission, and another half-dozen had brought ammunition. Some sixty more had dropped parachutists.

From one source the reports had been accurate. The 4th Brigade had been able to inform Divisional Headquarters that 'twenty-six planes' had been seen 'taking off from aerodrome'.[57] This was an observation that should have served to dispel much of the wilder optimism about the extent of the destruction that was being caused by the artillery.

Freyberg was forced to make what he could of this confused and contradictory information. His dilemma upon that evening of 21 May is well revealed in a signal sent to Cairo some time late that night or early on the following morning. After remarking that all appeared to be going reasonably well at Heraklion and Retimo, and that the Suda perimeter was intact, he went on to describe the day's fighting in more detail. For the first time he expressed some anxiety about events in the west. He recognized that the enemy had begun to make a particular effort in this part of the island and had indeed succeeded in forcing a limited withdrawal from Maleme. Bombing from the air was still very heavy and there had been many casualties. Late in the afternoon further drops of parachutists had been made on both sides of the 22nd Battalion's old defence lines, and at 5 p.m. 'thirty' planes had landed on the airfield itself, while others had put down on beaches. It was feared that the guns had been put out of action by air attack. He was bringing some of the Australian troops over from Georgeoupolis in order 'to strengthen the position' at Maleme and he hoped that the R.A.F. would do everything possible to crater the runway. But the situation here remained 'far from clear' and might be 'perilous as well'.[58]

This message makes it clear that he was still thinking of parachutists, coupled with planes landing upon the beaches, as the main source of enemy reinforcement. The 'thirty' troop-carriers, which were all that he had as yet understood to have come down on the runway, appear as a cloud no larger than a

[56] DP   [57] New Zealand Division War Diary   [58] Davin, p. 206

man's hand. The whole tenor of the day's reports had continued to confirm in him his belief that the capture of an airfield was no more than a subsidiary part of the enemy plan. It has been seen that he was to write later of this 21 May that it had been 'estimated that during the day 600 planes landed at Maleme aerodrome or its environs'.[59] He had not quoted this number in his signal to Cairo. Perhaps he had felt it to be scarcely credible.[60] Even so, such a tale, brought to him by his own staff, must have done much to sustain him in his original belief that the troop-carriers would crash-land all over the countryside. In August 1941 he was to maintain that it had not been thought possible for aircraft to put down in the riverbed west of the airfield at Maleme. Nevertheless, during that morning 'troop-carriers' had 'begun to land and also on the beaches west of the aerodome'.[61]

Since only thirty were said to have used the runway, and no more than a dozen or so had put down along the beach west of Platanias, it was natural for him to assume that many scores, if not hundreds, must have been crashing where they could, perhaps under the mountains, or out of sight on the far side of the Tavronitis. Once more the significance of the airfield itself was diminished by such a judgement. There could be no pressing need for its capture if the enemy were landing most of their troops without requiring to use it. Thus false information ensured that his view of the battle should remain set within the pattern of his own disastrous preconception.

How valuable to him on that evening would have been the knowledge that at most 850[62] parachutists had been dropped in the Western Sector during the day, all of them in the Maleme area, that less than 550 of them were still with their units and capable of fighting, that no more could be dropped in time to influence the battle, and that, apart from the dozen Junkers along the beach, most of which had come to disaster, together with the further seven which had floundered to a standstill among the whin-covered dunes near the river mouth, every troop-carrier had been forced to come in along the narrow half-mile runway at Maleme. Among so much that was misleading there had been

---

[59] See above, p. 274, n. 54

[60] The figure reappeared in Wavell's despatch: *Operations in the Middle East from 7th February 1941 to 15th July 1941*

[61] DP

[62] Allowing for about 250 'left-overs' not recorded in *Einsatz Kreta*

one clue to the truth. If the Junkers were indeed putting down safely in open country and along distant and unseen beaches, why had they persisted late that evening in accepting what appeared to be severe losses in their use of the airfield? But this was a question that nobody thought of asking.

In his acceptance of the Divisional plan for the counter-attack Freyberg was subscribing to a paradox. While overestimating the numbers of the enemy at Maleme he was yet sending insufficient force to deal with them. As night fell he must have believed, on the most conservative interpretation of the information available to him, that at least 1,500 fresh troops, and probably many more, much better armed than their predecessors, had arrived to reinforce the Storm Regiment. How then could he have hoped that two weakened battalions could succeed after the failure of the previous day when the Storm Regiment was still shaken and unsupported?

The truth must be that he did not yet choose to regard the matter as urgent. Perhaps he hesitated to enquire too closely at this stage into the strange confidence apparently felt by Hargest and Puttick. That he had already developed some misgiving about Maleme is made clear by his signal to Cairo. He may very well have realized that little could be expected of this counter-attack, while at the same time seeing the problem as one that he would later be able to face with success. Certainly the airfield at Maleme could not be allowed to nourish the enemy for long, even within the limited rôle which was all that he supposed it to have played so far. Soon he would round upon it from his secure base at Suda.

But this must wait. First he must deal with a threat still more pressing. He must ensure that his base itself should remain intact. Until the sea invasion had been defeated all else must take second place.

For now he had heard the invasion from the sea was imminent. It would fall upon the coast west of Canea. The news came from the sources that had proved so reliable in the forecast of the airborne attack. And apart from the slight change in the suggested landing area this was the plan that he had read in the captured Brigade Order. Here was confirmation of what from the first had been his greatest anxiety. Within an hour or two heavy armoured vehicles might be churning off the sand dunes by the Kladiso river mouth into the heart of his defence system. Once they were fairly ashore he would have no weapons capable of stopping them. True he had passed on his information to Cunningham. But the Admiral had never been optimistic about the Navy's prospect of intercepting the enemy flotillas. Recently his attitude had been somewhat more reassuring. Who could tell to what extent it would be justified?

The priorities that Freyberg accorded that night show well that all his care was for coast defence. Inglis recalls that as he left Force Headquarters, after the conference of brigadiers, the talk was of nothing but the sea.

And at 7.50 p.m. that evening a signal went out to the New Zealand Division:

> Reliable information. Early seaborne attack in area Canea likely. New Zealand Division remains responsible coast from west up to Kladiso River. Welch Battalion forthwith to stiffen existing defences from Kladiso to Khalepa.[63]

There was nothing more about Maleme.

[63] New Zealand Division War Diary

14

The Navy Intervenes: 21-22 May

The message from Freyberg came as no surprise to Admiral Cunningham. From the reports of long range reconnaissance aircraft he had known that groups of small boats were filtering southward through the Greek islands. When the airborne attack began he at once gave orders for light forces to patrol along the north coast of the island during the hours of darkness.

On the first night his ships encountered nothing more than six Italian motor torpedo boats. Soon after dawn, they retired under increasing attention from the air, passing through the Kasos Straits in the east and the Antikithera Channel in the west. But they could not escape the bombers. During the course of a high level attack by Italian planes the destroyer *Juno* blew up and sank within two minutes; the cruiser *Ajax* was damaged.

At dusk on the following evening, 21/22 May, they turned north again seeking in high expectation for the enemy. Soon they were to be rewarded.

Student's two invasion flotillas were now approaching the end of their voyage. They had little protection. After the calamity off Cape Matapan, at the end of March, the Italians had been in no mood to venture further with their injured naval forces. 'A renewed attempt to persuade the Italian Fleet to put to sea,' complained Air Fleet IV, 'in order to pin down British warships away from Crete', had 'failed due to the refusal of the authorities in Rome'.[1]

The Germans knew that their attempt to attack Crete from the sea must depend upon the *Luftwaffe*. During the long hours of daylight the ships had cruised in confidence over the blue water, while above them the planes roared in majestic succession. But progress had been slow. So far from disposing of the 'ample' resources attributed to them by the War Office the *Wehrmacht* had been hard-pressed to find craft that would be capable of passing

[1] *The Invasion of Crete*, report by Air Fleet IV

the shallows close to the shore. In the end it had resorted to Greek caiques. Even with sails hoisted to aid the feeble engines these clumsy vessels, each carrying about a hundred men with their equipment, could wallow forward at no more than a bare four knots, restricting the small steamers that accompanied them to their own laggard pace.

By the evening of the 20th, the western flotilla had reached the island of Milos. Ahead of it, there now lay seventy miles of open sea. Before dawn it had set out upon the last stage. For a time all went well. The captain of the Italian destroyer *Lupo* felt that it should be 'capable of reaching Maleme before dark'.[2] But during the afternoon the wind failed. When night closed upon them the men on board had caught only a glimpse of the mountains of Crete above the horizon. They still had thirty miles to go. And now they were in no doubt of their peril. In this strange contest of alternating hazards chance had turned against them. By day they had enjoyed complete security. At night the power of their enemies would be no less absolute.

First they heard, from far away, the changing note of heavy engines. Next they saw searchlights winking and probing in the darkness. Desperately they lowered their sails and waited in a silence broken only by the lapping of the black waters. The lights came nearer.

To us [a rifleman of the Mountain Troops was to recall later] these searchlights appear like fingers of death. Sharp cut against the darkness they grope blindly here and there over the water . . . for a moment they touch our mast tips in brilliant light, then wander on. Have they seen us? Or are we too small to be noticed? We don't know. The minutes crawl by while the hands of our watches appear to have stopped. Then without warning comes the harsh whisper of 'Warships'. Not another sound to be heard. But there the thing is right in front of us. A dark shadow high as a church tower – not moving. I have to turn my head to take in its great dark length. Suddenly the searchlights flash out again, drenching our tiny vessel in a light as bright as day, tearing us from the protection of the darkness and plunging us in the instant upon the brink of destruction. 'Everybody overboard.' As we leap into the water the first salvoes crash into us like a tempest, sending showers of wood and debris about our ears.[3]

The fatal glare of a searchlight fastened sooner or later upon most of these caiques – followed by the tornado of shells and bullets. Rear-Admiral Glennie, with a squadron of destroyers and

[2] *The Invasion of Crete*, report by Air Fleet IV   [3] Wittmann, p. 40

cruisers, had found them eighteen miles north of Canea. His ships, which had endured much during the day, now 'conducted themselves with zest and energy',[4] using radar to seek out their silent targets. At the end of a 'scrambling engagement'[5] at least a dozen caiques and three small steamers, all crammed with enemy infantry, had been left blazing or sunk by ramming and gunfire.

In his autobiography, written soon after the war, Cunningham maintains that 'some four thousand German troops were left to drown, and the first attempted invasion by sea was completely frustrated'.[6] This figure, now known to be too high, is quoted by Churchill.[7] The first reports of the German Twelfth Army gave the total of men in the convoy as 2,331.[8] Certainly the command in Athens at first believed that nearly all had perished. But in the dark night some of the caiques had escaped, helped by smoke from the Italian torpedo boats, and most of the men who had jumped into the sea, kept afloat by their lifebelts in the relatively warm water, were rescued on the following morning. 'An officer and thirty-five men'[9] of 100 Regiment were able to struggle ashore on Cape Spatha. Later a secret investigation by the Twelfth Army was to conclude that no more than thirteen officers, including the Commander of the Mountain Battalion, and 311 other ranks had been lost, an estimate which must be accepted.[10] But with the second of Cunningham's conclusions there can be no dispute. Scarcely a man had reached Crete. In the words of Air Fleet IV the problem of sending reinforcements by sea 'remained unsolved'.

That same night, as dawn was breaking, the eastern squadron of cruisers and destroyers, under Rear-Admiral King, began to sweep north-west from the Kasos Strait deep into the Aegean. Inevitably they were at once picked up by the *Luftwaffe*. Nevertheless, they held on boldly to the north. Soon they came upon several caiques. These proved to be the unfortunate outriders of the second enemy flotilla, held up for six hours by the late arrival of its escort vessels off the Piraeus. The delay was to prove its salvation. Had it approached the coast north of Heraklion before daylight its fate must have been certain. But it was not until 10 a.m. that one of King's destroyers reported the presence,

---

[4] Cunningham, p. 369, quoting Glennie   [5] Ibid., p. 369
[6] Ibid., p. 369   [7] Churchill, Vol. III, p. 268
[8] Davin, p. 487   [9] War Diary of 5th Mountain Division   [10] Davin, p. 486

behind an enemy smoke screen, of many more caiques and small ships.

Here was a tantalizing prospect. And also a singular dilemma. King realized that if he were to spend more time in the destruction of these vessels he must offer his ships to the full violence of the bombers. His ammunition was running down, and his mobility had been reduced by damage to one of the anti-aircraft cruisers. Already he had pressed north in daylight to within fifty miles of the mainland, further than had any part of the Fleet since the evacuation of Greece. Many hours remained before dusk. From far and wide, as he knew very well, the enemy aircraft were now concentrating upon him. Moreover his mission had been accomplished. The enemy flotilla could no longer hope to reach Crete that day. Surely he must now do all that he could to preserve his force. Reluctantly, therefore, he chose to break away to the south and west. Such a decision might be held to have interpreted exactly the mind of the Commander-in-Chief, whose main anxiety for many days past had been the avoidance of irreparable damage to the Mediterranean Fleet, except in the supreme necessity of support for the Army. In the end, his ships managed to reach the Kithera Channel only with the greatest difficulty.

Later he was to be criticized for this withdrawal, not only by the Prime Minister, but also, less comprehensibly, by Cunningham who maintained that 'the safest place' would have been amongst the enemy convoy'.[11] This may be doubted. There can be no analogy with those parachutists who had become intermingled with their enemies in Crete; upon their survival must depend the outcome of the battle. The situation of the troops in the caiques was very different. It was unlikely that the German authorities would feel the same qualms about their safety as about that of the parachutists. They were incapable of influencing the struggle on land, and, indeed, already in peril so great that no intervention could increase it, even had the Germans not seen before them that prize dearest of all to German hearts – the ships of the Royal Navy.

A pitiless ordeal now began for all the officers and men of Cunningham's command. At so short a distance from the mainland there could be no hope of escaping observation by enemy reconnaissance planes, even by swift withdrawal southwards

[11] Cunningham, p. 370

during the hours of daylight. Thus dawn on the 22nd found a major part of the Mediterranean Fleet at the mercy of the *Luftwaffe*. Over a wide area ships were sunk. Others were left crippled, the enemy planes swarming like bees about their mast tops. Lingering beside them, or turning back to help, were sister vessels whose captains were ready to face any risk in their determination to rescue survivors from the water, even to the extent of ignoring Cunningham's orders.

One reason for all these losses [he was to declare after the battle] was the disregard of a golden rule which we had long since found essential in all our previous encounters with aircraft, and that was never to detach ships for any particular tasks. The fleet should remain concentrated and move in formation to wherever any rescue or other work had to be done.[12]

In these circumstances a series of disasters fell upon the ships assembled west of Crete. The famous *Warspite*, veteran of Jutland, bearing the flag of Rear-Admiral Rawlings, was badly damaged, and the *Greyhound* sunk; a young seaman from this destroyer found himself in a boat with the First Lieutenant and eighteen men; as a plane came straight at them he dived into the water to avoid the bullets; when he came back to the surface he found that every man in the boat was dead. Admiral King, now the senior officer remaining in the area, instructed two more destroyers, supported by the cruisers *Gloucester* and *Fiji*, to pick up the survivors. Not until 3 p.m. did King learn that both the cruisers had expended nearly all their ammunition. Immediately he ordered them to withdraw. But it was too late. At 3.50 p.m. the *Gloucester*, now defenceless in the brilliant afternoon, was hit by a succession of bombs, set on fire, and sunk. Of her crew forty-nine officers and 673 ratings were lost. Those who did not go down with her were machine-gunned in the water.

Thus went the gallant *Gloucester* [wrote Cunningham of this incident in words which illuminate the stresses of the time and reveal the burden which lay upon the Commander-in-Chief], she had endured all things, and no ship had worked harder or had had more risky tasks. She had been hit by bombs more times than any other vessel, and had always come up smiling. As she left Alexandria for the last time I went alongside her in my barge and had a talk with her Captain, Henry Aubrey Rowley. He was very anxious about his men, who were just worn out, which was not surprising, as I well realized. I promised to go

[12] Cunningham, p. 373

on board and talk to them on their return to harbour; but they never came back . . . Rowley's body, recognizable by his uniform monkey jacket and the signals in his pocket, came ashore to the west of Mersa Matruh about four weeks later. It was a long way to come home.[13]

The *Fiji* almost escaped. Dusk was falling as a Messerschmitt 109[14, 15] swept out of a cloud in a shallow dive to drop a single bomb which blew in her bottom and brought her close to a standstill. Half an hour later another solitary plane emerged out of the gathering darkness that would have saved her. This scored a final hit. At 8.15 p.m. she rolled over and sank. Most of the crew were rescued by the *Kandahar* and *Kingston*.

That night it was reported to Cunningham in Alexandria that the battleships were 'empty'[16] of short-range ammunition. The cruisers he already knew to be in similar plight. He therefore gave the order that all ships at sea should return to Egypt to refuel. By the following morning a mistake had been discovered in the signal. According to the corrected version the heavy ships still had 'plenty' of ammunition. But it was now too late for them to return during the day of the 23rd. This meant that the 5th Destroyer Flotilla, which had sailed for Crete from Malta, must be left without aircraft protection. It had been intended that these destroyers, under the command of Captain Lord Louis Mountbatten of the *Kelly*, should try to find survivors from the *Gloucester* and the *Fiji*. Cunningham had now to make the painful decision that this hope must be abandoned. Mountbatten and his destroyers would have to undertake the night patrol north of Canea. There were no other ships to do it.

On the following morning, at about 8 a.m., after a night in which they had destroyed two caiques full of soldiers and fired a few shells at Maleme airfield, the *Kelly*, *Kashmir* and *Kipling* were attacked by twenty-four dive bombers.

The *Kashmir* went first, sinking almost immediately. A few minutes later the *Kelly* was hit by a heavy bomb while 'steaming at thirty-three knots'.[17] Still racing through the water, she capsized before curving to a standstill. Half an hour later she was gone. Commander St. Clair Ford, in the *Kipling*, turned back to search for survivors. For three hours he lingered upon the scene, his ship attacked again and again by bombers. By the early

[13] Cunningham, p. 371   [14] Ibid., p. 373
[15] Kurowski, p. 125, says that it was 'most unlikely' to have been a 'Messerschmitt 109'
[16] Cunningham, p. 373   [17] Earl Mountbatten, *Observer*, 20 Sept. 1964

afternoon no fewer than forty aircraft had struck at her with more than eighty bombs. Miraculously, she carried on unscathed until the morning of the 24th when she was towed into Alexandria after running out of fuel. Her commander had forgotten the 'golden rule'. For this 279 survivors, including Mountbatten, had cause to be thankful.

Cunningham had not known that, among all his difficulties, there existed two factors which would greatly help him in his task of coast defence. First there was the slow speed of the enemy flotillas. No doubt he had received from London the same advance information as that sent to Freyberg on 29 April, the appreciation that the enemy shipping would be 'ample for seaborne operations', with lighters for the transport of tanks, supplemented by further shipping sent from Italy. After this it must have come as a pleasant surprise to find, almost a month later, that the Germans were relying so heavily for their sea transport upon the ancient caiques, and that the final stage of their voyage, requiring at least twenty hours even with the help of a favourable wind, was leaving them in darkness, bereft of the protection of the *Luftwaffe*. The second factor in his favour was Mussolini's refusal to risk anything more than destroyers and other small surface craft in their defence. At this time, the Italian Navy was still a great deal more formidable than it has come to appear in retrospect. The gallant exploits of Prince Borghese's torpedo-boat flotillas had already brought spectacular and important successes, among them the crippling of the *York* in Suda Bay. By September 1943, no less than eighty-five out of 122 submarines had been lost in the fighting.[18] Despite Taranto and Matapan, the Italian Battle Fleet could have played a menacing part in the waters about Crete.

Had Cunningham known that the German attempt at sea invasion was to be handicapped in this fashion he might well have decided to hold his heavy ships further south, in closed anti-aircraft formations, detaching to race north at sundown only light forces which could return within the protection of the squadrons soon after dawn. This was the general plan towards which he was beginning to turn by the third day. But its effectiveness was now much diminished by the losses which had already befallen his widely scattered Fleet, and by the increasingly urgent need to land men and material.

[18] Böhmler, p. 33

The protection of the coast was not his only responsibility. No less vital was the matter of supply. Freyberg's anxieties about his communications, already sufficiently acute, had been further increased by the general paralysis which had afflicted his troops as a result of the airborne attack coupled with the parachute lodgments. Now he had begun to press for the delivery of reinforcement to Suda Bay. And to reach Suda even the fastest destroyers must hasten for many hours in daylight under the bombers.

Every evening Cunningham waited in his office in Alexandria, 'dreading the sound of the telephone bell which was usually the harbinger of more bad news'.[19] His ships and men were being harried as never before by this unimpeded onslaught from the *Luftwaffe*. The concentration against them from the air was far heavier than in the Norway campaign. Increasingly, it was evident that anti-aircraft guns alone could not give sufficient protection. Support was needed in the air itself. But he was operating 400 miles from his base. At this range the Royal Air Force could not have intervened effectively even if planes had been available. And the Fleet Air Arm could do little. The only aircraft-carrier was the *Formidable* which had 'built up her fighter strength to twelve Fulmars, though some were of doubtful utility'.[20] He had repeatedly asked for more aircraft. Yet he still had not sufficient planes even to carry out essential reconnaissance.

These difficulties were not understood in England. The messages arriving from London revealed that not only the politicians, but also the Chiefs of Staff, had failed to realize that a fleet, no less than a land force, must eventually become reduced to helplessness under continued and overwhelming assault from the air.

Why the authorities at home apparently could not see the danger of our situation in the Mediterranean without adequate air support [he was to write after the war], passed my comprehension.[21]

At 4 p.m. on the 23rd, as if to emphasize this lack of contact, the Admiralty sent directly to the *Glenroy* a signal countermanding his order for the ship to turn back; he had felt that it would be 'sheer murder to send her on'. Within an hour, he had reaffirmed his original decision, pointing out that if the ship had obeyed the Admiralty she would have arrived off Crete in daylight at the

[19] Cunningham, p. 390   [20] Ibid., p. 376   [21] Ibid., p. 351

'worst possible time for air attack'. Long after the war the sting of this incident still lingered, revealed in his acid comment, 'The less said about this unjustifiable interference by those ignorant of the situation the better.'[22]

It had become plain that the battle would be decided by the factors of reinforcement and supply. Thus far the Navy had amply fulfilled the first of its obligations to the Army. But now Cunningham was beginning to feel increasing anxiety lest this continued exposure to the *Luftwaffe* should cripple the Mediterranean Fleet. He signalled to London on the 23rd:

The operations of the last four days have been nothing short of a trial of strength between the Mediterranean Fleet and the German Air Force. . . . I am afraid that in the coastal area we have to admit defeat and accept the fact that losses are too great to justify us in trying to prevent seaborne attacks on Crete. This is a melancholy conclusion, but it must be faced. As I have always feared, enemy command of air, unchallenged by our own Air Force, and in these restricted waters, with Mediterranean weather, is too great odds for us to take on except by seizing opportunities of surprise and using utmost circumspection . . .[23]

The Chiefs of Staff replied that it remained essential to prevent German reinforcement from reaching Crete by sea even if this should mean that ships would have to operate north of the island by day. It was hoped that soon the Army would be able to overcome the airborne troops. After that it should also be able to deal with any attack from the sea. In the meantime the Navy would have to face the prospect of further losses. The Chiefs of Staff added that Cunningham should 'concert measures'[24] with the other Commanders-in-Chief, a comment which, in the light of the help that could be given at that time by the Royal Air Force, did little to enhance his already sadly frayed confidence in their judgement.

His indignation is revealed in his reply:

Their Lordships may rest assured that determining factor in operating in Aegean is not fear of sustaining losses but need to avoid loss which, without commensurate advantage to ourselves, will cripple Fleet out here. So far as I am aware, enemy has not succeeded in getting any considerable reinforcements to Crete by sea, if indeed he has sent any at all . . .[25]

[22] Cunningham, p. 375   [23] Churchill, Vol. III, p. 259
[24] Cunningham, p. 375   [25] Churchill, Vol. III, p. 260

Already he was pessimistic about the battle on land. Things appeared to be going wrong as a result of the German air operation alone. The Fleet might suffer further grievous injury yet have nothing to show for it. In three days, two cruisers and four destroyers had been sunk, and a battleship, two cruisers, and four destroyers severely damaged.

He went on to say:

We cannot afford another such experience and retain sea control in Eastern Mediterranean.

Writing in 1961 Captain Roskill, the Naval Historian, was in no doubt that such anxieties had been abundantly justified. He condemned the policies which in 1941 had exposed the ships of the Navy without air cover so close to enemy-occupied coast lines and concluded that the damage inflicted in these actions had threatened the whole conduct of the war.[26] Certainly, few would now deny that to have followed a scattered flotilla of caiques at high noon into the northern recesses of the Aegean would have been no less foolhardy, in relation alike to the needs of the moment and to the ultimate cause, than were the cavalry pursuits of Prince Rupert. Admiral King had been right after all. It is to be hoped that on reflection his august detractors may have found time to tell him so.

The danger from the sea, sharply suggested by the predicament of the Fleet, had never been as grave as Freyberg and the staffs in Egypt had been led to suppose. And herein lay a fateful paradox. From the start, Cunningham had insisted that he might not be able to protect the coast. Yet in this his success had been complete. How much better if his assurance had been greater and his achievement less. A few scattered caique loads of soldiers straggling on to the shore need have presented no very deadly problem. On the other hand, if Freyberg had been given good reason to place greater confidence in the Navy, much else might have been transformed.

Within such a perspective his attention would have been directed less compulsively toward the sea. Another requirement, not merely anticipated, but already active and pressing, would have leapt into relief. He would have seen that, come what might, as a first and clamorous necessity, the enemy must be cleared from Maleme.

[26] Roskill, Vol. III, p. 2

15

Counter-Attack: 21-22 May

At seven o'clock on the evening of the 21st, Hargest heard from Puttick over the telephone that he was to go ahead with the night attack on the airfield. As infantry reinforcement he would have the New Zealand 20th Battalion, detached from the 4th Brigade and sent forward in motor transport from its defensive position on the coast east of the Hospital. He could also expect support from artillery, and from three light tanks. Between midnight and 2 a.m. the Royal Air Force would drop some bombs, a prospect which was recorded in the 5th Brigade War Diary as 'great news', with the wry comment that not a British plane had been seen since the opening of the battle.

He decided to deploy the 20th across the coastal strip immediately west of Platanias, the Maoris extending the line south of the road. At 1 a.m. the two battalions would begin their three mile advance to Pirgos. Here the men would stop to rest for half an hour before delivering the final assault at 4 a m. After passing the cemetery at the far end of the village, the 20th would move to the left, into the protection of the lower slopes of Hill 107, with the Maoris going ahead to capture the heights. At the same time, the 21st would advance to occupy the high ground further south. Later in the day the 20th would take over from the Maoris, who would then return before nightfall, by covered routes, to their starting position at Platanias. The only rôle given to the 23rd was that of 'mopping up' enemy parties left in the rear of the advance. The Brigade would still be responsible for coast defence. To cover Platanias, one of the Maori companies would have to stay behind in the old position.

Thus the recapture of Hill 107, the key objective, was entrusted to a single battalion, reduced by the loss of a company, and wearied by an approach march in darkness across five miles of broken country. Indeed, both battalions would be dissipating their energies in encounters with stray Germans among the undergrowth on each side of the road before they could approach their real objective. No less strange was the order that the Maoris should return to their old position. The 20th could scarcely be expected to stand unsupported against the reinforced enemy in the trenches which the 22nd had been forced to abandon by the Storm Regiment alone. And once again the 23rd had been given no specific rôle. There had been no more activity from Gericke's men since their rebuff at the Pirgos cross-roads. Yet no attempt was to be made by Leckie to clear the Germans from the houses and trees in this area in preparation for the main assault. Nor was it suggested that the 23rd should attempt to add weight to the attack once it had passed. Leckie indeed was later to deny that he had received even the instruction about 'mopping up'.

In his preparation for this counter-attack Hargest wore the air of an utterly weary man. Many witnesses have referred to his exhaustion at this time. A Divisional Staff Officer, Colonel Gentry,[1] who visited him that evening, thought him so spent as to be 'unable to think coherently'.[2] Farran, who was in command of the three tanks, formed the same impression:

> We mounted the steps of an old farmhouse to receive orders from the Brigadier. He was a red, open-faced man, who looked like a country farmer, and it was obvious that he was suffering from acute fatigue. He asked us to wait for half an hour while he had some sleep. Disgusted, intolerant, we sat on the steps until he was ready . . .[3]

He had lost none of his sanguine temper. But now the virtue had gone out of it. Its roots lay in ignorance. A strange fatigue had blurred his perception. Once again he was entering upon a critical action with less than half his force engaged – and in a manner which must greatly handicap the two battalions upon which success would depend.

To the shortcomings in Hargest's plan there was soon added, from outside his control, another factor which before long began to outdo all else. At 9.15 p.m. Freyberg himself had told Puttick that the New Zealand 20th Battalion must not be released for the counter-attack until after its relief by the 2/7 Australian Battalion from Georgeoupolis. The 20th would then use the Australian

---

[1] Lieut.-Col. W. G. Gentry was G.S.O.1 to the New Zealand Division
[2] DP   [3] Farran, p. 95

transport for the move to Platanias. By 10 p.m. it was clear that the Australians had been delayed.

The trucks carrying the first of their companies had left Georgeoupolis, with about twenty-five miles to go, at five o'clock in the afternoon. They were at once heavily bombed. After they had covered the inland section of the journey the attack increased. The road now wound nakedly exposed across the cliff face high above the bay; the planes came slanting upon them from over the water.

A letter written by Major Marshall, second in command of the battalion, who was in the leading truck, gives a good impression of the journey:

We whizzed down the road and past the food dump and breathed again. Then we turned a corner and found half a dozen planes above with the obvious intention of attacking us somewhere. I stopped the column until I was sure Savige with A Company had caught up and then we sailed on. It was rather exhilarating. By this time I had got it into my driver's head that we were not stopping for anything. Consequently he drove his thirty-hundredweight truck at a hell of a bat swinging around curves on what seemed like two wheels. The planes had now obviously got on to us but the road was winding along a valley and there were few straight stretches. The planes cruised about these straight stretches waiting for us but fortunately had little luck. Twice I watched a plane single us out and bank and turn to machine-gun us along the straight and I told the driver to crack it up. It then became a race to the curve between us and the plane and curiously enough I had little fear. Excitement buoyed me up probably. Nevertheless, twice it was touch and go and we just sneaked around the corner in time and foiled the planes. We streaked along and I hoped the Bn was following . . .[4]

The last of the battalion did not reach Canea until after dusk. In the darkened town the companies were then misdirected. Marshall gained the impression that, despite these difficulties, the 'relief was finally completed about 11 p.m.' But such timing would have meant that there need have been no delay. Major Burrows, the commander of the 20th Battalion, was probably nearer the truth in believing that the first two companies had not arrived until midnight. Another hour had passed before they could take over their positions. Disappointed that his own men had not been asked to make the counter-attack Walker had done his

[4] Long, p. 235, entry in his diary later that year by Maj. H. C. D. Marshall

utmost to encourage the New Zealanders to get going earlier. In this he had met with no success:

Burrows would not move. From 10.30 p.m. I began urging him to. I spoke to Brigade at 11.30 about it, and told them that the relief was complete enough.[5]

Already it was plain to those officers who knew of the expected invasion that few if any Germans were likely to reach the coast that night. At 11.30 p.m. a thunder of guns had begun to sound over the water. Soon every man was watching the lights that were flickering along the horizon to the north, and the brief eruptions of red flame that licked the night sky, as the ships of Admiral Glennie set about their work of destruction.

At Maleme, and on the low hills that lined the Prison Valley, the Germans stood in silence and anguish, aware both of the fate of their comrades and the certainty that they could themselves no longer hope for reinforcement from the sea.

By the roadside in Platanias, Hargest was still waiting for the 20th. Suddenly, it had become highly unlikely that the Germans would be able to land that night in any significant strength. But it was no less clear that the threat alone had served them well. How much, indeed, was it continuing to achieve? The hours were passing. Yet there was no sign of any troops from the 4th Brigade. Not much time remained.

Near Canea Bridge, Burrows and Inglis had seen with satisfaction that the Navy was at work. At once they realized that little more need be expected that night from those Germans who had been so unfortunate as to have encountered the British Fleet at sea. Both drew the conclusion that there was no longer any need to wait for the arrival of the Australians. Now was the time to get moving with the 20th. Twice Inglis put this point of view to Puttick over the telephone. But Puttick would have none of it. To Inglis he continued to insist that the 20th must 'remain in position until relieved'.

Colonel Dittmer, still at Platanias with his Maoris, knew very well how necessary it was that his attack should go in while it was dark. Now that the front line was becoming defined the Germans would be able to enjoy the unopposed support of their aircraft from soon after dawn. He therefore told Captain Royal to move west with his company in order to clear up pockets of resistance

[5] DP, Letter from Lieut.-Col. P. G. Walker, 26 Jan. 1950

ahead of the main advance. This time Royal's men, a little weary after their eleven-hour route march of the previous night, found their task complicated by the sturdily independent Engineer Detachment, which had sown mines in front of its position and was inclined to shoot at sight. Royal quickly decided that, as before, he preferred the main road. Without much difficulty he was able to follow it as far as the turn to Dhaskaliana.

At last, Burrows and Inglis, on their own initiative, decided that the 20th would leave by companies as the Australians came in to take over from them. Nevertheless, it was already 2 a.m. before Burrows could arrive at Platanias. From Hargest, whom he found 'so exhausted that he could not complete one sentence at a time', he now learnt the details of his formidable task. Before taking over the high ground to the south he must begin by 'cleaning up all the German posts between the forming up place and drome, and also destroying guns and material on the drome itself'.[6]

At this stage, both Hargest and Burrows may well have begun to question how seriously this counter-attack was being regarded by Puttick and indeed by Freyberg himself. It was now 3 a.m. Only two of the 20th companies had arrived. Soon it would be morning. Even if these two companies were to start at once they could have little hope of reaching the airfield before daylight. Understandably, Burrows was reluctant to move without the whole of his battalion. Hargest rang Divisional Headquarters and asked 'Must the attack go on?' He was told 'It must'.[7] He therefore ordered Burrows to set out with his first two companies, leaving the rest to follow.

For nearly four hours the main body of the Maoris had been resting on their start-line. Out at sea, the last rumbles of the naval engagement had died away. They had watched the display with interest, and had speculated upon its significance. But they had not realized what was happening. It did not occur to them, or to their officers, who were no better informed, that the action in which they were about to take part might well determine the outcome of the battle for Crete. But one thing they understood very well – that they were starting far too late. Inevitably now, the planes must catch them in daylight before they could reach the airfield. Something had gone wrong.

[6] DP. Narrative by Maj. J. T. Burrows   [7] Davin, p. 215

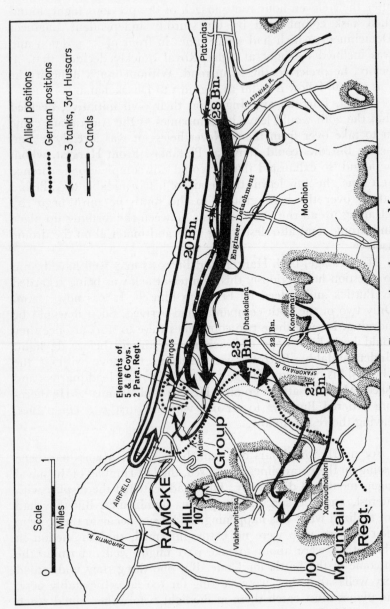

14. Maleme Counter-Attack: 21-22 May

At last the two leading companies of the 20th started to file out across the coastal strip. And at 3.30 a.m. both battalions began to move.

A narrow moon had long since faded from the sky, but some light still came from the brilliant stars. The men found themselves well able to pick their way among the stone walls and trees. Almost at once the right-hand company of the 20th was engaged by a strong-point in a house close to the beach. But it was soon evident that enemy resistance was likely to be less fierce than it had been during the day. After some of the Germans had been killed the others quickly surrendered to the company commander, throwing away their weapons 'to show that they meant it'.[8]

The New Zealanders were short of grenades. Often they found themselves forced to charge with the bayonet. As they moved further west, the width of the coastal strip broadened to about half a mile, and the going became more difficult among reeds, grape-vines, and bushes. Close to the road, casualties were caused by mines and booby traps, part of the defences established by the Engineers.

We went on meeting resistance in depth [Lieutenant Upham remembered later], in ditches, behind hedges, in the top and bottom storeys of village buildings, fields and gardens, on road beside drome . . . there was T.G. [tommy-gun] and pistol fire and plenty of grenades and a lot of bayonet work which you don't often get in war. The amount of M.G. [machine-gun] fire was never equalled. Fortunately a lot of it was high and the tracer bullets enabled us to pick our way up and throw in grenades. We had heavy casualties but the Germans had much heavier. They were unprepared. Some were without trousers, and some had no boots on. The Germans were helpless in the dark.[9]

But the night was almost over. Dawn was beginning to break behind them as they pressed into the denser growths of bamboo north of Pirgos.

After further exchanges with the long-suffering Engineers, who had continued to fulfil to the letter their instructions to shoot first and ask questions afterwards, the Maoris were making good progress south of the road. They were at full strength, their commanding officer, Lieutenant-Colonel Dittmer, had contrived to misunderstand Hargest's order that one of his companies should

[8] DP, Lieut. P. V. H. Maxwell
[9] Davin, p. 216, Lieut. C. H. Upham (later awarded the Victoria Cross for his work in Crete)

remain behind. Steadily the men filtered through the trees and houses, joined every few minutes by shadowy figures appearing out of the darkness; the armed Cretans had waited two days for this moment. Sudden resistance flared among the cottages and was quickly thrust down. From the road came help from the three tanks which fired at the flashes ahead of them. Again the main work was done with grenade and bayonet. And now the Maoris too found that the sky had begun to pale. It was full daylight before they reached Dhaskaliana. Ahead of them more planes had begun to land on the airfield, still some two miles away and hidden from view by the rising wooded country. They kept going. On the right the leading detachments entered the south-eastern outskirts of Pirgos where they found the enemy 'pouring out of the houses in confusion'. Further south they made their way across the Xamoudhokhori Road into the shallow valley of the Sfakoriako River, where they met opposition which increased every minute.

By this time the 20th had come upon the biggest group of survivors from the parachute drop of the previous afternoon. The men nearest to the road were held up in bitter fighting among shacks half-hidden in the undergrowth. Close to the shore two more companies plunged forward across gullies, and through clumps of bamboo, to reach the edge of the runway. 'With another hour,' Upham was to write, 'we could have reached the far side of the 'drome.'[10] But now it was bright morning. Most of the officers had been killed or wounded. They could go no further. In full view of the machine-gunners on Hill 107, and of the howling Messerschmitts which now filled the sky, they had no choice but to withdraw from the bare sand into the cover of the bamboos.

Worst of all was the task that had fallen to the three light tanks. Unable to cross the open country, the drivers had been forced to set out in single file down the road. A small detachment of New Zealanders accompanied them to give them the pace and to ward off skirmishers. On both sides the walls of bamboo stood thick and menacing at the edge of the tarmac, perfect cover for a point blank ambush. And Farran had already been told that the enemy were using some of the captured Bofors. He felt that to advance upon these guns in their 'thinly armoured perambulators' must mean 'almost certain suicide'.[11]

But at first all went well. Soon after dawn they reached the

[10] Davin, p. 216, Lieut. C. H. Upham   [11] Farran, p. 95

cross-roads east of Pirgos. Here they hesitated. The captured guns were said to be watching the road from somewhere close to hand. Impatient and angry, Captain Dawson, Hargest's vigorous Brigade Major, walked over to the sergeant in the leading tank and urged him on with the mocking comment that there was 'nothing to worry about except perhaps small-arms fire'.[12]

At this the sergeant pressed on down the central street. As he turned the last corner, his tank was hit by shells from two guns established in the walled cemetery by the roadside. Mortally wounded, the gunner fired back to knock out one of the enemy. Another shell then struck the tank in the middle as it tried to turn. 'I knew and had known all along,' Farran wrote later, 'that the leading tank would be destroyed.'[13]

And now they had been seen by the enemy planes. Farran and his corporal were helpless:

A swarm of Me 109s like angry buzzing bees beset our two tanks. Hot flakes of burning metal flew off the inside of the turrets into our faces. We tried to minimize their dives by halting under a tall tree but it was of no avail. Finally, like a wounded bull trying to shake off a crowd of flies, I crashed into a bamboo field.[14]

From within the thick cluster of trees and bushes that enclosed the road at the entry to the village, Burrows could only guess at the progress of his forward companies. Nor could he maintain contact with Dittmer and the 28th, which was cut off from him by the long street on his left, most of the houses still being occupied by the enemy. But he knew that in daylight it would not be possible to cross the airfield. He judged, therefore, that the time had come for him to put into operation the second part of his instructions, the withdrawal of his battalion from the right flank and its realignment behind the Maoris. Together the two battalions might still be able to recapture some of the high ground.

Upham set out with his batman to carry this order to the companies. 'When we reached the 'drome,' he wrote later, 'the planes were landing – some leaving too, and the parachutists,' Mountain Troops had he known it, 'were jumping out and getting straight into the battle.'[15]

In the confusion, the new orders were misunderstood by the commander of the company which had made the longest pene-

[12] DP, Narrative by Capt. R. B. Dawson   [13] Farran, p. 97
[14] Ibid.   [15] Davin, p. 219, Lieut. C. H. Upham

tration along the coast. He gained the impression that he was to withdraw to Platanias. This he did, taking part of another company with him, and thus opening a long gap along the shore. Only three companies of the 20th remained to cross the road.

The Maoris were now under heavy fire from the Germans hidden among the gardens and cottages on their right, while from their left, a storm of machine-gun bullets and mortar shells came down upon them from the heights. Immediately in front a cluster of olives grew thickly across the gashed red slopes leading to Hill 107. Here the Germans were established behind their Spandaus.

We could at times see German machine-gunners running up through the trees [says Major Dyer]. We collected in small groups and worked forward. Men were hit, men were maimed. The din of the fight was incessant. There seemed to be machine-guns behind all the trees. If we could silence one or two immediately in front we might break through.[16]

But it was not possible. Gradually the enemy pressure increased both from the air and on the ground. Late in the afternoon, Dittmer went back about three-quarters of a mile to appeal for help from the other two battalions. He met no encouragement. 'Both the 22 and 23 Bns,' he felt, 'had had a very thin time and were feeling the strain very much'.[17] Leckie believed that the whole of the 20th 'had withdrawn after the failure of the counter attack'. Both he and Andrew felt that no further progress could be made that day 'without more infantry, artillery and air support.'[18]

The men of the 23rd were less despondent than their leaders. Some of them had impulsively joined the Maoris. One platoon, moving across country through 'continuous machine-gun fire',[19] managed to get beyond Maleme village and reach the lower slopes. That the enemy on the hills cannot have been very numerous is well shown by the fact that one section from this platoon was able to move down to the road and across to the coastal strip where it found itself among the Germans who were firing at the forward companies of the 20th. Only then did the men realize that the advance had stopped. 'We had no option,' one of them reported later, 'but to make our way back.'[20] This also they succeeded in doing without loss.

[16] Dyer, p. 30   [17] DP   [18] Ibid., Leckie comments on Davin Draft
[19] Ross, *23 Battalion*, p. 72   [20] Ibid., p. 72

By the late afternoon, the Maoris had been forced to withdraw into the valley south of Pirgos. After a short pause they were rallied by their redoubtable sergeant-major, who led a bayonet charge upon a group of the enemy who had collected in a stone house. 'We cleaned up what turned out to be a patrol of about platoon strength,' he wrote of this episode, 'half . . . we speared and shot in the middle of the ridge, the other half, including their commander, in the vineyard'.[21]

Towards dusk, the Germans began to press again. Setting up a large swastika flag, held by two poles, they advanced on each side of it as though in a street procession. Covering fire poured in from each flank.

On seeing the enemy preparations the Maoris had retired to a reverse slope where they waited among the gnarled olive trunks. In the words of one of their lieutenants the attack then began with a 'bursting of flame from the grenades the Huns threw on the top – it shook us up a bit – then they came over'.[22]

Silently the Maoris rose. Dyer saw them as

. . . a scattered band of dark figures under the trees . . . with knees bent, and leaning to the right they slowly advanced firing at the hip. They did not haka, for this was not rehearsed. Instead there rose from their throats a deep shout 'Ah! Ah! Ah!' as they advanced firing. Then the cartridges in their magazines being exhausted, they broke into a run with bayonets levelled and their shouts rising as they went. . . . The air whistled and cracked with bullets. Men went down but they still charged. And the pride of the German army turned and fled.

From the crest the enemy could be seen bolting down the hill, 'plunging through the vines and over the stone wall'.[23] The Maoris walked back through the fallen bodies and the abandoned machine-guns to their line above the gully.

A mile away, Colonel Allen had not taken long to realize that whatever his orders might suggest the 21st was not going to get onto Hill 107 that day without fighting for it. At 7 a.m., on his own initiative, he had struck out boldly for the west. Contact with the enemy brought almost complete immunity from the *Luftwaffe*. By 8.30 a.m. he had overcome considerable opposition and occupied the wireless station at Xamoudhokhori. One of his

[21] Cody, *Maori Battalion*, p. 105, R.S.M. A. C. Wood
[22] Ibid., p. 106, Lieut. H. J. MacDonald   [23] Dyer, p. 73

lieutenants was able to establish a Lewis gun in the church tower. Two companies, one on each side of the road, then pressed on to Vlakheronitissa which they passed through without stopping to clear the Germans from the houses. Here they were only a few hundred yards from the summit of Hill 107. Taking part in this advance were detachments from D Company of the 22nd. Several of these men got back as far as their old positions on the east bank of the Tavronitis. Such enterprise on the part of the 21st during the afternoon of the first day, at a time when only Stentzler's two weary companies barred the way to the river bed, would have brought vital help to Andrew and the 22nd.

But now Allen was faced by the fresh Mountain Troops that had landed on the previous evening. His forward company commander had been killed. Moreover, he soon found that the main attack on his right had been held up. Towards evening he was forced to withdraw to 'Vineyard Ridge' north-east of Xamoudhokhori in order to avoid being cut off. Nevertheless, he had demonstrated the sort of advance that could be made, even in daylight under the *Luftwaffe*, by infiltrating within the German line.

Further back the news was brighter. Unable to find water without exposing themselves, in terror of their own planes, and with their ammunition exhausted, the few Germans surviving between Pirgos and Platanias quickly surrendered; during the early part of the day the Engineer Detachment had accepted the submission of sixty-five prisoners. The guns had continued to shell the airfield at every available moment, despite the searching attentions of the enemy aircraft. But they had not been able to give effective support to the infantry. Once the timing of the advance had begun to go wrong, the gunner officers had been unable to find out what was happening.

The counter-attack had failed. Indeed, it had made no impact before daylight. According to *Operation Crete* it was not until 7 a.m. that Gericke's men first noticed that the New Zealanders had 'attacked unexpectedly from Pirgos'.[24]

The move was unexpected only because it had come so late. During the early part of the night the Germans at Maleme had been highly apprehensive, especially after they had become aware of the disaster to their seaborne reinforcements. But from shortly

[24] *Einsatz Kreta*, Battle Report of XI Air Corps

after dawn they had enjoyed the support of their bombers and machine-gunning fighters. Even more important was the confidence inspired by their knowledge that behind them more troops were beginning to land upon the airfield, and that they would be able to do so without serious inconvenience throughout the day. They felt confident that they could deal with this limited attack, which the enemy, for some strange reason, had postponed for so long.

Several hours were to pass before the truth got through to Hargest. The messages that he sent to Puttick well illustrate both his ill-founded optimism and the failure of his communications. The first news had given him little enough to be cheerful about. Dawson came back to tell him that soon after dawn the Maoris and the tanks had been held up short of Pirgos under full-scale air attack. There had been no sign of the Royal Air Force, and the artillery reinforcement had not reached Platanias. In the light of this information it must have been with wry satisfaction that he learnt at 7.30 a.m. of the destruction of the sea invasion force; if the higher command had taken a chance on it he could have had the 20th three hours earlier.

Contact with his battalions had then failed again. He was forced to rely upon garbled reports from stragglers, and upon what he could observe through his field glasses from the hill behind his headquarters. This was not very much. Planes could be seen circling in the dust cloud above Maleme. At regular intervals others emerged with a swelling roar from below the ridges. The airfield itself, five miles away, lay hidden behind the roll of hills.

Encouraged, nevertheless, by his impressions from these dubious sources, his optimism took another bound forward. At first he had admitted that there was 'a steady flow of enemy planes landing and taking off'. But by 11.50 a.m. he was telling Puttick: 'Reliable reports state aerodrome occupied by own troops.' It seemed as though 'enemy might be preparing evacuation'. Failure of comprehension between the brigadier and his battalion commanders was complete. Not until the early afternoon did he emerge from this dream world. Now the tone of his messages changed. At 1.25 p.m. he reported that the position was 'confused'. The troops were 'not so far forward on left as believed'.[25] Dawson would go forward again to try to find out what was

[25] New Zealand Division War Diary

happening. Soon after this, he was forced to accept the fact that his brigade was back on a defence line south of Pirgos, while the Germans were steadily landing more men and equipment.

This was a situation that was changing the balance of the contest. It is not surprising that there has been much criticism of the senior officers involved. Less attention has been directed to the problems that presented to them at the time.

How, and why, did they fail? The courage of the four men most concerned was beyond question and their experience great. Two of them were holders of the Victoria Cross. Nor is there any parallel with those elderly majors and colonels of 1914 and 1915, relics of earlier colonial wars, who later faded from the scene as their incapacities were revealed. Hargest was to escape after capture at Sidi Azeiz and to live through further adventures, before his death in action at an age when many Members of Parliament younger than he, in England at least, were safe at home and doing well for themselves out of the war. Freyberg himself, the most battle-hardened fighting general in the western world, was to win fresh honours in the desert and in Italy.

It is clear that Hargest never understood how much hung upon the Maleme counter-attack. He was only dimly aware of what was happening in the rest of the island, and neither Puttick nor Freyberg had impressed upon him that this action might be of supreme importance. On the contrary, the last message to reach him that evening from Force Headquarters had spoken only of a sea invasion attempt and the need for constant vigilance along the beach. The warning was consistent with all his previous instruction. From the first, it had been emphasized that his brigade must bear a responsibility to coast defence equal to that of protection of the airfield.

Moreover, he knew that Freyberg believed the enemy troop-carriers to be capable of landing in open country away from the airfields. Indeed, he was probably under the impression, as Puttick had been, that many such landings had already been made under the mountains to the south. From what he had been able to see during the afternoon, it was plain that the Germans were now using Maleme for the landing of heavy planes, but he, too, may well have felt that they were doing so out of preference rather than necessity, and his natural optimism would certainly have disposed him to accept the tales of destruction wrought upon the runway by artillery and machine-gun fire.

Within this conception, recapture of the Maleme position, although obviously desirable, could not claim priority over coast defence. And it must also be important to clear up the parachutists surviving from the afternoon drop west of Platanias; these men would certainly become very active in the course of any beach-landing attempt. For the same reason there was the need to guard against infiltration from the Germans in the Prison Valley.

In his diary, Hargest left no details of his thoughts, but if his reasoning were along these lines his conduct of the counter-attack can be understood. It would explain his preoccupation with the isolated Germans near the road, and his instruction that a company of the Maoris should be held back to watch the southern flank. It would also make better sense of his order that the Maoris should return as soon as possible to Platanias. Here they would be available to deal with any Germans that might disembark from the sea. And it would have been unwise for him to have moved his own command post further west. By doing so he would have lost the telephone link with Divisional Headquarters and might well have become incapable of controlling a battle developing along the shore. The fact that he had asked only for one additional battalion for the counter-attack suggests that he expected no great opposition provided that the operation could be carried out at night. Later he seems to have felt that the delayed arrival of the 20th Battalion absolved him from all immediate responsibility for the recapture of the airfield and Hill 107. But under the cloud of his fatigue he showed no great concern about the matter. No doubt he felt that, with the sea invasion defeated, sufficient force would now become available to clear Maleme without much difficulty.

If he had been told during the afternoon of the 21st that he must recapture Hill 107 and reach the Tavronitis that night, or lose his brigade in the attempt, it seems likely that his first thought would have been to bring his two fresh battalions as close as possible to their objectives before deploying them. To do this, he would have had to begin moving the Maoris at dusk, bringing them straight down the road. There was no need to send them stumbling among the isolated Germans in the undergrowth. Any ambushes would have been dealt with at this stage; in fact, as Rangi Royal was to demonstrate for the second time, the Battalion could have been brought virtually intact to within half a mile of Pirgos. He would himself have gone forward with the Maoris, using a Bren-carrier, to direct the operation from the 23rd dug-out. After discussion with Leckie, he would probably have decided to switch the 23rd to the right flank while the Maoris drew up southward from Dhaskaliana along the Kondomari Road. Allen would have been told to prepare the 21st for an advance to the upper Tavronitis, and for Burrows he would have left a message to bring the 20th forward in the transport as far as the Dhaskaliana Turn. By perhaps 2 a.m., he would have decided that he could wait no longer. The 20th would have to be left to form a support group with the 22nd as it arrived.

With some three hours of darkness remaining he could then have launched his attack. The 21st was at a strength of only just 350 men, but the 23rd and the Maoris were not much reduced in numbers. Together they still made up a total of over 1,500 trained infantry. All three battalions had been engaged sufficiently only to whet their appetites. Thus far they had escaped the worst of the bombing. Moreover, they knew the ground far better than the Mountain Troops and the parachutists. It seems probable that they would have succeeded in occupying commanding positions upon Hill 107 by dawn, at the same time infiltrating into the ravine of the Tavronitis along its lower two miles. Once again, there was the prospect that the tangle of friend and foe along the whole area between the Tavronitis and Platanias would have made it impossible for the *Luftwaffe* to intervene successfully. All must now have hung upon the maintenance throughout the day of aimed fire upon the half mile of the runway. A single heavy machine-gun, nourished and protected upon the forward slopes of Hill 107, or firing from among the sand-dunes along the shore, could have prevented further landings by troop-carrier. Even had a few planes put down successfully the men on board could not have hoped to leave them alive.[26]

And what of Brigadier Puttick? It had been his responsibility, as commander of the New Zealand Division, to ensure that the counter-attack at Maleme should be mounted in sufficient strength. But, like Hargest and Freyberg, he was much pre-occupied with the sea invasion. Nor was this his only anxiety. He was no less apprehensive of further landings from the air. At

[26] Ringel, p. 88, says 'Any landing attempt under machine-gun fire would have been madness'.

the same time he remained convinced that the power of the *Luftwaffe* must render impossible all movement of his troops in daylight. Indeed, he continued to see dangers on every side. These were the fears that had from the start made him reluctant to use his reserves. Thus the claim that he had always believed that the 'real front' would be at Maleme is seen to lose its force. On the evening of the 21st he had refused to send Hargest even a small detachment to protect his isolated Brigade Headquarters from the south while the 28th Battalion took part in the counter-attack.

After the war, Puttick was to write:

The attempted seaborne attack on Canea defeated by the Royal Navy, comprising I believe at least 5,000 men, and of which we had definite warning from a source which proved completely reliable in several other instances, could not be ignored. A NZ success at Maleme, which at least was highly problematical in view of the weak forces available for it and the rapid enemy reinforcement in that area, would have been largely nullified by a German success at Canea, with all its implications.[27]

To this it must be said that during the late afternoon of the 21st he had told Freyberg that he proposed to back the counter-attack with only one battalion of his own reserve. He had not asked for further reinforcement. Nor is there any record that he declared the outcome to be 'problematical'. Rather does he appear to have given an impression of confidence. If he had felt serious doubt about it he could have asked for more force with which to carry it out. He might not have got it. But it was not his business to worry about what Freyberg could afford to give him.

In fact, it can now be judged that Puttick was not, that evening, very closely concerned about Maleme. This relative detachment would appear to have been based upon the two conceptions which he shared with Hargest, and which stemmed originally from Freyberg himself. He still believed that the Germans need not depend upon an airfield for their airborne attacks. And, secondly, like everyone else, he was convinced that the greater threat came from the sea. In his determination, later that night, that the Australians must complete their relief before he would release the 20th, Puttick was doing no more than interpret exactly the specific orders that had been given to him that afternoon by Freyberg. But at the same time he was refusing to recognize that,

before midnight, a fresh, and fundamental, event had transformed
the situation. The prospect of naval intervention had turned from
hopeful conjecture to visible fact. Although no further word had
come from Force Headquarters it was open to him to seek an
amendment over the telephone. He did not do so. Nor would he
take it upon himself to change Freyberg's orders in order to
exploit the advantages offered by the new development. No doubt
he feared that a few boatloads from the German convoy might
yet evade the Navy and make a landing.

It is of course easy to see how much he might have achieved
had he conceded less to fear of invasion across the beaches. There
would have been no need to abandon coast defence, scarcely
indeed to have jeopardized it. And at midnight time enough still
remained. A commander of more flexible spirit might have told
Hargest over the telephone to get the Maoris moving down the
main road, by-passing any opposition, to a start-line east of
Pirgos, at the same time ordering the 23rd and the 21st to concert
an attack with the Maoris at the earliest possible moment. Behind
them, the 20th could have been withdrawn on to the road to
await the arrival of the Australians with the necessary transport,
leaving a few men with automatic weapons to hold the positions
along the beach. This would have saved the hour which must
otherwise be lost while making the handover in detail. In the
meantime, the first two or three companies could have started
out on foot.

The difficulties were plain enough. Chief of them, as always in
Crete, was that of communication. The line to the 5th Brigade
Headquarters was working, but the lapses of Leckie's radio transmitter would have made it necessary for Hargest to have used one
of his staff officers, protected perhaps by a company of the
Maoris, to get the news through to the 23rd; indeed, after such
encouragement, it seems probable that he would, at last, have
gone forward himself. Much less serious was any threat that might
be offered by the isolated groups of parachutists surviving along
the seaward flank. Left where they were, their capacities would
certainly grow less while their discomforts increased.

There is no evidence that Puttick gave serious thought to any
of these possibilities. He knew that the Junkers would return
within an hour of their dawn take-off in Greece, and that if,
before that time, the Germans could not be dislodged from the
airfield, there was nothing that could prevent a stream of re-

inforcement from pouring in by air during the following day. Yet he never wavered in his conviction that his own duty remained clear. Not for him was it to concern himself with what might happen at Maleme in the morning, nor with what he had already seen to be happening upon the sea. Freyberg had given him his instructions. His first responsibility was coast defence. And thus once again a smaller, intangible and soon unrealized threat was allowed to obscure the infinitely greater but more remote reality.

At midnight on 21/22 May Freyberg had been offered a supreme opportunity.

The naval action had begun half an hour before. From his command post he watched the lighted horizon. Within a few minutes he knew that Cunningham's ships had not failed to make their rendezvous and were indeed intent upon their task. He can scarcely have doubted that, at most, no more than a handful of enemy vessels would reach the shore, and that any that might succeed must be greatly harassed and widely scattered. Suddenly it was clear that the Navy had, after all, arrived to redress the balance which for so long had been weighted by the *Luftwaffe* to the side of the enemy. By one of his staff he was heard to murmur, in words that reveal his exultation and relief, 'It's been a great responsibility – a great responsibility'.[28] Here was escape from what had always been the greatest of his fears, an enemy disembarkment of men and tanks from the sea, and that at a time when there was already reason to hope that the Chiefs of Staff had been right in their forecast that airborne troops would be unable to hold for long without seaborne reinforcement. Looking north into the night sky, he saw the flashes and heard the roll of the guns, and for the first time, after weeks of wearing strain and misgiving, he glimpsed the bright vision of victory.

And in this same moment, in this crisis of his life as a soldier, his inspiration failed him. The fleeting instant came and went, and not all the years of his courage and devotion availed him to recognize it.

Those who now look back with the advantages of after knowledge can scarcely forebear to speculate upon what might have been the outcome had he now turned eagerly to the second requirement of the night, bending all the power of his honoured leadership to ensure, while the darkness remained, that the

[28] Mr. Geoffrey Cox to the author, 1962

counter-attack at Maleme should be mounted with the utmost speed, weight, and resolution. It is easy to picture him at midnight in urgent telephone conversation with Puttick, the whole resources of the New Zealand Division pressed immediately into the attack, with Puttick going forward to Platanias, and Hargest set free to direct his brigade from the front line, 20th Battalion, and perhaps the 18th as well, setting out pell-mell along the road on foot, or with the help of such transport as might be sent after them, and the Australians thinning out along the beach as they arrived. Even the 1st Welch, which knew the ground, could still have been sent west; it had transport enough to get forward immediately with a company, and most of the battalion could have been assembled in time to march to Pirgos before dawn.

Today it can be seen that the counter-attack was from the first doomed to failure – by the delay with which it began, even more than by the weakness of the force committed to it. The roots of this failure lay in the conceptions, all of them thoroughly impressed upon his commanders in the west, with which Freyberg had begun the battle; his personal belief, unshared by Intelligence, that the operation of the German troop-carriers need not depend upon the use of an airfield; the expectation of the Chiefs of Staff that parachute drops might be continued indefinitely, and their conviction that the dominant need was to guard against a landing from the sea. Each of these anxieties had tended to conceal from him the importance of Maleme. Inevitably, therefore, even when relieved from the last of them, he had still felt no compelling need to switch his attention in the new direction.

Since the war, much has been written upon the events of this night, most of it paying no great attention to the facts. In 1952 Christopher Buckley recorded his view in dramatic terms:

Now to Freyberg came the realization that the clock was about to strike the vital hour. . . . He knew that if the Germans were granted another day for the landing of troop-carrying planes at Maleme airfield they would have built up such a strength that successful counter-attack would be impossible . . . it would demand every man, vehicle and gun that could be concentrated. . . . But Freyberg knew that this might not be enough.[29]

[29] Buckley, p. 220

None of this was true. A few, perhaps, of the New Zealanders at Pirgos had begun to have thoughts of this kind. And Stephanides says that some of the Cretans feared that if the counter-attack did not come soon it might be too late. But on that night of 21 May no senior officer in Crete had yet understood the significance of the enemy lodgment at Maleme. Freyberg was thinking in terms of a sandy strip where, according to his information, some thirty troop-carriers had succeeded, while many more had failed, in landing perhaps 300 men, a useful addition no doubt to the parachutists, and to the survivors from those other troop-carriers which he believed to have crashed elsewhere in the vicinity. But in this there was nothing to attract his particular attention. Sooner or later, of course, Maleme would have to be retaken, if not tonight within the next day or two. Thus far, however, possession of the landing-ground appeared to have been of no great help to the enemy. The airborne forces there seemed to be no more dangerous than they were in several other areas. At any moment, so he understood, there might be troop-carriers coming down in the Prison Valley. Provided that there was not much more air reinforcement it should be possible to clear up all these airborne lodgments once the sea invasion had been defeated. Until that had been achieved the security of his base must remain his first consideration.

I could not leave this covering position near Canea unheld [Freyberg was to write later in answer to criticisms about the delayed release of the 20th Battalion], because had the Germans landed as they planned we should have lost all our supplies and ammunition; besides the enemy lodgment would have cut the whole New Zealand Force off from Suda Bay. I gave the order; neither Puttick nor Inglis was responsible for the delay.[30]

With his memories of the First World War he had felt that 'the Australians coming in as they were at the moment of the attack could not occupy the defences in the dark without a proper hand over'.[31]

Student had been in no doubt about the danger. In 1947 he was to make the comment:

If the enemy had made a united all out effort in counter-attacking during the night from the 20th to the 21st or in the morning of the

[30] DP, Freyberg comments on Davin Draft, 5 Dec. 1949
[31] Ibid., Freyberg comments on the Battle for Crete, 31 Dec. 1949

21st, then the very tired remnants of the Storm Regiment suffering from lack of ammunition could have been wiped out.[32]

Later he was to tell Captain Liddell Hart that 'at this decisive period the British Command' was restrained by fear of a sea invasion and so 'did not take the risk of sending their forces to Maleme'.[33]

Clark maintains that the failure to use the stronger forces that were available ignored the 'salient fact – that if the airfield was not captured the frustration of the seaborne invasion and the preservation of communications were academic points, for the island would surely be lost',[34] and the *New Zealand War History* observes of the counter-attack that 'if it failed, it was only a matter of time before the island belonged to the enemy'.[35]

These comments take no account of the light in which Freyberg saw the situation as it arose. There had been no 'surely' about it. If he had felt on the evening of the 21st that failure that night would render it impossible ever to regain the landing-field, thus, indeed, making certain that it must be 'only a matter of time' before the island was lost, it is clear that his attitude would have been very different. From the start he would have used more of his reserve from Suda Area, and he would have added further weight to it after the reassuring appearances of the Navy at 11.30 p.m. Above all, he would have imparted to his commanders a sense of urgency. And it is scarcely conceivable that, even before the attack had started, he would have let fall that confident and revelatory aside 'It's been a great responsibility'.

The truth is that the failure of his information had continued to hide from him the reality of what was happening in the west. If this be accepted there can be no logic in criticism which blames him for reluctance to commit the uttermost of his reserve to this one action. Indeed his failure is seen to be no greater than that which is in some degree inseparable from the dilemma facing all commanders who find themselves bound to fight a defensive battle against a mobile enemy – the inability at the outset to recognize the *schwerpunkt* of the attack. He alone, despite the apparent confidence of Hargest and Puttick, had felt instinctively that within the confusion at Maleme there might lie a menace greater than he yet could know.

[32] Proceedings at the trial of Kurt Student, 1947

[33] DP, Letter from Student to Capt. B. H. Liddell Hart, 28 Nov. 1948

[34] Clark, p. 106   [35] Davin, p. 199

But these were doubts that he suppressed while he thankfully savoured the triumph of the British Navy. Like Napoleon after Quatre Bras and Ligny he allowed himself to become lulled into uncharacteristic inertia by his physical weariness, fatally combined with the sudden prospect of success. The hours passed. Briefly he slept. When he awoke it was to find that the vision had receded.

16

The Wider Scene: 22 May

At midnight on 21/22 May any detached all-seeing observer must have believed that nothing could save the Germans from defeat. All their parachute and glider troops had been committed. One of the sea invasion flotillas had been intercepted. The other was about to meet the cruisers of Admiral King. Only the few hundred exhausted survivors of the Storm Regiment stood between the airfield and the New Zealanders of Hargest's 5th Brigade. A few miles further east, thousands of unengaged infantry waited in their slit trenches with nothing to prevent them marching west in darkness along the open coast road.

Seven hours later the counter-attack had been held at Pirgos, and the troop-carriers were coming in again upon the runway. The invaders had struck their first effective blow.

Yet the odds against them were still heavy. In the Prison Valley they were closely contained, unable to approach Canea or Suda Bay. At Heraklion and at Retimo they had failed. Even at Maleme scarcely 2,000 remained alive and capable of fighting. Within ten miles of them Freyberg held some 7,000 trained infantry, in addition to the improvised units of Kippenberger's 10th Brigade and at least another 6,000 ancillary British troops bearing arms. If some of this strength could now be swiftly mobilized, and used to recapture the airfield, Student's last hope of sending reinforcement would at once be ended.

In rage and frustration, Heidrich had continued to drive 3 Parachute Regiment into a series of vain attacks upon the heights about Galatas. Now much of its strength was spent, despite the support of the Engineer Battalion, which had succeeded in reaching him, 'after an extremely exhausting night march during which it was engaged in constant fighting with enemy detachments on each side of the reservoir',[1] a phrase which

[1] *Einsatz Kreta*, Battle Report of XI Air Corps

reveals the efforts of the 8th Greeks and the Cretan villagers; ready enough, when it suited them, to rely upon the chivalry of their opponents, the Germans of this battalion had left their wounded near Alikianou in the care of 'medical orderlies and a Greek doctor'.[2] Even with this addition, the total of Heidrich's active force did not exceed 1,250. To his relief, he had not been faced by a counter-attack, but not a man had been sent to replace his losses, and little supply had reached him from the air. Already he had been forced to recognize that his own regiment was no longer strong enough to attempt any major aggression, and that for the moment he could expect no help from Student who would now plainly concentrate every effort upon Maleme. At best he might contribute to the attack from the west by offering a threat to the coast road; it could be little more than a gesture, since he dare not imperil his hold upon the Prison. On the morning of the 22nd he sent northward a detachment of 150 men under the command of Major Heilmann.

The New Zealanders at Galatas soon found that they were receiving unexpected support. Captain Forrester had stayed with the survivors of the 6th Greeks after leading them in their successful counter-attack among the olives on the first afternoon. Throughout the following day, still prolonging his social visit, he had continued to organize and arm them.

Now he and his followers made a dramatic reappearance. At about seven o'clock on the evening of the 22nd a group of Germans, covered by mortar fire, and supported by aircraft, began to make some progress up the slopes south-west of Galatas into the lines of the Divisional Petrol Company. This was the moment for which Forrester had been waiting.

Over an open space in the trees near Galatas [says Kippenberger, who was on Wheat Hill, a few hundred yards to the north-west], came running, bounding, and yelling like Red Indians, about a hundred Greeks and villagers, including women and children, led by Michael Forrester twenty yards ahead. It was too much for the Germans. They turned and ran without hesitation, and we went back to our original positions.[3]

A New Zealand driver was no less impressed by this phenomenon, and by its leading figure,

. . . clad in shorts, a long yellow army jersey reaching down almost to the bottom of the shorts, brass polished and gleaming, web belt in place and waving his revolver in his right hand. He was tall, thin-faced, fair-haired, with no tin hat – the very opposite of a soldier hero . . . a Wodehouse character. It was a most inspiring sight.[4]

On the same evening another party of about fifty Greeks, led by a New Zealand sergeant, stormed some houses on the crest of Pink Hill about a quarter of a mile below the village walls. The Germans were killed.

At the time the efforts of the Greek Regiments were under-estimated. Since the war their contribution has sometimes been exaggerated.

Had the course of the battle been differently conceived by the senior officers on the Island [says Clark], the Greeks might have been used with great effect in a counter-offensive – perhaps making the frontal attack with the New Zealanders operating on the flanks.[5]

This is to see the matter out of all proportion. What is true is that the Greeks and Cretans were contributing greatly to the defence of their island, and to an extent far exceeding anything that had been expected of them. On the third night Kisamos Kastelli was held by the force of Police which had destroyed the Muerbe detachment. South of the airfield, the company of parachutists on the Palaiokhora Road remained closely invested by the local Cretans, and near Pirgos the sharp-shooters who had disturbed the advance of the Germans around the fringe of the airfield now fought on with the New Zealanders. Above Alikianou the resolute 8th Greeks were far from 'hopelessly dispersed and disorganized'.[6] Stoutly aided by the men and women from the village, they barred entry into the hills. West of Canea the forces of King George were engaging something like a thousand of the enemy. Nor was their success any greater than that of their com-patriots further east. At Retimo the Police held the town, and at Heraklion almost every citizen had turned in fury upon the invader.

Our fighters' lack of rifles, automatic weapons and ammunition [says the author of a Greek account] may naturally cause everyone to ask how we carried on the contest so effectively against an enemy both fully equipped and more numerous. The answer to those who were not

---

[4] Davin, p. 235, Driver A. Q. Pope   [5] Clark, p. 138
[6] See Chapter 10, p. 187, n. 15, report by N.Z. Div. Cav.

present at the battle is that it was made possible mainly through the spirit, self-denial and contempt for death inspired by the ideal of our country; but also thanks to the abundance of enemy war material in machine-guns, quick firing weapons, rifles, ammunition and other supplies which came into our hands from the enemy from the first day.[7]

The book describes 'a characteristic . . . incident showing the spirit of the heroic people of Crete'. Accompanied by his young son, an elderly man left his village and went towards 'the sound of the fighting'. Neither had any weapons. First they 'threw rocks' at the enemy, but soon they had succeeded in arming themselves fully. Another young Greek, about to take part in a counter-attack, was found to have only two cartridges. Asked by his commanding officer how he expected to be able to face the Germans with all their modern equipment, he replied: 'It is true that I have only two cartridges in my pouch, but my spirit is there too.'[8]

These men and women well knew that in thus daring to defend their homes they risked a fate more bitter than death in the heat of battle. For soldiers in uniform there still existed rules of a kind. For fighting civilians, if they wore no distinctive emblem, not even international convention could offer protection if they should fall alive into the hands of their enemies. Yet they were un-deterred. Day after day they continued to use their miscellaneous weapons, not in the covert manner of camp followers as the Germans pretended, but in the front line. This was a factor that nobody had foreseen.

By contrast, from the moment of their arrival, the enemy troops had been under no illusion. On all sides they met a fanatical hatred. Nowhere could they count themselves safe. Danger lurked behind the rocks and trees, upon the roof-tops, and from the windows. And in every house they found the walls covered with pictures of the bristling Cretan fathers, their belts hung with pistols and daggers, a sharp reminder of the tradition which had so long demanded that every man in the island should bear arms.

Here in Crete the Germans were seeing the first stirrings of that new *Völkerschlacht*,[9] which would at length fall upon them from every side in concert with the avenging armies from east and west. They could not understand it. During a year of unbroken triumph they had known nothing but the cowed submission of their

[7] Mourellos, Vol. I, p. 412   [8] Ibid., p. 415
[9] 'Rising of the Peoples' – as eventually against Napoleon

victims. This unexpected defiance by a civilian population surprised and angered them. In 1941 rebellion seemed inconceivable.
Their reaction was typical and inevitable. Loudly they protested
their indignation. And very soon they had begun to talk of
atrocities and to announce reprisal. At 10 a.m. on 23 May the
5th Mountain Division issued a notice to all troops:

> The murder of a German airman on 22 May has proved that the
> Greek population, in civilian or German uniforms, is taking part in
> the fighting. They are shooting or stabbing wounded to death and
> removing rings from them, and also mutilating and robbing corpses.
> Any Greek civilian taken with a firearm in his hands is to be shot
> immediately, as is anyone caught attacking wounded.

And then, more ominously, in phrases soon to become familiar
throughout Europe:

> Hostages (men between 18 and 55) are to be taken from the villages
> at once, and the civilians are to be informed that if acts of hostility
> against the German army take place these will be shot immediately.
> The villagers in the area are to be informed that 10 Greeks will die
> for every German.

Once it had become clear that fighting was continuing at
Maleme the Cretans must have become well aware of their peril.
Indeed, it might have been expected that they would now vanish
discreetly from the scene. They did nothing of the kind. On the
contrary, they sought to answer threat with threat. The Greek
Commander fighting in the suburbs of Heraklion reported to
Chappel that German troops to the west of the town had been
using Cretan women and children as a protective screen. This
practice had ceased after he had sent a message threatening to
kill all his prisoners if it should continue.

On the second day the condition of the Germans in the two
eastern Sectors grew increasingly desperate. They found themselves cut off from each other in broken country, deprived of
reinforcement, and short of weapons, food, and ammunition.

At Heraklion, the parachutists outside the defence perimeter
were constantly menaced by the Cretan guerrillas. Three miles
east of the airfield, near Gurnes, a company was wiped out in
ferocious fighting. Soon another group of about thirty men
suffered the same fate. Colonel Brauer thus found it impossible to
co-ordinate attacks from east and west. By dawn on the 21st no

more than a single platoon had penetrated to the high ground east of the airfield. Here it was quickly isolated. Brauer judged that his only hope of bringing relief was to send his troops forward independently as soon as he could find them. This attempt was brought to nothing by the Black Watch, supported by artillery, mortars, and the tanks. On the following morning, the isolated platoon was overrun and its commander killed. He bore a name, Count Blücher, that was not unknown to the British Army.

South and west of the town the York and Lancs were guarding a difficult terrain that offered the Germans many covered approaches among the houses, vineyards, and dried stream beds. Captain Rabbidge felt some anxiety about supply. He had been told that his company must be careful with small-arms ammunition. Already he was using 'R.A.F. 303, tracer, and incendiary'.[10] But his men were in excellent heart. The Cretan Minister of Justice, who was watching the battle from a terrace, saw one of 'these soldiers of the White and Red Rose' stop for a moment to put a rose in his buttonhole before running on.[11]

The effectiveness of the Greek and Cretan troops had been much increased by their use of German arms. In response to a judicious display of swastika flags, one of the Australian units had been rewarded with 'machine-guns, wireless sets, mortars, a motor-cycle and sidecar, chairs and tables, a tent, and much food and ammunition.'[12] Most of the weapons were at once sent on to the Greeks.

Towards evening on 22 May, Brauer was forced to withdraw the survivors of his eastern group, now less than half a battalion in strength, to Ames Ridge, two miles south-east of the airfield, while the troops under Major Schulz, after their brief success on the quays at Heraklion, were driven off to the west. A report that a major of the Greek Army had earlier 'offered to surrender the town'[13] can have afforded them little consolation.

Before nightfall on that day, the bodies of 950 Germans had been collected within the British perimeter. To this could be added a further 300 corpses piled in the Greek Sector. 'Many more,' says the *Australian War History*, 'lay where they could not be reached without undue risk of coming under fire'.[14] Another

[10] Capt. T. V. Rabbidge to author, 23 Sept. 1961

[11] Sheffield, *The York and Lancaster Regiment*

[12] Long, p. 283   [13] *Einsatz Kreta*, Battle Report of XI Air Corps   [14] Long, p. 286

200 had been lost at Gurnes and in the surrounding hills. Thus of the 2,000 men who had jumped from their planes on the first afternoon some 1,450 were already dead. Others had been wounded or taken prisoner. At 5 p.m. on the 21st, eleven troop-carriers had come in east of Ames Ridge and dropped about 120 parachutists left over from the previous day. There had been no other reinforcement. Even with this small addition the number of Germans capable of fighting cannot have reached 600 on the evening of the 22nd. The casualties among the British and Australian troops had not exceeded fifty.

Only the heavy tanks had failed. They had started well. And neither had been damaged by the enemy. But the strain of so much activity had proved too much for them. Both had broken down.

At dusk on 20 May it had seemed that the airstrip at Retimo was about to fall to the parachutists. Despite their losses, and the failure of their radio contact with Athens, the airlanding troops had occupied almost the whole of the vital hill south-east of the runway. On the northern face only one section of Australians fired in gallant defiance at their enemies on the surrounding terraces. The Germans now held a position which stretched back from the beach, across the road, and along the eastern edge of the airfield. All night they pressed their advantage against the re-inforced company which was clinging precariously to the southern neck of the hill.

Campbell was in no doubt that if he could not recapture this height the airfield must be lost. And the certainty that he was alone lent spurs to his resolution. At dawn he attacked once more with the same company. It was driven back under an intense barrage of mortar bombs; both its commander and one of the lieutenants were wounded. He then sent across another company, under Captain Moriarty, who at 6.15 a.m. reported to him over the telephone that the Germans were pressing hard and that the position was 'very desperate'.[15]

He now had no further reserve. Already firing could be heard from the south where a party of the enemy had captured the dressing station at Adhele; if he were to take his last company from Hill D he must leave a wide gap through which they would be able to drive from this area straight up the wadis Bardia and

Pigi. Nevertheless, this was a risk that he decided to accept. In his own words:

The first attack by Channell was at dawn. When that failed I led round my remaining Company and told Captain Moriarty to take most of the troops in the area and clear Hill A at about 10 hrs. He was my most experienced remaining Company Commander. I then set off back to my Bde cum Bn HQ, but on the way took Captain Embrey 'B' Coy plus my Signal Pl (riflemen not signallers, as no signal equipment) and moved up wadi BARDIA as I feared the Germans would outflank me to the south and come NW against the south of Hill D, which was by this time undefended, and then thrust due North on to the airstrip.[16]

Moriarty had been given a force which included most of the 2/1 Battalion. As he well knew, all depended upon what he could do with it. Shortly before 8 a.m., he was much encouraged to see a German plane dropping bombs among the parachutists further up the hill. At this he decided to wait no longer. In a superb attacking surge he led his men up the slopes, among the rocks and boulders, to pour over the crest and down the terraces on the far side. This time success was complete. The survivors fled across the road, leaving their dead and fifty-nine prisoners.

Later in the day the two Australian battalions, aided by the Greeks, completed the destruction of the enemy along that part of the coastal strip that faced the defence positions, together with the parachutists who had collected in the south. Those that remained were now split into two groups. A mile and a half east of the airfield a few score fugitives had succeeded in making their escape from Hill A to find shelter in the olive oil factory at Stavromenos, and in the west a somewhat larger collection was held confined between the 2/11 and the Cretan Police, who had ejected them from the outskirts of Retimo.

The self-important Colonel Sturm had been taken prisoner with the whole of his staff. He was found still to be carrying his written orders. From these Campbell learnt that 1,500 men had taken part in the attack. By nightfall his Australians were back in their original lines, most of them equipped with enemy weapons. Several hundreds of the Germans were dead, and hundreds more taken prisoner or wounded. No reinforcement had reached them, and it was plain that the *Luftwaffe* was having great difficulty in

[16] Letter to author, 1 May 1960

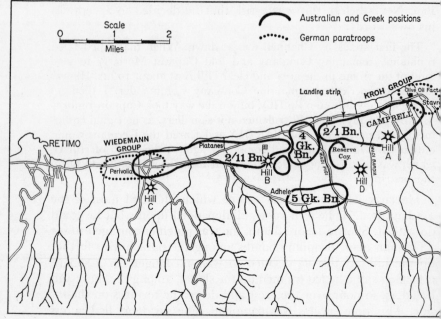

15.   Retimo: 10 a.m., 21 May

identifying its own men on the ground. Some captured Australians had been rescued, and the two tanks salvaged. That evening Campbell sent a message to Freyberg saying that the situation was well in hand.

During the eighteen hours that had followed the invasion, Campbell had fought an action which can today be seen as a model of what was required of the defenders in Crete. Too young to be prejudiced by inhibiting memories of the Great War, he had recognized from the start the paramount importance of immediate counter-attack, and he had understood that in the occupation of Hill A lay the key to the possession of the airfield. Three times, on the first evening, he had attempted to wrest it from the parachutists who had seized it by exploiting their original initiative, coupled with their superiority in numbers. All these efforts had come to nothing, despite the reinforcement which he had sent immediately. The tanks, from which so much had been expected, had disappeared. On the following morning another attack had been stopped almost at once, with the loss of most of the officers. The sound of firing from the south had then revealed that some of the Germans had made their way through the hills and were threatening him from this new direction. He had seen that this was the moment of crisis. Boldly collecting the whole of his reserve, while accepting the risk that the Germans in his rear might move north through the wide gap that he was leaving in his centre, he had left his Headquarters and gone himself to the foot of Hill A. Here he had organized a fifth attempt, this time successfully.

As at Heraklion, the air attack had been far lighter than at Maleme, but it was no less important that Campbell had reduced the pilots to impotence by putting his men among the Germans on the ground. Nor had he allowed himself to be deterred by unproductive anxiety about the possibility of further parachute drops, or of landings from the sea. He knew that if the entire Germany Army were to arrive at Retimo before noon, the loss of the airfield would follow no more certainly than it must if the parachutists already in action were allowed to increase their hold upon the height that commanded it.

Upon this understanding, he had controlled the battle in a manner that cannot fail to point a contrast with the direction of events at Maleme. And his men had supported him. Shedding on the instant those lawless airs which, a few days earlier, had dismayed their more sober English friends, they had responded to his leadership in the tradition established by their fathers at Gallipoli and on the Somme, devoting themselves with casual gallantry to the purpose of the hour. The risks had been great. They had ignored them, caring nothing for the reputation of their enemies, sure only of one another, and of the justice of their fight. Now their triumph was decisive.

On the 22nd the Germans landed a further three Mountain Battalions at Maleme.[17] By this time the airfield was 'littered with burning and broken-down aircraft', although 'cleared again and again, with the help of captured tanks, by a landing commando'.[18] And not only tanks. Prisoners, too, were driven in among the bursting shells and 'ordered to unload guns, shells, cases and stores'. Some refused. At this 'the officer in charge

[17] The Report by Air Fleet IV says that the landings at Maleme during the course of the 22nd were two Mountain Battalions, one Mountain Pioneer Battalion, elements of a Parachute Artillery unit, and one Field Hospital

[18] *Einsatz Kreta*, Battle Report of XI Air Corps

marched three aside and had them shot in the sight of the others'.[19]

Something of the speed and urgency of this operation is conveyed by the impressions of one of the Mountain Troops. Like most of his comrades he had been making his first flight:

We didn't need to open the door for it had flown open already. The first men jumped out of the moving plane with their heavy rucksacks flying behind them. The wind of the propellers blew the yellow dust in our faces; the Junkers was already moving again. A mortar bomb burst very close. The crash of the burst, the noise of engines, the dust and the shouting of the ground crews made our heads swim. We all found ourselves in an enormous bomb crater near at hand. Two more of the men off our plane came running. They had almost been taken back, but at the last moment they had jumped from the plane as it started up, leaving their packs behind. Only now could we have an undisturbed look at the aerodrome. Our Junkers was hardly away when the next one landed right in the middle of the thick dust. A cracking rending sound, more clouds of dust . . . crash . . . belly-landing. The undercarriage flies in huge bounds into the nearby water.[20]

Shells continued to burst all around, but the losses remained 'within bearable limits'.[21] After the battle XI Air Corps was to give the total dead of the 5th Mountain Division in Crete as 580. Of these, the great majority were killed during the later days of the fighting, and probably at least sixty in the planes that crashed along the beach towards Platanias on the first afternoon. These figures can be accepted, since they were issued in secret to the German High Command. They suggest that at most no more than a score or two of the Mountain Troops died on the airfield. The pilots had quickly realized that it was safer to come down on the runway, crowded as it was, rather than to make further attempts to crash along the shore.

By the morning of the 22nd Student knew that he had been right in subordinating all else to the exploitation of the Storm Regiment's success in the west. He now decided that the whole of the 5th Mountain Division would be sent to Maleme instead of to Heraklion. The eastern flotilla was recalled to the Piraeus. All idea of sending help by sea was abandoned. Heidrich was told that his men need only continue to pin down their opponents. The parachutists at Heraklion and Retimo were to do what they

---

[19] Proceedings at the trial of Kurt Student. The Court found this charge proved but sentence was not confirmed

[20] DP   [21] *Einsatz Kreta*, Battle Report of XI Air Corps

could to prevent enemy use of the airfields. In these three areas, the troops must shift for themselves, without reinforcement, largely deprived of air support, and supplied only by hazardous drops from the air.

The supreme effort of XI Air Corps was focused upon this narrow strip of sand at Maleme. Those troop-carriers that were still capable of flying took off again within minutes. From time to time it was still necessary to drag clear a machine that had been damaged. But these losses became fewer. While the organization of the bridge-head improved, the artillery fire against it was slowly extinguished by the *Luftwaffe*. All through the day the landing operation went on. Once more it remained immune from the New Zealand infantry.

For many who have studied the battle of Crete there has lain here a central mystery. Like those people in England who followed the course of the fighting during the last days of May 1941, first with confidence and later with bewilderment and disquiet, they cannot understand why it should have proved so difficult to mount an effective counter-attack at Maleme. Here was a small enemy force apparently at its leisure effecting a vital lodgment under the very noses of Freyberg's superior numbers. The local commanders were known to be men of courage and vigour. Why then were the days drifting by and no progress made? What strange unseen power had come to the aid of the enemy?

Only from the men who fought in Crete can the truth be known. And for them the matter has always been plain. With them there remains a single vision that surpasses all else—the memory of the absolute dominion held by their enemies in the air.

The predicament of the infantry in Crete remains unique in the history of war. Often in the past men have been asked to fight under worse handicap, sometimes without hope. But never before or since has such a vast concourse of close-support planes operated at will above a defenceless enemy exposed in the open. At Dunkirk it had been very different. Gort's weary divisions, owing their unrecognized debt to the distant squadrons of the Royal Air Force, had suffered few casualties as they waited day after day in their long queues among the sand-dunes. Nor was there ever again mounted a sustained attack of comparable type and intensity. The British-American command of the air, which developed after 1943, was never used in this way, partly because it was seldom unopposed, and partly because it had by that time been realized that measures could be taken by trained infantry even against such an onslaught as that delivered by the German aircraft in Crete. But, in this battle, the defence had neither the anti-aircraft weapons that might have held the planes at a distance, nor the wireless communications that could have spared the need for exposure, or ordered it better when it became unavoidable.

On the first day the soldiers of both sides, indistinguishable from the air, had fought in hundreds of small encounters while the German pilots had cruised in leisurely circles above them, unable to intervene. During these few hours a golden opportunity had been exploited to the full at Retimo, and to a lesser extent at Heraklion. At Maleme the moment had been allowed to slip away. By the morning of the 22nd the battle line had been clearly drawn through Pirgos, marked by flare signals and by wireless advice from the ground.

Now the air attack rose to a new crescendo. This is something to remember. After the battle it quickly became fashionable, or perhaps politic, to deprecate the effect of the German planes in Crete. It was conceded that they had shown themselves capable of imposing inconvenience upon the Navy, and of causing some annoyance to the daylight movement of transport. But to acknowledge that they might impair the activities of disciplined infantry was regarded as heresy. By the spring of 1941 this had become an article of faith in every Headquarters Staff and base depot in England and the Middle East. Less understandably much was done to nourish the illusion by several of the senior officers who returned to Egypt from Crete. Prominent among these was General Weston, who was to declare that the experiences of the troops in Greece, and later in Crete, had produced in them an absurd anxiety about the danger from aircraft. In his view machine-gunning from the air had nearly always proved quite ineffective, seldom causing any casualties. The judgement recalls Haig's opinion that the machine-gun was 'a much overrated' weapon.

During the battle Weston had not left Suda Area. Nor was the failure of morale among some of the troops closest to him any indication of the experience and reactions of the men who had been in the front line. Nevertheless, his opinions found a ready acceptance among critics who wished to know no better, and were later to acquire spurious validity as the passage of time silenced the voices of those who understood. By the end of the war so many planes had flown above so many battlefields that it had become difficult to appreciate that never again had there arisen the particular association of circumstance which had rendered paramount their influence in Crete.

Thus historians were encouraged to make the discovery that the infantry-support rôle of the *Luftwaffe* in Crete had been of no great account. In 1962 Clark dismisses it in a footnote, with a comment that its effect had indeed been 'emphasized'[22] by Freyberg, but that it had not upset anybody very much at Heraklion.

In fact, even at Heraklion, a company of the Leicesters was to be 'almost annihilated' when a supporting party, 'pinned by strafing aircraft',[23] failed to 'get up' in time to protect its rear. But this was unusual. For almost a week, after the first evening, the Germans were able to spare for the men of Chappel's brigade little more than a single bombing assault upon the town and a few desultory visits from troop-carriers bringing supplies.

The fury expended upon the west was infinitely greater. Nevertheless, its significance has remained unrecognized.

The Official Australian War Historian denies that British air inferiority was 'a decisive factor in Greece'. And he adds:

If so much as a platoon had altered its position because it had been attacked from the air, or if substantial casualties had been inflicted on the rearguard by aircraft, or the transport and supply of the force seriously impeded because they had destroyed its trucks, there would be support for such a contention . . . the German air force failed to achieve any of these results in Greece: its greatest success was the destruction wrought in the port of Athens.

Whatever may be thought of this there can be no justification for his further observation:

The time was then distant when air power, vastly stronger than that employed by the Germans in Greece, considerably more accurate in its fire and more closely co-ordinated, would be able to play a part comparable with, say, the artillery in an action on the ground.[24]

The time was one month distant. All the effects that he describes were achieved by the *Luftwaffe* along the strip of coast between Maleme and Canea. In the light of such latter-day

[22] Clark, p. 95, *n.* 1   [23] Underhill, *The Royal Leicestershire Regiment*, p. 51
[24] Long, p. 195

revelations it is instructive to learn the facts and to read the impressions of the men who were there. On 26 May the New Zealand 5th Brigade was to lose a further seventy men to air attack during the course of movements behind the line, and at Retimo machine-gunning planes were rewarded by thirty-nine casualties among two companies in the course of a single afternoon. At every level the sensations were the same, from the front-line infantry in the gully south of Pirgos to Freyberg himself, who was to write:

The enemy's control of the air made movement by daylight impossible. . . . I travelled usually as a pillion on a motor-bike, and had to run for my life on the road on many occasions.[25]

It soon became clear enough to Captain Dawson that machine-gunning from the air need not always be 'ineffective'. After Hargest had told him to find out what was happening to the counter-attack, he set out again along the coast road between Platanias and Pirgos. Of this journey, he wrote:

Left Bde in Bren Carrier with last W/T set and wireless operator and driver. Also some rations and amn. We were caught in Platanias village by Messerschmitts. The set was riddled and was useless; bailed out into coast side of road on to open ground but planes strafed us there also snipers from direction of coast. We then dashed for North side of road into a wheat field. Planes then strafed us there, and set fire to the wheat field which we had to vacate. This lasted approx. 40 mins. Then inspected carrier – it would go – found driver but couldn't find W/T operator – looked for him for a short while and shouted for him but no luck. Then as set was no good decided to get on up to 23 Bn.

The driver and I then went on in a series of dashes and bail outs to 23 Bn with ammunition and some rations. We turned the corner at the rd junction at about 40 mph much to the amusement of some 23 Bn people who could see us.[26]

The threat from the sky produced a cumulative impression. Least affected were those who had been in action and remained in close contact with their friends. But once a man found himself alone his feelings changed. Few were then immune against sudden panic.

I lost my head [Farran wrote of his sensations after the loss of his tank], I was so afraid that I could have burrowed into the ground. And

[25] DP, Freyberg comments on Davin Draft, 1952 (undated)
[26] Davin, p. 230, Capt. R. B. Dawson

so I ran . . . crashing through the undergrowth, tumbling into ditches, and all the time looking up at the sky at the black crosses on the aeroplanes. . . . I threw myself into a slit-trench on top of a German prisoner. I could feel his body quivering against my belly . . . I doubled across the road, but in a moment they were diving down again. I dashed into the open door of a stable and threw myself head first into an iron manger while the bombs carved a big crater in the road outside. It was not until it was over that I noticed that the other mangers were all occupied by New Zealanders in a similar state. I left for the open, running between patches of cover and crawling along ditches until I reached the squadron.[27]

Hour after hour the planes screamed in criss-cross patterns above the trees. Every man felt himself gripped by this menace from the air, watched in his every movement from an hour after dawn until a little before dusk, threatened with instant death if he should leave his shelter. In order to move fifty yards he might have to watch many minutes for his opportunity. Sound alone could not guide him since the noise was so great from all directions that a plane might pass unnoticed twenty feet above his head. However he chose his moment, the chances were that, before he could run more than a few strides, he would find the earth alive about his feet, the red pencils of tracer leaping upon him from the snub yellow noses of the Messerschmitts. If he should be caught a few yards from cover he might well be hunted to his death by half a dozen of them sporting with him as they pleased. Almost every newcomer to a slit trench plunged to safety among a shower of stones and branch fragments as the bullets swept across his path.

Even those who had less need to expose themselves felt increasingly the strain of the constant noise and danger. In his dressing station among the olive groves south of Suda Bay Stephanides found that

. . . the continuous noise and concussion made one feel sick and dazed, yet every nerve was on edge as in a nightmare. One's ears were cocked the whole time to judge the distance of each plane from the roar of its engines and the nearness of every bomb from the screech of its approach. And there was never any let-up of the tension.[28]

Fear was exaggerated by the sensation of impotence. Against these Messerschmitts, Stukas, and Dorniers, the men on the ground had no effective weapons. They quickly learnt that to fire

[27] Farran, p. 98   [28] Stephanides, p. 100

back with small arms served only to reveal their own positions. Streams of bullets might pass through the fuselages, but the tracer could be seen harmlessly turned aside by the armour that protected the engines and cockpits. For months they had been fed on propaganda which told them of the hundreds of Spitfires that were being turned out by Beaverbrook's Ministry. All the more bitter was it to find that these planes were not to appear in Crete. Among those of the officers who understood something of the difficulties of defending an island four hundred miles into the Mediterranean there was less disillusion. And the Australians and New Zealanders, with their healthy distrust of all official information, had scarcely expected anything better. But the soldiers from England felt that they had been deceived. In their indignation they were not disposed to discriminate.

Where are our air force? Disgraceful effort I think [wrote Sergeant Charles of the R.A.O.C. in his diary]. These planes can cruise along as slow and as low as they like, and do everything except land.[29]

Once more the letters R.A.F. were mocked with all the familiar variations. Here was yet another repercussion from that failure on the part of the Chiefs of Staff and the politicians to face and accept the truth of the situation while there was yet time. It would have been better to have admitted from the first that the Royal Air Force would be unable to give protection, even if this had meant the surrender of the same information to the Germans, who might then perhaps have drawn the conclusion that their attack need not include all the airfields. The risk would have been worth taking, since it must have encouraged resource and resolution in applying such remedies as were available, while lessening dismay at the harsh reality.

Certainly there was much that might have been done. Inglis was later to maintain that there had been 'ways of circumventing' the enemy control of the air by 'proper dispersion, timing of moves', and that the worst effect had been 'on the minds' of those commanders who had let it influence them unduly in their conduct of operations.[30]

There is justice in this criticism. Even from the west some of the planes were withdrawn intermittently to attack the Fleet. Little advantage was taken of their absence, partly for the reason that these brief lulls could be interrupted unpredictably at any

[29] Sgt. F. S. Charles, letter to author, 30 June 1961
[30] DP, Inglis to Kippenberger, 12 Feb. 1951

moment, but partly also because too much limitation was placed
upon the capacity of the troops to move unseen among the trees
and across the broken ground. Very soon the experienced infantry
learnt the knack of watching their opportunity to dash from cover
to cover. At Vlakheronitissa, Allen had shown that it was not
impossible to infiltrate across country in this way, above all while
in close contact with the enemy, and at Retimo, the one Sector
in which the defence sought constantly to engage the enemy
infantry closely in daylight, the *Luftwaffe* was enticed repeatedly
into bombing its own men. Here was the true rejoinder.

Inactivity brought its own damage to morale. Gradually the
attack from the air became the governing factor in the thought
and actions of every man between Suda and Pirgos. In all the
diaries written at the time there is revealed this growing obsession
with the enemy planes. The feeling was seldom that of simple fear.
Rather did it go beyond reason, the sensation of an animal,
trapped and helpless, sufficient to numb the stoutest heart. Men
felt it whose courage was never in question, men who continued
to give orders and to fight with no thought of surrender or withdrawal. What had changed in them was their spontaneity, and
their power of decision. A lethargy gripped them. They spoke in
low monotones, and replied to questions in sudden feeble
irritation. They became unrecognizable to their friends. Even the
placidly brave Hargest, whose cheerful fortitude had remained
untroubled by the shelling at Delville Wood, was to admit that
the air attack in Crete had induced in him 'a kind of dread'.[31] It
was as though the enemy had enlisted in his support the powers
of the supernatural.

These effects, though grave and increasing, had not much
reduced the value of the troops in the front line. More serious was
the crippling of administration by the grip upon daylight movement. Ammunition, food and weapons could be delivered only at
night. And always there was the handicap laid upon the con-
veyance of information. Telephone lines seldom remained intact
for more than a few minutes at a time, and the few wireless sets
repeatedly broke down. By the second day communication, even
by runner, had become protracted and uncertain. At no time
had there been any hope of the air reconnaissance that could have
revealed the truth of the German dependence upon Maleme. In
these circumstances, deprived increasingly of knowledge both of

[31] Mr. Geoffrey Cox to author, 1962

his own troops and of the enemy, Freyberg found it ever more difficult to control the battle.

More clearly even than appeared at the time, the *Wehrmacht* records reveal the extent to which the Germans were depending upon the *Luftwaffe*. During the 22nd they had added about 2,000 to their numbers in western Crete. It was not yet enough to make them safe.

That evening, the command of the troops in the west was taken over by Major-General Ringel, a regular soldier greatly experienced in mountain warfare, who had been the leader of the Nazi party in the old Austrian Army. As a tactician he was famous for his maxim 'Sweat saves blood'.[32] This principle he at once put into effect by ordering the main body of his Mountain Troops, under the command of Colonel Utz, to carry on with their lengthy march through the southern foothills 'firstly with the object of eliminating the enemy artillery', which aircraft of VIII Air Corps had 'failed to silence'.[33] Later they were to cut the coast road east of Platanias. A smaller group he directed to go in search of the missing Muerbe party. Other detachments were to secure his flanks by the capture of Kisamos Kastelli in the west, and Palaiokhora in the south. He did not reinforce his main front. For the immediate protection of his base from the east, he kept back only the available survivors of the Storm Regiment, now organized as a single battalion under the command of the resolute Ramcke.

Thus he boldly amplified the dispositions of the previous night. Like Ramcke, he revealed no qualms about weakening his protection over the airfield itself. Such confidence was not yet shared by his men. Many years later, Colonel Wittmann, one of the Mountain Troops battalion commanders, was to write of this evening:

On 22 May the sun sinks glowing into the sea – unbelievably beautiful, untouched by the sorrows and joys of men. Wearily the exhausted troops think back upon the uncertainties and anxieties of their day upon the island and wonder what the morrow will bring. But nobody mentions the torturing question which tugs at every heart, 'Shall we be able to hang on?'[34]

[32] Wittmann, *Die Gebirgstruppe*, Number 3, p. 6
[33] *Einsatz Kreta*, Battle Report of XI Air Corps
[34] Wittmann, *Die Gebirgstruppe*, Number 3, p. 5

17

The Vision Fades: 22-23 May

On the morning of 22 May Freyberg quickly found that his hopes had been premature. There was news from Egypt of the Navy's success against the German invasion fleet, but it was also clear that the counter-attack at Maleme had failed. Hour after hour he watched the steady flow of enemy troop-carriers. Although the airfield remained hidden behind the heights at Platanias, the Junkers could be seen coming in to land. And not only to land. Every few minutes the narrow shape of a plane would lift silently out of the haze, the wings suddenly broadening in silhouette as it banked to fly out low over the sea past the grey mass of Theodhoroi Island, while the roar of the take-off swept back across Canea.

Anxiously he sought to find some consistency in those fragments of news that were reaching him. Most of his information at this time came from the New Zealand Division. Until midday he continued to hear of Hargest's long enduring optimism. Perhaps he may have allowed himself to believe that the counter-attack was still making progress, and that at any moment the air taxi service would be interrupted. But the traffic continued with 'painful monotony'. By the early afternoon Hargest had begun to take a different view; the troops, after all, were 'not so far forward'[1] as had been thought; the Maoris had been forced to withdraw into the valley south of Pirgos.

The blazing sun beat down upon the Headquarters in the quarry, filling it with sweltering heat. A deceptive quiet now lay over the west while the *Luftwaffe* turned aside for another onslaught upon Cunningham's ships. Through his field glasses Freyberg could see little more than the soft line of the coast. The Messerschmitts, the Stukas, and the Heinkels had vanished. And of the fighting nothing could be heard apart from the occasional whisper of musketry, varied at long intervals by the distant crack

[1] New Zealand Division War Diary

of a gun. Only that sudden roar, repeated every few minutes, revealed the menace that was gathering. Bitterly he must have asked himself the strength and nature of this enemy lodgment, for so long little regarded, now suddenly become a deadly threat.

At one o'clock, he requested the New Zealand Division to estimate the numbers landed at Maleme, carrier-borne and by parachute, since the beginning of the operation. He had to wait more than five hours for an answer. When it came, at 6.40 p.m., it bore no relation to anything that he had heard before. A mere thirty planes were now thought to have 'dropped parachutes' on the 21st, while 139 had landed or crashed in the vicinity of the airfield.[2] This was an improvement on the previous guesses. But a little late. And still wide of the truth; in fact, almost exactly twice the real figure. More accurate, if somewhat limited, was a report from the 4th Brigade, observing better than the 5th Brigade although six miles further away, that so far during the present afternoon fifty-nine troop-carriers had put down 'between 1 p.m. and 4 p.m. . . . when landing stopped'.[3] Everyone within a dozen miles of Maleme knew that the landing had begun again early that morning. Nobody had done any counting before lunch.

Gradually, however, this information if no other, was improving. There was still much confusion over the relative strengths of the parachutists and airborne infantry that had arrived on the first two days. But it was now becoming easy to judge how many were being transported entirely by troop-carriers. Later that evening the New Zealand Division was to send a further report estimating the enemy landings as '20 May 2400 paratroops, 21 May 300 paratroops 300 airborne, 22 May 1500 airborne plus stores'.[4] And at 12.15 a.m. on the morning of the 23rd the brigades were told that the enemy strength was about '5 Bns with heavy mortars and some motor-cyclists vicinity Maleme aerodrome'.[5]

Now there could no longer be any doubt of what must be done if the island were to be saved. In his report Freyberg says of the situation on the afternoon of 22 May:

The vital question was whether we could attack and dislodge the

---

[2] New Zealand Division War Diary   [3] Ibid.

[4] Ibid. Appearing suddenly from such a welter of misinformation this was a revelation of astonishing accuracy. In the light of what is now known of their subsequent actions it can be judged in retrospect that probably both Puttick and Freyberg himself thought it too optimistic. It has been seen that it was the stuff about the '600 troop-carriers' on the second day that was later reported by Freyberg. Moreover this figure subsequently reached Wavell's despatch.

[5] Ibid.

enemy from the Maleme Aerodrome area. . . . The enemy had absolute air superiority; not only could he bomb any movement but he could call upon about 400 fighter ground straffers with cannon guns which would, and in fact did, prevent any movement during the hours of daylight. We had counter-attacked by night and succeeded but our success had been temporary only as we were bombed off again as soon as it was daylight. On the other hand the possession of Maleme landing-ground was vital and at 5 p.m. I gave orders for another counter-attack to dislodge the enemy.[6]

He gives no details of how he expected the attack to be made, simply noting the intention to 'concentrate the 4th Brigade to carry through this plan'. No doubt he felt that the New Zealand Division must have been aware all day of what would be required and had already put the necessary preparations in hand.

Puttick attended Force Headquarters to receive these orders. There is no record that he expressed any opinion about them or asked for reinforcement.

As he returned through Canea, he may have reflected that upon the next few hours must depend the vindication of the policy that he had followed since the beginning of the battle. Hitherto he had handled the 4th Brigade with extreme caution, on the first day resisting all pressure to use it in the Prison Valley, and on the night of the 21st releasing for the counter-attack no more than a single battalion, and that three hours too late.

Yet even now he was showing no great sense of urgency. Indeed, it was only at the express orders of Freyberg that he was at last proposing to engage this reserve that had been handed over to him on the first morning. He had made no attempt to move any part of it west in daylight, despite the disappearance of the *Luftwaffe*. The alternative must be an eight-mile flank marching at night across the Germans in the Prison Valley, some of them beginning to probe north against the coast.

It was not an inviting prospect. But here was the crisis by which must be judged his claim to have recognized from the first that 'the real front' would lie at Maleme. For this, ostensibly, had the enemy near the Prison been left so long undisturbed. It might be supposed, therefore, that he was returning to his Headquarters resolved to recapture Maleme at all costs, pressing into the attack every man not immediately required to watch the Prison Valley, the first assault to be made by the New Zealand 18th and the

[6] Freyberg Report, quot. Davin, p. 238

Australian 2/7th Battalions, together with the available companies of the 20th, and backed by the whole of 5th Brigade. The fact that he had not asked for help from the 1st Welch might be taken to indicate that he was confident that these forces would be enough for success.

Such, however, was not the impression that he now made upon his staff officers. Nor did he find awaiting him any great fervour of anticipation. 'As far as I remember,' says Colonel Gentry, the Divisional Chief of Staff, 'there were no considered plans for another attempt to recapture Maleme airfield on the night 22/23 May. It must have been well into the afternoon of 22 May before Div. H.Q. knew clearly how the original counter-attack had fared. The first proposal for a new attack came from Puttick on his return from Creforce Headquarters. I do not think that he had any intention of using part of 4 Bde which in any case would not have been easy then. My memory of the occasion is that Brig. Puttick had in mind spurring on 5 Bde to try again. Another attack that night would have been very difficult to organize.'[7]

The atmosphere was not improved by disconcerting news. In his Divisional Report Puttick himself says:

Arriving at Divisional H.Q. Divisional Commander found from situation reports that there was considerable enemy movement on 10 Inf. Bde Front and that the road between 4 and 5 Inf. Bde H.Qs. was commanded by an enemy detachment including a MG.[8]

He next moved on to the 4th Brigade, which was only a short distance away. From here the prospect looked no more cheerful. A Bren carrier had been 'detailed ready to take him to 5 Inf. Bde. H.Q.'[9] But while he was still with Inglis a message came from Hargest reporting that the troops near Pirgos had been 'severely attacked, were considerably exhausted, and certainly not fit to make a further attack'.[10] He could not know that this dejected assessment was based on evidence little better than that which had stimulated the earlier hope that the Germans were evacuating. While he still hesitated more reports told him of increased enemy activity in the Prison Valley. Again in the words of the New Zealand Divisional Report:

He learnt of a strong enemy attack against Galatas from the direction of the Prison, while enemy movement from south to NW of

[7] DP, Lieut.-Col. W. G. Gentry
[8] Davin, pp. 238 and 526, New Zealand Divisional Report, para. 97
[9] Ibid.   [10] Ibid., para. 98

Galatas indicated the probability of important enemy forces attempting to cut the Canea-Maleme road behind or east of 5 Inf. Bde. This road had already been commanded by enemy MG and mortar fire on several occasions.[11]

At this he waited to hear no more. All too clearly he saw the threat to his troops west of the Galatas Turn. Now that the time had come for him to mount his grand attack he felt bound to conclude that it was already too late. From the 4th Brigade Headquarters, just west of Canea, with the bright sunlight of late evening throwing long shadows across the road, he telephoned to Freyberg expressing his fears and urging that the 5th Brigade should be withdrawn. The Bren carrier which was to have carried him to Hargest still waited under the trees. It would not be needed. Never, since the action started, had he so nearly made the trip. But now he would not be going to Platanias.

For Freyberg this was a sombre moment. How brief had proved his hopes. The implication of what Puttick was saying was clear enough. If the 5th Brigade were to come back another five miles it would be difficult indeed to mount any further counter-attack. And in the meantime the Germans would be able to reinforce without so much as desultory artillery fire to inconvenience them. Yet he made no demur. Over the telephone he told Puttick 'in guarded language' that it certainly appeared as though the brigade 'should be withdrawn'.[12] Brigadier Stewart would come down to discuss the matter.

By 10 p.m. Puttick and Stewart had worked it all out. The 5th Brigade would occupy the line of the road east of Platanias, and thus link up with the 10th Brigade. The disorganized 22nd Battalion would be taken over by the 4th Brigade, the two Australian battalions, reformed under Vasey, remaining within the New Zealand Division to occupy the left flank near Perivolia. Forty-two vehicles, including ten three-ton lorries, would be used in the withdrawal to 'salvage all possible'. Thus the Division would once more present a solid front, based upon sound communications, and it would still be difficult for the Germans from Maleme to reach the Prison Valley except by the detour to the south.

But it was no less clear that unless some desperate throw could be devised the enemy would be able to build up undisturbed to such strength as might be necessary for victory. It was a decision,

[11] Davin, p. 339, New Zealand Divisional Report, para. 97   [12] Ibid., para. 98

Stewart was to say later, that 'virtually amounted to accepting the loss of Crete'.[13]

Scarcely two hours after Freyberg had given orders for the New Zealand Division to 'dislodge the enemy' from Maleme Puttick had concluded that such an action would be too dangerous. Indeed he could think only of continuing the retreat. This was a desperate course. It must be asked whether it was unavoidable.

In fact it was soon apparent that the reports from the 10th Brigade were greatly exaggerating German activity in the Prison Valley. The 'considerable enemy movement' during the day had been little more than patrol action, and the 'strong enemy attack against Galatas from the direction of the Prison' was merely the probing advance from the south-west routed soon after 7 p.m. by Forrester and his Greeks. Nor was anything more heard of the tale that the road to Platanias had been 'commanded by an enemy detachment including a MG'. The 'machine-gun' cannot have been part of the 'important enemy forces attempting to cut the Canea-Maleme road behind or east of 5 Inf. Bde.', since this formation, presumably that of Major Heilmann with his nine officers and 141 men, was not to reach Stalos, still a mile short of the road, until 7 a.m. next morning. The truth was that throughout the day Heidrich had been almost wholly concerned with consolidation. 'The positions already won were maintained', is all that Air Fleet IV says in its report of the day on the central front. There is no mention of the attack up the road towards Galatas.

Like all the senior officers under his command, Puttick had been misled by his information. For this he cannot be blamed. But it is also true that he had allowed himself too readily to become dismayed. While acutely aware of the difficulties of his task he had recognized little of its necessity. Instead he had seen nothing but threats and dangers on every side. Even before he had learnt of the signals from the 10th Brigade he was coming to believe yet again, to judge by the impression that he made upon his staff, that it would be too dangerous to engage the 4th Brigade west of the Galatas Turn. He cannot have told Freyberg of this feeling, since the General had supposed that he would use it for the attack. The fresh alarms that greeted him on his return to his Headquarters had been unfounded – as further inquiry might

[13] DP, Comment by Brig. K. L. Stewart

quickly have revealed. But he had made no attempt to confirm their accuracy. Their effect had been to deter him finally.

On the first night, Andrew had not waited for the darkness that would have enabled him to establish contact with his lost companies. Nor had either Hargest or Puttick gone forward to judge the situation for themselves. Had they done so they would have found, at every stage, that things were not as bad as was suggested by the tangle of rumour and false report upon which they had been relying. Their anxious hesitancy had contrasted with the bold and thrusting opportunism of Gericke, Meindl, and Ramcke. For this Kippenberger was to criticize them in forthright terms:

The failure in each case seems to me to have been that they answered all questions pessimistically, that they saw all dangers real, imagined, or possible, that none made any effort to dictate or control events, that they were utterly without any offensive spirit, and that invariably in each case they adopted a course that made victory impossible . . . not the kind of mistakes that all commanders make, selecting unsatisfactory start-lines, making the rate of advance too fast or too slow, failing to tie up lanes for supporting any neighbouring formations etc., but fundamental mistakes irretrievable by the valour and devotion of those under their command.[14]

Ironically it was Kippenberger himself who had completed Puttick's discouragement. If the messages from the 10th Brigade had said, as they might have said, 'Don't worry about us – we can keep them busy if they try to leave the Prison', the Divisional Commander might have felt less apprehensive about his flank.

In assessing the events of these three days, it must be remembered that by 1941 few of the leaders who had fought on the Western side in 1914–18 had yet learnt to make frequent visits to the front line. Unlike their opposite numbers in the German Army, they had still to learn the necessity to 'think two down',[15] in Montgomery's phrase, about the problems of their junior officers. Nor were the Germans to find it any easier, when their turn came, to improvise attacks at night while prevented from moving in daylight by the Allied air superiority. A Parachute officer who had fought in Crete believed that they lost their opportunity at Salerno for the reason that their 'counter-moves had to be restricted to the hours of darkness and were for the most part unable to keep pace with events on the field of battle'.[16] At

[14] DP, Kippenberger to Brig. H. B. Latham, 27 Aug. 1952
[15] Kippenberger, p. 349   [16] Böhmler, p. 63

Maleme, the senior officers had been facing not only complete enemy control of the air but also the continued threat of parachute attack, conditions that no soldier had ever met before. Always haunting them had been the feeling that the enemy could see everything, and that if they moved at night more parachutists would be dropped behind them on the following morning. Deprived of wireless communications, the one simple aid that might have done so much to help them, they had continued to hesitate until it was too late.

Out of their experience the young colonels and majors fashioned new techniques of command that were to prove worthy of the men they led, making of their Division perhaps the finest infantry unit in the world. If that Division had been already, in May 1941, what it was soon to become it is likely that Student's venture would quickly have ended where it had begun – among the whins and sand-dunes at the mouth of the Tavronitis.

The New Zealand War Historian makes no criticism of the decisions taken on the night of the 22nd. He believes that Puttick was 'probably right' in turning away from the idea of any further attack, and that the chance that remained was 'slender'. To have pursued it would have been 'little better than gambling and failure would probably have destroyed any hope of orderly withdrawal'.[17]

This cannot pass without challenge. Much of war is a gamble. Sometimes a gamble must be taken. There must be speculation as to what might have been the outcome had Puttick not so readily abandoned the task entrusted to him, or had the General himself overridden all objections.

First it must be said that Freyberg's orders should not have come as a surprise. He had the right to expect that Puttick and his Divisional Staff would have spent the day in active preparation for a further assault on the airfield. All should have been ready for the necessary movements to begin at dusk if not earlier. There was no reason for waiting, in the words of Gentry, until 'well into the afternoon' for news of 'how the original counter-attack had fared'. That it had failed was constantly proved by the steady flow of troop-carriers, no less than by the sudden pessimism of Hargest's message at 1.25 p.m. That it must again be attempted should have been no less certain. For here was the German

17 Davin, p. 239

strength, and if it were allowed to grow there need be no other. Already it had proved sufficient to thrust back the 5th Brigade from the airfield. It was therefore plain, as it had not been on the previous evening, that if this reinforcement by troop-carrier were allowed to continue there could be an end to further speculation upon the possibility that more of the enemy might come by boat, by crash-landing, or by parachute; if they were to come by magic carpet it could not render their ultimate victory more certain. The threat of invasion from the sea now fell into its true perspective. After the disaster of the previous night it was unlikely that the Germans would at once try the same thing again. But no matter if they did. This time the Navy must be trusted to deal with it.

There had been no news of what the Germans were doing at Maleme. Both Puttick and Freyberg may well have believed that they would improve their perimeter defences before venturing to strike east. It was scarcely to be expected that the fresh formations brought by the troop-carriers would at once be sent away to the south-east in a strength sufficient to threaten the communications of the 5th Brigade. But if they should be committed in this way nothing could better favour the prospects of a counter-attack upon the airfield mounted directly from the coast road. At 6 p.m. there was still time to bring to action at Pirgos that night the New Zealand 18th, the Australian 2/7, and the 1st Welch. The forty-two vehicles later ordered for the withdrawal were available to help their concentration, and Puttick knew that the way was clear within the 5th Brigade area, whatever might be his doubts about German encroachment between the Galatas Turn and Platanias. Even on foot the men could have reached Pirgos soon after midnight to start an attack not later than 3 a.m. with more than an hour of darkness remaining.

And now there would have been no uncertainty. No looking back. Every man would have realized that here was the crisis of the battle. Yet again the supreme object would have been, not the destruction of the Germans, but the occupation and consolidation of strong points from which to bring fire upon the airfield. The immediate opposition would have been little stronger than on the previous night. Ramcke's Storm Regiment was more firmly based in Pirgos and along the slopes to the south, but the men were greatly reduced, little more now than a single battalion, and weary after the desperate fighting. It is doubtful whether their number reached a thousand. In the darkness the three fresh battalions, backed perhaps by the New Zealand 23rd, would have offered a formidable challenge. Taking with them all that they could carry of food, water and ammunition, these splendid troops must have had a good hope of capturing some of the old gun-pits on Hill 107 and infiltrating through to the Tavronitis.

The effect upon the Germans must have been shattering. They stood to lose even more than their enemies. Encirclement of his 4th and 5th Brigades would have left Freyberg with an army beaten but not broken. Retreat through the mountains would have saved something from the wreck. Ringel had no strength to organize an effective pursuit. Many of the New Zealanders might well have escaped, as had most of the 22nd Battalion after the fighting on the 20th. But for Student the issue would have been all or none. From the first, even while he expected reinforcement by sea, he had recognized that failure to hold at least one airfield must mean defeat. No doubt the Utz battalions, followed by Heidrich's men from the Prison Valley, would have recoiled at bay into a raging mêlée among the hills south of the airfield. But this time the impotence of the *Luftwaffe* in such conditions would have been known. Within a day or two, Student might have contrived to scrape together in support the mixed group of 400 parachutists, 'remnants of the Air Division',[18] which he was to find two days later for Heraklion. Perhaps he might have persuaded Löhr to attempt a few more desperate Junker crashes along the shore west of the river. Yet, for so long as New Zealand small-arms fire could command the 800 yards of runway, his troops would have been deprived of the very life source of their action.

After the war, Freyberg was to maintain that by this stage the enemy had 'built up undisturbed across the river out of range a position which he could reinforce without interference'.[19] But how reinforce? There were no more parachutists. And in the words of Kippenberger, if he had lost Maleme he 'could have brought no more troop-carriers in until he had cleared a new landing-strip further west'.[20] It may well be wondered how such a landing-strip could have been constructed by some 3,000 men, dependent upon the hazard of supply by parachute, increasingly

[18] *Einsatz Kreta*, Battle Report of XI Air Corps
[19] DP, Freyberg comments on Davin Draft, 1952 (undated)   [20] DP

pressed from the east by superior numbers, and eagerly attended by the exultant Greeks and Cretans.

With a boldness sufficient to cause misgiving among their own men, first Ramcke, and after him Ringel, had decided upon a policy of calculated daring. The war correspondent Meyer, who was with a detachment of Mountain Troops, felt that the New Zealanders could not have understood the situation. 'Either they overestimate our forces or they suppose that we can go into an attack with a handful, a company of Mountain Troops.'[21] Wittmann considered that the threat to the southeast had been a bluff which had succeeded. It was their opponents who had 'lost their nerve'.[22]

Something of Freyberg's anxieties can be seen in the cable that he sent to the Middle East late that night. This has been summarized by the New Zealand War Historian. First he pointed out that 'at Maleme the enemy had kept on landing troop-carriers, not only on the airfield but on the beaches and in the area to the west'. He had been holding an extended line behind Maleme, and now strong enemy forces near the Prison south-west of Canea had attacked towards the coast. Already 'the troops at Maleme' were 'cut off'. Nor did he feel able to relax his precautions against invasion from the sea. 'Small ships' had put Germans ashore that day on the Akrotiri Peninsula. At any time further landings from the air or sea might again cut his communications.

Everything must now depend upon maintenance, and this, in his view, meant that there must be supply through the docks at Suda. Neither Tymbaki, nor Sphakia, the small fishing villages on the southern coast, could be used without lighters and transport. Moreover, they would have to be protected against the *Luftwaffe*. There was also the difficulty that the road across the island to Sphakia was not yet 'complete'.

In these circumstances he had felt it necessary 'to readjust present insecure position and make ready for secure defence'. The cable concluded:

I have decided (1) That I cannot continue to chance all rear areas and coastline and (2) That troops cannot fight without a rest. Am therefore taking up line which will lessen my responsibilities. Enemy is

[21] Kurt Meyer, *Battle for the Strongpoint of Crete*
[22] Wittmann, *Die Gebirgstruppe*, Number 3, p. 6

now approaching equality in numbers. . . . We can fight on as long as maintenance does not break down.[23]

Early on the following morning he reported to Cairo that the new line would run immediately to the west of Galatas. Once more he added a special plea for help from the Royal Air Force.

Here indeed is a change of tone. And once more it is possible to see the failure of information that was reaching Force Headquarters. In transit the tales of woe and disaster had magnified. The activities of the Heilmann detachment, stumbling about the foothills west of Galatas, together with the machine-gun and mortar fire said to have commanded the road 'on several occasions', were now transmuted into an attack which had 'cut off troops at Maleme'. Nor was there any truth in the story that 'small ships' had reached the Akrotiri Peninsula. The Welch patrols were to find no survivors from the sea. *Operation Crete* contains no suggestion of such a landing. The only hint of it appears in von der Heydte's description of the arrival within his battalion lines of a distracted young lieutenant declaring himself the only man left alive from a sunken caique.

But Freyberg was not the man to be daunted by rumour. Why then did he accept Puttick's opinion without question? How is it that he did not intervene directly in what he now knew to be the crisis of the battle? In modern times no senior general has led his men from the front line with more inspiration and skill. Everything in his record, both after and before this time, his methods during the arduous campaigns in the desert and in Italy, alike with his conduct as a junior officer during the First World War, would seem to proclaim that before accepting such a decision he would go forward to judge the situation for himself. All his instinct must have urged him to such a course. In half an hour he could have been at Canea Bridge. Why did he suddenly show a restraint, almost a diffidence, so foreign to his character?

There are several possible explanations. Even to his rich experience of war, airborne invasion was something new. And at first he had felt that, by leaving his command post, he must run the risk of losing control of the battle as a whole, a disaster

---

[23] Davin, p. 244 and Long, p. 241. In a footnote on this page Long makes a comparison of German and New Zealand strength. But the German figures that he gives apply not to 22 but to 24 May, by which time the balance had shifted decisively to the German side.

suffered three years later by the commander at Arnhem who was
cut off during many vital hours after running into an ambush.

It would have been an advantage [wrote Freyberg of the first day's
fighting in Crete] if I could have gone forward to the 5th Brigade
Headquarters and had a talk with the Brigadier on the spot, together
with General Puttick, but it was a very difficult journey to get to
Divisional Headquarters and the times I went there were extremely
hazardous. Little movement could be made by daylight.[24]

By the evening of the 22nd, however, all danger had passed.
An hour or two earlier Puttick had twice made the journey
untroubled by so much as a sniper, and the planes, which had
returned after their action against the Fleet, were again departing.
It is possible that Freyberg may still have felt reluctant to intervene directly in the control of the New Zealand Division. This
seems unlikely. There could no longer be any doubt that all else
must yield before his own obligation to overcome the threat from
the west.

Yet he did not go. In itself, this suggests a further explanation –
that he judged the battle already lost, that scarcely eighteen
hours after his moment of elation, as he watched the destruction of
the invasion fleet, he had come to believe that the unopposed
domination of the *Luftwaffe* must necessarily render the Germans
invincible.

There was little concrete reason for this abrupt loss of
confidence. Certainly he felt the continued oppression of the
overwhelming air attack, with its relentless strangle-hold upon
his communications and supply. And he was constantly aware of
the menace from the Germans in the Prison Valley. Later he was
to emphasize that he had been concerned from the first with the
possibility that the German parachutists in the vicinity of the
Prison might strike north to the coast past Kippenberger's relatively weak Brigade and so cut off all the troops further west.[25]
But, beyond these factors, it seems probable that a subtler
influence now bore upon him overwhelmingly. As he watched the
troop-carriers coming into Maleme, their numbers still increasing
despite the artillery fire, and the destruction of the seaborne convoys, he may have felt that the limitless resources of the Germans
made it certain that they would conquer Crete, since they were

apparently determined to do so, whatever setbacks might overtake them on the way. In words that he was to use later, they were 'determined to take Crete, and they were prepared to go to any length to get it'.[26] So far as he knew the whole of their vast armies lay idle on the Continent, with nothing to do but to capture this one island. Failure must inevitably strike a heavy blow at their prestige. They were unlikely to accept it. Come what might they would not neglect to 'commit enough troops for the job'.[27] It would, after all, as Wilson and Weston had said, 'only be a matter of time'.[28]

Neither then nor later did he appreciate that for this one action not even the vast German military machine, at the apogee of its power, could command success. It did not occur to him that the Germans had already dissipated against his own defences the particular strength that would enable them to strike again at any other point, and that they were now relying solely upon exploitation of their success at Maleme. In his despatch to Cairo he had shown that he was misled by more than false information. Here was revealed once more the old compulsive belief, unsupported now by any kind of evidence, that the troop-carriers, were landing 'not only on the airfield but on the beaches and in the area to the west'. If this technique could bring them success against Hargest's powerful brigade, why should they not be able to do the same thing wherever they might choose and thus make a German victory inevitable? He still did not understand their dependence upon the runway. Soon after the battle he was quoted as saying that the enemy had expected to capture the island with parachutists alone. And on 5 December 1949, he was to tell Kippenberger:

Had we captured Maleme . . . it would not have rested there; the enemy could at any time have concentrated their follow-up attack on either Retimo or Heraklion, and these garrisons, owing to lack of resources could not have sustained themselves for half the time that we did in Suda Bay area.[29]

Again and again he returns to this theme. By 1952 he is writing to Davin, 'In my opinion the Crete campaign was never in doubt'.[30] And to Kippenberger, in the same year,

If they had landed the force on places remote from the aerodromes,

---

[26] DP, Freyberg comments on Churchill Draft, 25 Mar. 1949   [27] Ibid.
[28] Appreciation by Generals Wilson and Weston on 29 April 1941. See chap. 4, p. 72
[29] DP, Freyberg to Kippenberger, 5 Dec. 1949
[30] Ibid., Freyberg to Davin, 3 Jan. 1952

they could have built up their excellently trained and equipped units without loss.[31]

To judge by these comments it seems that he was never to realize that, once the last of Student's parachute and glider troops had been committed on the evening of 21 May, nothing more could have been brought in except upon the one captured airfield. This is the reason why he had sent too few of his troops to Maleme, and those few too late. And it becomes easy to see why he did not himself go forward that night. There could have been little satisfaction or purpose in such a journey if he felt that any further counter-attack could do no more than expose his countrymen to deadly peril, with none of the compensating hope of victory. From the first he had nobly disdained to call attention to the particular danger borne by New Zealand in consequence of the presence in Crete of nearly the whole of her young army. But later he felt bound to admit:

There was another factor which weighed with me. I had the bulk of the New Zealand Division in Crete. If it were lost it would be a crushing blow to New Zealand.[32]

Yet all might have been changed on the night of 22 May, had he brought himself to act, as had always been his habit, not upon rumour and conjecture, but upon tested and confirmed reports. Despite this set-back at Maleme, he had solid grounds for encouragement. He had heard that, at both Heraklion and Retimo, the airborne troops had suffered nothing less than disaster. Their casualties had been so heavy that there seemed every prospect that a detachment of Chappel's troops, using the garrison transport, would soon be able to break through to the relief of Campbell at Retimo, thus clearing the way along the coast road between Heraklion and Suda.

Nor was there any evidence that the enemy had attained crushing strength at Maleme. A few minutes after midnight he was told there were about five battalions in this area, with another thousand parachutists still active in the vicinity of the Prison. This appreciation, which was roughly correct, accorded with the rate of troop-carrier landings that had been reported to him at 6.40 p.m. that afternoon. It scarcely justified the view that the Germans were 'approaching equality in numbers' even in terms of the New Zealand Division alone. Moreover, there was reason

[31] DP, Freyberg to Kippenberger, 3 Jan. 1952
[32] Ibid., Freyberg comments on Long Draft, 5 Dec. 1949

for believing that the parachutists in the Prison Valley could not by themselves establish a permanent block upon the coast road. They had shown that they were basing their security upon occupation of the Prison itself. Already it was clear that they had not strength enough to take the heights at Galatas, although this objective lay immediately in front of them, and was defended only by Kippenberger's improvised infantry with the help of a single trained battalion. To reach the road they must move in the open over three miles of country. It was also becoming plain that many of the earlier reports had been without foundation. Increasingly, it was evident that no parachutists had dropped at Maleme after the first evening, and none elsewhere in the Western Sector since the first morning. Campbell had told him that no reinforcement had been sent to rescue Sturm's failure at Retimo. At Heraklion, parachutes bearing unidentified objects had been seen falling in the distance, but only a few score had landed troops within sight of the perimeter after the evening of the first day. All this might have been taken to suggest that there were no more parachutists available. The possibility became clearer in the light of the fact that the landing operation at Maleme was being pursued with so much determination despite what appeared to be great hazards from the artillery. Here, too, was an indication that little success could be attending any attempts to crash-land troop-carriers somewhere out of sight. The Chiefs of Staff had always believed that the Germans would find it impossible to maintain a lodgment from the air without seaborne reinforcement. Now, as he knew, the invasion flotillas had been intercepted. There was thus good reason for him to arrive at the true conclusion – that the enemy would be unable to survive the loss of Maleme.

He made none of these deductions. At last he had information that was substantially correct. But now that he had it he could not believe it. And so he lost his opportunity. That evening a last hope remained that a supreme effort might wrest Maleme from the invaders. The fight must have been desperate. Yet it is plain that it would have been aided, far more than was suspected at the time, by the Greeks and Cretans. And how enticing was the reward. How much, indeed, must the very nature of the enterprise have appealed to the raw but ardent young soldiers who had crossed the world in search of just such an adventure. For sixty hours the Germans at Maleme had been practising a bluff, masked by the *Luftwaffe*, and sustained only by their own conviction of invincibility. Today it would appear that Freyberg should have called upon the 1st Welch and Australian 2/7 Battalions to mount an assault in concert with the New Zealand 4th and 5th Brigades. Transport was not essential. The men could have marched at 9 p.m. – as soon as the planes had gone; for the 4ht Brigade the distance to Pirgos was scarcely eight miles, and for the Welch no more than twelve. In retrospect it is easy to see the pity of this failure to move the forces of counter-attack in darkness along the open coast road. Starting at dusk Massena's seven battalions had covered fifteen miles before dawn to turn the battle of Rivoli. Nor would Freyberg's men have needed to carry more than the *Sansculottes* in Italy a century and a half earlier. As with every close encounter in Crete this too would have been an uncomplicated struggle between light infantry.

A night march on Maleme could still have changed the course of disaster, and Freyberg himself, going forward not merely to Divisional Headquarters, but to Platanias or even to Pirgos, there to put before his men the simple issue of victory or defeat, might very well that night have surpassed every other triumph in his great career, while inflicting upon the *élite* of the German Army their first great reverse of the war.

PART FOUR

VICTORY AND DEFEAT

'Stand for New Zealand.'

Colonel H. K. Kippenberger, at
Galatas, 25 May, 1941

18

Retreat to Galatas: 23-24 May

News of the withdrawal spread slowly to the west. First to hear of it were the men of the Field Ambulance on the high ground near Modhion.

On the third evening [wrote Captain Palmer, one of the Medical Officers] we all turned in to sleep in the unfounded belief that all was going well, a belief that was rudely shattered at about 1 a.m. when instructions to withdraw were received. At first many were frankly incredulous – so small is the individual unit's ability to gauge the progress of a modern engagement. We mostly believed the situation to be well in hand.[1]

But soon they were moving down the slopes with their wounded, passing on their way through the area so long disputed by the Engineers. All was quiet. It was still dark when they reached the coast road and turned east through Platanias and Ay Marina. Small craters pitted the dusty tarmac. Dead donkeys lay among the debris of shattered vehicles. Here and there a small white cottage smouldered among the trees, its scarred walls revealing where some group of parachutists had made a brief stand. Palmer noticed 'a fetid odour' that 'mingled with the night scents'. From time to time a mortar shell landed on the ridge to their right, but 'the road itself was at no time under fire'.[2] And no other sign came from the Germans. The 'machine-gun' which had caused Puttick so much misgiving remained silent.

Dawn had broken before the grim orders reached the front line. Again they were at first scarcely believed. Dawson, now utterly weary, once more appeared at the 23rd Headquarters, saying that he had some 'surprising news'. To this Leckie replied, 'What! Have they tossed it in?'[3] The other battalion commanders were no less confident that they could have held their positions. Lieutenant Thomas heard 'with horror' the order to withdraw,

[1] DP, Capt. D. B. Palmer   [2] Ibid.
[3] Ibid. Lieut.-Col. D. F. Leckie, 12 April 1951

and was afterwards to maintain that his men had 'seen so many of the enemy die that their morale was quite unshaken'.[4] They had been expecting that there would be another night attack, and that this time they would be able to take part in it. Already they felt sure that in this form of fighting they could master the Germans.

But the night had passed. Now they must turn back across the bare and arid ridges, away from Maleme, and Pirgos, and the sheltering glades of bamboo along the Sfakoriako river bed, away, too, from the matchless prize that they were leaving to their enemies – a strip of sand 800 yards long under the protection of its guardian hill.

As the sun rose the survivors of the Storm Regiment began to move forward cautiously from Pirgos. Here they came into the area where their III Battalion had been destroyed.

Frightful was the sight that met our eyes in this part of the battle-field [says Gericke]. Among the boughs of the olive trees could be seen the white silk of the parachutes with their tangles of twisted cords. Dead parachutists, still in their full equipment, hung suspended from the branches swinging gently to and fro in the light breeze – everywhere were the dead. Those who had succeeded in getting free from their harness had been shot down within a few strides or slain by Cretan volunteers. From these corpses could be seen all too clearly what had happened within the first few minutes after the beginning of the battle of Crete. Bodies lay singly or in small groups in the grass and along the road. The pockets of their uniforms had been torn open; equipment lay strewn in all directions, grenades, helmets, weapons, a bayonet stuck in the sand, ammunition boxes, packets of bandages, the stand of a machine-gun and close by it a heap of empty cartridge cases the sun glinting from their metal surfaces, a water container full of stinking water, fragments of torn paper, field postcards, photographs. Here and there among the debris lay a dead Englishman or a New Zealander. All alike, without regard to nationality, had turned black in the burning heat. Around them buzzed the fat blue flies.[5]

The airlanding troops, reduced to the strength of a single battalion, were greatly exhausted. For three days they had borne the full weight of a savage battle. Behind them, as they well knew, there was no reserve. Understandably they were inclined to wait, at least for the arrival of their heavier weapons. But by 7 a.m. Ramcke could see that the New Zealanders had begun to retreat,

---

[4] Thomas, p. 16　　　　　　　　　　[5] Gericke, p. 85

and he was able to judge, from the green flares which soared repeatedly against the dark background of the hills, that the Mountain Troops were making good progress in their flank march further south. At once he urged his men in pursuit. On this side of the front there was no need for concealment. Within an hour they were pouring down the coast road, while others made quick progress along the coastal strip through the gap left by the withdrawal of the New Zealand 20th Battalion. Only in the undulating country upon their right flank did they meet any opposition.

A small detachment of Maoris covered the retreat. It was commanded by Major Dyer, who remembered later:

The withdrawal from Maleme was not an orthodox affair. The army manuals lay down a pattern for a rear-guard action which is hardly ever carried out. In practice you give your enemy a knock; then run as hard as you can; and then he comes racing after you, you give him a surprise, and then you run again. . . . I looked for my command. It was not easy to see; just a thin line of men extended to about ten paces and lying behind trees. We arranged that our first 'bound' would be to a shoulder of the hills nearly half a mile back and that we would make a stand there. We could see the Germans moving from tree to tree. So when their machine-guns and mortars opened up we let those trees have it. . . . It was then six-thirty and I planned to reach Platanias at ten o'clock. Then judging that the battalion was well clear we passed the word along the line and ran.

As usual the pilots found it difficult to identify targets within a fluid battle line; the Maoris had little trouble from the planes. Gradually they worked their way back across the slopes. By midday they had reached the wooded creek west of Platanias, their pursuers investing them closely from both flanks. To reach safety they still had to cover the last few hundred yards up the face of the ridge.

The enemy was now on to us [says Dyer], men were hit, a sergeant was decapitated by a Bofors shell. We must get up that hill . . . we were practically within our main position, it was every man for himself.[6]

All but a few managed to get home over the crest.

Once more the line held firm. But before evening two of the Mountain Battalions, probing south-east of Platanias, had begun to establish a link between the Ramcke Group on the left and

[6] Dyer, p. 60 et seq.

Heidrich's Brigade in the Prison area. A third battalion, part of 85 Mountain Regiment under Colonel Krakau, was taking a wider sweep under the mountains to the south, where it encountered unexpected resistance from the 8th Greeks above Alikianou. At Stalos, the Heilmann detachment from the Prison Valley had been held up all day by spirited patrol activity from the 10th Brigade. It was still well short of the road.

In front of the Germans rose the steep heights of Platanias. Ringel saw them as 'a strong terraced ring of rocks which like a fortress barred the way to the important Naval base of Suda'.[7] At first he thought that the British, 'having learnt from the battle at Maleme',[8] would attempt to hold this position in strength. But he was quick to recognize that the 'fortress' extended no more than a mile or so inland from the coast, and that further south the going was easier.

Of this Hargest was no less aware. Nor could he be happy about his immediate front on the main road, where the Ramcke group, supported by the captured Bofors, and now too by some of their own light artillery, became increasingly active. Moreover, with the two sides again distinguishable from the air, the planes were menacing every movement of his brigade in the open. For the first time since the beginning of the battle, he had been able to judge for himself the condition of his men. Among them he met Leckie, 'unwashed and thin but magnificent'.[9] No doubt he found them in far better fettle than he had dared to hope. But he remained vividly conscious of the strain under which they had been fighting. And he was still overestimating their losses. That evening, in an untimed message, he sent to Divisional Headquarters an assessment of unit strengths in which the 21st Battalion was thought to be down to 170, the 22nd to 110, and the 23rd to 250. By 2.50 p.m. he had already expressed doubts about his capacity to hold the line at Platanias. Indeed, it was true that the danger to the left flank, so long foreseen and feared before it existed, had now become reality. His apprehensions were shared by Puttick who agreed that the brigade should continue its withdrawal.

After darkness had fallen the men set out again along the coast road.

We withdrew under orders soon after midnight carrying our

---

[7] Wittmann, *Die Gebirgstruppe*, Number 3, p. 7   [8] Ibid
[9] DP, Hargest's Diary

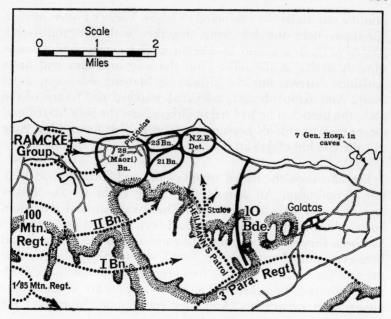

16. The Germans move on Platanias and Galatas: 23 May

wounded on improvised stretchers [says Thomas], down a steep cliff face and then along a difficult clay creek bed to the road. Then we marched until nearly dawn. I was very impressed by the continued discipline. . . . Mile after mile we trudged. Everyone was tired. All were vaguely resentful, although none of us could put a finger on the reason. Those of us who could bear the strain better carried the rifles and Bren guns of those who were fatigued.[10]

Most of the wounded had been left behind in the care of their doctors and orderlies. Of the eight trucks which had been detailed to evacuate them only three survived the journey. But some of the guns were saved, several of them snatched from the hands of the enemy. Eight French and Italian 75 mm. pieces were brought back safely, together with two Bofors and two two-pounders.

From the coast, a mile west of the Galatas Turn, the line now ran south along the ridges and across the Prison Valley to the hills beyond Perivolia. Puttick had brought forward his 4th Brigade to take over the right wing, leaving the diminished 10th Brigade to hold its positions down to the Prison Road. All this part of the

[10] Thomas, p. 20

front he put under the command of Inglis. Vasey's two Australian battalions held the left wing, together with the 2nd Greek Regiment and a group of Cretan civilians who had become robustly active in the hills. Thus the way to Canea and Suda remained barred. But the airfield at Maleme was eight miles away. And Kippenberger, who had watched the return of the 20th, the battalion he had led in Greece, saw the men 'dazed and weary to exhaustion'. Looking at them he 'felt for the first time . . . the coming of defeat'.[11]

For four days the mixed troops of the 10th Brigade had been full of optimism. All around them they could see the bodies and graves of their dead enemies. The parachutists at Heraklion and Retimo, so they understood, had been 'cleaned up', and they had been very ready to believe the rumour that the Germans had been evacuating from Maleme. Now it was suddenly plain that all the time the battle in the west had been going against them. With this realization they became more sharply aware of their own hunger and exhaustion. And they spoke more bitterly of the absence of the R.A.F.

The regular infantry, although tired and disappointed, were the least dismayed. In the improvised units, morale was best maintained among those who had been able to taste some success in their encounters with the Germans. The Cavalry Detachment, together with the Divisional Petrol Company, still held out among the olives on each side of the Prison-Galatas road, despite casualties which had cost them about a third of their number. Both groups were led by Major Russell, whose continuing sang-froid was much appreciated at 10th Brigade Headquarters.

All this time John Russell was a sheer joy [Captain Bassett, the Brigade Major, was to write after the battle]. A Brigade Major appointment Code name was then 'M', signals jargon for which is Monkey, and he'd ring up and say 'Is that Monk of Moto – hello dearie, got any cigarettes . . . oh by the way . . . there are about a hundred Jerries coming up the road at us'. I'd get excited and say we'd send up reserves and he'd drawl, 'Don't bother, old boy, Ian Bullivant's just dying to gobble them up'. I got to the stage of almost praying whenever the phone went that it would be him instead of some frantic despairing anxiety from another battalion.[12]

But there were some in the Composite Battalion upon whom

[11] Kippenberger, p. 61   [12] DP, Capt. B. I. Bassett

the strain was beginning to leave its mark. With neither the training nor the equipment of infantry they had done their best. But they had no regimental loyalty to sustain them and they had suffered 190 casualties. Inevitably, they were disconcerted to learn that the 5th Brigade had been forced to retreat. Kippenberger began to notice 'an increasing number of cases of slightly wounded men being brought in by three or four friends in no hurry to go back'.[13]

Nor was much more to be expected of the Greeks and Cretans at Galatas. Their primitive arms could scarcely serve them further in the open against the modern weapons of the enemy.

For the moment, the Germans made no serious attack against the new line. But the planes screamed along the coast road and across the ridges that led from Galatas down to the sea, while the troop-carriers flowed endlessly into Maleme, and north of the Prison, the enemy infantry, untroubled by any need for concealment, could be seen cross-marching in columns just out of range of small arms fire. Clearly a major assault was in preparation.

At Force Headquarters Freyberg was absorbed by an anxiety which had never ceased to be one of his major preoccupations, and which now threatened to surpass all others. At the moment when the Germans had survived their own crisis in the face of the same problem he found himself increasingly distracted by the threat to his reinforcement and supply.

He had asked that a battalion of the Queen's Royal Regiment, now on its way from Egypt, should be transported directly to Suda. But on the 22nd he had heard from the Commander-in-Chief in Cairo that it had become 'impossible to land any troops in Suda Bay'. After 'consulting with the Navy' Wavell had decided that no more ships could be expected to survive the long journey along the north coast. He was, however, 'trying to arrange for a commando to land on the south coast and cross the hills northward to help,'[14] and he continued: 'If you report that the situation at Maleme is really serious hope to arrange for R.A.F. to send fighters to strafe enemy tomorrow till ammunition and petrol exhausted and then land within your protection.'[15] The message had concluded by saying that the defence of the island was having a great effect upon the enemy who clearly were experiencing their own troubles.

[13] Kippenberger, p. 60   [14] Davin, p. 243   [15] Long, p. 241

To this Freyberg replied that 'The situation at Maleme', a phrase that was something of a euphemism now that the front line had receded eight miles from the airfield, was indeed 'really serious',[16] and that all possible air support was required. At the same time he insisted that a commando coming from the south would have little chance of getting through in time to help the forces in the north. As for a landing at Palaiokhora, which had also been suggested, this was out of the question, since the small harbour had in all probability already been taken by the enemy.

Later in the day, he was told from Cairo that an effort would be made to get reinforcements to him through Tymbaki. It was suggested that he might be able to 'move troops from Retimo to Canea, replacing them with troops from Heraklion, and in Heraklion making good the loss by replacements from Tymbaki'.[17]

Here was a name that had suddenly appeared in these despatches. Tymbaki lay on the south coast, in the gulf of Mesara. It was to this tiny fishing port that Brigadier Brunskill, on 17 May, had proposed to send a reconnaissance party. Two days later the few inhabitants had been startled by the arrival of a battalion of the Argyll and Sutherland Highlanders, accompanied by three of the new heavy tanks from the 'Tiger' convoy. The whole party had been abruptly decanted on the bare and precipitous coast. Nobody had told Freyberg that they were coming. Some Staff Officer in the Middle East had sent them to guard the Mesara Plain against parachute attack. Now it was hoped that they might get through to Heraklion along a route that looked promising on the maps to be found in Egypt. But it was a little late in the day to be pioneering this primitive track as a supply road.

Freyberg at once pointed out some of the practical difficulties. The distance between Tymbaki and Heraklion was forty-five miles. Galatas lay a further seventy-five miles to the west, while at Retimo the Germans still held a block on the coast road. In addition to the pressing need for new men, weapons, and equipment, there was a rapidly worsening shortage of food. Already the troops were on limited rations. Soon it would become necessary to cater for nearly half a million Cretans. Again he insisted that it was essential that at least some of his stores should continue to come through Suda. He was trying to establish a supply line between Canea and Sphakia. He gave no details but, as he had already pointed out, the road to Sphakia was not 'complete'.[18]

[16] See above, p. 357   [17] Davin, p. 243   [18] Ibid., p. 273

This was to put it mildly. Perhaps he had not, even now, learnt the whole truth. In fact it ended in a mile and a half of goat track, impassable to vehicles, leading down the open face of an escarpment.

In another signal, on the same day, he had protested that further consideration should be given to the possibility of sending the battalion of the Queen's Royal Regiment to Suda instead of to Tymbaki.[19] And on the following day, in much the same words as Brunskill had used in a memorandum on 2 May, he added that he was coming to believe that his force could be maintained only by frequent deliveries carried in small ships rather than by large convoys.[20]

Already it was all too clear to him that the noose drawn around the island by the *Luftwaffe* had begun to tighten fatally.

On 23 May Force Headquarters lay shrouded under the black smoke which billowed up from the burning ships in the harbour. It was not a happy moment for the arrival of a personal message to the General from the Prime Minister in Great Britain:

The whole world watches your splendid battle on which great things turn.[21]

But Freyberg knew, as he was to write later, that 'however splendid the battle might appear in the eyes of the world' the situation was in fact fast deteriorating.[22]

Even in London it was now realized that the enemy had succeeded in gaining a foothold and that a hard struggle was in progress. Churchill had given a further report to the House of Commons on the 22nd: 'It is a most strange and grim battle that is being fought. Our side have no air, because they have no aerodromes, and not because they have no aeroplanes, and the other side have very little or no artillery or tanks. Neither side has any means of retreat.' But he could not believe that the landing of effective reinforcement could be beyond the power of the Royal Navy. On the following day he cabled to Wavell:

Crete battle must be won. Even if enemy secure good lodgments fighting must be maintained indefinitely in the island, thus keeping enemy main striking force tied down to the task. This will at least give you time to mobilise Tiger Cubs [Tanks in convoy 'Tiger'] and

[19] Davin, p. 243   [20] Ibid., p. 274
[21] Freyberg Report, quot. Long, p. 241   [22] Ibid.

dominate situation Western Desert. While it lasts it also protects Cyprus. Hope you will reinforce Crete every night to fullest extent. Is it not possible to send more tanks and thus reconquer any captured aerodrome? Enemy's exertions and losses in highest class troops must be very severe. He cannot keep it up for ever. . . .[23]

The Chiefs of Staff were no less insistent upon the need for reinforcement:

Our difficulties in Crete are great, but from all the information we have so are those of enemy. If we stick it out enemy's effort may peter out. It seems to us imperative that reinforcements in greatest strength possible should be sent as soon as possible to island to ensure the destruction of the enemy already landed before they can be seriously reinforced. The vital importance of this battle is well known to you, and great risks must be accepted to ensure our success.[24]

But generalities about the problems of the enemy were a poor substitute for appreciation of the facts and action appropriate to them. There was still no understanding that Student had used all his airlanding forces, and that for three days the key to victory had lain in an absolute concentration of effort by land, from the air, and by shelling from the sea, upon his airfield bridgehead.

Cunningham was reluctant to engage the Fleet further, perhaps to its total destruction, in a cause which he feared already lost. He made no attempt to stage an effective bombardment at Maleme. But, in the matter of transport, he continued to perform more than he would promise. During the night of the 23rd two destroyers bringing ammunition, *Jaguar* and *Defender*, got in and out of Suda Bay.

On the 24th Freyberg exposed plainly to Wavell the depth of his misgiving. The enemy was attacking fiercely towards Suda, using artillery as well as dive-bombers, while the troop-carriers still roared in and out of Maleme. The pressure was increasing steadily. He had been forced to reorganize his position that evening and he feared that some of his men, together with many of the wounded, had been cut off on the previous night. The troops still in action were very 'tired'.[25] Everyone had been much encouraged by a Blenheim attack on Maleme, but the situation at the front had now become uncertain.

The appearance of the Blenheims had indeed brought a ray of comfort. Their departure had been followed by some satisfying

[23] Churchill, Vol. III, p. 260   [24] Ibid.
[25] Davin, p. 293

'crumps' that told, so it was hoped, of the explosion of delayed-action bombs. But the truth was that the enemy had been caused no more than trifling inconvenience.[26]

An attempt to send twelve Hurricanes to Heraklion had ended in disaster. Of the six in the first flight, two had been shot into the sea by British warships before the naval gunners could recover from their astonishment at seeing friendly aircraft. Three more had been so badly damaged that they could scarcely limp away towards Egypt. Only the last succeeded in reaching Heraklion where to the garrison it appeared, in Buckley's phrase, like 'Noah's dove'. It was at once destroyed on the ground. Five of the second flight were immediately shot down or badly damaged by enemy fighters. A single survivor remained briefly intact.

This unexpected gesture by the Hurricanes had been made possible by the use of extra fuel tanks, a contrivance which found little favour with the pilots since it drained the machines of power and frequently led to disastrous engine failure.

The additional tanks gave the Hurricanes a range of 900 miles compared with the normal range of 600 miles [wrote one of the few men to get back.] There were two additional tanks. . . . The port tanks emptied first, then the starboard tank. Air locks were liable to develop owing to bad refuelling or severe bumps in the air and throw the system out of commission. You never knew when the port tank emptied if the starboard tank was going to feed through. If the starboard tank refused to work over the sea, that was the end.[27]

It had been a pitiful expedient, ill-considered, ineffective, and careless of the lives it wasted. Thus it was fully in keeping with the times. Nevertheless, the troops had drawn a cynical, if modified, encouragement from these visitations. They had scarcely expected to see the R.A.F. again.

In both Cairo and London the means of salvation seemed clear enough. If the new line at Galatas could now hold successfully for a day or two, might it not be possible to mobilize an effective striking force from the strong garrison at Heraklion, together perhaps with some Australians from Retimo, while feeding reinforcements into Tymbaki? This was the 'side-stepping' technique already suggested by Wavell in his dispatch of the

[26] The report of Air Fleet IV says: 'Enemy aircraft made their first appearance over the island on 23 May. Five Bristol Blenheims attacked Maleme airfield in the afternoon without causing much damage'

[27] Hetherington, p. 91

22nd. Such hopes were further encouraged by the fact that in both the eastern Sectors the enemy had been further rebuffed.

At Retimo, a private battle had now been raging for three days. Sturm's men had received little help from the *Luftwaffe*. Indeed the Dornier pilots were unable to distinguish between the combatants, and had repeatedly attacked the airborne troops between the airstrip and the town, inflicting losses which the German Report was to acknowledge as 'considerable'. They had not been able to deliver replacements for the damaged wireless apparatus. The Germans on the ground were still reduced to drawing signals in the sand.

The Australians had been little better served by their own communications. The line to Suda had gone, and there had been no contact with Heraklion. During the confusion of the first day Campbell had destroyed his ciphers lest they fall into the hands of the enemy. All exchange of messages with Force Headquarters had been made through a primitive code, with the use of such substitutions as 'potato' to mean 'tank'.[28] Nor was this his only problem. By the 23rd the rations that were left would last for no more than four days. And the number of wounded had already reached 450, most of them Germans.

Yet nothing deterred him. Not for a moment did he rest upon his success. Although daylight movement on the roads 'invited an instant swoop by a Messerschmitt', he had 'found that they did not come down for a lonely motor-cyclist',[29] and that he could keep up his necessary contacts by riding alone about his command, moving repeatedly from flank to flank, and organizing counter-attacks to east and west. The two tanks, now retaken, had been manned by improvised crews. In turn, he and Sandover took on the perilous task of guiding them through the darkness along the coast road. 'It is not easy,' he was to comment later, 'to induce even the bravest man to take a tank into action after only one night's experience. . . . How they learned enough to make it work always amazed me'.[30]

In the east, where the Germans had become strongly established in the olive-oil factory at Stavromenos, the Australians had suffered a heavy blow. While reconnoitring forward, Moriarty had fallen to a sniper's bullet, twenty-four hours after his triumph upon Hill A. On the next evening Campbell mounted an attack along two converging gullies, 200 Greeks in one party and forty

[28] Campbell to the author, 1 May 1960   [29] Ibid.   [30] Ibid.

Australians, under Captain Mann, in the other. The Greeks failed to start. The Australians crawled forward as far as they could and then rushed into the open. Many fell. Mann was seriously wounded. The survivors, under a corporal, were forced to shelter below a bank a few yards short of the factory walls. Campbell himself, close by as ever, shouted to them to stay where they were. After dark they were able to withdraw.

Leaving the Greeks to hold the factory under fire, Campbell turned his attention to the other flank, where there was now a clearly defined line of battle. Once again, the German planes were able to intervene effectively. On the afternoon of the 23rd, fifty aircraft attacked for five hours across the area between Perivolia and Platanes, causing thirty-nine casualties, nearly all by machine-gun fire, among two companies of 2/11 Battalion. The parachutists then came forward with the setting sun behind them. They made little progress. 'Our forward troops', wrote an Australian, 'stood up and shot them down like rabbits'.[31] Privates Johnson and Symmons had both been hit early in the afternoon. But they kept their Bren gun firing until the end of the action. That same evening Symmons died of his wounds.

The severity of their losses had now induced in the Germans a spirit very different from that in which they were later to celebrate victory. Campbell remembers them as a 'gallant and chivalrous foe'. They had

> . . . lost many dead, so many that we were quite unable to bury them until I accepted an offer from our German prisoners to bury them themselves. These P.O.Ws played the game and, after collecting their dead scattered amongst the vineyards etc., they returned to their cage.[32]

The Medical Officer of 2/11 Battalion was allowed forward to dress the wounded under the enemy machine-guns, and at Stavromenos a three-hour truce was arranged and scrupulously observed.

Two days later, Campbell mounted another attack against the olive-oil factory, sending forward one of the tanks and giving supporting fire from the 75 mm. guns, which had not been discovered by the searching aircraft, despite the lack of cover among the straggling vineyards on the exposed forward slopes. Now the Germans were ready to surrender. Captain Embrey and his men

---

[31] Long, p. 266   [32] Campbell to the author, 1 May 1960

'jumped the wall' and stormed the buildings. Another eighty-two prisoners were captured.

For the moment, Campbell could do no more. All efforts to break westward were handicapped by the lack of heavy weapons, and by the shortage of shells. It was impossible to shift the Germans from their fortified positions among the houses and gardens on each side of the road. In an attempt to help the Greeks and Cretan Police in their attack from the west, Freyberg had sent a company of the Rangers from Suda. Without artillery they could make no better progress. On the night of the 24th Campbell heard of their failure in a wireless message from Force Headquarters. The Rangers had 'come a gutza'.[33] No doubt the German Intelligence officers were duly puzzled – 'belly-flop' might have been easier for them.

Despite this set-back, Campbell was soon laying plans for a further effort to reduce the road block, the only success that still eluded him. By the 25th there were '500 German prisoners penned in a cage under the southern side of Hill D'.[34] Not without reason, Freyberg had sent him a signal which said simply, without code and for all to hear, 'You have done magnificently'.[35] The Germans must have felt inclined to agree.

At Heraklion, Chappel had been less vigorous. Like Campbell, he had been unable to rely upon his contact with Suda, despite the submarine cable that linked the two ports. Such communication as he had with Freyberg came largely by way of Cairo. No record remains of the messages that passed through his Headquarters, Nevertheless, there is indirect evidence to show that for several days Freyberg made continued efforts to spur him into an attempt to send a relieving force to the west. Thus on 23 May Freyberg included in a cable to the Middle East a message which said:

Heraklion now in touch by road with ARGYLL and SUTHER-LANDS and I have ordered them to concentrate battalions and tanks at Heraklion preparatory to reinforcing Suda garrison if possible by road.[36]

Communication between Force Headquarters and Retimo, and also, he believed, between Retimo and Heraklion, had been interrupted by the enemy. He had ordered the two garrisons to make contact and he was confident that they would do so.

---

[33] Campbell to the author, 1 May 1960   [34] Long, p. 267
[35] Ibid., p. 265   [36] Long, p. 241

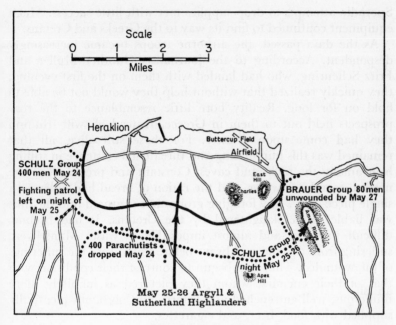

Scale
0   1   2   3
Miles

Heraklion

Buttercup Field
Airfield

SCHULZ Group
400 men May 24

Fighting patrol
left on night of
May 25

East
Hill

Charlies

BRAUER Group 80 men
unwounded by May 27

400 Parachutists
dropped May 24

SCHULZ Group
night May 25-26

Apex
Hill

May 25-26 Argyll &
Sutherland Highlanders

17. Heraklion: 24-26 May

But Chappel had understood neither the extent of his own victory nor the predicament of his enemies. With all the parachutists committed, the sea invasion abandoned, and the airfield still in the hands of the defenders, Student had been powerless to send reinforcement to Heraklion. Indeed, the plight of the airborne troops in this Sector, like that of their comrades at Retimo, reveals the fate which would have befallen his whole Division had the Storm Regiment not succeeded at Maleme. On the second evening, 150 of the parachutists left over from the previous day had been dropped east of Ames Ridge, and on the morning of the 24th, 'after the situation at Maleme had been got under control', some '400 men' were put down west and south of the town. This group had been made up of 'those remnants of the 7th Air Division which had remained behind'.[37] That was all. Until the 28th not another man would arrive to join the few hundred survivors from the first day. Moreover, the help given by the *Luftwaffe* declined as it turned almost all its energies to support of the ground forces in the west, and to the attempted destruction of the British Fleet.

[37] *Einsatz Kreta*, Battle Report of XI Air Corps

Sporadic attempts to drop supplies met with little success. Much equipment continued to find its way to the Greeks and Cretans.

As the days passed, the airborne troops became increasingly despondent. According to the journalists Gunther Muller and Fritz Scheuring, who had landed with them on the first evening, they quickly realized that without help they would not be able to hold on for long. Reality bore little resemblance to the rosy prospects held out to them in Greece. Instead of swift triumph they had come upon disaster. For those still alive, all that remained was this humiliating and threatened existence in stifling heat among the rocks and caves. Constant and pressing was the need to search for water, and the ration of bread had fallen to a single piece daily. Any foraging group that ventured into the hills was liable to be slaughtered by the Cretans. It had become difficult to shave and almost impossible to wash. Many were suffering from diarrhoea. Always before them were the sufferings of the wounded. They had begun to contrast their condition with that of their enemies, whom they pictured as infinitely more numerous, well entrenched and armed, and no doubt plentifully supplied with food, beer, and cigarettes.

By the end of the third day their wireless sets were failing and ammunition was running short. Contact between the widely scattered battalions could be maintained only at night by runners seeking arduous and perilous pathways among the menacing rocks and ravines. There was no news from the other Sectors. This suggested that their comrades in the west must have fared as badly as themselves. They were very conscious of fighting upon an island. Suppose the British Fleet should land fresh troops in the port, perhaps bringing tanks? That must be the end. Without the *Luftwaffe* there could be no protection. And what had happened to the Stukas and fighter bombers?[38]

Student was himself no less concerned about their prospects. He had never supposed that any airborne force, equipped only with its own light weapons, could long hope to sustain an action unaided against an established enemy. Now he feared for the survival of his cherished troops at Heraklion and Retimo and determined upon their rescue at the earliest possible moment.

None of this was suspected by Chappel, whose own strength had greatly increased. At noon on the 23rd, two of the new tanks

[38] DP, Reports by journalists Gunther Muller and Fritz Scheuring

'clambered over the road block'[39] south of the town – the third, less than a week after leaving the workshops in Alexandria, had broken down at Tymbaki. During the next two days they were followed by the main body of the Argyll and Sutherland High-landers, short of their mortars, and indeed armed 'only with what they could carry', but otherwise fit and ready for action. The garrison now included more than 3,100 well equipped fully trained British and Australian infantry, backed by a thousand ancillary British troops, the three Greek battalions, and the many armed Cretans who had gained daily both in weapons and in thirst for revenge. Everywhere there was an abundance of German arms and equipment. 'Henceforward,' says the Australian War Historian, 'there was not a platoon that did not possess more than its normal quota of weapons'.[40] Almost untouched in casualties, and immensely heartened in confidence, the defenders were indeed 'stronger than before'.[41] Of the parachutists who faced them, hungry, scattered, and exhausted, scarcely a thousand remained in action.

Chappel did little to exploit this disparity.

During the day [wrote one of his officers] the valley would ring to the volleys of rifle and machine-gun fire sent hurriedly across it by both sides, but after darkness set in shooting ceased; for by a tacit and mute understanding no firing took place at night; it would have inconvenienced both sides equally. For this was the time when what had to be done was done, when the casualties were evacuated, the dead were buried, the rations and ammunition distributed, and the men were able to walk about and stretch their legs'.[42,43]

Such passivity must have surprised the Germans who no doubt expected night attacks upon their western and southern road blocks. Instead they were allowed to regain the initiative. On the afternoon of the 25th the bombers returned and reduced Heraklion to rubble. That night, acting upon orders that had reached him direct from Athens, Major Schulz successfully led his western group of parachutists in a long night march to the east, the light in the sky above the burning town casting their shadows in grotesque shapes upon the hill-sides as they picked their way along the narrow paths and goat tracks. By the following morning

---

[39] DP, Lieut. J. F. G. Terry, 22 April 1949   [40] Long, p. 283   [41] Ibid.

[42] Mr. Gerald Barry, 'The Parachute Invasion,' *Blackwoods Magazine*, Feb. 1944

[43] Others preferred to fight at night. Capt. C. R. Croft found it 'interesting to watch the Cretans creeping out of the town in the evening with antique guns, like a lot of farmers off for an evening's shooting', letter to the author, 26 Feb. 1963

most of the Germans were concentrated within a single group. Schulz had been able to occupy Apex Hill, capturing it after considerable loss, from a platoon of Australians. From this position it would be possible to command the airfield by light artillery. In the west only the wounded and the dead remained, together with some 'fighting patrols' left behind to 'conceal the departure'.

Why had Chappel not employed part of his force to break out in the direction of Retimo and Suda? Before the action began he had been instructed by Freyberg to do everything possible to ensure that communication along the coast road should be maintained. To help in this task he had been given an allotment of vehicles, generous for those days, sufficient to transport a battalion. On the 23rd Freyberg had again ordered him to make an attempt to reinforce the Suda garrison by road. Unlike the Australians at Retimo he enjoyed a great advantage in numbers. It was true that he had complied with Freyberg's request to send on by lighter to Suda the two new tanks, together with one of his own patched-up Matildas and two field guns. But he still had available a fair armament of heavy weapons. With much less relative strength at his disposal, Campbell had struck repeatedly. Chappel had not attempted a real blow. His transport remained unused.

There is nothing to reveal his thoughts during these days. He took nobody into his confidence.[44] The battalion commanders had little contact with him. From the start, he had been out of sympathy with the officers of the Black Watch.[45] Nor did the men gain from him any urgent sense of purpose. Indeed he had no great facility for contact with European troops, a consequence perhaps of the fact that he had served for many years in India.[46]

But it is easy to understand some of the doubts that must have restrained him. Like Freyberg, he had no trained staff. And after the brief exchange on the 23rd the link with Suda had again become uncertain. 'Our intelligence of and communication with Freyberg was nil,' wrote Captain Fleming, an officer who had been appointed to his Headquarters.[47] At all times his primary obligation had been to deny the airfield and harbour to an enemy

[44] Capt. C. R. Croft felt that he was 'a man who kept his own counsel', letter to the author, 26 Feb. 1963
[45] Maj. Neville Blair to the author, 1962
[46] Capt. R. W. Fleming to the author, 21 May 1962
[47] Ibid.

who was supposed to have available a large and indefinite reserve of airborne troops, together with a force of ships capable of landing on the beaches. He had no means of knowing that while the rest of the island held nothing could threaten his security at Heraklion, that the German airborne effect was spent, nearly half the parachutists dead, and the invasion flotillas defeated. Much that he was hearing pointed to the opposite inference. Every day parachutes could be seen falling outside the perimeter. It was natural to suppose that they carried men. But, like Freyberg, he was misled more by what he feared than by what he knew. Thus he, too, quickly became the victim of reports which told of troop-carriers landing successfully upon the beaches and in open country.

Here again was the misconception that was doing more than all else to damage the conduct of the defence of Crete. In Wavell's despatch, submitted to the Secretary of State for War on 5 September 1941, it appears in confident terms:

> At Heraklion the enemy . . . continued to land troops in the valley to the east, outside the range of our defences, and was gradually accumulating a large force there.[48]

By 1947 Christopher Buckley felt himself able to write that

> . . . on the second day about 30 troop-carriers were reported to have made beach landings over on the west side . . . in the area under control of their ground forces beyond East Beach . . . the enemy managed continually to land troop-carriers several miles to the east out of range of our field guns.

In this way a 'formidable force' was gathering. Soon it would have been 'strong enough to take the initiative and attack'.[49] All the Regimental Histories came to echo this view. 'By now, however,' says the Historian of the York and Lancaster Regiment, 'the Germans had built up a very large force in the east of the island and an all-out attack by them was obviously becoming imminent'.[50] In 1950 Churchill followed the same line: 'The German strength east of the airfield grew daily.'[51] And a year later Cunningham, faithfully reflecting the belief of the soldiers, wrote of 'constant enemy reinforcement'.[52]

[48] Wavell Despatch: *Operations in the Middle East from 7th February 1941 to 15th July 1941*
[49] DP, Buckley Draft for *Greece and Crete 1941*
[50] Sheffield, *The York and Lancaster Regiment*, p. 83   [51] Churchill, Vol. III, p. 263
[52] Cunningham, p. 383

With the passage of time, this legend acquired the trappings of verisimilitude. In 1952 Buckley accepted it without a trace of scepticism in his book:

German aircraft were now making unopposed landings on the relatively smooth surface of Mallia Beach fifteen miles along the coast to the east – yet another instance of the extent to which the enemy was dispensing with the airfields which at one time had appeared to be essential to his success in Crete.[53]

Inaccuracy and paradox could scarcely be more tightly packed within a single sentence. *Operation Crete* contains not a word to suggest that aircraft ever landed at Mallia or anywhere else within eighty miles of Heraklion. Any that may have done so, perhaps by necessity after sustaining damage, certainly played no part in the German plan. Nor had Freyberg ever believed that the airfields would be 'essential' to the enemy's hope of success. The pity was that he had not done so – since in fact they were.

These mistaken impressions about the enemy operation at Heraklion, strangely uncontested by any account written in English, can have reached Middle East Headquarters only from Chappel himself and must, therefore, be taken to explain the inertia that followed so quickly upon his vigour of the first evening. Fleming recalls that 'all our units were convinced' that the 'build-up' of enemy troops was 'taking place continuously'.[54] Such is the power of misinformation transmitted by hearsay.

Yet the Sector Commander had received at least one report which might have led him to doubt the authenticity of popular rumour. On the 23rd he sent two companies of the Leicesters on reconnaissance to the east. They saw no evidence of troop-carriers. Indeed, they brought back the news that the Germans were not numerous in the area, although they seemed to be very heavily armed with machine-guns. A few months later something of the truth was to emerge, only to lie unrecognized for many years in the records of a field interrogation centre. Colonel Brauer, captured in Libya, remembered the days that he had spent in the hills east of the airfield at Heraklion: 'Eventually we were at our wit's end. I had but eighty men left of my eight hundred, no food, little ammunition.'[55]

There is another question that must puzzle the historian. Why did Chappel make no attempt to defend Apex Hill? Since he

[53] Buckley, p. 258   [54] Capt. R. W. Fleming to the author, 21 May 1962
[55] Fergusson, *The Black Watch and the King's Enemies*, p. 91, recollections of Col. Brauer

believed the Germans to be concentrating dangerously in the east it might have been expected that he would use this strong point to block any movement by the western group of parachutists across his southern flank, hastening to destroy them in detail before they could join their fellows, while at the same time maintaining his contact with Tymbaki. It is strangely paradoxical that the policy which he adopted, while difficult to understand in the light of what he thought to be the condition of the enemy, was nevertheless well suited, so far as it went, to meet the situation which he had failed to recognize. For the truth was that there was no need for him to worry about the Germans outside his defence perimeter except in so far as they might block his communications. They could be supplied only by hazardous drops from the air, and the Greeks and guerrillas could be relied upon to make their existence increasingly uncomfortable. Moreover, no great prescience was needed to conclude that there was little prospect that the Royal Air Force would make an effective return to Crete for many weeks to come. It therefore mattered not at all that groups of the enemy might for a time command the runway from entrenchments in the hills. All that need concern him was to ensure that the Junkers should not land upon it.

In the light of such reasoning he might have judged it high time to carry out the second part of his instruction. A single battalion, travelling in the vehicles at night, together with perhaps three or four guns, could have overcome any minor blocks upon the road short of Retimo. In fact the way was clear as far as Stavromenos. Such a force, after lending Campbell any necessary help, might then have returned to Heraklion or pressed on to Suda as required by Freyberg.

Events were to determine that it was at Maleme that things were to go wrong. And it can now be seen that any reinforcement from Heraklion must have come too late had it not begun to arrive by the 22nd. In order to achieve this, Chappel would have had to break the Germans west of the town, and send his motorized relief column to Retimo, on the first or second night. At this time it seemed likely that there were many more airborne troops still to come, and probably a sea landing as well. Understandably enough his attention remained concentrated upon these forbidding prospects. He would do nothing that might weaken his hold upon the aerodrome and harbour. He knew that the forces at his disposal were much less strong than those already available between Maleme and Canea, and that he could expect little mercy if Heraklion should fall while the rest of the island held. Thus he never attempted the daring and immediate action that might have maintained his communications and enabled him to send reinforcement to the west. Today it seems that he could have done it. But it would have taken a bold man to try.

All through the 24th it remained quiet from the Prison Valley to the sea. It was a convenient moment for a demonstration by the *Luftwaffe*. Increasingly enraged by these impudent Cretans, who had presumed to defend themselves with such courage and success, the Germans determined to demonstrate the price of such defiance. How better than by reducing the town of Canea to ashes?

From half a mile away Sergeant Charles looked on with indignation:

Then came bombers wave after wave [he wrote in his diary]. It seemed interminable. Bombs rained down and in order to catch the panic-stricken people who broke cover, there were bursts of machine-gun fire. The sets of waves had a break of 10 minutes or so in between and during that time odd Stukas would fly down the roads and lanes towards the town and machine-gun and bomb fugitives; then others after a short period would rake the woods near by with gun fire. Great clouds of dust rose high in the air and spread all over the countryside. A gusty wind was started and birds flew about in bewilderment. This lasted for over four hours – and I should think almost the whole town was destroyed. I felt sick . . . to think of all the innocent people being indiscriminately slaughtered. . . . The raids petered out and finished about 20.00 hours leaving flames leaping high into the sky.[56]

Captain Stephanides, who was in the village of Tsikalaria, two miles away, saw that 'the whole of Canea seemed to be ablaze'. Tongues of red and yellow flame were 'writhing like gigantic boa-constrictors. . . . The villagers, too, were gathered in stunned silence watching that holocaust'. He could 'sense that to them it was like the end of a world. Canea was the only town that many of them had ever known. . . . Some of the men had tears streaming down their faces and others shook their fists and cursed the Germans.'[57]

To those who sought to follow the battle from afar, the realities

---

[56] Sgt. Charles, letter to author, 30 June 1961   [57] Stephanides, p. 100

of the situation, the distance between the Sectors, the lack of transport, the primitive routes, the menace to daylight movement, the paralysing failure of communication, all remained hidden. Freyberg saw these handicaps grow hour by hour in ominous significance. But, as the line steadied west of Galatas, he still had some hope of help from the garrisons in the east. This is shown by his signal to Chappel of the 23rd. At the same time he knew that if the island were to be saved he must also have substantial and immediate support from Egypt.

Clark and others, echoing Churchill's exhortation to 'send more tanks and thus reconquer any captured aerodrome', have written much to the effect that a few heavy armoured vehicles might still have retaken Maleme and thus reversed the fortunes of the battle. Freyberg himself was to admit: 'It is a pity that all the Infantry tanks that were sent to us were not concentrated to hold Maleme, as the few "I" tanks working were of little use anywhere. It would have been better to get the whole six tanks together in one detachment.'[58] In fact, had he done so, it seems likely that he might have chosen to send them to Heraklion – to guard the only modern airfield in the island. Certainly all might have been different had it been possible, on the first day, to launch half a dozen new Infantry tanks out of the smoke and dust against the lightly-armed enemy collecting close to the Tavronitis Bridge; instead Andrew had been given only his two crippled derelicts. But once the Germans had become established in Pirgos the moment for a dramatic stroke by armour had passed. So much was ensured by two factors. Between Suda and Maleme tanks could scarcely have moved a yard in daylight without destruction by aircraft, while at night they could not have left the narrow coast road. With the noise of their approach sounding far ahead through the darkness they would have faced certain ambush in the village. There was no need even for the Germans to throw up barricades. They had heavy mortars, and light guns, capable of blowing off a track, as they were to show at Retimo; whereupon their automatic weapons, firing from among the houses and trees, could make certain that no repair would be possible.

Freyberg needed infantry, at least a brigade of fresh troops, together with heavy artillery. He required them immediately. And they must be landed under his hand at Suda.

These demands were beyond the capacity of the Royal Navy.

[58] DP, Freyberg comments on Davin Draft, 1952 (undated)

In his despatch Wavell was to write that by the 24th

. . . no merchant ship had any chance of survival within 50 miles of the island, and the only means of sending reinforcements was by fast warships which could reach Suda Bay under cover of darkness, disembark their troops and get clear of the island before dawn. This limited both the number and type of troops that could be sent, even if such reinforcements had been available. It was, for instance, impossible to send any more guns by this method.[59]

Thus the daily 'five to six hundred tons' of stores, most of it to come through Suda, that Freyberg had considered the minimum necessary for maintenance had shrunk progressively, first to the bare hundred tons landed under the 'umbrella', and now to the fevered discharge of an occasional destroyer sneaking at midnight down the bay. Events were failing to justify Churchill's expectation that Wavell could 'reinforce far more easily' than could the enemy.

Anxiously, Cunningham was doing his best. He had relented slightly in his refusal to send ships direct to the north of the island; the first 200 men of a Commando detachment of two battalions were to arrive safely in Suda on 24 May. But the battalion of the Queen's Royal Regiment, together with part of the 16th Infantry Brigade, had failed to get through. These units were being carried by the convoy which Cunningham had instructed to return, in defiance of the direct order from the Admiralty insisting that it should continue.

By the night of 23/24 May Freyberg's Intelligence Staff had greatly increased their efficiency. From 'captured documents', coupled with calculations based on 'the rate of landings' from the air, and with information from a 'completely reliable source', they now produced for him a report which was remarkably accurate. There were errors in detail, and some misunderstanding of the German organization, but in essentials it got very near the truth. It correctly identified all the German objectives and assessed that a total of 15,550 men had landed on the island from the air, 6,450 in the vicinity of Maleme, 5,800 in a central group attacking in the Prison Valley and at Retimo, and the rest at Heraklion.[60] The enemy losses on land were thought to be 'approximately 3,340'. It was believed that very little had been

[59] Wavell Despatch: *Operations in the Middle East from 7th February 1941 to 15th July 1941*
[60] DP, Intelligence Appreciation, 24 May 1941

brought by sea.[61] Perhaps more important than anything else in this report was the suggestion, here clearly made for the first time, that no more than one airlanding division was taking part, and that only 600 parachutists were 'still to land'.[62]

The casualties suffered by the defence had not been overwhelming. As more survivors filtered back from Maleme, the number of unwounded men answering the 5th Brigade roll calls continued to rise steadily. The figures for the 22nd had swollen from 110 to 383, and the 250 members of the 23rd identified at Platanias had now increased to 438. The four infantry battalions still had an active strength of 1,574. In an assessment of casualties made on the 24th, Freyberg's staff arrived at a total of '1909', with 'killed 396, wounded 1,118, missing 395'. Some three-quarters of these were from the New Zealand Division.

After some rumination upon these two sets of figures Intelligence in Cairo was able to point out that the defence still enjoyed a considerable numerical superiority, apart from the help that was being given by the Greeks and Cretans. From Egypt, indeed, it seemed plain enough that the main need was to use every possible resource to prevent the Germans from landing seaborne reinforcements.[63]

But Freyberg knew that mere numbers did not matter. All that counted was combined strength at the vital point. Even reinforcement could not help him now unless it were supported to the utmost by the Royal Air Force and the Navy. Perhaps, while the halt in the German advance continued, he may again have begun to feel a hesitant renewal of hope. Might it not be possible to send a substantial force of bombers on a night raid to Maleme? And surely it was reasonable to hope that in this moment of extremity the Navy might at last contrive an action in which the vulnerable airfield could be shelled at night from the sea; apart from a shot or two from the ill-fated *Kelly* during the night of the 22nd no such bombardment had been attempted. The effect upon the enemy would at least be disconcerting. To the defending infantry it could not fail to bring encouragement. Without this support he could do nothing. The time when he might have won the battle from his own resources had already passed. Enemy fighters could operate directly, if they should need to do so, from their new base, a mere twelve miles from the docks at Suda. And steadily the

[61] DP

[62] Ibid., Creforce G.S.I., 24 May 1941   [63] Ibid.

German strength was increasing. Like a bewildered Titan, he could do little more than contemplate events which he was powerless to control, while across the widening gulf that separated him from Egypt and London there poured a stream of admonition urging him into courses which he already knew to be impossible.

Late on the evening of the 24th he moved his Headquarters to Suda Point on the southern shore of the bay. As he passed slowly through Canea the town was covered by a choking mist lit by a yellow glow from the dying fires. Piles of masonry, festooned by telephone wire, had fallen into the streets, partly obliterating the scattered debris of flight, the broken carts, the heaps of clothing, and the household utensils. In unexpected corners, the corpses lay like drunken millers, wearing their powder of white dust.

That night his despatch to the Middle East was composed in sombre tones. It may be noted by historians, and by all others who decry the importance of the *Luftwaffe* at Crete, that it is dominated by his concern for the effects of this heavy and sustained bombardment from the air. He began by saying that the enemy seemed likely to renew their attack at any time. The fresh positions that he had taken up should give his troops a better hope of offering effective resistance in depth. At this moment, however, he would like to make the position quite clear. On the whole he felt that they had beaten the highly lauded parachutists, particularly in man to man encounter, but the fighting had been very heavy. Indeed 'the scale of the air attack was far greater than anything he had ever visualized. He did not believe that the enemy would ever again use his parachutists in a similar operation'. Nevertheless, 'the battle continued and a further attack was to be expected in which the enemy would use heavy bombs to try and blast his way through. Tired though they were the troops could be counted on to do their best; but the result would be in the balance.'[64] He ended his cable by insisting yet again upon the ferocity of the air attack on the front line and on Canea.

There was not much comfort in the reply that came from the Commander-in-Chief of the Middle East:

Guts and determination of yourself and troops under your command

[64] Davin, p. 293

are splendid example to all. We have evidence that Germans have great difficulties. R.A.F. have inflicted considerable damage on enemy. We are doing our best to help you.[65]

It was true that the Germans had experienced 'great difficulties'. But these difficulties were now largely over. At last they could see the end of their troubles. During four days of hard-won success, the survivors of the Storm Regiment, shaken by the unexpected strength of the resistance and by their own losses, had been slow to overcome their misgivings, while Heidrich's men in the Prison Valley, like their comrades at Heraklion and Retimo, had begun to think of defeat. These fears had been increased by the *Wehrmacht* communiques, which had continued to avoid reference to any land fighting in Crete. There was, therefore, much relief, on the evening of the 24th, when news spread among them of a Special Announcement which had been released from the German Broadcasting stations during the afternoon. Airborne Troops, it was now proclaimed with fanfare and trumpet, had been in action in Crete since 20 May. Tactically important positions had been captured, and the attack reinforced by army units. Already the west of the island was safe in German hands. In the words of the 6th Mountain Division War Diary:

The situation appeared to be sufficiently under control to allow information on the fighting to be issued from now on.

How could they ever have had any doubts? At Heraklion and Retimo the hard-pressed parachutists quickly recovered all their old bounce and soon were demanding surrender of the garrisons. Everywhere there were renewed promises of wholesale slaughter in reprisal for 'atrocities'.

With Maleme secure Ringel had declined to mount further piecemeal attacks. From a tactical point of view, he could afford to wait for the arrival of fresh troops and artillery before launching upon the line at Galatas a prepared assault which should bring him to the head of the bay. In fact, he had no time to spare. As usual his infantry would be relying upon the *Luftwaffe* for close support. Even more desirable was the need for bombers to prevent the British Navy from putting a last minute reinforcement ashore at Suda. But the Chiefs of Staff in Germany were insisting to Student, who had been turning a 'deaf ear' to their

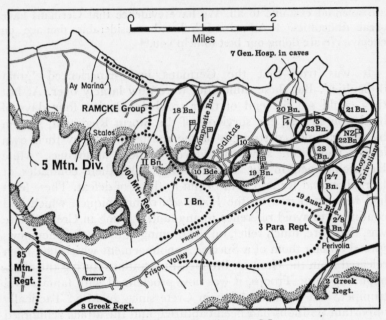

18.   Galatas: Evening, 24 May

exhortations, that Air Fleet IV must return north for the attack upon Russia. They had expected that the planes would be able to begin the move on the 25th, by which time the campaign in Crete should have been over. Now they feared that this delay must lead to the postponement of 'Barbarossa'.

Ringel had every reason for believing that he had become strong enough to complete his victory. Most of the 5th Mountain Division had arrived to supplement the survivors of the Airlanding Division. He determined, therefore, that on the 25th he would fight a battle that should decide the fate of the island. Since he dare press no further upon either flank while the New Zealanders held the central heights, his first objective must be to break the line at Galatas. At the same time, faithful to his maxim that sweat saved blood, he would thrust a deep flanking movement past the Greeks at Alikianou and through the mountains to the southeast.

Not all his strength was available for the front line. With their primitive equipment, the Greeks and Cretans in the west were engaging more than three battalions of Germans. A Motor Cycle

group was probing south towards Palaiokhora, while a Mountain
Pioneer Battalion, under Major Schaette, was held up along the
approaches to Kisamos Kastelli. Even more important was the
effort of the soldiers of the 8th Greek Regiment above Alikianou.
From behind their rocks and bushes on the foothills, helped by
men and women from the village, and reinforced by 'twenty
valiant reservists',[66] they continued to pick off their enemies as
they tried to find a way up the exposed slopes. Clifford Wilson,
the young New Zealand liaison officer, had been shot while trying
to cross open ground between defence posts, and the Regiment
had long since been given up for lost by the men behind them,
and by Freyberg's Headquarters. Yet these valiant Greeks still
barred the way into the hills.

Despite these diversions Ringel had assembled a powerful
combined force for the Galatas assault. The units of the 7th Air
Division had lost much of their striking power, but the men
remained eager to share in a victory which they now felt to have
been brought within reach by the arrival of the Mountain Troops.
South of the Alikianou-Canea Road were the depleted battalions
of 3 Parachute Regiment. Although encouraged by the radio
communiqué, and by contact with the relieving battalions on
their left, Heidrich's men were much reduced physically, as were
all those Germans in Crete whose supply had depended upon
delivery by parachute. Von der Heydte, who had breakfasted
that morning on 'a gulp of water and a morsel of biscuit', expressed
his concern in terms that recall the impressions of the journalists
at Heraklion:

> The meagre rations, coupled with unaccustomed heat, was under-
> mining their resistance more than they realized. The faces of some of
> them had grown taut, almost shrunken, their eyes lay deep in their
> sockets, and their beards, unshaven now for five days, accentuated the
> hollowness of their cheeks. Others were suffering from diarrhoea as a
> result of drinking stagnant water.[67]

Heidrich himself, with 'nerves stretched to breaking point', had
once more urged his troops against Galatas. On the 23rd von der
Heydte had watched from the far side of the valley as II Battalion
'the forward elements, widely spread out, emerged from the
olive-grove half-way up the slope'. But soon 'the sight of the
parachutists moving up the slope became less and less frequent,

<hr>

[66] Mourellos, Vol. I, p. 360   [67] von der Heydte, p. 130

13*

while the downwards traffic steadily increased'.[68] The attack had failed. Its commander was brought back, wounded in the stomach, to die in the Field Hospital at the Prison.

The men of the Storm Regiment had been supplied directly along the coast road. But they were weary after five days of desperate fighting, and dismayed by losses that far exceeded their worst expectations. Early on the 25th Student himself had flown to Maleme. A few hours later he went out to their lines east of Platanias. Almost all of them he knew by name. By capturing the airfield they alone had saved his campaign from disaster. No doubt he was pleased with them, and they perhaps were duly gratified by this special attention. But Gericke does not mention the visit. That night, as they wrapped themselves in their blankets, they had been thinking less of generals than of their own exhaustion, of the fate of friends, and of the unbroken enemy who lay before them within the folds of the hills.

Ringel decided to strike his first blow in the centre, where the two battalions of Mountain Infantry led by Colonel Utz waited beside their stacked mortar bombs. These troops were fresh and superbly armed. Distributed to every company were twenty heavy and light machine-guns, an abundance of automatic pistols, rifles with telescopic sights for the specialist marksmen, and for every man as many grenades as he could carry.

They were not underestimating their task. They knew that a regiment of parachutists had been repulsed upon the heights that faced them. To their right the Prison stood white and solid among the trees. From its gates, the road wound upwards to Galatas. Hidden by the olives was a bare knoll crowned by a cemetery and cypresses. Both sides, like the two armies at Gettysburg, had named it Cemetery Hill. Here the dead lay huddled to the red earth below the graveyard walls. Across the front ran a shallow ravine. Into this jutted the three features known to the New Zealanders as Ruin Hill, Wheat Hill and Pink Hill. On the far side of the low ground, scarcely half a mile away, the incline rose to the crest of the ridge that linked the coast road with Galatas. The grey stone walls of the hill-top village, curling about the enclosed houses, stood out like the battlements of a fortress.

Further back, near Platanias, Ringel held in reserve two more fresh battalions of infantry, together with a regiment of artillery.

[68] von der Heydte, p. 122

Finally he would still have, for this day at least, his usual massive support from the air.

Awaiting this formidable concentration of arms the New Zealanders could place in their front line only 400 relatively fresh troops. During the night of the 23rd Inglis had brought forward the reduced New Zealand 18th Battalion to relieve the harassed Composite Battalion on the forward hills and slopes. Kippenberger had found it 'heartening to see the 18th come in – looking very efficient and battle-worthy – in painful contrast with the columns of clumps in which my unfortunate quasi-infantry got about'.[69] But Lieutenant-Colonel Gray, the commanding officer of this half-strength battalion, had been given a front that stretched a full mile and a half from the coast to the west of Galatas. Moreover, the line ran through country closely covered with thick scrub and entered by steep gullies.

In making this precarious disposition Inglis had been left with no choice. Behind him the 5th Brigade must be given a few more hours to rest and to reorganize. Already he had committed most of his command to the front line.

Indeed the whole of the New Zealand Division was much weakened, in material as well as in men. There was a shortage of all types of ammunition. Only seventy-two three-inch mortar bombs remained. Most of the guns had been lost. Even worse, there were not enough grenades, that weapon that was proving so deadly among the bushes and ravines. Communications were as bad as ever. Every daylight movement was at once pursued from the air, and the steady drain in casualties had led to a further loosening of control among the untrained infantry. It was with diminished confidence that the men of the Composite Battalion set about scraping such shelter as they could find along an exposed ridge half a mile east of their old position.

On the 24th the men enjoyed a brief respite from air attack while the bombers concentrated upon Canea. By the late afternoon, the flames had begun to die down but smoke still gushed in black columns from the wrecked town. The day had been overcast and surprisingly cool, with a hint of rain. Now the sun burst above the cloud beyond Maleme, drenching the sky in red and yellow, and turning to pink the flat water of the inlets by the coast road.

[69] Kippenberger, p. 61

Grimly, in the fading light, the New Zealanders saw to their weapons and ammunition and filled their water bottles. After nightfall, they watched briefly, exhausted and silent, as the enemy flares clustered more thickly than ever before in the west. The following day would be a Sunday, the sixth day of battle, 25 May. Few of them knew it. Their thoughts led no further than the certainty that the enemy was stronger than before, and that within an hour of dawn the planes would once more be crowding the sky above them.

Upon Kippenberger and the other senior officers there bore unexpressed an added awareness. Behind them in the darkness it might be that more men and equipment were arriving in Suda Bay. Despite all appearance perhaps it would still be possible to mount a counter-blow. But, if the island were to be saved, such a stroke could no longer be delayed. West of Canea they must already be greatly outnumbered by the enemy. And if the line at Galatas should give way all would be lost. For with it must go Suda and the last hope of reinforcement.

19

Riposte in the dusk: 25 May

On the morning of the 25th, the New Zealanders crouched under
the mortars that fountained out of the valley to the west. From
Galatas down to the sea the planes fled across the tree-tops as
though in terror of their own bombs, the spurting pillars of smoke
and debris pursuing them in giant strides along the ridges. During
the night the cloud had drifted to the horizon. Now the sun
glared from a cobalt sky, burning the red earth of the olive
plantations to a fine powder which swirled in choking clouds
above the newly opened craters. At about one o'clock the Stukas
and Messerschmitt fighter-bombers concentrated their assault

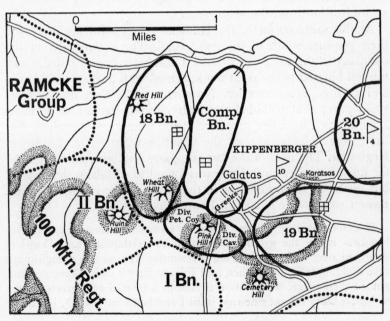

19.   Galatas: Noon, 25 May

upon Galatas itself. A few minutes later the Germans began to feel their way forward along the whole front. Kippenberger heard the sudden 'crackle of musketry'. Soon it 'swelled to a roar, heavily punctuated by mortar bursts'.[1]

Everywhere the defenders met the attack coolly with aimed fire. From behind the twisted olive trunks, the drivers and artillerymen of the Russell detachment sniped with deadly effect, cutting down the green figures as they darted from the shadows among the trees to waver in the patches of dazzling light. Here the Mountain Troops met with no better success than the parachutists before them. Some were borne down by the heat, to lie trapped in sweltering ovens among the unshaded rocks. But, as the afternoon lengthened, the 18th Battalion found itself increasingly hard-pressed along its much extended line. Ready as usual to make his own decision, Gray had decided that he could not afford to maintain occupation of Ruin Hill, the westernmost prominence of the hill cluster below the Galatas ridge. Quickly the enemy moved forward onto this vantage point and from it brought enfilade fire upon his men further north. This forced them back and left a gap in his centre through which there now began an infiltration from the north-west.

At this same moment, the Ramcke group suddenly increased their pressure south of the coast road. The commander of the company in this area was wounded and his successor killed. Gray himself hurried to the right flank, armed with a rifle and bayonet and crying, 'No surrender. No surrender.'[2] With him went a small party that included the padre, cooks, clerks and batmen, accompanied by a few members of the Composite Battalion. But they were helpless against the superior weapons of the Storm Regiment. The men of the lost company had been cut off on the far side of open ground. Gray was forced to withdraw, leaving all but twelve of them killed or in the hands of the enemy. Captain Bassett went to see what was happening:

It seemed an easy job, but I was no sooner out than flights of dive-bombers made the ground a continuous earthquake and Dorniers swarmed over the guns blazing incessantly. It was like a nightmare race dodging falling branches, and I made for the right Company and got on their ridge, only to find myself in a hive of grey-green figures so beat a hasty retreat sideways until I reached Gray's H.Q. just as he

---

[1] Kippenberger, p. 63　　　　　　[2] DP, Pte. W. H. Bishop

was pulling out. I had to admire the precise way he was handling the withdrawal. . . . A bomb landed amongst us.[3]

These Germans quickly threatened to force their way straight down the road into Canea. To prevent this, Kippenberger sent across 140 men of the 20th, his own old battalion, whom Inglis had moved forward earlier in the afternoon. They blocked the gap. 'For the rest of the evening' Kippenberger found it 'a comfort to hear their fight going steadily on'.[4]

But messages from other parts of the field told him that the situation was worsening:

John Russell reported that he was being hard-pressed and a trickle of stragglers was coming back past me. I sent Brian Bassett on foot to tell Inglis the position and say that I must have help. There were nearly 200 wounded at the Regimental Aid Post, close to Head-quarters. Our two trucks worked incessantly, taking them down to the Advanced Dressing Station in loads like butchers' meat.[5]

Now there came mounting pressure in the centre as the Utz troops pressed forward in the glare of the setting sun. Wheat Hill, overlooked by the abandoned Ruin Hill, was swept by a continual rain of fire from small arms, mortars, and artillery. Kippenberger walked a few hundred yards forward over the crest and watched 'the rain of mortar bombs'. In a hollow, almost hidden by under-growth, he came on a 'party of women and children huddled together like little birds', who looked at him silently with 'black, terrified eyes'.[6] Twice runners got through from Wheat Hill asking permission to withdraw. Twice he sent back refusals. By 7 p.m. only the survivors of two companies held their positions, the grenades flashing in the dust as the enemy pressed around them 'almost at arm's length'.[7] A few minutes later they too, those that could still move, began to come back under the protection of a covering platoon, among them Major Lynch of 'C' Company, who had fought with his men from a forward trench.

At this moment the enemy in the south started another move against the Russell detachment in an attempt to 'storm the heights during the last hour before darkness'. This attack broke into the defence line, but Russell's cavalrymen kept up their fight.

Not a New Zealander takes as much as a step backwards [says the journalist Meyer, who was with I Battalion of the 100 Mountain Regiment], one lanky young fellow heaves himself out of his slit

[3] Davin, p. 301. Letter from Capt. B. I. Bassett, 6 June 1941
[4] Kippenberger, p. 64   [5] Ibid.   [6] Ibid.   [7] Davin, p. 303

trench. He has taken out two hand grenades, one in each hand, while that in his left hand explodes prematurely and tears the hand off, the other he throws at the feet of the advancing Germans who are not more than three strides from him.

At last, 'in the failing light', the Mountain Troops gained the summit of Cemetery Hill and saw in the distance 'the roofs and gardens of Canea and the gleam of Suda Bay'.[8]

Galatas itself still held. The Germans had worked their way forward among the trees and scrub that encircled the low mound of Pink Hill. Here the men of the Petrol Company continued their resistance under the orders of Captain Rowe, the Brigade Supply Officer – a scratch collection of drivers and fitters, yet every man a soldier, facing the best of Hitler's infantry. Two platoons came over from the 19th Battalion, and Lieutenant Carson, who had played cricket for New Zealand, brought some drivers. Lieutenant Dill, with a platoon of gunners, held out on the western spur. A few Greeks, with no bayonets to fit their rifles, fought on under a young officer called Michael.

Dill and his men saw the attack developing around them. The bushes that grew on the open face of the slope gave some cover from observation, but there was no protection from the bullets, nor from the screaming plunges of the dive-bombers. And after the withdrawal of the 18th Battalion an intense machine-gun fire began to pour in upon them from their right. Rowe kept his head. He waited as long as he dared. Then, at the last possible moment, he withdrew his men into the protection of Galatas, the platoons giving each other covering fire with the steadiness of veterans. The enemy came quickly through the trees into the streets behind them. This mixed group of men, scarcely a quarter of them trained as infantry, had done much to save the day from disaster, for now night was approaching and the enemy effort in the south had begun to fade. Many did not come back. In the moment of declaring 'If a man believes he will be hit, he will', Dill[9] had been fatally wounded. The gallant Michael was last seen defending a ditch below the walls.

Further north, the 18th Battalion was in serious disarray. About a hundred had been killed, and the trickle of stragglers from the centre was turning into a stream. Most of the wounded, abandoned among the rocks and gullies, were falling into the hands of their enemies. Those whose injuries had not brought

[8] Kurt Meyer, *Battle for the Strongpoint of Crete*   [9] Davin, p. 307, Sgt. M. H. R. Hill

them to the ground stumbled painfully up the slope between the shivered trees, too spent to care for the bullets that scattered the dust about their feet. Several of these men staggered under the weight of a friend. Soon they were followed by others, some 'on the verge of panic',[10] as yet unwounded, but dazed by the heat and the intensity of the fire. Almost the last to return was Gray, looking 'twenty years older than three hours before'.[11] At this moment Kippenberger himself walked among them shouting 'Stand for New Zealand',[12] while 'swarms of Germans'[13] had begun to appear along the crest of the ridge, where dusk now lay among the trees. Kippenberger was told that the Composite Battalion had 'nearly all gone', although they had 'only been getting "overs" '.[14] Once more the right flank was in danger this time from the rear. And on the left the Russell Detachment was almost cut off by the Mountain Troops who had got into the village behind them.

But help was on the way. Both Inglis and Hargest had responded immediately to the request for reinforcement. The 4th Brigade Band and the Kiwi Concert Party were the first to arrive. They were joined by some Divisional Signallers, among them a captain who was much impressed by the 'red patch' worn by a young lieutenant whom he now met for the first time. Explaining that he was only a Signals officer he suggested that the subaltern should make the dispositions. 'Only a Signals officer,' was the reply, 'what the hell do you think I am? I'm only a bloody bandmaster.'[15]

Kippenberger set them all to line a stone wall which ran north from Galatas under the brow of the hill. Behind and below it, in the protection of the dead ground where the road wound out of the village on its way down to the coast, the men of the 18th Battalion were able to pause and draw breath. After a few minutes, Kippenberger moved them on a few hundred yards further to the east, telling them to form a reserve position along the next ridge at Karatsos, where 'a white church gleamed in the evening sun'.[16] To patch the forward line he sent up elements of the 4th and 5th Brigades as they continued to appear – another company of the 20th to support the rest of their battalion on the coast road, and before long most of the 23rd to plug the gap in the centre. And suddenly there was relief of another kind. From half a mile down

[10] Kippenberger, p. 65   [11] Ibid.   [12] Ibid.   [13] Ibid.
[14] Ibid., p. 64   [15] DP   [16] Kippenberger, p. 65

the road a troop of Australian artillery, using four Italian seventy-
five millimetre guns, began to fire over open sights into scattered
groups of the enemy who were mustering among the houses and
gardens in the northern outskirts of Galatas. Hastily the Germans
withdrew.

The men of the 23rd had been resting among the olives south of
the hospital while the sounds of battle drew nearer. In retreat,
and out of contact with the enemy, the threat of air attack had
troubled them far more than the tumultuous onslaughts which
they had endured so cheerfully at Pirgos. For much of the day a
Heinkel had hovered over their area.

It was alarming now [says Thomas] to see how this affected some
of the men. They would cringe close to the ground and huddle around
the trunk of an olive tree . . . their eyes opened unnaturally wide. Tired
and frightened men lose their sense of proportion, and if one crossed
an open space between trees with a Stuka anywhere even within sound
urgent and panic-charged shouts would be hurled from all directions.
'Get down, you bloody fool. Do you want us all to be killed.'[17]

At 5 p.m. these anxieties were quickly dispelled by the news that
they were needed to stop the enemy advance. Wearily, but with
a return of spirit and resolution, they trudged back to the Galatas
Turn and inland up the twisting switch-back road. Terrified
fugitives appeared out of the trees on their right and rushed
through them to the rear. As they mounted the last rise, Leckie
was wounded in the leg by a machine-gun bullet. They left him
lying against the bank. But now the planes were thinning at last.
Once more they would be meeting the enemy on level terms.
Already the flashes of the mortar shells had turned to brilliant
orange in the gathering darkness. Beyong Galatas flare after flare
mounted against a violet sky. A few hundred yards short of the
houses they came upon Kippenberger, 'a slight figure, pipe in
mouth, standing unconcernedly on the road'.

From Farran, who had made a reconnaissance in his tank, the
forward commander had learnt that the village was 'stiff with
Jerries'.[18] They were 'in all the cottage windows, in the orchard,
behind chimney-stacks, and in the school-yard'.[19]

Since early that afternoon, Kippenberger had been watching
the gradual disintegration of his force. Now he decided that he

[17] Thomas, p. 20, and Ross *23 Battalion*, p. 75   [18] Kippenberger, p. 67
[19] Farran, p. 101

'must hit or everything would crumble away'.[20] Galatas must be retaken. He asked Farran to lead the way with his two tanks, and told Major Thomason, replacing Leckie, to follow with two companies of the 23rd, one on each side of the road. On their left Gray would give what support he could with those few dozen survivors of the 18th who had not withdrawn to Karatsos. Quickly the word went round. It was plain that this would be a desperate venture. Thomas saw that the members of his platoon looked 'tense and grim'. He wondered if they were 'feeling as afraid' as he was. He then noticed that his strength had increased. In the gloom he made out several unfamiliar faces. 'We've got some reinforcements' said his sergeant.[21]

Indeed from every side men were appearing silently to join the attack, 'the flower of those left from the day's fighting',[22] they are called by the New Zealand War Historian. Forrester was there, still bare-headed and carrying only a rifle and bayonet, and Carson, accompanied by the remnants of his patrol. Bassett had gone across to join Gray. Two of the volunteers had lost brothers during the day. All had been forced to leave friends, dead or wounded, in the hands of the enemy. For six days they had felt the chagrin of defeat. Now it had come upon them, in a quick surge of desperation and anger, that they were about to strike back. Thomas suddenly realized that this was to be 'the biggest moment'[23] of his life. It was not quite dark. But already the stars were bright. Tracer whipped and crackled about the slopes. From the village looming above them the men heard confused shouting and an occasional shot. They fixed bayonets and waited.

Farran had discovered that two of his crew were wounded. They were 'dragged out'[24] and replaced by a pair of sapper volunteers who 'understood Vickers guns'.[25] After a 'ten minutes' course of instruction'[26] they were ready. It was 8.10 p.m. Kippenberger gave the order to go. Farran climbed back into his seat, waved briefly at the tank behind him, and pulled down the turret lid. The two tanks raced their engines and roared up the road. First at a walking pace, then at a run, 200 men followed them up the hill.

As the tanks disappeared into the first buildings of the village in a cloud of dust and smoke [says Thomas], the whole line broke spon-

[20] Kippenberger, p. 66   [21] Thomas, p. 23   [22] Davin, p. 312
[23] Thomas, p. 23   [24] Kippenberger, p. 67   [25] Farran, p. 102
[26] Kippenberger, p. 67

taneously into the most blood-curdling shouts and battle-cries. The effect was terrific. One felt one's blood rising swiftly above fear and uncertainty until only inexplicable exhilaration, quite beyond description, remained.[27]

Gray heard that cry as he waited in the eastern outskirts of the village, 'the deep-throated wild-beast noise of the yelling charging men as the 23rd swept up the road'.[28] It reached the men in the tanks above the noise of the engines. To one of them the 'howling shouting of the infantry sounded like the baying of dogs. As it rose and fell it made my flesh creep'.[29] And away to the south, on the far side of the Prison Valley, von der Heydte heard it too.

Now fire spurted from windows and doorways, from behind walls and from the roof-tops, while mortars crashed on to the road and among the plots and gardens, but already harmlessly, too far to the rear. The attack surged on. Many of the enemy, taken by surprise, were still inside the houses. For some of them life ended with the clatter of a grenade through a window. But those who reached the open fought savagely against this enemy that had come upon them like shadows, recognizable only by their flat helmets. Man against man fought for life in the narrow streets. Pistols flared in the darkness. Bayonet crashed on bayonet. Some tore at each other with their bare fists. A tall German seized one of his enemies by the throat using him as a shield. At once another New Zealander split the German's skull with a butt stroke. His victim, a company cook, picked himself up and went on with the others. Soon the narrow streets were filled with the dead and dying.

Beside his shattered tank Farran lay wounded in a gutter at a corner of the main street. The New Zealanders came past him at a scrambling gallop. Among them was Thomas who went on to lead a charge across the square:

Screams and shouts showed a desperate panic in front of us and I suddenly knew . . . that we had caught them ill prepared and in the act of forming up. . . . By now we were stepping over groaning forms and those which rose against us fell to our bayonets.

Beyond the square another group of Germans came at them head on:

The enemy were ten paces away in line. There were only four now, and before I could aim at the biggest he stumbled and fell. They were

---

[27] Thomas, p. 24
[28] Davin, p. 313, *n.* 4, Letter from Lieut.-Col. Gray, 24 July 1941   [29] DP

right on us. A bayonet glinted not three yards from my pointing pistol. As I pulled the trigger, even as that helmetless figure plunged down towards my groin I saw a mop of fair curly hair, a young face with teeth bared in a savage shout. My pistol jarred in my hand. On the instant that I noted the shudder that shook his frame, something like a sledge hammer hit me on the thigh, lifted me up and back.[30]

Now Thomas too lay helpless. Through the noise of battle he could hear Farran shouting encouragement. 'A very English voice calling "Good show New Zealand, jolly good show. Come on New Zealand".'[31]

The company on the left of the road, supported by the 18th, were fighting their way over rough walls and through alleys and back gardens.

A machine-gun held up the attack for a minute or two [says the 23rd Battalion War History], until Private David Seaton broke the spell by striding forward firing his Bren gun from the hip. While he kept up steady bursts, others edged round to a flank and knocked out the machine-gun with grenades. Seaton was killed.[32]

Nearby the Germans had formed a strong point in a house. Lieutenant Cunningham threw a grenade which 'burst harmlessly on a roof, scattering slates in all directions'.[33] He next rolled another grenade along the cobble-stones. It burst in a doorway of the house. 'As the German occupants dived out Private Lydiate shot four of them while Cunningham despatched the officer with his pistol.'[34] Before long this company too had reached the square. Brief resistance in the village school was quickly broken by Sergeant Hulme using grenades. The enemy were now in flight. The New Zealanders drove on until the village had been cleared to the top of the Prison Road.

The price had been heavy. As always, in street fighting, it was largely the best that had been lost. Of the company that came in behind the tanks all the officers and most of the N.C.Os. were dead or wounded. But Russell and Rowe had seized their chance and extricated 'what were left' of the Divisional Cavalry and the Petrol Company. Kippenberger had achieved his purpose.

The position was now stabilized for the night [he wrote after the war], and there was nothing left of 10 Brigade. I told Thomason

[30] Thomas, p. 26   [31] Ibid., p. 28   [32] Ross, *23 Battalion*, p. 80
[33] Ibid., p. 81   [34] Ibid.

where everyone was, and more tired than ever before in my life, or since, walked down the road . . . to report to Inglis.[35]

In this day's work he had found himself as a senior commander in the field. Exploiting his meagre resources to the utmost, he had given the orders which led to the blocking of the advance on the right and checked the beginnings of rout in the centre. No less significant had been his 'Stand for New Zealand' as he walked among the men stumbling back in terror, and his casual attitude on the road, pipe in mouth, under the machine-gunning planes. His demeanour, at once both instinctive and deliberate, had served to bring fresh courage to men at breaking point. Later he was to pay tribute to the efforts of Bassett, 'undefeatable, gay, tireless, dazzlingly gallant'.[36] He had less praise for the improvised units, scarcely recognizing even the valiant stand of the Petrol Company on Pink Hill. And he was to remain harsh in his criticism of the brave but wayward Gray for his failure to maintain occupation of Ruin Hill, conceding nothing to the difficulty of disposing 400 men in thick country over a front of a mile and a half, nor to the fact that Gray himself had fought with blazing courage in every part of the field. These uncharacteristic failures of generosity cannot detract from his behaviour at Galatas. For the first time he had found occasion to display those qualities which were soon to mark him as the outstanding New Zealand soldier of the Second World War. Faced with swiftly developing disaster, he had been cool and courageous, calculating and decisive.

The counter-attack had indeed been a notable feat of arms. Freyberg was to describe it as 'one of the great efforts of the New Zealanders in the defence of Crete'.[37] But how plain is the paradox that springs from it. After six days and nights of hard fighting these two companies of the 23rd had erupted with passionate verve and spirit against fresh troops more than double their number. If these same men had been called upon to deliver such a stroke at Maleme on the first night the outcome of the whole battle might have been very different. They would have had the support of the rest of their battalion, and on the western edge of the airfield the Gericke group had been exposed in the open, unprotected by walls and houses. Even upon the second night, against stronger opposition, the 21st, 23rd and the Maoris

[35] Kippenberger, p. 68   [36] Ross, *23 Battalion*, p. 62

[37] Ringel, pp. 164 and 166, says that 'three companies' of the Mountain Troops had 'reached the northern edge of the village', with another company in the houses behind them.

attacking together in such style as this, without waiting for the 20th, must surely have broken through to the Tavronitis.

Back at the 4th Brigade Headquarters Kippenberger found Inglis conferring with his Battalion Commanders 'in a tarpaulin-covered hole in the ground, seated at a table with a very poor light'.[38] What was to be done now? At 10 p.m., in a signal marked 'IMPORTANT', Inglis asked Puttick to come forward to discuss the matter. No doubt he hoped that Freyberg might be prevailed upon to send reinforcement. Kippenberger felt that at least two fresh battalions would be required. But Puttick did not come himself. It was Gentry, his staff officer, who next 'lowered himself into the hole' to find a weary group in the 'fug and smoke', some of them 'nodding half-asleep'.[39] He brought no suggestion of support for a counter-attack.

Not much was said. If there were to be any effort to improve the position it would have to be made by the Maoris, already reduced to a strength of 477 by their efforts south of Pirgos. The difficulties were plain; an attack in darkness, by men who did not know the ground, across rolling featureless country covered by olives and cleft by transverse ravines, and on a front far too wide. The task was impossible. The attempt would lead only to the loss of a fine battalion, while further weakening the line which must be held on the morrow.

But if the right flank could not be restored the return of daylight must find Galatas indefensible, exposed from both sides and naked under the bombers. Reluctantly, Inglis acknowledged the inevitable. There must be a general withdrawal beyond Karatsos to a shortened defence position aligned on the right of the Australians. Gentry took this decision back to Puttick who quickly agreed. He had made preparations for such a move. All knew that he was accepting defeat.

Indeed he was already looking further ahead. At 2.45 a.m. on the 26th he wrote to Hargest:

My dear Hargest,

I think you and Inglis have done splendidly in a most difficult situation. All I have time to write now is to say that in the unfortunate event of our being forced to withdraw we must avoid Canea and move well south of it towards Suda. Brig. Stewart says he will in that event try to organize a covering force across the head of Suda Bay through which we would pass, south of the Bay, of course. This information is highly confidential to you but will indicate a line to follow in event of dire necessity.

Would you kindly pass one copy to Inglis.

Good Luck,

Yours ever,

E. Puttick.[40]

Here was a line of thought that was to attain much significance during the next two days. But Puttick was not in general command. And there might still be other considerations beyond those of immediate tactical efficiency.

Soon the weary New Zealanders were once more trudging eastward through the darkness. Behind them Galatas lay in silence save only for the small muffled sounds of the wounded. Towards midnight a Cretan girl, about twelve years old, stole out from the broken masonry. She crouched over the bodies in the gutters, covering them with rugs and carpets and returning, where she found response, to offer drinks of sweet goat's milk.

Among the shadows cast by the young moon a man lurked on business of his own. Sergeant Hulme,[41] one of those who had learnt that day of the loss of a brother, was seeking vengeance. In the German reports of the fighting around Galatas there is indignant reference to the use of parachute uniform by the New Zealanders. The accusation is justified. Hulme had thrown all caution to the winds in adopting a device for which he could expect no mercy if he should be captured. From the first he had fought as a solitary hunter, stalking his quarry upon long, lonely patrols. Now he had taken to wearing a camouflage overall removed from a dead parachutist, together with a German sniper's hood which he pulled down over his face. All night he prowled alone about the outskirts of Galatas, a mile in front of the new defence line. As dawn broke he exploited his deadly advantage to pick off three Germans who were feeling their way forward to investigate a food dump.[42]

For twenty-four hours Freyberg had known that the island

---

[40] Davin, p. 340

[41] Sgt. A. C. Hulme, later awarded the Victoria Cross for his exploits in Crete

[42] 'In the morning light,' says Kurowski, p. 193, 'the village presented a grim picture. The fallen, friend and enemy, lay one upon another, Germans and New Zealanders together, their weapons still locked in their clenched fists.'

could not be held. Of the situation on the night of the 24th he was to write in his Report:

At this stage I was quite clear in my own mind that the troops would not be able to last much longer against a continuation of the air attacks which they had had during the previous five days. The enemy bombing was accurate and it was only a question of time before our now shaken troops must be driven out of positions they occupied. The danger was quite clear. We were gradually being driven back on our back areas, the loss of which would deprive us of our food and ammunition. If this heavy air attack continued it would not be long before we were driven right off our meagre food and ammunition resources. I really knew at this time that there were two alternatives, defeat in the field and capture, or withdrawal. Without tools, artillery and transport we could not readjust our rearward defences.[43]

The R.A.F. attacks on the airfield at Maleme had been no more than belated pin-pricks. They could not alter events. And now a cable told him that a night force of destroyers had failed to reach Maleme in time to bombard it before daylight. It was little consolation to hear from Wavell that the Greek King and his party had arrived safely in Alexandria and that Wavell himself, as yet scarcely aware of what was happening in Crete, had returned from Iraq. The message assured him that his splendid fight was having a profound effect upon the balance of the forces in the Middle East. Every effort was being made to send reinforcement but there were, of course, certain difficulties and the weather had been bad. The R.A.F. would do everything that it could. Already the enemy had lost many aircraft, together with a large proportion of his trained troops. The survivors must be weary and dismayed. 'Instead of an easy win they were confronted with the prospect of a costly defeat.'[44]

For two days Freyberg had hesitated to reveal the full gravity of the situation. But the moment had come when the truth could no longer be denied. In the words of his Report:

On the night of Sunday 25th I sat writing my cable to the C-I-C after having watched a savage air attack on the forward troops by dive-bombers, heavy bombers, and twin-engined fighters with machine-guns and cannon guns. This is what I had written:

'Today has been one of great anxiety to me here. The enemy carried out one small attack last night and this afternoon he attacked with little success. This evening at 1700 hrs bombers, dive-bombers and ground straffers came over and bombed our

[43] Freyberg Report, quot. Davin, p. 294   [44] Davin, p. 328

forward troops and then his ground troops launched an attack. It is still in progress and I am awaiting news.'

To this he added a sentence which he underlined. It reveals a last flicker of hope.

'If we can give him a really good knock it will have a very far-reaching effect.'[45]

While he was writing, news arrived from Puttick, who had not yet heard of Kippenberger's counter-blow at Galatas.

Heavy attacks about 2000 hrs. [said the message] have obviously broken our line. Enemy is through at Galatas and moving towards Daratsos.[46]

The Divisional Commander went on to give details of a new defence position, adding his hope that a mixed force of Marines and armed gunners would be able to provide support along the river through Canea Bridge. He concluded by saying that the reports reaching him indicated that the 'men (or many of them)' were 'badly shaken', and that it seemed probable that all the guns would be lost. He was 'exceedingly doubtful' whether he could 'hold the enemy tomorrow'.[47]

Freyberg now made an alteration in his signal to Wavell. Striking out the last sentence of his draft telegram he added in its place:

Later: I have heard from Puttick that the line has gone and we are trying to stabilize. I don't know if they will be able to. I am apprehensive. I will send messages as I can later.[48]

At this moment of anxiety and failure, he still found time to reply to Puttick in a message characteristic in its generosity and firm encouragement. At 4 a.m.:

Dear Puttick,

I have read through your report on the situation. I am not surprised that the line broke. Your battalions were very weak and the areas they were given were too large. On the shorter line you should be able to hold them. In any case there will not be that infiltration that started before. You must hold them on that line and counter-attack if any part of it should go. It is imperative that he should not break through . . .[49]

Crete was lost. But it was to be some time yet before this could be understood in Cairo and London.

[45] Freyberg Report, quot. Davin, p. 325
[46] The village of Karatsos was sometimes referred to by the N.Z. officers as Daratsos
[47] New Zealand Division War Diary   [48] Freyberg Report, quot. Davin, p. 326
[49] New Zealand Division War Diary

20

The loss of Force Reserve:
26-27 May

Freyberg was now confronted by a dilemma. Should he at once
set about organizing an evacuation? Or must he prolong a vain
resistance until all hope of escape was lost? Neither Wavell nor
any of the authorities at home, deceived by the failure of communication, had begun to understand that no other choice
remained. With less reason, some historians have shown the same
inability to recognize the facts. They have applied their diligent
arithmetic to every man in khaki who lurked among the olive
groves somewhere in the vicinity of Suda, while forgetting that
thousands of these troops were neither armed nor trained, and
upon this frail evidence have sought to imply that Freyberg
accepted defeat too readily.

Clark maintains that a further counter-attack should have
been made on the 26th 'with strictly limited objectives – the
restoration of the line of the "heights", with the inclusion of Ruin
Hill'. If this had succeeded it was 'just possible that the enemy
would have been forced to recognize a stalemate'.[1] Somewhat
incongruously he adds that 'the line had been restored'[2] by the
success of Kippenberger's action.

This is fantasy. On both flanks, the New Zealanders had been
driven back two miles. All that remained was a precarious salient
which daylight must expose to the mercy of the planes. But there
was another element which far transcended in importance the
tactical situation at Galatas. The answer to any suggestion that a
continued defence of the island was still possible lies in the single
word – supply. Freyberg was later to point out that his 'cable of
23 May' should have made it plain that 'the end was in sight from
an administrative point of view alone'.[3] For a week already no

[1] Clark, p. 156   [2] Ibid., p. 158
[3] DP, Freyberg comments on Davin Draft, 1952 (undated)

more than a dribble of men and light stores had reached Suda. Even this was more than Wavell and Cunningham could guarantee. Indeed, Wavell had told him that delivery to Suda had become impossible, and was later to comment in his despatch that 'no merchant ship had any chance of survival within fifty miles of the island'. This meant that there could be no hope of receiving further heavy equipment even at Heraklion or on the south coast. By contrast it was clear that more than 3,000 Germans were arriving each day by air. At any moment they would have the support of light tanks landed at Kisamos Kastelli. Already they must be stronger than the defenders in the western half of the island. Not even a return to Maleme could redress the balance.

The truth was that, since the morning of the 23rd, Student had known that his victory was secure. The relief of his airborne troops at Retimo and Heraklion had become his main concern. For their sake he was intent upon pressing urgently to the east despite the advantage that must continue to swing overwhelmingly in his favour. Not that he had need for delay. By the morning of the 26th some 8,000 men were available for the front line at Galatas – the major elements of five brigades, together with two regiments of artillery and numerous ancillary troops, many of them as yet scarcely engaged, with above them the unresisted *Luftwaffe*.

The New Zealanders who faced them were far reduced in numbers, weary to exhaustion, and some of them, as Puttick had acknowledged, 'badly shaken'. After a week of uninterrupted fighting they greatly needed rest. On their left the Australians were increasingly occupied. And ominous news had come from the hills in the south. Soon after midnight on the 25th a liaison officer had brought Freyberg a warning that the 2nd Greeks were 'about to break'.[4] Further back were the miscellaneous survivors from Greece, few of them trained as infantry, scarcely organized, and armed at best with a rifle. Last of all there remained Force Reserve, about 1,200 men of the 1st Welch, the Northumberland Hussars, and the Rangers. Clark finds it 'almost incredible that these battalions had not been put into the Galatas position at least twenty-four hours earlier'.[5]

The 1st Welch, certainly, might have played a critical part much earlier – at Maleme. But the Rangers were at half strength, and the Northumberland Hussars had lost almost a third of the 279

[4] Davin, p. 326, Maj. H. G. Wooler   [5] Clark, p. 159

men with whom they had begun the battle. Neither, in any real sense, was a 'battalion'. Not surprisingly, Freyberg felt that 'with the exception of the Welch Regiment and the Commando' his troops in the west were 'past any offensive action'.[6]

On the first and second nights, while the vital hours slipped by at Maleme, the great prize had lain, unrecognized, almost within his grasp. On the third night it was still within reach. But, one after another, these opportunities had been cast away. All that now remained was the hope that some of his army might again see Egypt. Even this prospect must have been remote had the 8th Greeks not sustained their magnificent fight at Alikianou. On the 20th they had gone far towards destroying the Engineer Battalion of 3 Parachute Regiment. During the succeeding days they had held their positions in the foothills against the gathering strength of Krakau's 85 Mountain Regiment, 'troops that in the Greek campaign had stormed the toughest defences on the Metaxa Line'.[7] Throughout this time they had remained cut off, with no hope of supply, and with no knowledge of what might be happening in the rest of the island. In order to continue their resistance, they had been forced to equip themselves almost entirely with the weapons of their enemies. Until after the war this feat of courage and endurance remained known only to the Germans. Today it can be acknowledged in admiration and affection by every soldier who fought with the men of Greece and Crete. It was not until the evening of the 25th that these Greeks, and their Cretan supporters, were at last dispersed by three infantry battalions augmented by a Reconnaissance Unit.

With these troops Ringel was seeking to capture Stilos, a village lying in a fold of the hills, six miles south from Suda Bay, on the road which led across the mountains to Sphakia. From here they were to push north to the Bay, thus completing the encirclement of their enemies at Canea and Suda, while at the same time hastening to the rescue of their comrades at Retimo. In order to hold the New Zealanders and Australians fully engaged west of the Kladiso he had inserted 141 Mountain Regiment between the Heidrich and Krakau groups. Its commander, Colonel Jais, had orders to drive over the foothills through Perivolia to Suda.

Thus, with every hour that passed, the New Zealand Division was coming nearer to destruction. If it should be lost nothing could save the troops at Suda. One course alone might still rescue

---

[6] Freyberg Report, quot. Long, p. 248   [7] Kurowski, p. 195

some part of the force in the west – an immediate retreat behind a rearguard followed by embarkation. This Freyberg understood. It was well that he did so.

During the morning of the 26th he expressed this view in a cable to the Middle East:

I regret to have to report that in my opinion the limit of endurance has been reached by the troops under my command here at Suda Bay. No matter what decision is taken by the Commanders-in-Chief from a military point of view our position here is hopeless. A small, ill-equipped and immobile force such as ours cannot stand up against the concentrated bombing that we have been faced with during the last seven days. I feel I should tell you that from an administrative point of view the difficulties of extricating this force in full are now insuperable. Provided a decision is reached at once a certain proportion of the force might be embarked. Once this sector has been reduced the reduction of Retimo and Heraklion by the same methods will only be a matter of time. The troops we have with the exception of the Welch Regiment and the Commando are past any offensive action. If you decide in view of whole Middle East position that hours help we will carry on. I will have to consider how this would be best achieved. Suda Bay may be under fire within twenty-four hours. Further casualties have been heavy, and we have lost the majority of our immobile guns.[8]

Later in the afternoon he sent a further message in which he acknowledged for the first time that he was pinning his hopes upon an evacuation from Sphakia, and that his immediate concern was for the supply that would be necessary to sustain a withdrawal across the island. The front west of Canea had broken and the 'men were falling back in disorder'.[9] He was trying to establish a new line south of Canea to cover the unloading of the stores that were expected to arrive in Suda that night. He hoped that it would be possible to move some of the rations and ammunition to Stilos. At best, however, the situation could be stabilized for no more than a short time. He would then attempt to withdraw southward to the coast at Sphakia and Port Loutro. He feared that his casualties had been heavy.

But he could not yet set the retreat in motion. 'There was no question of our retiring further,' he was to say in 1952, 'until we got answers to my cables to General Wavell.'[10] And answers were

[8] Long, p. 248   [9] Davin, p. 365
[10] DP, Freyberg comments on Davin Draft, 1952 (undated)

not easy to get. He was finding it difficult to induce the Commander-in-Chief and his staff to 'face up to the fact that Crete could not be held . . . they would not say stand and fight it out, nor would they contemplate evacuation'.[11] Later he was to blame himself 'for not having forced General Wavell to make a decision on the 25th'. His difficulties were increased by the delays which had now developed in his exchanges with Cairo. The move to the southern shore of the Bay had cut him off from the submarine cables to Alexandria and Heraklion. He was now dependent upon wireless contact. This was always precarious. As he wrote later, 'Crete, because of its mountains, was bad for wireless reception'. Yet the link was vital. 'Decisions were being asked for hourly, and "Creforce" Main H.Q. had to be situated well back to avoid constant movement of our wireless lay-out, and on the top of a hill because of the bad reception in the valleys.'[12] He did his best to ensure that no whisper of his real purpose should become known, understanding well, in his own phrase that 'once the word "withdrawal" is used no more fighting takes place'.[13] Three people, Brigadier Stewart, his Personal Assistant, and his Cipher Officer had learnt from him that he 'contemplated evacuation'.

Nevertheless, food dumps along the route had to be established if the troops were not to starve during the retreat. He had cabled for 'eighty tons of meat and biscuit to replace the stores which had been lost', and had been told that a pair of destroyers would be sent to Suda carrying more Commando troops together with food and ammunition 'if the tactical situation allowed'.[14] It thus became of paramount importance that he should 'keep Suda and prevent it from being under fire on the night of the 26th'.[15]

He determined that a line must be maintained west of the Kladiso throughout the following day. The Australians would continue to hold the left flank, while the centre would be filled by Suda Brigade. This was a group about 2,000 strong under the command of Lieutenant-Colonel Hely. It included the 'Royal Perivolians', a mixed party of riflemen whose regimental honours had been accorded by Weston in recognition of their defence of

[11] DP, Freyberg comments on Long Draft, 5 Dec. 1949

[12] Ibid., Freyberg to Kippenberger, 3 Jan. 1952

[13] Ibid., Freyberg comments on battle for Crete, 31 Oct. 1949

[14] Ibid.   [15] Ibid.

King George's villa on the first day. On the right, Force Reserve would take over from the New Zealand Division.

This decision he revealed early in the afternoon of the 26th to Brigadier Inglis whom he had summoned to his Headquarters:

I told him that the line must be stabilized and that I proposed to put him in command of Force Reserve with his Brigade Staff and send them forward to relieve the N.Z. Division. I visualized them taking over the position which the Welch Regt had themselves prepared astride the road to the west of Canea.[16]

He had already instructed the officers commanding the three battalions to report to Force Headquarters.

Only Major Boileau of the Rangers had arrived. After a short delay, it was decided that Inglis should go back to the New Zealand Division and that the commanding officers should join him there. The details of the relief could then be arranged on the spot where it would take place.

Inglis thereupon returned to Puttick, who found this news highly disconcerting. If there were to be no general withdrawal during the night the assumption must be that it would be necessary to hold throughout the following day in order to avoid a precipitate retreat under air attack. But he felt the line must break before another nightfall. In his view, not only the New Zealand Division, but Suda Brigade and the Australians as well should go back to Suda that evening as soon as it was dark. He determined to say as much to the General. Neither telephone nor wireless communication could be established with Force Headquarters, which had now reached Suda Point four miles along the southern shores of the bay. And no truck could be found for him. He set out on foot.

An hour later he met Freyberg by chance in Suda, not 'at the quarry',[17] as described by Clark; it was now almost two days since Force Headquarters had left the Akrotiri Peninsula. At once he explained his anxieties, and suggested that instead of waiting for the relief it would be best to withdraw as soon as possible to a position at the head of Suda Bay where the Force Reserve and the Commandos could hold a covering position.[18] Freyberg recognized that the suggestion was sound from a tactical point of view. But there was another consideration which was essential for the survival of his whole force. Could he keep Suda open and

[16] DP   [17] Clark, p. 160   [18] DP

The Garden battlefield

(Imperial War Museum)

The coast road leading west through Pirgos; early June 1961

(*Author*)

Canea after the bombing

(*Imperial War Museum*)

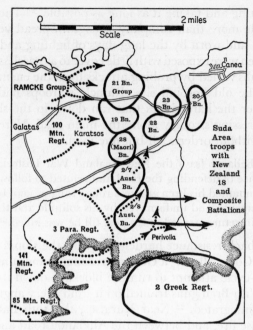

20.   German Move East from Galatas: 26 May

prevent it from being under fire on the night of the 26th? The withdrawal must bring the Germans within a mile of the docks, and so endanger the landing of the Commandos and the supplies. He had therefore ordered everybody to hold on where they were. At the same time, he had told Puttick of his decision to put General Weston in command of the Western front with control of his Marines, the Australian Brigade, and the Force Reserve.[19]

Puttick returned to his Division. This time he got a lift from Lieutenant-Colonel Duncan of the Welch who was trying to find Inglis. The news when he got back was no better. Vasey had reported that the Germans were 'working round' the left flank, and the 5th Brigade had described the situation as 'dangerous'. It was now 4.30 p.m.

West of the Kladiso it had been a hard afternoon. Indeed a company commander of the 19th Battalion, later to reach the rank of brigadier after surviving much desperate fighting, was to remember this as 'the worst day of the war'. It had become 'just

[19] DP

14

a case of sitting and taking it as long as possible'.[20] The battalions were in little more than company strength. Spread very thin on the ground, and worn by the long days of fighting and by lack of sleep, the men were exposed with little cover to a ceaseless cascade of mortar bombs varied by probing attacks from the enemy infantry.

East of the old hospital site, Ramcke's troops had begun to advance over the bare ridges that ran down to the shore. They were also pressing strongly along the main road. Here a platoon withdrew without orders. All but one man.

Sergeant Bellamy [says the New Zealand War Historian] grasped the importance of defending the road and refused to follow the others. Instead, he mounted his Bren gun in a rough sangar, kept up fire on all enemy movements, and undismayed by his solitude and the fierce fire he received in return, stayed at his post till he was killed.[21]

Further back resistance hardened. From the slopes on the left Lieutenant Cockerill saw 'a German reconnaissance unit mounted on a motor-cycle attempt to run the blockade down the centre of the road. With Bren guns trained on it from every angle, this unit literally disintegrated.'[22] Near Karatsos, the 19th Battalion was under intense fire, and between the Alikianou road and Perivolia the Australians had been forced into local withdrawals. But much more disconcerting was the continued movement of enemy troops through the Greek positions in the foothills. Late in the afternoon, machine-gun fire from the south began to come in over Divisional Headquarters as though to emphasize the danger from this flank. Puttick's anxieties were increased by the news that the battalions of the 10th and 4th Brigades were finding it difficult to reorganize. The Composite Battalion was scattered, and contact with the 18th had been lost. Hargest had been 'staggered' to find his brigade 'in front again' after 'less than a day's rest'.[23] Both he and Inglis were convinced that it would be 'very dangerous'[24] to rely on their troops after that day. The number of stragglers was increasing. Some had drifted as far as Suda, where perhaps they found consolation in the sight of their General on the back of a speeding motor-cycle 'holding tight with one hand and the other holding his hat on his head'.[25]

[20] DP, Capt. C. L. Pleasants   [21] Davin, p. 333
[22] Ibid., p. 336, Lieut. K. C. M. Cockerill   [23] DP, Hargest Narrative
[24] Ibid., Lieut.-Col. Gentry reporting the views of Brigadiers Hargest and Inglis to Col. Stewart in a note dated 26 May 1941
[25] Davin, p. 355, Lieut. C. A. Borman, retiring under orders with Divisional Signals

But the front had not 'broken' as Freyberg feared. The troops 'coming back in disorder' were not from the forward battalions. The main line still held. It had been expected that the Germans would launch a full-scale assault out of the sun during the late afternoon. This they forbore to do, partly because Ringel preferred his technique of encirclement, and partly in consequence of a failure of liaison with the *Luftwaffe* which had led to the killing of Mountain Troops both near Galatas and around Alikianou. Nor were they finding it easy to make progress.

The enemy is offering fierce resistance everywhere [says an entry in the 5th Mountain Division War Diary dated 26 May]. He makes skilful use of the country and of every known method of warfare. Mainly snipers, M.G. nests, and positions partially wired and mined. . . . His camouflage from the air is perfect. . . . Armed bands are fighting fiercely in the mountains, using great cunning.

By contrast, the German planes could now operate with increasing profit. Pinned upon their narrow front, and forced to move reserves in the open, the defending infantry were more than ever at their mercy. It was now that the 5th Brigade lost seventy men to air attack, and the 18th Battalion suffered a further dozen casualties. Private Pankhurst of the 23rd Battalion was luckier than many:

As we were making our way up a small gully C Coy were coming down causing a lot of congestion. A Hun fighting Messerschmitt crossed this gully firing his guns. I felt the heat of the bullets pass my face and the leaves were dashed from the trees under which I was crouched . . . so I was out of the gully, and it's just as well I did for that darned plane came down the gully a few minutes later (not across it as it did the first time) and cleaned up fifteen men with one burst from its guns.[26]

A young officer was caught up in the same sport:

The German aircraft had so little to do that they chased Ellis and me over a hill firing all the time until we managed to shelter over the brow, and the two aircraft, M.E. 110's, turned round and chased us up the other side.[27]

General Weston might maintain that machine-gunning from the air had nearly always proved quite ineffective,[28] and a generation later historians would find it easy to believe him. At the time there were others who had cause to think otherwise.

[26] Ross, *23 Battalion*, p. 86   [27] Davin, p. 335, Lieut. K. C. M. Cockerill
[28] See above, p. 324

A few minutes before the arrival of Puttick, at about 3 p.m., Freyberg had told Weston that he was to command the western front:

I informed General Weston of the orders I had given Brigadier Inglis and I advised him to put in the Force Reserve to stabilize the line and relieve the N.Z. Division that night.[29]

According to Lieutenant-Colonel Wills, his staff officer, Weston decided to supplement this plan by occupying the 'bottle-neck' position at Suda docks with 'fresh troops' at daybreak on the 27th, in order to enable 'N.Z. Div to get away'. East of the docks there would be a further 'stop position' at the point where the mountains came down close to the water. Through this gap he intended that the rearguard should make its escape. But he would not move Force Reserve forward until he had 'ascertained the local situation at first hand from Brig. Puttick'.[30]

At 5.45 p.m. Weston, accompanied by Wills, duly appeared at the New Zealand Division Headquarters. Here they found Puttick more than ever convinced that the line was breaking. In a memorandum that he was preparing at the moment of Weston's arrival he had written that his brigadiers on each flank were reporting their 'total inability to hold their fronts after dark'. Any attempt to maintain the forward position would 'prejudice the possibility of holding a line further back behind which the Fwd tps could reform'. Moreover there was the special danger from the left flank. The German movement in the foothills might succeed in turning north to the Akrotiri Peninsula, thus cutting the narrow line of retreat.[31] He now told Weston of these apprehensions, and repeated his suggestion that the Welch should hold a covering position south from the tip of the bay.

Weston spoke to Vasey on the telephone. Shortly before noon the Australian had told Hargest that his men were 'fresh and . . . could hang on indefinitely'.[32] But this confidence had quickly evaporated at the sight of the movement round his left flank. Now he confirmed Puttick's view. Later Vasey was to recall this conversation:

About 1800 hrs Gen. Weston rang me from H.Q.N.Z. Div and I informed him of the situation and told him that I considered that it

[29] DP
[30] Ibid., a 'brief narrative' by Lieut.-Col. J. Wills, G.S.O.I. Suda Force
[31] New Zealand Division War Diary   [32] Davin, p. 341, Brig. Hargest's Diary

was not possible for me to retain my present posn or the line of the
wadi about 1000 yards in the rear of it until dark on the 27th May
i.e. for a period of about 30 hrs, and that I considered it necessary for
me, in conjunction with the N.Z. Div to withdraw to a shorter line
east of Suda Bay. Gen. Weston stated he was unable to give a
decision on this, but he would represent the matter to Gen.
Freyberg.[33]

Weston then went back to look for Freyberg. In the New
Zealand Divisional Report the time of his departure is noted
as 6.10 p.m. Wills believes it to have been not earlier than 7 p.m.

Certainly it was not until 9.30 p.m. that evening that Weston
was at length able to find the General and to tell him of Puttick's
continued anxieties. Freyberg did not change his mind. He again
insisted that he had decided to relieve the New Zealand Division,
bringing forward the Force Reserve, while at the same time
holding the southern part of the line with the 19th Australian and
Suda Brigades.[34] Weston had already warned the three reduced
battalions of the part that they were to play that night. He now
sent them their final orders to move.[35]

Less than an hour later, at 10.15 p.m., the two generals met
again. In order to 'make absolutely certain that the line was
holding',[36] Freyberg had gone forward to visit Weston in his new
Headquarters at 42nd Street. This was a sunken track that ran
south to the foothills from the main road at a point a mile west
of the docks; it owed its name to the fact that the 42nd Field
Company had been stationed in the neighbourhood before the
invasion. He told Weston of his proposal to Wavell that a withdrawal should be made through Sphakia.[37] At the same time he
sent a strongly worded order to Brigadier Vasey and Lieutenant-
Colonel Hely insisting that the line was to be held at all costs.[38]
The explanation for this special order appears in Freyberg's
Report:

I had seen General Weston (at 22.15 hrs) and been told by him
that the Australians were coming back but that the N.Z. troops were
holding the line. I at once sat down and wrote an order that the
Australians were to continue to hold their line.[39]

While he was at 42nd Street he 'saw the Australians in position
and they appeared absolutely confident'.[40] The phrase is taken

[33] Davin, p. 344   [34] DP   [35] Ibid.   [36] Ibid.
[37] Ibid.   [38] Ibid.   [39] Freyberg Report, quot. Davin, p. 346
[40] Long, p. 251

by the Australian War Historian to mean that he saw Vasey's brigade. But this cannot be true. The 2/7 and 2/8 Battalions were not to reach 42nd Street, together with the New Zealanders, until some hours later. Indeed Freyberg was to return to Egypt still under the impression that they had remained forward after the retirement of the New Zealanders.

There is no explanation for the fact that Weston should have told him that 'the Australians were coming back'. It has been seen that Vasey's recollection of their telephone conversation was to be very different. He had merely said that he 'considered' that a move to the east of Suda, 'in conjunction with the N.Z. Div', would be necessary. He had understood that Weston was 'unable to give a decision on this, but would represent the matter to General Freyberg'.[41]

Stranger still was the fact that another two hours were to pass before Weston attempted to inform Puttick of the final decision from Freyberg that the line must be held. Not until 1.10 a.m. did he send a despatch rider with a message which said:

BRIG PUTTICK

G.O.C. in C has ordered that 4 N.Z. Div must hold present positions tonight 26/27 May until relieved by 1 Welch, NH and 1 Rangers. These latter units received orders to move about 2000 hrs and they should move up about midnight.

0110 hrs. W. H. Wills Lt-Col G.S.O. 1 Suda Area H.Q's.[42]

In terminology it was a little confused. The phrase '4 N.Z. Div', remarks the New Zealand War Historian charitably, was 'presumably a loose way of saying 5 Bde'. It seems more likely that the digit '4' had been written in error for '2',[43] since elements of both the 4th and 10th Brigades were still in the forward area, and Freyberg's intention had been to bring back the New Zealand Division as a whole. But the general sense was clear enough. The line was to stand fast until relieved. Neither Weston nor Freyberg had understood that Puttick still regarded the Australian Brigade as part of his Command.

Freyberg now returned to Suda Pier, picking his way along the shattered quayside through a silent group of walking wounded, among them many stragglers whose hopes had been raised by the appearance of the mine layer *Abdiel* and the two destroyers *Hero*

---

[41] See above, p. 407
[42] New Zealand Division War Diary
[43] The New Zealand Division was officially entitled the Second New Zealand Division, although only one division ever became operational in the West.

and *Nizam*. These ships had carried the vital supplies. They had also brought Colonel Laycock, who was in charge of the Commandos, together with the main body of his force, which now reached a strength of two battalions of 400 men each. Freyberg told him that if he did not get his troops off the docks they would be 'heavily dive-bombed at daylight'. He explained that there was no longer any hope of holding the island. The Commandos would be needed as part of the rearguard.

As he was leaving, he ordered the despatch to Retimo of a Motor Landing Craft loaded with ten tons of rations. It was to hide up near Suda Point during the following day before continuing on the night of the 27th. Well before that time, so he supposed, he would have Wavell's permission to abandon the island. He would then be able to give Lieutenant Haig, the young officer in charge, a message for Campbell explaining the situation and ordering the retirement of the Retimo garrison to the south coast. In the meantime, however, he said nothing to Haig of this intention. Nor did he tell him specifically that he must wait until dusk on the 27th.

It was past midnight before he started back to his Headquarters at Suda Point. Here he hoped to find a response to his urgent message of the late afternoon. Despite the catastrophe which he could see approaching, this had been for him a more congenial day, better to his taste than he had found it sitting in isolation in his quarry. As the rattle of small-arms began to echo through the olive groves at Suda, and the signs of panic and defeat appeared on every side, he was back again on familiar ground. He knew that every man must now depend upon him, as his brigade had depended upon him during the German onslaught in March and April 1918. He alone could save something from disaster.

A reply had arrived from Cairo. 'The gist of the telegram I received,' he was to say later, 'was that General Evetts was arriving by Sunderland as L.O. and that I would find him useful as he was an expert in "I" tanks'.[44] The signal went on to suggest that the retreat should continue to Retimo and that the east of the island should be held. He 'did not derive much comfort from this helpful advice'. As he pointed out, it 'indicated complete ignorance of the strength of the Retimo road blocks and the latest reports of a German sea landing at Georgeoupolis'.[45]

Many years later, he was to recall that 'at this time we were

[44] DP   [45] Long, p. 254

having a good deal of difficulty with the Middle East'.[46]

The Germans had not yet landed at Georgeoupolis. But they still held the road block at Retimo. And it was plain that they might put small parties ashore at any moment. If they did, they could scarcely expect to find easier victims for ambush than exhausted men without food, water, transport or ammunition, constantly hunted by the *Luftwaffe* and spread out over the seventy miles of exposed coast road which lay between them and the first hope of relief at Heraklion.

At one o'clock in the morning, Freyberg despatched an answer in which he sought to clarify the situation beyond misunderstanding. He began by saying that it was apparent that the true 'situation was not understood in Egypt'.[47] The garrison at Retimo was short of food and ammunition and was cut off by road from all directions. In the Western Sector the lack of gun tractors had led to the loss of the artillery. Despite a large ration strength the number of his effective troops was very small. Most of them had never been fit to take part in any kind of offensive action; among these there had now been a serious fall in morale. The front-line infantry were near exhaustion and had been constantly battered by the overwhelming *Luftwaffe*. In such circumstances the suggested plan for withdrawal on Retimo could lead only to certain catastrophe. There was indeed only one hope of saving some of his force. The troops must hide up during the day and withdraw at night to selected beaches. He therefore again proposed urgently that the retreat should be made towards the south. It would help if more commandos could be landed to assist the rearguard. At the same time it must be remembered that Retimo was also in danger unless the men there could be rescued at once. As for the ideas about tanks, he would like to point out that armoured vehicles, operating in daylight under the dive bombers, could scarcely hope to survive for more than a few minutes. Finally, as in so many of his signals, he returned to the subject of the enemy air onslaught. After every successful counter-attack his troops had been quickly blown out of their new positions by a renewed deluge of heavy bombs. What they required above all was air support.

If he had known of the drama that was developing west of Canea his anxieties would have been all the greater.

[46] DP, Freyberg comments on Davin Draft, 1952 (undated)
[47] Davin, p. 366

After Weston had gone, Puttick waited hour after hour without further word. By this time a wireless link had been established with Force Headquarters. But he had no contact with Weston's new command post at 42nd Street. Twice he signalled to Suda Point asking for news. Freyberg had not returned. Nothing was known of any further development. The replies were not helpful. At 10.15 p.m. he was told simply that he was under the command of Weston who would 'issue orders'.[48]

His dilemma can be imagined. He remained convinced of the necessity for immediate withdrawal, believing that every hour must increase the probability that 'the enemy movement round Vasey's left flank . . . would cut the line of retreat at the head of Suda Bay'.[49] At best his troops would be caught by the *Luftwaffe* in daylight while moving through the bottle-neck along the Bay. For all he knew, Weston might have been killed by an attack from the air on his way back. The cover of night, that boon so precious to the defenders in Crete, would be lost before fresh orders could reach him from Suda Point. At 10.30 p.m. he decided that he could wait no longer. He ordered a withdrawal to begin at half past eleven. He sent Captain Bell, an Intelligence Officer, to Weston with a message which stated his intention:

New Zealand Division urgently awaits your orders. Cannot wait any longer as bde comds represent situation on their front as most urgent. Propose retiring with or without orders by 1130 hours (11.30 p.m.) 26 May . . .[50]

A few minutes later he heard over the telephone from one of Vasey's staff officers that a runner had just brought from Freyberg the signal that the 19th Brigade must maintain its position 'at all costs'. Whether or not he found this information disconcerting he at once, in the words of the New Zealand War Historian, took 'full responsibility for countermanding General Freyberg's orders'.[51] Only a few minutes earlier he had 'telephoned Hargest and Vasey personally',[52] to authorize the retirement which they had been expecting since early that morning. The movement had hardly begun. But he did nothing to arrest it. And so he came to behave in a manner that was in total contrast with his usual punctilious deference to higher authority. On the first day he had

[48] New Zealand Division War Diary
[49] DP, Puttick comments on McClymont Narrative
[50] Davin, p. 348   [51] Ibid., p. 349
[52] DP, Puttick comments on McClymont Narrative

failed to make use of the 4th Brigade, although fully empowered to dispose of it as he pleased. Now, when all discretion had been refused, he defied his own nature and, in the teeth of Freyberg's explicit instructions, led his men to the rear. The Australians went too, together with Suda Brigade and the Greeks in the hills.

Another three hours were to pass before he received the message for which he had waited so long. At 1.45 a.m. a signal was handed to him while he was in his car on the way to Suda. It was the order that Weston had written at 1.10 a.m., with its confirmation that the New Zealanders were to hold until relieved by Force Reserve.

After much wandering in the dark, Captain Bell had 'eventually found'[53] Weston's Headquarters at 42nd Street. Here his tale of the withdrawal attracted less interest than he had expected. He made a note at the time: 'General Weston and his staff of M.N.B.D.O. are hopelessly out of touch with the situation.'[54] After the war he was to recall that he had experienced 'difficulty in getting access to General Weston personally that night. I think Weston was asleep when I arrived but my message was certainly delivered, if not to General Weston himself then to his G.S.O.I.'[55]

In his Report Weston makes no mention of the visit of Captain Bell. But to judge by the timing of subsequent messages it seems probable that at about 1 a.m. somebody must have thought it worth while to awaken him with the news that the New Zealanders were coming back – and with them the Australians and Suda Brigade. At this it occurred to him that Force Reserve might shortly be finding itself in a position of considerable embarrassment.

This withdrawal obviously left the Welch, N.H., and the Rangers in a very difficult position [he says in his report], and I sent a signal to them ordering them to withdraw immediately along the Suda Road. Some difficulty was found in getting D.Rs to take this message but two were despatched at about 0130 hours.[56]

Scarcely had he settled back to sleep when more visitors arrived. This time it was Puttick himself, together with Hely. After the war Puttick was to recall their conversation. He had asked why no orders had been sent to him. To this Weston replied

[53] DP, letter from Capt. R. M. Bell, dated 1 Mar. 1951, quoting notes that he had made under the heading 26 May 1941
[54] Ibid.   [55] DP, Capt. R. M. Bell, 1 Mar. 1951
[56] Weston Report, June 1941, quot. Davin, p. 361

that it was 'no use sending orders as Div Comd had made it very
clear that NZ Div was retiring whatever happened'.[57] This re-
mark, comments the New Zealand War Historian, can only have
been promoted by exhaustion since, if Weston 'had really believed
that the retirement would take place whatever happened, his
action in sending Force Reserve forward would be quite incomprehensible'.[58] Such is the reasoned view. Or, just possibly, he may
have felt that the sacrifice of Force Reserve could be justified in
the hope of delaying the Germans – and then changed his mind.
But all the evidence suggests that he was past the capacity to
make any considered calculation. Rather is it likely that his
comment was no more than a tart reference to Puttick's 10.30 p.m.
message about retirement 'with or without orders', and that it
can be taken as confirmation that this message had indeed
reached him a few minutes earlier. Weston himself says of this
meeting no more than that the two officers informed him of the
situation. Whereupon he directed them both to 'report to General
Freyberg'.[59] There is no record that anyone asked Puttick
whether he might have thought of notifying Force Reserve of
what he had done.

While Puttick and Hely set out for Suda Point, and Weston
resumed his interrupted sleep, the men of Force Reserve were
deploying beyond Canea Bridge. Their appointed commander
was not with them. Brigadier Inglis, still with his fellow New
Zealanders, was moving east through Suda on his way to Stilos.

For a week the men of Force Reserve had been fighting a series
of small actions scattered about Akrotiri and the outskirts of
Canea. They had killed and captured some 250 of the enemy and
had themselves suffered about the same number of casualties.
Little news had reached them from the battles at Maleme and
Galatas. Along the shores of the peninsula the surf had still
sparkled among the rocks and inlets, reminding them of home,
and women, and holidays in the sun. But these memories had
grown more remote with each day that passed. Gradually they
had begun to understand the meaning of that recurring roar
swelling and fading from the west, and to realize with sharpening
awareness that it carried a promise of death.

On the morning of the 26th, at about eight o'clock, the Rangers had been told that they would be required that night to take over defensive positions from the New Zealanders west of Canea. For this operation, like the Northumberland Hussars, they would 'come under command 1/Welch'.[60] By the early afternoon the three depleted battalions were concentrated and ready.

Until late in the evening, Duncan had stayed at the New Zealand Divisional Headquarters trying to find out what was to happen.

> There was some strong language at the Conference [he wrote later]. I was hanging about on the fringe and heard some of it. Everyone, including Inglis, pressed for the holding of the rear line. In fact Inglis informed me he had made a recce of it. Weston would not alter his wish to hold the forward line. It was pointed out to him (Weston) that if he sent Force Reserve forward he would never see them again.[61]

Soon after Weston had departed, Duncan returned to his battalion. Inglis did not accompany him. Some time later, Weston's final orders reached the Welch Headquarters; according to Major Gibson, second in command of the battalion, it was 'probably considerably later'[62] than 10 p.m. before Duncan learnt that the original plan was unchanged. Force Reserve was to relieve the New Zealanders west of Canea Bridge. On the left, south of the Prison Road, would be a 'mixed force known as the Royal Perivolians . . . and on their left again some Australian troops'.[63] The last words of the order were:

> Final evacuation from Sphakia on South Coast.[64]

Shortly after midnight the men of Force Reserve began to move off the Akrotiri Peninsula down the steep road into Canea. Under the fading moon, the stricken town lay dark and empty and reeking with the stink of death. Every few minutes a red flash lit the sky as a shell rumbled overhead from one of the Naval guns at Suda. Scattered fires cast wavering shadows across the broken houses, while the flames murmured softly among the debris. There was no other sound and no movement anywhere.

With difficulty the troops picked their way past the bomb craters and the burning vehicles. Some had heard the whisper of

---

[60] DP, letter to Gen. Freyberg from Maj. A. R. W. Low of 'The Rangers', dated 5 Aug. 1941

[61] Lieut.-Col. A. Duncan, letter to the author, dated 4 Feb. 1963

[62] DP, Report by Maj. J. T. Gibson of the Welch Regiment, dated 12 Aug. 1941

[63] Ibid.   [64] Ibid.

evacuation. They did not speak of it. The Rangers, short of equipment and at half strength, and the 200 men of the Northumberland Hussars, well knew the ordeal that must await them in a
pitched infantry battle. But the 700 soldiers of the Welch
Regiment felt themselves as good as any in Crete. They would
have preferred an attacking part with a prospect of victory. But
they were glad enough to enter the fray in any capacity. They
moved west with grim and sober confidence.

Gibson caught a glimpse of two New Zealanders as he was
crossing Canea Bridge. It did not occur to him to say anything to
them as he was 'expecting to see New Zealanders'.[65] That night
he was to see no more of them.

The Rangers and the Northumberland Hussars took up unprepared positions close to the river, while the Welch filed out
into the olive groves, and over the ridges, to occupy the trenches
which they had dug four weeks earlier. Soon they were a mile
beyond the bridge, with the battalion spread in a wide arc convex
to the west, its right flank on the sea and its left across the
Alikianou Road. In the darkness the men stumbled over the
bodies of the unburied dead, and they noticed that much of the
equipment which they found was German. But they saw not a
living man, neither friend nor enemy. By 2.30 a.m. 'everyone was
in position'.[66] The moon had set and the night was black and
silent. To one at least of the officers there came unbidden the
memory of words spoken two days before in the House of
Commons and quoted over a dying wireless set: 'Neither side has
any means of retreat.'[67]

The first stragglers from Suda, the outriders of defeat, were
already far to the south, climbing the mountain road to Sphakia.
And in London the Prime Minister, awake and active as usual at
this hour, was sending another exhortation to the Middle East.
It was timed at 1.35 a.m.

Victory in Crete essential at this turning point of the war.

And it added:

Keep hurling in all aid you can.[68]

In the circumstances it was not one of his happiest phrases.

Throughout that week-end all available ships of the British

[65] DP, Report by Maj. J. T. Gibson, dated 12 Aug. 1941   [66] Ibid.
[67] See above, p. 359, Churchill in the House of Commons, 22 May 1941
[68] Churchill, Vol. III, p. 262

Navy in the North Atlantic had been converging upon the wounded *Bismarck*. 'Poring over the charts' in Church House he had 'followed every shift and change in the drama'[69] with a zest made all the greater by his thirst to see revenge for the *Hood*. This diversion had done nothing to diminish the anguish with which he continued to contemplate the struggle in the Eastern Mediterranean. But now his contact with events in Crete had so far declined that it matched the impotence with which he still sought in vain to influence them.

During the early hours of the morning, a few of the enemy filtered through to the southern outskirts of Canea on the heels of Suda Brigade. In this area a small detachment of the Welch was guarding the battalion transport. At dawn there were some harsh encounters among the trees. Sergeant Creighton remembered later:

One of the drivers asked me if he could go for a short walk to stretch his legs. He went, but did not return. Presently two little Greek boys came out of the wood, one of whom had been shot in the back by a German. We grabbed our rifles and moved stealthily into the wood. I hadn't got far when I saw a German officer about fifty yards from me. He was immaculately dressed, with beautifully polished helmet and boots. He wore no equipment but was holding an automatic pistol in his left hand. He waved the pistol and shouted in English, 'Come on boys'. I saw no other movement and I think he was bluffing. I shot him in the chest and he fell dead.[70]

As it grew lighter Welch patrols began to probe left up the stream of the Kladiso. At once they clashed with Germans. They found no sign of supporting troops. Along the front all remained quiet. But an hour after dawn shots were heard from the direction of the Canea-Suda road. Here was that disconcerting alarm signal familiar to all soldiers, the sound of firing where no firing should be, briefly at first, then repeated and sustained, soon proclaiming beyond all doubt that the enemy had penetrated far to the rear.

At 7 a.m. Messerschmitt fighters, with guns blazing, searched both banks of the river. They did little damage. After their departure, the hot, still morning was again uneasily silent. Invisible to each other, the men on each side listened for the snap of a twig or the sound of a footstep on the roadway.

[69] Chandos, p. 345

[70] De Courcy, *History of the Welch Regiment*, p. 61, Sgt. T. Creighton

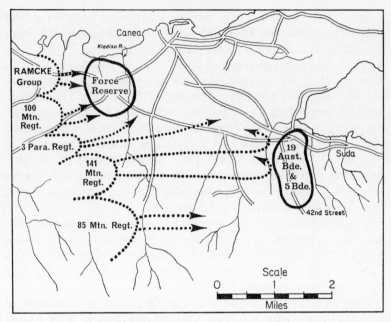

21. Canea–Suda: 11 a.m., 27 May

Five German Regiments stood poised for the advance on Suda.
The Ramcke Group of the Storm Regiment remained astride the
coast road. Ranged in order to the south were the Utz battalions
of the 100 Mountain Regiment, 3 Parachute Regiment, 141
Mountain Regiment, under Colonel Jais, and Krakau's 85
Mountain Regiment in the foothills south of Perivolia.

At first the Germans did not understand that the New
Zealanders had withdrawn. It was not until 6.45 a.m. that Jais
heard over the telephone from Ringel that Utz had lost contact
with the enemy south of Platanos, a village on the Canea-
Alikianou road. He was told to take his regiment through to the
head of Suda Bay and so cut off the enemy's retreat. At 7.30 a.m.
he started to advance, his leading battalion pushing confidently
forward with its companies widely deployed among the olives.
About an hour later, Ringel launched a general assault backed by
many machine-guns and mortars.

On a front that was a full mile and a half long, the 1,200 men
of Force Reserve now faced at least 4,500 Germans thrusting not
only from the west but into the open left flank. Duncan quickly

realized that the attack was making unopposed progress in the
south. He could not know why. He had heard nothing from
Weston since the arrival of the final order to move. 'Right from
the start' his Headquarters had been 'trying to make contact with
Weston's H.Q. by wireless'. But his operators 'never got them',
and 'no message of any sort got through'[71] from Suda. His runners
could no longer find a way past the infiltrating Germans, and the
Bren-carriers that might have run through them down the road
had all been taken from him a few days earlier. That morning
they would have been 'worth their weight in gold'.[72] At nine
o'clock he sent back a captain with the news that there was no
resistance on his left and that the enemy was advancing on Suda.
This officer failed to reach 42nd Street.

It made little difference. Weston had long since written off the
men whom he had sent out into the darkness on the previous
night. At this moment he and his staff were setting out for Neo
Khorion, eighteen miles away on the road to Sphakia. He had
left no instructions about Force Reserve.

The Germans now found that there had been no lessening of
the opposition along the coast. At 10 a.m. Ramcke told Ringel
that the enemy had 'reoccupied the positions . . . which he had
evacuated yesterday'. He made a request for 'Stuka raids',[73] while
urging his men to renew their attacks. At the same time the Utz
battalions pressed forward towards the Kladiso. The scattered
Welch companies were quickly penetrated. Fire poured in upon
them from all sides. Communication failed. One after another,
the runners were killed as they tried to cross open ground carrying
their messages. By noon it was clear to Duncan that his battalion,
already nearly surrounded, was being cut to pieces where it
stood.

From his command post, under a bank two hundred yards west
of the bridge, he could hear that saddest of changes in the clamour
of battle – the sounds that tell of the weapons of friends borne
down by those of the enemy; everywhere the stabbing of the rifles
and Brens was being slowly extinguished by the tearing rattle of
the Spandaus and the churning and crash of the mortars. He
decided that he must try to bring back B and D Companies from
the left flank. With great difficulty orders were got through to
them. At last a few men began to come running in groups out

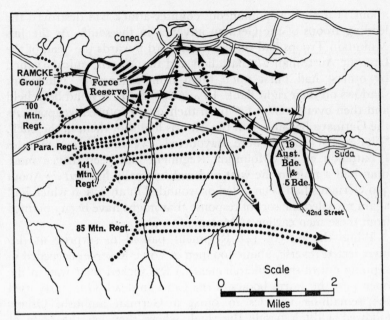

22.   Encirclement of Force Reserve

of the trees, splashing through the shallow water of the river and dropping for a moment behind the stone walls to fire at their pursuers before stumbling on. The Mountain Troops were close behind. Grey uniforms could be seen among the sun-dappled plantations east of the stream. Duncan told Gibson to take the survivors through Canea in small parties, and to reorganize on the Suda road. With them he sent those that could be reached of the Rangers and the Northumberland Hussars.

Some passed south of the town, out of range, now, of the mortars. But under the blazing sun, now directly overhead, the dusty orchards were alive with the unseen enemy. Machine-guns chattered abruptly from the thickets, and long bursts of fire swept among the leaves. The scattered groups of khaki figures moved steadily from cover to cover. After about an hour they reached a clearing among the olives. And suddenly they were aware that on the far side a line of riflemen lay silently awaiting them. At first they thought themselves trapped. For a time they hesitated, then cautiously came nearer. The helmets were flat.

This was the defence line at 42nd Street. Two hours earlier, at about 11 a.m.,[74] a spontaneous counter-attack had destroyed the leading troops of the German advance in the south. As the Jais Mountain Troops had turned northward towards the head of the bay, the Australian 2/7 Battalion and the Maoris, quickly joined by others, had burst upon them from among the patchwork shadows on their right flank. In a savage fight they had been held and then overcome by fire from their own captured weapons. As the Germans began to run the Maoris had shot them in the back. 'Those that stayed were bayoneted.' Within a few minutes I Battalion of 141 Mountain Regiment had been driven more than half a mile to the west and was 'virtually finished'.[75] About 300 Germans had been killed or wounded in an action which had again revealed the sort of response that might have been obtained from these men earlier at Maleme.[76]

While the rest of 141 Regiment paused in surprise at this unexpected reverse, about 400 men of Force Reserve succeeded in slipping out of their encirclement. A few picked their way in the open past the warm bodies of the German dead. One party used the remaining vehicles to burst a German ambush. Others followed a ditch beside the road, where they left the body of the Welch quartermaster, the veteran of 1917.

Duncan had stayed behind. Early in the afternoon, with the Germans all around, he was joined at the Kladiso Bridge by those members of C and D companies who had been able to escape the fire that was sweeping the ridges on the right. At this point all the main elements of the German assault were now converging. Kurt Meyer had accompanied the advance of the Utz battalions northward along the bed of the stream. He saw them break from the undergrowth and run towards the bridge:

We bring to bear all the machine-gun fire that we have in order to cover the last seconds of our comrades' advance. A croaky hurrah breaks out from half-dried throats. Hand grenades fly. The defenders tear their machine-guns round . . . and set them in the face of the attackers, but the German machine-pistols are quicker. With hand grenades and bayonets the yellow shadows spring out of their holes and defend themselves. They won't surrender. Nearly fifty . . . cover

[74] There are varying reports about the time of this attack. The War Diary of the 141 Mountain Regiment says that III Battalion, which was some way behind I Battalion, first reported 'heavy enemy counter-attacks' at about 11.25 a.m.

[75] Davin, p. 378

[76] The 141 Mountain Regiment War Diary says of I Battalion that 'most of the officers and many other ranks had been killed or wounded'

with their bodies this last bulwark before Canea. Only four men, pale and shattered, are taken as prisoners.[77]

Some 200 of the Welch, together with a few dozen of the Rangers and Northumberland Hussars, remained with their Commanding Officer, who was now manning a Bren gun. They fought back through the main street of the town. The bullet marks that today fleck the walls of the houses, clustering about every window and doorway, bear evidence of a bitter resistance that did not end until late in the afternoon among the rocks and boulders of the Akrotiri Peninsula. From 42nd Street Hargest watched their last stand.

Up on Suda Hill enemy bombers and fighters were blasting at a village to our surprise until we found that the Welch Regt and Rangers, who had gone out to beyond Canea with the mistaken idea that they could hold the line Vasey and I had left, had been smashed to bits in a few minutes and had been driven up to the hill village where they were annihilated. Whoever sent them should be shot.[78]

And far to the west, in their gun pits on a small knoll near the old Hospital Peninsula, part of a Welch platoon under a sergeant, held on into the following morning. Captured New Zealanders watched in admiration. A wounded officer saw a Bren gun team which

fired bursts all day. . . . Then must have run short of ammo. One man got out and in full view of the Germans walked 100 yds round the hillside – walked with no intention of hurrying though bullets were hitting the bare hillside. We could see every strike at his feet and above him on the slope. He got into a gun-pit, emerged with two Bren mag carriers and walked back at the same pace – bullets and mortars. The gun went into action again. . . . Patients cheered the inspiring sight.[79]

Throughout the morning Ringel had continued in his belief that the 'main enemy force'[80] still lay before him in Canea. And 141 Mountain Regiment had been expecting that, by cutting the Suda Road, they would achieve 'a great victory'.[81] Indeed the War Diary of the 5th Mountain Division, as though in explanation of the relative slowness of the advance, contains the entry:

We were opposed in this sector by a battalion of English *élite* troops

[77] Kurt Meyer, *Struggle for the Strongpoint of Crete*   [78] DP, Hargest's Diary
[79] Davin, p. 372, Report by Capt. R. S. Sinclair
[80] 5th Mountain Division War Diary   [81] 141 Mountain Regiment War Diary

(Welshmen) who had been ordered to hold their position to the last man.

Not until 'about midday' did Ringel first gain 'the general impression . . . that the enemy intended to abandon Canea and Suda Bay'.[82] He now again urged Jais to press forward to the head of the water. This the Mountain Troops succeeded in doing by about 3 p.m., while von der Heydte came in from the south to occupy the town. But Kurt Meyer noted that the 'total of prisoners' was 'very small'.[83,84]

As with so much that went wrong in Crete, the breakdown of communications was the root cause of the disaster that befell Force Reserve. During many critical hours, there had been neither wireless nor line contact between the New Zealand Division and Weston's new Headquarters at 42nd Street. In the face of a signal relaying further insistence from Freyberg that he must stay until relieved, Puttick could scarcely have withdrawn. Had he, nevertheless, finally determined that he must defy this order, he could still, if he had possessed a radio transmitter, have notified Suda Area in time for Weston to have stopped the movement of Force Reserve.

Further complication had been introduced with the change in command. By putting Weston in charge of all the forces in the Canea-Suda area Freyberg had hoped that the scattered New Zealand Division could be given an opportunity to reorganize under its Commander. Moreover, it had seemed at first that the troops making up the rearguard would assemble in Suda and would largely be British. These considerations had scarcely justified the change at such a critical time. More comprehensible is the explanation assumed at the time by Gentry and confided

[82] 5th Mountain Division War Diary

[83] Kurt Meyer, *Struggle for the Strongpoint of Crete*

[84] Gericke, p. 120, describes the scene in Canea. 'The houses are burnt black where the fires have raged, and the great bomb craters have made the streets almost impassable. Women and children run hither and thither among the wreckage, and between them dart dogs and cats. Thick clouds of smoke rise from a burning oil installation. And over all hangs the burning heat. Pitilessly the sun blazes down. Now the streets fill with parachutists, thankful that they have succeeded after all, and happy to be among the survivors. . . . Hundreds of the English march as prisoners through the streets, and mixed with them are the Italians, themselves just freed from imprisonment, in torn dirty uniforms, their unabashed southern temperament overflowing as they weep with joy, dancing and singing and kissing the parachutists. . . . Suddenly the released German prisoners appear and run to mix with the seething crowd in the central square.'

later to Kippenberger, that Freyberg had 'lost confidence' in Puttick.[85]

The confusion created by the change in command had been aggravated by the fatigue of the men concerned. In no phase of the battle are the characters of the leading officers in Crete more clearly revealed than on this day and night of 26 May. Freyberg himself, shedding his earlier uncertainty, had continued to grow in stature with every moment that brought the enemy nearer. Turning his back at last upon the disastrous advice still reaching him from Cairo and London, he had remained calm amidst the gathering panic that surrounded him. With little hope of the outcome, but with the utmost resolution, he had chosen for himself the single course which he now knew to be right.

Others had become less sure of their actions and of themselves. Both Weston and Puttick were professional soldiers, rigid in outlook, and reluctant to take any serious initiative without higher authority. As the situation worsened each had behaved in a manner that seemed to the other as incomprehensible as it was unforgivable. In their dismay, bereft suddenly of the comfort and support of that military order upon which they had always relied, they had allowed themselves to become stampeded into actions which could not fail to be disastrous since they had not sufficiently calculated their consequences.

From a legalistic point of view, Puttick had been given no reason to complain of lack of orders. Categorically he had been told to stand until relieved. Weston had refused to absolve him from that responsibility. But in leaving him hour after hour without further news, after consenting to question Freyberg's decision, Weston had shown a singular lack of imagination. Above all, he had failed to understand the confiding yet independent spirit of the New Zealanders. He may even have believed that in thus postponing further reference to an order which Puttick had already twice contested he was making easier acceptance of the inevitable. This, however, cannot explain a delay so protracted that the final instruction for the relief could not have reached the New Zealand Headquarters until an hour after the intended arrival of Force Reserve.

Certainly Weston was staggered by the outcome. It seems never to have occurred to him that Puttick might come back at his own discretion 'with or without orders'. Such waywardness outraged the conceptions of a lifetime. Indeed it seems to have brought him suddenly to despair. There was no gaiety left in him now, nor any of that brisk good sense which he had shown during his brief command of the island.

General Weston came to me on the 27th [Freyberg was to write later], and said that owing to the terrible conditions and the appalling casualties that we should have we must capitulate and all surrender.[86]

Something of this collapse of confidence can be seen in his attitude to the fate of Force Reserve. It would appear that some weeks later he was requested to furnish more information about the events of the night of 26/27 May. Already he had revealed that the vital message recalling Duncan had been entrusted to a pair of despatch riders found after 'some difficulty'. On 3 July 1941, in an addendum to his Report, he revealed that, although the official records of the orders issued in Crete had been lost, copies of some of them had later been recovered and the officers and men concerned interrogated.

The two despatch riders are again mentioned:

These D.Rs have since been interviewed and the fact that the message was delivered to the Welch H.Q. has been established. The D.Rs arrived back at Suda H.Q. at 0345 hours.[87]

The implication is plain. Little notice had been taken of these men until their evidence was sought for an inquiry in Egypt.

Why had they not been closely examined upon their return to 42nd Street? Had this been done it must surely have been realized that they had been unable to find Force Reserve. Wills formed the impression, no doubt upon the strength of what they told him, that it had never reached its position but had been 'caught moving up'.[88] It can only be assumed, therefore, that the despatch riders never went beyond the town. Certainly the manner of their instruction, as related by Weston, does not encourage the belief that any great attempt had been made to impress upon them the significance of their task. And it was no light thing to ask two young soldiers to ride alone through the night, upon noisy motor cycles, into what they believed to be

---

[86] DP, Freyberg letter to Brigs. Puttick and Hargest, dated 27.6, almost certainly 1941
[87] Weston Report, Addendum, 3 July 1941, quot. Davin, p. 361
[88] DP, a 'brief narrative' by Lieut.-Col. J. Wills, G.S.O.I. Suda Force

territory occupied by the enemy. The dark and menacing streets
of Canea must once more have appeared utterly deserted, with
nothing to indicate that an hour earlier twelve hundred men had
passed through to the west. Nevertheless, it was unfortunate that
Weston, or his staff, had not sent to accompany them at least one
experienced officer, fully informed of all that hung upon the
success of his mission, under orders to stake his life upon finding
Duncan. Such an enterprise was less desperate than appeared at
the time. It would indeed have been entirely simple. The road led
straight over Canea Bridge into the heart of the position to which
Force Reserve had been directed. Nor is there reason to suppose
that any living German was in contact with it that night.[89]

Now the truth can be known from Duncan:

No message to withdraw was received by me from any source.
I would have been off like a 'scalded cat' if I (it) had. I was quite
aware how precarious our position was.

Long after the battle, when he heard about the despatch riders,
it occurred to him that they must have gone to 'the people on our
left' whom he believed to have been 'actually in position at one
time during the night'.[90]

In the light of what he was hearing from his brigadiers, it is easy
to sympathize with Puttick's conviction that the New Zealand
Division must withdraw during the night if it were to avoid
destruction. He may well have been thinking of his experience in
the First World War. Many times, in 1914 and 1918, battalions
had been lost unnecessarily because their commanding officers
had not dared to act upon their own initiative after runners
had failed to reach them with orders to retire. And here was
this stiff-necked Englishman behaving in just that rigid and
unthinking way that Dominion Troops had learnt to fear. Nor
was it only the New Zealanders who were in danger. Puttick still
believed himself to be responsible for the Australians as well. In
these circumstances, influenced further no doubt by the fact that
his instructions for the withdrawal must by now be passing
through the battalions, he had felt no hesitation in making his
counter-order to Vasey, even after hearing over the telephone that
Freyberg had said that the Australians must stand where they
were. Thus, to some extent, it was misunderstanding, brought

---

[89] Not a shot was fired at the troops of Force Reserve as they moved west along it
between midnight and 2 a.m. Observed by the author

[90] Lieut.-Col. A. Duncan, letter to the author, 4 Feb. 1963

about by the sudden switch in the chain of command, that had encouraged him to destroy not only the centre but also the left flank of the line upon which Freyberg and Weston had hoped to hold through the following day.

But in taking it upon himself to move east Puttick had automatically incurred a further responsibility which he did not fulfil. It has been said that the affairs of Force Reserve were nothing to do with him. This remained true only for so long as he continued to obey his own orders. Once he had decided to go against them he might have asked himself what result must follow if Freyberg and Weston were in fact still pursuing their original plan. Nothing would have been simpler than to send an officer walking down the main road to Canea with instructions to meet the relieving force, if indeed it should appear, and to explain the new situation to the Commanding Officer. This he failed to do.

The third actor in this drama was Inglis. He was a man very different from Weston and Puttick. After his service in the First World War he had for twenty years been exercising a swift and flexible intelligence upon his practice of the law. As a soldier he was now resolved to place these same mental qualities at the service of his country, and in this capacity he had quickly found himself impatient of his superiors. Particularly galling to him in Crete had been Puttick's reluctance to engage his reserves in the Prison Valley and at Maleme. Not without reason, he believed that promotion might soon afford him more scope to exercise those talents of which he was confidently aware. In sombre contrast with such hopes there had come to him out of the blue this totally unexpected commission offering little more than the probability of death or capture upon a forlorn venture among strangers. But the order was unequivocal. And from Freyberg himself. What can be said of his failure to obey it?

In truth there can exist for him only one justification – that he believed the order to have been cancelled. This was the explanation that he offered after the war. He refers to the moment when Weston was leaving the New Zealand Headquarters to return to Freyberg with Puttick's plea for an immediate retirement on Suda:

As Weston was about to go I tackled him about the 'new Brigade'. He was hurried and worried and very short with me; but I gathered that he intended to use these troops himself and not through me. In any event, neither then nor at any other time did he give them any orders through me, and I did not attempt to make confusion worse confounded by giving them any myself.[91]

He can scarcely claim, however, that there is anything here to show that Weston, when importuned in this way, had released him from Freyberg's specific order.

At 4.30 p.m. Duncan had arrived to join him at the New Zealand Headquarters. It might be supposed that he would at once have conferred urgently with the Commanding Officer of the 1st Welch, since this battalion formed the heart and centre of Force Reserve. Together the two of them could have looked at the ground and sought out Hargest in order to discuss the take-over. He could have no reason for postponing all activity on the chance that Puttick might succeed in his agitation for withdrawal. Yet he did nothing. By 7 p.m., or perhaps somewhat earlier, Weston had departed, still refusing to accept Puttick's application. It thus remained probable that Force Reserve would be required to relieve the New Zealanders in the way that Freyberg had described to him. Now surely was the time for him to hasten to the Akrotiri Peninsula and there take over his new command.

Why did he still not go? Why indeed had he not left the New Zealand Division during the two hours that preceded Weston's visit? He seems to have felt that some explanation is required, although none would be necessary if he were content to rest on the assumption that Weston had released him from his obligation. In fact he offers several. Among them is the suggestion that he 'wanted to make sure that 4 Bde was not left out in the cold'.[92] He also says that he was waiting for the Force Reserve Commanding Officers, and that, in his 'own view', because they did not all arrive, he 'never got command of the Composite Bde at all'.[93] Again:

Nothing was done at Force H.Q. (while I was there) as regards the actual assumption of command of the 'new Brigade' or its organization. It was left to me to fix-up when the C.Os reported to me, and the Gen sent me off with the assurance that he would have them report to me at N.Z. Div.[94]

[91] DP, Inglis to Kippenberger, 16 May 1951   [92] Ibid.
[93] DP, comments by Inglis on Davin Draft, 15 Mar. 1951
[94] DP, Inglis to Kippenberger, 16 May 1951

But Boileau of the Rangers, whom he had met at Force Head-quarters, might be presumed to have returned to his men. And Duncan was already with him. Did the validity of Freyberg's order hinge upon the appearance of a major commanding 200 men of the Northumberland Hussars? Had it been necessary to wait two vital hours for this officer? He adds: 'There was no possibility of my going off to look for the units because I had to move on my flat feet.'[95] This is scarcely accurate. Duncan was there. Puttick could have told him that Duncan had a car. Duncan had spent nearly four weeks on the Akrotiri Peninsula and knew exactly where to find all three of the battalions. Indeed, as he could have made clear, they had been concentrated since early afternoon and were ready to move. The figure of Duncan threatens the whole structure of this defence.

The Commanding Officer of the 1st Welch, whose 'admiration for the New Zealanders' had always been 'unbounded', [96] did not know why he had been told to report to Inglis. While 'hanging about on the fringes' of Puttick's headquarters, he had gathered that a senior officer might be appointed to Force Reserve. But, again in his own words: 'Once the idea of F.R. [Force Reserve] holding the rearward line was ruled out I was never in any doubt as to who was commanding – A.D. [Lieut.-Col. A. Duncan] was given the honour! I received my orders, part verbal and backed by a short message with no information in it. I issued orders to Rangers and N.H.'[97]

In his despatch Weston says nothing of this affair. His orders at 8.30 p.m. and 10 p.m. were addressed to 'Force Reserve'.[98] Perhaps he was assuming that the place of a Force Commander was with his men. But it has been seen that Duncan's recollection is that these last brief orders, 'with no information', were ad-dressed to him. By this time Weston may have accepted the fact that nothing was going to persuade Inglis to assume the rôle which he had been given. The New Zealand War Historian notes that the Rangers and the Northumberland Hussars had been 'placed under command' of the 1st Welch, and adds: 'This seems to confirm that General Weston did not intend to use Brigadier Inglis'.[99] But the evidence for such a deduction is destroyed by the fact that this notice, as shown in the summary of the Rangers'

[95] DP, comments by Inglis on Davin Draft, 15 Mar. 1951
[96] Lieut.-Col. A. Duncan, letter to author, 4 Feb. 1963
[97] Ibid.   [98] Weston Report, quot. Davin, p. 358   [99] Davin, p. 358, n. 2

War Diary, was received at 'about 0800 hours',[100] whereas it was not until the early afternoon that Freyberg told Inglis of his new appointment, a decision which clearly superseded all previous arrangements.

The truth must be that Inglis had based his actions throughout, as had Puttick, not upon provisional acceptance of an order already twice confirmed, but upon the ill-placed and mistaken conjecture that it would be rescinded.

The final word in this controversy must surely lie with Freyberg himself. After reading criticisms by Inglis of Weston's behaviour on 26 May 1941, he wrote, in 1951:

> I discount very heavily the remarks of one officer whose responsibility it was to command the Force Reserve, a responsibility from which he was not relieved.[101]

Inglis did well later in the war. In 1942 he led the New Zealand Division out of its encirclement at Minqar Qaim after Freyberg had been wounded. Certainly his courage had never been in question. But when he looks back upon his career he will find little cause for satisfaction in the events of 26 May 1941. It may be surmised that in giving him command of the 'new brigade' Freyberg had been counting on his special knowledge of the situation west of Canea, and that if he had been with Force Reserve that night he would have been able to avert the disaster which destroyed it. His contact with his countrymen would have ensured that he knew the truth of what was happening, and with five hours of darkness remaining, there would still have been time for him to have halted his men in Canea, while awaiting from Weston the authorization that would have enabled him to bring them back in safety to 42nd Street.

Yet some gain emerged from chaos. The resistance of Force Reserve until far into the afternoon of the 27th ensured that by nightfall no great pressure had developed against Suda. If the Australians and Suda Brigade, together with Force Reserve, had attempted to hold the forward position, as Freyberg had intended, it seems likely that the line must have crumbled while some hours of daylight remained. Without the Australians it might then have been difficult to hold a firm defence position at 42nd Street. Any such failure must have compromised the retreat.

[100] War Diary of 'The Rangers', 26 May 1941
[101] Freyberg comments on Davin Draft, 1952 (undated)

Moreover, the New Zealand 4th Brigade would have been delayed some three hours in its march to Stilos. Thus, if Puttick had not taken his dramatic decision, the Germans might well have succeeded in completing their encirclement of Freyberg's main force.

As it happened, thanks above all to the Greek resistance at Alikianou, coupled with the fact that Ringel had not yet realized that the retreat was moving south, the weary New Zealanders were to arrive at Stilos a few hours before the enemy. There was still a chance that the bulk of the retreating troops might be able to slip through the mountains to Sphakia.

21

Wasted Victories: 28-30 May

'During the afternoon'[1] of the 27th Freyberg at last received an acknowledgment that the island must be abandoned. In making this decision Wavell was acting upon his own initiative. At 9.30 a.m. he had sent a signal to London pointing out that the situation in Crete had become 'most serious'; the Canea front had 'collapsed', and it was unlikely that Suda Bay could be held for 'another twenty-four hours, if as long'. Boldly throwing back the Prime Minister's words he had added that there was 'no possibility of hurling in reinforcements', a comment which can have done little to restore his lost favour. He had then given Freyberg's view that immediate withdrawal to the south of the island offered 'the only chance of survival'[2] to the men in the vicinity of Suda. Thus the evacuation which he had thought impossible a month earlier must now be attempted under the noses of the victorious enemy.

For ten hours he had waited for a reply while the War Office sought to avoid recognition of the inevitable. But that evening the Cabinet accepted that 'all hope of success was gone'.[3] At 7.30 p.m. he was told that the Navy would rescue as many men as could be embarked.

This was a bad time for the Commander-in-Chief in Cairo. Darkening prospects faced him on all sides. He had been reluctant to intervene in Syria, where the Vichy French were every day committing themselves more closely to the Germans. Once more he had been overruled by the Prime Minister who had added a brusque, though not yet final, warning of the dismissal upon which he had already decided. That morning, by an unexpected stroke, Rommel had captured the Halfaya Pass. In Iraq, Rashid Ali and his followers, supported by a German air base, still held Baghdad; a few hours later the brigade group from Palestine was to begin its precarious advance against the insurgents. Here

---

[1] Davin, p. 389   [2] Churchill, Vol. III, p. 262   [3] Ibid.

was a swift and cruel reversal of fortune. At the beginning of March Wavell had been triumphant throughout the Middle East. Now the tale of disaster seemed no less complete. Little wonder that he afterwards felt that 27 May had been for him 'the worst day of the war'.[4]

When he received authority to break off the battle, Freyberg's first thought was to tell Campbell to retire from Retimo across the mountains to the south coast. He dared not send this vital message by wireless; even disguised within the primitive code it might give away the plan of the withdrawal. Nor could it be sent by runner on a journey which had been taking three days. But this was a difficulty that he had foreseen. He gave instructions that the order should be carried to Retimo by Lieutenant Haig, whom he believed to be waiting with his Motor Landing-craft near Suda Point.

There were other anxieties closer at hand. He had not yet understood the extent of the contribution that had been made by the Greeks and Cretans, but it must have been with sadness that he read a letter from General Scoulas, the General commanding the Greek Army in Crete. It had been written on the previous evening. With dignity and restraint, the message expressed the tragedy of a nation:

At Stylo – Apocoronon   26 May
Higher Command C.O. Crete
To the C.-in.-C. Allied Forces at Suda

We have the honour to inform you that, according to the information which we have collected, the position of the Greek Forces is so difficult that they have begun to disintegrate at many points, as a result of the hard and constant struggle which has been waged for so many days.

This must be attributed to the lack for many days of war material, food supplies, and red cross material.

The enemy air force acting with conspicuous brutality while it is itself safe owing to the lack of friendly aircraft is razing to the ground cities and villages without pause, destroys the morale of the fighting forces and civilians; the army despite all this had maintained its spirit up till now and destroyed single Units.

According to the statements made by Mr. Churchill, which we had the honour to hear also from your lips, it was necessary for the successful conduct of the struggle to await the timely despatch of impressive forces, which if sent at this the last moment will have

[4] DP, Observation to Freyberg who was staying with the Wavells after Crete

proved decisive for victory. Otherwise the end of the struggle in Crete is revealed as near at hand and disastrous.

Achilles Scoulas.[5]

As usual there was no news from the front line. Freyberg understood that the enemy had 'found an unheld gap between 19 Aust. Bde on left and 1 Welch'.[6] It was becoming clear that the Welch had been destroyed, and it must have seemed to him that the Australians had suffered the same fate while holding on, according to his instructions, in their position below the foothills at Perivolia.

For many hours he had heard nothing of the New Zealand 5th Brigade. From Puttick, who apparently had not told him of the Australian withdrawal, he had learnt that Hargest's battalions had reached 42nd Street just before dawn; but now it was rumoured that they had been surrounded during the afternoon. Another story told of German vehicles landing from the sea a few miles east along the coast.

Already the organization of the retreat had broken down. At 6 a.m. that morning he had dismissed Weston's anxieties and given him command of the rearguard. Soon afterwards Weston had vanished; later it was to appear that he had moved south to establish his Headquarters at Neo Khorion, and then had found it impossible to return 'owing to the extreme difficulty of movement on the road'.[7] But at Force Headquarters it was thought that he had been captured. There seemed to be no hope of order within this confusion. It was with a heavy heart that Freyberg set out that night on the long road to Sphakia.

In fact the day had gone well at 42nd Street. The two brigades were still in position. During the move back, Vasey and his Australians had crossed to the right, and were now astride the road, while the New Zealanders blocked the gap as far as the foothills. Weston had not put them there. At 8 a.m., he had astonished two of Hargest's battalion commanders by telling them that they were 'fools to stay'.[8] They had remained only at the insistence of Puttick who had suggested to Weston, during his visit of the previous night, that the defence would need 'every man available at dawn'.[9]

[5] DP   [6] Ibid.   [7] Weston Report, quot. Davin, p. 374
[8] Davin, p. 375, Lieut.-Col. G. Dittmer and Lieut.-Col. J. M. Allen
[9] DP, Puttick comments on McClymont Narrative

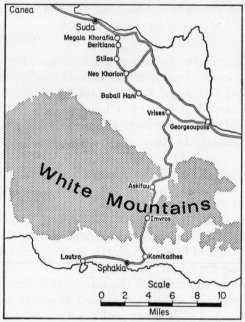

23. Retreat to Sphakia

It was well that they did so. The 'stop line' which Weston had
intended to form from 'A' Battalion of the Commandos, together
with a Marine detachment, the ships' company of H.M.S. *York*,
and some stray units from the dock area, could not have struck
back to check the encirclement of Force Reserve. Indeed it could
scarcely have prevented the Germans from breaking through
before evening and pressing east along the road above the
bay.

Desperately weary, hungry and thirsty the New Zealanders
and Australians had arrived at 42nd Street a little before daylight
thinking only of their need to drink, and wash, and then to rest.
A few hours later, most of them took part in the charge which so
shook the leading battalion of 141 Mountain Regiment and served
to release four hundred of the men who had been cut off to the
west. Moreover, by standing firm all day among the olives, they
had won time for the retreat to get under way. Upon the efforts of
these two depleted brigades, together with such help as might be
available from the Commandos, must now depend the hopes of
those thousands who had taken the road to the south.

Street scene at Galatas

(from Mourellos)

Ramcke parachutists advance along the coast

(Imperial War Museum)

Germans enter Canea

(Imperial War Museum)

British cemetery at Suda; early June 1961

(Author)

Through the blazing afternoon the men at 42nd Street watched the enemy infantry moving across their southern flank.

The enemy's pressure was meant to hold us [wrote Hargest], while he poured troops over the hills to cut us off. By 4 o'clock 1,200 men . . . with mules and guns had gone over the hills and were a constant concern. We could not stop it as our guns had gone right to the rear with Division and we now had really nothing but our own weapons.[10]

No word came from Puttick or Weston. At dusk Hargest decided that it was time to be moving. He had struck up a good understanding with Vasey. Together they brought back their battalions in good order onto the road.

Soon the weary column was passing through Suda, where 'A' Battalion of the Commandos lingered among the docks. On their left, as they plodded along the road above the bay, the men could see the broken shapes of the vessels in the harbour, dark against the moonlit water. Three miles short of Suda Point they reached Megala Khorafia, and at last turned south.

. . . there was silence [one of the officers remembered later], broken only by the tramp of feet. Our greatest hardship was the lack of water and the fact that we could not smoke. Over the rise and down into a huge valley, the road getting worse all the time. At the bottom we see lights. These turn out to be burning stumps of olive trees which glow hotly in the breeze which fans them. . . . A plane is heard overhead – 'Keep still'. A yellow flare lights up the countryside and we are a huddled column on the roadway. How long does it take to burn out? It seems an age but shows one thing – a well.[11]

All knew that they were racing against time, and that at any moment they might come upon an ambush. But the night remained silent. A little before dawn they came to Stilos. Here they fell to the ground in exhausted sleep.

The Commandos were not far behind them. At nightfall the men of 'A' Battalion had heard that they were to delay the Germans for as long as they could. One of them noted that the news was received with 'little enthusiasm', and that Laycock, who in most circumstances was a gay and approachable character, had become 'very worried and frivolous'.[12] They were fortunate. The Jais troops in Suda made little attempt to move against them that night.

During the early hours of the morning they too were able to retire along the winding cliff road. But dawn was breaking as

[10] DP, Included in McClymont Narrative
[11] Davin, p. 382, Capt. J. P. Snadden   [12] DP, Pte. Anthony Cheetham

they approached Megala Khorafia, and now the enemy were beginning to filter out of the hills to their right. These Germans were in no great strength; to that cynical observer whose appraising eye had fallen upon Laycock during the previous evening they seemed to be 'more scared than we were and fewer'.[13] Nevertheless, many of the Commandos might well have been cut off had it not been for the timely appearance on the road of the three heavy tanks that had been brought by sea from Heraklion, still under the command of Lieutenant Terry.

West of Suda there remained only the dead, the captives, and the wounded who could not walk. Many of these, packed together in Field Dressing Stations, were hearing for the first time the voices of their enemies. Others lay alone – on the floor of some deserted cottage, in ditches, behind walls, or in the open among the olives, their wounds turning to gangrene, and their rage of thirst fading at last to dreams of home as they slid into delirium and death.

Ringel had not yet suspected that his enemy might be attempting to escape to the south. He was still intent upon an advance along the coast road. In his orders for the 28th he insisted that the enemy was to be pursued 'eastwards through Retimo to Heraklion without a pause'. The first objective would be 'Retimo and the relief of the paratroops fighting there'.[14] He had strengthened the 95 Motor Cycle Battalion with various mobile formations of artillery, engineers, and anti-tank gunners, to form a striking force under Colonel Wittmann, the commander of 95 Artillery Regiment. These troops would head the advance. The Air Division was to stay behind to guard the coast between Maleme and Canea, at the same time clearing the Akrotiri Peninsula. On the right flank, the Mountain Regiments were to accompany the advance to the east, their task being that of flank protection and support for the relief of Retimo. Ringel made this very plain. He signalled to 85 Mountain Regiment:

> Do not let yourselves be drawn away southwards. Leave protected posts to the south of you. 100 Mountain Regiment will relieve them as soon as possible. Your objective is still Retimo.[15]

He might have had better information about the direction of the retreat had not most of the *Luftwaffe* been withdrawn on 26 May. Recognizing that the crisis in Crete had been overcome,

[13] DP   [14] 5th Mountain Division War Diary   [15] Ibid.

the German High Command was hastening to complete its mobilization against Russia. Scarcely one plane was appearing now, where two days before there would have been fifty. And those that came were often deceived as the men of Freyberg's army froze with chameleon skill into the countryside at the first sound of engines in the sky.

During this same day and night of the 27th, Krakau's three reinforced battalions, emerging at last from the grip that had been laid upon them by the 8th Greeks, had been struggling eastwards, in burning heat, across the 'steep broken and pathless'[16] hills. At dawn on the 28th a detachment from II Battalion began to climb the ridge west of Stilos. They were too late. Most of Hargest's Brigade had already arrived. The alarm was given and two companies of the 23rd, 'many of whom had already dropped off to sleep', were roused in great haste and brought scrambling to the top of the ridge. From behind a stone wall they opened fire 'just when the leading elements of the enemy were approaching some 15 yards away'.[17] The attack was beaten off and most of the enemy killed.

If these Germans had arrived twenty-four hours earlier they must have fallen like wolves upon the helpless mass of the retreat. Among those thousands who had made their way through the narrow pass to the south, not one knew that he owed his safety to those few anonymous Greeks and Cretans who had continued their fight day after day, unrecognized by their friends and with little hope for themselves, on the hillsides above Alikianou.

A few hundred yards south from the bay, a bridge carried the road across a ravine. Here two companies of the Maoris, together with the Spanish Company of the Commandos, had been left to fight a delaying action. Laycock had pointed out that the position might very easily be turned, and that his men had no heavy weapons, but the order to make a stand here was 'confirmed by Force H.Q.'[18]

Soon after dawn, the Germans began to cross the road south of the block. The sight proved too much for the Spaniards who showed no disposition to linger. This was not their kind of fighting. Indeed, the Commando troops were ill-suited to the test that now

---

[16] 85 Mountain Regiment War Diary   [17] Ross, *23 Battalion*, p. 89
[18] DP, Brig. R. E. Laycock to Davin, 17 Sept. 1951

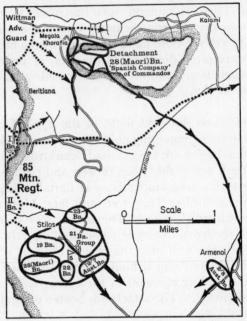

24.   Rearguards at Megala Khorafia and Stilos

faced them. This was quickly apparent to the men from Maleme
and Galatas who had hoped for support from regular infantry.
Instead they saw these strange characters in baggy shorts and
bandeaus, their belts hung about with dirks and daggers and
throttling ropes, and their training, so it appeared, more appropriate to the silent assassination of a drowsy night watchman on
some deserted dockside than to the serious business of holding the
Germans in the open.

The performance of the Maoris at Megala Khorafia was very
different. Captain Royal had sited them for all round defence.
Without difficulty they were able to hold the enemy at a distance
for six hours. From the heights above the bridge they could see
an unbroken column of German transport passing east along the
coast road. Not until the early afternoon did Royal break off the
engagement. Keeping his men well in hand he then led them in
a wide withdrawal to the south-east.

For two days now the retreat had been moving south. Sphakia
lay a full thirty miles beyond Stilos, and the primitive road

wound across a savage range of the White Mountains. In the lead were the troops from Suda, the men without leaders or arms who had spent the weeks awaiting transport to Egypt. They had never felt themselves part of the battle. At the first whisper of evacuation they had set out with relief upon a march which promised refuge from the planes and might lead them to safety. Some had re-captured the football crowd jollity that had been seen on the quaysides at the time of the arrival from Greece. There were jokes again, and laughter, and some ragged attempts at singing. But soon they fell silent as the heat began to drain their strength. Their soft feet quickly blistered, and they looked with envy at the trucks and lorries that jerked and laboured past them up the sharp slopes. Riding in these vehicles were some who pretended injury, indifferent to the drawn faces and blood-stained dressings of the wounded who staggered below them in the dust.

With the return of daylight most of them wandered aside to find protection among the trees and gullies. Those who kept going on the road walked like men playing a game of musical chairs, lingering near every wall or culvert before straining onward to the next promise of cover from the planes. At the distant sound of aircraft the shout 'Take cover, take cover' echoed from group to group to start a shambling gallop among the rocks. Any man who moved as the planes came closer was pursued by curses, while shouts of 'Keep still, keep still', rang down the petrified ravines. Night brought no lessening of the same obsession. The flash of a match or torch at once evoked harsh cries edged with panic, and was quickly followed by a fusillade of shots aimed at the light.

Second only to this absorption with the planes was the need for water. In the burning heat every mouthful drunk was a luxury long anticipated and thankfully savoured. No man knew when he would again be able to fill his bottle. As the road climbed into the mountains the wells became fewer, each surrounded by its crowd of jostling troops.

Freyberg was to write of this 'nightmare' journey:

There were units sticking together and marching with their weapons, but in the main it was a disorganized rabble making its way doggedly and painfully to the south. . . . Never shall I forget the disorganization and almost complete lack of control of the masses on the move as we made our way slowly through the endless stream of trudging men.[19]

[19] Freyberg Report, quot. Long, p. 253

When he arrived at his new Headquarters, established in a cave above Sphakia, he found that the wireless operators were having difficulty with their fading batteries. No response had yet been heard from the Middle East. Anxiously he waited for several hours until the messages began to come through. He then made arrangements for the evacuation, and at the same time requested urgently that direct contact should be made with Retimo from Egypt. That morning he had been disconcerted to learn that Haig had set out in his Motor Landing Craft before hearing of the vital message for Campbell. And now no response could be obtained from signals sent northwards.

Next he turned his attention to the direction of the last stages of the withdrawal. Ten miles above the beach, the twisting road emerged from the highest point of the pass to enter a green and fertile plateau among the mountains. This was the Askifou Plain. He ordered that a rearguard action should be fought in the narrows of the pass, and that the plain itself should be guarded against parachute attack by the New Zealand 4th Brigade. The Operation Instruction ended with the sentence:

It cannot be too strongly stressed that immediate action is necessary, should parachutists be landed.[20]

The lesson of Maleme had not been missed.

Far back at Stilos the New Zealanders of Hargest's 5th Brigade were nearing exhaustion. For eight days they had fought a gruelling battle. During that time they had eaten little but bully beef and biscuit. They had scarcely slept. Many had taken part in two night counter-attacks. Some had marched four times until dawn. In daylight they had been menaced by a deadly attack from the air, and lesser spirits had long since made off with the transport that should properly have been at the disposal of the wounded and the rearguard. They expected little help from the Commandos. Vasey and his two Australian battalions were still with them. But there was no one else. And still no orders. It was a time for leadership.

Commanders do not bring wisdom and insight to every phase of their direction. Often their decisions remain wavering and contradictory until the issue is decided by chance, or by some single stroke, fatal or triumphant. Later every blemish fades when

[20] 4th Brigade Op. Instruction, 27 May 1941

touched by the accolade of victory, or all appears blameworthy when marked by the stigma of defeat. In extremity their resources may prove no less surprising than their lapses when fortune has favoured them. These simple truths would scarcely merit restatement were it not that some historians have ingenuously sought to apportion absolute merit and blame between Wavell, Freyberg, Puttick, Hargest and the other leaders in Crete.

Freyberg's failure of appreciation on the 21st and 22nd had ensured that a battle already half lost could never be regained. But on the 26th he had cast off uncertainty. By ignoring the potentially fatal advice from Cairo, and instead directing the retreat southward, he had made the only decision that could offer any hope of escape from the west of the island. Even this prospect must quickly have faded but for Hargest, who at Maleme had seemed jaded beyond all recovery. He now imposed his authority upon the rearguard. His lack of grip and urgency on the first and second days had pointed the way to disaster. It might have been expected that by the time he reached Suda he would have been incapable of command. Yet in retreat his eye had sharpened and his judgement grown harder. East of Galatas he had fought his brigade with a new control and resolution. Like Freyberg he had come to grips with a situation that he could understand.

At dawn on the 28th he and Vasey were faced with a dilemma. Should they hang on at Stilos until dusk? Or should they risk a move back in daylight? The two brigadiers called a conference of their battalion commanders.

At 9 we met [says Hargest]. The alternatives were simple. Would we risk staying and becoming engaged in battle and so surrounded or would we march out in daylight in view of the Hun planes and their ground strafers.[21]

Opinion was divided. All around them they could see reminders of the *Luftwaffe*. On the previous day the village buildings had been reduced to rubble. The road was pitted by bomb craters, and littered with the wrecks of burnt-out vehicles, many of them still tangled with the bodies of the dead. But it was clear that they could not again 'hope to fight all day and march all night'.[22] He and Vasey were for marching. At 10 a.m. they began to move out.

The road ahead lay exposed among the barren foothills. If the planes returned there would soon be many more wounded left to

[21] Davin, p. 398, Hargest's Diary   [22] Ibid.

die among the burning rocks. Dizzy with fatigue they struggled
on. Each man, like a patient passing under an anaesthetic, felt his
perceptions blunted one by one, leaving unimpaired, and constantly aware, only the sense of hearing that would warn him of
the familiar murmur in the sky. But the slow minutes passed
and then the hours. Miraculously no sound came from above
the hills. Hargest rode up and down the line in a Bren carrier
before moving on to the cross-road village of Babali Hani, six
miles beyond Stilos, where he stopped and waited for his men.

At last they came, fast but together, keeping to the sides of the
road – thirsty, almost exhausted, but they kept on – they knew
the issue.[23]

After a short rest they moved on through the heat of the early
afternoon, past the scattered evidence of defeat, the abandoned
vehicles and equipment, the helmets, valises, and gaping packs.
Many now found that the soles had worked loose from their boots.
Others had replaced their worn socks with field dressings. The
narrow road wound in gentle undulations across the parched
countryside, between dusty patches of cultivation bearing
vegetables or short brown oats. From the slopes above came the
scent of lavender, cistus, and wild thyme.

Near Vrises, six miles from Babali Hani, they entered a small
valley watered by a mountain stream. Here there were olives
again, with oaks and plane trees that gave shelter from the sun.
The fragrance of flowering jasmine and mimosa mingled with the
stink of filth and sweat. Outside the cottages where they had been
given their last dressings the dead rested on their stretchers, and in
every patch of shade, tumbled in attitudes scarcely to be distinguished from those of death, lay the men who could go no
further.

'D' Battalion of Layforce had been left to fight a defensive
action at Babali Hani, where the valley was a mile and a half
across and thickly covered with olives. The field of fire scarcely
reached a hundred yards, but, since the men had only short-range
weapons, this was little disadvantage. Lieutenant-Colonel Young,
the Commanding Officer, had established his main position on
each side of the road, which at this point lay under the protection
of high ground to the east, and had placed the weakened 2/8

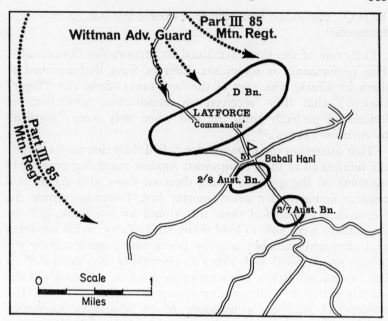

25.   Babali Hani

Australian Battalion to cover his left rear. He was hoping that there might also be armoured support.

Although the three heavy tanks from Heraklion had found it impossible to cross the broken country they had been able to operate from the road, moving largely at night. In this way they had played a useful part between Megala Khorafia and Stilos. With the slackening of the enemy air effort they had contrived to creep in daylight from cover to cover among the clumps of trees that lined the wayside. But they had continued to suffer from their own defects. Like the rest of the long awaited 'Tiger cubs' they had been inadequately serviced in England.[24] Less than ten miles from Suda two of them had broken down.

One of my tanks developed a major engine trouble [wrote Terry later], and on my orders the crew destroyed the tank and made their own way on foot to the coast. It was in this preliminary skirmish that Brigadier Laycock commanding the Commandos got cut off, and he and his B.M. squeezed into my two tanks and were brought back to

[24] Connell, p. 484, Wavell to C.I.G.S., 30 May 1941

the H.Q. The second tank developed trouble and was, on my orders, destroyed.[25]

Only one of the three remained to support the Commandos. This performance is somewhat different from that ascribed to them by Clark, who says of the '*new* tanks (from the "Tiger" Convoy)' that they 'received no maintenance whatever, yet functioned perfectly until the end when they were "scuttled" by their own crews'.[26]

That afternoon the Commandos belied their detractors despite the limitations of their equipment. Against mounting pressure of numbers on the ground, Young directed them in a skilled and resolute action under heavy mortar fire. Towards evening the Germans began to feel their way round his left flank, but the Australians were able to hold them, while Terry, in his surviving tank, brought valuable help by positioning himself among the foliage on the road and 'firing at everything that moved'.[27] At last the sun fell below the western mountains, and darkness slid quickly across the valley extinguishing the sounds of battle. The action had engaged a battalion of 85 Mountain Regiment, and had drawn down from the coast the whole of the Wittmann Battle Group. It seemed that many Germans had been killed among the trees. The Commandos had lost only three dead and twelve wounded. At 9.15 they successfully broke contact with the enemy and set out to follow the New Zealanders and Australians.

Slowly and painfully under the bright young moon the men of the rearguard drew on towards the White Mountains, aware of nothing but the need to keep going to the next halt. Behind them flames licked the sky above the village of Vrises, which had been set alight that evening by a late raid. Soon they began to climb. There was no talking. No man attempted to keep step with his fellow. Each plodded alone, in silence save for the drag of boots on the rough surface of the road, and the occasional click of a rifle butt against a water bottle. By midnight the flames at Vrises had been left far behind and the moon had set. Like ghosts the men wandered in the starlit gloom. Some lay exhausted against the rough stone walls, their cigarettes shining like 'rows of glow worms'. Others slept briefly across the grass verges, responding

[25] DP, letter from Lieut. J. F. G. Terry to Davin, 22 April 1949
[26] Clark, p. 98
[27] DP, letter from Lieut. J. F. G. Terry to Davin, 22 April 1949

only with a 'muttered curse or just a grunt or a snore'[28] as those still moving stumbled across their legs.

At the foot of the main pass they suffered a cruel outrage. The Engineers had brought down a fall of rock into the defile. Many hundreds, left on the wrong side of the demolition, were forced to scramble on hands and knees over the face of the mountain before they could regain the road on the further side. Even the fittest found that it took them nearly two hours to make this detour. For many it called for an effort that was now beyond them, and for the wounded it meant the end of hope. The rest went on in a new mood of bitter resolution. Loyalties grew narrow. Here and there some stalwart carried equipment for a friend, but there was little help for those who found themselves among strangers. Ears were deaf to anonymous voices that cried for water, and eyes looked stonily away as men from other units fell in exhaustion.

In a series of hairpin curves the road wound upwards, each short deceptive fall leading only to a steeper rise from the next bend. Hour after hour the men struggled on. Ahead of them reared the black shape of the mountains, unbroken and inexorable.

But relief came at last. The night air grew sharp with the promise of mountain snow, and pungent with the scent of lentisk and pine, and as the sky lightened, they could see that the road fell away through a narrow gorge, and that no mountains lay beyond the gap. Thankfully they moved through the defence lines of the New Zealand 4th Brigade into the unexpected haven of the Askifou Plain, a place of woods and fields, and of birds singing in the dawn above tumbling streams, with all around the aromatic Cretan herbs and shrubs, myrtle and sage, rosemary, rue and fennel. Smell is the most evocative of senses. Every man who was to reach home would carry with him the memory of this sudden fragrance quickening in the morning dew. For years he might forget, until suddenly and without warning, in some summer garden in New Zealand, Australia or England, he would be reminded of this long-past moment of his youth.

The garrison at Heraklion, for so long engaged below its strength, and still scarcely touched in casualties, was now to suffer grievous loss in vain, and without the opportunity to strike a blow in its own defence.

[28] Stephanides, p. 123

Freyberg's signals to the Middle East show that he still maintained intermittent contact with Chappel. Thus, on 26 May, he informed Wavell that information from Heraklion, delayed by communication difficulties, had been received on the previous day. He had learnt from this that on the evening of the 25th enemy troop carriers had dropped stores east and west of the town, and that a few minutes later the Germans had launched an assault from the west. A counter-attack had met with little success. It had been 'frustrated by an ambush and by low-flying fighter aircraft'.[29]

That night the Schulz Group had begun its move east past Apex Hill.

On the 27th Chappel sent a message to Freyberg through Cairo. He reported that the Germans had increased the number of their automatic weapons and were apparently preparing an attack. A little belatedly he enquired whether he should seek to open the roads to the west or south. It was as though he asked permission to fight the enemy. A few hours later a cable from Middle East Headquarters spared him further speculation. He was told to arrange an evacuation for the following night. Warships would reach Heraklion at 'about midnight' and would leave by 3 a.m. 'at latest'. They would be able to carry a maximum of 4,000 troops. This meant that there would be scarcely space enough for the British and the Australians, and none for the Greeks and Cretans. For the rest of the night he kept the news to himself.

At dawn he summoned his senior officers and told them what must be done. Once more this was the harsh necessity to abandon friends to the mercies of an enemy, the insoluble dilemma that for centuries has faced British commanders in the early stages of a Continental war. Quickly the arrangements were made. All was done in stealth and secrecy. Vehicles were damaged, and timed charges left in stores and dumps. Routes were reconnoitred. Towards noon the enemy received a small reinforcement, the second since the beginning of the battle; XI Air Corps had 'succeeded in organizing a further battalion of Parachute Rifles from the remnants of various units'.[30] At the same time aircraft bombed the perimeter. But the Germans remained, as they had always been, much weaker than Chappel's garrison. They still made no move on the ground.

[29] Davin, p. 363
[30] *Einsatz Kreta*, Battle Report of XI Air Corps

Soon after nightfall the battalions began to file through the town towards the harbour.

It was an eerie business [says the Black Watch historian], trailing down in the darkness, past the well-known landmarks, past the airfield, the Greek barracks, and the Club, where many a good party had been enjoyed with the hospitable people of Heraklion. Nobody could get out of his mind the people who had welcomed their Scottish comrades so warmly, who had fought beside them so bravely and who were now being abandoned, on tiptoe at midnight, and without warning, to the vengeful enemy.[31]

Behind them they left a scene of desolation.

Heraklion [wrote one of the Australian Medical Officers] was one large stench of decomposing dead, debris from destroyed dwelling places, roads were wet and running from burst water pipes, hungry dogs were scavenging among the dead. There was a stench of sulphur, smouldering fires and pollution of broken sewers.[32]

The rescue force was composed of the cruisers *Orion*, *Ajax* and *Dido*, together with six destroyers, under the command of Rear-Admiral Rawlings. It had sailed from Alexandria at 6 a.m. on the 28th. At 5 p.m. it was attacked by bombers while 'racing through a choppy sea'[33] south of the Kaso Straits. Before darkness could bring its usual protection the *Ajax* had been damaged, and forced to turn back, and another bomb had narrowly missed the destroyer *Imperial*. The squadron then reached Heraklion without further incident.

More than 4,000 men were taken aboard, the destroyers ferrying them from the jetties to the cruisers. Room was found for all the British and Australians, apart from those of the wounded who had been cut off outside the perimeter at Knossos, and a small detachment guarding a road block. Despite 'pitch darkness'[34] all went very well. The Germans suspected nothing.

At 3.20 a.m. the ships sailed.

Twenty-five minutes later [in the words of Admiral Cunningham] things started to go wrong. The *Imperial's* steering gear failed, obviously having been damaged by her close miss the night before. She narrowly avoided colliding with both cruisers. It could hardly have happened at a more inopportune moment; but as the force must try to clear the Kaso Straits before daylight, it was no time for indecision. Rawlings at

[31] Fergusson, *The Black Watch and the King's Enemies*, p. 88

[32] Long, p. 291, Capt. P. A. Tomlinson

[33] MacIntyre, p. 75   [34] Cunningham, p. 383

once ordered the *Hotspur*, Lieutenant-Commander Brown, to embark the troops and ship's company from the *Imperial*, and to sink her. Easing to 15 knots Rawlings steamed on, leaving the *Hotspur* to her task, which was successfully accomplished by 4.45.[35]

Alone now, and carrying 900 troops, *Hotspur* pressed on desperately to the east. To those on board it seemed certain that daylight would find them exposed and isolated within a few miles of the enemy airfields at Scarpanto.

Their relief can be imagined [says Cunningham] when, in the grey light of the dawn, they saw the shape of ships ahead of them. Rawlings had waited.[36]

But an hour and a half had been lost. And now, as they entered the Kaso Straits, there was a price to be paid. At 6 a.m. the first German aircraft appeared and began an assault which was to continue for eight and a half hours. Within a few minutes the destroyer *Hereward* was hit and sunk close to the Cretan shore. In the confusion Lieutenant Mann, an Australian barrister and Rhodes Scholar, was 'an inspiration to all', delaying his own escape until 'all floating material had been used'.[37] He was drowned.

The men in the water were machine-gunned by a Stuka, but an Italian Red Cross seaplane then brought them under its protection. Later most of them were rescued by Italian motor-torpedo boats; the Italian Navy had 'not forgotten'[38] the help given to their own survivors after the battle of Matapan. Worse was to come. Shortly before 9 a.m. both the *Dido* and the *Orion* were hit by dive-bombers, and Captain Back of the *Orion* was fatally wounded by an explosive bullet. At 10.45 *Orion* was attacked again, this time by eleven Junkers 87. A bomb pierced her bridge to explode on the stokers' mess-deck. Among the troops and crew 260 were killed and 280 wounded. For some hours the ship limped out of control and on fire.

On one of the destroyers Corporal Johnstone of New South Wales was a close observer of this desperate encounter. His description well illustrates the trial through which the Navy was passing:

These destroyer commanders are out on their own. As soon as the planes appear overhead you can feel the boat lift out of the water as she puts on speed. Then the deck rolls over at an angle of about 45 degrees. Then back it comes again and down goes the other side as

[35] Cunningham, p. 383   [36] Ibid.   [37] Long p. 292
[38] Surg.-Lieut. P. C. Steptoe to the author, 1963

she zigzags, turns and squirms at 40 knots, trying to spoil their aim. Down comes the Stuka and lets his bomb go at about 500 feet. The commander watches the bomb, judges where it is going to fall, turns his boat almost inside out and generally manages to dodge it. Meanwhile every gun is firing all the time and the noise is deafening. The 6-inch and 4-inch guns shake the whole boat and the multiple pompom is going like a steam hammer. Four-barrelled multiple machine-guns mounted on each side of the ship add to the general din. Besides all these a lot of our boys had their Brens mounted on deck and were doing their best to add to the row . . . occasionally as the bomb was coming down I glanced at the sailor sighting and firing the pom-pom and I didn't see the slightest sign of emotion on his face, even though the bomb only missed by about three feet and lifted our boat out of the water.[39]

At noon two Fulmars of the Fleet Air Arm brought encouragement. But there was still no protection from the Royal Air Force. Operating far beyond their normal range, the fighters had been unable to keep their delayed rendezvous. It was not until late into the afternoon that the ships at last drew clear of the *Luftwaffe* to reach Alexandria at 8 p.m. On the bridge of one of the cruisers a piper of the Black Watch stood alone to play them in, the searchlights holding him in their beams.[40] Of the 4,000 troops that had left Heraklion '800 had been killed, wounded, or captured'[41] on the way home; 'over 200'[42] of the Black Watch were dead.

Cunningham went down to the docks to meet the ships. It was a moment of grim significance, not only for those who had now reached Egypt, but no less, in consequence of its effect upon the Naval Commander-in-Chief, for the thousands of exhausted men who still waited in Crete. During the days that followed, and for the rest of his life, he would

. . . never forget the sight of those ships coming up harbour, the guns of their fore-turrets awry, one or two broken off and pointing forlornly skyward, their upper decks crowded with troops, and the marks of their ordeal only too plainly visible.[43]

At dawn on the 27th Campbell and his Australians at Retimo made yet another attack towards Perivolia. This time both tanks took part, each under the command of an infantry officer, in an attempt to support Sandover's 2/11 Battalion. But once again they proved highly vulnerable. According to one of the Australian

[39] Long, p. 292, Cpl. N. M. Johnstone   [40] Spencer, p. 283   [41] Playfair, p. 143
[42] Fergusson, *The Black Watch and the King's Enemies*, p. 92   [43] Cunningham, p. 384

infantrymen the first of them 'penetrated the enemy line some 150 yards and was then hit by what appeared to be a mortar bomb. It burst into flames'. The second was only a few yards from the Germans when it struck a land mine which knocked off a track and bogged it down. Mortar shells then blew off the top of the turret, smashing the officer's fingers, and putting the guns out of action.

Despite this discouraging start, one of the platoons broke into the German position. To bring them support, Captain Honner, who was commanding a company, ordered a section of nine men 'to move to a low stone wall fifty yards ahead round a well about twenty-five yards from the German line to cover with Bren fire an attack across the open'. He watched them as they raced forward.

The leader, Corporal Tom Willoughby, was nearly there before he fell. The man carrying the Bren went down. Someone following him picked it up and went on until he was killed, and so the gun was relayed until it almost reached the well in the hands of the last man, and he too was killed as he went down with it. Eight brave men died there . . .[44]

On the following night Sandover tried again, launching two of his companies towards Perivolia, one on each side of the road which led into the village from the south-east. At 3.20 a.m. they moved off into the darkness. But before they could cover a quarter of a mile the Greeks on the left opened fire prematurely. This warned the Germans. The assault pressed on, bombing from house to house, against a vigorous enemy. Caught between machine-guns firing on fixed lines the Australians suffered many casualties. One of the company commanders was killed, and all but two of his officers were wounded; the forty-three men who survived were forced to withdraw at dawn. The other company pressed through the German lines into the outskirts of Retimo before moving south to return through the foothills. The enemy position still held.

Without heavy weapons or mortars, and with very few grenades, Campbell could do no more. Except for the reduction of this road block at Perivolia his victory had been complete, and these Germans too must soon be forced to surrender unless quickly relieved.

But now, through no fault of their own, time was running out

[44] Long, p. 268, Capt. R. Honner

for the Australians themselves. They still did not know that the New Zealanders had been defeated in the west. On the 26th a liaison officer had returned to Retimo from Canea, but he had heard no hint of evacuation. Twenty-four hours later Lieutenant Haig arrived in his Motor Landing Craft. He brought welcome rations, but no news. Nor had he any idea that Freyberg had intended to entrust him with a message. All that he had been told was that he himself was to go south across country to Sphakia.

This hint was far from sufficient to induce Campbell to neglect his original orders. His own wireless set was still working – more effectively, indeed, than the feeble apparatus at Sphakia. On 28 May he was able to tell Force Headquarters of the safe arrival of 'Sailor Haig'. But the operators at Sphakia could get no message back across the mountains. At Retimo the receiver remained silent. In bitter anguish Freyberg again asked for help from Cairo. The Royal Air Force did what it could. Three times aircraft from Egypt tried to deliver messages ordering a retreat to the south coast. None succeeded. Not until the 29th did Campbell learn from the BBC News Service that the situation in Crete was 'extremely precarious'. At the same time the Greeks began to bring reports that a large German force was approaching from the direction of Heraklion. He now had food to last only one more day. His last hope, therefore, must lie with the Navy. Every twenty minutes that night a beach patrol flashed a message out to sea. No reply came from the darkness.

Soon after dawn next morning the sound of many motor-cycle engines was heard from beyond Perivolia, and at 9.30 Wittmann's infantry appeared, accompanied by three tanks and some field guns. Campbell knew that the end had come. For three days his men had been on half rations. They had very little ammunition, and Sphakia lay a full three days march away across the mountains.

The only hope [he wrote later] would be every sub-unit for itself, which would, I knew, result in many being shot down, because, though olive trees are excellent cover from aerial observation, their widely dispersed bare trunks offer little protection against ground observation. I considered that the loss of many brave men to be expected from any attempt to escape now, and the dangers and penalties to which we must expose the Cretan civilians, were not warranted by the remote chance we now had of being evacuated from the south coast.[45]

[45] Long, p. 273

Over the telephone, in a conversation interrupted by heavy rifle fire, he explained his decision to Sandover, telling him that he thought that 'the show' at Heraklion had 'packed up'.[46] By this time the 2/11th Battalion area was under pressure from the tanks, and the German gunners could be heard calling out 'The game's up, Aussies'.

Sandover told his men to destroy their weapons. Any who cared to do so could make a break for it. He was going himself. A few minutes later, accompanied by a small party which contained several wounded, he set off for the hills. Gradually the firing died. Campbell tied a towel to a stick and walked alone down a track towards the airfield and the Germans.

For the loss of 'about 120' dead the Australians had killed some 700 of their enemies, burying 500 of them. At the same time they had taken 500 prisoners.[47] Scarcely 200 of Sturm's Regiment remained unwounded and at large. No less than the commanders in the other Sectors, Campbell had feared from the first that the Germans would land parachute reinforcements. But his reaction to this threat had differed from that of Puttick and Chappel. So far from inducing him to hold his hand, lest he should be left without reserve, it had spurred his determination to destroy his enemies at the earliest possible moment. Henceforward this was to be recognized universally as the classic technique for dealing with an airborne landing; at Arnhem it was to prove the secret of the German success.[48] Despite all difficulties Crete would not have been lost had the willing infantry at Maleme and Heraklion been led in similar fashion.

But all Campbell's efforts must have been unavailing against so formidable an enemy had they not been supported by the matchless courage and sustained aggression of his men.

[46] Long, p. 273   [47] Ibid., p. 275   [48] Hibbert, *The Battle of Arnhem*, p. 64

22

The Cost of Defeat

Soon after his arrival at Sphakia Freyberg wrote a brief testament of his views upon the battle. He entrusted it to his personal assistant, Lieutenant John White, who was to carry it immediately by ship to Alexandria. It began:

We have had a pretty rough time. The troops were not beaten by ordinary conditions, but by the great aerial concentration against us. The 'I' tank was suggested as a counter but they would not last more than a few minutes in the open being dive bombed. The bombing is what has beaten us, the straffing having turned us out of position after position. Bombs of heavy calibre from heights of about 200 feet simply blew our people out of the ground . . . if we get away with 25% of our original strength we shall be very lucky. . . . We were handicapped by lack of transport, communications and lack of staff. Everybody tried hard in most difficult circumstances. I am sorry Crete could not be held.

And it ended with a sentence typical of the man:

It was certainly not the fault of the troops.[1]

At the same time, on the morning of the 28th, he issued an Operation Order. This laid down that 1,000 men were to be taken off that night, 6,000 on the following night, 3,000 on the night of 30 May and 3,000 on the night of the 31st. But he did not believe that this programme, or anything like it, could be achieved. In another signal he told Wavell that he had been unable to disengage the front and that it was very unlikely that the bridgehead would hold until the night of the 31st. It was therefore essential that the embarkation should be carried out as quickly as possible. Only a few New Zealanders and Australians remained in formations capable of fighting. 'An optimistic view of their numbers', he thought, 'would be under 2,000, with three guns'.[2] There were, however, large numbers of unorganized

[1] DP   [2] Davin, p. 414

stragglers. On the following night he would concentrate on the evacuation of fighting troops. If any remained after that he would tell them to disperse westwards along the coast towards Ay Rumeli. He was certain that the 29th would be the last night on which planned embarkation would be possible.

His fears were fully shared in Egypt.

After the disasters which had befallen the Heraklion convoy, the Middle East commanders felt great anxiety about this much bigger operation that must now be conducted from Sphakia. Further air attack on the same scale might achieve the virtual annihilation of the Fleet in the Eastern Mediterranean, while at the same time bringing death by drowning to thousands of soldiers. Nevertheless, Admiral Cunningham was in no doubt that rescue must be attempted. 'We must not let them (the Army) down,' he signalled to the Fleet, while declaring to his staff 'It takes the Navy three years to build a new ship. It will take three hundred years to build a new tradition. The evacuation will continue.'[3] In London, General Ismay, Churchill's representative on the Chiefs of Staffs Committee, was much impressed. He felt that it 'might have been Nelson speaking'.[4]

Shortly before midnight on the 28th, as the ships of Rear-Admiral Rawlings were reaching Heraklion, the destroyers *Napier*, *Nizam*, *Kelvin*, and *Kandahar* arrived off Sphakia. They found confusion on the primitive quayside. Lieutenant Sutton of the Royal Navy had crossed the island on foot from Maleme. Never had he felt more inclined to appreciate the virtues of his own Service. He noticed 'chaos and terribly slow working until various naval officers from the ships and awaiting evacuation intervened'.[5] But by 3 a.m. 1,100 men had been taken safely aboard. With them went Lieutenant White who had added a brief footnote of his own to Freyberg's memorandum:

After days of work it was not possible for my General to make a full report. He is very tired but going strong. Immediately after dictating the above he left during the closing stages of the evening Blitz to go to General Weston's H.Q. Also Brigadier Puttick's. He definitely needs a rest but he would be very annoyed to know I had said so.[6]

[3] Churchill, Vol. III, p. 265   [4] Ismay, p. 205
[5] Lieut. A. W. F. Sutton, letter to Rear-Admiral, Mediterranean Aircraft Carriers, June 1941
[6] DP, Lieut. J. C. White, Personal Assistant to G.O.C. in Crete

When the destroyers had gone, it was quickly discovered that in their safe offices in Alexandria the quartermasters had blundered. The ships had carried few of the food concentrates that were so desperately needed by the men who had crossed the White Mountains. Instead there were bags of flour and cases of matches.

Freyberg assigned command of all the fighting troops to Weston, while retaining management of the evacuation under the direct control of his Headquarters. It was not a happy arrangement. Weston protested that in his capacity as commander of the rearguard he had already made the 'arrangements for embarkation',[7,8] and that he could 'not accept any interference in these duties' if he were to retain responsibility.

Before these misunderstandings could be resolved, the ration dumps had been plundered by the swarms of men who lurked about the little port in the hope of being taken aboard one of the ships. Only then were adequate guards posted. Later, Maori ration parties arrived to carry back small-arms ammunition thrown into blankets, and to collect what was left of a small consignment of bully beef. Their efforts, helped by a few sturdy volunteers, made possible an issue of some three tins for each fifty men among those troops who were still fighting, and for those who waited in orderly groups under their officers. For many it was all the food that they would taste during the next three days.

If Freyberg had known the truth of the situation on the German side he would have felt less pessimistic about the prospects of the evacuation. Strong elements of three German brigades had been threatening the Commandos at Babali Hani. But on the following morning, Ringel had sent the bulk of these troops on to the east. With them had gone Student himself, still thinking first of his parachutists at Retimo and Heraklion and 'waiting sleepless through the night' for news of their fate.[9] Colonel Jais of 141 Mountain Regiment now reported that 'captured English officers'

---

[7] DP, letter from Weston to Freyberg, 07.30 hrs., 29 May 1941

[8] Handsomely enough Weston was to write in his Report: 'I was able to have little influence on the rearguard operations until Thursday (29th) owing to the extreme difficulty of movement on the road . . . the fact that the rearguard actions were efficiently and successfully conducted was due mainly to the excellent co-operation between N.Z. Brigadiers and Col. Laycock', quot. Davin, p. 374

[9] Kurowski, p. 226

were were saying that troops had been brought from Egypt three days earlier to 'cover withdrawal of the main body of the English force to the south coast and its embarkation there'. The task of the rearguard now facing the 5th Mountain Division, thought Jais, was to 'gain as much time as possible for the main body of the English to withdraw to the south coast of Crete and embark'.[10]

This message in no way diverted Ringel from his main purpose. For the pursuit southwards he detached only the two battalions of 100 Mountain Regiment under Colonel Utz. These troops had been much battered at Galatas. Moreover, their commander was a convinced disciple of the Ringel technique; wherever possible he avoided a frontal approach. Weston had noted that the procedure was always the same. High ground was seized on the flank of the withdrawal and machine-guns quickly brought into action. Mortar fire was then directed onto the main position while snipers pushed forward to concealed hide-outs close to the front line. At the same time flanking parties were thrust well out into the mountains with the object of cutting in behind the rearguard.[11]

The method was safe, effective – and slow.

The grim and menacing debouches from the Askifou Plain would certainly offer Utz no incentive to depart from his normal technique. For several days Freyberg's diminishing force should be able to hang on in its bridgehead below the mountain passes.

But neither Freyberg nor Cunningham could be aware of Ringel's reluctance to press his attack southward. Freyberg indeed felt that the situation was 'as bad as it could be'. While on a visit to Weston's Headquarters he noted that there was 'no food on the hills where most of the troops were situated', and he was greatly concerned about the supply of water.[12]

On the 29th he was given some encouragement. In the stifling heat of the pass the Germans were sharply rebuffed on the serpentine road. Helped by three light tanks of the 3rd Hussars and three Australian Bren carriers, the New Zealand 23rd and 18th Battalions fought until the late afternoon in a series of small actions that sent the sound of shots ringing round the mountain sides.

Eight miles behind them 8,000 men of every arm had found

<hr>

[10] 141 Mountain Regiment signal to 6th Mountain Division, 29 May 1941

[11] DP   [12] Ibid.

refuge, most of them in the Komitadhes Ravine, already known as Rhododendron Valley. Here the southern face of the mountains was cleft by savage gorges, the vertical walls excluding all but a few minutes of the noonday sun. Water trickled in these cool and shadowed depths, and the rich Mediterranean vegetation swarmed in scented riot about the boulders and narrow terraces. Among the stragglers from the broken battalions of infantry were stranded sailors, ground staff from Maleme, Greeks, Cretans and Cypriots, and, wandering unregarded in the throng, two Greek girls in khaki shorts. Soon they were joined by the Commando Spaniards, arriving in twos and threes from their barbecues in the hills.

For several days these men had been thrown upon their own resources, deprived even of those limited rations which had reached the organized units. Many were starving, their haggard faces lined with dirt and dust, sores running from cracked lips into a stubble of beard. Among them were the best and the worst. Some had fought in the front of the battle and now found themselves separated from formations which had been captured or dispersed. Few of these had lost faith or enthusiasm. There were complaints of individual officers, and contempt for the High Command in Egypt, and for those politicians who had promised air support. But, as always, Churchill was exempted from blame. The general feeling was that Crete had been just one more set-back, perhaps the last before the tide would turn. It would all be different as soon as they had a few planes of their own. Like so many British soldiers in adversity, they had quickly fabricated for themselves a brighter image, scarcely accepting it as real, but adopting it for comfort in present trouble. Men told each other that it was 'all over in the Desert' where a great and successful offensive had required the support of every available aircraft. Clearly recognizable among these stauncher characters were others who had long since discarded all thought of comrades and friends. For the moment their spirits too were high, as each glimpsed the prospect of personal survival and escape.

Such order as there was in Rhododendron Valley had been achieved by the efforts of Major Bull, a schoolmaster before the war, and now a New Zealand gunner. Deferring all thought of his own escape, he imposed a genial authority upon this turbulent rabble, organizing them into groups of fifty, and arranging a primitive system of supply.

On the night of the 29th the evacuation went well. Those fortunate enough to be chosen made their way through Sphakia to the ships.

It was an eerie experience [says Stephanides] as we groped our way along the streets of that murdered and deserted village, skirting huge bomb craters or clambering over masses of rubble and smashed brickwork. Every now and then the men in front would come to a sudden halt, and then the whole column would stand stock-still for several long minutes before gradually moving on again. Now that deliverance seemed so near, everybody's nerves were on edge; people were cursing and swearing at each other at the slightest provocation in venomous whispers. I wondered – and others no doubt, were thinking along the same lines – if something would not happen at the very last moment to prevent our getting away. I wondered too if enemy planes might not suddenly pounce down on us and start their usual bombing and machine-gunning. Each time the column stopped, I wondered if some hitch had occurred, and if we were going to be told that the ships would not come for us after all. Yet, in a way, I did not feel things anywhere near as keenly as I would have done normally; I was so exhausted that I lived in a kind of daze, rather as if I were following the doings of someone else in a cinema film. As a matter of fact, to me the one concrete and all-pervading reality was the pain in my feet. . . . At last after many delays, we neared the beach, and I could make out the shadowy outlines of several ships looming faintly through the night some distance from the land. Smaller craft flitted about in the darkness, and crowds of soldiers and sailors jostled each other on the shore. From time to time a pale light flashed out at sea and was answered by another light from the water's edge. Finally we were on the beach and moving along a rough jetty with sailors all around us; the next moment, though I cannot remember how, we were filing aboard an iron self-propelling invasion-barge manned by several officers and ratings. What struck me most when we set foot on the barge was the efficiency of everything. We seemed to have been translated to another world where everything was more civilized, .rimmer, cleaner, better run – even the officers' uniforms were neat. Orders were given in a calm, matter-of-fact manner, there was brightly polished machinery around us and a bell which clanged to the engine-room with a very reassuring sound. Everybody relaxed almost instantaneously. . . . Once more the unanimous refrain was on everybody's lips, 'Thank God for the Navy'.[13]

Admiral King had arrived off Sphakia with a substantial force of cruisers and destroyers, the *Phoebe*, *Perth*, *Glengyle*, *Calcutta*,

[13] Stephanides, p. 155

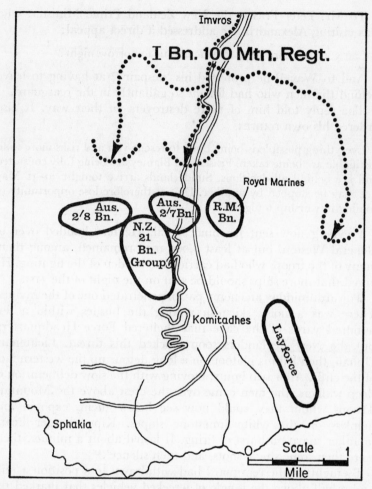

26. Sphakia: 30 May

Coventry, Jarvis, Janus and *Hasty*. At 3.20 a.m. he set out on the return voyage carrying 6,000 passengers. Soon after dawn, R.A.F. fighters arrived over the convoy to ward off the dive-bombers. With this protection every man reached Alexandria.

Freyberg failed to learn the full extent of this success. He was told that Admiral King had been able to take no more than 3,500 men. On the 30th he signalled again and again to the Middle East in words which reveal his state of mind.

To Mr. Peter Fraser, the New Zealand Prime Minister, who was visiting Alexandria, he addressed a direct appeal:

Can you get more ships to evacuate us tomorrow night?

And to Wavell he protested his 'despair'[14] at having to leave behind the men who had fought so gallantly in the rearguard.

The reply told him of more destroyers on their way. It also ordered his own return:

Everything possible is being done to rescue you and risks more than justifiable are being taken. Fraser and Blamey are being fully consulted and are behind all decisions. Sunderlands arrive tonight 30–31 May . . . may be stopped by weather. Do not therefore lose opportunity of coming in warship tonight.[15]

Freyberg now sent his final signal. He had handed over to General Weston, but at least 7,000 men remained, among them many of the troops who had carried the burden of the fighting. He urged that more ships should be sent on the night of the 31st.

Towards midday an enemy patrol penetrated one of the ravines. There was a noisy skirmish among the bushes within a few hundred yards of the cave that sheltered Force Headquarters. But the New Zealanders soon blocked this threat. Lieutenant Upham then led his platoon on a long detour up the western face of the cliffs. After two hours, moving with the slow deliberation of sleep walkers, the men came over the crest above the Mountain Troops whom they could now see below them, exposed and helpless on the white limestone slopes. Kippenberger heard 'another sharp outburst of firing. It lasted about a minute, there were then some single shots, and then silence'.[16]

By nightfall the rearguard had withdrawn to a position a mile and a half above the tangle of wrecked vehicles that marked the end of the road. Vasey's two battalions of Australians, helped by a battalion of the Royal Marines, still held secure control of the central pass.

There was nothing more that Freyberg could do. His anguish was increased by the fact that he must leave the island while many of his troops were still fighting, and by his conviction that there was little hope for them. His thoughts were for the men who still held out on the escarpment. At 11 p.m., while Italians from

[14] Davin, p. 437   [15] Long, p. 301
[16] Kippenberger, p. 75

Rhodes were beginning to creep into the eastern part of the island,[17] he and his staff were taken out to their flying boat.

My feelings can be imagined better than described [he was to write of this departure]. I was handing over a difficult situation with the enemy through in one place almost to the beaches from which we were to make our last attempt to get away the remnants of the fighting force that still held out, tired, hungry and thirsty on the heights above.[18]

Nine days exactly had passed since that fateful moment of exaltation when he had read across the northern sky the signs that revealed the destruction of the enemy invasion flotilla. He did not know it yet, perhaps was never to understand it, but that had been his moment of failure. He had fought the battle with all the steadfast valour and generosity of spirit that were natural to him. It had not been enough.

During this night of the 30/31st the destroyer *Kandahar* developed a mechanical defect while approaching Sphakia, and *Kelvin* was damaged by a bomb. Both were forced to return. The destroyers, *Napier* and *Nizam*, took off another 1,400 troops, including most of the New Zealand 4th Brigade. An attempt by the Royal Air Force to drop supplies from the air was unsuccessful.

All through the following day the perimeter remained unshaken. With a return of something of his old spirit, Weston ordered the Australians, Marines and New Zealand 21st Battalion to remain on the 'top storey' along the escarpment. For 'duty on the ground floor' he brought down the main body of the 5th Brigade to guard the western ravines immediately north of Sphakia village.[19] The enemy made little progress. A few aircraft ranged about the hills, machine-gunning into the caves, and dropping occasional bombs into the gullys. They did nothing to diminish the rising hopes of the defenders.

At 4 p.m. Weston reported to the Middle East that about 9,000 troops were left, and that again more of them might have been taken off on the previous night had the capacity of the ships been known in advance. It was not easy to move men 'at short notice over difficult country. He had 'every hope that Sphakia could be used again on the night of 1st-2nd June'.[20]

[17] Halder's Diary, 30 May 1941   [18] Freyberg Report, quot. Davin, p. 438
[19] Davin, p. 432   [20] Davin, p. 445

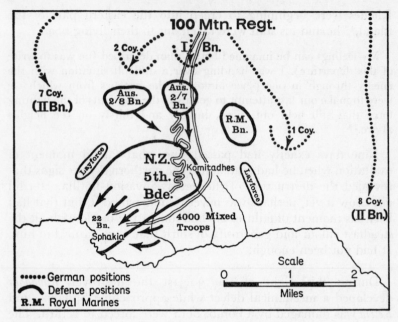

27. Sphakia: 31 May

But now hard decisions were being taken in Egypt. Cunningham was reluctant to risk any more cruisers in the evacuation. For the night of the 31st he had intended to send only the three destroyers *Kimberley*, *Hotspur*, and *Jackal*, together with the mine-layer *Abdiel*; this despite the fact that reports by officers reaching Alexandria were now revealing that German pressure against the bridgehead was not as great as Freyberg had feared, and the revelation that the number of men remaining was larger than had been thought; Cunningham found that 'the figures had suddenly been increased by 5,000'.[21] Among them were most of the New Zealanders.

The predicament of his countrymen greatly disturbed Mr. Fraser, who was still in Alexandria. During the afternoon of the 30th he visited the Naval Commander-in-Chief and 'repeated a number of times that a further effort should be made to evacuate a larger number of our men from Crete'.[22] Cunningham agreed.

[21] Cunningham, p. 389

[22] DP, Mr. P. Fraser to the Editor-in-Chief of the New Zealand War Histories, 10 May 1948

He would send back the cruiser *Phoebe*, still on her way from Sphakia to Egypt, thus increasing by some fifteen hundred the number of men who could be carried.

That night, 30 May [says Fraser], between 11 and 12 p.m. Admiral Cunningham, with his officers, came down to the dock at Alexandria to meet the *Phoebe*, and gave the necessary instructions for her to be turned about and sent back to Crete to rescue as many of our men as possible.[23]

Cunningham had intended to relieve the ship's company, but by now the sailors had seen the condition of the men who were still waiting. All volunteered to return.

At 6 a.m. on the following morning Fraser again went to the Fleet Headquarters in Alexandria. This time he was accompanied by Freyberg. They requested that the commander of the *Phoebe* should 'take aboard at Sphakia every man he could pack on to his ship'.[24] This would slightly increase the total of 3,500 men whom it had been intended to bring away that night.

As the result of our deliberations [says Cunningham of this meeting], it seemed that Rear-Admiral King's five ships would be able to bring off most of the troops assembled at Sphakia, so a message was sent telling him to fill up to capacity.[25]

Freyberg can scarcely have felt the same assurance. He knew very well that a lift on this scale would not be anything like enough to carry 'most of the troops'. But neither Cunningham nor Fraser suggests that he made any request that more ships should be sent on the next night as well. The Admiral was therefore given no stimulus to prolong the evacuation from the source most likely to have influenced him. The pessimism that had from the first darkened Freyberg's hopes for the bridgehead still maintained its baleful effect.

And so Cunningham came to decide that this must be his last effort. He informed the Admiralty that he 'had called a halt after the evacuation that night, and that even if Rear-Admiral King's ships were to suffer no damage in the operation in which they were then engaged, the Mediterranean Fleet would be reduced to two battleships, one cruiser, two anti-aircraft cruisers, one mine-layer and nine destroyers fit for service'.[26]

[23] DP, Mr. P. Fraser to the Editor-in-Chief of the New Zealand War Histories, 10 May 1948

[24] Ibid.   [25] Cunningham, p. 387   [26] Ibid.

Many hours were to pass before this decision became known at Sphakia. At 4 p.m. that afternoon Weston had no suspicion of it as he sent his message revealing that 9,000 troops remained, and that he had 'every hope' of using the port on the night of 'the 1st-2nd June'. When news of this report reached Cunningham he must have heard it with a qualm. But he did not allow it to change his mind.

Wavell was now forced to tell Weston that this must be the end. By ironical chance he could do so only with the help of the Navy. Cunningham recalls that he was asked to 'pass on' the necessary signal, the 'naval wireless being the only means of communication'. He understood that the Army Commander-in-Chief was 'authorizing the capitulation of any troops who had to be left behind'. Since this would mean 'an irrevocable decision to cease the evacuation' he gave the message his 'most careful consideration before finally deciding to send it on'.[27]

Nevertheless, its contents cannot greatly have surprised him since they expressed the inevitable consequence of his own refusal to send more ships.

In London, late on the evening of the 31st, the Prime Minister heard with dismay that the rescue operation was to be abandoned after that night. At 10.20 p.m. he telephoned to the Vice-Chief of Naval Staff protesting that five thousand men could not be left behind without some further attempt to save them. Before midnight the Admiralty had urged Cunningham to go back once more, emphasizing the improvement that had followed the intervention by the long-range aircraft from Egypt.[28] He remained unmoved. On the following day he was to tell the Admiralty that he had been afraid that the waxing moon might allow the enemy to bomb at night, that all available air cover had been required for the protection of Tobruk, and that the remaining troops at Sphakia would probably have been forced to capitulate before he could reach them.

It seems unlikely that these reasons alone sufficed to deter him. Two months earlier the Germans had made use of the full moon in their onslaught against the shipping in the Piraeus. But at

[27] Cunningham, p. 387

[28] At this moment the Admiralty, sensing a change in the situation, was more perceptive than the man on the spot. The signal from London 'presumed that work of aircraft' had 'contributed largely' to the recent success. It added 'H.M. Government assume that this air support will also be available for further day operation'

Sphakia it would be several days before it would shine much beyond midnight. Certainly the *Luftwaffe* had not appeared in darkness since the beginning of the evacuation. Nor had any particular emergency arisen that could demand the use of all available aircraft at Tobruk. And it was not within his province or capacity to decide how long the troops would be able to hold on in their bridgehead. Rather was there every reason for him to accept the confident assessment of the situation that was now being made by Weston. The fact that Freyberg's expectations had already been so much exceeded could in itself have been taken as a pointer that some fresh factor was operating.

But Cunningham was haunted by his vision of the Heraklion convoy. In all his thoughts and calculations he saw the crippled ships that had come slowly up the harbour at Alexandria, and the 'ghastly shambles' of the mess-deck in the *Orion*.[29] He understood only too well the pitiless ordeal of his devoted sailors, and he feared to tempt providence too far. The Fleet had lost nearly 2,000 dead in the actions around Crete, and this without the consolation of inflicting injury upon the enemy. He was very conscious that, without air cover, his men had been fighting at a bitter disadvantage. By comparison with this the action off Norway had been 'child's play'.[30] Like Jellicoe at Jutland he felt that he stood to lose more than he could gain. Long after the war he was to think of May 1941 as 'a period of great tension and anxiety such as I have never experienced before or since'.[31] And in his despatch covering the operations around Crete he wrote:

It is not easy to convey how heavy was the strain that men and ships sustained. Apart from the cumulative effect of prolonged seagoing over extended periods it has to be remembered that in this last instance ships' companies had none of the inspiration of battle with the enemy to bear them up. . . . They had started the evacuation already over-tired and they had to carry it through under conditions of savage air attacks such as had only recently caused grievous losses in the Fleet. . . . More than once I felt that the stage had been reached when no more could be asked of officers and men, physically and mentally exhausted by their efforts and by the events of these fateful days. It is perhaps even now not realized how nearly the breaking point was reached.[32]

The crews would not have disputed these sentiments. Indeed

[29] Cunningham, p. 384   [30] Signal to the Admiralty, 26 May 1941
[31] Cunningham, p. 390
[32] Cunningham's despatch to the Admiralty dated 4 Aug. 1941

there were some who were now finding the strain intolerable. Several men had jumped overboard rather than leave Alexandria. Many had found fresh courage in the admiration and gratitude of the rescued soldiers, but all had come to dread the order to go back into the area controlled by the *Luftwaffe*. They had begun to suspect that their own Commander-in-Chief, like the politicians and everybody else, had failed to understand the significance of this new element in the war at sea. In the words of a destroyer commander: 'It was Cunningham we were afraid of.'[33]

Yet the comparison with Jutland is not exact; at the worst Cunningham could not lose the war in a single night. Nor was the danger now as great as he supposed. He was not to know that most of the *Luftwaffe* had been withdrawn, but in his absorption with the fate of the Heraklion convoy he had not taken sufficient account of the shorter distance from the south of the island that was enabling his ships to cover many scores of miles in darkness. Moreover, by this time, a tenuous liaison had been established between the Royal Air Force and the Naval Staff in Alexandria. This made it possible for fighters from North Africa to bring their scanty, but vital, protection at dawn. Later he was to acknowledge that Group Captain Pelly, the officer responsible, had been 'a tower of strength', and that this belated arrangement had saved 'many casualties'.[34] At the time he showed little faith in what was no more than a hasty improvisation; he could not forget the missed rendezvous above the Kaso Strait. At this stage of the war few of the high commanders had much understanding either of the capacities or the difficulties of the other Services.

Thus he had reached the decision that must seal the fate of all who remained in Crete, a decision that he now sustained despite the confident expectations of the officer now in command at Sphakia, coupled with his own knowledge that not a ship or a man had been lost during the first three days of the southern evacuation. His attitude can readily be understood. But it accords ill with his criticism of Rear-Admiral King's earlier reluctance to scour the northern Aegean in daylight. The reward offered now, no less than the rescue of 5,000 British and Imperial troops, was far greater, and the risk that he declined much less. It seems unlikely that Nelson would have approved.

No copy of Wavell's last order has been found. Nor is it known

[33] Lieut. Pat Lawford to the author, 18 June 1963   [34] Cunningham, p. 382

exactly when it was sent. But by 6 p.m. Weston knew the worst. His answer, despatched at the time, shows his reaction. After the final evacuation 5,500 would be left, all of them exhausted by lack of food. In these circumstances further resistance must be impossible. Unless they could be supplied it was clear that their only hope of survival lay in capitulation. What action was he to take?[35]

To this there was no reply. The battery of the only remaining wireless set had run down at last. But the question itself throws some light upon the instruction that must have prompted it. It shows that Cunningham's recollection is mistaken. The Middle East Command had shirked the responsibility of ordering capitulation. That unhappy duty had been left for Weston to take upon himself.

A big ship would take off 3,500 tonight, after that nothing [wrote Hargest]. We sat stunned by it. We had expected two or three more nights of it but this was to be the end.[36]

Weston made his final selection. Since there was no more need of fighting troops to guard the perimeter, the New Zealand 5th and the Australian 19th Brigades would have the priority which they had fairly earned by their long fight west of Canea and in the rearguard. There might be room for some of the Marines, and perhaps a few representatives from each group among those troops who had waited so long in the ravines. The rest must capitulate. One of the Commando colonels would make contact with the Germans as soon as the ships had gone.

Towards dusk Hargest marshalled his Brigade. He was resolved to use force if necessary to ensure that his men should make the escape to which he felt them entitled. 'We had borne the burden and were going aboard as a Bde and none would stop us.'[37] He had 1,100 men. Many came begging to join them. Some were New Zealanders – gunners, engineers, and medical orderlies with no one to look after them. He did not accept them all. 'If they came without rifles I turned them down cold – they were stragglers. Never had I such a day.'[38] Weston had told him to clear Sphakia and post a beach cordon. He gave the job to the 22nd Battalion who went about it 'with fixed bayonets'.[39] It was a long way from Maleme.

[35] Davin, p. 446   [36] Ibid.
[37] DP, Hargest's account in McClymont Narrative   [38] Ibid.   [39] Ibid.

16

As it grew dark the Brigade closed up and began to come down from the hills 'in a solid block and at a slow pace so that none could break in'.[40] All had shaved. They wore helmets and haversacks. Every man carried a weapon. They moved in silence save for the creaking of their equipment and the rattle of pebbles as they stumbled down the rocky path. Other men got to their feet to watch them pass. There were murmurs in the darkness, 'It's the New Zealanders, the New Zealanders'. But most of the watchers stood without sound or movement among the shadows cast by the rising moon. Their envy was touched with admiration. They felt no resentment against these soldiers in the silent column. It was their day today, and good luck to them. But whose day tomorrow? And indeed few of those who passed that night to freedom were to survive the war.

Very different was the experience that awaited Vasey's Australians. These were the men who had held the perimeter at the top of the escarpment. They had done it with the same casual confidence as their fellow Australians had shown at Retimo. And with the same success. It had not occurred to them to speculate upon the overwhelming strength which the enemy must now be able to bring against the rearguard. Each day they had counted sufficient in itself – and the worst had not been realized. Without difficulty they had been able to stop everything that the Germans had brought against them in the pass. Beyond this they had troubled themselves no further. They deserved their reward.

Utterly weary they began to come down from their positions at 9 p.m. Some were so exhausted that they 'fell to the ground and slept'.[41] In great anxiety, knowing that they fought a race against time, their officers sought to press them on.

But the order and discipline of the beachhead, so long barely preserved, was now beginning to dissolve. The men in the ravines had learnt that many of the official parties had been arriving too late at the quayside, and that large numbers of stragglers and deserters had been taken aboard at the last moment after defying orders and setting out for Sphakia on their own. For any man determined upon escape at all costs the problem had not been difficult. Some had made off upon the pretext of searching for rations. Others, adopting the old device of wrapping themselves with bandages, had limped in among the wounded. Scores had

[40] DP, Hargest's account in McClymont Narrative   [41] Long, p. 306

simply evaded the pickets and crept at dusk into the outskirts of the port where they had waited for an opportunity to steal aboard one of the lighters. Every night there had been places available for those who happened to be on hand. During the fighting, as in all fighting, some men had lost for ever, in ten minutes of action, a reputation acquired in twenty years as a peace-time soldier. These last hours at Sphakia had brought a test no less severe. Many failed – among them some of whom failure had been least expected. The truth appears with remorseless clarity in the conflicting recollections of those who were there. Few see their actions as they appear to others.

On this night of the 31st, as the pickets melted away, hundreds of troops began to pour in exasperation down the narrow path to the beach. Arriving at last from the top of the escarpment, the Australians found their way 'blocked with men sitting down', and their passage questioned by individuals who 'represented themselves as Movement Control Officers'.[42] For the 2/7th Battalion the delay was fatal. When at last the men reached the quayside it was too late. Still 'quiet and orderly in their ranks', they heard 'the sound of anchor chains through the hawse'.[43] Sixteen had managed to get away. The rest joined Colonel Walker as he sat in bitter dejection and weariness upon the stone sea wall.

With them many more of the best had been left behind – the Commandos who had been at Babali Hani, most of the Marines, and the survivors of Force Reserve; Laycock's Intelligence Officer had noted 'the heartening appearance on the last day when discipline everywhere was low, of a small detachment of the Welch Regiment under a captain, marching in with their equipment in perfect order'.[44] Of the men who had fought the heavy tanks under Lieutenant Terry only two had been taken. And in the ravines many had followed the example set by Major Bull, continuing to wait their turn with stoic discipline and restraint. Some had repeatedly declined the offer of a place in a boat, returning again and again to Rhododendron Valley carrying rations for those too weak to move. Major Burston, an Australian gunner who had been entrusted by Weston with responsibility for the guides, had refused to leave without his men. Happy indeed were those who had allowed themselves no time for reflection,

[42] Long, p. 306, report by Brig. G. A. Vasey
[43] Ibid., p. 307, report by Maj. H. C. D. Marshall
[44] DP, letter to Davin from Mr. Evelyn Waugh, 7 Sept. 1951

when offered some quasi-legitimate chance of escape, but had chosen instead the only course that might some day allow them again to face their friends.

Starving as they were, these troops could have mounted a formidable resistance had there been any prospect that the ships would return. The Australians were too spent to return to their old position at the foot of the central gorge, but thousands of resolute men still had arms and ammunition to command the exposed slopes leading down from the escarpment. Within their restricted perimeter, knowing that their freedom depended upon it, they would certainly have defended themselves with ferocity throughout another day.

In fact the Germans were not yet ready to press any further attack. For thirty-six hours the two weakened German battalions had been held up in their central advance along the road. And no help had come from the north. The cautious Utz had found, as Freyberg had done, that he could not maintain wireless contact across the barrier of the mountains. He was forced to rely upon liaison officers for his communication with Ringel. In the meantime he had to make his own decisions. To have pressed the frontal attack against the strong position held by the Australians within the gorge would have outraged all his principles. Moreover, as he had quickly realized, it would be unlikely to succeed.

He had therefore divided his force, accepting the certainty that this must mean delay. Leaving I Battalion to hold the centre he had sent a company of II Battalion upon a wide flanking movement through the mountains to the west, and another company down a ravine four miles to the east. In the blazing heat they made slow progress over the wild precipitous country. By the evening of the 31st neither group had reached the coast. But during the late afternoon a party from I Battalion had succeeded in manhandling a light infantry gun on to a central height. From here it could be seen that there were still strong opposing forces in the vicinity of Komitadhes and Sphakia. Utz felt that it would be unwise to attack without strong artillery and air support. He decided 'not to attack at all on 1 June, but to use that day to complete the encirclement'. Any general assault would be postponed until 2 June.[45]

Thus one more sufficient effort by the Fleet must have suc-

[45] Col. Utz, 100 Mountain Regiment War Diary, 31 May

ceeded in rescuing another 5,000 troops. As at Gallipoli, not a living man need have been left in the bridgehead. For once the Royal Navy had not dared to the end. The bombers which had made their onslaught upon the Heraklion convoy were claiming their last victims.

By 2.45 a.m. the ships had gone. Again all who sailed in them were to come safe to Egypt. A quarter of an hour later Lieutenant-Colonel Young of the Commandos was reading Weston's last order. It was addressed to 'The Senior Officer left on the Island', a post which Laycock had declined. It authorized capitulation.

The position must be considered in the light of the following facts:
1. There are no more rations available and men have had no food for three days.
2. The wireless set can only last a few hours and the risk of waiting for further instructions from H.Q. M.E. cannot be accepted.
3. The decision to give priority in withdrawal to fighting troops has reduced numbers below the minimum necessary for resistance.
4. No more evacuation is possible.
5. You will collect as many senior officers as possible and make known to them the contents of this order.
6. You are ordered to make contact with the enemy and arrange capitulation.[46]

Nothing could better illustrate the confusion that had paralysed the Staffs in Alexandria and Cairo. Over a period of four nights fifteen ships of the Royal Navy had made nineteen visits to Sphakia. The food stores which they had delivered had been grotesquely ill chosen, and nobody had thought of providing replacements for the single wireless set upon which all communication depended.

On Sunday 1 June the Mediterranean dawn changed swiftly to a perfect summer morning. Below the escarpment the pale sparkling sea lay calm and empty to the horizon, no trace remaining to recall the fevered traffic of the night. Everywhere it was quiet. Many did not know that the evacuation had ended. They heard the news with surprise and anger; some with despair. Exhaustion which had been borne while hope continued seemed suddenly insupportable. Men collapsed to the ground and lay without moving. A few, bolder or less weary than the rest,

[46] Davin, p. 447, from copy in possession of Lieut.-Col. G. A. D. Young

gathered what they could find of food and weapons and set out east along the coast. Others contrived to man the three Motor Landing Craft which had been used as ferries by the Navy. With petrol sufficient only for a hundred miles, and with little food or water, they chugged away one by one upon the long and desperate voyage to North Africa.

A little before nine o'clock the Germans began to come out of the hills. Briefly there was an appearance of macabre goodwill, even the sound of accordions. But suddenly the aircraft that had been requested by Utz swooped out of the blue sky above the mountains. Ignoring the white signals and the swastika flags, four Stukas and four fighters bombed and machine-gunned along the shore, killing friend and enemy alike. After this there was no more firing. The Mountain Troops squatted on the hillsides taking photographs, while their officers, carrying towels, walked in holiday mood through the crowds of men down to the beach.

Towards midday they began to collect their prisoners, and to drive them back into the gorge. In uniforms scarcely recognizable Britons, Australians, New Zealanders, Greeks, Cypriots and Spaniards, like men in a dream, staggered about the burning slopes, scarcely hearing the strange and raucous cries of their enemies. For them the way lay back along the cruel road they had followed in hope a few days earlier, away from the shelter and comfort of Rhododendron Valley, with its false promise of escape, back to the heat and the glare, the dust and the stench of Suda and Canea, Galatas and Maleme, where the blackened corpses of their friends still lay among the olives under the indifferent sun.

Major-General Freyberg with Admiral Cunningham on board
H.M.S. *Phoebe* after evacuation of Crete

(from Cunningham, *A Sailor's Odyssey*)

Epilogue

With the capture of Crete, Hitler had secured his southern flank. Most of his Balkan divisions were free to move north for the great assault upon the unsuspecting Russians, and he need no longer fear any immediate threat to the oil wells at Ploesti. Moreover, he had provided cover for his campaign in North Africa. But the manner of his victory had carried implications far beyond the Mediterranean. Both sides had learnt much that was to influence them for the rest of the war.

In the eyes of the world the airborne troops had achieved a triumph that was both spectacular and unique. What might they not attempt next? Everywhere the friends of Britain were disconcerted. In support of the operation the *Luftwaffe* had shown that it could challenge and outdo the British Navy across nearly two hundred miles of sea. Did this mark 'a revolution in the art of war?'[1] Were the same techniques now to be used in support of an invasion across the English Channel? 'If Hitler takes Crete one thing alone is certain,' the London *Evening Standard* had proclaimed on 24 May, 'the next island to be assaulted is our own'. Until the last moment the outcome had been awaited with confidence. Now British arms had suffered yet another heavy blow.

The Prime Minister faced sharp criticism. He did his best to conceal his dismay. 'Suppose we had never gone to Greece and had never attempted to defend Crete,' he asked during the course of a debate in the House of Commons on 10 June, 'where would the Germans be now? Suppose we had simply resigned territory and strategic islands to them without a fight. Might they not, at this early stage of the campaign in 1941, already have been masters of Syria and Iraq and preparing themselves for an advance to Persia?' As on a similar occasion a generation earlier, during the debate after Gallipoli, he could not reveal all that he knew, nor much that would justify him. He could not acknowledge that the preparations for the defence of Crete had been pitifully and needlessly inadequate; significantly, he made no

[1] Playfair, p. 148

reference to the feeble apologia offered to him by the Chiefs of Staff for the fact that the airfields had been left intact. Nor could he tell the House that only his direct intervention, coupled with the failure of Hitler and his staff to recognize their opportunity, had prevented the Germans from establishing themselves in the Levant. Not until many years later would his countrymen begin to learn something of those hard strategic decisions, many of them carried by argument and conviction in the face of initial remonstrance from his professional staffs, that no less than the magic of his public leadership had served to save the world.

In Cairo, an Interservices Committee of Inquiry was appointed. It drew attention to the lack of activity in the island during the six months of occupation, and emphasized that 'no attempt had been made to construct pens or similar works to protect our aircraft on the ground'. These criticisms were resented by the supporters of Wavell, their justified admiration for the man rendering them incapable of judging events upon their merits. Nor was Freyberg enthusiastic. Although the conclusions that were offered did much to absolve him from blame, he was reaching an age at which he had begun to feel that eminent generals should not be subjected to appraisal by officers of inferior rank. The report was suppressed and still has not been published.

In Australia and New Zealand there were hard words about war direction in the Middle East. But there was no unproductive recrimination. At home, on 2 June, the *Manchester Guardian* suspected that 'the weight, speed and cunning' of the German attack from the air had been 'underestimated'. It was the best public comment. For the people of England, massive incomprehension quickly supplied its customary reassurance. On 28 May, as Freyberg's rearguard struggled towards the White Mountains, a letter to the *Daily Telegraph* discussed the merits of double pay for Sunday labour in wartime, and a fortnight later *The Times* carried a column about the Fourth of June at Eton.

Some indication of the fighting in Crete is given by the unusually high proportion of dead to wounded. In the island, the British and Empire forces lost 1,742 dead, 1,737 wounded, and 11,835 prisoners. Another 800 were killed, wounded, or captured after embarking from Heraklion. The casualties in the Royal Navy were 2,011, with the remarkable figure of 1,828 killed. Thus rather more than 18,000 British and Empire Servicemen were lost

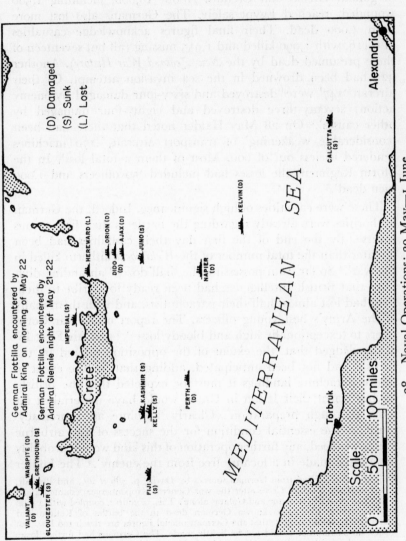

German Flottilla encountered by
Admiral King on morning of May 22

German Flottilla encountered by
Admiral Glennie night of May 21–22

(D) Damaged
(S) Sunk
(L) Lost

VALIANT, WARSPITE (D)
(D) GREYHOUND (S)
GLOUCESTER (S)

FIJI (S)

PERTH (D)

KELLY (S)

KASHMIR (S)

IMPERIAL (S)

HEREWARD (L)

ORION (D)

DIDO (D) AJAX (D)

JUNO (S)

NAPIER (D)

KELVIN (D)

CALCUTTA (S)

Crete

MEDITERRANEAN SEA

Tobruk

Alexandria

Scale

0   50   100 miles

28. Naval Operations: 20 May—1 June

during the action on land and sea. Of these about 4,000 were killed. To this must be added the deaths of an unknown number of gallant Greeks and Cretans. About 18,000, including 1,500 wounded, reached Egypt safely. The Germans also lost more than 4,000 dead. Their final figures acknowledge casualties of 6,116, with 1,990 killed and 1,955 missing (all but seventeen of these presumed dead by the *New Zealand War History*). Another 327 had been drowned in the sea invasion attempt. Of their aircraft '147' were 'destroyed and sixty-four damaged by enemy action; seventy-three destroyed and eighty-four damaged by other causes'.[2] On 28 May Halder noted that there had been 'considerable weakening' of transport aircraft, '170 machines rendered useless out of 600. Most of them a total loss'. In the Storm Regiment the losses had included '50 officers and 1,000 men dead'.[3]

These were casualties of high significance. Indeed, the German authorities were already regarding the battle as their first serious reverse. By the end of the first day their casualties had been 'greater than the total number of the *Wehrmacht* hitherto killed in the war'.[4] So far from possessing the 'half dozen' airlanding divisions that British Intelligence had been ready to ascribe to them they had lost almost half their parachutists, and with them many of the Army's best young officers. The report of XI Air Corps refers to 'exceptionally high and bloody losses',[5] and Air Fleet IV acknowledged that 'the extent of the opposition offered by the British' had not been anticipated, adding that 'in the event of future parachute landings it must be expected that the British, having learnt their lesson in Crete, would have undertaken far more thorough preparation'. Clearly 'absolute air supremacy' must be 'the essential condition for the success of any airborne attack'. Indeed, any further operation of this kind would 'probably have to be made in a locality free from the enemy'.[6] The Führer

[2] Figures summarized from German sources by Davin, p. 486 *et seq.*, and Playfair, p. 146 *et seq.* Visiting Crete after the war General Kippenberger 'counted 4,400 German graves in Maleme and Galatas alone'. This, of course, coupled with a total of something like 2,000 known German dead in the battles of Retimo and Heraklion, would suggest that the German official figures are much too low. But such an assumption should not be lightly made. The Germans had further losses during the resistance fighting in the island. Above all it must be remembered that the German figures quoted here were known only to high authorities in the army; soldiers do not deceive themselves in the matter of their own casualties.

[3] Halder's Diary, 28 May 1941. Ringel, p. 128, says '200 out of 650 Ju 52' were lost

[4] Connell, p. 465

[5] *Einsatz Kreta*, Battle Report of XI Air Corps   [6] Air Fleet IV Report

was 'most displeased with the whole affair'.[7] On 20 July he told
Student 'Crete proves that the days of the paratroopers are over.
The paratroop weapon depends on surprise – the surprise factor
has now gone'.[8]

On the British side the more perceptive observers were quickly
aware that some comfort might be drawn from disaster. 'After
what you did in Crete,' Mr. Fraser told the New Zealanders who
had got back to Egypt, 'it is unlikely that any German parachutists will ever land in the United Kingdom'.[9] The truth of this
was soon widely recognized. All reports showed that a few dozen
fighter aircraft would have sufficed to spread havoc among the
slow moving Junkers. It was not yet known that Hitler had used
virtually all his parachutists in Crete, but, after the beginning of
his attack on Russia, it was plain that for a time, at least, he
would need to divert a large proportion of his air strength to his
new eastern front. The battle for Crete had demonstrated in
London no less than in Berlin that there was now no prospect that
parachute troops could offer a serious threat to the British Isles.

None saw their limitations more clearly than Hitler. In
November 1945 Student told his interrogators: 'After Crete
I proposed that we should make an attack on Cyprus in order to
obtain a jumping-off ground for an air and paratroop attack on
the Suez Canal. . . . Hitler rejected it because of the losses we
received in Crete.'[10]

But, despite his misgivings, Hitler had not given up all hope
of further airborne operations. A year later, in April 1942, he was
'persuaded to adopt a plan for capturing Malta'. Student would
command a combined airborne force made up of his own
'Parachute Division, three additional regiments that had not yet
been organized as a division, and an Italian parachute division'.
An Italian naval expedition was then to bring in 'six to eight
divisions by sea'. This was a serious threat. If it had succeeded,
it must greatly have increased the menace of Rommel's final
thrust against Egypt from El Alamein. In July Student 'flew to
Berlin for the final conference'. Again he was disappointed. 'When
I went in to see the Führer he simply turned it down flat. "The
affair will go wrong and cost too many lives," he said.'[11]

---

[7] Interrogation of Gen. Student, War Office Intelligence Review, Nov. 1945
[8] Ibid.   [9] Address to N.Z. Forces, 7 June 1941
[10] Interrogation of Gen. Student, War Office Intelligence Review, Nov. 1945
[11] Ibid.

Crete, as Student was forced to realize, had been 'the grave of the German parachutists'.[12] Freyberg's men had achieved more than they knew.

. . . the victory of our defeat [concludes the New Zealand War Historian] was that never again, against Cyprus or elsewhere, were the parachutists launched from the air *en masse* to gain victory at the cost of crippling losses.[13]

The British Official Historian goes further. He suggests that 'the loss of Crete at such a high cost to the Germans was almost the best thing that could have happened'.[14] Such a view cannot fail to provoke two questions. First, could the Germans have been beaten? And second, what effect might this result have had upon the course of the war?

To the first of these questions the answer must be yes, despite all subsequent denials. In 1949 Freyberg maintained that if a staff appreciation had been made it must have decided that it would be 'impossible to hold the island with the forces available'.[15] It may be supposed that Wavell had reached the same opinion before the beginning of the attack, and a few weeks later the Committee of Inquiry decided that 'the major lesson of the campaign was that to defend with a relatively small force an island as large as Crete, lying under the permanent domination of enemy aircraft and out of range of our own, was impossible'.

This conclusion, although it at last recognized the significance of unopposed air power, did not take sufficient account of German difficulties and mistakes. Nor could the Committee of Inquiry know that it was essential to the enemy High Command that most of the *Luftwaffe* should be withdrawn a thousand miles to the north before the end of the first week of the campaign in Crete.

The truth is that Wavell could have rendered the island impregnable using the forces available, without air support, and with no addition to his heavy equipment. It is easy to say, and it may well be true, that half a dozen fully serviced infantry tanks at Maleme could have ensured the destruction of the Storm Regiment on the first day, or that a battery of 25-pounders, skilfully camouflaged about the perimeter, could have smashed the troop-carrier reinforcement, as the Howitzers and the heavy mortars of General Giap's Vietnamese were to smash the French

---

[12] Davin, p. 464   [13] Ibid.   [14] Playfair, p. 148
[15] DP, Freyberg comments on Churchill Draft, 25 Mar. 1949

landing-field at Dien Bien Phu. But this is to forget that, through all that bitter spring, tanks and guns were as precious to him as aircraft. Inevitably, he had been chary of committing them to risks even greater than those they had already survived on their perilous journey to the Middle East. The real indictment against Wavell is that a few simple measures, taken during the six months of occupation before the battle, could have deprived the enemy of any hope of success – the construction of roads across the island, the improvisation of landing facilities in the south, the preparation for the destruction of the northern airfields, and the arming of the Cretans.

Nobody can doubt the great moral qualities of this unusual General, his courage and honesty, and the stoicism which enabled him to bear all rebuffs with fortitude. In the spring of 1941 these virtues could not compensate for the failure of his professional judgement. Despite warnings that should have been sufficient, he had encouraged the dispatch of the doomed expedition to the mainland. It cannot excuse him that others made the same mistake. His had been the main responsibility. He had not understood that, under the overwhelming German air superiority, only Crete could provide a base from which to threaten the Balkans. Nor had he seen, until too late, that the island itself could not be safe if the enemy should capture Greece. For this reason he had given no thought to its defence. Finally, beset by difficulties on all sides, he had hesitated to face the vital issues that were arising in Syria and Iraq.

It is possible that the complex problems then bearing upon the Commander-in-Chief would have proved too much for any man. More certain is it that he was now already too old for them; no matter that the Prime Minister, an exception to all rules, was nine years his senior. Wavell's most devoted biographer has written of him that in 1939 'He did not go to his fate with a light or eager heart – the season for such feelings was gone for him'.[16] Whatever his attributes, command in the Middle East at that time was no place for any man in such a frame of mind as this. Many voices have spoken for Wavell. Much has been made of the unfair pressures brought to bear upon him from home, and of the temperamental difference that divided him from his political leader. Certainly no general of the Second World War can be more sure of his reputation as a fine soldier and honourable man.

[16] Connell, p. 206

These considerations should not divert attention from the fact, that in all essentials at this time, Churchill was right and Wavell wrong.

Yet Crete might still have been held. The German plan had contained three flaws. First, Student would have done better to have concentrated the main weight of his assault upon one Sector, either in the west, as Löhr had suggested, or at Heraklion; diversionary attacks at other points along the coast, coupled with continual sweeps along the road by his fighter aircraft, and small drops of parachutists to form road blocks, would have ensured that no reserves could have arrived in time to prevent the relatively easy capture of the necessary airfield and harbour. Second, he had not understood that the slow pace of the sea transports must lead them into deadly danger, since they would be unable to reach the island in daylight under the protection of the *Luftwaffe*. Finally, by committing almost all his airlanding troops on the first day, he had deprived himself of the opportunity to reinforce at the critical point with these vitally important specialists. At his Headquarters in Germany, Halder noted in his diary on 28 May that it had been a 'mistake' to mount the invasion in 'three equal Sectors'. There had also been 'mistakes in reconnaissance' which had made 'the drops very difficult', and the timing of the sea invasion attempt had been 'too late and even then postponed'. In consequence 'any possibility of surprise' had been lost.

These failures had opened a series of brilliant opportunities to the defence. Andrew, Leckie, Hargest and Freyberg himself, had each held victory within his grasp, only to allow his vital moment to pass. And for the same essential reasons.

At every level they had been betrayed by their communications. Sector was divided from Sector, and Service from Service. For days at a time Freyberg lost contact with Heraklion, and he seldom knew what the Navy was doing. His exchanges with the Royal Air Force in Egypt took days rather than hours. In the end none of this mattered. Two of the Sectors achieved their local victory, and the Navy held the shore inviolate, while no form of communication could have called up an air power which did not exist. What proved fatal was the collapse of the short-range contacts; and this was a deficiency that could have been foreseen and remedied. On the first morning, the lost observers west of the Tavronitis were unable, before their deaths, to report that silent drop of a thousand men along the shore; the company commander guarding the western slopes of Hill 107 at Maleme could not pass back news of his successful day; and Lieutenant Beaven had no means to tell Andrew that the enemy had indeed been in Pirgos but that 'only the dead remained'. No less disastrous was the failure of transmission that cut off Hargest from his forward battalions. These failures were critical. 'The truth is,' wrote one of Freyberg's staff after the war, 'that a hundred extra wireless sets could have saved Crete'.[17]

Even under this handicap, Hargest and his battalion commanders might have succeeded had they not allowed themselves to be seduced from their usual robust efficiency by the strangeness of this new form of attack from the air. At dusk on the first evening, groups of Germans were still fighting in isolation at many points between the Tavronitis and Platanias. If Andrew had followed his instinct he would certainly have sent patrols to search for his lost companies with orders that they should hang on. Next morning the sounds of their continuing struggle, in the type of resistance later to be seen from the Japanese, must have lent wings to the feet of their friends in the 23rd and 21st Battalions who could scarcely have been restrained from attempting their relief without further delay.

And now surely guidance would have come from the Brigade Commander. The danger from the sea had given Hargest some reason to hold his Headquarters as far back as Platanias. He had none for failing to go forward to Pirgos at the first hint of withdrawal by the 22nd. No doubt he had not understood the significance of what Andrew had tried to tell him over the radio telephone. But at least he knew that help was needed at Maleme; indeed he had sent two companies as reinforcement. And he had been told that everywhere else in his area the battle was under control. If he had gone to Pirgos after the communication link had broken down he must have realized that immediate counter-attack had become urgent. With the withdrawal of the 22nd the situation had deteriorated seriously, but not yet critically. For himself, as for all the forces in Crete, it was a tragedy that during these vital hours on the night of the 20th, and the morning of 21 May, he should have failed to discover the truth of what was happening.

[17] Singleton-Gates, p. 159, quoting Mr. Geoffrey Cox, *Evening Standard*, June 1962

Nor can Leckie be exonerated. After the disconcerting arrival of Andrew, he could have asked Allen to support him with the 21st, and then moved west on his own initiative, with his largely undamaged battalion, to take over many of the positions on Hill 107 before the Germans could reach them. If a handful of his men had survived the second day, enough to serve a single heavy machine-gun on the forward slopes, the landing of the Mountain Troops would have become impossible. That evening Student would have faced defeat. The same result would still have been probable if Hargest and Puttick between them had contrived to bring two full-strength battalions into action during daylight on the 21st or before dawn on the 22nd. On the first night a battalion counter-attack could have decided the battle. Hargest had sent two companies. On the second night a brigade would probably have done it. Puttick had sent two battalions – and these too late. On the third night a reasonable hope still remained. Freyberg had accepted Puttick's advice, acquiescing in the withdrawal that made defeat certain.

For Freyberg the supreme moment of crisis had come at midnight on the 21st. Despite all vagaries of communication, he now knew the outline of the German plan and of its failure both at sea and in all the airborne landings, save that at Maleme. Interpreted with imagination and insight, here was enough for him to have sent out that night, without stirring from his quarry, the orders that would have brought victory. Twenty-four hours later he could still have left Kippenberger to watch the Germans in the Prison Valley, and gone himself with his reserves along the open coast road to Pirgos, staking everything upon a final effort to drive back onto Hill 107, and so perhaps achieving a triumph that would have outdone all the exploits of his youth.

But he did not suspect the German dilemma. Intelligence had told him much. It had not told him enough. While remaining the victim of his prejudices about the capacity of powered aircraft to crash-land in open country, he did not know that the last of the parachutists had been committed. Thus he had failed to understand the total dependence of the Germans upon Maleme. Never daunted, but constantly bewildered, he was unable to grip the unique problem that faced him. Before the battle his chief anxiety had been for landings from the sea; he had been confident that, come as they might, he could defeat the airborne troops alone. But soon, like all his senior commanders except Campbell at Retimo, he had fallen under the spell of the omnipotent *Luftwaffe*, seeing things worse than they were, and becoming preoccupied with threats which never developed and with dangers that never existed. In the moment of defeat close contact with the enemy served for a time to restore his old grasp, and enabled him to rescue something from the wreck. But at Sphakia his uncertainty returned, unlike anything that he had felt before or ever was to feel again. Once more he saw the situation more darkly than the facts warranted, acquiescing without protest in the naval decision that led to the loss of 5,000 prisoners.

And here, too, Cunningham had failed at the last in a test less formidable than many that he had faced earlier with equanimity and success.

It is tempting to speculate for a moment upon what might have been the outcome if another hand had directed the battle from the quarry above Canea. Montgomery was never to face a problem that remotely resembled this. Nevertheless, it seems possible that his dedicated professionalism might have conjured order out of chaos. Would he not, for example, before the battle started, have insisted upon the provision of sufficient radio equipment? And it is easy to imagine that some eager young officer in a Bren-carrier would have reached Leckie's headquarters during the night of the 20th, and from there brought back news of the uncertainties within the 5th Brigade. Was there not, perhaps, already in the island a young Lieutenant-Colonel whose methods could have turned the scale? Unprejudiced by memories of an earlier and vastly different war, Campbell had understood the paramount necessity for immediate counter-attack before the enemy could reinforce. Moreover, he had seen that swift infiltration among the parachutists offered the best protection from the *Luftwaffe* in daylight. At Maleme every reaction above company level had been too slow, and at Heraklion, after his good start, Chappel had lapsed into inertia. Campbell alone had seized the initiative and held it from the beginning. To judge by what he did at Retimo it seems certain that on the morning of 21 May, at the first hint of danger to the airfield at Maleme, he would have ordered that the 23rd and 21st should attack westward in daylight to meet the Germans in head-on collision across the airfield and on the slopes of Hill 107. Such uncomplicated urgency might well have prevented the landing of the Mountain Troops and so brought victory.

For Student the situation had been saved partly by his own realization that his last hope lay at Maleme. But no less important for him had been the qualities of the men in his 7th Air Division – 'the toughest fighters in the German army' Hitler called them later, 'tougher even than the Waffen S.S.'[18] And he had been supported with the utmost spirit and resolution by his commanders, in particular by Meindl, Gericke, Stenzler and Ramcke, and by all those lieutenants and N.C.Os who had hung on, fortified by their radio contact, in their small groups east of the Tavronitis.

After the fighting had ended the Germans repeatedly told their prisoners that they had been beaten not through any fault of their own but by the failure of their leadership. At the time this suggestion was properly derided. Now it is seen to be true. A distinguished British general has remarked of the fighting outside Tobruk that 'the Germans of all ranks were more highly professional than the British'.[19] Much the same can be said of the struggle for Crete. In flexibility of mind, and speed of decision and action, the German battalion and brigade commanders, had outdone the officers who had opposed them. The fact is not surprising, nor anything to the dishonour of men leaving their peace-time occupations to make war against opponents whose every thought and ambition for many years had been devoted to nothing else. And there had been a shining exception. At Retimo Campbell's performance had been unsurpassed on either side. It is no less true that few had failed in the front-line. Here there had been qualities that could more than compensate for lack of experience. 'The British units were fully fit for action and fought with extreme courage and tenacity,' says *Operation Crete*.[20] The long waste of courage had not yet begun. New Zealanders believe that their soldiers 'never fought better than in Crete',[21] and Campbell's Australians, meeting the Germans on level terms, had beaten them to a standstill. With good reason the men of Andrew's forward companies had felt themselves the victors at the end of the first day, and at Galatas and 42nd Street the counter-attacks had revealed the spirit that was not released until too late.

[18] Clark, p. 49   [19] Carver, p. 255   [20] *Einsatz Kreta*, Battle Report of XI Air Corps
[21] Davin, p. 463

What of the suggestion that victory could not have secured a permanent occupation, and that it would have been too costly and difficult to maintain a second defence?

The answer to this can be well illustrated by interpreting in the light of later events the explanation that Churchill gave to the House of Commons on 10 June 1941:

> Our Army was to destroy the airborne attacks, while the Navy held off or destroyed the seaborne attacks. But there was a time limit. The action of the Navy in maintaining the northern seaguard without adequate air defence was bound to be very costly. We could only stand a certain proportion of naval losses before the northern seaguard of the fleet would have to be withdrawn. If meanwhile the Army could succeed in biting off the head of the whole terrific apparatus of the airborne invasion before the naval time limit, or loss limit, was reached, then the enemy would have to begin all over again, and having regard to the scale of the operation, the enormous unprecedented scale of the operation, and the losses he would have to incur, he might well for the time being have at least broken it off. At any rate, there would have been a long delay before he could have mounted it again. That was the basis on which the decision was taken.

Twelve days later Hitler invaded Russia. Immediately it became clear that there would have been more than a 'long delay' if the parachutists had not succeeded in Crete. Any aircraft returning from Russia to support a renewed assault would have found a very different situation. Those essential preparations that had previously been neglected would now surely have been completed, and once the Royal Navy could enjoy the protection of aircraft based in the island there would never again have been a time when the Germans would have dared an invasion by sea alone. Had they failed in the last week of May 1941 their chance of capturing Crete would have gone for ever. It is also clear that if Freyberg had succeeded, immense advantage would have followed, far more than Churchill had recognized when he suggested that to hold Crete after losing Greece could be no more than 'a consolation prize'.[22] It was no light gain to have destroyed the enemy's *élite* division, and to have demonstrated the short-comings of airborne attack. Yet much greater prospects had been lost.

For the next three years Hitler attached the utmost importance to the maintenance of his hold on Crete. First he used the island to support Rommel's operations in the Western Desert. By the end of 1942 he knew that he could no longer hope to enter the Middle East, but there was no lessening of his conviction that Crete was vital to the firm defence of his southern flank. As his fortunes declined this preoccupation increased. In 1943 it made him all the readier to accept the false information planted by British Intelligence in their coup 'Mincemeat'. On 12 May, a few weeks before the landings in Italy, his ambassador in Madrid told him that the Allied attack would be 'directed in two main thrusts against Crete and Peloponnese and against Italian mainland'.[23] Similar advice came from many other sources, from the navy minister in Greece, and from Switzerland, most of it based on the finding of false papers attached to the wrist of the body dressed as a British officer that had been washed ashore at Hulva in Southern Spain.

> . . . even more dangerous [he decided] than the problem of Italy, which in the worst case we can always somehow tidy up, is that of the Balkans. If a landing takes place in the Balkans, let us say in the Peloponnese, then in a foreseeable time Crete will go. . . . I have therefore decided whatever happens to transfer one armoured division to the Peloponnese. As things are, it can only be taken from the west.[24]

And this, he felt, would certainly not be enough. 'As soon as any real danger of invasion appears within the next few days or weeks,' he wrote to Mussolini on 19 May, 'a large number of German divisions must be sent immediately to the Peloponnese'.[25] All this at a moment when he was doing his utmost to scrape together every division that he could find for the great battle at Kursk that was to follow in July.

Four months later not even the full scale invasion of Italy had lessened his concern for the Balkans, Greece and the Aegean. At a conference in his Headquarters on 24 September 1943, Field-Marshal von Weichs and Admiral Dönitz urged evacuation of Crete and the other Aegean islands. He replied that he could 'not order the proposed evacuation of the islands on account of the political repercussions that would necessarily follow'. And he went on to point out:

> The attitude of our allies in the south-east, and also of Turkey, is determined exclusively by their confidence in our strength. To abandon the islands would create the most unfavourable impression.[26]

[23] Deakin, p. 347   [24] Ibid., p. 351   [25] Ibid., p. 354
[26] Bullock, p. 655, Führer Conferences on Naval Affairs, 24 Sept. 1943

These fears of a British return to the Continent through the Balkans, amounting almost to an obsession, must have been greatly increased had the British remained in Crete. Wavell's successors in the Middle East would have been able to use the occupation to exploit their mounting air and sea power in the way that MacArthur was to use New Guinea, first as a bulwark against any further enemy advance, and later as a base for the return north. Hitler might then have felt impelled to weaken his forces in Italy to an extent that would have made significantly easier the task of the Allies in their advance up the Peninsula. And every month that passed must have brought a deepening of his original anxieties over the threat to the Ploesti oil wells, and to the integrity of his southern flank.

But if 'Operation Mercury' had failed, perhaps the greatest effect would have been felt immediately. On 22 May Halder wrote in his diary:

It has become very unlikely that the air striking forces employed in Crete will be available for 'Barbarossa' at the time arranged. Postponement of the start of 'Barbarossa' may perhaps become necessary.

This was the first of a series of notes on the same theme. By the following day the wording had become more definite: 'Deferment of "Barbarossa" to be expected.' Such was still the Staff view on 27 May: 'O.K.W. is demanding a hold-up in the starting date of "Barbarossa".' But on the 30th there was a change. At the Morning Conference it was reported that the English in Crete were 'trying to escape' from the south coast. The Führer's decision was awaited. Later in the day another entry began in italics:

Führer's Decision, Starting date to remain as 22.6[27]

To judge by this record of the feeling at his Headquarters it seems that even slight prolongation of resistance in Crete might have persuaded Hitler into a further postponement of 'Barbarossa', and so significantly lessened the strain upon the Russians during their winter crisis a few months later. Certainly, the defeat of his cherished airborne troops at this moment, when he was about to start his greatest campaign, would have been a stunning blow for him. Eighteen months before Stalingrad and El Alamein, Freyberg's men would have opened the first crack in the German myth of invincibility, bringing pleasure and relief to all the western world, with echoes of the tale carrying encouragement into

[27] Halder's Diary, entries for 22, 23, 27 and 30 May 1941

the occupied countries, and reaching perhaps even to some of those Russians who were about to face their own grim trial.

Thus a successful defence of Crete might have exerted both immediate and sustained influences upon the course of the war comparable with those brilliant prospects that had once seemed to beckon from Gallipoli.

The chivalry which Lieutenant-Colonel Campbell had ascribed to his beaten enemies did not outlast their triumph. Waiting only for the return of those of their fellows who had been taken prisoner, they quickly sought pretext for murder.

At Kisamos Kastelli they had been greatly frustrated. The Greeks and Cretans, many of them unarmed, supported by a handful of New Zealanders, had held them back from the primitive harbour until the 27th. Only then had a full battalion reached the quayside and made possible the landing of a few light tanks. They wanted revenge. One of their Medical Officers had seen 'mutilated' German corpses and 'taken photographs of them'.[28] This was enough. 'The sharpest retaliatory measures,' records *Operation Crete*, 'were taken by the troops themselves'.[29] Despite protest by the New Zealanders, and even by some of the rescued parachutists, about 200 hostages 'were shot'[30] in the town square.

Later the Germans held an enquiry. The Commission concluded that 'from all investigations it appeared that no enemy soldiers had been guilty of mutilation'. All 'crimes' were attributed to 'fanatical civilians'. The presiding judge emphasized 'the fair way in which the British and New Zealanders had fought'.[31,32] Today the Cretans maintain that the young German soldiers, in their first experience of battle, had been deceived by the effects of heat upon the dead. They deny that atrocities of any kind were practised by the defenders during the fighting.[33]

But the Germans needed no excuses to do as they pleased in an occupied country. Nor did they feel any need to await the arrival of their trained executioners. Parachutists formed the first firing parties. Germans had behaved in this way in the France of 1870, and during the first weeks of apparent victory in the Belgium

---

[28] DP, report by Dr. Unger to the Chief Medical Inspector of *Luftwaffe*

[29] *Einsatz Kreta*, Battle Report of XI Air Corps

[30] Long, p. 240   [31] Report by Dr. Unger

[32] *Einsatz Kreta*, Battle Report of XI Air Corps. Appendix II says that released German prisoners had maintained 'unanimously' that they had been well treated.

[33] To the author 1961

of 1914. Later the stories of such deeds had been disbelieved – for this was still thought to be a civilized nation. But now in Crete, as in the rest of Europe, there followed a reign of infamy un-dreamed of in the modern world. Soon the S.S. arrived to prepare their cold rituals of murder among the olives. Hundreds of hostages were seized, tortured and killed.[34]

Most of the surviving German officers gained quick advance-ment after their success in Crete. Some were to meet the New Zealanders again. Familiar names reappear in accounts of the Allied attack on Cassino, where Heidrich was commanding the reconstituted Parachute Division, now fighting as infantry. With him was Heilmann, leading 3 Parachute Regiment. The 5th Mountain Division was a few miles away. Also in Italy were Gericke, in charge of a detached Battle Group, and Ramcke who had led a brigade at El Alamein. Von der Heydte, whose barely disguised distaste for the leaders of the régime was said to have blocked his promotion, was captured by the Americans in December 1944 while taking part in the unsuccessful parachute landing in support of the Ardennes winter offensive.

For some of the victors of 1941 the end of the war brought sharp retribution. By a strange chance Student had been in Holland not far from Nijmegen, when the Allied airborne attacks began on 17 September 1944. He watched with envy as the hundreds of planes started to carry out the sort of operation which for so many years had exemplified his dream of war. And then, like Freyberg on 20 May 1941, 'the operation orders . . . carried by an American Freight Glider' fell into his hands, thus providing him with 'most valuable knowledge regarding the enemy's intentions'.[35] After the German defeat he was accused of War Crimes committed under his direction during the battle of Crete, and was found guilty on three counts, including that of the killing at Maleme of 'several British prisoners-of-war'.[36] He was condemned to five years imprisonment. His responsibility, how-ever, remained in doubt; the sentence was not confirmed. For Field-Marshal Löhr there was no escape. On 27 December 1947 he was shot by a firing squad for his part in the murder of Yugo-

[34] Llewellyn Smith, p. 163

[35] DP, Student to Liddell Hart, 28 Nov. 1948

[36] Trial of Kurt Student, extracts from the War Crimes Law Reports, Trial and Law Report Series No. 33

slavian civilians, a destiny which must have seemed to him bizarre had he dreamed of it during the halcyon days of 1941.[37]

Among those defenders of the island who returned to Egypt many did not live to see the outcome. Allen, of the New Zealand 21st Battalion, was killed in North Africa, and of those who had fought at Galatas not only Russell, but Gray, Bassett, Carson and Lynch were all dead before 1944. From the village square at Galatas, Thomas and Farran were carried to an Aid Post where the Germans found them on the following morning. Both recovered to escape from Greece and play a distinguished part in the fighting in Europe. Forrester survived to rejoin his regiment, his exploits at Galatas long remembered by the New Zealanders.

The thousands who were transported to Germany were drained of all illusion. One memory sustained them; after the war the Prime Minister was to write of his 'gratitude to those unknown friends', the men taken in Crete, who had told the Germans of their 'absolute confidence'[38] in his leadership. Among their fellow prisoners, these men found themselves marked and honoured for their particular claim to the word that had become universal in all the slave camps of Europe. Frenchmen, Russians, Serbs, Greeks, Dutchmen, Croats, Norwegians, knowing nothing of each others' languages, held in common the name of 'Churchill' to pass between them as a 'talisman of hope'.[39]

None of Freyberg's colonels and brigadiers had failed in anything more than capacity to meet the strange demands of this new type of war. But some did not again command in the field. Others, together with many who had been of junior rank in Crete, achieved fresh honours in battle. Kippenberger had first clearly revealed his quality during the bitter fighting in the sun at Galatas on 25 May. On his return to Egypt he was soon given a brigade, and at Cassino he commanded the New Zealand Division until both his feet were blown off by a mine. Upham was awarded a bar to the V.C. that he had won for his exploits near Pirgos. Both Campbell of the 22nd, whose company had surveyed the Tavronitis from the western slopes of Hill 107, and Burrows who had brought the 20th to their delayed counter-attack, were commanding brigades by the beginning of 1945. Sandover, the Australian, who had led 2/11 Battalion at Retimo, achieved the

[37] Davin, p. 80, *n.* 4   [38] Churchill, Vol. III, p. 269
[39] Author, under pseudonym, letter to *The Daily Telegraph*, 20 July, 1947

same promotion; he had escaped from the south coast east of
Sphakia after crossing the mountains with his handful of men.
His senior officer at Retimo was less fortunate. Campbell had
brought further distinction to Australian arms, only to spend the
next four years in German prisons. He was not forgotten. After
his return to Australia he was promoted to Major-General before
his retirement into civilian life.

Freyberg himself, wounded yet again during the retreat to
El Alamein, continued to serve with his New Zealanders in North
Africa and in Italy until the end of the war. His reading of a
battle was again unfailingly shrewd, and his courage no less
famous than it had been a generation before. He was regarded
with respect and admiration by his fellow generals, and in awe and
affection by all under his command. He always maintained that
Crete could not have been held, and he was ready to offer many
reasons, not always the same reasons, why this must be true. He
did not care to talk about it. Those who were closest to him felt
the word 'Crete' was written upon his heart. Perhaps, without
fully acknowledging it even to himself, he may have realized that
here was the one flaw in his long and devoted service, a brief
failure of judgement that came to its crisis during the hours
before dawn on 22 May 1941.

It was recognized that he might have limitations 'above the
level which suited him so supremely well'.[40] Nor is it likely that
he could have been persuaded to leave the New Zealanders. He
never again held an independent command. On 29 September
1945 he returned to Suda, and at a Memorial Service he paid
tribute to the men who had fallen in the battle. 'History will do
justice to the part they played,' he said. 'It will be belated justice.
Gallantry in failure, no matter how great it may be, has tardy
recognition. May 1941 was a difficult period of the war, certainly
our most difficult. We had little equipment and no allies. Looking
back on our long and eventful war, the fight to hold Crete was the
hardest and most savage campaign of the New Zealand Division.'[41]

In June 1946 he began a highly successful six-year term as
Governor-General of New Zealand. When this was over he
returned to England as a member of the House of Lords, to
become Lieutenant-Governor of Windsor Castle. He died in
1963. No man has had a better right to end his life as a Queen's
Champion.

[40] Obituary, *The Times*, 6 July 1963   [41] Davin, p. 523

Today most of the rubble has been cleared from Canea and the old bustle has returned to the streets and market places. But, outside the town, the bare ridges roll westward as silent and deserted as they were when Wavell's soldiers came, as though on holiday, to explore the island. Once again the sun can travel half across the sky before any vehicle appears to raise the dust along the coast road, and at noon in early summer only the cicadas sound among the thickets. At Maleme the runway is overgrown by scrub and bushes; scarcely a trace is left to tell of the desperate encounter that was fought there in May 1941. Bullet marks fleck the pillars of the Tavronitis Bridge and a broken stone hut marks the old R.A.F. Camp, but the wreckage of the planes has long since vanished. Any soldier who returns with memories of the battle can walk for an hour along the river bank, and climb among the strong young trees that cover the western face of Hill 107, without the movement of any living thing to disturb his solitude. As he stands for a moment half expecting that some yellow-nosed Messerschmitt will come sweeping out of the sun, it dawns upon him finally that only the bridge and the sky and the shape of the hills are still unchanged.

Among the Cretans memories of the battle are merged with age-old tales of the numberless struggles that have rent the island since the beginning of civilization, and these tales blend with the mythology that was celebrated in the heroic poems of Homer. Already the airborne invasion and the German occupation seem no more than a fragment of this infinite past despite the lingering evidence that reveals the savagery of this last invader, the lone survivors of families, the broken overgrown villages, the ossuaries that hold the bullet-marked bones of the hostages, and the court-yards and olive groves that once rang with cries and shots as the firing parties went about their work. After so many centuries of struggle against the peoples of the mainland, and the many bitter conflicts that have raged among themselves, they are not greatly inclined to settle their hatred upon this most recent enemy. It is not in any spirit of pointless desecration that they have emptied the German graves, but because 'the land is too precious to hand it over to the dead'.[42] Like the Turks they think it natural to accept the anonymity of death, for themselves as for others.

They have made no attempt to forget the unforgettable. The Parachute Memorial, with its great black eagle, still stands against

[42] Prof. James A. Notopoulos, letter to the author, 17 Sept. 1964

the hillside near the Galatas Turn, not far from the bridge where the soldiers of the Welch Regiment gathered for their last fight, and in the villages the men of middle-age converse with visitors in halting German. Some of them were boys in 1941, too big to be killed in their mothers' arms and a little young to stand beside their fathers in front of the pointing rifles, but a convenient head-patting height for adoption by some *Obergefreiter*, to be rewarded with chocolate, and to pass a year or two hanging about the camps of the victors. Nobody cares to mock them for these tarnished loyalties of childhood.

The dead of Freyberg's army remain undisturbed. They lie in their cemetery between Canea and Suda, a mile from the quays that welcomed them when they first set foot upon Crete in the spring of 1941. Here the red earth is sheltered by a glade of cypress, and the white headstones face east down the long narrows of the bay to the distant inlet where the morning mists close over the bright water.

Bibliography

UNPUBLISHED SOURCES

1. Davin Papers (DP)

These comprise the large collection of documents used by Mr. D. M. Davin while he was writing his book *Crete*, published in 1953 as part of the official history of New Zealand in the Second World War. The papers were assembled largely during 1947 and 1948. It follows that most of the undated comment or opinion quoted under this source was expressed at some time in one of these years. All the material has of course already been used by Davin. In the present book many quotations from it are published for the first time.

The material can be divided into three main groups:

a) The McClymont Narrative. This consists of some 2,000 paragraphs, with hundreds of recorded impressions, annotations and footnotes prepared by W. G. McClymont as the basis for Davin's book. Also the very important New Zealand and Australian Unit Signals and War Diaries.

b) Detailed comment, mostly from leading figures in the battle, made at the invitation of the New Zealand War historians. These include observations by General Freyberg on draft histories relating to the campaign, among them proofs submitted to him by Mr. Winston Churchill who, in 1949, was completing Volume III of *The Second World War*, by Mr. Gavin Long, author of the Australian War History of the battle in Crete, and by Davin himself. A narrative by W. E. Murphy, *N.Z.A. on Crete*, and a draft of Christopher Buckley's book on the same subject, *Greece and Crete, 1941*, fall into this category.

c) German documents, reports and War Diaries, including: *The Invasion of Crete*, Report of Air Fleet IV, 28 November 1941.
Einsatz Kreta (Operation Crete) (and appendices), XI Air Corps Battle Report, 11 June 1941.
War diaries and reports of the 5th and 6th Mountain Divisions, together with reports of 85, 100 and 141 Mountain Regiments, 2 Parachute Regiment, and Wittmann Group (German Military Documents Section, Washington, Translations by Mr. W. D. Dawson of the New Zealand War History Branch). No War Diaries of the 7th Air Division or the Storm Regiment are available.

Notes on German officers (compiled from biographical files, translated by Mr. W. D. Dawson).

2. Material collected by the author.

Letters, opinions and personal diaries made available to the author by participants in the battle from England, Germany and Crete, together with photographs taken by the author in Crete (June 1961) and from German War Film in the possession of the Imperial War Museum.

PUBLISHED SOURCES

This list is not comprehensive. Sources quoted in the text, and referred to in the footnotes, are indicated by an asterisk.

GENERAL

AITKEN, ALEXANDER, *Gallipoli to the Somme (Oxford University Press 1961).

AVON, THE EARL OF, *The Eden Memoirs, The Reckoning (Cassell 1964).

BARCLAY, C. N., *On Their Shoulders: British Generalship in the Lean Years 1939-42 (Faber 1964).

BARRY, GERALD, *The Parachute Invasion (Blackwoods 1944).

BEAVERBROOK, LORD, *Politicians and the War 1914-1916 (Oldbourne 1960).

BONHAM CARTER, LADY V., *Winston Churchill as I Knew Him, Vol. I (Eyre & Spottiswoode 1965).

BRYANT, ARTHUR, *The Turn of the Tide: War Diaries of Field-Marshal Viscount Alanbrooke (Collins 1957); Triumph in the West completing the War Diaries of Field-Marshal Viscount Alanbrooke (Collins 1964).

BUCKLEY, CHRISTOPHER, *Greece and Crete 1941 (H.M.S.O. 1952).

BULLOCK, ALAN, *Hitler, 'A Study in Tyranny' (Odhams 1952).

CARVER, MICHAEL, *Tobruk (Batsford 1964).

CHANDOS, LORD, *Memoirs of Lord Chandos (Bodley Head 1962).

CHUIKOV, MARSHAL V. I., *The Beginning of the Road (MacGibbon & Kee 1963).

CHURCHILL, WINSTON S., *The Second World War, Vol. II (Cassell 1949); The Second World War, Vol. III (Cassell 1950).

CIANO, COUNT, *Ciano's Diary 1939-43 (Heinemann 1947).

CLARK, ALAN, *The Fall of Crete (Blond 1962).

CODY, J. F., *28 (Maori) Battalion, Official History of New Zealand in the Second World War 1939-45 (War History Branch, Department of Internal Affairs, Wellington, New Zealand, 1956).

COLVIN, IAN, *Chief of Intelligence* (Victor Gollancz Ltd. 1951).

COMEAU, M. G., **Operation Mercury* (Kimber 1961).

CONNELL, JOHN, **Wavell, Scholar and Soldier* (Collins 1964).

CUNNINGHAM, VISCOUNT, OF HYNDHOPE, **A Sailor's Odyssey* (Hutchinson 1951).

DAVIN, D. M., **Crete (Official History of New Zealand in the Second World War 1939–45)* (Oxford University Press 1953).

DEAKIN, F. W., **The Brutal Friendship, Mussolini, Hitler and the Fall of Italian Fascism* (Weidenfeld & Nicolson 1962).

DE COURCY, CAPTAIN J., **The History of the Welch Regiment 1919–1951* (*The Western Mail*, Cardiff 1952).

DE GUINGAND, MAJOR-GENERAL SIR FRANCIS, **Operation Victory* (Hodder & Stoughton 1947); **Generals at War* (Hodder & Stoughton 1964).

DYER, MAJOR H. G., **The Way of the Maori Soldier* (Stockwell 1957).

FARRAN, ROY, **Winged Dagger* (Collins 1948).

FERGUSSON BERNARD, **The Black Watch and the King's Enemies* (Collins 1950); **Wavell, Portrait of a Soldier* (Collins 1961).

FIELDING, XAN, **The Stronghold* (Secker & Warburg 1963).

FLEMING, PETER, **Invasion 1940* (Hart Davies 1957).

GARNETT, DAVID, *The Campaign in Greece and Crete* (H.M.S.O. 1942).

GIBSON, MAJOR T. A., *Assault from the Sky, Crete 1941* (Journal of Royal United Services Institution, May 1961).

GUEDALLA, PHILIP, **The Duke* (Hodder & Stoughton 1931); *Middle East 1940–42, A Study in Air Power* (Hodder & Stoughton 1944).

GWYER, J. M. A., **Grand Strategy*, Vol. III, Pt. 1 (H.M.S.O. 1964).

HARMELING, LIEUTENANT-COLONEL HENRY, **'Armor v. Paratroopers,'* *U.S. Army Combat Force Journal*, Vol. IV, No. 7, 1954.

HECKSTALL-SMITH, ANTHONY and BAILLIE-GROHMAN, VICE-ADMIRAL, **Greek Tragedy* (Blond 1961).

HENDERSON, JIM, **22 Battalion, Official History of New Zealand in the Second World War 1939–45* (War History Branch, Department of Internal Affairs, Wellington, New Zealand, 1958).

HETHERINGTON, JOHN, **Airborne Invasion* (Schindler, Cairo 1944).

HIBBERT, CHRISTOPHER, **Corunna* (Batsford 1961); **The Battle of Arnhem* (Batsford 1962).

HOWELL, WING-COMMANDER EDWARD, **Escape to Live* (Longmans 1947).

ISMAY, GENERAL LORD, **The Memoirs of Lord Ismay* (Heinemann 1960).

KEMP, P. K., **Victory at Sea 1939–45* (Muller 1957).

KENNEDY, SIR JOHN, **The Business of War* (Hutchinson 1957).

KIPPENBERGER, MAJOR-GENERAL SIR HOWARD, **Infantry Brigadier* (Oxford University Press 1949).

LEASOR, JAMES, *War at the Top, Experiences of General Sir Leslie Hollis* (Joseph 1959).

LIDDELL HART, B. H., *The Other Side of the Hill* (Cassell 1948); *Memoirs*, Vol. I (Cassell 1965).

LLEWELLYN SMITH, MICHAEL, *The Great Island, A Study of Crete* (Longmans 1961).

LONG, GAVIN, *Greece, Crete and Syria, Australia in the War of 1939–45*, Series 1, Vol. II (Canberra, 1953).

MACINTYRE, DONALD, *The Battle for the Mediterranean* (Batsford 1964).

MAJDALANY, FRED, *Cassino, Portrait of a Battle* (Longmans 1957).

MOOREHEAD, ALAN, *Gallipoli* (Hamish Hamilton 1956); *African Trilogy* (Hamish Hamilton 1944).

MOURELLOS, J. D., *Battle of Crete*, Vol. I, 1950 (Erotocritous, Heraklion 1950).

NEWMAN, BERNARD, *The Captured Archives* (Latimer 1948).

PAPAGOS, GENERAL, *The Battle of Greece* (Scaziglis, Athens).

PLAYFAIR, MAJOR-GENERAL I. S. O., *The Mediterranean and Middle East*, Vol. II (H.M.S.O. 1956).

ROSKILL, CAPTAIN S. W., *The War at Sea*, Vol. III (H.M.S.O. 1961).

ROSS, ANGUS, *23 Battalion, Official History of New Zealand in the Second World War 1939–45* (War History Branch, New Zealand, 1959).

SHEFFIELD, MAJOR O. F., *The York and Lancaster Regiment 1919–1953* (Gale & Polden Ltd., Aldershot, 1956).

SHULMAN, MILTON, *Defeat in the West* (Secker and Warburg 1947).

SINGLETON-GATES, PETER, *General Lord Freyberg, V.C.* (Joseph 1963).

SPENCER, JOHN HALL, *Battle for Crete* (Heinemann 1962).

STEPHANIDES, THEODORE, *Climax in Crete* (Faber & Faber 1946).

TERRAINE, JOHN, *Haig: The Educated Soldier* (Hutchinson 1963).

THOMAS, W. B., *Dare to be Free* (Wingate 1951).

TUCHMAN, BARBARA W., *August 1914* (Constable 1962).

UNDERHILL, BRIGADIER E. W., *The Royal Leicestershire Regiment 17th Foot: A History of the Years 1928–1956* (Published by the Regiment, Glen Parva Barracks, South Wigston, Leics., 1958).

UREN, MARTYN, *Kiwi Saga* (Collins, Auckland, 1943).

URQUHART, MAJOR-GENERAL R. E., *Arnhem* (Cassell 1958).

WALLER, LIEUTENANT-COLONEL R. P., *With the 1st Armoured Brigade in Greece* (Journal of the Royal Artillery, July 1945).

WAUGH, EVELYN, *Officers and Gentlemen* (Chapman & Hall 1955).

WHEELER, HAROLD, *The People's History of the Second World War January-December 1941* (Odhams).

WILMOT, CHESTER, *The Struggle for Europe* (Collins 1952).

WOOLLCOMBE, ROBERT, *The Campaigns of Wavell, 1939–1943* (Cassell 1959).

Quotations from *Battle of Crete* (Mourellos), translated by B. H. Kemball-Cook, M.A.

GERMAN

ABSHAGEN, K. H., *Canaris (Hutchinson 1956).

BÖHMLER, RUDOLPH, *Monte Cassino, A German View (Cassell 1964).

DOBIASCH, SEPP and FLECKHER, MAJOR, Gebirgsjager auf Kreta (Berlin, 1942).

GERICKE, WALTER, *Da Gibt es Kein Zurück (Fallschirmjager-Verlag, Munster Westf, 1955).

GUNDELACH, DR. KARL, Decisive Battles of World War II, edited H. A. Jacobsen and J. Rohwer (Deutsch 1965).

HALDER, COLONEL GENERAL FRANZ, *Halder: Kriegstagebuch (W. Kohlhammer, Stuttgart, 1963).

HEYDTE, BARON VON DER, *Daedalus Returned (Hutchinson 1958).

KUROWSKI, FRANZ, *Der Kampf um Kreta (Maximilian Verlag, Herford und Bonn, 1965).

MULLER, GUNTHER and SCHEURING, FRITZ, *Sprung uber Kreta (Stalling Oldenberg 1944).

RINGEL, GENERAL JULIUS, Hurra die Gams (Leopold Stocker Verlag, 6th Edition, 1965).

STUDENT, GENERAL KURT, *Crete ('Kommando,' South African Ministry of Defence, March 1952).

WARLIMONT, W., *Inside Hitler's Headquarters (published in English, Weidenfeld & Nicolson 1962).

WESTPHAL, LIEUTENANT-GENERAL SIEGFRIED, The Fatal Decisions (Joseph 1956).

WITTMANN, VON A., Von Kreta, der Insel der Rätsel (Die Gebirgstruppe, Vol. III, Munchen, 1954).

Quotations from Da Gibt es Kein Zuruck, Halder: Kriegstagebuch, Hurra die Gams, Der Kampf um Kreta, and Von Krete, der Insel der Ratsel, translated by the author.

GERMAN SERVICE PUBLICATIONS

MEYER, KURT, Battle for the Strongpoint of Crete (War Correspondent with 100 Mountain Regiment, 1941).

MULLER, GUNTHER and SCHEURING, FRITZ, War Correspondents at Heraklion.

GERMAN MOUNTAIN TROOPS CORPS H.Q., Gebirgsjäger in Griechenland und auf Kreta (Berlin, 1941).

GERMAN AIR FORCE HANDBOOK 1944, Wie Wir Kämpfen (Parachute Engineers in the Battle of Crete).

DESPATCHES

Operations in the Western Desert from December 7th 1940 to February 7th 1941, General Wavell's Despatch (Supplement to The London Gazette, 25 June 1946).

Operations in the Middle East from February 7th 1941 to July 15th 1941, General Wavell's Despatch (Supplement to *The London Gazette*, 3 July 1946).

Air Operations in the Middle East from January 1st 1941 to May 3rd 1941, Air Chief Marshal Longmore's Despatch (Supplement to *The London Gazette*, 19 September 1946).

Air Operations in Greece, 1940–1941, Air Vice-Marshal J. H. D'Albiac's Despatch (Supplement to *The London Gazette*, 9 January 1947).

Transportation of the Army to Greece and Evacuation of the Army from Greece, 1941, Admiral Cunningham's Despatch (Supplement to *The London Gazette*, 19 May 1948).

The Battle of Crete, Admiral Cunningham's Despatch (Supplement to *The London Gazette*, 24 May 1948).

ARTICLES

HORROCKS, LIEUTENANT-GENERAL SIR BRIAN, *Great Commanders* (*Sunday Times*, 20 July 1958).

MOUNTBATTEN, ADMIRAL LORD, *Mountbatten Speaks on World War II* (*Observer*, 20 September 1964).

TREVOR-ROPER, H. R., Article on Hitler's Policies in 1940 (*Sunday Times*, 16 May 1965).

NOTES

Germany's 7th Airlanding Division (Air Division) was composed exclusively of trained parachutists and glider troops. Later, in the British Army, the term 'airborne' came to be applied, in general, only to such specialist units. Nevertheless, in the strictest sense, the whole of the force that captured Crete was 'airborne', including the Mountain Troops who were transported by Junkers 52 to Maleme airfield.

All German times have been converted to British Summer Time by the addition of one hour.

In general, except where specific reference is made to some later period, the military ranks described are those held at the time of the battle.

The strength of a German Regiment is roughly that of a British Brigade.

As far as possible, abbreviations have been avoided in the text. But some appear in quoted passages. For this reason a short glossary is appended.

ABBREVIATIONS

AA   Anti-Aircraft.
AMES   Air Ministry Experimental Station (Cover description for radar station).

Bde	Brigade.
BGS	Brigadier, General Staff.
BM	Brigade Major.
CIGS	Chief of the Imperial General Staff.
C-in-C	Commander-in-Chief.
CO	Commanding Officer.
Coy	Company.
DAQMG	Deputy Assistant Quartermaster-General.
FPC	Field Punishment Centre.
GHQ	General Headquarters.
GOC	General Officer Commanding.
GSO 1	General Staff Officer (1st Grade).
HQ	Headquarters.
LMG	Light Machine Gun.
LO	Liaison Officer.
ME	Middle East.
MG (mg)	machine gun.
MLC	Motor Landing Craft.
MNBDO	Mobile Naval Base Defence Organization.
MO	Medical Officer.
NH	Northumberland Hussars.
OC	Officer Commanding.
RAP	Regimental Aid Post.
RASC	Royal Army Service Corps.
RE	Royal Engineers.
Regt	Regiment.
RM	Royal Marines.
RMO	Regimental Medical Officer.
2 i/c	Second-in-command.
WD	War Diary.

INDEX

Heraklion (cont.)
142, 373; attacks on, 202–4, 206–9,
225, 322–3
Bombing of, 367
Defence, 30, 44, 70, 97, 109–10, 117,
202–3
Docks and harbour, 34, 117; to be
used for supply route, 358
Evacuation from, 446–9, 454, 465–6,
471; casualties, 474
Garrison, 31, 46, 58, 70, 117, 140, 361,
366–7, 398
German attacks, plans, 87–88, 104–5,
139, 142, 194, 480; first attack,
200–9, 216, 223–4, 227, 229–30,
251, 253–4, 264–5, 275, 312, 321–5,
344–6, 356; further attacks, 340,
365, 367, 369–71, 445–7, 451–2;
number of parachutists engaged,
161, 202, 214, 259, 374; remnants of
Air Division dropped, 340, 365
Germans in Sector, citizens' attitude
to, 314–15; condition of, 316–18,
365–8, 377, 379; relief efforts, 398,
410, 436, 445–7, 455
Hurricanes arrive, 131, 361
Naval operations, 281; convoy losses,
447–9, 454, 465–6, 471, 474
Hereward, H.M.S., 448
Hero, H.M.S., 409
Hetherington, John, cited, 361
Heydt, Baron von der, 81, 193, 342, 390,
422, 489; cited, 83, 88, 138–9, 142,
184, 187, 252, 267, 379–80
Heywood, General T., 47
Hibbert, C., cited, 70, 452
Hill, Professor A. V., 21
Hill, Sergeant M. H. R., 386
Hill A., 210, 212–13, 215–17, 319–21, 362
Hill B., 212–13
Hill C., 212
Hill D., 212–13, 318–19, 364
Hill 107 (Kavzakia Hill), 125–7, 148,
152, 490, 492; battle for, 162–71,
174–8, 230–47, 259–60, 481–3; held
by enemy, 266, 270, 296–300;
attempt to recapture, 256–7, 289,
299–300, 303–4, 340
Hitler, Adolf, 2–8, 15–16, 21–22, 24, 67,
80–81, 103, 253; and invasion of
England, 2–3; and Crete, 43–44, 86,
268, 473, 476–7, 484–7; and attack
on Russia, 3–4, 6–8, 15–16, 24, 477,
485, 487
Hitler Youth Movement, 83
Holland, 2, 82, 86, 106, 215
Home Guard, 107
Honner, Captain R., 450
Hood, H.M.S., 416
Hospital Peninsula, 156–7, 185, 191, 221,
421

Hospitals, 102, 136, 229, 289, 404;
7th General Hospital, 74, 92, 114,
155, 185, 220, 273
Hostages taken by Germans, 316, 488–9,
492
Hotspur, H.M.S., 448
Howard, Corporal E. A., 155
Howell, Wing-Commander Edward, 131,
148–9, 151, 170, 230, 239; cited,
149–50, 239
Hulme, Sergeant A. C., 391, 394
Hulva, Spain, 486
Hungary, 81
Hurricanes (aircraft), 17–18, 24, 39, 45,
60, 62, 99, 129–32, 134, 361
Hussars, 3rd, 113, 120, 174, 198, 456

Imperial, H.M.S., 447–8
Imperial General Staff, 9
India, 2
Inglis, Brigadier L. M., biographical,
120–1, 426, 429; commanding 4th
Brigade, 120, 190–2, 194–7, 222,
292–3, 309, 328, 334, 356, 381;
attends conference of brigadiers,
272, 278; put in command of Force
Reserve, 402–4, 406, 413–14, 426–9
Intelligence Service, 102–8, 132, 194,
224, 228, 374–5, 482; German, 103,
201
Interservices Committee of Inquiry, 474
Invasion of Crete (Report of Air Fleet IV),
cited, 219, 279–80, 321, 336, 361, 476
Iran (Persia), 6, 473
Iraq, 6, 29, 31, 42–43, 395, 431, 473, 479
Ironside, General, cited, 107
Ismay, General Lord, 27–28, 454
Italy, 4, 279, 448, 460–1, 486–7
British victories over, 2, 12, 29, 57
Invasion of Greece: see under Greece
Naval forces, 80, 89, 141, 279–81, 285,
448, 477
Parachute troops, 477, 489
Prisoners of war, 93, 197

Jackal, H.M.S., 462
Jaguar, H.M.S., 360
Jais, Colonel, 399, 417, 420, 422, 435,
455–6
Janus, H.M.S., 459
Japan, 2, 3
Jarvis, H.M.S., 459
Jews, 83
Jodl, General, 5, 86
Johnson, Private H. C., 363
Johnson, Captain S. H., 174, 237, 239,
244–5
Johnstone, Corporal N. M., 448–9
Joint Planning Staff, in London, 4, 9, 32,
41, 60; Middle East, see under Middle
East